English

Writing and Skills

CORONADO EDITION

HOLT, RINEHART AND WINSTON
THIRD COURSE

Critical Readers and Contributors

The authors and the publisher wish to thank the following people, who helped to evaluate and to prepare materials for this series:

Charles L. Allen, Baltimore Public Schools, Baltimore, Maryland
Kiyoko B. Bernard, Huntington Beach High School, Huntington Beach, California
Sally Borengasser, Rogers, Arkansas
Deborah Bull, New York City, New York
Joan Colby, Chicago, Illinois
Phyllis Goldenberg, North Miami Beach, Florida
Beverly Graves, Worthington High School, Worthington, Ohio
Pamela Hannon, Kirk Middle School, Cleveland, Ohio
Carol Kuykendall, Houston Public Schools, Houston, Texas
Wayne Larkin, Roosevelt Junior High School, Blaine, Minnesota
Nancy MacKnight, University of Maine, Orono, Maine
Catherine McCough, Huntington Beach Union School District, California
Kathleen McKee, Coronado High School, Coronado, California
Lawrence Milne, Ocean View High School, Long Beach, California
Al Muller, East Carolina University, Greenville, North Carolina
Dorothy Muller, East Carolina University, Greenville, North Carolina
Arlene Mulligan, Stanley Junior High School, San Diego, California
John Nixon, Santa Ana Junior College, Santa Ana, California
Jesse Perry, San Diego City Schools, California
Christine Rice, Huntington Beach Union School District, Huntington Beach, California
Linda C. Scott, Poway Unified High School District, Poway, California
Jo Ann Seiple, University of North Carolina at Wilmington, Wilmington, North Carolina
Joan Yesner, Brookline, Massachusetts
Seymour Yesner, Brookline Education Center, Massachusetts
Arlie Zolynas, San Diego State University, San Diego, California

Classroom Testing

The authors and the publisher also wish to thank the following teachers, who participated in the classroom testing of materials from this series:

David Foote, Evanston High School East, Evanston, Illinois
Theresa Hall, Nokomis Junior High School, Minneapolis, Minnesota
Carrie E. Hampton, Sumter High School, Sumter, South Carolina
Pamela Hannon, Proviso High School East, Maywood, Illinois
Wayne Larkin, Roosevelt Junior High School, Blaine, Minnesota
Grady Locklear, Sumter High School, Sumter, South Carolina
William Montgomery, Hillcrest High School, Jamaica, New York
Josephine H. Price, Sumter High School, Sumter, South Carolina
Barbara Stilp, North High School, Minneapolis, Minnesota
Joseph Thomas, Weymouth North High School, East Weymouth, Massachusetts
Travis Weldon, Sumter High School, Sumter, South Carolina

Teachers of the Huntington Beach Union High School Writing Program

Cassandra C. Allsop	Carol Kasser	Catherine G. McCough
Eric V. Emery	Patricia Kelly	Kathleen C. Redman
Michael Frym	Stephanie Martone	Christine Rice
Barbara Goldfein	Lawrence Milne	Michael D. Sloan
Joanne Haukland	Richard H. Morley	S. Oliver Smith
Don Hohl	John S. Nixon	Glenda Watson
Sandra Johnson		

Dorothy Augustine, District Consultant in Writing

English

Writing and Skills

CORONADO EDITION

W. Ross Winterowd
Patricia Y. Murray

HOLT, RINEHART AND WINSTON

AUSTIN NEW YORK SAN DIEGO CHICAGO TORONTO MONTREAL

The Series:

English: Writing and Skills, First Course

English: Writing and Skills, Second Course

English: Writing and Skills, Third Course

English: Writing and Skills, Fourth Course

English: Writing and Skills, Fifth Course

English: Writing and Skills, Complete Course

Also available for each title:

Teacher's Edition

Workbook

Test Book

Teacher's Resource Binder

Computer Test Generator

Computer Scoring Program

W. ROSS WINTEROWD is the Bruce R. McElderry Professor of English at the University of Southern California. Since 1975, Dr. Winterowd has traveled widely as a writing consultant for numerous schools in North America.

PATRICIA Y. MURRAY is Director of Composition at DePaul University in Chicago. Dr. Murray taught junior and senior high school English in the Los Angeles city schools. She is also a consultant in curriculum development and teacher training.

Printed in the United States of America

ISBN 0-03-014643-7

Contents

1   *Writing*

6   *Writing an Expository Composition*

7   *Writing a Research Report*

11 Writing for the Business World

2 *Grammar and Usage*

12 Nouns

13 Pronouns

14 Verbs

15 Adjectives

3   *Mechanics*

28 Understanding Your Language

29 Vocabulary and Spelling Skills

30 Speaking and Listening Skills

1
Writing

1 Discovering the Writing Process

The Writing Process

Racy, yellow, and gleaming with chrome, a sports car on the showroom floor is a *product*, something made from precise specifications and completed to perfection. All the steps it took to complete the product—shaping the ideas, designing the blueprints, assembling the parts, adding the finishing touches, and driving the test runs—all those steps are the *process*. No car can be produced in one step alone; similarly, no piece of writing can be prepared for an audience without first going through the three steps of the writing process.

The writing process always consists of three stages—*prewriting*, *writing*, and *postwriting*.

Prewriting includes all the preliminary things you do to get started writing. In this chapter you will learn a variety of prewriting techniques designed to help you to stimulate your own flow of ideas. Once you begin to generate ideas, you have started to encourage the creative thinking process.

The writing stage involves putting your ideas into sentences and then into paragraphs. As you write, you may explore various ways to express your ideas. The forms you select will be linked to your purpose for writing and to the specific needs of your audience.

To shape your writing explorations into a final product, the next stage—postwriting—becomes crucial. Postwriting includes changing or adding to your first draft. It also involves sharing your writing with an audience and having others help you revise and edit your compositions. Finally, postwriting means polishing the final product by proofreading and making corrections in grammar, mechanics, and spelling.

Sometimes you will write simply for practice, just as a baseball player needs to practice before a game; thus, you may not take everything you write through all the stages of the writing process. Some compositions, however, you will want to polish, like the shiny yellow sports car in the showroom window. These compositions will take more time and should undergo the entire process of prewriting, writing, and postwriting.

Prewriting: Discovering Ideas for Writing

Perhaps you have had the experience of using a diving board to spring into the water. In the same manner, writers use prewriting methods as springboards for writing. These methods, or strategies, can help get ideas flowing before you write. Because getting started is often difficult, the prewriting stage is important. It is a stage of warming up—of discovering what you know and what you need to know. Prewriting can involve listening to and discussing ideas, as well as reading and responding to literature, reports, articles, and the writing of others. In addition, prewriting involves observing, using your senses, and incorporating your experiences into your writing.

The prewriting strategies you use will vary depending on the nature of the writing assignment and on your personal preferences. You will discover the prewriting methods that work best for you only by experimenting. The following section will acquaint you with a variety of strategies for discovering your ideas, for organizing information, and for getting started in writing.

The *word cluster* below is an example of one method for getting ideas on paper. It also "clusters" a variety of prewriting strategies.

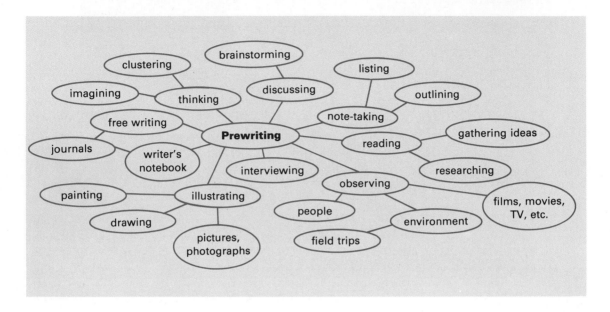

Think and Discuss

1. Which prewriting methods in the word cluster above have you used? Which methods have helped you the most to get started in writing?

2. How might your prewriting methods differ for a character description than for a news article about the same person? For a research report than for a short story?

Making a Word Cluster

Clustering is a prewriting method of discovering ideas to write about by grouping words into clusters.

To begin a *word cluster*, take a blank sheet of paper and, in the middle of it, write your subject. Then think of ideas associated with the subject, and write those ideas around it. Connect words and phrases to the subject and to each other if they are related. As you can see in the model word cluster on the next page, related ideas begin to form branches or word groups within the cluster.

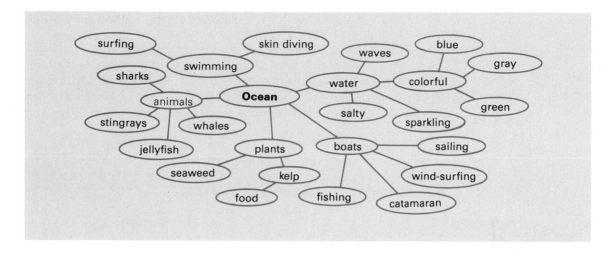

Clustering can help you organize your ideas and narrow your topic for writing. For instance, suppose you want to write a composition about the ocean. Whole books could be written about the ocean; the problem is to find a narrower focus for your composition. Clustering can help. Notice how the branches in the word cluster above lead in several different directions. You could write a composition about any one of the branches in the word cluster. You might want to write about sailing, about sharks, or about ocean plants we can eat. The word cluster offers many directions for writing.

Writing Practice 1: *Clustering Ideas*

Make a word cluster for your high school. Write the name of your school in the middle of a sheet of paper. Then, around it, write any ideas or thoughts you associate with your school. Connect related words and phrases. Then select one branch of your word cluster and write a paragraph about it. For example, you might want to write about your gymnasium, the homework policy, your favorite teacher, or your first day as a freshman. The possibilities for topics are unlimited.

Brainstorming

Brainstorming means producing as many ideas as you can about a subject.

Brainstorming is somewhat like clustering in that you associate words and ideas around a central subject; however, in brainstorming, there is no set pattern for writing your ideas. Usually, ideas you brainstorm are listed or jotted down as notes.

The best way to brainstorm is with a group of people. Record all suggestions, no matter how wild, without judging them; sometimes the most outrageous idea may spark a more sensible one. During the brainstorming session, the group discovers what each member can contribute. These collective ideas may generate new knowledge and new directions for writing.

Suppose, for instance, that you are a member of a school newspaper staff. Your committee needs to come up with a new name for the paper. As a group, you decide to brainstorm a list of names. Your list might look something like this:

1. The Rambler
2. Daily Dribble
3. Signals
4. The Crusader
5. Teen Times

6. The Spectator
7. Gazette
8. The Patriot
9. Quad News
10. High School Herald

From this list, your group might select a title; or you could use parts of titles to make up a new one. For instance, the committee might combine parts of titles from examples 5 and 8 and come up with "The Patriot Times."

Another kind of brainstorming, one that can be done alone, involves listing details about a subject and then making connections between items in the list. Suppose you want to write a description of a person you know. You can get started by making a list, following no particular order:

Jenny

Has brown hair
Is learning to bowl
Walks two miles to school each day
Prefers dancing to studying
Speaks with a soft, Southern accent
Plans to become a veterinarian

These are basic details, and you need to expand them if you want to make Jenny as interesting to your reader as she is to you. To do this, let your mind make some further associations with each item in your list. Perhaps Jenny's brown hair makes you think of other things that are brown, such as coffee with just a little milk in it. Jenny's learning to bowl may remind you of a funny incident involving Jenny at the bowling alley. The fact that she walks two miles to school each day may make you think of her health in general, her athletic ability, her pastimes, her fondness for the outdoors, and so

on. Later, you can organize your associations and use them in your description.

Brainstorming works best when you let your thoughts flow freely, without any particular design or pattern to them. As you brainstorm, you will probably find that you know much more than you thought about your subject. You may also find that there are things you need to research in order to write a complete report, description, or story.

Writing Assignment I: *A Character Description*

A. Prewriting

Brainstorming Ideas: Form a group of four or five students and select one member to record the ideas you share. As a group, brainstorm a list of people whom you all know. You may want to include some of the following subjects.

1. A movie or TV star
2. A singer or musician
3. A figure from history
4. An athlete

5. A local or national politician
6. An author
7. An artist
8. A character from a book

Together, select one person or character from your list. Then brainstorm any ideas or thoughts that you associate with this person. Include information related to physical features, personality traits, habits, talents, activities, likes and dislikes, and so on. After each member has contributed as many ideas as possible (in five minutes or less), the recorder should read the list of ideas to see how thoroughly you have covered your subject.

B. Writing

A Descriptive Paragraph: Using some of the ideas from the list, each group member should write a paragraph describing the subject. It is not necessary to include all the ideas that were brainstormed. Rather, focus on one particular aspect of the subject, such as his or her talents, athletic ability, disposition, personality, or contributions to society.

C. Postwriting

Sharing Your Writing: When all members have completed their paragraphs, share your compositions in small groups. Note similarities and differences in style and content if members of the group wrote about the same subject.

The Who? What? When? Where? Why?How? System

For information on interrogative pronouns and adverbs, see pages 328, 391, 416-417.

A simple system for gathering information asks six basic questions: *who? what? when? where? why? how?*

Imagine that you have just witnessed an awards ceremony at your school and have been asked to report the event for your school paper. Since you were present during the ceremony, you should be able to put the story together, but as you begin to write, you discover that you cannot remember many details. The six basic questions can help you recall details of people, events, and circumstances.

Who? *Who* were the students involved in the ceremony?
What were their names?
(If you did not know their names, how would you find out?)
Who conducted the ceremony?
Who were the speakers?

What? *What* took place during the ceremony?
What were the awards?

When? *When* did the ceremony take place?
What time of day, day of the week, year was it?
In what order did the events take place?

Where? *Where* did the ceremony take place?
(Think of details to describe the setting accurately.)
As parts of the ceremony took place, *where* were the students receiving the awards, the speakers, the band, the audience?

Why? *Why* did the ceremony occur?
(What had the students done to earn the awards?)
Why did some of the students cry when they received their awards?

How? *How* was the ceremony conducted? In what manner or spirit did it take place?
How were the awards distributed?

Writing Practice 2: *Six Basic Questions*

Looking back over the past year, think of an important event at school that had special meaning for you. Perhaps you remember a ceremony, a game that your team won, your first high school dance, or a speech that you gave. Select a subject that you can clearly recall. Using the *who? what? when? where? why?* and *how?* system, make a list of questions associated with the event. Think of as many specific details as you can in listing your questions. Save your list of questions for the next Writing Practice.

Free Writing

Free writing **is a method for getting your ideas on paper as quickly as they come to you.**

When you write freely, you relax; observations and memories flood your mind, and you let them flow onto paper, not worrying about grammar, punctuation, or spelling. You write all ideas that come to you, without evaluating or even glancing back over your writing until the end of the free writing session.

Model: *Free Writing About an Important Event*

In the following model, Angie did some free writing about an event that changed her life—having to wear a back brace. Through writing, she remembered how she felt about the day that changed her life.

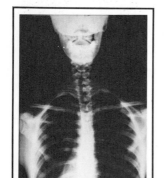

As soon as my mom and I walked into the doctor's office, the nurse told me to put on a gown for my X-ray.

Fifteen minutes later, the doctor clipped the X-rays to a board and measured the degree of curve in my spine. Then came the bad news. "When the curve gets this bad, we have to do something about it." I tried not to hear the doctor's words. My face was pale and I was holding back tears because I knew what he was going to say next. "The best choice is a Milwaukee brace." I just couldn't help it. I broke into tears.

The doctor left the room and my mom tried to calm me down. To me, it was the end of the world. I imagined looking terrible, my friends leaving me, feeling isolated. But the doctor introduced me to a girl in the next room who had been wearing the brace for six months. She told me she was able to do everything. That helped. Still, the whole experience was a nightmare.

Writing Practice 3: *Free Writing*

In Writing Practice 2, you wrote a series of questions about an important school event. Read over your questions again and try to recall the event. Imagine the scene, *where* the event occurred, *who* was there, *when* it took place, *what* happened, and *how* you felt at the time. Then let your thoughts flow onto paper by free writing about the event. Save your free writing for the next Writing Practice.

Purpose and Audience

The phone rings. You answer it. A friend wants to go jogging. You quickly jot a note:

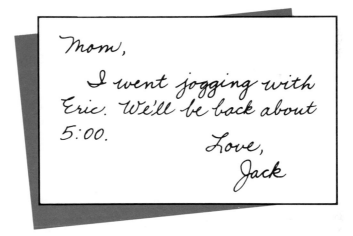

Mom,

I went jogging with Eric. We'll be back about 5:00.

Love,
Jack

The purpose for your note is simple—to *inform* your mother of where you went and when you will be home. You wrote the note to an audience of one—your mother.

Effective writing reveals awareness of purpose and audience.

Purpose **in the context of writing is your reason for writing.** *Audience* **is the person or persons to whom you write.**

A writer's purpose, whether it be to inform, explain, describe, entertain, or persuade, guides what the writer does during all stages of the writing process. For example, purpose directs what kind of prewriting is necessary. Whereas a word cluster might be useful in writing a descriptive paragraph, notes or an outline would be more helpful in writing a research report.

Once you have established your purpose for writing, you will need to consider your audience—those to whom you are writing. If you were running for student body president, you probably would prepare your campaign speech very carefully: you would direct your language to the students at your school, gear the issues in your platform to meet their needs, and anticipate questions they might ask. Like speakers, writers also must be sensitive to the needs of their audience. They must consider who is most likely to read what they write, and then anticipate the readers' background and knowledge of the subject. The audience will determine the kind of language the writer uses. Abstract or complex language is appropriate for older, educated readers. Short, simple words and sentences are appropriate for younger readers. Details and examples should also be chosen with your audience in mind.

In this book, you will write for various purposes and for a variety of audiences. Sometimes you will write for your peers and classmates and share your compositions in student response groups. Sometimes you will write for yourself alone.

Writing Practice 4: *Changing Purpose and Audience*

In Writing Practice 3 you did some free writing about an event that was important to you. Using the same topic, complete the following two exercises.

1. Write a letter to a friend describing the event and telling why it was important to you.

2. Write a brief article about the same event as if it were to be published in the school newspaper. In the article, include essential facts and details, leaving out most of your personal feelings and responses.

Kinds of Writing

Think back to your early years when you first held a pencil or crayon in your hand. Do you remember writing on the walls, marking up your sister's or brother's homework, or scribbling in the pages of a book? It is human nature to experiment by making your mark. You may have observed the delight in the face of a young child drawing, experimenting with colors, shapes, and forms. Good writers and artists continue to play with language by experimenting with ideas and expressing these ideas in creative ways.

Writing is a process of discovery. You can't know what the product will be like until the last word is written. Sometimes you may think a piece of writing is going in one direction, only to discover that it leads elsewhere. It often takes time to discover what you know and how to express it. Like the child experimenting with colors, you can experiment with words by writing in different ways.

There are many different kinds of writing that you use every day. You might jot a note to your parents, write a letter to a friend, make a list of things you need, fill out a form for a bike race, take notes for a reading assignment, or write a report for one of your classes at school. Most of the writing you do falls into four basic categories—*description, narration, exposition,* and *persuasion.* Whenever you describe the characteristics of a person, place, or thing, you are using description. If you tell your friends about the fun you had on a trip to the mountains, you are narrating or telling a story. You would also use narration to write a short story, based on either fact or fiction or a combination of the two. Exposition involves writing to inform or explain. Expository writing presents information, explaining through the use of facts, ideas, or examples. Persuasive writing involves getting readers to agree with your opinions. You may recall a time when you wanted to do something, but your parents refused to let you. As a result you tried to persuade them to change their minds.

Most of the writing you will do throughout this book will involve varying combinations of these four kinds of writing. In the chapters that follow, you will learn how to select the kind of writing that best suits your purpose and your audience. For example, if you recently visited Washington, D.C., our nation's capital, you could write about your experiences in any of the ways noted on the next page.

Kind of Writing	Purpose	Audience
a letter	to inform and entertain	a friend
a composition telling about your trip	to express ideas and narrate experiences	your classmates
a paragraph describing the Capitol building	to describe	your English teacher
an essay on the House and the Senate	to explain by comparison/contrast	your social science teacher
a short story based on your experiences	to narrate and entertain	your readers (peers, parents, friends, etc.)
an editorial for the school newspaper	to explain an opinion	the student body
a letter concerning a political issue of importance to you	to persuade	your congressman

Writing Practice 5: *Identifying Kinds of Writing*

Look through newspapers, magazines, and books to find examples of each of the four kinds of writing—description, narration, exposition, and persuasion. Examples you select may include a combination of these four kinds. Use the following suggestions in locating your examples. Select one example and share it with your classmates.

1.   Find an example of description in the travel section of your newspaper or in a story from a book or magazine.

2.   Look for narration in your favorite story.

3.   Locate exposition in an encyclopedia or textbook about a subject that interests you.

4.   Find an advertisement or an editorial in a newspaper for your persuasive example.

Writing Practice 6: *Selecting a Kind of Writing*

Think about a special place where you have been. Perhaps you have visited another city or a place of interest in your community, such as a park, sports arena, theater, or museum. Choose one of the following exercises and write a paragraph about your experiences. Save your paragraph for the next writing assignment.

1. A paragraph *describing* the place.

2. A paragraph *telling* about your visit.

3. A paragraph *informing* your readers about something you learned from your visit.

4. A paragraph *persuading* someone else to visit the same place.

Postwriting

S uppose you were going to wash the family car. First, you would gather your materials, including soap, water, and a sponge or washcloth. Then you would wash the car. Afterwards, you might pay particular attention to the details of shining the chrome and wiping the water spots off the windows. If the surface of the car still appeared dull, you would probably want to polish it. Polishing and waxing a car can be hard work and take time, so you might enlist the help of friends or family members. Finally, after the scrubbing and polishing, the product of your hard work would glisten with cleanliness.

You might compare the process of writing to washing a car. Prewriting includes gathering ideas and information in the same way

you collect your materials to wash the car. Writing the first draft is the actual washing and scrubbing part of the process—the "getting-it-down" part of writing. The postwriting stage involves standing back and looking objectively at the writing product to see how it can be polished. It means wiping away the streaks and flaws. It means paying attention to detail, clarifying language, and adding ideas and information. The result of the polishing is the pride of creating a product to be shared and admired by others.

Revising

Revising is an important part of postwriting. The word *revision* means "to see again." Revising a composition involves seeing it again by rereading it, and then making the necessary changes to improve it.

During the revision process, you stand back and objectively consider the expression of your ideas from the reader's point of view. You must anticipate what the reader knows, fill in gaps of information, and add details that will help the reader understand the contents. You must also consider the use of language and decide whether it will be clear to the audience.

Revision includes more than making surface changes in spelling or mechanics. You may automatically make corrections as you write. But the main focus for revising a draft should be on contents—on the expression of ideas, the organization of information, and the clarity of language. The changes you make depend on these factors.

Most good writers and authors experiment with ideas on paper; they may revise and rewrite a draft several times until they are satisfied with the final product. As they write, they will cross out words and phrases, rewrite sentences and paragraphs, rearrange information, add new details, select better words, and so on. In other words, a writer will rethink an original draft by reshaping and reworking it until the words accurately express his or her thoughts.

Because revision is the messy stage of writing, you will find it helpful to use the following editing marks in making changes. These marks will guide you in rewriting your final draft.

Editing Marks

═	use a capital letter
/	use a lower-case letter
⊙	add a period
⋀	add a comma
ᕠ	add quotation marks
⋀	add something
ℓ	remove or delete something
⟲	move a section
⁋	indent a paragraph
⬭	spell correctly

Model: A Revised Composition

The following composition is a first draft that the writer revised using editing marks. Read the composition and note how the writer made changes to improve the draft. Then read the final draft.

17

¹ ~~As I looked back to~~ the day ~~when~~ I learned to swim ~~it was pretty special~~, ^to me ² I was ⑪ (eleven) years old then and the only one at school who couldn't swim ~~because~~ I was scared to death of water. ³ ~~It was~~ that summer ~~that~~ my dad decided to teach me to swim, ^in our neighbor's pool⊙ ⁴ ~~Luckily that year I had just met someone who had a swimming pool who became my best friend.~~ ⁵ ~~My parents were really good friends with them.~~ ⁶ ~~So one day we went over there.~~ ^After he coaxed me into the pool, ⁷ At first he told me to put my face under the water. ⁸ Then, he had me kick my legs⊃ as I held on to the side. ⁹ Finally, he made me ~~let go and~~ go around in circles kicking while he held my stomach. ¹⁰ ~~He led me~~ ^We went out farther and farther. ¹¹ When we ~~were at the~~ ^reached 5 ft (five foot) mark, he let go. ¹² I ~~paneked~~ ^panicked and went under. ¹³ ^As he pulled me up, Everyone watching laughed! ¹⁴ All day long I kept practicing. ¹⁵ Their laughter was ~~humileating~~ ^humiliating and made me determined to learn to swim. ¹⁶ ~~Finally~~ ^By evening, I had the courage to swim by myself. ¹⁷ That day ~~was so scary for me.~~

¹⁸ ~~But it really~~ taught me an important lesson, ¹⁹ A lesson I had to learn by myself. ²⁰ You can ~~acomplish~~ ^accomplish anything if you believe in yourself.

Overcoming a Fear

The day I learned to swim was special to me. I was eleven years old then and the only one at school who couldn't swim. I was scared to death of water. That summer my dad decided to teach me to swim in our neighbor's pool.

After he coaxed me into the pool, he told me to put my face under the water. Then, as I held on to the side, he had me kick my legs. Finally, he made me go around in circles kicking while he held my stomach. We went out farther and farther. When we reached the five foot mark, he let go! I panicked and went under. As he pulled me up, everyone watching laughed! Their laughter was humiliating and made me determined to learn to swim.

All day long I kept practicing. By evening, I had the courage to swim by myself. That day taught me an important lesson, a lesson I had to learn by myself: you can accomplish anything if you believe in yourself.

Think and Discuss

1. Look back at the rough draft and reread sentences 1 and 2 only. Compare these two sentences with the first three sentences in the revised draft. What changes in words and sentences did the writer make? How do these changes improve the introduction?

2. The writer divided the second long sentence into two shorter ones. How does this change show a greater use of sentence variety and sentence lengths?

3. Reread sentences 4, 5, and 6 in the rough draft. Do you find this information in the revised draft? Why do you think the writer chose to omit these sentences? What important piece of information from the omitted sentences was added to sentence 3?

4. The phrase, "After he coaxed me into the pool," was added to sentence 7. How does this addition give the reader a better picture of what was happening.

5. In sentence 8, the writer uses the transitional word *then* to connect ideas in sentences 7 and 8. Find three other transitional words and phrases the writer uses to link sentences and ideas. What are they, and how do they help connect ideas?

6. At sentence 14, the writer made two important changes. What are they? How do these changes show a shift in the writer's attitude about learning to swim as well as a change in time reference? How are they reflected in the organization of the composition?

7. The writer concludes the draft, beginning with sentence 17 and ending with sentence 20. Find a sentence fragment in this group of sentences. What simple change does the writer make to correct the error? How does the writer's use of the colon help to connect ideas in the conclusion and give emphasis to the theme or lesson of the composition?

Using a Checklist for Revision

Revision is essentially a process of asking questions about a piece of writing. The questions you ask should reflect your own personal standards for writing, the needs of your audience, and basic criteria for good writing. These questions will also vary, depending on the nature of each writing assignment. For example, a particular writing assignment might require you to describe an activity using strong action verbs. As you reread and revise your composition, you should ask yourself if you have used active verbs throughout. If not, you should substitute better verb choices.

The following checklist is one that you can use to revise any composition. More specific checklist questions are included after certain writing assignments throughout this text. This checklist also appears at the back of the book for easy reference.

Checklist for Revision

1. Did I express my ideas in a clear and interesting way?

2. Should I add new details, examples, or information?

3. Can I omit or leave out unnecessary details?

4. Is the content organized clearly?

5. Does each paragraph include a main idea with supporting sentences that develop this idea?

6. Have I used a variety of sentence patterns and lengths?

7. Are my sentences clear and complete?

8. Did I link sentences and ideas by using transitional words and phrases?

9. Are there better word choices I can make (concrete nouns, descriptive adjectives, and active verbs)?

10. Does the style of my writing reflect my own ideas?

11. Does my writing form a circle by showing a relationship between the introduction, the body of the composition, and the concluding statement?

12. Am I satisfied with my writing?

See the Proofreader's Checklist on page 23 for questions concerning grammar, mechanics, and spelling.

Writing Practice 7: *Revising a Composition*

Use the preceding checklist to revise the paragraph you wrote in Writing Practice 6 about a special place. Use editing marks to make changes in content, organization, and language. Save your revised paragraph for a later Writing Practice when you will make final corrections in grammar, mechanics, and spelling.

Student Response Groups

Because you must consider the knowledge and needs of your audience when revising a composition, you may find it helpful to involve other readers in the revision itself. There are several ways to acquire audience response. You can work with an "editing partner"—a classmate, parent, friend, or teacher. If you work with a classmate, you can exchange papers or read your compositions aloud. The two of you can help each other revise and improve your rough drafts. You can also work with a small group of classmates (usually three to five people) in a student response group. The larger group increases your audience and gives you a wider range of responses for revision.

Whatever the size of the group, it is important to use consideration when working with others. You need to be sensitive to the feelings of others when responding to their writing. Follow these guidelines when working in student response groups.

Student Response Guide

1. **Be positive:** First, look for and comment on the positive features of a composition.

2. **Be polite:** Make helpful and constructive suggestions; ask considerate questions if something is unclear.

3. **Be specific:** Select one or two areas that need improvement and make specific suggestions to help the writer make changes.

Writing Practice 8: *Responding and Revising*

Form a student response group or work with an editing partner to read and revise the composition you wrote in Writing Practice 6. Follow the standards in the Student Response Guide. As a group, refer to the Checklist for Revision on page 20 to evaluate one another's compositions.

Proofreading

Proofreading **is the final act of making corrections in sentence structure, grammar, mechanics (punctuation and capitalization), and spelling.**

You will probably make corrections as you write and revise. However, new errors may occur as you change parts of the original draft, making it necessary to proofread your final draft after all other changes have been made. It is also wise to proofread your final copy since errors can occur during recopying.

Refer to the following checklist when proofreading a composition. This checklist can also be found at the back of the book.

Proofreader's Checklist

1. Have I indented each paragraph?

2. Did I use capital letters where they were needed?

3. Did I punctuate each sentence correctly?

4. Have I corrected any sentence fragments or incomplete sentences?

5. Do related verbs, nouns, or pronouns in each sentence show agreement in kind and number?

6. Are all words spelled correctly?

7. Can my writing be read easily?

Writing Practice 9: *Proofreading a Paragraph*

Proofread the composition you wrote and revised in the last few Writing Practices. Make the necessary corrections in sentence structure, grammar, mechanics, and spelling using the preceding Proofreader's Checklist. You may also want an "editing partner," either a classmate, parent, or friend, to proofread your composition as well.

Sentence Combining:
Using Connectors

Achieving Sentence Variety

Perhaps you have heard the expression "Variety is the spice of life." This means that without variety, life would become dull and boring. Human beings seem to need variety for amusement and stimulation. This need is reflected in our language. For instance, you may have heard a speaker who spoke in a monotone voice, whose speech was dull and predictable, and who reflected no enthusiasm for what he or she was saying. Your reaction? Boredom. Disinterest. Fade out! In contrast, you may have heard another speaker who aroused your attention by exhibiting enthusiasm and using interesting, clear, and appropriate language; he or she did not repeat the same old, lifeless ideas and clichés.

As in speech, the language you use in your writing needs to have spark and individuality. One way you can bring life to your writing is by adding a dash of sentence variety. Because sentences are the core of the English language, you need to know how to use them effectively. You can manipulate sentences in a variety of ways to fulfill your purpose for writing and to communicate your message to your reader.

Throughout this book, you will find sections entitled *Sentence Combining*. These sections will provide experience in writing a variety of sentence patterns.

Using Connectors to Join Sentences

For information on conjunctions, see pages 458-467.

Several words in the English language make effective connections between two sentences of equal importance. The first group of connecting words is *and, but, or, for, yet, so,* and *nor.* Study the following models to see how two sentences have been joined into one through the use of these connectors.

Sentences: Dad fixed the hot water heater.
I repaired the faucet. (*and*)

Combined: Dad fixed the hot water heater, *and* I repaired the faucet.

Sentences: The movie is interesting.
I may have to leave early. (*but*)

Combined: The movie is interesting, *but* I may have to leave early.

Sentences: Al will have to open the gate.
We cannot drive into the park. (*or*)

Combined: Al will have to open the gate, *or* we cannot drive into the park.

The word in parentheses, called a *signal*, is the connector that you should use.

Unless the combined sentences are closely related and very short, place a comma before the connector in the combined sentence.

The three men in that boat caught seven fish, *for* they remembered to bring the right bait.

Nor follows the same pattern as the other connecting words, but it causes a change in word order. In addition, since *nor* means "not," the word *not* in the second sentence is removed:

Sentences: Susan had not finished her homework.
She had not completed the list of jobs her uncle had asked her to do. (*nor*)

Combined: Susan had not finished her homework, *nor* had she completed the list of jobs her uncle had asked her to do.

25

Another kind of connection between sentences of equal importance can be made by using a *pair of connecting words*, such as *either . . . or*.

Sentences: Those are Holland bulbs.
I never saw tulips before. (*either . . . or*)

Combined: *Either* those are Holland bulbs, *or* I never saw tulips before.

When joining sentences with *either . . . or*, place a comma before the *or* in the combined sentence.

Exercise 1: *Joining Sentences*

The following sets of sentences can be joined with one of the sentence connectors in this lesson. In some cases you are given a connecting word in parentheses; for the other sentences use the connector that you think makes the most sense. After studying the examples, join the sets of sentences, writing the new sentences on a sheet of paper.

Examples

a. The starter gave the signal to begin.
The horses were off. (*and*)
The starter gave the signal to begin, and the horses were off.

b. The attorney spoke very quietly and politely.
The witness was frightened anyway. (*but*)
The attorney spoke very quietly and politely, but the witness was frightened anyway.

1. The grapes were ripening in the fields.
The leaves were turning reddish brown. (*and*)

2. The curtains flapped noisily in the wind.
I had left the window open. (*for*)

3. Jane looked behind every stick of furniture.
She could not find the missing button. (*but*)

4. Medicine bottles should be labeled.
People can tell what is in them. (*so*)

5. You leave this room right now.
I'll throw you out. (*either . . . or*)

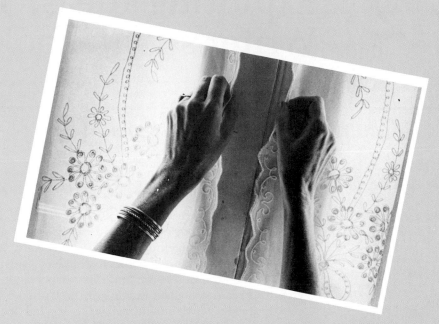

6. Early settlers along the Maine coast suffered from the harsh winters.
   They never lost their spirit.

7. Robert rubbed his eyes with both hands.
   He could not believe what he saw.

8. Hannibal had no other way to move against Rome with his army.
   He crossed the Alps on elephants.

9. Marsha was never very well known outside her hometown.
   We thought of her as our most outstanding citizen.

10. The old Dalmatian dog dozed in the sun.
    The yellow cur known as Butter scratched noisily at the kitchen door.

Writing Practice:*"Variety Is the Spice of Life"*

Think about the expression, "Variety is the spice of life." Write a paragraph that explains what this expression means to you. When you have finished writing, go back over your paragraph and look for ways to combine sentences, perhaps using some of the connectors in this lesson. Vary your sentences by beginning them in different ways. Also vary the length of your sentences, making some short and others longer.

2 Exploring Ideas: The Writer's Notebook

Keeping a Writer's Notebook

A *Writer's Notebook* is a personal record of ideas, observations, words, responses, events, dreams, and insights.

Some writers keep journals just for themselves; they do not expect anyone else to read this writing and so record private thoughts and feelings they do not want to share. Other writers, however, keep notebooks for readers. Most Presidents, for example, have kept notebooks and the notebooks of the first settlers to cross the prairies and mountains of the United States have given readers interesting insights into what life was like for these pioneers.

Your Writer's Notebook can be like a scrapbook; you will use it to save things of importance to you. You may record ideas, words, poems, possible writing topics, or anything you think you might use for future writing assignments. You can also use it for spontaneous or free writing. Periodically, you might want to share an entry from your notebook with others, so do not record private thoughts or feelings.

Writing About Your World

When writing in your Writer's Notebook, you write about a subject you know better than anyone else in the world: yourself—what happens to you and what you feel.

Each of us has many experiences every day to write about. Think of your Writer's Notebook as an idea bank where you deposit only those experiences and ideas that are important to you. Besides describing the experiences, you can also explain how and why they seem meaningful to you.

Model: A Writer's Notebook Entry

In the entry on the following page, the writer records an experience and explores its meaning.

On my way to school today, I stopped to watch two little kids playing in a mud puddle. One of them would fall face down in the mud, get up laughing, and then shove the other one in. Every inch of those kids, including their hair, was covered with black, oozy mud. They might be in trouble when they got home, but right then all they cared about was that mud puddle. I thought about all the puddles I used to play in, and for a few seconds I was tempted to join those kids. I didn't, but I haven't stopped thinking about them. Maybe I'm just a kid at heart.

Think and Discuss

1. What details does the writer use to describe the children?

2. Why was this experience important to the writer?

Writing Practice 1: *A Writer's Notebook Entry*

In your Writer's Notebook make a list of your activities on a recent day and circle the one event, feeling, or thought that was most important to you. If you like, consider using one of the following eight suggestions.

1. a moment when you stopped to look closely at something—a tree, the sky, a person—that you had looked at only casually before

2.   an experience that helped you better understand yourself or others

3.   a moment when you felt you really communicated with another person

4.   an important decision you made during the day

5.   a moment when you thought about what you would like to do in the future

6.   a story, poem, or play that impressed you and made you think or feel a certain way

7.   a television or radio program that gave you a new insight or understanding of something

8.   a funny or unusual person, thing, or event you observed

Think about the one event, feeling, or thought that you circled as most important from your list. Then write about it in your Notebook. Assume that you are describing it to your classmates. Include details that will make the situation come alive for them.

Using Specific Details in a Writer's Notebook

One reason for keeping a Writer's Notebook is to capture important moments in your life, much as a camera would capture them. Yet the Writer's Notebook is even better than a camera, since the camera records only things you can see, and most events in your life involve the other senses: taste, touch, hearing, and smell. For instance, think of an event you enjoyed recently, such as a picnic, a bicycle trip, or a walk in the city on a clear, cool autumn day. What sense experiences did you have? Was there some especially good food or drink? What did it taste like? If you took a walk through the city, you may remember the hard feel of concrete beneath your shoes, the sound of jump ropes slapping on the sidewalk, and the aroma of the hot dogs the vendor on the corner was selling.

You can also record your thoughts and feelings about the occasion in your Writer's Notebook. No camera can preserve as effectively as your words the feeling you had when you saw the Pacific Ocean or the Rocky Mountains for the first time or the feelings of excitement and nervousness on your first day of high school.

When you write a notebook entry for readers, part of your purpose is to share something of yourself with your audience. Using specific details to describe your thoughts can help you do this.

Model: *Using Specific Details in a Writer's Notebook*

Read the following account of a backpacking trip from Michael Parfit's ''The Road Less Traveled.'' As you read, look for details the writer uses to record the experience.

Tuesday morning. A beginning. Like a kid crying ''Salvation!'' I expect a miracle from the first steps, a sudden relief of worldly burdens the first time I turn a corner and cut away from the road. It never happens. I have put on the pack, 35 pounds, tied on Vibram-soled boots, crossed a small river called the Manzana, walked for an hour and a half and so far feel only continued restlessness, the urge to push faster than my new weight will let me, and, from a fold of sock, the start of a little pain. Perhaps it's like meditation, or tennis, the inner game: Ask too much of it and you lose it all, double-faulting into the wind. There's more release than grasp in the sport, and it all comes slowly, like the accumulating miles.

The trail winds along the Manzana, named after apple trees but lined with oaks. It is summer, the dry season in this part of the country, and the river is low and warm, making its way languidly from pool to pool, thick with algae the color of straw. There are small, hungry trout in these pools, and when I stop for a drink they gather around my immersed fingers and nibble at my nails and my ring. The sensation is strange, like being kissed by tiny people, and it creates a false but delightful feeling of communication.

I flip a white pebble in the pool and watch them fight over it, then share some crumbs of my "gorp," a mixture of nuts, raisins, granola and M&M's, which they devour like piranhas. Most of them, of course, will die as the river shrivels in the summer's heat, so there's no point in becoming too attached. Still, when the sun finally persuades me to remove my boots and swim in the pool, the little trout kiss my feet.

Later, drying on a rock, I study the "topo" map, a maze of contour lines speckled with interesting names: Cold Spring, Manzana Narrows, Big Cone Spruce Camp, White Ledge, Hurricane Deck, Sulphur Spring, Sweetwater Canyon, the Sisquoc River. The last holds more promise than just the ring of its Chumash Indian name: It is the heart of this wilderness, and so becomes my goal.

You begin a backpack determined to subvert normal, goal-oriented existence to the point of walking onward with nowhere to go, and then find that goals are necessary to keep you going. Without them, you'd sit down on a rock after a mile, pant, and eat all your gorp. So I find my devotion to reaching the Sisquoc grows as my body tires.

I am climbing, weaving back and forth up a slope covered with manzanita, the red-skinned savage bush, and dry grass, on which occasional scarlet buglers, small elongated wildflowers, blare silent messages to invisible bees. I had forgotten, as I always do, that the most intense experience of a backpack is its labor. I am not spending my day examining the sublime filigree of nature; I'm spending it in toil, sweat running down my back and in my eyes, watching only the dust of the trail a yard ahead, not for the detail of its diatomacious soil, but for loose obstacles.

But here is an interesting paradox. The longer I trudge, committing myself to the achievement of the Sisquoc, and the more

important the goal becomes to the maintenance of the hike, the less it really matters, except as a device, like a shoehorn to pry me out of laziness and get me moving. If I rest a minute, the desire to get there fidgets at my ankles, but once I'm up and hurting, it disappears in the intensity of the moment.[1]

Think and Discuss

1. In his description of backpacking, Michael Parfit uses specific details to record the experience. In the first paragraph, for example, he names the day of the week, describes his feeling when he begins, and gives the weight of his pack. What are some of the other specific details in Michael Parfit's account?

2. Throughout his account Michael Parfit is concerned with communicating to readers how it feels, both emotionally and physically, to backpack. In the first paragraph he mentions a slight pain beginning from a fold in a sock. What are some of the many other details of emotional and physical feelings the writer uses?

3. By recording his thoughts and feelings, Michael Parfit shares something of himself with his readers. You know, for example, that he begins his hike with a certain amount of impatience—he wants to experience a sense of freedom instantly. What else do you learn about the writer from this account?

Writing Assignment I: *Using Specific Details in a Notebook Entry*

A. Prewriting

Gathering Ideas for Writing: Think about an outdoor experience you have had. Perhaps you recall a simple experience such as walking with a friend, or fishing in a lake or river. Or go back to the event, feeling, or thought you wrote about in Writing Practice 1.

One way to recall the incident you have chosen is to imagine yourself in a dark movie theater. Suddenly your memorable experience flashes onto the screen. Relax for a few moments and relive the entire experience, perhaps closing your eyes to capture the sights, sounds, and feelings more completely. Keeping this memory in mind, ask yourself questions, such as the following ones, to gather as many specific details about the experience as you can. As you answer your questions, make notes in your Writer's Notebook.

1. Where were you? What made this location unique?

2. When did the experience occur? What was the time of day or the season?

3. What did you see, hear, smell, touch, or taste?

4. Who was involved? How did these people look? What were they wearing?

5. Exactly what happened? Why did it happen? How did it happen?

6. How did you react? Why did you feel this way?

Suppose, for example, that you have decided to write about a street carnival in your neighborhood last summer. Your list of details for the first two questions might look like the following ones.

1. Where were you? What made this location unique?

    at the Tenth Street summer carnival
    the street looked different without cars or trucks
    lots of small booths with gaudy banners of crepe paper

2. When did the experience occur? What time of day? What season of the year?

    hot, humid summer day
    just about sunset
    the carnival lights had just come on

Notice that each question asks *who? what? where? when? why?* or *how?* Using combinations of these six questions will help you probe your memory for the details that make writing vivid and realistic.

B. Writing

An Important Moment: Using your notes as an aid, develop a Writer's Notebook entry about your experience. Include vivid details about what you saw, heard, smelled, touched, or tasted. Write as though you are flashing an image of this event onto a movie screen for your reader.

C. Postwriting

Sharing an Experience: Read your entry to a classmate or to a small group of classmates. Share with each other how you were able to visualize or imagine certain features of your experiences through the use of words. Circle the specific details in your writing that your audience liked.

Observing Your World: Noting Sensory Details

You learn about the world around you through your five senses: sight, touch, taste, smell, and hearing.

Sensory details, **details you observe with your senses, have the same effect in writing that color does in painting: they make your writing more vivid.**

How well do you note sensory details? How would you describe a common object, such as an orange? If you said that it is about the size of a tennis ball, yellowish-red in color, and round, you would be using only your sense of sight and ignoring touch, taste, smell, and sound. Your description would be more complete if you thought of questions such as the following ones.

1.   How does the outside of an orange smell? How does the orange smell when it is cut open? When it is squeezed?

2.   If you put your ear close to the orange, what kind of sound do you hear when you squeeze it? What about the sound of an orange when you rub your thumb across the surface?

3.   How does the orange feel when you rub your fingers over the outside? What is its texture? What happens when you press your fingernail into the surface?

4.   How does the orange taste when you put your tongue on the outside? How does the white layer just below the surface taste? How does freshly squeezed orange juice taste?

Specific sensory details, when carefully selected, can focus readers' attention on parts of an experience a writer wants to emphasize. For example, in the following paragraph from Annie Dillard's book *Holy the Firm,* the writer describes how moths fly into the candle that she is using as a light for reading.

Model: Using Sensory Details in a Writer's Notebook

As you read, notice Annie Dillard's use of specific details. Where does she focus her readers' attention?

Moths kept flying into the candle. They would hiss and recoil, lost upside down in the shadows among my cooking pans. Or they would singe their wings and fall, and their hot wings, as if melted, would stick to the first thing they touched—a pan, a lid, a spoon—so that the snagged moths could flutter only in tiny arcs, unable to

struggle free. These I could release by a quick flip with a stick; in the morning I would find my cooking stuff gilded with torn flecks of moth wings, triangles of shiny dust here and there on the aluminum. So I read, and boiled water, and replenished candles, and read on.[1]

Think and Discuss

1. The focus in the preceding paragraph is on the plight of the moths as they fly into the candle. Annie Dillard achieves this focus by using sensory details to describe the moths' struggle. What specific details does she use for of the senses of sight, sound, and touch?

2. Notice that she does not describe the candle, her cooking pans, or the book she is reading. Why do you think she only describes the moths? How is her description similar to a camera focusing on the plight of the moths?

3. Turn back to Michael Parfit's account from "The Road Less Traveled" on pages 31–33. Skim over it again and note the sensory details he uses to give his reader a vicarious experience of his backpacking trip. Identify the specific words and phrases for each of the senses. How does his use of sensory detail compare with Annie Dillard's description of the moths?

4. The topics of Annie Dillard's description and Michael Parfit's account are different both in scope and purpose. How do these differences affect the focus of each piece?

[1]From *Holy the Firm* by Annie Dillard. Copyright © 1977 by Annie Dillard. Reprinted by permission of Harper & Row, Publishers, Inc., and Blanche C. Gregory, Inc.

Writing Assignment II: *Sensory Details in a Notebook Entry*

A. Prewriting

A Sensory Detail Chart: Imagine that you are a part of the photograph on page 37, perhaps shivering on a cold park bench beneath the tree. What is it in this scene that is most important to you—the tree, the birds, the building in the background, or perhaps your own feelings as you observe the scene? What sights, smells, tastes, sounds, and textures do you experience?

In your Writer's Notebook make a sensory detail chart by dividing the page into five columns. Label each column with one of the five senses—sights, smells, sounds, textures, tastes. Observe the photograph closely and try to imagine what sensory sensations you would experience if you were actually there. In the appropriate column list vivid sensory words and phrases that describe your reactions.

For example, if you were sitting in a small corner grocery store in your neighborhood, your chart might look like the following one.

Sights	*Smells*	*Sounds*	*Textures*	*Tastes*
Dark wooden door	Tangy aroma of fresh oranges	Tiny bell when front door opens	Feel of rough wood planks under bare feet	Bitter sourness of long dill pickles
Spots on the floor where varnish has worn away	The sweet-ness of soaps in the third aisle	Whirring of grocery cart wheels	Whiff of cold air when cooler opens	Tart apple cider
		Cash register		

Compare your list with those of your classmates.

Observing Your World: Think about a part of your world that you observed at a time when you were especially sensitive to your environment. Perhaps it was a fleeting experience such as Annie Dillard's observation of struggling moths by candlelight. Perhaps it was a walk in the snow as in the photograph. If possible, visit the spot you have chosen and list your sensory observations on a chart, as you did in the preceding assignment. Divide a page of your Notebook into five columns, labeling each column with one of the five senses. Then list the sensory details you observe. During your visit use *who? where? when? why?* and *how?* questions to gather specific details.

B. Writing

A Description Using Sensory Detail: In your Writer's Notebook, write a description to share with your teacher and classmates about a part of your world that you have observed closely. Include some of the specific sensory details from your sensory detail chart. Concentrate, however, on focusing your reader's attention on important parts of the experience. Incorporate as much sensory detail into your description as possible without losing the focus of your composition.

C. Postwriting

Noting Sensory Detail: Share your entry with a small group of classmates. Comment on one another's use of specific, sensory detail. Circle the details your audience liked in your writing. Insert new details that are needed. Have someone in your group summarize in his or her own words the focus of your description. See how closely this description matches your idea of the focus.

Making Comparisons

As you are noting details and recording them in your writing, you will probably write many comparisons, such as the following ones.

Like a small child on the night before a birthday, she waited impatiently for the long hours to pass.

With his quick, nervous ways and twitching nose, he resembled nothing so much as a giant rabbit.

The elderly man's voice creaked like footsteps on a bare, wooden floor.

Her touch was as strange and unexpected as that of a mouse brushing past in the dark.

Using Similes

A comparison using the words *like* or *as* is called a *simile*.

Writers often use similes to help their readers understand things that may not be familiar to them. A good simile often calls to mind a sight, sound, odor, taste, or texture. For example, you may not know much about a kiwi fruit, a teletype machine, or rattlesnake meat, but when you read the following similes, you have some idea of what these objects are like.

A kiwi fruit is like a fuzzy lime.

A teletype machine is like an electric typewriter operated by remote control.

Rattlesnake meat tastes like chicken.

To use similes well, you must be certain that the two things being compared have similar qualities. A kiwi fruit and a fuzzy lime share common characteristics of shape, color, and texture. Teletypes and typewriters are both machines that print out words. Rattlesnake meat and chicken have a similar taste.

Writing Practice 2: *Similes*

Choose five of the following items. Write two or three sentences describing each sensation. In each description include at least one simile.

1. The sight of a spider crossing a spiderweb
2. The sight of a tall, lighted building against the night sky
3. The color of an article of clothing you have on today
4. The sound of the bell at the end of a school day
5. The sounds you hear in the country or city at dawn
6. The texture of very fine hair when it is clean (or dirty)
7. The feel of spilled sugar on a kitchen floor under your feet
8. The taste of a cold drink on a scorching day
9. The smell of your favorite food cooking
10. The sound of a child crying at night

Using Metaphors

A *metaphor* is a direct comparison, made without *like* or *as*.

For example, the sentence "The stars are like candles of the night that flicker in the sky" is a simile, but the sentence "The candles of the night flicker in the sky" is a metaphor. The following is another example.

Simile: The Mississippi River is like the main artery of the United States. It winds its way from Minnesota to the Gulf of Mexico.

Metaphor: The main artery of the United States winds its way from Minnesota to the Gulf of Mexico.

Model: A Poem Using Metaphor and Simile

Metaphors are often used in daily conversation because they are an economical and colorful way to convey meaning. Poets often use metaphors because, like similes, they can create vivid images. What is the metaphor in the following poem? What is the simile?

The Courage That My Mother Had [1]

The courage that my mother had
Went with her, and is with her still:
Rock from New England quarried;
Now granite in a granite hill.

The golden brooch my mother wore
She left behind for me to wear;
I have no thing I treasure more:
Yet, it is something I could spare.

Oh, if instead she'd left to me
The thing she took into the grave!—
That courage like a rock, which she
Has no more need of, and I have.

—*Edna St. Vincent Millay*

As with similes, the things you compare in a metaphor must share characteristics. You can describe stars as candles because stars and candles both shine and appear to flicker. You can call a river an

---

[1] "The Courage That My Mother Had" from *Collected Poems* by Edna St. Vincent Millay. Copyright © 1954 by Norma Millay Ellis. Reprinted by permission of Norma Millay Ellis, Literary Executor.

artery because an artery carries blood to parts of the body, just as a river carries another vital fluid, water, to many parts of the country. What characteristic does the mother's courage in the preceding poem share with New England stone?

Good poets use metaphors to give a fresh insight into experience. For example, before reading ''The Courage That My Mother Had,'' you may not have imagined courage as a type of New England rock; now, however, you might have a new way of looking at that particular quality. When writing in your Writer's Notebook, use fresh comparisons that will give your readers this type of insight.

Writing Practice 3: *Metaphors*

Choose five items from the list in Writing Practice 2. Either rewrite some of your similes as metaphors, or write new metaphors from the list. Then choose one of your metaphors and develop it into a paragraph in your Writer's Notebook. Include the metaphor somewhere in your paragraph.

Free Writing

You can also use your Writer's Notebook for free writing.

Free writing **is a method for getting your ideas on paper as quickly as they come to you.**

Imagine an electrical circuit between your brain and your pencil, with continuous energy, in the form of ideas, flowing through the circuit. Attempt to capture these ideas on paper by continuously filling the page with words, phrases, and sentences, without stopping to make corrections.

Writing in this manner helps you discover your ideas and loosens you up for other types of writing. You can often use parts of your free writing for a more structured composition. For example, from your free writing, you might discover a focus for a specific writing topic.

Writing Practice 4: *Free Writing*

Reread the poem entitled "The Courage That My Mother Had." Respond to the word "courage" in your Writer's Notebook. Write any thoughts that come to mind about this word.

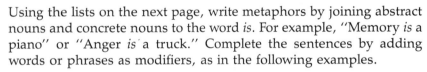

Developing Language

For more information on nouns, see pages 300-319.

You can use your Writer's Notebook to play with language.

The following language game is based on the nature of nouns. Some nouns are *concrete*, naming things that can be seen, touched, smelled, heard, or tasted—things that can be known through the senses (*tree*, the color *green*, the *aroma* of a pine tree). Other nouns are *abstract*, naming concepts or emotions (*democracy*, *square root*, *sadness*).

Writing Practice 5: *Concrete and Abstract Nouns*

Using the lists on the next page, write metaphors by joining abstract nouns and concrete nouns to the word *is*. For example, "Memory *is* a piano" or "Anger *is* a truck." Complete the sentences by adding words or phrases as modifiers, as in the following examples.

Memory is a piano, *keeping the thoughts of music in its keys.*

Anger is a truck, *filled with emotion and speeding out of control.*

Follow these rules to write metaphors.

a.   From the left-hand list choose six abstract nouns.

b.   Place the word *is* after each abstract noun.

c.   From the right-hand list choose six concrete nouns and place each one after an abstract noun and the verb *is*.

d.   Insert a comma after the concrete noun and write a modifier that you think gives some explanation of why the abstract noun *is* the concrete noun. Complete all six sentences in this manner.

43

Abstract Nouns	Concrete Nouns
anger	zebra
beauty	yellow
cleanliness	X-ray
death	waffle
error	village
falsehood	uncle
growth	truck
happiness	salt
injustice	rock
joy	quill
knowledge	piano
legality	orange
memory	nightingale
nature	mountain
opinion	leopard

"I found myself in a small room. Soundlessly the doors slid shut after me and a sequential series of numbers on the wall began to light up - one after another. Some sort of countdown, I figured, or perhaps a trick. I became aware of a faint whirring sound and got the weird feeling I was being taken for a ride. Yet I was standing still! A fist tightened inside my stomach and I felt sick. My ears began to pop like cheap gum. Pop! Pop pop pop! This case was beginning to take on bizarre proportions, all right."

Drawing by Ziegler; © 1975 by the New Yorker Magazine, Inc.

Writing From a Different Point of View

In the Jack Ziegler cartoon to the left, the character describes an elevator from an unusual point of view, which makes the elevator seem sinister and mysterious.

Describing a familiar object or event in an unusual light is one way to loosen up your style in your Writer's Notebook.

Writing Practice 6: *Point of View*

First, select an·object or event from the following list (or use one of your choice). Then decide how you want the object or event to seem—perhaps funny, sinister, ridiculous, sad, or deeply important. Finally, write a description in your Writer's Notebook of the object or event in such a way that it takes on that characteristic.

1. An escalator
2. A bicycle
3. A game of tennis or some other sport
4. A parade
5. A trip to the grocery store
6. A whispered conversation
7. A tree
8. A television being turned on

Writing Practice 7: *Traveling in Time*

A Writer's Notebook is a good place to explore your imagination. Suppose that you could live for one day as any character from history. You could be a famous explorer, scientist, writer, ruler, composer, diplomat, inventor, or performer; or you could choose to be someone whose name has been lost in history—a cavewoman, Phoenician sailor, child of Atlantis, or crusader. What character would you choose? Write an entry in your Writer's Notebook describing your day as this person, telling what the person observes in his or her world, as well as what the person does and thinks.

Writing Practice 8: *Explaining a Utopia*

You can explore ideas as well as imaginary worlds, in your Writer's Notebook. For example, many writers have been fascinated by the idea of *utopia*—a society perfect in every way. What in your opinion makes something perfect? You can think of a perfect school, family, friendship, society, country, or experience of any kind. Write an entry in your Writer's Notebook explaining your utopian subject.

Sentence Combining: Using Adverbs and the Semicolon

Adverbs That Connect Sentences

For more information on adverbs, see pages 414-435.

Another group of sentence connectors includes adverbs such as *however, therefore, instead, besides, furthermore, nevertheless, consequently, moreover, on the other hand, indeed,* and *in fact*.

The purpose of these adverbs is to show special kinds of relationships between two sentences. *However, instead, on the other hand,* and *nevertheless* show that one idea is followed by an opposite idea. *Therefore* and *consequently* suggest that a conclusion is being made. *Besides, furthermore,* and *moreover* signal that some additional point, idea, or detail will follow. *Indeed* and *in fact* help emphasize the writer's point.

These sentence connectors are more formal than *and, but,* and *or;* they require the use of a semicolon just in front of them and are usually followed by a comma.

Sentences:	The nurse hurried down the corridor. She was too late to stop the intruder. (*however*)
Combined:	The nurse hurried down the corridor; *however,* she was too late to stop the intruder.
Sentences:	Four ocean liners took up most of the harbor. The Coast Guard had to alert other incoming ships to anchor somewhere else. (*consequently*)
Combined:	Four ocean liners took up most of the harbor; *consequently,* the Coast Guard had to alert other incoming ships to anchor somewhere else.
Sentences:	Harry tried unsuccessfully to untie the rope around his ankles. There was no way he could do so. (*indeed*)
Combined:	Harry tried unsuccessfully to untie the rope around his ankles; *indeed,* there was no way he could do so.
Sentences:	Carlos and Rita wanted to travel by car to Ontario, Canada. They rented a car for the month. (*in fact*)
Combined:	Carlos and Rita wanted to travel by car to Ontario, Canada; *in fact* they rented a car for the month.

Exercise 1: Using Adverb Connectors to Join Sentences

On a sheet of paper, combine each of the following pairs of sentences with a semicolon and one of the adverb connectors (*however, therefore, instead, besides, furthermore, nevertheless, consequently, moreover, on the other hand, indeed,* and *in fact*). When signals are not given, use the connecting adverb that you think makes the most sense. Study the examples before you begin.

Examples

a. Behind him hoofs rang on the sharp stones.
    They pierced his eardrums with their intensity. (*in fact*)

    Behind him hoofs rang on the sharp stones; in fact, they pierced his eardrums with their intensity.

b. The experience was a wild nightmare of fright and pain.
    Sue Wong recovered more rapidly than one might think possible. (*however*)

    The experience was a wild nightmare of fright and pain; however, Sue Wong recovered more rapidly than one might think possible.

1. The site appeared to be too rocky for a safe landing.
    The control tower had to alter our course toward a better landing place. (*therefore*)

2. Joan wants to take ice-skating lessons next winter.
    She has to work this summer to make money. (*consequently*)

3. The grove of juniper down by the stream may live in spite of the fire.
    It may die quickly. (*on the other hand*)

4. Eduardo likes to paint, cook, and work at carpentry.
    He likes to teach others to do these things, too. (*moreover* or *in addition*)

5. My mother was always devoted to her job.
    She seldom took a vacation. (*indeed* or *in fact*)

6. It seemed foolish for Jason to make such a fuss.
    It wasn't going to matter to anyone else.

7. The path you want to take is grown over with weeds, thistles, and burrs. You should take the path down by the river.

8. Sweden and Norway are warm during the day in the summer

but chilly at night.
You should take a light sweater.

9. The tourists wanted to ride down the river in a canoe.
The tour guide urged them to take a motor launch.

10. The Berlin Wall was erected in the early 1960s.
It still divides East Berlin from West Berlin.

Using a Semicolon to Connect Sentences

For more information on semicolons, see pages 561-562.

A close relationship between two sentences can be shown by using a semicolon alone. The resulting sentence presents a nice balance between two equally important ideas:

Sentences: Mary was older than he.
She was wiser, too. (;)
Combined: Mary was older than he; she was wiser, too.

Sentences: The desks were arranged in careful order.
Not one was out of line. (;)
Combined: The desks were arranged in careful order; not one was out of line.

Exercise 2: Joining Sentences with Connectors or a Semicolon

For each of the following sentences, decide whether you want to join the two sentences by using a connecting word or a semicolon alone. Some of the sentences have signals to suggest how to make the connections; use your own sentence sense for the others. After studying the examples, write the combined sentences on a sheet of paper.

Examples

a. The cowhand at the chute pulled the bars and jumped for the fence.
Twenty ponies crashed through the opening and out into the night. (;)

The cowhand at the chute pulled the bars and jumped for the fence; twenty ponies crashed through the opening and out into the night.

    b. World Studios features tours of movie sets.
        Acme Studios lets visitors onto soundstages to see actors at work.

        World Studios features tours of movie sets; however, Acme Studios lets visitors onto sound stages to see actors at work.

1.   I enjoy reading poetry.
       Mystery novels entertain me more on a lazy summer afternoon. (*on the other hand*)

2.   Ann did not want to go to her recital.
       She had not rehearsed. (*for*)

3.   His plan to escape promised to be unworkable.
       He went ahead with it. (*nevertheless*)

4.   Shopping for gifts can be a trying experience.
       It can be great fun. (*on the other hand*)

5.   To be at peace with the world is wonderful.
       To be at peace with oneself is even greater. (;)

6.   A position in this company requires excellent qualifications for any job.
       Assembly line workers are underpaid.

7.   Helen MacInnes writes exciting adventure stories.
       Jessamyn West entertains with remembrances of the past.

8.   Colonel Tad Lawson, the American prosecutor, and Hans Rolfe, the German defense counsel, were important figures in the Nuremberg trials.
       Richard Widmark and Maximilian Schell played their parts in the movie *Judgment at Nuremberg*.

9.   Mr. Ward delivered a bitter tongue-lashing to the public.
       They voted for him in the next election.

10.   She pulled in behind the last car and turned off the motor to listen.
       There was not a sound.

Writing Practice: *Revising a Notebook Entry*

Look over the entries you have made in your Writer's Notebook. Select one entry that you think can be improved by sentence combining. Revise the entry using some of the sentence connectors you have learned about. Remember to vary both your sentence lengths and your sentence patterns. Rewrite the revised entry in your Writer's Notebook.

3 Developing Paragraphs

Building a Paragraph

A paragraph is a group of sentences that relate to the same topic or idea.

Just as sentences are the building blocks of paragraphs, paragraphs are the building blocks of larger compositions, reports, letters, and books. The purpose of a paragraph is to isolate one main idea and develop it with clarity.

A *topic sentence* is a single sentence that states the main idea of the paragraph. *Supporting sentences* develop the main idea of each paragraph through the use of details, facts, examples, and reasons.

Writers use paragraphs for many reasons. In written conversation, a new paragraph is begun whenever there is a change in speakers. In longer compositions and books, paragraphs help the reader make the transition from one idea to another. In expository writing, paragraphs separate one complete unit of thought from another. The paragraphs you will learn to write in this chapter include a main idea and a series of sentences that explain or develop that idea.

Unity in a Paragraph

If you have ever been a member of a team, you know that a team functions best when all the members work toward the same goal; in other words, they are unified. The same is true of paragraphs. A paragraph is clearer to the reader when all the sentences relate to the same topic; that is, when the paragraph is unified.

A reader can easily locate the main idea in a unified paragraph because every sentence in that paragraph supports or develops the central idea.

Model: *Paragraph Unity*

What is the main idea in the following paragraph?

Topic

Supporting Sentences

(1) SCUBA, self-contained underwater breathing apparatus, was invented in 1943 by two French navy divers, Jacques Cousteau and Emile Gagnan. (2) This invention was a watershed in undersea exploration, since divers were no longer tied to the surface by their air lines. (3) Also, because of the development of simple equipment, diving is no longer an expensive activity limited to professionals or military experts. (4) Divers now search the seas for scenes of beauty to photograph; such a frivolous use of diving time would not have been possible in pre-SCUBA days. (5) SCUBA gear is easy to learn to use, and there are now sport divers of all ages all over the world.

Think and Discuss

1. Which sentence states the topic of the paragraph?

2. How does the second sentence support the topic sentence?

3. What specific reasons do sentences 3–5 give for the importance of the invention?

In the entire paragraph there is no sentence that does not discuss SCUBA equipment, and after the second one there are no sentences that do not discuss the *importance* of SCUBA equipment.

Topic sentences do not always come at the beginning of a paragraph. Many paragraphs begin with details or illustrations and end with a topic sentence. Regardless of where the topic sentence comes in the paragraph, however, all details must develop the topic in a unified paragraph.

Writing Practice 1: *A Unified Paragraph*

The following paragraph is *not* unified because it contains details that do not develop the topic or that seem out of place. Rewrite the paragraph to make it unified. Delete or leave out sentences that are off the topic.

Have you ever thought about what hard work cooking is? Before you can even begin, you have to spend time planning meals and shopping. Most grocery stores today offer a great variety of products. Then the groceries have to be brought home, sorted, and put away. Many fruits and vegetables have to be washed and peeled before they can be cooked. Vegetables should not be cooked at too high a temperature because the vitamins will be destroyed. In addition, meats sometimes require special preparation, like tenderizing. When you finally get to actual cooking, you find that recipes are often difficult to follow. Then, frequently, in the middle of preparing a meal, you discover you are out of something and have to make a special trip to the store. Too frequent trips to the store are a drain on the country's energy resources. Another way to conserve energy is

to cook food in covered utensils. If all this isn't enough, there's all the cleaning up to do at the end. If the meal tastes good, though, it makes the work seem almost worthwhile.

Coherence in a Paragraph

Readers should be able to move easily from one point to another within the paragraph. When they can do this, the paragraph is *coherent*.

In a coherent paragraph details supporting the topic are arranged in some sort of *logical order;* that is, they are arranged the way they are for a reason. In a paragraph describing a person, place, or thing, details are often arranged as they appear in space (*spatial organization*). When you tell a story, you can use *chronological organization,* telling what happened first, then what happened after that. Chronological and spatial organization can also be used in an expository paragraph, as in the following instructions for inspecting a used car.

Model: Combining Chronological and Spatial Organization

Before buying a used car, you should inspect it carefully. Examine the engine first, for engine repairs can be costly and inconvenient. In checking the engine, look at the exhaust smoke. If it is blue, the piston rings may be worn. Check the dipstick also. Heavy oil is sometimes used to make a mechanically defective engine run more smoothly. After examining the engine, inspect the body. Look for dents, scrapes, and rusted metal. Any body-repair cost should be added to the selling price. Open and close the doors to determine if the body is aligned. The frame of a car that has been in a serious accident may be bent out of shape; if this is the case, the doors may not hang or shut properly. A close scrutiny of the interior may also reveal evidence of the kind of care the car has received. Inexpensive seat covers may hide torn upholstery and broken springs. Next consider the make and model of the car. Popular makes and models have a higher resale value. One more word of advice: if you know little about automobiles, take along a friend or a mechanic to advise you. Buying used cars involves some risk. If you want to get the most for your money in a used car, be alert and cautious.[1]

[1]From *From Thought to Theme*, Second Edition by William F. Smith and Raymond D. Liedlich. Reprinted by permission of Harcourt Brace Jovanovich, Inc.

Think and Discuss

1. What specific words in the paragraph signify chronological order? How does the importance of each detail relate to its position in the paragraph?

2. How does the writer use spatial organization in the paragraph? In what order are the parts of the car discussed?

Transitional Devices

The use of *transitional words and phrases* can also improve coherence. By showing relationships among ideas, these words act as bridges between parts of the paragraph.

The following examples are of transitional words and phrases and the relationships they sometimes show.

Relationship	Transitional Words and Phrases
Sequence or Time:	after, afterward, as soon as, at first, at last, before, before long, finally, first (second, third, etc.), in the first (etc.) place, in the meantime, later, meanwhile, next, soon, then
Addition:	also, and, another, besides, furthermore, in addition, likewise, moreover, other
Contrast:	but, even if, even so, however, despite, instead, nevertheless, on the contrary
Example:	for example, for this reason, that is
Result:	accordingly, as a result, consequently, for this reason, hence, therefore

Parts of a paragraph may be linked in other ways. *Pronouns* link words and sentences when they refer to a noun or an idea in another sentence.

John spends many hours working on *his* car. *It* is a hobby he truly enjoys.
[*His* refers to John. *It* refers to *working on his car.*]

Parts of a paragraph can be linked by *nouns* when they are repeated from one sentence to another.

The explorers encountered *difficulty* on the last part of their journey. This *difficulty* was the result of high winds and bitter cold.

Words and ideas can also be *rephrased* and *repeated* from one sentence to another.

Everyone in the class looked forward to the annual *class outing*. On this *yearly expedition* previous classes had gone to a large amusement park, a national forest, and the seashore.

Model: *Use of Transitions*

The following paragraph about the 1971 balloon flight of two men, Chauncey Dunn and Karl Stefan, shows how words and phrases can be used to link ideas in a coherent paragraph.

Then[1] suddenly the sunlight reappeared and I popped above the clouds. *The great expanse of whiteness*[2] looked as flat as an unused landing field. The 14,000 foot top of Longs Peak was the only sign of the earth that showed. *Then*[3] I noticed a jetliner two to three miles away flying east. The pilot's voice crackled over my radio and he identified himself as Japanese Airlines Flight 113. Was I still over Colorado? Because of my disorientation I really wondered where I was. *Soon*[4] the *aircraft*[5] was out of sight but *our*[6] conversation continued. *After*[7] questions of what a balloon was doing at 30,000 feet in jet territory and where a *JAL jet*[8] was going had been answered, weather information and congratulations ended our conversation. I was assured by *the pilot*[9] who was enroute to Chicago that I was in fact still over Colorado. *Then*[10] it was time to concentrate on the flight upward. [*superscripts and italics added.*]*

(1) transitional word

(2) *clouds* rephrased

(3) transitional word

(4) transitional word
(5) *jetliner* rephrased
(6) pronoun reference to author and pilot
(7) transitional word

(8) *Japanese Airlines Flight 113* rephrased

(9) noun repeated

(10) transitional word

*From *Ballooning* by Peter Dixon. Copyright © 1972 by Peter Dixon. Originally appeared in *Ballooning* magazine. Reprinted by permission of Peter Dixon.

Writing Practice 2: *Identifying Transitional Words and Phrases*

Reread the paragraph on page 53 about buying a used car. List all the transitional words and phrases you can find in the paragraph.

Developing Paragraphs with Details

One way to develop an expository paragraph is through the use of supporting *details*.

In descriptive writing, specific details used to describe a person, place, or object help the readers visualize what you describe. In expository writing, specific details can also help readers understand the information you explain.

When you explain how to do something, the specific details will be steps in a process. For example, the following paragraph is about hitting a forehand groundstroke in tennis. As you read, note the steps involved in this process.

Model: Explaining a Process

There are different ways to hit forehand groundstrokes in tennis. Any way is all right if you get the ball back over the net. It's all the better if you can return the ball consistently with some power and grace. Here is one way that is easy to learn and to use. Grip the racket as if you were "shaking hands" with it. As the ball comes toward you, twist your body (shoulders, hips, and arms) backwards in a natural movement. Keep your wrist fairly straight (bent neither up nor down). Lock your wrist in this position—don't let it move during your stroke. Keep your elbow comfortably straight. When the ball is at the top of its bounce (neither rising nor falling), uncoil your body forward naturally, your arm rising as you "come through" the ball. Contact the ball about in line with your toes or slightly ahead of them. Keep your eyes at the point of impact until the stroke is completed. Follow through by ending with your upper arm roughly parallel to the ground. All of this describes an "ideal" stroke. When you are actually on the court, don't think about how to stroke the ball. Let your body do it for you. Trust your body to find and use the most efficient, graceful, and accurate way.

Notice the specific details used to explain each step in the process of hitting a forehand groundstroke. The writer tells readers, for example, that you should "grip the racket as if you were 'shaking hands' with it." What other specific details does the writer use?

Writing Assignment I: *Explaining a Process*

A. Prewriting

Selecting a Topic: Think about the different kinds of things you know how to do well. Make a list of five or six items in your Writer's Notebook. Select one topic that you will explain to your classmates in an expository paragraph.

Organizing a Paragraph: Decide on the best order for explaining the process using either chronological or spatial organization or a combination of both. In your notebook list the steps in the order in which you want to write them.

B. Writing

How to Do Something: Using your list as a guide, write an expository paragraph that explains how to do something. Explain each step in the process, giving enough specific information for your readers to be able to repeat the process. Use transitional words and phrases to link sentences and ideas.

C. Postwriting

Clarifying the Process: Share your paragraph with a classmate. Ask your partner to repeat in his or her words the same process that you have explained in your composition. Make a note of those parts that are unclear to the reader. Then use the following checklist to revise your paper. After revising your paragraph share it with a larger group of classmates if possible.

Checklist for Revision

1. Does the topic sentence clearly state what process will be explained?

2. Did you include all the steps?

3. Are the steps logically organized?

4. Does each step include enough specific details and information for the reader?

5. Are there transitional words and phrases that link sentences and help the reader follow the steps?

Developing Paragraphs with Examples

Examples help support or explain a topic because they are specific. A science teacher may ask you to give an example of a mammal, and you will name a *specific* mammal, like a cat or dog. When you ask your parents to increase your allowance, you may give them examples of specific things you have done around the house, such as cleaning up your room or taking care of your younger sister, to support your point.

Expository paragraphs are often developed through the use of examples, which give specific information about a general topic.

Model: Development with Examples

As part of a Bicentennial project, students interviewed people from all over the United States and published the results in the book *I Wish I Could Give My Son a Wild Raccoon.* The following passage is an excerpt from an interview with a man named Charles Schroeder.

Topic
Supporting Sentences

I'd like to believe that an ordinary person like myself plays some part in the entire picture of American history. I'd like to believe that things I did as a youngster may be important and pass those on to others. If I could, I'd pass on how to make a frog gig and how to catch catfish in the river when it's beginning to rain, and how to make stink bait out of the lining of a cow's stomach.

Supporting Sentences

I wish I could pass on the sight of a group of desert bighorn sheep coming to graze near where I was camping a few years ago; the view of the desert fox, things that have since disappeared. I wish I

Supporting Sentences

could give my son a wild raccoon to teach him the joys of learning about animals. I'd like to give him that Christmas when I had only ninety-seven pennies to spend, and I bought my father a box of smoking tobacco and my mother a plaque of the Lord's Last Supper and I bought my sister some cheap perfume from the ten-cent store. I wish I could pass on to him a belief that what he's doing is important: an idea that the part of America that he grew up in will be just as important as the one I'm telling you about today. I wish I could pass all of that on to him, and to you.[1]

Topic

Think and Discuss

Charles Schroeder made a general statement: he would like to pass on to his children the things that were important to him when he was young. Then he gave specific examples of how to make a frog gig and how to catch catfish.

1. What are some other things Schroeder wanted to pass on?

2. In the beginning, Schroeder is speaking to a general audience; then he narrows his wishes to just one person. Who is this person?

3. How does the final sentence complete the piece in a personal way?

Writing Assignment II: *An Expository Paragraph with Examples*

A. Prewriting

Composing a Wish List: Make a list of things you would like to pass on either to a younger brother or sister, to someone you know, or to your own children someday. Include items that you have learned or experienced in some way. Go beyond material possessions.

B. Writing

Pass It On: Write an introductory paragraph that tells why you wish to pass on certain things to the specific person or persons you chose. Then write a second paragraph that includes examples of those things you wish to pass on. End with a final sentence that concludes the paragraph in a personal way.

---

[1]From *I Wish I Could Give My Son a Wild Raccoon* by Eliot Wigginton. Copyright © 1976 by Reading Is Fundamental. Reprinted by permission of Doubleday & Company, Inc.

C. Postwriting

Polishing a Final Draft: Read your draft to a partner or to a small group of classmates. Use the Checklist for Revision below to respond to one another's compositions. Make the necessary revisions and proofread your final draft using the Proofreader's Checklist at the back of the book.

Checklist for Revision

1. Does the first paragraph introduce the topic and identify the person to whom the composition is written?

2. Does the second paragraph include enough specific examples to develop the topic?

3. Does the composition conclude with a personal statement that finishes the piece effectively?

Developing Paragraphs with Reasons

I f someone asks you *why* you disliked a movie, you are being asked to support your opinion. If you say that you did not like the movie because the characters did not seem like real people, you are supporting your opinion with a *reason*.

When you write a paragraph explaining a fact or an opinion, you can develop the paragraph by giving reasons that are specific. Your reasons should be specific so that your readers will know exactly what you mean. You should also include enough reasons in your paragraph to support or explain your opinion.

Model: Paragraphs of Opinion

Which of the following paragraphs do you think has a better chance of convincing a school board to sponsor school dances every Saturday night?

1

Topic
Supporting Sentences

I think the school board should sponsor school dances every Saturday night. They would be a lot of fun. Besides, they would keep the students out of trouble.

2

Topic
Supporting Sentences

I think the school board should sponsor dances every Saturday night. Weekly dances would have many benefits. For one thing, recreational opportunities in the community are limited, and dances would provide the students with much-needed social events. Also, dances are educational because the students attending them learn manners and social skills. Then, too, if students are attending a school dance, they will not be tempted to engage in undesirable activities. In spite of all these benefits, dances are inexpensive and would not increase the school's budget by much.

Paragraph 2 would have a better chance of convincing the school board to sponsor weekly dances because the writer has given specific reasons why the school board should sponsor these dances.

In an expository paragraph developed with reasons, the reasons may be arranged from the most important to the least important or from the least important to the most important.

Model: A Paragraph Using Reasons

How are the reasons arranged in the following paragraph?

Topic
Supporting Sentences

Exercise, in moderation, offers both physical and mental benefits. It tones your muscles and thus helps to make your body more attractive. If you want to stay slim and trim, exercise can help control your weight, and if you do not increase the amount of food you eat, you may even lose weight. Exercise also can leave you with an overall feeling of well-being. It can even help you feel better about yourself as you demonstrate self-discipline and work toward a goal. Most important, exercise can help keep you healthy. Vigorous exercise strengthens your lungs and heart and will help you to have more energy, perhaps even lengthening your life.

Think and Discuss

1. How many specific reasons does the writer give to support the topic? What are they?

61

2. Which reason is the most important one? Where is this reason placed in the paragraph?

3. Why do you think the writer gives the most important reason last?

For Your Writer's Notebook

Have you ever wondered why students have a three-month summer vacation or why a football team is allowed four downs to advance the ball rather than three or two? Perhaps you are curious about why freshmen and sophomores in your school are required to attend study hall while students in the upper grades are not. In your Writer's Notebook make a list of questions such as these. Choose one question you can investigate by interviewing a coach, teacher, or school official or by using library resources. Then write an entry stating the question and the reasons you uncovered in your research that answer it.

Writing Practice 3: *A Paragraph Using Reasons*

Complete the preceding Writer's Notebook assignment. Then write a well-organized paragraph using the notes and information you wrote in your Writer's Notebook. Identify the topic of your paragraph in a clear topic statement. Support your topic by giving at least three specific reasons. Bring your paragraph to a conclusion in the final statement.

A Basic Paragraph Pattern

Most expository paragraphs contain a restricted topic sentence and illustrations.

Illustrations are supporting sentences that develop the main idea of the paragraph by providing examples, data, descriptive details, or reasons. A restricted topic sentence is one that has been narrowed to a specific topic.

Suppose a writer chooses *newspapers* as a subject. If the writer began the paragraph at this point with only the subject *newspapers* in

mind, the finished paragraph might look as unfocused as the following one.

Newspapers provide valuable information. Writing for a newspaper is demanding but interesting work. Some of the newspapers in our city have gone out of business in the past few years. Today people often watch television for news rather than read a newspaper. A good newspaper has a variety of sections and provides something of interest for everyone.

Because there are thousands of statements the writer could make about the subject *newspapers,* the successful writer knows that the paragraph must be restricted to one main idea about newspapers. Once the topic is restricted, the writer adds specific illustrations. These illustrations give the reader a better understanding of the paragraph's main idea. A paragraph about newspapers, with the restricted topic "A good newspaper provides sections to interest every kind of reader," might be developed with illustrations like the following ones:

Illustration: The first section of a newspaper usually provides complete reports on national and international news.

Illustration: However, sports fans often turn directly to the sports section to learn how their favorite teams are doing.

Illustration: Another section of the paper often contains recipes and articles about food that are of interest to cooking buffs, like my uncle.

Illustration: Many people enjoy the business section, which provides information about the stock market and developments in the world of finance.

The finished paragraph, which would include the restricted topic and the four illustrations, would look like this:

A good newspaper provides sections to interest every kind of reader. The first section of a newspaper usually provides complete reports on national and international news. However, sports fans often turn directly to the sports section to learn how their favorite teams are doing. Another section of the paper often contains recipes and articles about food that are of interest to cooking buffs, like my uncle. Many readers enjoy the business section, which provides information about the stock market and developments in the world of finance.

Writing Practice 4: *Using a Basic Pattern*

On a sheet of paper, develop each of the following paragraphs by supplying the information called for. In three of the paragraphs, you are given a subject and are asked to supply the topic and illustrations. For the fourth paragraph you are asked to use your own subject, topic, and illustrations. Then select one of the paragraph patterns and write the entire paragraph, using the illustrations and appropriate transitional devices. Save your paragraph for the next Writing Practice.

1. Subject: Music
   Topic:
   Illustration:
   Illustration:
   Illustration:

2. Subject: Part-time jobs
   Topic:
   Illustration:
   Illustration:
   Illustration:

3. Subject: My favorite sport
   Topic:
   Illustration:
   Illustration:
   Illustration:

4. Subject:
   Topic:
   Illustration:
   Illustration:
   Illustration:

5. Subject:
   Topic:
   Illustration:
   Illustration:
   Illustration:

Variations on the Basic Paragraph Pattern

Many paragraphs have a variation of the *Restricted Topic-Illustration* form. For example, a writer may introduce the main idea of a paragraph in a topic sentence, then restrict or narrow the topic in a second sentence. This paragraph form is known as the Topic-Restriction-Illustration *(TRI)*.

Models: *Paragraphs with Different Forms*

The following paragraph is an example of the *TRI* paragraph pattern in which the second sentence restricts the topic:

> (*Topic:*) Peanut butter is a common American food. (*Restriction:*) Americans eat this spread in a variety of interesting and unusual ways. (*Illustration:*) For example, many people enjoy peanut butter spread on celery, carrots, or bananas as a nourishing snack. (*Illustration:*) Almost everyone has encountered the famous peanut butter and jelly sandwich, but some people enjoy peanut butter and pickle sandwiches or peanut butter and bacon sandwiches. (*Illustration:*) In some parts of the South, peanut butter soup is an old favorite. (*Illustration:*) One of the most unusual peanut butter combinations is my aunt's special recipe for peanut butter eggnog.

A variation is to reverse the *TRI* (*Topic-Restriction-Illustration*) order, giving the illustrations first. A slight rewording makes the paragraph smoother:

> (*Illustration:*) Almost everyone has encountered the famous peanut butter and jelly sandwich, but fewer people have ever eaten a peanut butter and pickle sandwich or a peanut butter and bacon sandwich. (*Illustration:*) Many people enjoy peanut butter spread on celery, carrots, or bananas as a nourishing snack. (*Illustration:*) One of the most unusual peanut butter combinations is my aunt's special recipe for peanut butter eggnog. (*Topic:*) Peanut butter is a common American food. (*Restriction:*) Americans eat this spread in a variety of unusual and interesting ways.

The following paragraph shows yet another organization.

> (*Illustration:*) Almost everyone has encountered the famous peanut butter and jelly sandwich, but fewer people have ever eaten a

peanut butter and pickle sandwich or a peanut butter and bacon sandwich. (*Topic*) Peanut butter is a common American food. (*Restriction:*) However, Americans eat this spread in a variety of unusual and interesting ways. (*Illustration:*) Many people enjoy peanut butter spread on celery, carrots, or bananas as a nourishing snack. (*Illustration:*) In some parts of the South, peanut butter soup is an old favorite. (*Illustration:*) One of the most unusual peanut butter combinations is my aunt's special recipe for peanut butter eggnog.

Writing Practice 5: *Varying Paragraph Patterns*

Using the paragraph you wrote in Writing Practice 4, vary the form so it no longer follows the *Topic-Illustration* pattern. Change your paragraph by using the *TRI* pattern or one of the variations of this pattern. You may need to leave out or insert transitional words, such as *also, but, for example,* or *however,* to connect sentences within the paragraph.

Developing Paragraphs by Comparing and Contrasting

You have probably never seen a breadfruit, but if you read that a breadfruit is about the size and shape of a large pear, you would have some idea of what this unusual fruit is like. When you tell how a breadfruit is like a pear, you are *comparing* the two fruits.

A breadfruit is different from a pear in some ways. It is not sweet, it has an uneven surface, and it is green in color. When you point out ways in which two things are different from each other, you are *contrasting* those things.

A good way to convey information to a reader is by comparing and contrasting ideas and things, pointing out both the similarities and the differences.

This method is especially useful if one of the ideas or things is unfamiliar to the reader. When developing a paragraph in this manner, begin by making a rough list of ways the two items are similar and different. For example, the following list is of ways a student's junior high school and high school are alike:

The schools are in the same town and serve the same students.

Students take courses in English, math, social studies, and science.

Teachers assign homework at both schools.

Students meet regularly in homerooms.

Students are assigned to study halls.

The following list is of ways the junior high and high school are different.

Oswego High School is almost three times as big as Thompson Junior High School.

The high school offers many elective courses in which students can enroll.

Junior high teachers give students time in class to begin their homework. High school teachers usually don't.

Juniors and seniors in high school are not required to attend study hall.

In junior high, homerooms meet every day; in high school, homerooms meet once every two weeks.

Models: *Paragraphs That Compare and Contrast*

The comparison and contrast paragraph may be developed in either of two ways. One way is to discuss everything the two subjects have in common first and then to discuss the ways the two subjects differ, as the following paragraph shows.

Restricted Topic

Illustrations

Thompson Junior High School and Oswego High School are alike in many ways, but they are also different. Both schools are in the same town, and most of the students from the junior high school will also attend Oswego High. Students at both schools study the same basic subjects: English, math, social studies, and science. Teachers at both schools give homework and assignments in these classes and expect the students to complete the work. In addition, both schools assign students to a homeroom and study hall. One of the most noticeable differences between the two schools is that the high school is almost three times as big as the junior high, so that at first many students feel a little lost. At Oswego students can choose interesting electives, such as auto mechanics, printmaking, and child guidance, which aren't offered in junior high. However, high school courses involve more studying at home because the teachers usually don't set aside class time for students to do their homework. At the high school, juniors and seniors are not required to attend study hall. Finally, unlike junior high, where students meet in homeroom every day, high school students have homeroom only once every two weeks.

Another way to compare and contrast is to discuss the two items point by point, telling both likenesses and differences for each point. The following paragraph is an example.

Topic
Restriction

Illustrations

My best friend is always complaining because he has eleven brothers and sisters. He thinks I am lucky because I'm an only child, but I'm not so sure. I think things are about even. When it comes to working around the house, we both seem to have about the same amount of work to do. There's more to do around his house, but there are also more people to do it. At my house there's less work to do but no one to share it. The only difference I've noticed in this area is in his favor. If he doesn't do something he's supposed to do, there's a chance his parents won't notice. When I don't do something, you can be sure my parents will know about it. Another thing he's always complaining about is holidays. He says things get very hectic when his married brothers and sisters bring their families home. I don't see much difference there. With four grandparents and as many aunts, uncles, and cousins as I have, my house looks like Grand Central Station decorated for the holidays. I do see his point about clothes, though. I always look forward to those shopping trips and new clothes. There are so many sizes to pass around in his family that Bill says he hasn't had anything new in six years. Come to think about it, I'm not so sure I would trade places with him, after all.

Sometimes, a topic calls for development through either similarities or differences alone. Look at the topic to decide whether to develop the paragraph through similarities, through differences, or through both. For example, a topic like *John and Ann are somewhat alike, but in many ways you would never know they are related, much less twins* requires bringing out both similarities and differences. Similarities alone should be used with a topic such as *My dog acts just like a human.* A topic such as *My new high school is nothing like my previous one,* however, needs development with differences.

Writing Assignment III: *A Comparison/Contrast Paragraph*

A. Prewriting

Looking Back: Think about how your life as a student used to be when you were in junior high or middle school. In your Writer's Notebook make a list of the important experiences you remember as a student at that time. You may want to divide your list into categories, such as *Positive experiences* and *Negative experiences.* Focus your ideas on your experiences as a student and not on the entire scope of your personal life.

Looking at the Present: Think about the changes you have experienced as a high school student. In your Writer's Notebook, jot down any ideas that come to mind about changes you've experienced, such as in your study habits, in your interests or activities, in your attitudes, or in your plans and goals for the future.

B. Writing

My Life as a Student Then and Now: Decide whether you want to develop your composition by comparing similarities first and then contrasting differences or by interweaving the two. Write a first draft comparing and contrasting your life as a student in junior high or middle school with your life as a high school student now.

C. Postwriting

Revising and Proofreading: Read over your first draft with a partner or classmate. Check your writing against the items in the Checklist for Revision on the next page. Be aggressive about making necessary changes in your writing. Comparison/contrast paragraphs are not easy to write and often need to be reworked many times.

After you are satisfied with your revision, exchange papers with your partner and proofread each other's paper for correct grammar, mechanics, and spelling. Use the Proofreader's Checklist at the back of the book.

> ## *Checklist for Revision*
>
> 1. Does the topic statement concretely identify the main idea of the paragraph?
>
> 2. Did the writer clearly develop both similarities and differences?
>
> 3. Are there transitional words and phrases that link ideas together to produce a coherent composition?
>
> 4. Are there extraneous or unnecessary details that are off the topic and need to be deleted?

For Your Writer's Notebook

Write an entry in your Writer's Notebook about some of the ways you and your closest friends are different. Consider the differences in your interests, families, goals, and temperaments. Perhaps you are the oldest child in your family and have a lot of responsibility, but your friend is the youngest and feels too protected. Do you enjoy a spine-tingling horror film on a Friday night, while your friend prefers zany comedies? You may be a person who speaks out and expresses strong opinions, while your friend is very careful with words. Think about how you handle these differences. Do they make your friendship more exciting? Do they sometimes lead to problems for you and your friend?

Developing Paragraphs Through Anecdote

The anecdote is a single incident that provides an interesting, specific illustration of the paragraph topic.

A brief story, or *anecdote,* can be used to develop and explain the point of an expository paragraph.

Model: An Anecdote

In the following paragraph, Margot Fonteyn, the ballerina, tells an anecdote about her mother.

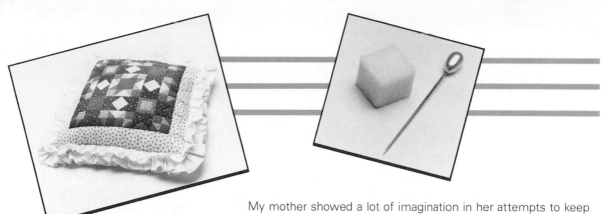

Topic
Restriction
Illustrations

My mother showed a lot of imagination in her attempts to keep me from getting bored and so annoying her. One simple trick, which worked well until I was about six years old, was the cushion, the pin and the lump of sugar. It involved first sending me to fetch a pin, which she then put on the floor under a cushion. If I sat on the cushion long enough without speaking, the fairies would transform the pin into a lump of sugar. If I looked at the pin myself, the fairies wouldn't come near. If I spoke, the transformation would take longer. From time to time, my mother would come into the room and look under the cushion. "Oh dear," she would say, "it's still a pin. I'll come back in a minute to see if they've changed it." Then she went off and finished baking the cake, or whatever she was occupied with, and when it was done she looked under the cushion again and exclaimed, "Look now! There's a lump of sugar; the fairies have changed it at last."[1]

Margot Fonteyn relates that her mother used imagination to keep her from getting bored. To illustrate she tells one anecdote, or story, about a trick her mother used. Notice that the writer develops the anecdote with specific detail, telling step by step about this trick of her mother's, even recording what her mother said when she looked under the cushion.

Writing Practice 6: *An Anecdote from the Life of a Student*

In the last writing assignment you compared and contrasted your former life as a student in junior high or middle school with your life as a high school student now. Read over your composition and the notes you made for this topic in your Writer's Notebook. Identify one idea for a paragraph using an anecdote or brief story from your student life. Write a new paragraph focusing on the anecdote alone. Introduce the topic in a new topic statement. Then write about the anecdote in detail.

---

[1]From *Margot Fonteyn: Autobiography* by Margot Fonteyn. Copyright © 1975, 1976 by Margot Fonteyn. Reprinted by permission of Alfred A. Knopf, Inc., and W.H. Allen & Company, Ltd.

Sentence Combining: Using Clauses

Connecting Sentences with Subordinators

For information on subordinate clauses, see pages 514-531.

In the last *Sentence Combining* section, you learned how to use adverbs to connect sentences. A different group of connecting words join ideas of *unequal importance*. You indicate the less important idea by introducing it with words such as *because, although, since, after, before, if, as if, just when, as soon as, even though,* and *until.*

These words are called *subordinators* because they make the string of words that follow them less important than the rest of the sentence. (Subordinators are also called *subordinating conjunctions*.) The less important part of the sentence is *subordinate* to the main part, and a subordinate part cannot stand alone as a simple sentence.

Sentences: Josie is my friend. (*because*)
            I will give her a helping hand.
Combined: *Because* Josie is my friend, I will give her a helping hand.

The word *because*, the subordinator in the preceding model, shows a cause-and-effect relationship between the two original sentences: *Because* Josie is my friend (cause), I will give her a helping hand (effect).

The following are more examples of sentences joined by subordinators.

Sentences: Everyone crept into the cellar.
            The tornado hit. (*before*)
Combined: Everyone crept into the cellar *before* the tornado hit.

Sentences: You take time to look for them. (*if*)
            You can find exciting ideas in books.
Combined: *If* you take time to look for them, you can find exciting ideas in books.

Notice that when the signal appears at the end of the first sentence, the subordinator is placed at the beginning of the combined sentence. When the signal follows the second sentence, the subordinator appears in the middle of the combined sentence. If the subordinator appears at the front of the first sentence, use a comma to separate the joined sentences.

Sentences:	It is impossible to describe the litter in Doheny Park. (*since*) I'm not going to try.
Combined:	*Since* it is impossible to describe the litter in Doheny Park, I'm not going to try.

When the subordinators *though* and *although* appear in the middle of the combined sentence, place a comma before them. Do the same with *since* if it means "because."

Sentences:	Greg's receiving the prize pleased me. I'm his greatest fan. (*since*)
Combined:	Greg's receiving the prize pleased me, *since* I'm his greatest fan.

Exercise 1: Using Subordinators to Join Sentences

On a sheet of paper, combine the following pairs of sentences on this page and the next with subordinators. Where there are no signals, use the subordinator you think best. Study the examples before you begin.

Examples

a. John was a young man. (*when*)
   He learned a skilled trade.
   When John was a young man, he learned a skilled trade.

b. Gloria swerved sharply to the right.
   The approaching car missed her narrowly. (*so that*)
   Gloria swerved sharply to the right so that the approaching car missed her narrowly.

1. I am afraid of bees. (*even though*)
   I will help gather the honey from the hives.

2. We planned a picnic near the lake.
   We knew it might rain. (*although*)

3. You open Pandora's box. (*if*)
   All the evils in the world will fly out.

4. Everyone pitched in and helped with the housework.
   We could get to the show on time. (*so that*)

5. The night guards had checked the grounds. (*after*)
   They sat down and ate their midnight snacks.

6. This problem can be solved.
   We agree upon a method of solving it.

7. They filled up the entrance to the cave with rocks.
   They heard the posse entering the canyon.

8. You listen to the beat of the music.
   You will never learn to dance.

9. Rice grows well in California.
   We usually think of the South as the rice-growing region.

10. Anyone breathes a word of this story.
    I will deny telling it to you.

Writing Practice 1: *Combining Sentences*

The following paragraphs sound choppy and are hard to read. Improve them by combining sentences in any way you choose. Rewrite your revised paragraphs on another sheet of paper.

> Pale light filtered through the clouds. The wind blew from the lake. The day was dreary and dismal. The young man was in a good mood. He was on his way to the bus station. He was headed for Florida. He wanted to spend a week in the sunshine. He had saved his money for the trip. He had looked forward to the journey for six months.
>
> After a forty-five-minute walk in the cold wind, the young man arrived at the bus station. He purchased his ticket. He bought a magazine to read. He sat on a bench. He waited for the announcement that the bus was ready for boarding. A lady who sat next to the young man in the station was listening to a portable radio. When the man heard, "And now, the news," he listened carefully for the weather report. The announcer gave this news: "The first hurricane of the season is heading toward Florida."

Joining Three or More Sentences in a Series

For information on clauses see pages 512-531.

In this section you will practice joining three or more sentences together. The first sentence in each set is called the *base*. This base sentence will remain as it is, and the other sentences will be added to it, as the following example shows.

Base Sentence:	She gave him a warm smile.
Add:	S~~he~~ laid her hand on his arm.
Add:	S~~he~~ looked deep into his eyes.
Combined:	She gave him a warm smile, laid her hand on his arm, *and* looked deep into his eyes.

In the preceding example the first three sentences are combined. The repeated word *She* has been taken out; the word *and* has been added before the third sentence to join the three sentences. Commas have been added to help make the combined sentence readable.

In the following example the signal (,) tells you to put a comma before that added sentence. The signal (*,and*) means to write the word *and* along with the comma before the last added sentence. The cross-out signal over a word (she) means to remove that word from the combined sentence.

Base Sentence:	The fire raced up the stairwell.
Add:	T~~he fire~~ reached into the upper hallway. (,)
Add:	T~~he fire~~ consumed everything in its path. (*,and*)
Combined:	The fire raced up the stairwell, reached into the upper hallway, *and* consumed everything in its path.

When two sentences are added to a base, the resulting sentence can be punctuated in several ways. A comma separates the added elements from the base, and the new word groups are often separated from each other with a comma plus *and*.

Base Sentence:	As the bobsled zoomed around the corner, David waved his arms.
Add:	Da~~vid~~ shouted encouragement to the racers. (,)
Add:	H~~e~~ pounded his companion on the back. (*and*)
Combined:	As the bobsled zoomed around the corner, David waved his arms, shouted encouragement to the racers, *and* pounded his companion on the back.

However, when one or more of the new elements has a verb form ending in *-ing*, the punctuation often varies. These elements are often separated by commas alone or by other conjunctions, such as *but*.

Base Sentence:	Twenty-four wagons struggled to the top of the pass.
Add:	Their frames were creaking. (,)
Add:	Their canvas tops were billowing in the wind. (,)
Add:	Their water barrels were spilling over with every jolt. (,)
Combined:	Twenty-four wagons struggled to the top of the pass, their frames creaking, their canvas tops billowing in the wind, their water barrels spilling over with every jolt.

Base Sentence:	The lizard managed to free itself.
Add:	The lizard was leaving its tail behind. (,)
Add:	The lizard was saving its life. (but)
Combined:	The lizard managed to free itself, leaving its tail behind *but* saving its life.

Exercise 2: *Joining Three Sentences*

On a sheet of paper, combine the following sentences, using the signals where given. Study the example before you begin.

Example

a. The child hid in a closet.
   The child was frightened of the dark. (,)
   The child was hoping to win the game. (*but*)
   The child hid in a closet, frightened of the dark but hoping to win the game.

1. Carolyn swung back and forth in the swing.
   She noticed we were watching her. (,)
   She began to pump the swing even higher. (,*and*)

2. Phil gave Sandy a sidelong glance.
   Phil turned away quickly. (,)
   Phil hurried across the driveway. (,*and*)

3. Carefully he put the wood on the fire.
   He shook down the ashes. (,)
   He lit the kindling. (,*and*)

4. The horses were heading for the home stretch.
   They were jockeying for the front position. (,)
   They were not noticing the roar of the crowd. (,)

5. The bride threw her bridal bouquet.
   ~~She was~~ hoping Cynthia would catch it. (,)
   ~~She was~~ knowing Estelle would. (,but)

6. Anna approached the springboard.
   She walked gracefully to the end.
   She made her most beautiful drive.

7. Shirley has no more manners than a street urchin.
   She is sticking her tongue out that way.
   She is making a terrible face.

8. A path led from the gate.
   It wound through a cypress grove.
   It ended by the lily pond.

9. Pop reached behind the door.
   He grabbed the flyswatter that he kept hanging there.
   He whirled toward the intruder.

10. Mama stood stiffly in front of her doorstep.
    Her arms were crossed over her bosom.
    Her body was blocking the entryway.

4 Describing and Narrating Experiences

Elements of the Personal Narrative

I f you've ever listened to yourself talk to others, you might have been surprised at the number of times the word *I* popped into your conversation. Yet, what better frame of reference do you have than your own experience? It is natural for you to tell your own story.

A *personal narrative* is a form of writing in which the writer relates an event, incident, or experience in his or her own life.

The events of a personal narrative are most often presented in chronological order, the order in which they actually occurred in time. Effective narration, however, goes beyond a simple retelling of facts or events; it also incorporates vivid descriptive details as well as the thoughts, feelings, and reactions of the writer.

This type of writing is similar to Writer's Notebook entries. Indeed, a notebook is an excellent source of ideas for personal narratives. Unlike notebook entries, however, where your ideas tend to flow unstructured on the page, the personal narrative has a tighter organization. The writer must focus on one particular incident or experience and develop it around a central theme. The central theme is the main idea of the composition, to which the incident relates.

In the following excerpt about an Indian girl, the writer focuses on one memorable incident with her mother. She develops the incident by adding descriptive details about her surroundings, herself, and her mother. She also includes a conversation which helps the reader understand the mother's character. Throughout the narrative, the writer weaves in her own thoughts and feelings.

Model: A Personal Narrative

Gertrude Bonnin, whose Native American name was Zitkala-Sa, was a Dakota Sioux. In the following selection, "Impressions of an Indian Childhood," she describes a conversation that revealed to her some of the pain her mother suffered. As you read, determine why the writer has chosen to write about this incident and how the incident

might have influenced her. Also look for the details the author uses to make the incident interesting for readers.

A wigwam of weather-stained canvas stood at the base of some irregularly ascending hills. A footpath wound its way gently down the sloping land till it reached the broad river bottom; creeping through the long swamp grasses that bent over it on either side, it came out on the edge of the Missouri.

Here, morning, noon, and evening, my mother came to draw water from the muddy stream for our household use. Always, when my mother started for the river, I stopped my play to run along with her. She was only of medium height. Often she was sad and silent, at which times her full arched lips were compressed into hard and bitter lines, and shadows fell under her black eyes. Then I clung to her hand and begged to know what made the tears fall.

"Hush; my little daughter must never talk about my tears;" and smiling through them, she patted my head and said, "Now let me see how fast you can run today." Whereupon I tore away at my highest possible speed, with my long black hair blowing in the breeze.

I was a wild little girl of seven. Loosely clad in a slip of brown buckskin, and lightfooted with a pair of soft moccasins on my feet, I was as free as the wind that blew my hair, and no less spirited than a bounding deer. These were my mother's pride—my wild freedom and

overflowing spirits. She taught me no fear save that of intruding myself upon others.

Having gone many paces ahead I stopped, panting for breath, and laughing with glee as my mother watched my every movement. I was not wholly conscious of myself, but was more keenly alive to the fire within. It was as if I were the activity, and my hands and feet were only experiments for my spirit to work upon.

Returning from the river, I tugged beside my mother, with my hand upon the bucket I believed I was carrying. One time, on such a return, I remember a bit of conversation we had. My grown-up cousin, Warca-Ziwin (Sunflower), who was then seventeen, always went to the river alone for water for her mother. Their wigwam was not far from ours; and I saw her daily going to and from the river. I admired my cousin greatly. So I said: "Mother, when I am tall as my cousin Warca-Ziwin, you shall not have to come for water. I will do it for you."

With a strange tremor in her voice which I could not understand, she answered, "If the paleface does not take away from us the river we drink."

"Mother, who is the bad paleface?" I asked.

"My little daughter, he is a sham,—a sickly sham! The bronzed Dakota is the only real man."

I looked up into my mother's face while she spoke; and seeing her bite her lips, I knew she was unhappy. This aroused revenge in my small soul. Stamping my foot on the earth, I cried aloud, "I hate the paleface that makes my mother cry!"

Setting the pail of water on the ground, my mother stooped, and stretching her left hand out on the level with my eyes, she placed her other arm about me; she pointed to the hill where my uncle and my only sister lay buried.

"There is what the paleface has done! Since then your father too has been buried in a hill nearer the rising sun. We were once very happy. But the paleface has stolen our lands and driven us hither. Having defrauded us of our land, the paleface forced us away.

"Well, it happened on the day we moved camp that your sister and uncle were both very sick. Many others were ailing, but there seemed to be no help. We traveled many days and nights; not in the grand, happy way that we moved camp when I was a little girl, but we were driven, my child, driven like a herd of buffalo. With every step, your sister, who was not as large as you are now, shrieked with the painful jar until she was hoarse with crying. She grew more and more feverish. Her little hands and cheeks were burning hot. Her little lips were parched and dry, but she would not drink the water I gave her. Then I discovered that her throat was swollen and red. My poor child, how I cried with her because the Great Spirit had forgotten us!

"At last, when we reached this western country, on the first weary night your sister died. And soon your uncle died also, leaving a widow and an orphan daughter, your cousin Warca-Ziwin. Both your sister and uncle might have been happy with us today, had it not been for the heartless paleface."

My mother was silent the rest of the way to our wigwam. Though I saw no tears in her eyes, I knew that was because I was with her. She seldom wept before me.[1]

Think and Discuss

1. When Gertrude Bonnin writes that "a wigwam of weather-stained canvas stood at the base of some irregularly ascending hills," she is using specific details to help the reader visualize her home. What other details in the first paragraph give a clear picture of this place?

2. The writer describes her feelings when she says she was "keenly alive to the fire within." What do you think she means? What are other phrases that describe the writer's feelings?

3. What specific details does the writer use to describe herself as a child of seven? What comparisons does she make?

4. Gertrude Bonnin states that her mother was "sad and silent" and that her lips were "compressed into hard and bitter lines." What does the writer learn about her mother's sadness and worry, which is the central theme of the essay?

5. The selection describes a brief conversation between mother and child. Why is this conversation memorable for the writer? Why do you think she chose to write about it? How does it relate to the essay's central theme?

Writing Assignment I: *Personal Narrative*

A. Prewriting

Selecting a Topic: Think about a specific incident in your life that left a strong impression on you. If you like, choose one of the following topics.

1. Your first day as a freshman
2. An experience when you learned something about yourself or someone else
3. A disastrous cooking experience
4. A competition or contest
5. The hardest thing you ever did
6. A bicycling or hiking trip
7. A childhood experience from an older point of view
8. A decision you have reached

Listing Events and Details: To ensure that your writing reaches a conclusion, you might list the major stages in your experience. Divide

---

[1]From "Impressions of an Indian Childhood" by Gertrude Bonnin, in *The Atlantic Monthly*, January 1900.

a sheet of paper into two columns, labeling one *Events* and the other *Details*. Put the conclusion of the episode at the bottom of the page. Then begin at the top and space the other three or four steps in your experience evenly down the page, leaving several lines between each stage. In the *Details* column, beside each stage of the experience, brainstorm to come up with as many specific details as you can. (Brainstorming involves immediately putting down all the ideas that come to mind without stopping to evaluate them.)

If you listed the events and details about an evening when the power was off for several hours, your chart might look like the following one.

Events	Details
1. Storm began at 4:30.	Trees bending in the wind White streaks of lightning Crash and boom of thunder
2. Lights went off at 5.	Everything black I had just started dinner. Couldn't find flashlight Banged my knee on kitchen table
3. People started gathering in hall and coming to the door.	Landlady asked if we were all right. Neighbor lent us a candle. Mr. Sanchez turned on a portable radio in hall.
4. Catastrophe turned into a picnic.	Mrs. Sanchez built fire in her fireplace and invited us to her apartment. Mr. Vitali brought some hot dogs.
5. No one wanted the fun to end when the lights came on.	I took some popcorn. We sang songs. Everyone told stories about other bad storms. Mrs. Vitali told the children a ghost story. We all went home feeling good.

B. Writing

A Personal Narrative: Write a sketch about the incident you have chosen. Relate the events of the incident in chronological order. Include details that tell when and where the incident occurred, who was involved, and what happened. Conclude with a brief statement about the meaning the incident had for you.

C. Postwriting

Revising Your Personal Narrative: You revise to improve your writing by making it clearer and more interesting. Revising a paper may mean rewriting a few words, a few sentences, a paragraph, or even the entire paper.

To revise and proofread your personal narrative, use the following checklists, evaluating your paper for each of the items. If your writing is weak in one or more of these areas, rewrite as much of your paper as necessary to correct each weakness.

Before you revise you may want to share your paper with a partner or a small group of classmates. Consider their responses and suggestions in making your final revision.

Checklist for Revision

1. Does the narrative keep the readers interested?

2. Is the narrative organized in a time sequence that helps readers follow the events?

3. Do specific details make events, characters, and places seem real?

4. Does the narrative build to a conclusion that includes your personal thoughts and feelings about the incident?

Checklist for Proofreading

1. Have I used clear and correct sentence structure?

2. Is each word spelled correctly?

3. Are words capitalized correctly, including all proper nouns?

4. Have I used singular verbs with singular subjects, and plural verbs with plural subjects?

5. Is each sentence punctuated correctly?

For Your Writer's Notebook

In "Impressions of an Indian Childhood," Gertrude Bonnin discusses an incident from her early childhood that gave her new insight into her mother's nature. Think of some experience, perhaps a brief conversation, that revealed something about someone in your family. Maybe you visited a favorite great-aunt or helped your grandfather with some task and learned something in the process. Write about the experience in your Writer's Notebook, remembering to include interesting, specific details about what happened, where the event occurred, and who was involved.

Organizing Your Personal Narrative

S ince a personal narrative is the story of some part of your life, it is easy to organize. You can simply tell about the events one after another in the order they happened, as you did in the previous assignment.

Arranging events as they happen in time is called *chronological organization.*

Events may be arranged in a straightforward, chronological fashion, or they may be in a different order. If, for example, you want to tell about your experience with a history test, you might tell first about preparing for the test on Monday, then about taking it on Tuesday, and finally about finding out the results on Wednesday. You might prefer to organize your narrative in the following way.

1. Taking the test (Tuesday)

2. Preparing for the test (Monday)

3. Finding out the results (Wednesday)

With the preceding organization the narrative begins in the middle, goes back to the beginning, and concludes with the final events. Another way of organizing the events would begin with the ending and move backward to the beginning. One of the reasons writers sometimes use an order other than straightforward, chronological order is to capture the reader's interest right away. If the middle or end of a story is more exciting than the beginning, the writer may begin at one of these points and move backward to finish the story.

Writing Practice 1: *Organizing Events in a Narrative*

The following narrative is organized with the events in the order of their happening. Read this narrative carefully and then rewrite it, giving it a new organization. Change any part of the narrative as you think necessary to fit the new organization.

1.   Monday was a day of work for me. I had not studied my history lesson, and on Tuesday I was faced with a big test on the American Revolution. Every spare minute during the school day, I tried to fill my mind with facts about the Revolution. After school I crammed from 4 P.M. until midnight, when I flopped into bed exhausted.

2.   Tuesday morning when my grandmother dragged me from bed, I was still tired. I hurried through breakfast and rushed off to school an hour early so that I could study some more for the test. When Mr. Humphrey, our history teacher, passed out the test, I nearly blanked out. The test was about the Declaration of Independence. I couldn't think of what it said or who wrote it, and I couldn't remember any of the dates.

       Finally I was able to scribble down some information. I remembered that Thomas Jefferson primarily wrote the Declaration of Independence and that it was adopted on July 4, 1776, but when the test hour was over, I knew I had done a bad job, and I felt sick. I wondered if I would flunk the test.

3.   Wednesday morning I waited nervously for Mr. Humphrey to hand back the test, afraid to get mine. As Mr. Humphrey went up and down the rows of students, passing back the test, I became more and more anxious. When my turn came, I put my test on my desk written side down, so that I couldn't see the grade.

       After a minute or two I fearfully peeked at the front of my paper. Written on it was a large, red *D*. That was the lowest grade I had ever received in history, and I was nearly crushed. It took me several minutes to push back the tears that were flooding my eyes. I felt terrible.

From this experience I learned that cramming is a bad way to study, and I will never do it again. That *D* I got on my history test taught me an important lesson about how to learn.

Writing Practice 2: *An Important Event*

Think of an event during the past year or so that was important to you. It may not have been a "headline" event; in fact, you and your family or friends may be the only ones to know about it. Then write a narrative about this event, using sensory details and details about thoughts and feelings when appropriate. Organize your narrative either chronologically, as the events actually happened, or in some other order.

Selecting Details

For information on expanding your vocabulary, see pages 652-664.

Interesting personal narratives are informative, filled with details that help readers learn to know the writer and understand or visualize what he or she is saying.

Effective writing includes details that show rather than tell the reader what something or someone is like.

Writers can add "showing" details to a piece of writing by using sensory description or by giving examples. They might also relate an interesting anecdote or incident that emphasizes a point they are suggesting.

Models: Show-not-Tell Paragraph

The following two passages are written about the same topic. As you read them, notice which paragraph uses more "showing" details.

1

One person who means a great deal to me is my friend Alice. She is my neighbor, and we do a lot of our chores together. When I first met Alice, I had trouble understanding her speech, but now I understand her perfectly. Alice is a person I really respect; she cares about people and worries about them. Alice also loves animals and is very kind to them. I'll never forget the stray cat she brought home. She really loves that cat, and the cat follows her everywhere. It's hard to explain exactly what Alice means to me. I guess what I like about

her is that she thinks of other people. I can remember so many times when she has been more thoughtful than I've been. She notices so many things that I just forget about. I wish everybody could meet Alice and really get to know her—the world would probably be a better place.

2

Alice is mentally retarded, and if she's excited, she sometimes speaks unclearly. At first I was nervous about that, but I learned to listen carefully, and we've become good friends. I've discovered that Alice is one of the most considerate and sensitive persons I know. Last month, for instance, a stray kitten was hit by a car on our street. Alice picked up the scrawny kitten and gently carried it to her house, stroking its gray fur and soothing it. The veterinarian patched up the kitten's wounds, but Alice really nursed it back to health. For two days Alice fed it milk with an eyedropper and held it on her lap until it could stand. Now that cat, Annie, follows her everywhere.

Alice amazes me with her perceptiveness. One afternoon last winter we were both outside shoveling our sidewalks. I was tired and did a hasty job, but Alice, as usual, shoveled up every scrap of snow. When I waved to her and said I was going in, Alice shook her head vigorously and pointed to the two or three still-icy patches I'd ignored. Then she mentioned Mrs. Engel, another neighbor. Alice knew that Mrs. Engel, who was ninety-one, walked along our sidewalks and that the icy patches I'd skipped would be dangerous for her. Alice won; I spent thirty more minutes doing a good job on the sidewalk, and my friend nodded her approval. Then just last week, she wouldn't let me mow the lawn until I had changed my shoes. I was wearing thongs, and she said that wasn't safe. She was right, of course; I just hadn't thought about it. I wish everyone could meet Alice—the world would probably be a better place.

Think and Discuss

1.   What details does the writer add to the second paragraph that show rather than tell what Alice is like?

2.   Which paragraph tells more about the writer?

Details about your life may be of several different kinds. They may be *sensory*—sight, sound, smell, touch, and taste—or *data* and *facts*.

Data are measurements of things: *there are seventeen cows and three bulls in the herd; last month the lowest temperature in Estes Park was −21°F.* *Facts* are statements that can be proved through data or observation: *the population of Los Angeles is decreasing; the room is empty.*

Other important details in your narrative are your thoughts and feelings. Without these your reader will learn only about the things you do and not about the kind of person you are.

Writing Assignment II: *A Personal Narrative*

A. Prewriting

The Facets of Our Lives: If you have ever observed a diamond closely, you will notice that the more facets or sides it has, the more it shines. Our lives, too, have many facets. Think about the different facets of your life—your life as a son or daughter, a sister or brother, a friend, a student, a neighbor, an athlete, and so on.

Make a list of all the facets of your life. Select one to develop into a personal narrative. You might consider using an experience from the following list.

1. Your life as a freshman

2. Your life as a younger, middle, or older sibling

3. Your life as an athlete

4. Your life as an absent-minded person

5. Your life as a shy person

A Creative Angle: Good writing is original and creative; it points out fresh details or develops unusual ideas that the average person might miss. Experts know that creativity depends on playing with topics in a relaxed way or approaching ideas from a new angle. You can then use basic *who? what? when? where? why?* and *how?* questions to approach your topic more creatively. Suppose you have decided to write about your life as an athlete. Brainstorm to gather as many details as you can about your athletic abilities and experiences. Use creative questions like the following ones to approach your topic creatively—from an unusual angle.

1. What animal are you most like as an athlete? How are you like a graceful gazelle? In what ways are you a lumbering bear?

2. What color describes your athletic experiences? Why are your experiences like this color?

3. What song describes you as an athlete? How is the song appropriate?

4. What vegetable comes to mind when you think of your athletic experiences?

Of course, these are not logical questions, but creative ideas begin in fanciful ways; they are new, unusual, and out of the ordinary. Let your thoughts wander playfully. Perhaps you are calm in emergencies or in threatening situations, and "blue" is the color you pictured. That is a good start; stick with that idea and think of all the "blue" situations you were in where you acted in a calm and coolheaded way.

Perhaps these new details about your coolness under fire will give you a fresh and amusing point of view. The other creative questions may lead to interesting similes and metaphors for your paper.

B. Writing

One Facet of My Life: Write a personal narrative about one facet or side of your life, using the topic you selected in the prewriting exercise. Try to describe your experiences from an unusual angle. Allow your readers to get "under your skin," so that they can identify with this facet of your life.

C. Postwriting

Identifying the Writer: In small groups, read someone's paper anonymously to the members in your group. See if they can identify the writer by the style and details he or she used in the composition.

Selecting and Organizing Details of Description

When writing about places and things, you can use *spatial organization*; that is, you can arrange details by the way they appear in space.

You can describe a room as your eyes move from left to right, or right to left, or from floor to ceiling. A large object, such as a car, can be described from the front to the rear or from the inside to the outside. If you are describing a larger area, you can begin with the details closest to you and then move to those farther away.

For example, details in the following paragraph about a decaying Victorian house are arranged spatially. The description begins with gables jutting out from the roof and follows the lines of the house.

Model: Spatial Organization

Around the corner from my apartment building is a decaying Victorian mansion that has been split up into small, drab apartments. Like a shabby duchess, the red brick mansion still reigns proudly over the lesser buildings crowding in on both sides, and I love to sit in the park across the street, daydreaming about the building's past. The mansion is three stories high but seems even taller. Two narrow white gables jut out toward the street from the steep slate roof. I can imagine the lace curtains that might have hung in the tiny windows of those gables and the well-dressed children that once pushed them aside to peer into the street below. Four long, narrow windows are spaced evenly across the second floor. The middle windows are actually French doors that open onto a small balcony with a low wood railing. I'm sure those doors once opened out of glowing, chandeliered hallways, but today the balcony holds an outdoor grill, a bag of charcoal, and two blue plastic chairs. A spacious wooden porch supported by a half dozen round pillars runs across the front of the mansion. Portions of the wood railing and trim are missing or broken, but a trace of elegance is still visible in the fluted scrollwork at the corners of the roof. The porch is littered with dead leaves, plastic garbage bags, and a battered baby stroller, but if I close my eyes, I can imagine white wicker settees and hanging flower baskets. The small yard behind the mansion's bent, twisted iron fence is a hodgepodge of elegant past and tawdry present. Dry grass and weeds choke the tangled, overgrown bushes daubed with shriveled, brown roses. Someone pulls at the creaking hinges of the rusty gate. I expect to see a slender gentleman with a dark hat and a gold-headed walking cane, but it is a young man in a black T-shirt with an armload of groceries who walks up the steps and opens the front door.

Think and Discuss

1. How are the details in the above paragraph arranged—from top to bottom, from one side to another, or in some other way?

2. How does the writer use her own imagination, thoughts, and feelings to make the description more interesting?

Writing Assignment III: *Personal Narrative Using Description*

A. Prewriting

Clustering Descriptive Details: Choose something important to you, such as a certain tree you like to sit under, your bicycle, or a wristwatch or ring you wear. If possible, observe the object closely, noting the spatial details of size, shape, and appearance. Make a word cluster using the details. Add another branch to your word cluster that lists details showing the importance of the object to you. For example, the following word cluster shows one way to organize details about a rowboat.

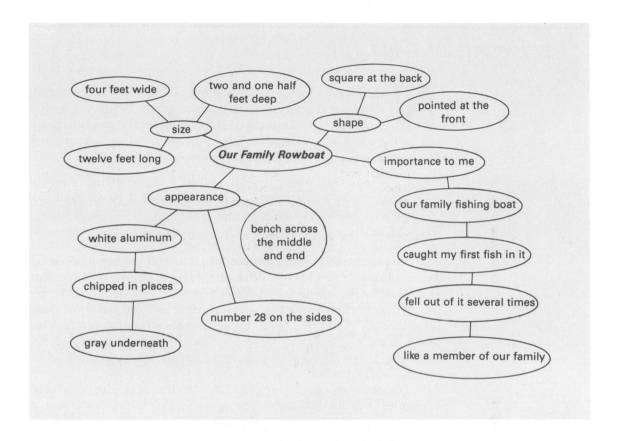

B. Writing

A Descriptive Narrative: Using your word cluster as an aid, write a descriptive narrative about the object you have selected. Include the spatial details in your description. Tell the reader why this object is important to you.

C. Postwriting

Revising and Proofreading in Response Groups: Read your descriptive narrative to a small group of classmates. Ask members of your group to describe in their own words the object or place you described in your narrative. If they cannot visualize your object or place, you will need to add more details.

After you have completed your final draft, proofread your paper using the Proofreader's Checklist at the back of the book. Then have an editing partner from your group proofread your paper again. Make the necessary changes and corrections in your final draft.

Details of Dialogue

Narration is more likely to seem real to readers when details about the characters' speech are included. When you write a sentence like "John asked if he could be the last one to try out for the part," you write *about* what John said; but you can also use his exact words, as in the following example.

> "Say, Mr. Wong," John said in a high-pitched, nervous voice, "would you mind . . . that is, would it be all right if I, uh . . . could I please be last?"

Dialogue **is the exact words spoken by a character.**

As you can tell from the preceding example, dialogue can make an event seem more realistic. When recording dialogue, try to capture real speech. For example, speakers often do not finish sentences before they are interrupted by someone else, and you can show these interruptions in your dialogue. Remember also that the situation has much to do with the way people speak. You would not speak the same way when asking your principal a question as you would when visiting with friends.

Dialogue should be appropriate for the age, character, and background of the speakers. The speech of children, for example, sounds different from that of adults; a shy person probably has speech habits different from those of a more outgoing person. Southerners often use words and phrases that Northerners and Midwesterners do not. These groups also pronounce some words differently.

The following dialogue is from Frank Gilroy's play *The Next Contestant*, about a man named Walter Cartright, who is a contestant on a quiz show called *The Big Challenge*. As you read, think about whether the dialogue seems real to you.

Model: *Dialogue*

> *SCENE: stage right is a radio studio; stage left, a girl's room. AT RISE: A program is in progress. An M.C. is at the mike. The girl's room is blacked out.*
>
> **M.C.:** And now, on The Big Challenge, we bring up our next contestant, Mr. Walter Cartright. (*WALTER appears, takes his place before the mike; there is applause from the audience.*) How do you do. Nice to have you with us.
> **WALTER:** Thank you; it's nice to be here.
> **M.C.:** Where are you from, Walter?

WALTER: I'm from New York.

    M.C.: What do you do for a living?

WALTER: I sell business machines.

    M.C.: Have you any idea what we're going to ask you to do?

WALTER: No, sir.

    M.C.: Well, let me tell you it's a beaut. (*Laughter from the audience. WALTER smiles.*) I understand you're engaged. Have a house picked out?

WALTER: Yes, sir.

    M.C.: Furnished?

WALTER: Somewhat.

    M.C.: Well, then you might be able to use a new Hydro-Surf Spray washer and dryer, a complete bedroom suite designed by Viking, a Royal console radio, TV and stereo?

WALTER: Yes, sir. We could sure use them all right.

    M.C.: Well, they're yours, along with other gifts too numerous to mention, provided you meet your Big Challenge . . . Are you ready?

WALTER: Yes, sir.

    M.C.: All right, here it is . . . We challenge you, Walter Cartright, to call up an ex-girlfriend who knows you're engaged and get a date with her. You can say anything you want with the exception you can't tell her that you're on this program or that you've broken your engagement. (*Some audience laughter.*) Do you accept your Big Challenge?

WALTER: (*Hedging.*) Which old girlfriend? (*Laughter.*)

    M.C.: That's up to you.

WALTER: Where would I call from?

    M.C.: Right here. From the Big Challenge Isolation Booth. (*A booth is wheeled out.*) We'll be able to hear everything that's said by both of you . . . but you won't be able to hear us.

WALTER: I don't know.

    M.C.: A Hydro-Surf Spray washer and dryer. A Viking bedroom suite. A Royal console. Plus the Big Bonus Jackpot . . . if you meet your challenge.

WALTER: Gee, I don't know.

    M.C.: Well, let's get your fiancee's opinion. (*Looks out in the audience:*) Will Walter's fiancee please stand up? (*Spots her:*) There she is. And very pretty. (*To WALTER:*) What's her name?

WALTER: Doris.

    M.C.: (*To DORIS:*) Doris, you've heard the challenge. Is it all right with you if Walter tries it? . . . She's nodding her head. She says yes. That's a game little girl. (*Applause for DORIS. M.C. turns to WALTER.*) Well, Walter, what do *you* say?

WALTER: Okay, I'll try it. (*Applause.*)

    M.C.: What's the name of the girl you're going to call?

WALTER: (*Ponders.*) Catherine Horton.

    M.C.: When was the last time you saw her?

WALTER: About a year ago.

    M.C.: She knows you're engaged?

WALTER: Yes.

   M.C.: Okay, let's get started. What's her number?

WALTER: Murray Hill 4-2325.

   M.C.: All right, you go in to the Big Challenge Isolation Booth and dial the number. (*WALTER* enters the booth.)

   M.C.: (*To the audience:*) Hasn't seen the girl in a year but remembered her number like that. Watch out, Doris![1]

If the preceding dialogue seems real, it is because the writer captured the characters' vocabulary and manner of speaking.

Use the dialogue to stage a Reader's Theater in your class. Volunteers should read the dialogue aloud with expression as if they are performing on stage.

Writing Practice 3: *Dialogue*

With a small group of classmates write a dialogue for a real or an imaginary conversation, similar to the one you have just read. Try to make the dialogue sound natural and fit the situation, being certain that it is appropriate for the age, background, and personality of each speaker. You might want to use one of the following situations.

1. Mark, age five, is watching the gas station attendant check the oil in the car. Create a dialogue that might occur between Mark, who asks many questions, and the teenage attendant, who finds Mark an amusing child.

2. Your grandfather has stopped at your house for a Saturday afternoon visit. You are listening to your favorite rock or country and western records with one of your friends. Create the dialogue that might occur as your friend politely tries to explain to your grandfather why the music is so appealing.

---

[1]From *The Next Contestant* by Frank D. Gilroy. Originally published by Samuel French, Inc. Reprinted by permission of Frank D. Gilroy.

Describing a Person

One of the most famous roles of the actor Hal Holbrook is that of Mark Twain. When he walks onto a stage dressed in character, audiences feel they are actually seeing and hearing Mark Twain. Hal Holbrook prepared carefully for this role by studying newspaper clippings about the famous writer and by listening for many hours to an old recording of Mark Twain's voice. To prepare himself to portray this famous American, Hal Holbrook became interested in more than Mark Twain's physical appearance. The actor also studied the writer's movements and speech, facial expressions, posture, and mannerisms—just as you will need to do when you describe characters.

By giving details about appearance, body movements, manner of speaking, and the many other ways in which one person differs from another, you will make your characters come alive for readers.

Asking yourself questions such as the following ones will help you think of details for descriptions of people.

Physical Appearance

How tall is the person?
How much does he or she weigh?
What are the person's facial features?
What type of clothes does he or she usually wear?
Are the clothes in any way unusual?
What kind of hairstyle does the person wear? Does it reflect his or her personality?
What is the color of the person's eyes and hair?
What is the person's complexion like?

Body Movement and Posture

How does the person walk? Stand?
What hand gestures does he or she habitually make?
How are the hands and body held when the person is at rest?
Does he or she have a habit such as constantly adjusting eyeglasses or a lock of hair?

Facial Expression

What does this person look like when smiling? Frowning?
Does he or she have any unusual facial expressions?
Is the person's face especially expressive, or does it seem to hide emotions?

Voice and Speech

Does this person have a particularly high- or low-pitched voice? Is the voice pleasant or unpleasant?
What are his or her speech habits? Does the person speak rapidly or slowly? What dialect does he or she speak?

Personality

What activities does this person enjoy? Dislike?
How does he or she react to other people?
How do other people react to him or her?
How does the person behave when angry? Happy? Sad?

What you say about a person will depend on your purpose, so you will not use all of these details when you write a character description. Sometimes, you will be more interested in personality than in physical appearance, and at other times you will want to concentrate on manner of dress or on just one physical feature, such as eyes. Before beginning to write a character description, ask yourself what you most want your reader to know about your character, and select your details with this purpose in mind.

Like other descriptions, your description of a person will be more vivid if you use specific, sensory details. A sentence such as *His eyes were blue* does not tell you as much about a character as does a sentence such as *His eyes were the pale blue of a robin's egg.*

Model: Character Description

In the following excerpt from her autobiography, *I Know Why the Caged Bird Sings*, Maya Angelou tells about an important woman in her life, named Bertha Flowers.

In Stamps, Arkansas, I met, or rather got to know, the lady who threw me my first life line.

Mrs. Bertha Flowers was the aristocrat of Black Stamps. She had the grace of control to appear warm in the coldest weather, and on the Arkansas summer days it seemed she had a private breeze which swirled around, cooling her. She was thin without the taut look of wiry people, and her printed voile dresses and flowered hats were as right for her as denim overalls for a farmer. She was our side's answer to the richest white woman in town.

Her skin was a rich black that would have peeled like a plum if snagged, but then no one would have thought of getting close enough to Mrs. Flowers to ruffle her dress, let alone snag her skin. She didn't encourage familiarity. She wore gloves too.

I don't think I ever saw Mrs. Flowers laugh, but she smiled often. A slow widening of her thin black lips to show even, small

white teeth, then the slow effortless closing. When she chose to smile on me, I always wanted to thank her. The action was so graceful and inclusively benign.

She was one of the few gentlewomen I have ever known, and has remained throughout my life the measure of what a human being can be.

Momma had a strange relationship with her. Most often when she passed on the road in front of the Store, she spoke to Momma in that soft yet carrying voice, "Good day, Mrs. Henderson." Momma responded with "How you, Sister Flowers?"

Mrs. Flowers didn't belong to our church, nor was she Momma's familiar. Why on earth did she insist on calling her Sister Flowers? Shame made me want to hide my face. Mrs. Flowers deserved better than to be called Sister. Then, Momma left out the verb. Why not ask, "How *are* you, *Mrs.* Flowers?" With the unbalanced passion of the young, I hated her for showing her ignorance to Mrs. Flowers. It didn't occur to me for many years that they were as alike as sisters, separated only by formal education.

Although I was upset, neither of the women was in the least shaken by what I thought an unceremonious greeting. Mrs. Flowers would continue her easy gait up the hill to her little bungalow, and Momma kept on shelling peas or doing whatever had brought her to the front porch.

Occasionally, though, Mrs. Flowers would drift off the road and down to the Store and Momma would say to me, "Sister, you go on and play." As I left I would hear the beginning of an intimate conversation. Momma persistently using the wrong verb, or none at all.

"Brother and Sister Wilcox is sho'ly the meanest—" "Is," Momma? "Is?" Oh, please, not "is," Momma, for two or more. But they talked, and from the side of the building where I waited for the ground to open up and swallow me, I heard the soft-voiced Mrs. Flowers and the textured voice of my grandmother, merging and melting. They were interrupted from time to time by giggles that must have come from Mrs. Flowers (Momma never giggled in her life). Then she was gone.

She appealed to me because she was like people I had never met personally. Like women in English novels who walked the moors (whatever they were) with their loyal dogs racing at a respectful distance. Like the women who sat in front of roaring fireplaces, drinking tea incessantly from silver trays full of scones and crumpets. Women who walked over the "heath" and read morocco-bound books and had two last names divided by a hyphen. It would be safe to say that she made me proud to be Negro, just by being herself.

She acted just as refined as whitefolks in the movies and books and she was more beautiful, for none of them could have come near that warm color without looking gray by comparison.[1]

---

[1]From *I Know Why the Caged Bird Sings* by Maya Angelou. Copyright © 1969 by Maya Angelou. Reprinted by permission of Random House, Inc.

Think and Discuss

1. To make Bertha Flowers seem real to her readers, Maya Angelou describes the way she looks, smiles, and walks. What else does the writer describe about this character?

2. Maya Angelou uses many specific details in her description of Bertha Flowers, for example, "her skin was a rich black that would have peeled like a plum if snagged." What are other examples of specific details used to describe this woman?

3. Do you think Mrs. Henderson's dialogue sounds real? Explain what you learn about Bertha Flowers from the one time she speaks in this excerpt.

4. Why do you think Maya Angelou is embarrassed by the way her grandmother (Momma) speaks to Bertha Flowers?

5. A good character description gives you an idea of what the person being described is like. In your own words, describe the kind of person you think Bertha Flowers is and why you think she is so important to Maya Angelou.

Writing Assignment IV: *Character Description*

A. Prewriting

Listing Descriptive Details: Make a list of the ten most important people in your life. Select one person from your list to write about.

Using the questions on page 99, list or make a word cluster of descriptive details about this person. Include details relating to character and personality, as well as physical appearance.

B. Writing

A Character Description: Write a character description of the person you selected. Decide what aspects of personality and appearance you want to emphasize, and focus on these details in your description. Tell your reader why this person is important to you.

C. Postwriting

Sharing and Polishing a Character Description: Share your character description with a small group of classmates. After you have read your description, ask your classmates to describe in their own words both the physical appearance and the character of the person you wrote about. If their descriptions are either incorrect or vague, you will need to add more specific details to your description.

Revise your composition using the suggestions from your group and the checklist below. Then proofread your final draft, using the Proofreader's Checklist at the back of the book.

Checklist for Revision

1. Does the character description include details relating to physical appearance, body movement, facial expression, or speech quality?

2. Are there details that show the character of the person through his or her mannerisms, conversation, or responses?

3. Are the writer's own feelings and reactions to the individual evident in the composition?

Sentence Combining: Joining Sentences in a Series

New Ways to Add Sentences in a Series

Adding sentences in a series does not always mean attaching the elements to the *end* of the base sentence. For instance, each of the following sets of sentences can be combined in two ways.

Base Sentence: The gardener moved carefully through the rosebushes.
Add: The gardener was talking softly to herself.
Combined: *Talking softly to herself,* the gardener moved carefully through the rosebushes.

or

The gardener moved carefully through the rosebushes, *talking softly to herself.*

Base Sentence: They walked on.
Add: They were looking at the stars.
Add: They were not noticing the open trench in front of them.
Combined: *Looking at the stars,* they walked on, *not noticing the open trench in front of them.*

or

They walked on, *looking at the stars, not noticing the open trench in front of them.*

Exercise 1: Combining Sentences in Varied Ways

On a sheet of paper, combine the following sets of sentences by adding to the front or back of the base sentence. Let the sense of the final combined sentence be your guide. Some signals are provided; when they are not, make the combinations as you think best. Study the example before you begin.

Example

   a. The terrified child quieted down.
     ~~The terrified child~~ was pacified at last.
     ~~The terrified child~~ was whimpering only now and then.
     Pacified at last, the terrified child quieted down, whimpering only now and then.

1. Jake didn't show up for his date.
   ~~Jake was~~ not caring to go to the movies.

2. The soldiers came home.
   ~~The soldiers were~~ singing.
   ~~The soldiers were~~ tired but proud.

3. The plane rode out the storm.
   Its motors ~~were~~ sputtering.
   Its intake valves ~~were~~ clogged.

4. The sleeve of his jacket was torn from the shoulder.
   ~~The sleeve was~~ unraveling rapidly.

5. Karl checked the runner on first base.
   He ~~was not~~ wanting to lose this inning. (,)
   ~~He~~ threw the final pitch. (,and)

6. The hot-air balloon burst into flames.
   The balloon was wobbling dangerously from side to side.
   The balloon fell among the crowd of spectators directly below.

7. Fearless Fosdick leaped on his horse.
   Fearless Fosdick was trying to escape from Monty Goodheart.
   Fearless Fosdick galloped headlong into the cabin door.

8. The editor was looking through the newspaper.
   He was clipping items of interest.
   He was jotting down ideas.

9. The car was carefully checked.
   It was hoisted on the rack.

10. They had to be guided by the stars.
    Their compass was not working.

11. The clouds moved rapidly across the sky.
    The clouds were tall and dark.
    The clouds brought stormy weather.

12. The volcano erupted in the night.
    The volcano was emitting clouds of gas and ash.
    The volcano was causing people to abandon their houses.

13. The earthquake destroyed many buildings.
    The earthquake lasted only seconds.
    The earthquake killed 10 people.

14. The ocean was a mass of whitecaps.
    The winds were blowing strongly across the ocean.
    The ocean was too rough for gulls to float on it.

15. The fish swam in its bowl.
    The fish was looking bored.
    The fish was waiting to be fed.

16. The frog hopped into the water.
    The frog was looking for something to eat.
    The frog was keeping its skin wet.

17. The bird trilled and warbled.
    The bird was one of a chorus.
    The bird was greeting the sunrise.

18. The lizard began sunning itself on a rock.
    The lizard was choosing a warm spot.
    The lizard moved out of the shadows.

19. The kitten dashed about the yard.
    The kitten was chasing a moth.
    The kitten was amusing everyone who watched.

20. Lightning struck the radio tower.
    The lightning was accompanied by thunder.
    The lightning was appearing to split the sky.

Writing Practice 1: *A World Without Television*

The last chapter included an entry for your Writer's Notebook about a world without television. If you have written the entry in your notebook, go back and revise it using the sentence combining methods you know. If you have not written it, write a quick draft, then revise it by varying your sentence patterns. Check your composition for variety of sentence beginnings and lengths.

Special Connectors: The Colon, Dash, and Parentheses

For more information on punctuation, see pages 548-581.

Many writers find that three punctuation marks, the *colon*, *dash*, and *parentheses*, give them another way to join sentences. These three punctuation marks have special uses, however, and should not be overused. The following examples show their most common use in combining sentences.

Colon

Each bake-off contestant is to bring supplies as follows: two large pans, a wire eggbeater, and a cookie cutter.

No matter what Gloria told him, he would never forget what worried him most: her failing health, her loss of memory, and her lack of exercise.

In the preceding two examples, the sentence base is followed by a *list* that names or illustrates the idea in the base.

Dash

One use of the dash shows a sudden change in thought:

At that moment Zeno—no, it was Tiger—came crashing through the gate.

Without the dashes the sentence would be confusing:

At that moment Zeno no, it was Tiger came crashing through the gate.

Another use of the dash is to separate a list at the front of a sentence from the rest of the sentence:

Happiness, wealth, fame—these were the only things Jack wanted out of life.

Parentheses

Writers use *parentheses* to enclose added information that they do not want to detract from the rest of the sentence. While the dash emphasizes an interruption, parentheses de-emphasize it.

Mr. Beaker (wouldn't you know he had a large hat?) walked into the room and demanded our attention.

First she lived in Fremont (that's in Nebraska, not Iowa) and then in Miami (that's Florida, not Ohio).

Notice that the information inside the parentheses is not capitalized and that punctuation belonging to the whole sentence comes outside the parentheses.

The signals for these combinations are (*colon*), (*dash*), (*paired dashes*), and (*parens*).

Exercise 2: *Joining Sentences with Colons, Dashes, and Parentheses*

On a sheet of paper, combine each sentence set. For the first five sets, follow the signal. For the last five sets, you must decide which punctuation is best. Study the examples before you begin.

Examples

a. On our treasure hunt we had to find four things.
These things were a ball-point pen, two bird feathers, a paper cup, and a red rock. (*colon*)

On our treasure hunt we had to find four things: a ball-point pen, two bird feathers, a paper cup, and a red rock.

b. Such were the gifts we treasured most.
We treasured a music box, a set of knives, and a hand-carved statue.

A music box, a set of knives, and a hand-carved statue—such were the gifts we treasured most.

1. Carl tipped the cab driver, and we were on our way.
The tip was about one dollar, I think. (*parens*)

2. The small boy got two white rabbits for his birthday.
Maybe they were gray. (*parens*)

3. You surely haven't forgotten the basic documents of American history.

The documents are the Declaration of Independence, the Constitution and the Emancipation Proclamation. (*colon*)

4. Mom believed my story and gave me an extra dollar on my allowance.
But did I really fool her? (*paired dashes*)

5. These were the major ingredients of the delicious enchiladas.
The ingredients were chili, chicken, cheese, and onions. (*dash*)

6. I don't know why John is so mean.
He's my brother.

7. Red meat is full of protein.
   Vegetarians, of course, do not eat red meat.

8. Several beautiful birds were perched on the wire.
   The birds were cockatoos, parrots, macaws, and mynahs.

9. By the end of the week, there were sixteen inches of snow on the ground.
   Some people claimed it was more.

10. These are the things I enjoy most about summer.
    I enjoy sleeping late, having time to read, and swimming for hours.

Writing Practice 2: *Revising for Sentence Variety*

Select one composition you wrote at the beginning of Chapter 3. Use the sentence combining techniques you have learned to revise your composition.

5 Understanding Expository Writing

The Uses of Expository Writing

Expository writing, which explains thoughts, explores ideas, and presents information, is the writing you encounter most often in your everyday life. In this section you will read about its many uses.

Models: Different Kinds of Exposition

Expository writing is used to give directions.

> To get to Foshay Junior High School, take the Harbor Freeway to the Santa Barbara Avenue exit and then drive west on Santa Barbara to Western Avenue. Foshay Junior High School is on the corner of Santa Barbara and Western.

Expository writing is used to explain a process (how to do something or how something works).

> To dial a long-distance number directly, you should do the following: (a) Look up the area code of the city in the front pages of your telephone book; (b) Dial *1*, then the area code, and then *555-1212,* which is the long distance information number; (c) Give the operator the name of the city you are calling and the name of the party you are trying to reach; (d) When the operator gives you your party's telephone number, write it down; (e) Break the connection by placing the receiver in its cradle; (f) Pick up the receiver again and dial *1,* then the area code, then the party's number. For example, to reach Mr. Bert Watanabe in Salt Lake City, obtain the proper number in the way just described, and then dial *1-801-555-7766.*

Expository writing is used to make reports.

Report on the Laketon Area Recycling Center

> Our group's assignment was to report on LARC, the Laketon Area Recycling Center. LARC is a nonprofit organization staffed by volunteers. The center is located at the corner of Jackson and Mill Streets and is open 9–3 on Saturdays. The center accepts newspapers, aluminum, tin cans, and miscellaneous metal for recycling. We were surprised to learn that motor oil can also be

recycled. Because LARC is run by volunteers who are always busy, it is important to follow the Center's directions for recycling.

Newspapers should be tied in bundles or placed flat in grocery bags. (Magazines are not accepted.) Items such as aluminum or tin cans and bottles should be carefully rinsed. Aluminum boxing tins, pop-top cans, and foil should be crushed to take up as little space as possible. Remove lead, metal or plastic caps, and labels from glass bottles. The paper labels should also be removed from tin cans. Cut out both ends of tin cans and flatten each can with your foot. Used motor oil can be collected in any closed containers, such as bleach bottles. Sorting glass, tin, and aluminum into separate bags or boxes also helps the center and saves the volunteers' time.

We also learned that the center welcomes teen volunteers. If you can volunteer at least three hours a month, call Anna Rivera at 555-7470.

Expository writing is used to present information through the use of facts or data.

Phillis Wheatley[1]

Phillis Wheatley was the most popular black writer of colonial times. Kidnapped from Africa at the age of eight and sold as a slave to a master in Boston, she started writing poetry as a teenager. She called her first poem, "To the University of Cambridge, In New England, 1767." "An Elegiac Poem on the Death of George Whitefield" was the first of her poems to be *published*. It praised the famous English minister George Whitefield. This poem became her most popular and was published in newspapers in Boston, Philadelphia, and New York. It was also *reprinted* many times.

Phillis Wheatley became famous. People began to talk about her writing. The news of Phillis Wheatley's poetry spread to England and to the rest of Europe.

Expository writing is used to explain opinions.

Schools need to establish a policy of homework for a purpose. Students resent having to fill an hour or two of their time each night with meaningless busy work. If, however, they are assigned homework that has a specific purpose and teaches them something beyond what they have learned in the classroom, then they are less inclined to feel that their time is wasted. Students need to understand the purpose and merit of each homework assignment. They also need to understand how the quality of their homework assignments will affect their final grade. If homework has purpose and merit for both teacher and student, then it is time well spent.

---

[1]From *A History of Black Americans* by William L. Katz and Warren J. Halliburton. Reprinted by permission of Harcourt Brace Jovanovich, Inc.

Expository writing is used to form definitions.

> What does the verb *to read* mean? If you run your eyes over the page, noticing every word carefully, but cannot give the meaning of what you have looked at, then you have not read. On the other hand, if you can tell or explain the meaning of the words and sentences, then you have actually read. The verb *to read*, then, can be defined as "getting meaning from print."

Writing Practice 1: *Expository Paragraph*

Only when writing accomplishes its purpose is it effective. If expository writing is effective, you should be able to follow the directions or understand the process or idea being explained. Explain why each of the three following pieces of exposition is ineffective and then rewrite one of them, adding any information you think might be necessary, until it does a good job of giving information.

1. *Scrambled Eggs*

   Some flour
   About one tablespoon water
   Salt and pepper

   > Mix all these ingredients together and then cook in a hot pan with some margarine or butter. Oh yes, add diced ham or sausage, if you like.

2. *To Get to My House*

   > Drive two or three blocks down the street and turn left. Continue down that street for several miles. On the right you will see a lovely old farmhouse that was bought by a family with four children. They plan to move from the city and live here. Anyway, somewhere around the farmhouse you will see a road. I live down that road.

3.   *Report of the Planning Committee*

> We looked at a lot of places. Some of the people we talked to were really nice and were a big help, but we finally decided to have the dance at the school gym. The civic center and the hotel would cost too much. Besides, no one would want to drive that far in bad weather.

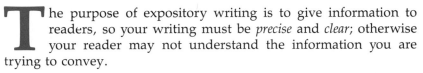

Purpose and the Way You Write

The purpose of expository writing is to give information to readers, so your writing must be *precise* and *clear*; otherwise your reader may not understand the information you are trying to convey.

Precise writing is specific, not general or vague; it gives information exactly.

Imprecise expository writing is not likely to be effective. The difference between one-third cup and one-fourth cup in a recipe can mean the failure of a dish; directions that read "two blocks" instead of "three blocks" may cause you to become lost. On the other hand, precise writing, such as the report on the recycling center which you read in the preceding section, gives exact and complete information.

Clear writing can be easily understood by readers.

Clear writing is also carefully organized so that there is a logical flow of ideas. In a recipe, for example, the ingredients are listed first; instructions for combining the ingredients follow; and instructions for cooking the dish are last.

The report about the recycling center is clear because it is well organized. The writer begins by defining LARC, giving its location, hours of operation, and materials that can be recycled. Finally, the writer describes the procedure for preparing materials to be brought to the center.

Clear writing has no unnecessary details.

A recipe for peanut butter soup with a history of the peanut in the middle of a list of ingredients would be confusing. Directions to a town that include a description of the town's founder would be hard to follow. Unnecessary details detract from the topic. Clear writing includes details that are related to the topic and develop the main idea.

Model: An Expository Article

In the following excerpt from an article describing a meeting of people concerned with endangered animals, Emily Hahn reports on a presentation made by James Antrim and Lanny Cornell of Sea World. As you read, notice how the writer organizes specific details in the report.

The next offering was mainly a series of slides, presided over by James Antrim, curator of mammals, and Lanny Cornell, vice-president for research and veterinary husbandry, at Sea World, a marine establishment just outside San Diego. Their topic was the reproduction of sea otters in captivity. To start with, Antrim told us a few things we should know about sea otters, such as that they date back to an ancestor that lived probably a million years ago. He told us what they weigh when they are born (three to five pounds) and when they grow up (a maximum of ninety-nine pounds for males, seventy-two for females). Their vibrissae, or whiskers, are very useful for finding food in the water. Unlike other marine mammals, they have no blubber, and depend for protection on very closely growing fur and a high metabolic rate. Although there are certain differences between the sea otters of the California coast and those of Alaska, they are all one species. In the eighteenth century, before their fur became a popular trade item, there were probably between a hundred thousand and a hundred and fifty thousand animals in the population, which ranged from Kamchatka and the northern Japanese islands to the west coast of North America as far down as Baja, California. The greedy fur trade nearly wiped them out. From 1741 to 1911, when a moratorium was enacted, an estimated million pelts were taken, but the species has made a comeback. The California population is now between eighteen hundred and two thousand animals, according to the latest official report. This population is classified as threatened under the Endangered Species Act of 1973—especially since it is concentrated in central California and could be wiped out by some environmental disaster, such as a large oil spill.[1]

Specific details

Specific details

Specific details

[1]From "The Eleventh Hour" by Emily Hahn from *The New Yorker*, September 1, 1980. © 1980. Reprinted by permission of The New Yorker Magazine, Inc.

Think and Discuss

1. Which sentence states the topic of the report?

2. What kinds of facts and data does the writer include concerning the sea otters?

3. What is the writer's purpose in specifying these facts and data about otters in this report?

Writing Practice 2: *Expository Writing*

As practice in expository writing, complete one of the following exercises. Be sure to make your writing as precise and clear as possible, and proofread what you have written to avoid errors in spelling and punctuation. Use the Checklist for Proofreading found at the back of the book.

1. Write directions for traveling from your house or apartment to your school for a person who does not know your city or area.

2. Write the procedure for preparing a simple meal, such as scrambled eggs and toast or canned soup and a peanut butter sandwich.

3. Prepare a list of hints for saving energy in the home.

4. Imagine that you are part of a committee assigned to investigate the possibility of having school during the summer, and vacation during the months of December, January, and February. In your report list the advantages of (a) having school during the summer and having vacation during the winter; (b) having school during the winter and having vacation in the summer. End your report with your recommendation and summarize your reasons for making the recommendation.

Finding Subject Matter

You are an expert on many subjects, though you may not realize it. For example, you probably know very little about economics, but you know almost everything about your own finances: how much money you now have and how much you can expect during a month or year; expenses that your funds must cover; plans that you have for spending your money on pleasure; and so on. You are probably not an authority on architecture, but you know which houses or buildings in your neighborhood appeal most to you, and you could explain why, if you gave the matter some thought. On the basis of your own knowledge, you are indeed an expert on many, many subjects.

In the following sections you will be writing on subjects that you already know about, subjects that you can explain through your own experience. In a later chapter you will learn how to use outside resources to learn about subjects.

Writing Practice 3: *Identifying What You Know*

In your Writer's Notebook make a list of ten subjects you know something about. Include a variety of subjects with which you have had some personal experience. You may want to include a few of the following suggestions on your list. Save your list for the next Writing Practice.

1. Sports
2. Music
3. Literature
4. Careers
5. Homework
6. Friendship
7. Fads
8. Computers

Focusing Your Writing

Interesting and informative writing gives specific details about a subject.

If the subject is too broad, you will not be able to supply many specific details about it in a short paper; instead, you will use the entire paper to make general statements, and your writing will lack focus. For example, the subjects you listed in Writing Practice 3 are probably too broad for a short paper. However, they have one thing in common: each contains many small topics that cover less than the original subject. The following examples show how subjects can be narrowed to become good topics for writing.

Subject: The history of the United States
[This subject covers hundreds of years, from the time America was first discovered to the present.]

Topic: The Fiesta of Five Flags celebration in Pensacola, Florida, a commemoration of the settlement of Pensacola
[The subject has been narrowed to *one* city and to one event.]

Subject: The exploration of outer space
[This subject covers an infinite area and many years.]

Topic: My visit to the Air and Space Museum in Washington, D.C.
[This subject has been narrowed to *one* person's experiences on *one* occasion.]

Subject: Literature
[This subject covers millions of books and thousands of years, from the first spoken or written stories to the present.]

Topic: Why I like *Roughing It*, by Mark Twain
[This subject has been narrowed to *one* person's experiences with *one* book.]

Subject: Sports
[This subject covers all sports played in the entire world, from the beginning of history to the present.]

Topic: Some safety rules for bicycling
[This subject has been narrowed to *one* aspect of *one* sport.]

Writing Practice 4: *Narrowing a Topic*

Using the ten subjects you selected in the previous exercise, list two specific topics for each subject that you might use as a basis for writing a short paper from your own experience.

Example

Subject: School

Topic: The hectic life of a freshman

Topic: The homework policy of our school

Gathering and Recording Information

O nce you have chosen a subject and developed a topic from it, the next step is to gather information about your topic. One way to do this is to use a system for gathering information, such as one of the prewriting methods discussed in the first chapter. Another way is to read through your Writer's Notebook for ideas that you have recorded there.

One method for taking notes about a subject is to record each idea on a separate slip of paper, on a 3 × 5 card, or on sheets of scratch paper cut into four sections. Notes will be a help to you later when you begin organizing your writing. The following sample shows the way a note on the topic *A Day in the Life of a Television Addict* might look:

> The late morning and early afternoon hours frustrate me because I must choose between soap operas and game shows, and I like them both.

Sometimes your notes will be words or phrases:

My interest in mystery series

Commercials

The intellectual stuff on educational channels

Notes may also be sentences:

Why am I so fascinated by game shows?

I can miss two or three episodes of a soap opera and still know what's going on when I tune in again.

Notes may be paragraphs:

There is one big problem with television mini-series. In every episode after the first one, several minutes at the beginning are devoted to finding out what went on in the other episodes, and then at the end several minutes are spent previewing what is to come. Too much time is spent going over past episodes and previewing future ones.

Each note is an idea for writing. When you begin to write, you can throw out the ideas that are not useful, and organize the ideas you want to keep.

Writing Practice 5: *Taking Notes*

Select one topic from the list you made in Writing Practice 4 to write about. Use the directions that follow to take notes on the specific topic you have selected.

1. Use the basic questioning method to develop ideas concerning your topic, and make notes of these ideas: Why am I interested in this topic? What do I know about it? What do I need to find out about it? Where and how will I get this information? What have I learned about the topic that I want to communicate to others?

2. For two or three days make notes of every idea you have about your topic.

3. Save the stack of notes you accumulate in this exercise for the next Writing Practice.

Planning Your Writing

Suppose that you have fifty slips of paper containing notes relating to your topic. You could begin to write, taking the first note from the stack, explaining and developing the idea on it, and then going to the second slip and doing the same. The resulting essay, however, would be puzzling to readers, for they would not be able to discover how ideas relate to one another. On the other hand, you could look through your collection of notes and begin to separate them into stacks, grouping together those ideas that are related to one another. This would be an excellent way to start to organize your writing.

As you read the following notes, collected over a three-day period for an essay entitled "A Day in the Life of a TV Addict," think how you might organize them.

1. What is a typical day on the tube like? How much time is given to each kind of show? Is the schedule balanced among kinds of shows, or is too much time given to some and not enough to others?

2. Characters on soap operas all seem to be doctors or lawyers.

3. Movies are usually spoiled by too many commercials.

4. I spend so much time watching TV that many times I don't get my homework finished.

5. Last night I watched a National Geographic special on Alaska.

6. Nature shows

7. The game shows and human greed

8. Why do I like certain characters?

9. Evening talk shows have much empty time.

10. I have always liked to travel. Maybe that's why I like TV shows about different places in the world. I am especially interested in nature, wildlife, and the wilderness.

11. TV hosts annoy me. They're too smooth, too self-satisfied.

12. Ridiculous situation comedies

13. Last night I watched a show on how the human heart works.

14. On Thursday, December 28, the 6 P.M. to midnight lineup on three major networks was as follows: news, 6 hours; adventure show, 1 hour; special, 1 hour; detective shows, 4½ hours; musical variety, 30 minutes; documentary, 30 minutes; drama, 2 hours; comedy, 2½ hours; talk show, 1 hour.

15. Has TV changed since I began watching? How? Is it better or worse? Why?

Writing Practice 6: *Organizing Notes*

Some of the sample notes about television shows seem to relate to the same idea. For example, notes 1 and 14 relate to the kinds of shows on television and to the amount of time devoted to each kind. On a sheet of paper, list in separate columns the ideas that seem to cluster together. Then organize your own notes from the previous exercise in the same manner.

The Informal Outline

An *informal outline* shows the arrangement of major ideas and supporting details.

The purpose of an informal outline is to remind you of what you want to say and the order in which you want to discuss your ideas.

If you arranged your note cards into stacks according to related ideas, read through each stack and rearrange the cards until the order makes sense to you. When you actually begin writing your outline, you will probably decide not to use some of your notes, and you may think of new ideas to add. The following informal outline is based on the television notes in the preceding section.

A Day in the Life of a TV Addict

The Definition of TV Addict
    Hours spent in front of TV set
    Neglected homework
    Knowledge of TV

Game Shows
    Human greed
    Foolish contestants
    Smooth hosts
    Too easy questions

Soap Operas
    Characters as doctors or lawyers
    Female characters as housewives
    Talkativeness of characters
    Unhappiness of characters

Night Shows
    Ridiculous comedies
    Occasional good documentary
    Too many commercials
    Empty time on talk shows

The Lesson from Television
    Room for improvement on TV
    Need for discriminating viewing

The only "rule" for organizing an informal outline is to arrange it in a way that will help you organize your paper. The items in the preceding outline are not marked with letters or numbers, but you can easily tell which are the main ideas because the details supporting them are indented slightly under the headings.

Writing Practice 7: *An Informal Outline*

Using the notes you assembled for the previous exercise, prepare an informal outline. Begin by putting notes related to the same ideas together, and then use the stacks to help you with the outline.

Considering Your Audience

The purpose of expository writing is to get information and ideas from a writer to a reader. For this reason, you must keep your audience or readers in mind as you plan and write your exposition.

Your audience affects *what* you say and the language you use in writing.

Which of the following two sets of directions is written for a person unfamiliar with the location?

1. The Martin Luther King, Jr., Expressway is the major highway running north and south through town. Head north on this highway. On your right, approximately two miles before the city limits, you will see a small shopping center called Lakeview. Take Exit 6, one mile past Lakeview, off the expressway.

2. Go north on King. Take Exit 6 past Lakeview.

The second set of directions is written for a person familiar with the area. The reader of these directions must know that *King* is the *Martin Luther King, Jr., Expressway* that runs north and south through the town and that *Lakeview* is a shopping center located within sight of the expressway. Although the second set of directions is much shorter than the first, it is still an effective piece of communication if the reader knows the area.

In expository writing it is important to give your audience all of the information they need to understand your subject, but it is also important not to bore them by giving them information they already know. Before you begin writing, ask yourself how much your audience knows about your subject. For example, you can probably begin a report for your classmates on the pharaohs of Egypt without explaining what a pharaoh is or where Egypt is located, because your classmates probably know these facts. You could not, however, expect first-graders to know them. A report for first-graders would have to contain more basic information than a report for your classmates.

Models: Expository Paragraphs for Two Different Audiences

The following two paragraphs were written by a college professor for ninth-grade readers of a book about writing. Which paragraph is the more effective piece of communication between a college professor and ninth-grade students?

1

The example, considered as an analogue of the concrete universal, functions both illustratively and developmentally in that a reader apprehends it as a particularization of an abstraction and is forced to interpret it through the creation or intuition of a subsidiary category of examples. This cognitive process inevitably impacts support of and development for a topic.

2

Examples help support topics. Even one example often brings a topic to life. For instance, if I write, "Most addictions, such as the addiction to tobacco, are harmful, but there are also positive addictions," my readers will have very little idea what I mean. But notice what happens if I give just one example of a positive addiction: "The addiction to exercise helps keep a person healthy, both mentally and physically." Now the reader will know what sort of thing a positive addiction is and can supply other examples: "Oh yes," (the reader will think), "there are many positive addictions. An addiction to running strengthens the heart. An addiction to studying brings success in school. An addiction to clarity helps make writing effective."

The first selection is not an effective piece of communication between the college professor and the ninth-grade students simply because most ninth-grade students could not understand it. One reason for this difficulty is that the paragraph contains many technical words, like *analogue, concrete universal,* and *subsidiary.* Technical words are those used by people with special training or knowledge to communicate with peers. If this college professor were writing for another professor, these words would be appropriate; otherwise, they are not.

The second selection is more effective in this situation, because it uses terms that are common to a ninth-grade student. The writer also uses many examples to help the reader understand and visualize the point being made.

Writing Practice 8: *Considering Your Audience*

For more information about considering your audience, see pages 672-675.

This is an exercise to give you practice in adjusting your writing to your audience. Using the informal outline you wrote in the preceding Writing Practices, develop your topic, or one section of your topic if it has several, into an expository paragraph directed to your classmates. Then choose a different audience, perhaps one listed below, and rewrite the same paragraph, adjusting the language to your new audience.

1. A six-year-old brother or sister of a friend
2. A foreign exchange student from another country, who knows almost nothing about life in America
3. A senior citizen who is volunteering in your school
4. A new student in your class who has transferred from a nearby town

Writing Practice 9: *Response Groups*

Read both your paragraphs to a small group of classmates. Do not tell them which one was written for them as the audience. After reading each paragraph, have them tell you which one was written for them. Then see if they can guess the audience for whom you wrote the second paragraph.

Select one paper to revise and proofread using the comments and suggestions from your group.

For Your Writer's Notebook

Historians and psychologists often comment on the powerful impact television has on American life. One way to understand the medium's influence is to consider what society might be like if television had never been invented. Write a notebook entry about a world without television, thinking carefully about how different life would be. You might discuss how American society would be changed. Would Americans be less violent? Would they know less about other countries and world affairs? Would they be healthier because they would be outdoors and would exercise more? If you prefer, you might limit your entry to how your own life would be affected. How would you use the time you now spend watching television? What would you miss most? Consider both the beneficial and harmful effects of a world without television.

Sentence Combining:
Using Adjectives, Who, and Which

Building Sentences by Insertion

Inserting sentences involves taking *part* of one sentence and putting it into a *base sentence*. The part that is inserted may be changed in some way. The following examples show how insertions are made.

Base Sentence: The Snoop Sisters used to be on television.
Insert: The television was national.
Combined: The Snoop Sisters used to be on *national television*.

Notice that the words *The television was* in the second sentence have been removed because it would be impossible to repeat those words a second time and still have a good sentence.

Base Sentence: A young man stood before the mirror.
Insert: The young man was handsome.
Combined: A *handsome* young man stood before the mirror.

In the previous example the word *handsome* has been inserted into the base sentence because it describes the young man. If there were another sentence to insert, the result might be the following combination.

Base Sentence: A young man stood before the mirror.
Insert: The young man was handsome.
Insert: The mirror was cracked.
Combined: The *handsome* young man stood before the *cracked* mirror.

When there are no labels, you should be able to decide which sentence is the base sentence and which sentences are to be inserted into it.

Exercise 1: Combining Sentences by Insertion

On a sheet of paper, combine the following sentences after first studying the example. The first sentence in each set is the base sentence.

Example

   a. The woman looked for shelter.
      The woman was <u>frightened</u>.
      The shelter was <u>safe</u>.
      The frightened woman looked for safe shelter.

1. The vase contains roses.
   The vase is <u>Chinese</u>.

2. A telescope is an instrument.
   The telescope is <u>powerful</u>.
   The instrument is <u>delicate</u>.

3. Blackbirds were sitting on the telephone pole.
   There were <u>five</u> blackbirds.
   The telephone pole was <u>tall</u>.

4. Juan's car has a tire.
   Juan's car is <u>new</u>.
   The tire is <u>flat</u>.

5. The package was left in the mailbox.
   The package was <u>strange</u>.
   The mailbox was the <u>Joneses'</u>.

Exercise 2: Combining Sentences by Insertion

The signals for this exercise are (,), (*and*), and (,*and*). Place the punctuation and conjunction that correspond to the signal before that part in the combined sentence. On a sheet of paper, combine each set of sentences with the base sentence. Study the examples before you begin.

Examples

   a. The house showed signs of neglect.
      The house was old.
      The house was weather-beaten. (,)

      The old, weather-beaten house showed signs of neglect.

   b. Frank's new jacket was a bargain.
      The jacket is black.
      The jacket is white.

      Frank's new black-and-white jacket was a bargain.

1. The attorney defended the case well.
   The attorney was skilled.
   The case was difficult.

2. The child looked longingly into the window.
   The child was small.
   The child was dirty. (,)
   The child was bedraggled. (,*and*)

3. Oscar was a loving puppy.
   Oscar was frisky.
   Oscar was healthy. (,)

4. When the plane landed, he fought for a glimpse of the survivor.
   The plane was crippled.
   The plane was battered.
   The plane was single-engined.
   The glimpse was brief.
   The glimpse was covert.
   The survivor was lone.

5. The adults discussed the value of programming.
   The adults were concerned.
   The value was educational.
   The value was entertaining.
   The programming was children's.
   The programming was for television.

Inserting Who and Which

For information on relative pronouns, see pages 329-331.

With the inserting process you can add groups of words to tell *who* or *which* a person or thing is, as follows:

Base Sentence: I admire Beverly Sills.

Insert: Beverly Sills is a famous opera singer. (*who*)

Combined: I admire Beverly Sills, *who is a famous opera singer.*

The last sentence has been formed by combining the information about who Beverly Sills is with the first sentence. Notice that the words *Beverly Sills* in the second sentence have been removed because it would be impossible to repeat those words a second time in a good sentence. Notice also that the word *who* has been added in the combined sentence because it relates *a famous opera singer* with *Beverly Sills.*

The same process can be used to insert information about *which* person or object is being discussed, as the following examples show. The combining signal follows the insert sentence. In these examples commas separate the inserted information from the rest of the sentence.

Base Sentence: The dictionary was discarded.

Insert: The dictionary was missing the A's. (*which*)

Combined: The dictionary, *which was missing the* A's, was discarded.

Exercise 3: Using who and which to Combine Sentences

On a sheet of paper, combine the following sets of sentences. Use the signals when given. Consider the first sentence the base sentence. Study the examples before you begin.

Example

a. I sent a gift to Aunt Margaret.
    Aunt Margaret is my favorite aunt. (*who*)

    I sent a gift to Aunt Margaret, who is my favorite aunt.

1.   When we take the trolley in San Francisco, the driver lets me work the brakes.
      The driver is my older brother. (*who*)

2. The metric system is not difficult to learn.
    The metric system will eventually replace our present system of weights and measures. (*which*)

3. Art Buchwald writes humorous articles for many newspapers.
    Art Buchwald is a syndicated columnist. (*who*)

4. The seventh-graders could hardly wait until they became eighth-graders.
    The seventh-graders had worked hard at their studies all year. (*who*)

5. Hiromi's pocket calculator helped her master the arithmetic problems.
    The arithmetic problems were extremely difficult. (*which*)

6. The city council voted against building a superhighway through the middle of town.
    The city council was unhappy with rising costs.

7. The city council voted against building a superhighway through the middle of town.
    The middle of town was too congested as it was.

8. Miss Marple successfully solved the mystery and named the criminal.
    Miss Marple is a famous Agatha Christie sleuth.

9. Although Alice Wu excels at many things, much of the credit must go to her parents.
    Her parents encouraged her to do her best.

10. My cousin Matt used to live in Squirrel Flats; now he lives in Seattle, Washington.
    Squirrel Flats is a wide spot in the road.
    Seattle, Washington, is a large metropolitan area.

Writing Practice: *Comparing Compositions*

Look over the writing assignments that you completed in Chapter 5, Understanding Expository Writing. Select one composition and revise it to vary the sentence patterns. Join sentences that are too short by inserting sentence parts and by using other sentence combining methods you have learned. Divide sentences that are too long.

Read both your first draft and your revised composition to a small group of classmates without telling them which one is revised. Then ask them to choose the one they think exhibits greater sentence variety.

Writing an Expository Composition

Writing a Composition

If you understand the purposes of exposition and have practiced writing several kinds of expository paragraphs, you are now ready to put your ideas together in an expository composition. Even though the purpose of expository writing is to explain and inform, this does not mean that you cannot include your personal experiences and ideas. On the contrary, expository compositions can be lifeless and dull without the addition of the writer's style and personal touch. In the following sections, you will learn to organize and write an effective expository composition based on your experiences.

The Thesis Statement

Suppose that you have been assigned a subject for writing: *Leisure activities*. A subject such as this one is not effective as the basis for a successful composition because it includes too much: leisure activities in all parts of the world, through all of history, and of all kinds—in fact, everything about leisure activities. From that subject, however, it is easy to develop a topic for writing: *My volunteer work at the local museum*. From a subject such as *Animals*, you can develop a topic such as *Raising turkeys* or *The "zoo" in my backyard*.

Even though these topics might serve as good bases for papers, they still lack something. Anyone might ask, "What about your volunteer work at the local museum?" "What about raising turkeys?" "What about the 'zoo' in your backyard?" The writer could answer these questions with a thesis statement.

A *thesis statement* declares the *purpose* of a paper and gives it focus, direction, and sharpness.

Subject: Leisure activities

Topic: My volunteer work at the local museum

Thesis Statement: Working as a museum volunteer, I have learned about life in the past, become acquainted with the services a museum offers to the community, and discovered new talents in myself.

Now the purpose of the paper is clear.

Subject: Animals

Topic: Raising turkeys

Thesis Statement: Raising turkeys is a profitable but risky way to make a living.

The writer will explain both the profits and the risks.

Subject: Animals

Topic: The "zoo" in my backyard

Thesis
Statement: A close observer will find that my backyard contains a
real zoo of insects, birds, and amphibians.

For information on
complete and
incomplete sentences,
see pages 534-546.

The writer with the preceding thesis statement will give the
reader a close look at all the animal life to be found in the backyard.

A thesis statement may or may not appear in your paper, but it
serves as a "guidance system" for your writing in that you select only
those ideas and details that relate to your thesis statement. A thesis
statement is always written as a complete, declarative sentence.

Writing Practice 1: *Selecting a Topic*

In your Writer's Notebook make a list of five to ten activities that you
enjoy doing in your leisure time. The following list gives examples:

1. Playing in a band
2. Photography
3. Volunteer work
4. Odd jobs
5. Reading mystery stories

6. Sports activities
7. Cheerleading
8. Singing in a choir
9. Bicycling
10. Family outings

Select five subjects from your list and narrow them to topics
suitable for a short paper. For each topic, write a thesis statement that
serves as a "guidance system" for selecting details, as in the following
examples. Save your list for the next Writing Practice.

Examples

Subject: *Hobbies*
Topic: *My experience as a spelunker*
Thesis
Statement: *Exploring caves, or spelunking, is an exciting experience.*

Subject: *School*
Topic: *Driver education courses in my school*
Thesis
Statement: *Our school should offer more driver education courses.*

Writing the Introduction

P roducers of television shows know that viewers will switch channels if the beginning of a program is uninteresting. At the same time, viewers must get the information they need to understand what happens later in the show. Program openings must be both interesting and informative.

Your job as a writer is similar to that of a television producer. The introduction of your composition must interest your reader and also give some idea of what your paper will be about. In most short papers the introduction will be the first paragraph, and it can include a statement of the thesis.

Models: *Introductions for Expository Compositions*

The following examples show ways to make your introduction interesting to your readers while giving them the information they need to understand your paper.

Use specific, sensory details.

That first day, the museum seemed a strange and ominous place filled with fantastic objects. A wooden hay fork suspended from the ceiling spread a grotesque shadow across the floor, and my footsteps echoed as I moved past an old cookstove covered with mysterious iron kitchen appliances. In the carpentry shop I fingered the rough wooden walls and stared at the sharp-toothed saws. My work as a volunteer at the West Chicago Historical Museum has taught me about all these objects, and I am now as familiar with the museum as I am with my own room. Working as a museum volunteer, I have learned about life in the past, become acquainted with the services a museum offers to the community, and discovered new talents in myself.

Begin with an interesting anecdote.

Filled with apprehension about my own abilities, I arrived early for my first day as a museum volunteer. My first task was to unpack and clean a box of antique tools, recent donations to the woodworking exhibit. The tools, wrapped in old, yellowed newspapers were caked with cobwebs and grime. I worked steadily for an hour cleaning several wooden planes until their dark walnut gleamed. I don't remember when I got absorbed in reading the old 1903 newspapers the tools were wrapped in, but suddenly I turned to see the museum director behind me, smiling in amusement. My anxiety about being caught with my nose in the newspapers vanished when he laughed and said I seemed to have the makings of a real historian. We spent the next fifteen minutes together, flattening out the crumpled sheets of newsprint and reading headlines and funny, old advertisements to one another. Relaxed and intrigued by what I was learning, I realized working at the museum was going to be fun.

Begin with a question.

Do you know that West Chicago was once called Turner Junction? Are you aware that many museums can help you write a family history? Could you explain your city's history to a group of adults? Through my work as a youth volunteer at the West Chicago Historical Museum, I have learned about life in the past, become acquainted with the services a museum offers to the community, and discovered new talents in myself.

Begin with a point of view that is opposite to the one you express in your thesis statement.

When I told my brother I was going to work as a youth volunteer at the West Chicago Historical Museum, he laughed. He was convinced I would find the work dull and would soon quit. He was wrong; I have never thought of quitting. I have learned so much that my hours at the museum always seem to fly past. Through my museum work I have learned about life in the past, become acquainted with the services a museum offers to the community, and discovered new talents in myself.

Think and Discuss

1. In the first paragraph the writer creates a mood through the use of sensory detail. What is the mood at the beginning of the paragraph? What specific words and phrases help create this mood? At what point in the paragraph does the mood begin to change?

2. The second paragraph also uses sensory detail and creates a different kind of mood through the use of an anecdote. How is the mood in the second paragraph different from that in the first? When does the mood change? What details does the writer use to help the reader visualize the scene?

3. The third paragraph uses questions to get the reader's attention. The kinds of questions used to introduce a topic are very important. How do these particular questions appeal to the reader?

4. Presenting an opposite point of view in the fourth paragraph provides contrast and helps the reader identify with the writer. How does this introduction lend a personal perspective to the exposition?

Writing Practice 2: *Writing an Introductory Paragraph*

Select one of the topics and thesis statements you wrote in Writing Practice 1. Write an introductory paragraph for an expository composition. You may want to use an idea from one of the introductory paragraph models presented in this chapter. Do not, however, be limited to the methods of introduction you have read about. Use your imagination to invent a good opening.

Writing the Body

The body of a good composition is *unified* and *coherent*.

When each paragraph in the body develops one main part of the thesis, the composition has unity. When readers can move easily from one idea to another in the composition and clearly understand the relationship between those ideas, the composition has coherence.

Chapter 5, the chapter on writing paragraphs, discusses how to build a unified paragraph using the TRI (Topic-Restriction-Illustration) method. This method can also help you write a unified composition. Think of each paragraph as a restriction of the topic that presents and develops one main point. In the following informal

outline, the writer has restricted the topic (Volunteer work at the museum) to three main points: learning about the past, learning about the museum services, and learning about self. In the body of the paper, each restriction will be developed with illustrations in a separate paragraph. Because each paragraph's main idea is a distinct restriction of the thesis statement, the final composition will be unified.

After a writer decides how the thesis statement will be restricted, he or she can develop an informal outline that lists each restriction and the details that will illustrate it. The following informal outline is for the model essay on pages 135–137. Notice that all the details under the heading *Learning About Museum Services* are illustrations of services the museum provides. Organizing an informal outline, in which supporting details relate clearly to each restriction and each restriction relates clearly to the thesis statement, helps the writer produce a unified composition.

Thesis Statement
At the museum I've learned about life in the past, become aquainted with services a museum offers to the community, and discovered new talents in myself.

Learning About the Past
City's history
Railroad's influence
Work done by hand

Learning About Museum Services
Slide programs
Resources for family historians
School demonstrations
Student projects

Learning About Myself
More skillfulness
Less shyness

Model: An Expository Composition

The following composition is developed from the preceding informal outline. As you read, notice how the writer develops each of the topics in the informal outline.

This introductory paragraph ends with the thesis statement.

Do you know that West Chicago was once called Turner Junction? Are you aware that many museums can help you write a family history? Could you explain your city's history to a group of adults? Through my work as a youth volunteer at the West Chicago Historical Museum, I have learned the answers to these questions and many others. I have learned about life in the past, become acquainted

This paragraph develops the outline heading *Learning About the Past*.

This paragraph develops the outline heading *Learning About Museum Services*.

with the services a museum offers to the community, and discovered new talents in myself.

Cleaning and caring for the exhibits on the first floor of the museum has taught me about West Chicago's history. From a large railroad exhibit I have learned that the city did not exist until 1849, when the Galena and Chicago Union Railroad, the first railroad to run a line west from Chicago, helped to form it. By the time the population reached 2,000, five railroads ran through town, and the impact of the railroads on West Chicago and other towns was enormous. In fact, a large, round West Union clock is included in this exhibit because the telegraph lines established by the railroads helped create the first time zones. Town jewelers corrected clocks and watches by the signal transmitted over the telegraph lines every day exactly at noon. I've also learned, from the other exhibits on carpenters, blacksmiths, and farmers, that until 1918 most work in West Chicago was done by hand.

In addition to learning about the city's history, I have realized during my year as a volunteer that a museum is more than a building full of antiques. The West Chicago Museum provides many valuable services for the community. For example, Dr. Jerry Musich, the museum director, often presents slide programs about the city's history to clubs and church groups. Amateur historians interested in their family roots often find photographs of relatives in the museum's photo collection. As an additional service, the museum will copy these on the large copy camera. Sometimes, teachers bring their classes to the museum for special demonstrations, and sometimes, Dr. Musich goes out to the schools. Another way the museum serves the community is by allowing older students to use the museum records to find information for history reports and projects, and every year the museum awards a prize to the student with the best project. Last year some students used museum resources to plan a walking tour of West Chicago's historical homes; now the museum provides their map for tourists.

These paragraphs develop the outline heading *Learning About Myself*.

Just lately I have realized that working at the museum has also taught me something about myself. I once thought I was very clumsy, but now I know that I am actually adept at many tasks. Last week, for example, someone donated an 1858 tailor's iron to the museum. Because the iron weighs sixteen pounds, it is difficult to handle, but I easily took it apart, cleaned it, and reassembled it. Perhaps my most important insight into myself is that I can overcome my shyness and fear of speaking before groups. Last year when I tried to give a speech in English, I ended up blushing and could not remember what I wanted to say. After I had answered the telephone and talked with adult volunteers for a week or so, Dr. Musich asked me one day to show a small boy and his father through the museum. At first I was nervous, but I had barely begun when the little boy asked me if the metal object with the long handle was a pogo stick. I explained that it was a hand-pumped vacuum cleaner from 1913 and helped the boy pump the handle up and down. After that they both asked me questions, and I became so involved in answering them that I forgot my nervousness.

My volunteer work began because the director said he needed some helpers, and I thought I could earn a scouting merit badge for community service. I know I have served the community; I am just beginning to discover how the museum has helped me. I have learned much about the city, about what the museum does, and about myself. Now I am thinking that museum work might be a good career choice.

A *coherent* composition moves smoothly from idea to idea without awkward breaks. *Transitional devices* help readers make connections between the thought in one paragraph or sentence and that in the next paragraph or sentence. The *italicized* words in the following sentences link statements in the model essay on museum volunteer work.

1. *In fact*, a large, round Western Union clock is included in this exhibit because the telegraph lines established by the railroads helped create the first time zones.

2. *For example*, Dr. Jerry Musich, the museum director, often presents slide programs about the city's history to clubs and church groups.

3. *Another way* the museum serves the community is by allowing older students to use the museum records to find information for history reports and projects.

Think and Discuss

1. Besides the previous examples, what other transitional devices does the writer use throughout the composition?

2. How does the thesis statement at the end of the first paragraph tie the paragraphs in the body of the composition together?

3. The model composition discusses *what the writer has learned* from the museum volunteer work. How is this idea restated throughout the composition, and what has the writer learned from this experience?

4. How does the last paragraph provide an effective personal conclusion?

Writing Practice 3: *Writing the Body of a Composition*

Using the introduction you wrote in Writing Practice 2, write three or four paragraphs in which you develop the thesis statement. You may want to organize your thoughts first by making an informal outline or a word cluster, by doing some free writing in your Writer's Notebook, or by using any other prewriting method to get started. Do not write the concluding paragraph yet; save your composition for the next Writing Practice.

Writing the Conclusion

Because the *conclusion* is the last impression you leave with your readers, it can strengthen or weaken your entire paper. When you write your conclusion, think back to your thesis. What is the most important idea or feeling you want to leave with your reader? In your conclusion you might restate this idea or feeling in a new and interesting way.

In the composition on pages 135–137, for example, the writer tells about volunteer work at a local museum. The writer could use an ineffective conclusion such as, *In conclusion, my volunteer work has been a valuable experience. I have learned about history, about museum work, and about myself.* These sentences emphasize what the writer has learned through work as a museum volunteer but are not interesting to the reader because they merely repeat what the writer has already said.

Models: Concluding Expository Paragraphs

Adding specific sensory details can make the conclusion more interesting, as the following example shows.

I no longer spend my Saturdays watching old movies on television or calling my friends at home to see if they can think of anything interesting to do. Now I am at the museum by 10, and by

noon I have dusted the exhibits and am all ready to tell early visitors about West Chicago and its history as I show them around the first floor. If your Saturdays are often boring, and you would like to discover more about your city and yourself, perhaps you should think about working as a museum volunteer. I guarantee you will enjoy the museum more than television reruns.

Some papers may need special kinds of conclusions. In a paper explaining how to do something, the most important idea is the process or product. Your conclusion should emphasize this process or product.

If you follow these steps, you should produce an almost perfect loaf of whole-wheat bread. While the bread is still warm, cut and butter a slice. One taste will tell you why many societies describe bread as "the staff of life."

In a paper explaining your reasons for an opinion, the conclusion should emphasize your opinion.

Although many adults are reluctant to trust a teenage driver with their cars, much evidence shows that teenagers can be the safest drivers on the road. Of course, no one can guarantee that any driver will behave responsibly, but a responsible teenage driver can be one of the safest in the world.

Writing Practice 4: *A Concluding Paragraph*

Write a conclusion for the paper you wrote in Writing Practice 3. Develop a concluding paragraph that is interesting to the reader and reflects your thoughts and ideas as a writer.

Revising Your Expository Composition

An artist usually sketches a picture before adding the details, colors, and finishing touches. Sometimes an artist may make several sketches before deciding on one to use. The writing process is similar; the writer often composes several drafts before producing the final one.

Before revising, you may need to set your composition aside. By rereading it later, you may gain a fresh perspective. You might also want to get the reactions of others before making changes.

If necessary, review the section on revising in Chapter 1.

Writing Practice 5: *Responding, Revising, and Proofreading*

Share your paper with a small group of classmates. Evaluate one another's papers, using the following checklist. Ask each group member to identify the strongest feature in your composition and the one part that most needs improvement. Revise your draft using the group members' comments as guides. Then proofread your composition for correct grammar, mechanics, and spelling. Use the Proofreader's Checklist at the back of the book.

Checklist for Revising an Expository Composition

1. Does the composition have an interesting introductory paragraph that includes a clear and well-developed thesis statement?

2. Is the thesis statement adequately developed in the body of the composition?

3. Does the composition include sufficient information and details for the reader?

4. Does each sentence in a paragraph support the main idea?

5. Are there transitional words and phrases to link sentences and ideas?

6. Is the language clear and precise without unecessary details or sentence fragments?

Sentence Combining:
Inserting Clauses

Inserting Who, Whom, Which, *and* That

For more information on clauses, see pages 512-531.

The additions *who* and *which* do not always require commas. When they are used to identify a person, an idea, or an object so precisely that commas would change the meaning of the sentence, do not use commas. You can see the difference by comparing these sentences.

The old elm, which was standing near the curb, was cut down.

The old elm that was standing near the curb was cut down.

In the first sentence, *which was standing near the curb* could be removed without seriously changing the meaning of the sentence. There is apparently only one old tree in the vicinity. In the second sentence, however, the meaning is slightly different: only the old elm that was standing near the curb (not the old elm across the street or the other old one in the yard) was cut down.

For information on pronouns used as adjectives, see pages 390-392.

In Exercise 1 you will find the signals (*who*), (*whom*), (*which*), and (*that*). In formal usage *that* is used to introduce a series of words essential to the meaning of a sentence, and the words are not set off by commas. With *who*, *whom*, or *which*, however, you must decide for yourself whether the words are essential and add commas if they are not.

The boy *who came for dinner* stayed late.	[essential]
Dan, *whom we invited to dinner*, stayed late.	[nonessential]

Exercise 1: Combining Sentences with Who, Whom, Which, and That

On a sheet of paper, combine the following sentence sets. Use signals where indicated. Use commas to set off nonessential information. Study the example before you begin.

Example

a. We paid close attention to the traffic light.
   The traffic light was on the far corner. (*that*)
   We paid close attention to the traffic light that was on the far corner.

1. That lion was the most popular attraction.
   That lion was the oldest in the circus. (*which*)

2. All the broken test tubes must be taken outside.
   The test tubes are on this table. (*that*)

3. Blinded by the bright snow, the explorer tried to light the lantern.
   The explorer still had the use of his hands. (*who*)

4. The specially equipped explorers could live on Mars.
   NASA had trained the explorers. (*whom*)

5. Forest fires are a menace to our national parks.
   Forest fires are often set by careless campers. (*which*)

6. Allan was leaning against a freshly painted wall.
   Allan was looking very unhappy.

7. The chef tossed the pizza into the air, only to see it stick to the ceiling.
   The chef had been working only one day.

8. The clock is half an hour behind the clock.
   The clock sits on my dresser.
   The clock stands in the hallway.

9. A lesson is less difficult and much more fun than a lesson.
   A lesson allows me to be creative.
   A lesson makes me memorize rules.

10. The sailors vowed they would learn to swim.
    The Navy rescue team saved the sailors from drowning.

Inserting *Whose,* Where, When, *and* Why

In this section you will combine sentences by inserting the words *whose, where, when,* or *why* in place of the repeated word or words in the insert sentence. This process is the same as using the (*who*), (*which*), and (*that*) signals, as the following examples show.

Base Sentence: Lisa was able to identify the locker.

Insert: The thieves had hidden their tools in the locker. (*where*)

Combined: Lisa was able to identify the locker *where the thieves had hidden their tools.*

143

Base Sentence:	The pilgrims were searching for that person.
Insert:	That person's gift to them was wise advice. (*whose*)
Combined:	The pilgrims were searching for that wonderful person *whose gift to them was wise advice.*
Base Sentence:	The drivers were unable to tell the dispatcher the reason.
Insert:	They had lost the truck for that reason. (*why*)
Combined:	The drivers were unable to tell the dispatcher the reason *why they had lost the truck.*

Exercise 2: *Combining Sentences with* Whose, Where, When, *and* Why

On a sheet of paper, combine the following sets of sentences. Use signals where indicated. Study the examples before you begin.

Examples

a. I knew a woman.
   The woman's goodness was a marvel. (*whose*)
   I knew a woman whose goodness was a marvel.

b. Will the searchers be able to find anyone?
   Anyone can lead them into the cone of the volcano.
   Will the searchers be able to find anyone who can lead them into the cone of the volcano?

1. Oh, I do long for the time.
   At that time I can get these braces off my teeth. (*when*)

2. Because it involves a family secret, Aunt Leah wouldn't tell us the reason.
   For that reason no one ever saw Uncle Jacob. (*why*)

3. Carefully the camera zoomed in on the actor.
   The actor's face had been made up to look like the face of the Hunchback of Notre Dame. (*whose*)

4. The crown jewels were displayed in the same room.
   A man had been arrested. (*where*)

5. My favorite was the lion with the lion tamer.
   The lion performed in the cage. (*that*)
   The lion tamer's only equipment was a whip and a chair. (*whose*)

6. Actually, it is not necessary to fill out the application at this time.
   At this time we are so busy with other duties.

7. I'm concerned that you can't give one good reason.
   One good reason is that there are twenty expensive pens missing from this box.

8. Pollsters were asking people these questions at the time.
   Popular opinion was against sending aid to foreign countries at the time.

9. The leader of the marching band was looking for the person.
   The person's job was to carry the flag.

10. Now I remember the reason.
    For that reason I was supposed to tell Carlos to meet his brother after work.

Writing Practice 1: *Identifying Sentence Patterns*

Review the model expository composition in Chapter 6. As you reread the composition, select six sentences that you think represent good examples of sentence variety. Write these sentences on a sheet of paper, underlining connecting words and parts of sentences that have been combined with or inserted into a base sentence.

Writing Practice 2: *Revising for Sentence Variety*

Reread the expository composition you wrote to complete the writing assignment in Chapter 6. Check your composition for sentence variety, using the following checklist.

Checklist for Sentence Variety

1. Look at the first few words in each sentence. Do the sentences begin in different ways?

2. Check the length of sentences. Are there long sentences that need to be divided or short sentences that can be combined?

3. Is there a variety of sentence patterns?

7 Writing a Research Report

Kinds of Reports

A *report* is a factual account.

People who write news stories are called *reporters* because they write factual accounts of events. Salespeople write sales reports, giving facts about sales made over a period of time. Teachers turn in attendance reports with facts on the number of students attending classes each day. Bank officials must issue regular reports about the financial status of the bank. In school you write book reports, reports for science and social studies classes, and perhaps reports for a club or an organization of which you are an officer.

In a report you may give not only facts, but also your opinion about the facts. In a book report, for example, you may explain why you thought a novel was interesting. You might add to a financial report your opinion that the club's treasury is too low. For the most part, however, a report contains factual information.

Sources of Information

A *source* is a book, magazine, newspaper, pamphlet, or anything else that gives you information for a report.

If you write about a recent backpacking expedition, your source is your experience during the hike. If you write about a person, your source might be a magazine article, a book, or an interview.

A short report for which you have only one source is a *summary*. Reports that use more than one source are *research reports*.

In many ways writing a research report is no different from writing a composition or an essay. In each case you choose and limit a subject, and gather and organize information. The main difference is with the research report you are using others' ideas; therefore, you must give your sources the proper credit.

Writing a Summary

I f you tell a friend the highlights of a movie, you are giving a summary of a movie. If you write a book report describing the most important events in the story's plot, you are writing a summary of a book.

A *summary* is a condensed or shortened statement of the ideas in a book, article, story, speech, or other selection; it includes only the most important facts and ideas.

To help you select what to summarize in a book or article, use the *who? what? when? where? why?* and *how?* questioning system. Before you begin, however, read the entire story to discover which details are important. On your second reading, begin taking notes. This time ask yourself the *who? what? when? where? why?* and *how?* questions. Remember that some questions may not apply to the article you are summarizing. An article on dolphins, for example, may not mention people. When you finish taking notes, however; you should have the answers to the important questions about the story.

Make reading notes brief and write them in your own words, leaving out examples and unimportant details. For example, suppose an author writes, "I was always hardworking. When I was young, I had not only an after-school job but also a paper route." A statement that the author was always hardworking is a sufficient summary; the information about the author's jobs is unnecessary.

After taking your notes, set the article aside and write the summary from the notes alone. The summary should be one-fourth to one-third the length of the original. When you finish, compare your summary with the original. Have you left out any main ideas? If so, add them.

Identify each of your sources by recording the following information at the top of your summary.

For a Book

Author:	Lerone Bennett, Jr.
Title (underlined):	Before the Mayflower: A History of the Negro in America, 1619–1964
Page numbers:	183–219

For a Magazine Article

Author:	Patricia Skalka
Title (in quotation marks):	"The Girl Who Wanted to Run"
Name of magazine (underlined):	Reader's Digest
Date of magazine:	June 1980
Page numbers:	82–87

For an Encyclopedia Article

Author (if given):	David Byer
Title (in quotation marks):	"Falashi Jews of Africa"
Name of encyclopedia:	Encyclopaedia Judaica
Volume number:	VI
Page numbers:	162–168

Model: A Summary

The following entry about the first American railroad locomotive is given in its complete form and then in summary. Read the original and then the summary. After you have read the summary, compare it to the original to see what details were omitted. The selection is adapted from John Latrobe's *Personal Recollections of the Baltimore and Ohio Railroads.*

In the beginning, no one dreamed of using steam to power the railroad. Horses were to do the work. Even after the line was completed to Frederick [Maryland], relays of horses pulled the cars from place to place.

When steam was first used on the Liverpool and Manchester Railroad [in England], it attracted great attention here. But using an English engine on an American roadbed was difficult. An English roadbed was almost straight. An American road had curves, some of them quite sharp. For a brief time it was believed that this feature of the early American railroads would prevent the use of locomotive engines here. But Peter Cooper of New York proved that it could be done.

Mr. Cooper was sure that steam could be adapted to the curved roadbeds which he saw would be built in the United States. To test his belief, he came to Baltimore, which then had the only roadbed on which he could experiment. He had another idea, which was that the crank could be gotten rid of. He built an engine to demonstrate both of these points. The machine was no larger than the handcars used by workers to move from place to place. And as I now recall its appearance, the only wonder is that so insignificant an object should ever have been regarded as capable of producing results. But Mr. Cooper was wiser than many of the wisest around him. His engine could not have weighed a ton [.9 metric ton], but he saw in it a principle which the 40-ton [36.3-metric ton] engines of today have demonstrated.

Mr. Cooper decided to try a trip to Ellicott's Mills. An open car was attached to his engine and filled with the directors of the railroad and some friends, myself among them. Thus the first journey by steam in America was begun. The trip was most interesting. The curves were passed without difficulty at a speed of 15 miles [24 kilometers] an hour, and we went up the grades fairly easily. The day was fine, the people were in the highest spirits. Some excited gentlemen of the party pulled out memorandum books and at the highest speed—which was 18 miles [29 kilometers] an hour—wrote their names to prove that it was possible to do so even at that great speed. The return trip from Ellicott's Mills—a distance of 13 miles [21 kilometers]—was made in 57 minutes. This was in the summer of 1830.

But the triumph of this *Tom Thumb* engine was not completely successful. The leading stagecoach proprietors at the time were Stockton & Stokes. On this occasion they drove a gallant gray horse of great beauty and power from town to Ellicott's Mills on the second track (for the company had laid two tracks to the Mills). The horse, attached to another railroad car, met the engine on its way back.

From this point it was decided to have a race home. The start was even, and away went horse and engine, the snort of the one and the puff of the other keeping time. At first the horse had the best of it, for his "steam" could be applied to the greatest advantage immediately, while the engine had to wait until the rotation of the wheels set the blower to work. The horse was perhaps a quarter of a mile [.4 kilometer] ahead when the safety valve of the engine lifted and the thin vapor coming from it showed that there was too much steam. The blower whistled, the steam blew off in clouds, the engine went faster, the passengers shouted, and the engine gained on the horse until it reached him. The race was neck and neck, nose and nose—then the engine passed the horse, and a great shout of hurrah hailed the victory.

But it was not repeated. For just at this time when the horse's master was about to give up, the band which drove the pulley which drove the blower slipped from the drum. The safety valve ceased to scream. The engine began to wheeze and pant. Mr. Cooper, who ran the engine himself and also kept the fire going, cut his hands attempting to put the band back on the wheel. He tried to build up the fire with light wood. But the horse gained on the machine and passed it. Although the band was presently put back and steam again did its best, the horse was too far ahead to be overtaken and won the race.

But the real victory was Mr. Cooper's even so. He had believed in steam power and had demonstrated its use beyond a doubt.[1] [bracketed information added]

Summary

The railroad cars on the first American railroad were drawn by horses from Baltimore, Maryland, to Frederick, Maryland. Even though steam locomotives were already in use in England, they were believed incapable of being used on the curved American tracks.

New Yorker Peter Cooper solved this problem. He designed a small, light locomotive called the *Tom Thumb*, which was able to operate on American tracks. This locomotive was the forerunner of modern locomotives.

The first trip of the *Tom Thumb*, in the summer of 1830, covered the 21 kilometers between Baltimore and Ellicott's Mills at speeds up to 29 kilometers per hour.

Later a race was held between the *Tom Thumb* and a horse, each drawing a railroad car. The horse led the race at the beginning but was later passed by the locomotive. However, the horse won the race when the *Tom Thumb* broke down and fell too far behind to catch up.

Of course, though the horse won the day, steam power won the race in the end.

[1]Adapted from *Rise of the American Nation*, Volume 1, Heritage Edition by Lewis Paul Todd and Merle Curti. Copyright © 1977 by Harcourt Brace Jovanovich, Inc. Reprinted by permission of the publisher.

Think and Discuss

1. The summary says that the first trip of the *Tom Thumb* was made between Baltimore, Maryland, and Ellicott's Mills. What sentences in the original version supply this information?

2. A summary will not always capture the flavor of the original work. In the description of the race between the *Tom Thumb* and the horse, some of the excitement has been lost in the summary. What three sentences in the original helped to provide this excitement?

3. The summary states that steam engines were used in England before they were used in the United States. Why was the country important to mention in the summary, while the company was not?

4. The summary indicates that the *Tom Thumb* raced against a horse. What additional information about this horse exists in the original but not in the summary?

5. Find three or four additional details about the first trip taken by the *Tom Thumb* that are not given in the summary.

Writing Practice 1: *A Summary*

Write a summary of the following selection, "A True Instinct for the Beautiful" by Rachel Carson. Read the selection first and then read it again, taking notes the second time. Write a summary from your notes after your second reading.

> A child's world is fresh and new and beautiful, full of wonder and excitement. It is our misfortune that for most of us that clear-eyed vision, that true instinct for what is beautiful and awe-inspiring, is dimmed and even lost before we reach adulthood. If I had influence with the good fairy who is supposed to preside over the christening of all children I should ask that her gift to each child in the world be a sense of wonder so indestructible that it would last throughout life, as an unfailing antidote against the boredom and disenchantments of later years, the sterile preoccupation with things that are artificial, the alienation from the sources of our strength.
>
> If a child is to keep alive his inborn sense of wonder without any such gift from the fairies, he needs the companionship of at least one adult who can share it, rediscovering with him the joy, excitement and mystery of the world we live in. Parents often have a sense of inadequacy when confronted on the one hand with the eager, sensitive mind of a child and on the other with a world of complex physical nature, inhabited by a life so various and unfamiliar that it seems hopeless to reduce it to order and knowledge. In a mood of self-defeat, they exclaim, "How can I possibly teach my child about

nature—why, I don't even know one bird from another!''

     I sincerely believe that for the child, and for the parent seeking to guide him, it is not half so important to *know* as to *feel*. If facts are the seeds that later produce knowledge and wisdom, then the emotions and the impressions of the senses are the fertile soil in which the seeds must grow. The years of early childhood are the time to prepare the soil. Once the emotions have been aroused—a sense of the beautiful, the excitement of the new and the unknown, a feeling of sympathy, pity, admiration or love—then we wish for knowledge about the object of our emotional response. Once found, it has lasting meaning. It is more important to pave the way for the child to want to know than to put him on a diet of facts he is not ready to assimilate.[1]

Writing Practice 2: *Summarizing an Article*

Find a magazine or newspaper article that interests you. Read the article the first time to digest the information. On the second reading, take brief notes about the important details, answering *who? what? when? where? why?* and *how?* Write the notes in your own words except when you want to quote something exactly as written. Use your notes to write a summary of the article. At the top of your summary, list the important information about the source of the article, as in the example on page 148.

For Your Writer's Notebook

> Write a notebook entry in which you react in some way to the article "A True Instinct for the Beautiful." Remember an experience you had as a young child in which you were sharply aware of something that was very beautiful, exciting, or unusual in nature. Perhaps you saw a mountain or an ocean or a desert for the first time. Perhaps you saw a very young animal or closely observed the patterns on a butterfly or flower. Perhaps you planted some seeds and watched them grow. Who shared your experience with you? What did you feel? What did you learn? If you choose not to write about an experience as a young child, write about a more recent experience with nature.

Steps in Writing a Research Report

Writing a research report involves more steps than writing a summary. First you must choose a subject. Then you must focus your topic and gather information about it. Finally you must bring information from several sources together into an organized report. Because you are creating something original by bringing together information from several sources, your report will be more than just the sum of the facts you have taken from your sources.

Choosing a Subject

Sometimes, the subject of your research report will be assigned by your teacher; at other times, however, you will choose your own subject. When selecting your own subject, be certain you can find enough information for a good report. No matter how interesting a subject may seem, you will not be able to write an acceptable report unless you can find sources to provide the information you need.

For more information on finding information, see pages 609-613.

Imagine that you have just returned from a visit to a marine park, where you were impressed by the performing dolphins. You know something about dolphins and think they would be an interesting subject for a research report. However, before you decide on the subject of dolphins, you go to the library, where you find two books about dolphins. When you consult the *Readers' Guide to Periodical Literature*, you find articles in several magazines you know are in your library; therefore, you decide that dolphins would be a good subject for your research report.

Writing Practice 3: *Selecting a Subject*

Brainstorm a list of possible subjects for a research report. Select a variety of subjects in different content areas, such as social science, art, mathematics, music, and health. (See the sample subject list below.) In your Writer's Notebook make a list of the subjects you might want to explore for a research report. Select the subject that interests you the most and begin to gather sources of information about it. Using the card catalogue and the *Readers' Guide* in your school or community library, find at least two articles and two books with information about your subject. Record the important information about each source in your Writer's Notebook, following the example on page 148. Save this information for the next Writing Practice.

Sample Subjects for Research Reports

Social Sciences
Gold mining
Egyptian pharaohs
The Great Wall of China
The American electoral process

Art
The color spectrum
Navaho sand painting
The inventions of
Leonardo Da Vinci

Mathematics
Minicomputers
The Chinese number system
The metric system
The duodecimal system

Health
The effects of alcohol on
the brain
Biorhythms
The right way to jog

Music
The life of John Lennon
The harpsichord
Mozart
Rock 'n' roll in the 50's

Science
Common uses for solar
energy
Endangered animals
Space suits

Limiting the Subject

L imiting the subject for a short research report is like limiting the subject for an expository paper. If you do not remember how to limit your subject and develop a thesis statement for an expository paper, review the section on this subject in Chapter 6.

As you look over the information sources that are available, think about how to limit your subject. You may decide on a specific topic in the initial stages of research. On the other hand, you may find it necessary to do more reading and note-taking before a topic and thesis statement begin to emerge.

The following example illustrates how a research report on Egyptian pharaohs might be limited.

Subject:	Egyptian pharaohs
Topic:	Tutankhamen
Thesis Statement:	Tutankhamen, the youngest Egyptian Pharaoh, was responsible for major religious reforms in Egypt.

Writing Practice 4: *Limiting the Subject*

Read an article in an encyclopedia about the subject you selected in Writing Practice 3. As you read, think about how you can limit your subject by focusing on a specific topic. Also, read over the articles and books you gathered in the previous Writing Practice. Depending on your subject, you may need to find information from a variety of sources, including newspapers, magazines, books, periodicals, and pamphlets.

When you think you have found a focus for your research report, write a specific topic and thesis statement in your notebook. Keep your list of sources and your thesis statement for the next Writing Practice.

The Bibliography Card

For each source you use in preparing your report, make out a separate card listing the title, author, publisher, date of publication, and any other information you need to identify the source. This card is called a *bibliography card*. Later, when you write a *bibliography*, or list of sources used in your report, you will use these cards, so it is important to write them correctly now.

The following bibliography card is for a book. Notice that the punctuation marks separating the items of information have been emphasized to help you become familiar with their use in a bibliography entry.

Bibliography card number

Author, title, place of publication, publisher, and date of publication

Steauit, Robert. The Dolphin, Cousin to Man. New York: Sterling Publishing Company, 1968.

A bibliography card for a book should contain the following information in the order presented.

1. Author or editor, last name first. (If a book has two or more authors, only the name of the first author is written with the last name first.) Notice that a period follows this information.

2. Complete title of the book, underlined and followed by a period.

3. Place of publication, followed by a colon. (If two or more places are listed, use only the first.)

4. Publisher, followed by a comma.

5. Date of publication, followed by a period. (Always choose the most recent publication date.)

6.   A number in the upper right-hand corner. (Bibliography cards are numbered sequentially.)

Here is a bibliography card you might prepare for an article from a weekly or monthly magazine:

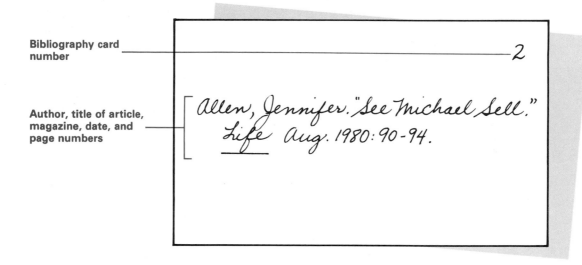

Bibliography card number

2

Author, title of article, magazine, date, and page numbers

Allen, Jennifer. "See Michael Sell."
Life Aug. 1980: 90-94.

A bibliography card for a monthly or weekly magazine should contain the following information in the order presented.

1.   Author (unless the article is unsigned). (Notice that a period follows this information.)

2.   Title of the article, enclosed in quotation marks and followed by a period.

3.   Name of the magazine, underlined.

4.   The day, month, and year of publication. (Notice that no punctuation separates these items, but the year is followed by a colon.)

5.   Page numbers, followed by a period.

6.   A number in the upper right-hand corner.

Writing Practice 5: *Preparing Bibliography Cards*

Prepare a bibliography card for each source for your research report. Follow the examples that are given for bibliography cards.

Asking Questions

The next step is to write out a list of questions that you want to answer in your report. Skimming through a variety of sources on your topic will help you develop questions. You may also use the *who? what? when? where? why?* and *how?* questioning system to organize your ideas. For example, an outline of questions for a report on dolphin communication might look like the following one.

Dolphin Communication

Why have dolphins always been a fascinating subject for study?

How do dolphins communicate?
> What sounds to dolphins make?
> How do dolphins combine sounds to make messages?

What are the similarities between dolphin communication and human communication?
> How do dolphins hold conversations?
> How does dolphin communication change as dolphins grow older?

Writing Practice 6: *Questions About the Topic*

After reading one or more articles on your subject, write a list of questions to guide you as you look for more detailed information. Use the *who? what? when? where? why?* and *how?* questioning system.

Taking Notes

The next step in report writing is to take notes from the sources you have located. The questions you developed in Writing Practice 6 will help you decide whether specific information is important and should be put on a note card. For example, if your topic is communication among dolphins, you probably will not want to record information about the first American zoo that had a dolphin exhibit. Use the index at the back of a long book to look up sections or pages that relate to your specific topic. Examine the chapter titles to identify chapters that relate to your topic, and read the material first to be certain it is relevant. Make your notes as brief as possible but do not leave out important details.

It is dishonest to record another person's words in a research report as if they were your own, so be certain that you take notes in your own words. Sometimes, you will want to write down exactly what an author says about a topic; when you do so, put quotation marks around the author's exact words. Doing this will help you avoid accidentally copying from your sources.

Your report will be much easier to organize if you record only one piece of information on each card. Later, you can arrange your cards to fit the organization of your outline, putting all the cards relating to your first main point in one stack, those relating to your second point in another stack, and so on.

Be certain that each bibliography card has a number (the circled number in the upper right-hand corner of the models). Place the corresponding bibliography card number in the upper right-hand corner of each information card. This eliminates the task of rewriting information about your source on every note card. If *The Mind of the Dolphin* is bibliography card number 1, every note card with information from this source will have the number 1 circled in the upper right-hand corner. Then write the page number from which you have taken the information under the bibliography card number. If you wish, you can write a topic heading on each card in the upper left-hand corner of the card.

The following note card contains information from *The Mind of the Dolphin.*

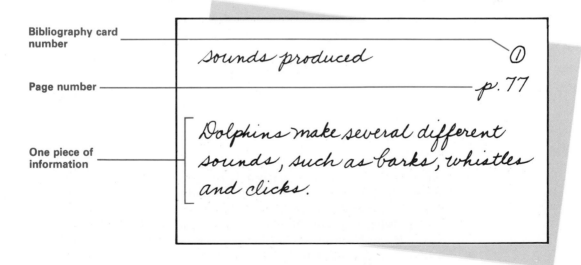

Bibliography card number

Page number

One piece of information

sounds produced ①
p. 77

Dolphins make several different sounds, such as barks, whistles and clicks.

When you have taken notes on each of your sources, consult the list of questions that you intend to cover in the report. Sort your note cards into piles that correspond to the questions on your list. Is there enough information to develop each of the questions? Has your reading raised any new, interesting questions? Now is the time to look up the information you need to complete the report.

Writing Practice 7: *Taking Notes*

Using a minimum of three sources (excluding encyclopedias), prepare and organize a set of note cards for a short research report on the topic you have previously selected.

Writing a Thesis Statement

After organizing your note cards, write a thesis statement for your report. The thesis statement should state the main idea suggested by the information you have organized. *Dolphins, like humans, seem to have a highly developed language* reveals exactly what your paper will be about. A thesis statement also lets the reader know what *not* to expect in your paper. For example, a paper using the thesis statement above would probably not include information about whale communication or about the old dolphin T.V. star *Flipper*.

The Formal Outline

A formal outline will help you organize your information to explain your thesis statement.

A *formal outline* lists each of the points you intend to discuss in your report and the order in which you intend to discuss them.

A formal outline differs from an informal outline in several ways. First it uses a regular numbering system made up of Roman numerals (I, II, III), uppercase (capital) letters, Arabic numerals (1, 2, 3), and lowercase letters. An outline divides the points you cover in a paper. Whenever you divide anything, you must have at least two parts. If you have a *I* in your outline, you must also have a *II*. If you have an *A*, you must have a *B*.

All the headings in your outline must be written either as complete sentences or as words and phrases. An outline with sentences is a *sentence outline*; one with words and phrases is a *topic outline*. If you have written any headings in sentence form, all the headings should be in sentence form. If any headings are words and phrases, all headings should be words and phrases, as the following topic outline for a research report on dolphin communication shows.

Dolphin Communication

I. Knowledge about dolphins
   A. Air-breathing mammals
   B. Highly developed language

II. Dolphin language
   A. Combination of whistles and clicks
   B. Research by Dr. Rene Guy Busnel
   C. Research by Dr. John Dreker

III. Similarities with human communication
   A. Meaning requires combination of sounds
   B. Conversations between dolphins
      1. Turn talking
      2. Sound used as name
   C. Language development in dolphins

IV. Human and dolphin communication
   A. Dolphins taught by hand signals
   B. Dolphins taught by computer sounds

V. Results of dolphin study
   A. Current knowledge about dolphin language
   B. Predictions for future

A sentence outline has the same organization with only the wording of the headings changed, as the following sample shows.

Dolphin Communication

I. For centuries dolphins have been a fascinating subject for study.
   A. Centuries ago dolphins were recognized as air-breathing mammals.
   B. More recently scientists have discovered that dolphins have a highly developed language.

II. Scientists have discovered how dolphins communicate.
   A. Dolphins communicate with whistles and clicks.
   B. The research by Dr. Rene Guy Busnel demonstrated combinations of whistles and clicks made by dolphins.
   C. The research by Dr. John Dreker identified thirty-two different dolphin whistles.

III. (etc.)

Writing Practice 8: *Thesis and Outline*

Reread the note cards you have organized into stacks, and write a thesis statement. It should state the main point and the purpose of your paper in one complete, declarative sentence. Then organize the cards within each stack. These will be the basis of your formal outline. Each question that guided your research can be one or more divisions of the outline, as the sample outlines (p. 161) show. Write your outline, being careful to follow correct outline form.

The Rough Draft

The *rough draft* is the first copy of your report.

To write the rough draft place your thesis statement, outline, and notes in front of you. Follow the pattern of organization you used in your outline, remembering, however, that your goal is to write a clear, well-organized report on your topic, not necessarily to use all your material. Often a note you took earlier will not fit with the organization of the final paper. If you have such a note, discard it as you write your rough draft.

***Parenthetical documentation* gives authors credit for their ideas and tells readers where to locate important information or exact quotations that you have used.**

When you refer to the source of your information you are *documenting* that source. You should use parenthetical documentation in your report to inform your reader where you found material that you quoted exactly. You should also reference any very unusual or specific facts or theories developed by an author. If several sources mention the same idea, that idea is considered general knowledge and does not require a parenthetical reference.

Parenthetical documentation has the following features.

1. The reference is placed in parentheses at the end of any sentence in your report that either quotes or uses an idea from a specific source. Sentence punctuation (a period, question mark, or exclamation point) *follows* the parenthetical reference. If you are using a direct quotation, the parenthetical reference follows the end quotation mark but still comes before the sentence punctuation. This example shows a parenthetical reference for a direct quotation.

    Some experts see this as "the most revolutionary discovery in the field in the last ten years" (Anderson 26).

2. Since complete information about your sources appears in your bibliography, a parenthetical reference is short, giving just enough details about the source so that your reader can find it easily in the bibliography.

3. Parenthetical documentation usually includes the last name of the author whose work is referenced and the page number where the information can be found in the source. As you will see, sometimes the book's or article's title is also necessary to clarify which work you are referring to.

4. The author's name, the source's title (if appropriate), and the page number are enclosed in parentheses.

The following sample sentence from the model research report that appears on pages 165–167 shows the correct use of a parenthetical reference.

> In similar research Dr. John Dreker identified at least thirty-two different dolphin whistles but could not match the whistles by themselves to specific messages (Stenuit 80–89).

Sources can be documented within a report in different ways. The parenthetical documentation form developed by the Modern Language Association is widely used by writers and researchers.

When you write a research report, ask your teacher whether you should use this form or one of the many other acceptable forms of documentation.

The following sample parenthetical references illustrate the MLA form. Pay special attention to the punctuation used.

For a Book

1. If the book has only one author, and your bibliography includes only one book or article by this author, put the author's last name and the page number where you found the information in parentheses. Notice that there is no comma after the author's name and no abbreviation for *page* (*p.* or *pp.*) before the page number.

    (Stenuit 80–90)

2. If the book has two authors, however, include both authors' last names in the parenthetical reference. Use *and* between the names.

    (Groh and Miller 10)

3. Sometimes you will use more than one source written by the same person for your report. In this case, if you used only the author's last name in your parenthetical documentation the

reader would not know which source was being referenced. When your bibliography lists more than one work by the same author, include the title of the book in your parenthetical documentation. (Sometimes a shortened version of the title is used.) The title follows the author's name and a comma. Underline the book's title.

(Lilly, Mind of the Dolphin 79)

For a Weekly or Monthly Magazine

1. When an author is given for an article in a magazine and your bibliography lists only one work by this author, use the same parenthetical documentation form you would for a book. Include the author's last name and the referenced page number in parentheses.

    (Black 91)
    (Caldwell and Caldwell 62)

    If your bibliography lists more than one work by the same author, again provide the title after the author's name. The title of a magazine article is enclosed in quotation marks.

    (Carp, "Fishing" 31)

2. If no author is given for the magazine article you used, the title (or a shortened form) is substituted for the author's last name in parenthetical documentation. Remember to enclose the title of a magazine article in quotation marks.

    ("New Ways to Listen" 9)

For a Newspaper Article

1. As with a magazine article, the parenthetical reference for a newspaper article where the author is given (and you use only one source by the same author) includes just the author's last name (or authors' last names, if there are two) and the page number where you found the information. Unlike magazines, however, newspapers often number pages by sections, using a letter to identify each section. Instead of referring to page 12 of a newspaper, you would also need to show which page 12 you mean: A12, B12, or C12. If the newspaper you use as a source numbers its pages by sections, make sure you include the section letter as well as the page number in your documentation.

    (Sullivan C1)

2. If the newspaper article is unsigned, use the title or the main

word or words from the title to reference your source. (When using a shortened form of the title, remember to use the word under which the article is alphabetized in your bibliography.) Like the title of a magazine article, the title of a newspaper article is enclosed in quotation marks.

("Tall Ships" B6)

If you use the author's name in the body of your report (*According to Black . . .* or *Carp says, . . .*) you do not need to repeat the author's name in your parenthetical reference. Simply follow the quotation or information with the correct page number in parentheses, as the following example shows.

In her article, Anderson calls this "the most revolutionary discovery in the field in the last ten years" (26).

Writing Practice 9: *The Rough Draft*

Using the thesis statement and formal outline you have already prepared, write a rough draft of your research report. Include parenthetical documentation in your draft. Read the following model on dolphin communication before you begin writing. Then follow the procedure for writing a rough draft discussed on page 162.

Model: A Short Research Report

Dolphin Communication

For over twenty-five centuries the dolphin has been a fascinating subject for study. Even the earliest researchers realized that dolphins are not fish but air-breathing mammals with lungs like those found in dogs, horses, and humans. More recently scientists have discovered that dolphins and humans share another important characteristic: dolphins, like humans, seem to have a highly developed language.

To communicate with each other dolphins use a combination of whistles and clicks. Because each of these sounds is made in a separate area of the dolphin's nose, a dolphin can make more than one type of sound at once. While working on the French research ship *Calypso*, Dr. Rene Guy Busnel matched forty combinations of clicks and whistles made by dolphins to what appeared to be forty different messages. In similar research Dr. John Dreker identified at least thirty-two different dolphin whistles but could not match the whistles by themselves to specific messages (Stenuit 80–89).

165

Dolphin language seems similar to human language in at least three ways. First, as Dr. Dreker's research shows, the sounds dolphins make do not have meaning until they are combined with other sounds. This is similar to human language, where a single sound means nothing by itself but can be combined with other sounds to make different messages. Second, dolphins seem to hold conversations just as humans do.

To prove the theory of dolphin "conversation" Dr. John Lilly put two dolphins in separate pools, where they could not see or hear each other, and connected the pools with a device like a telephone. When this device was turned on, the dolphins communicated constantly by producing combinations of clicks and whistles. When the device was off they stopped communicating. Unable to hear one another, each dolphin produced only one simple whistle—something like the names used by CB operators when they announce that they are on the air. The dolphins were calling for someone to talk to (Caldwell and Caldwell 60)! Researchers know that all dolphins seem to have a "signature" whistle or other sound that they use in the same way a human being uses a name (Sullivan C2).

The manner in which dolphins and humans learn their language is the third way their communication systems appear similar. Young children usually speak in very simple sentences that become more complicated as they mature. In the same way dolphins use more and more complicated patterns of signals as they become older (Lilly 79).

The similarity in dolphin and human communication has led some researchers to believe that humans might someday communicate with dolphins. Researchers at the University of Hawaii are now working to establish communication between humans and dolphins. The scientists first taught the two dolphins who are part of the study to recognize the names of objects placed on the surface of the water. Communication with one dolphin was carried out by means of arm signals; the other dolphin was taught by means of sounds transmitted through the water by a computer. Through arm signals the first dolphin has learned over twenty-five words. Phoenix, the dolphin trained through sounds, can correctly carry out simple statements such as "Phoenix-Ball-Fetch-Gate" and now even imitates the sounds made by the computer (Sullivan C1).

Researchers have already learned a great deal about dolphin language. They know what sounds dolphins use to communicate, how they produce the sounds and then combine them to produce messages, and how the patterns of signals change as the dolphins mature. With more study perhaps scientists will one day succeed in "translating" the dolphin language. Science fiction writers have already written about humans who could communicate with dolphins; the reality may not be far away.

Bibliography

Magazine article

Caldwell, David K. and Melba C. Caldwell. "The Dolphin Observed."

Natural History Oct. 1968: 58–65.

Book

Lilly, John Cunningham, M.D. The Mind of the Dolphin. New York: Doubleday, 1967.

Book

Stenuit, Robert. The Dolphin, Cousin to Man. New York: Sterling, 1968.

Newspaper article

Sullivan, Walter. "Scientists Move Toward Dialogue with Dolphins."

The New York Times 22 April 1980: C1–2.

Think and Discuss

Review the sample topic and sentence outlines on *Dolphin Communication*. Notice how the major points in each outline are developed in the report. The outline form served as a way of mapping and organizing the final research paper.

Reread the report and answer the following questions.

1. How is the subject of the report identified in the first sentence so that the reader's interest is aroused?

2. Locate the thesis statement in the introductory paragraph. How does it limit the topic and give focus to the report?

3. There are several examples of dolphin research used in the report. How does this information help develop the topic?

4. Identify several transitional words and phrases the writer uses to link sentences and paragraphs.

5. How does the concluding paragraph summarize the topic in an interesting way and leave the reader with something to think about?

6. Notice where the writer used parenthetical documentation in the report. Where do these references appear?

7. Where does the bibliography appear? What information is included in the bibliography? How is this information different from that given in parenthetical documentation?

Revising the Rough Draft

Think of the rough draft of your research report as a working copy. Most likely, you will need to make several changes. As you read it over, you may find entire paragraphs that need to be moved, topic sentences that need further development, and gaps of information that need to be filled. You may also find unnecessary information to delete. Making such changes will help improve your final report. You may even find it necessary to write several drafts. You may also find it helpful to read your draft to others and to ask them to identify areas that need to be rewritten or details that should be added or deleted.

If necessary, review the section on revising in Chapter 1.

Writing Practice 10: *Revising the Rough Draft*

Revise your rough draft. Ask a friend, parent, or classmate to listen to your report and make suggestions for improving it. Use the following checklist as a guide in making changes.

Checklist for Revising a Short Research Report

1. Is the subject limited to a topic that can be developed in a short research report?

2. Does the introductory paragraph include a thesis statement that gives focus to the report, and is it adequately developed throughout the report?

3. Is the information presented in a logical order? Does the report include the basic points in the outline?

4. Does the report include factual information from a variety of sources that develops and explains the topic?

5. Is there a concluding paragraph that summarizes the information and the topic in an interesting way?

6. Are there effective transitions between paragraphs?

7. Is the wording clear? Are there short sentences that could be combined or long sentences that need to be divided?

8. Are important ideas, facts, and quotations credited in accurate parenthetical documentation?

After you have completed your revision, proofread your report for correct grammar, sentence structure, mechanics, and spelling, using the Proofreader's Checklist at the back of the book.

The Final Draft

The *final draft* is a revision of the rough draft.

Before you write the final draft, be certain you have covered all the points about your topic in the rough draft and that you have arranged them in the best possible order. If not, rearrange or add to your material at this point.

169

As you rewrite your paper, check to make sure you have used parenthetical documentation where necessary and that you have punctuated these references correctly. See pages 165–166 for examples of parenthetical documentation.

Writing Practice 11: *The Final Draft*

Type or neatly write your final draft, carefully incorporating the changes you made in your rough draft. Include parenthetical documentation where appropriate. Remember that these references come before the punctuation at the end of a sentence. Proofread your final draft again. Then ask someone you know to act as your editor and proofread your final report.

The Bibliography

The final step in writing a research report is to prepare a complete bibliography.

A *bibliography* is a list of sources that have been used in preparing your report. It tells your readers where they can find more information about your topic.

To prepare the bibliography, arrange your bibliography cards in alphabetical order according to the last name of each author. If a source has no author listed, alphabetize it by the first major word in the title. On a separate sheet of paper write the bibliography directly from the cards you have already made. When an entry takes up more than one line, indent all the lines after the first. If you use two sources written by the same author, do not rewrite the author's name for the second entry. Instead, use three hyphens for the author's name in the second entry and in all other entries by that author. For example, the following bibliography entries are for two reference books by Ernle Bradford. Note that an abbreviation of the publisher's name is used. *Harcourt* is an abbreviated form of Harcourt Brace Jovanovich.

Bradford, Ernle. Cleopatra. New York: Harcourt, 1972.

---. Mediterranean, Portrait of a Sea. New York: Harcourt, 1971.

To be certain you have written your bibliography correctly, check the instructions for writing bibliography cards on pages 156–157. Use the sample bibliography on page 167 as a guideline.

Writing Practice 12: *Organizing the Bibliography*

Using a form that your teacher approves, prepare a bibliography for your report. Remember to

1. alphabetize sources by the author's last name, or if no author is given, by the first major word in the title;

2. indent the second line of an entry five spaces to the right; and

3. for two or more sources by the same author, use three hyphens for the author's last name after the first entry.

Refer to the sample bibliography at the end of the research report on dolphin communication on page 167.

Sentence Combining: *Using* with, -ing, *and Possessives*

Inserting With

For information on prepositions, see pages 438-455.

Another way of showing more about a person, an idea, or a thing is to modify (describe) it further by using a *with* phrase, as the following examples show.

Base Sentence: John's bike was in a lateral skid.
Insert: The bike had a loose wheel. (*with*)
Combined: John's bike *with a loose wheel* was in a lateral skid.

Base Sentence: She was in excellent physical condition.

Insert: She had no other desire than to stay in good health. (*with*)

Combined: She was in excellent physical condition, *with no other desire than to stay in good health.*

or

With no other desire than to stay in good health, she was in excellent physical condition.

Notice that *with* phrases can appear in different positions in the sentence. When a *with* phrase modifies one word, however, it should be near that word for the meaning to be clear.

Base Sentence: Hair is beautiful.
Insert: Hair has shiny highlights. (*with*)
Combined: Hair *with shiny highlights* is beautiful.

Commas usually set off nonessential *with* phrases, especially when they appear at the beginning or end of a sentence.

Exercise 1: Combining Sentences by Inserting With

On a sheet of paper, combine the following sets of sentences. Use the signals where given. Study the examples before you begin. (Remember that the first sentence is always the base.)

Examples

a. He was tall and slender.
   He had narrow shoulders and a long neck. (*with*)
   With narrow shoulders and a long neck, he was tall and slender.

b. The caribou traveled their ancient migratory route.
   The caribou had their young at their sides.
   The caribou, with their young at their sides, traveled their ancient migratory route.

1. A person is needed.
   A person has talent. (*with*)

2. The orangutan looked out of its cage at us.
   The orangutan had a newborn baby. (*with*)

3. You can't be very warm in that jacket.
   That jacket has three large holes in the back. (*with*)

4. Put this patient in the first-floor ward.
   The first-floor ward has the other pneumonia cases. (*with*)

5. Jenny is an intelligent, sensitive woman.
   Jenny has white hair and kindly eyes. (*with*)

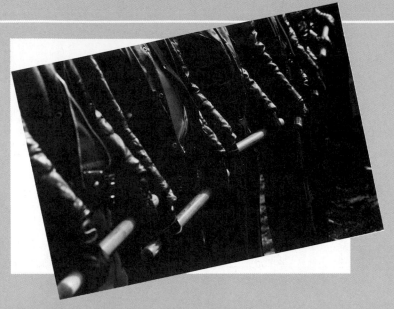

6. The guards stood scowling at us.
    The guards had their nightsticks firmly grasped in their hands.

7. Ramona was clearly in danger.
    Ramona had no chance to know why.

8. Ms. Chiang told us the same old story.
    The old story had a new ending.

9. The eight-year-old child inherited money from her grand-parents.
    The eight-year-old child had a rare bone disease.

10. The driver of the car did not see the truck.
    The truck had a flashing yellow light.

Inserting -ing

For information on present participles, see pages 496-497.

The (-ing) insertion involves changing the form of a word in the combined sentence. You can change a verb into a modifier, for instance, by using the -ing form, as in the following examples.

Verbs	Modifiers
A girl *smiles*.	a *smiling* girl
A boy *whistles*.	a *whistling* boy
Two roosters *crow*.	two *crowing* roosters

To make the (-*ing*) combination, change the main verb in the insert sentence to its -*ing* form and then insert the new modifier into the base sentence before the word it describes.

Base Sentence:	That dog must have fleas.
Insert:	That dog scratches. (-*ing*)
Combined:	That *scratching* dog must have fleas.

Base Sentence:	The train was winding its way slowly though the mountains.
Insert:	The train clattered. (-*ing*)
Combined:	The *clattering* train was winding its way slowly through the mountains.

Notice that the verb (was winding) in the previous insert sentence has the -*ing* form too. When the word *clattering* describes the train, however, it is being used as a modifier.

Exercise 2: Combine Sentences by Using -ing

On a sheet of paper, combine the following sets of sentences by making the (-*ing*) change. In the first five sets the word to be changed is *italicized*; for the others you must first locate the word to be changed and inserted. Study the example before you begin. Use your dictionary for help with spelling changes.

Example

a. The cat likes to sit on this cushion.
   The cat purrs. (-*ing*)
   The purring cat likes to sit on this cushion.

1. A committee of four honored us on our arrival.
   The committee *greets*. (-*ing*)

2. Ms. Marsh's assignment was not easy.
   The assignment was *to write*. (-*ing*)

3. The Presidential candidate went on a long tour of the nation.
   The candidate *speaks* on the tour. (-*ing*)

4. Judge Korhn, the judge in the arson case, handed down a stiff jail term.
   The judge *sentences*. (-*ing*)

5. My dining room table has two legs on either end that open to support extra leaves.
   The legs *extend*. (-*ing*)

6. Dirk Chang's club went on a long and difficult tour of the Rocky Mountain National Park.
   The club hikes.

7. There on the sidewalk, sitting on the curb, holding two skinned knees in both hands, was the child.
   The child weeps.

8. Mosquitoes swarmed above the lake and around our campfire, making it impossible for us to enjoy the outing.
   The mosquitoes buzz.

9. Watch out for those propellers as you board the plane.
   The propellers whir.

10. We stood there looking ridiculous, holding our sides and laughing as if the joke had really been funny.
    Our sides ache.

Inserting the Possessive Form (Pos)

The (*pos*) change transforms a word into its *possessive* form. Words like *Mary*, *calf*, *apple*, and *love* become *Mary's*, *calf's*, *apple's*, and *love's*. The following sentence sets demonstrate how this change is made. The expressions that begin with *belong to*, *by*, and *of* become the possessive.

For more information on possessives, see pages 302, 311-313.

Base Sentence:	There goes a little lamb.
Insert:	The lamb *belongs to* Mary. (*pos*)
Combined:	There goes *Mary's* little lamb.

Base Sentence:	This is a painting.
Insert:	This painting is *by Mary Cassatt*. (*pos*)
Combined:	This is *Mary Cassatt's* painting.

If the word to be made possessive is plural, use the plural possessive form.

Base Sentence:	The Constitution protects rights.
Insert:	The rights *belong to the citizens*. (*pos*)
Combined:	The Constitution protects the *citizens'* rights.

Exercise 3: Combining Sentences by Using the Possessive Form

On a sheet of paper, combine the following sentence sets by using possessives. The first sentence in each set is the base. Study the examples before you begin.

Examples

a. A helping hand would be welcome right now.
The helping hand belongs to a friend. (*pos*)
A friend's helping hand would be welcome right now.

b. The problem is how to find a job.
The problem belongs to Marcia.
Marcia's problem is how to find a job.

1. You can't always tell by a cover what will be inside.
The cover belongs to a book. (*pos*)

2. A niece is my first cousin.
The niece is of my mother. (*pos*)

3. The manes and tails were braided and decorated for the show.
The manes and tails belonged to the horses. (*pos*)

4. The court was extremely worried about the condition.
The condition belonged to the judge. (*pos*)

5. A first responsibility is to the voters.
The first responsibility belongs to a representative. (*pos*)

6. Does a tool kit include a left-handed monkey wrench?
The tool kit belongs to a plumber.

7. Masts dotted the bay with bright colors.
The masts were of sailboats.

8. A share of the cash had mysteriously disappeared.
The share belonged to Susan.

9. This sculpture shows the skill.
The skill is of the artist.

10. Beautiful lakes remain the main tourist attraction.
The lakes are of Switzerland.

Review: *Combining Sentences*

The following sentence sets require you to use more than one combining skill at a time. Follow the signals as you have been doing in the previous Sentence Combining sections. The first sentence in each set is the base. After studying the example, write each new sentence on a sheet of paper.

Example

a. The man was eating a sandwich.
His companion was drinking a soda. (*,and*)
The man was strange.
The man was little. (*,*)
The man had a gray fedora. (*with*)
The sandwich was ham.
His companion hulked. (*-ing*)
The soda fizzed. (*-ing*)

The strange, little man with a gray fedora was eating a ham sandwich, and his hulking companion was drinking a fizzing soda.

1. The investigators planned to make the raid on the cabin.
The investigators had worked on this case a long time. (*who*)
The raid was final.
The cabin was a mountain one.
This raid would end the robbers' careers. (*which*)

2. Concentration makes my head hurt.
Relaxation makes me feel fine again. (*;*)
Concentration is intense.
Concentration is difficult. (*and*)
My head is poor.
Relaxation is calm.

3. Cruz seemed to know everybody.
Cruz seemed to know everything. (*and*)
Cruz was president last year. (*who*)
The president was of our class. (*pos*)
Knowing everybody and everything made others dislike her a little. (*which*)

4. Don is known around here as a person.
He is never satisfied. (*because*)
As a person he complains. (*-ing*)
He is always wanting something better than the things he has now. (*;*)

5. The lady swept to the edge of the crowd.
   She pushed her way around the barriers. (,)
   She thrust her arms above her head. (,)
   She called for order. (,*and*)
   The crowd was noisy.
   Her arms waved. (-*ing*)

The next five sentence sets provide no signals, so apply any of the sentence-combining skills you think work best in creating one sentence out of each set. (There may be more than one way to make interesting and sensible combinations.) Consider the first sentence as the base sentence. On a sheet of paper, write each new sentence.

6. A steel drum provides a way to clean a hoe.
   A steel drum provides a way to clean a shovel.
   The drum is half-filled with water.
   The way is handy.

7. As they walked up the trail, they saw the horse.
   The trail was long.
   The horse was spotted.
   The horse was standing still.

8. Grandmother Banks remembered that Todd had lived a life during his years.
   Grandmother Banks belonged to the Republic of Texas.
   Todd's life was fruitful.
   Todd's years were eighty-odd.

9. They skipped along.
   They were excited.
   The sunshine was warm.
   They were hoping to find their friends.
   Their friends had professional footballs.
   Their friends were waiting for them in the park.

10. The brownstones were once beautifully maintained.
    The brownstones were of the city.
    The brownstones are four- and five-story houses that formerly housed the wealthy.
    Many of them are now in poor repair.

Writing Practice: *Revising a Research Report for Sentence Variety*

Reread the report you wrote for the Writing Assignment in Chapter 7, Writing a Research Report. Check your report for variety of sentence patterns, and use several Sentence Combining techniques to revise it.

179

8 Imaginative Writing: The Poem

Playing with Words

"Stop that playing around. Be serious."

Many people think that playing is something only children should do. Adults who "play" are wasting time. For many other people, though, playing is very serious business. Scientists "play" with ideas, and the results improve lives in many ways. Artists are people who have not forgotten how to play: composers play with sounds to create new forms, photographers with light and shadow, writers with words.

In the following sections you will learn how to play with words to create word images, puns, and poems.

Model: *A Humorous Poem*

Writers often make people laugh by using words in unexpected ways. As you read the following poem, think about how the poet uses words unexpectedly.

A Love Song[1]

Do I love you?
I'll tell you true.

Do chickens have lips?
Do pythons have hips?

Do penguins have arms?
Do spiders have charms?

Do oysters get colds?
Do leopards have moles?

Does a bird cage make a zoo?
Do I love you?

—*Raymond Richard Patterson*

---

[1]"A Love Song" by Raymond R. Patterson. Copyright © 1970 by Raymond Richard Patterson. Reprinted by permission of the author.

The first two lines of "A Love Song" are like a message on a valentine card. You expect the writer to answer *yes* to the question in the first line, but gradually you realize the poet is saying *no* in an amusing way.

Poets are not the only people who play with words to create humor, as the following humorous lines show.

1. Oil spills are the grime of the century.

2. *Lapse*: What we get when we sit down.

3. *Melancholy*: A dog that won't eat anything but cantaloupe.

4. Q. What's the best way to drive a baby buggy?
   A. Tickle its feet.

5. Q. What did Paul Revere say when he passed a London barbershop?
   A. The British are combing.

This form of wordplay is known as *punning*. A pun is a play on words because it contains at least one word that has two or more meanings or associations.

Sometimes, one word sounds very much like another word with a very different meaning. For example, in the first of the sample puns on the preceding page, the words *grime* and *crime* sound very much alike. You have probably heard the expression *the crime of the century* but did not expect to see *grime* in place of *crime*. The word *grime* fits into the meaning of the sentence, however, and the result is a pun.

In the second pun the word *lapse* sounds like *laps,* which people have only when sitting down. How does the word *lapse* relate to sitting down?

Advertisers often use puns to attract attention.

In a boarding kennel: Howliday Inn

In a used-book store: Secondhand Prose

In a pet shop: Canaries for Sale. Cheep

In a tire store: We Skid You Not

In a watch store: We Give You a Good Time

Writing Practice 1: *Wordplay*

Select one of the following "wordplay" exercises.

1.   In the poem on page 180, the poet "sets up" his readers by asking a question that seems to have one answer and really has another. Write a question of your own that seems to have one answer. Then answer the question in an unexpected way by asking humorous questions.

2.   Write a pun, which may or may not be an advertisement. To help you get started think of words that sound alike but have different meanings.

way/weigh   This diet will work—
No two weighs about it.

The Feeling of Words

For information on
adjectives, see pages
386-413.

The first scene of a movie shows a dark, deserted countryside. Lightning flashes through the sky, and dark clouds drift across the face of the moon. These images suggest that something frightening or strange is about to happen, by creating a *mood* of suspense.

Artists who work with visual media, such as film, photography, and painting, know they can use light and shadow to create feelings.

What type of mood do light and shadow create in the photograph on page 182?

Model: Mood in Poetry

Writers often use words to create a special mood or feeling. What mood does the following poem create?

Velvet Shoes[1]

Let us walk in the white snow
    In a soundless space;

With footsteps quiet and slow,
    At a tranquil pace,
    Under veils of white lace.

I shall go shod in silk,
    And you in wool,
White as a white cow's milk,
    More beautiful
    Than the breast of a gull.

We shall walk through the still town
    In a windless peace;
We shall step upon white down,
    Upon silver fleece,
    Upon softer than these.

We shall walk in velvet shoes:
    Wherever we go
Silence will fall like dews
    On white silence below.
    We shall walk in the snow.

—Elinor Wylie

[1]"Velvet Shoes" by Elinor Wylie. Copyright 1921 by Alfred A. Knopf, Inc.; renewed 1949 by William Rose Benet. Reprinted from *Collected Poems* by Elinor Wylie by permission of Alfred A. Knopf, Inc.

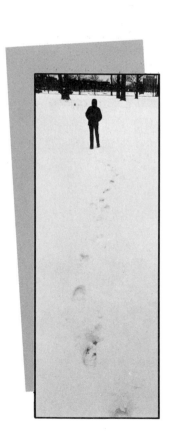

Think and Discuss

1. Adjectives like *white, soundless, quiet, slow, tranquil,* and so on create a special kind of mood in the poem "Velvet Shoes." How would you describe the mood? What other words in the poem contribute to this mood or feeling?

2. How is the mood in the photographs on this page different from that in the poem? In what way is it the same? What words would you use to describe the mood in the photographs?

Writing Practice 2: *Creating Mood*

In your Writer's Notebook make a list or word cluster of adjectives that describe the photograph at the top of this page. Using specific adjectives like *sparkling, glistening,* or *joyous,* write a description that captures the feeling you get from the photograph.

The Sounds of Words

Writers also play with the sounds of words. Poets and song writers especially use repetition of sounds to create a pleasing effect and mood. For example, in the poem "Velvet Shoes" on page 183, the poet repeats the *w* and *s* sounds throughout the poem. Notice how the repetition of sounds in the following lines creates a mood of stillness and peace.

> *Let us walk in the white snow*
>   *In a soundless space;*
> *With footsteps quiet and slow . . .*
>
> *I shall go shod in silk,*
>   *And you in wool,*
> *White as a white cow's milk . . .*

The repetition of the same initial sound in words is called *alliteration.*

Poets often use alliteration to create interesting sound patterns. They use these sound effects to emphasize both the meanings and the moods of poems.

Model: Alliteration in Poetry

Read the following poem by Robert Francis aloud, concentrating on the sounds of the words.

The Base Stealer[1]

Poised between going on and back, pulled
Both ways taut like a tightrope-walker,
Fingertips pointing the opposites,
Now bouncing tiptoe like a dropped ball
Or a kid skipping rope, come on, come on,
Running a scattering of steps sidewise,
How he teeters, skitters, tingles, teases,
Taunts them, hovers like an ecstatic bird,
He's only flirting, crowd him, crowd him,
Delicate, delicate, delicate, delicate—now!

—*Robert Francis*

---

[1]"The Base Stealer" from *The Orb Weaver* by Robert Francis. Copyright © 1948 by Robert Francis. Reprinted by permission of Wesleyan University Press.

Notice the repeated *t* sounds in *teeters, skitters, tingles, teases,* and *taunts.* These sounds suggest the action and tension of the baseball player who moves quickly on and off the base. What other examples of alliteration can you find in the poem? How does the poet also use the repetition of words as well as sounds to create a feeling of tension and suspense?

"The Base Stealer" on the preceding page is an example of a free verse poem: it does not follow a specific form or rhyme scheme.

Model: *Rhyme in Poetry*

The following poem, "Swift Things Are Beautiful," uses both rhyme and word sounds to emphasize meaning and mood. The words of the first stanza have different sounds from those of the second stanza. As you read the poem, notice the change in sound and mood.

Swift Things Are Beautiful[1]

Swift things are beautiful:
Swallows and deer,
And lightning that falls
Bright-veined and clear,
Rivers and meteors,
Wind in the wheat,
The strong-withered horse,
The runner's sure feet.

And slow things are beautiful:
The closing of day,
The pause of the wave
That curves downward to spray,
The ember that crumbles,
The opening flower,
And the ox that moves on
In the quiet of power.

—*Elizabeth Coatsworth*

Which stanza contains quick, brief sounds? Which stanza contains slower, lingering sounds? How do the sounds in each stanza reflect the poem's meaning?

When the sounds at the ends of words are repeated, the result is *rhyme*.

Elizabeth Coatsworth's poem uses rhyme in every other line of the first stanza: *deer* and *clear, wheat* and *feet*. How is rhyme used in the second stanza?

Writing Practice 3: *Creating a Poem*

Reread the poem "Swift Things Are Beautiful." Make a word cluster in your Writer's Notebook of the things you think are beautiful. See if you can find two different groups or categories of beautiful things to contrast, such as "swift things" and "slow things" in the poem. Then play with the words in your word cluster by rearranging lines and phrases to create either a free verse or a rhymed poem.

Model: *Sound Play in Song Lyrics*

Rhyming and alliteration can be found in the lyrics of most songs. How many examples of both forms of sound play can you find in the following song by Joni Mitchell?

Both Sides Now[1]

Bows and flows of angel hair,
And ice-cream castles in the air,
And feather canyons everywhere,
I've looked at clouds that way.
But now they only block the sun,
They rain and snow on everyone,
So many things I would have done,
But clouds got in my way.
     I've looked at clouds from both sides now
     From up and down, and still somehow
     It's cloud illusions I recall;
     I really don't know clouds at all.
Moons and tunes and ferris wheels,
The dizzy dancing way you feel
When every fairytale comes real,
I've looked at love that way.
But now it's just another show,

You leave 'em laughin' when you go.
And if you care, don't let them know,
Don't give yourself away.
    I've looked at love from both sides now,
    From win and lose, and still somehow
    It's love illusions I recall;
    I really don't know love at all.
Tears and fears and feelin' proud
To say I love you right out loud,
Dreams and schemes and circus crowds,
I've looked at life that way.
But now old friends are acting strange,
They shake their heads, they say I've changed,
Well, something's lost but something's gained
In living every day.
    I've looked at life from both sides now,
    From win and lose and still somehow
    It's life's illusions I recall;
    I really don't know life at all.

—*Joni Mitchell*

Writing Practice 4: *Word Sounds*

Think of a scene that involves sound or a definite lack of it, or select one of the following scenes. Then write a brief description of the scene, using words that will recreate either the sound or a sense of silence for your readers.

1. A supermarket on a busy Saturday morning

2. A carwash

3. A roller-skating rink

4. A deserted automobile junkyard

5. A sixteenth-birthday party

6. Your classroom at 4 A.M.

7. A Saturday morning children's cartoon show on television

8. A city street just after a blizzard

9. A dentist's waiting room

10. Describe the sounds suggested by the photograph on page 190.

For Your Writer's Notebook

The poem "The Base Stealer" on page 185 captures the tension a baseball player feels as he tries to move from one base to another. Think of some experience you know well enough to describe, from sports or from some other field. Perhaps you can capture the noise and movement you feel every day riding home on a bus or the subway, or the harmonious, relaxed feeling you have during band practice. Focus for a few moments on the experience you choose. Then use specific details to capture those movements in a notebook entry.

Writing Sense Poems

If you have ever been to a carnival, fair, or amusement park, you have probably experienced the feeling of all your senses working at once; the bright lights, rides, games, screams, tempting smells, and excitement fill your senses. When writers want to capture such an experience, they often use words that appeal to our senses.

The words and phrases writers use to describe what they see, hear, smell, touch, taste, and feel are called *sensory details*.

When poets want to describe a sensory experience, they often write *sense poems*. Such poems contain concrete descriptive words to help readers experience the poet's subject.

Model: Sensory Details in Poetry

In the following lines from Karl Shapiro's poem "Auto Wreck," notice how the poet captures both the *sights* and *sounds* of the ambulance's approach.

[from] Auto Wreck[1]

Its quick soft silver bell beating, beating,
And down the dark one ruby flare
Pulsing out red light like an artery,
The ambulance at top speed floating down
Past beacons and illuminated clocks
Wings in a heavy curve, dips down,
And brakes speed, entering the crowd.
The doors leap open, emptying light;
Stretchers are laid out, the mangled lifted
And stowed into the little hospital.
Then the bell, breaking the hush, tolls once,
And the ambulance with its terrible cargo
Rocking, slightly rocking, moves away,
As the doors, an afterthought, are closed.

—Karl Shapiro

[1]From "Auto Wreck," copyright 1942 and renewed 1970 by Karl Shapiro. Reprinted from *Collected Poems 1940–1978* by Karl Shapiro, by permission of Random House, Inc.

Think and Discuss

A poet who writes a good sense poem does not *tell* you about a person, place, or thing but recreates the subject of the poem, using vivid sense images. When you finish reading a good sense poem, you should be able to close your eyes and experience what the poet is writing about.

How does the poet create sensory images in the poem "Auto Wreck"? What specific words and phrases does he use to recreate both the sights and sounds?

Writing Assignment 1: *A Sense Poem*

A. Prewriting

Clustering Sensory Detail: Look at the photograph on the previous page. Pretend that you are one of the riders on the roller coaster. Or recall the scene you wrote about in Writing Practice 4. What did you see, hear, smell, touch, taste, and feel? Make a word cluster of your ideas in your Writer's Notebook. Include specific words and images that appeal to several senses.

B. Writing

Playing with Words: Play with the ideas from your word cluster by rewriting your words into a sense poem. Rearrange lines and phrases until you have captured the experience. It is not necessary to follow a rhyme pattern unless you choose to do so.

C. Postwriting

Listening for Sound Effects: Read your poem aloud, perhaps to a partner, and listen for the sounds of the words and the rhythm and flow of lines. Add sensory details where needed. Substitute concrete words that evoke more vivid images. Delete unnecessary words and phrases. Write your final poem in your Writer's Notebook and share it with a small group of classmates.

Haiku: A Special Sense Poem

A poem is an especially compact, concentrated piece of writing. A good poet chooses each word in a poem carefully and often revises the poem several times, eliminating nonessential words. The following examples are two versions of the same poem. In which version does the poet use words more economically and with greater impact?

1.

On a windy day in winter,
I am walking in the rain.
The strong wind pulls at my umbrella,
Making it want to walk backwards.

2.

Windy winter rain. . .
my silly big umbrella
tries walking backward.[1]

—*Shisei-jo*

The second poem is an example of *haiku*, a Japanese verse form that does not rhyme but has a fixed number of syllables (seventeen). In haiku, the first and third lines each contain five syllables; the second line has seven syllables. (Often when a haiku is translated into English, its syllable count changes from seventeen.) Read the following haiku aloud until you can recognize the number of syllables in each line.

Softly the breeze blows:
far clouds draw apart, and for
an instant—the moon.[2]

—*Tino Villanueva*

Because a haiku is so short, this form is often used to capture a single memorable experience from nature. Imagine taking a snapshot of a beautiful sight: fireworks against a dark sky; lightning flashing on a soft, spring night; a golden moon setting behind sharply etched skyscrapers. The camera clicks, and you have captured an instant of beauty. Think of a haiku as a camera recording an instant like this.

Models: Haiku

As you read the haiku on the next page, try to visualize and hear what the poets describe using concrete sensory details.

The lightning flashes!
And slashing through the darkness,
A night-heron's screech.[1]

—*Matsuo Basho*

Above the veil
of mist, from time to time
there lifts a sail.[2]

—*Gakoku*

Writing Practice 5: *Haiku*

Write a haiku about one of your own experiences in nature or about
one of those listed below. Remember to use five syllables in the first
and third lines, and seven in the second line. Share your haiku with
your classmates. Illustrate it with a photograph, drawing, or magazine picture and display it in your classroom.

1. The sight of a spider crossing a spiderweb

2. The sound of a cricket on a hot, still afternoon

3. Soft rain that starts to fall on a spring evening

4. A beach shortly before a heavy rainstorm

5. A rose that has just begun to open

6. A bird in flight

7. Leaves that have turned color in the fall

8. A waterfall

9. A field of corn or wheat

10. Bees buzzing around a flower

Using Figurative Language

Another way writers play with words is by creating imaginative
comparisons. For example, in the first line of his poem "Arithmetic,"

---

[1] "The Lightning Flashes" by Matsuo Basho, translated by Earl Miner in the *Princeton Encyclopedia of Poetry and Poetics*, edited by Alex Preminger et al. Copyright © 1965, Enlarged Edition Copyright © 1974 by Princeton University Press; Enlarged Princeton Paperback Edition. Reprinted by permission of Princeton University Press.

[2] "Watching" by Gakoku from *An Introduction to Haiku* by Harold G. Henderson. Copyright © 1958 by Harold G. Henderson. Reprinted by permission of Doubleday & Company, Inc.

Carl Sandburg writes, "Arithmetic is where numbers fly like pigeons in and out of your head." Numbers do not actually, or literally, fly around in anyone's head, but the poet's imaginative comparison does suggest the feeling a student might have during a long math assignment. The poet's comparison is an example of *figurative language*—that is, language that is not literally or actually true but that imaginatively represents one item in terms of another.

Figurative language can take many forms. When Carl Sandburg writes that numbers fly in and out of one's head "like pigeons," he uses a *simile*.

A *simile* uses the word *like* or *as* to make an imaginative comparison between two basically different things.

Model: Simile in Poetry

In the following poem find the two similes Burton Raffel uses to describe the construction of a skyscraper.

**On Watching the Construction
of a Skyscraper**[1]
Nothing sings from these orange trees,
Rindless steel as smooth as sapling skin,
Except a crane's brief wheeze
And all the muffled, clanking din
Of rivets nosing in like bees.

—*Burton Raffel*

---

[1]"On Watching the Construction of a Skyscraper" by Burton Raffel from *The Antioch Review*, Vol. 20, No. 4 (Winter 1960–61). Copyright © 1961 by The Antioch Review, Inc. Reprinted by permission of the Editors.

Another form of comparison writers use frequently is the *metaphor*.

A *metaphor* compares two unlike things directly without the helping word *like* or *as*.

Models: Metaphor in Poetry

In Alice Walker's poem "Mysteries," a person's eyes are compared to widely open flowers. Since the comparison is direct, and *like* or *as* is not used, this is metaphor.

Mysteries[1]
Your eyes are widely open flowers
Only their centers are darkly clenched
To conceal Mysteries
That lure me to a keener blooming
Than I know,
And promise a secret
I must have.

—Alice Walker

How many metaphors are in the following poem?

Fireworks[2]
Not guns, not thunder, but a flutter of clouded drums
That announce a fiesta: abruptly, fiery needles
Circumscribe on the night boundless chrysanthemums.
Softly, they break apart, they flake away, where
Darkness, on a svelte hiss, swallows them.
Delicate brilliance: a bellflower opens, fades,
In a sprinkle of falling stars.
Night absorbs them
With the sponge of her silence.

—Babette Deutsch

Sometimes, an entire poem is built around a metaphor, creating an *extended metaphor* that involves several comparisons. Have you ever felt that you had more than one self: a kind, well-behaved self and an impulsive, mischievous self; or a quiet, inward self and an outgoing, boisterous self? The poem on the following page, "In Mind," uses extended metaphor to describe this experience. The poet compares

---

[1]"Mysteries" from *Revolutionary Petunias and Other Poems* by Alice Walker. Copyright © 1973 by Alice Walker. Reprinted by permission of Harcourt Brace Jovanovich, Inc., and the Julian Bach Literary Agency, Inc.

[2]"Fireworks" by Babette Deutsch from *Collected Poems 1919–1962*. Reprinted by permission of Adam Yarmolinsky.

the two selves she feels inside to two very different women. How does she describe the two women? What does this description tell you about her two selves?

In Mind[1]
There's in my mind a woman
of innocence, unadorned but

fair-featured, and smelling of
apples or grass. She wears

a utopian smock or shift, her hair
is light brown and smooth, and she

is kind and very clean without
ostentation—
⠀⠀⠀⠀⠀but she has
no imagination.
⠀⠀⠀⠀⠀⠀⠀And there's a
turbulent moon-ridden girl

or old woman, or both,
dressed in opals and rags, feathers

and torn taffeta,
who knows strange songs—

but she is not kind.

⠀⠀⠀⠀⠀⠀⠀⠀⠀*—Denise Levertov*

Personification is a form of indirect comparison in which human qualities are given to nonhuman objects or ideas.

Model: *Personification in Poetry*

Dan Roth uses personification in his poem "War" when he compares the climbing of the sun (a nonhuman object) to a soldier who must move cautiously because of mortar fire.

War[2]
Dawn came slowly,
almost not at all.
The sun crept over the hill
cautiously
fearful of being hit
by mortar fire.

⠀⠀⠀⠀⠀⠀⠀⠀⠀*—Dan Roth*

Model: *Figurative Language in Poetry*

Walter de la Mare combines three forms of figurative language (simile, metaphor, personification) in his poem "Silver." He also creates a mood through the use of word images and sound patterns (alliteration). Read the poem aloud; listen for the sounds of words and imagine the silvery scene the poet portrays.

Silver[1]

Slowly, silently, now the moon

Shoon means "shoes."

Walks the night in her silver shoon;
This way, and that, she peers, and sees
Silver fruit upon silver trees;
One by one the casements catch
Her beams beneath the silvery thatch;
Couched in his kennel, like a log,
With paws of silver sleeps the dog;

Cote is a small shelter for doves.

From their shadowy cote the white breasts peep
Of doves in a silver-feathered sleep;
A harvest mouse goes scampering by,
With silver claws and a silver eye;
And moveless fish in the water gleam,
By silver reeds in a silver stream.

—*Walter de la Mare*

[1]"Silver" by Walter de la Mare. Reprinted by permission of The Literary Trustees of Walter de la Mare and The Society of Authors as their representative.

Think and Discuss

1.   What object is personified or given human characteristics in the poem "Silver"? What are the human qualities assigned to it?

2.   Find examples of metaphor and simile in the poem.

3.   Select several phrases that show the use of alliteration.

4.   What word images help the reader visualize the scene?

Writing Practice 6: *Using Figurative Language*

Write a poem, using figurative language: simile, metaphor, or personification. The following suggestions may be of help.

1.   Reread "On Watching the Construction of a Skyscraper" on page 194. This poem uses similes to let the reader experience sensory details: the steel of the building is "smooth as sapling skin," and the rivets are "nosing in like bees." Think of a process you have observed, perhaps a building being constructed, students piling out of school at the last bell, waves breaking on a dock, cars packed in and honking at rush hour, or a single bird settling on a branch. Write a poem using similes to describe the sights and sounds you noticed.

2.   Reread the poem "Mysteries" on page 195. This is a love poem that does not use the word *love*; instead, it describes a person's eyes in a way that makes them seem special and mysterious. Write a love poem to a real or an imaginary person. Begin your poem with a metaphor (it can be serious, beautiful, sad, humorous). If you like, you may use the person's eyes to begin your metaphor: "Your eyes are . . ." Or you may write, "Your heart is . . ."; "Your voice over the telephone is . . ."; "Your freckles are . . ."; "Your smile is . . ."; "Your gym shoes

are. . . ." Anything about the person or anything belonging to the person can be used as the starting point for your metaphor.

3. Reread the poem "Fireworks" on page 195. This poem uses multiple metaphors—"a flutter of clouded drums," "fiery needles," "chrysanthemums"—to describe the sights and sounds of fireworks. Choose a subject and think of as many different ways as possible to describe it. What does it look or sound like? What does it remind you of? You may choose the subject *fireworks* or any other subject that inspires you: a starry night, a rainstorm, a concert, a train, an earthworm crawling out of the ground, or trees swaying in the wind. Write a multiple metaphor poem describing your subject.

4. Reread the poem "Silver" on page 197. Personification helps the reader experience a scene by imagining that an object in the scene has human qualities. For example, you could describe a forest as if the trees were a group of people. What kind of people would they be? What would they be feeling? You could describe snow falling and melting as if it were aware of the brevity of its life. What would the snow say if it could speak? You could write about a tornado or hurricane as if it were a person deliberately destroying everything. What kind of a person would it be? What would go through the person's mind as he or she ripped up houses and flooded cities? Choose one of these subjects or any other subject that seems appropriate: tears, a harvest moon, a vending machine, tires, a boat, or a worn-out jacket. Write a poem personifying the subject you choose.

For Your Writer's Notebook

The poem "In Mind," on page 196, describes two different aspects of one personality by describing them as two different women. In your notebook write about different aspects of your own mind. Perhaps you are serious and quiet in class but aggressive and loud on the basketball court. Perhaps you have an inner and an outer self or a reflective self that emerges late at night when you are alone. You may want to use comparison to describe your different sides. Is your mind inhabited by a fun-loving child, a purring cat, or a growling, moody bear that hibernates most of the time? Perhaps a whole menagerie of selves inhabits your mind, or your mind changes like the seasons or the weather. Use metaphors and concrete details to explain the unique characteristics of your selves.

Sentence Combining: Inserting Phrases and Clauses

Inserting *Where, When, and How Phrases*

For information on phrases, see pages 490-509.

Adding information about *where, when* or *how* is done by attaching a phrase to the base sentence, as the following examples show.

San Francisco is a town.
San Francisco is a town *in California*. [tells *where*]

Jimmy packed his suitcase and left for Washington, D.C.
Jimmy packed his suitcase *early in the morning* and left for Washington, D.C. [tells *when*]

Marty skated across the ice.
Marty skated across the ice *skillfully*. [tells *how*]

The *where, when,* and *how* additions, which may be single words or groups of words, often begin with the words in the following list.

Where	*When*	*How*
at	after	carefully
beside	at	sadly
beyond	before	slowly
by	during	well
in	in	[*and most single how*
near	on	*words that end in* -ly]

Notice that the additions can sometimes be placed in more than one position within a sentence.

Base Sentence: The monster smashed the mirror.

Insert: The mirror was smashed with one blow of its huge, misshapen hand. (*how*)

Combined: *With one blow of its huge, misshapen hand,* the monster smashed the mirror.
or,
The monster smashed the mirror *with one blow of its huge, misshapen hand.*

Exercise 1: *Inserting with* Where, When, *and* How

On a sheet of paper, write a combined sentence for each of the following sets. Place the *where, when,* or *how* information where it makes the best sense in the final sentence. Study the example before you begin.

Example

   a. Beef prices rose rapidly.
     Prices rose during the first part of this year. (*when*)
     Beef prices rose rapidly during the first part of this year.

1.   The villagers washed their clothes.
     They washed in the muddy river. (*where*)

2.   Solomon knows his duties and performs them.
     He performs his duties well. (*how*)

3.   Ms. Perez practices backgammon.
     She practices daily. (*when*)

4.   Jason could see the puff of smoke rising.
     It was rising beyond the clearing.

5.   He cleaned the floor to remove all traces of the spilled drink.
     He cleaned the floor carefully.

Exercise 2: *Inserting Multiple Phrases*

The following sets of sentences require inserting more than one kind of information. Make each combination in any way that you can, but use all the information provided. After studying the example, write each new sentence on a sheet of paper. Only the first five sets are signaled.

Example

   a. Francis Scott Key saw the flag waving.
     It waved in the early morning light. (*when*)
     It waved proudly. (*how*)
     Francis Scott Key saw the flag waving proudly in the early morning light.

1.   Oxford is an ancient university.
     Oxford is in England. (*where*)
     Oxford is near the Berkshire Downs. (*where*)

2. My motorcycle broke down.
   It broke down at 2 o'clock. (*when*)
   It broke down at the corner of Chestnut and State. (*where*)

3. George played hockey this afternoon.
   He played hockey at Grangerfield Stadium. (*where*)
   He played in his new uniform. (*how*)

4. The cows came home, lowing.
   They were lowing softly. (*how*)
   They came home to the barn. (*where*)
   They came home slowly. (*how*)

5. The sleek rocket sped.
   It sped silently. (*how*)
   It sped toward Mars. (*where*)

6. The Cincinnati Reds played baseball.
   They played every night.
   They played for a month.
   They played well.

7. The anteater slurped up the nest of ants.
   It slurped greedily.
   It slurped with its tongue.

8. Mae Meier packed her bags and stormed.
   She packed angrily.
   She packed with little regard for neatness.
   She stormed out of the house.

9. Daniel figured out the problem.
   Daniel figured slowly.
   Daniel figured painfully.
   The problem was in the textbook.

10. He lay there, looking.
    He lay with his arms folded.
    His arms were folded over his chest.
    He was looking at the ceiling.
    The ceiling was cracked.

New Ways to Use Old Signals

In this section the base sentence itself contains a signal, *something*, and does not become a finished sentence until words from the insert sentence replace the signal.

Base:	Please show me *something*.
Insert:	This gadget works. (*how*)
Combined:	Please show me *how this gadget works*.

When you see the signal *something*, insert some part of the following sentences. For instance, the signal (*how*) tells you to insert information that tells *how* something is done in place of the signal *something* in the base sentence. The signals (*who*), (*where*), (*what*), (*why*), and (*when*) work in similar ways.

Base:	I saw *something*.
Insert:	Someone had just come through the door. (*who*)
Combined:	I saw *who had just come through the door*.

Base:	Have you found *something*?
Insert:	George was looking for *something*. (*what*)
Combined:	Have you found *what George was looking for*?

Base:	I wondered *something*.
Insert:	The hole in my sock kept getting larger for some reason. (*why*)
Combined:	I wondered *why the hole in my sock kept getting larger*.

Exercise 3: *Combining Sentences in Various Ways*

On a sheet of paper, combine the following sets of sentences. Use signals where given. Study the examples before you begin.

Examples

a. The explorers discovered *something*.
   The mummies had been stolen from the pyramid. (*why*)
   The explorers discovered why the mummies had been stolen from the pyramid.

b. The scientists were unable to predict *something*.
   The leg on the *Viking* space lab would be repaired. (*when*)
   The scientists were unable to predict when the leg on the *Viking* space lab would be repaired.

1. Is this any way to find out *something*?
   The other kids already know something. (*what*)

2. The student was trying to find out *something*.
   A transistor radio works somehow. (*how*)

3. A speaker stood before the microphone and announced *something*.
   Someone would be leading the Antarctic expedition. (*who*)

203

4. Our class finally determined *something*.
   The annual picnic will be sometime. (*when*)

5. Did you ever find out *something*?
   Marya changed her name to Mary for some reason. (*why*)

6. It is just impossible to tell *something*.
   Her grade card is somewhere.

7. If we all make a big effort, we can find out *something*.
   Something needs to be done immediately.

8. Keeping his eyes fixed downward, Ken tried to explain *something*.
   He had embarrassed his family at the restaurant.

9. *Something* is not yet determined.
   Rita and Raoul will be here sometime.

10. *Something* remained a mystery.
    Someone had sent the patients small portable radios.

Writing Practice: *Re-creating Sentences*

In this exercise the sentences of professional writers have been "taken apart" and are listed below each other just as the practice sentences have been. By following the signals, you can re-create the writers' original sentences.

The first three sentences are adapted from *My Side of the Mountain* by Jean George. On a sheet of paper, combine each set into one sentence. The first sentence is the base sentence.[1]

1. Frightful and I settled down to *something*.
   We lived in snow. (*ing*)

---

[1]From *My Side of the Mountain* by Jean George. Copyright © 1959 by Jean George. Reprinted and adapted by permission of E. P. Dutton, and The Bodley Head.

2. We went to bed.
    We went early. (*when*)
    We slept late. (,)
    We ate the mountain harvest. (,)
    We explored the country. (*,and*)
    We explored alone. (*how*)

3. Oh, the deer walked with us.
    The foxes followed in our footsteps. (,)
    The birds flew over our heads. (,)
    The birds were of the winter.
    Mostly we were alone in the wilderness. (*,but*)
    The wilderness was white.

Sentence sets 4–7 are adapted from *To Kill a Mockingbird* by Harper Lee.[1]

4. Maycomb was a town.
    Maycomb was old.
    It was a town sometime. (*,but*)
    It was tired.
    It was old.
    I first knew it. (*when*)

5. In weather the streets turned to slop.
    The weather was rainy.
    The slop was red.
    Grass grew on the sidewalks. (;)
    The courthouse sagged in the square. (,)

6. Somehow, it was hotter then.
    A dog suffered on a day. (*colon*)
    A dog was black.
    A day was summer. (*pos*)
    Mules hitched to Hoover carts flicked flies in the shade of the oaks on the square. (;)
    The mules were bony.
    The shade was sweltering.
    The oaks were live.

7. Ladies bathed before noon.
    They bathed after their naps. (,)
    Their naps were at three o'clock.
    By nightfall they were like teacakes. (*,and*)
    The teacakes were soft.
    The teacakes had frostings of sweat and talcum. (*with*)
    The talcum was sweet.

Sentence sets 8–12 are adapted from sentences in *Never Cry Wolf* by Farley Mowat.[1]

8. My head came slowly over the crest.
    There was my quarry. (*dash + and*)

9. He was lying down.
    He was evidently resting after his singsong. (*,*)
    His singsong was mournful.
    His nose was about six feet from mine. (*,and*)

10. We stared at one another.
    We stared in silence. (*how*)

11. I do not know *something*.
    Something went on in his skull. (*what*)
    His skull was massive.
    My head was full of the most thoughts. (*,but*)
    The thoughts disturbed. (*ing*)

12. I was peering straight into the gaze of a wolf.
    The gaze was amber.

[1]From *Never Cry Wolf* by Farley Mowat. Copyright © 1963 by Farley Mowat. Reprinted by permission of Little, Brown and Company in association with the Atlantic Monthly Press, and the Canadian Publishers, McClelland and Stewart Limited, Toronto.

The wolf was fully grown.
The wolf was arctic.
He probably weighed more than I did. (*,who*)
He was certainly a lot better versed in techniques than I would ever be. (*,and who*)
The techniques were close-combat.

Sentence sets 13–18 are adapted from a short story by Mark Twain, "The Californian's Tale."[1]

13. It was a land!
    The land was lonesome.

14. There was not a sound in all those peaceful expanses of grass and woods.
    There was the drowsy hum of insects. (*but*)
    There was no glimpse of man or beast. (*;*)
    There was nothing to keep up your spirits. (*;*)
    There was nothing to make you glad to be alive. (*and*)

15. At last, in the early part of the afternoon, I felt *something*.
    I felt a most grateful uplift. (*join*)
    I caught sight of a creature sometime. (*when*)
    The creature was human.

16. This person was a man about forty-five years old.
    He was standing at the gate of one of those cottages of the sort already referred to. (*,and*)
    The cottages were cozy.
    They were little.
    They were rose-clad.

17. However, this one did not have a look.
    The look was deserted.
    It had the look of being lived in. (*;*)
    It had the look of being petted. (*and*)
    It had the look of being cared for. (*and*)
    It had the look of being looked after. (*and*)
    So had its front yard. (*;and*)
    The front yard was a garden of flowers. (*,which*)
    The flowers were abundant.
    The flowers were gay. (*,*)
    The flowers were flourishing. (*,and*)

18. I was invited, of course.
    I was required to make myself at home. (*,and*)
    It was the custom of the country. (*dash*)

[1]From *$30,000 Bequest and Other Stories* by Mark Twain. Reprinted by permission of Harper & Row, Publishers, Inc.

9 Writing the Short Story and Play

Elements of a Story

The *Odyssey*, written in Greek about 700 B.C. by the blind poet Homer, is still one of the world's most popular stories. It has been adapted for comic books and children's books; Kirk Douglas starred in a film version of the story. Almost every library has a copy of the *Odyssey*, and it is in most bookstores. In fact, the *Odyssey* has been a "best-seller" for more than 2,600 years.

For a work to retain its popularity for more than 2,000 years, it must contain certain ingredients that interest readers. Indeed, the *Odyssey* contains the same basic elements found in today's best-sellers and in any good short story: *plot, conflict, character*, and *setting*.

Audiences become involved in the *plot*, or series of events, that concludes when Odysseus reaches home after a ten-year voyage. During the trip the hero faces many *conflicts:* he struggles against the sea, with supernatural beings like the Sirens, and even with forces within himself. Another reason the *Odyssey* has almost universal appeal is that it is about interesting *characters*, such as Odysseus, the great Greek warrior; Athena, the crafty goddess; and Telemachus, Odysseus's teenage son. Also, the story takes the reader to unusual *settings*, such as the Underworld and the cave of the one-eyed giant.

Stories are written for many reasons. The *Odyssey* was probably composed to entertain people and to emphasize values such as courage and loyalty. Today many stories examine one character's personality or look closely at contemporary life. Whatever their purposes, good stories involve plot, conflict, character, and setting. In this chapter you will learn how to write short stories using these elements.

Action and Plot

Action and *plot* refer to the sequence, or order, of events in a story.

Plots may be very simple or very complicated; in fact, there may even be more than one plot in a story. Whether the story line is simple or

complicated, the reader must be able to identify events, their order, and their importance. In some instances the reader must not only identify events and actions that are directly stated, but also interpret an event that is only suggested.

Plot

Suppose that last night you watched on television a popular detective program that emphasized action. During the show your favorite character ate in a restaurant, received a call from a friend, drove her car to a deserted park, entered an abandoned warehouse, and solved a kidnapping. These events by themselves do not make a story. It is the relationship between events and the reasons for their happening that makes the story. Notice how a story emerges when the reasons for a character's actions and the relationships among the events are added: at the beginning of the program, the detective is eating in a restaurant when she receives a phone call. You can tell from her side of the conversation that a friend who fears his sister has been kidnapped asks for help. Then you know that the detective is driving across the city *because* she is supposed to meet her friend. You learn that the detective goes to the deserted park *because* that is where the meeting is to take place.

At the end of the story, the detective enters an abandoned warehouse *because* she has a clue that the victim is being held there. The surprise in this story is that the kidnapper is the friend who called in the first scene. The friend asked the detective for help *because* he thought this action would keep the detective from suspecting him.

The plot of an effective story reveals a series of events that build to a *climax*, or point of highest interest. In the detective story described above, the climax would probably occur when the detective enters the abandoned warehouse to find the kidnapped victim.

After the climax, there is usually a *turning point*; from then on, the events in the story lead to the end.

Writing Practice 1: *Showing Relationships Between Events*

Select five events from the list below, or make up five of your own. Arrange the events in any order, but think about how they relate to one another. Write a paragraph using the events. Include specific characters in your paragraph and add any other details you want. When you finish, you will have the beginning of a story.

a. Three people meet for lunch in a diner at a truck stop in New Jersey.

b. A person walks two German shepherds in a city park.

c. A fire burns out of control in a heavily wooded area.

d. A person with a briefcase walks into a bank.

e. Six people have a meeting on a ship several miles off the coast of San Francisco.

f. A person sits alone in a bus station.

g. Officials at Fort Knox, where much of the country's gold supply is kept, report an attempted robbery.

h. An explosion at a large airport causes great confusion and long delays of air traffic.

i. A large city suddenly loses its power and is plunged into darkness.

j. A detective looks through police records for the past twenty years.

Characters

Characters, **who are the actors in a story, can be people, animals, creatures, or inanimate objects such as robots.**

In a movie or film a character's physical appearance is immediately obvious to the viewer because the character can be seen; however, the total personality of the character is only gradually revealed through his or her words, actions, expressions, and relationships with others. Story writers do not always have the advantage of pictures to portray their characters. They must use words to make their characters come alive for the reader. Their words must give clues about the physical features as well as the personality of each character introduced. As in films, writers reveal characters best by *showing* what they are like rather than by telling about them. Story writers reveal their characters through the use of dialogue or conversation and by describing their physical traits, actions, responses, and relationships with others.

To help you in writing about characters in your short story, review the section "Describing a Person" in Chapter 3.

Writing Practice 2: *A Character Description*

Think of a character you would like to use in a short story and decide what kind of person you want him or her to be. Then describe this character, using these directions and answering the questions.

1. Describe the person's physical appearance. For a list of physical traits to include in your description, see the section "Describing a Person" in Chapter 3.

2. Describe the person's background. What type of home does he or she come from? What kind of education or job does the person have?

3. Make a list of four or five events in which your character might become involved. How do these actions reflect the kind of person he or she is?

4. Think about how this character might sound when talking. Before you do this, think about how he or she talks. Does he or she have any distinctive habits, such as speaking very quickly or very slowly? How about an accent? Does the character use slang or speak formally? How does his or her manner of speaking reflect the character's personality?

Think of a second character you might use in a short story. Place this character in a scene with the first character, perhaps in a bus terminal or doctor's office, and then write a short dialogue between the two characters. In your dialogue, tell something about the first character by showing how the characters react to each other.

Conflict

For information on action verbs, see pages 355-356.

Conflict in a short story is a tug-of-war that results when two or more people or forces pull against each other. This pulling of opposing forces sets up a dramatic tension that makes the story interesting.

Conflicts may be *external* (physical) or *internal* (mental or emotional).

While external conflicts usually involve much physical action, internal conflicts take place within the characters' minds. Because action is easier to show than thought, most television programs feature external conflict.

The most common kinds of conflicts in short stories are people against people, people against nature, people against society, and people against themselves. The following examples are of conflicts from stories and plays you may have read.

Conflicts	*Examples*
People vs. People	A son punishes his parents by running away from home; one man hunts another like a wild beast; jurors debate the guilt or innocence of a man on trial.
People vs. Nature	In a world of the future, people fight a hostile environment; deadly snakes are loose on a ship at sea; survivors of an airplane crash work together to overcome bitter cold.
People vs. Society	A man is hanged as a spy; a woman fights against racial prejudice; a man goes to jail for a crime he did not commit.
People vs. Themselves (Mental or Emotional Conflict)	A young girl struggles to accept the divorce of her parents; a man must make a quick decision to save his son's life.

In some stories there is a resolution of the conflict. The turning point of the story that leads to this resolution, or end of conflict, is the *climax*. In old westerns the conflict was usually person against person—sheriff against outlaw. Often the turning point, or climax, of the film occurred when the two faced each other in a gunfight. Sometimes, the resolution of the conflict came only with the death of one character.

In many stories, however, the resolution is not so simple or obvious, especially when the conflict is an internal one. In these stories, as in real life, the conflicts are often never really resolved; instead, the character may emerge with a new understanding of life, a wiser person because of the experience.

Writing Practice 3: *Conflict in a Story*

Using the character you described in Writing Practice 2, make a list of possible situations when conflict would result. Include situations that involve conflict with people, with nature, with society, and within the character.

Select one conflict situation and decide how it will be resolved or what new understanding the character will gain from the experience. Write down the character's thoughts during the conflict and how the conflict will be resolved or what will be learned from it.

Setting

Setting in a story means more than just the time and place in which the story is set; it is the whole background, including weather, plants and animals, and the customs and traditions of the people.

Writers often use specific, sensory details to create a vivid setting. Refer to Chapter 3 for a review of sensory detail.

Model: Setting and Sensory Details

What specific details in the following passage from Langston Hughes' book *Not Without Laughter* help the reader visualize the setting?

> With a tremendous creaking and grinding and steady clacking of wheels the long train went roaring through the night towards Chicago as Sandy, in a day coach, took from his pocket Annjee's two letters and re-read them for the tenth time since leaving Stanton. He could hardly believe himself actually at that moment on the way to Chicago!
>
> In the stuffy coach papers littered the floor and the scent of bananas and human feet filled the car. The lights were dim and most of the passengers slumbered in the straight-backed green-plush seats, but Sandy was still awake. The thrill of his first all-night rail journey and his dream-expectations of the great city were too much to allow a sixteen-year-old boy to go calmly to sleep, although the man next to him had long been snoring.[1]

---

[1]From *Not Without Laughter* by Langston Hughes. Copyright 1930 by Alfred A. Knopf, Inc. Reprinted by permission of Alfred A. Knopf, Inc.

Think and Discuss

1. How does the first sentence introduce both setting and character? What specific words are used that appeal to the sense of hearing? What phrase gives you an image of the train?

2. In the second paragraph, find other examples of sensory details that appeal to different senses. What details do you learn about the character?

Sometimes, the setting of a story serves as a reflection of a character's state of mind. A violent storm in a horror story, for instance, might suggest mental turmoil, while a clear, bright day might reflect a character's joy or contentment.

Model: Setting and Character

What do the details of setting in the following selection suggest about Frankie, the main character in Carson McCullers' novel *The Member of the Wedding*?

> It happened that green and crazy summer when Frankie was twelve years old. This was the summer when for a long time she had not been a member. She belonged to no club and was a member of nothing in the world. Frankie had become an unjoined person who hung around in doorways, and she was afraid. In June the trees were bright dizzy green, but later the leaves darkened, and the town turned black and shrunken under the glare of the sun. At first Frankie walked around doing one thing and another. The sidewalks of the town were gray in the early morning and at night, but the noon sun put a glaze on them, so that the cement burned and glittered like glass. The sidewalks finally became too hot for Frankie's feet, and also she got herself in trouble. She was in so much secret trouble that she thought it was better to stay at home—and at home there was only Berenice Sadie Brown and John Henry West. The three of them sat at the kitchen table, saying the same things over and over, so that by August the words began to rhyme with each other and sound strange. The world seemed to die each afternoon and nothing moved any longer. At last the summer was like a green sick dream, or like a silent crazy jungle under glass. And then, on the last Friday of August, all this was changed: it was so sudden that Frankie puzzled the whole blank afternoon, and still she did not understand.[1]

---

[1] From *The Member of the Wedding* by Carson McCullers. Copyright 1946 by Carson McCullers; copyright renewed © 1974 by Floria V. Lasky. Reprinted by permission of Houghton Mifflin Company, Laurence Pollinger Limited, and The Estate of the late Carson McCullers. Published in Great Britain by Barrie & Jenkins, Ltd.

Writing Practice 4: *Story Setting*

Think about a setting for the character you have already described. Where will your character be when the story begins? Make a word cluster in your Writer's Notebook for the setting of your story. Imagine that you are there. What can you see, hear, smell, touch, taste, and feel? In your word cluster include sensory details, images, and any ideas that come to mind. Then write a brief description of the setting using your word cluster. Save your description for a later Writing Assignment.

Point of View

S uppose you and your six-year-old brother watch a parade together and then both tell a relative about it. Even though each of you saw the same parade, your accounts of the event will differ because you are telling them from different *points of view*. In this same way, every storyteller has an individual point of view.

In a story the storyteller is called the *narrator.*

The narrator may or may not be a character in the story. One common point of view in which the author does not pretend to be a character is called *omniscient narration. Omniscient* means "all-knowing." Omniscient narrators write as if they possess a magical ability to know what all the characters are thinking and feeling. An omniscient narrator can also describe what is happening in two different places at the same time.

Model: Omniscient Point of View

Morley Callaghan uses the omniscient narrator point of view in the following excerpt from the story "All the Years of Her Life." Notice that the writer is able to tell his readers both Alfred's and Mrs. Higgins' thoughts. In this scene Mr. Carr has caught Alfred, his teenage employee, shoplifting and has called his mother.

> Alfred knew how his mother would come rushing in; she would rush in with her eyes blazing, or maybe she would be crying, and she would push him away when he tried to talk to her, and make him feel her dreadful contempt; yet he longed that she might come before Mr. Carr saw the cop on the beat passing the door.
> While they waited—and it seemed a long time—they did not speak, and when at last they heard someone tapping on the closed

door, Mr. Carr, turning the latch, said crisply, "Come in, Mrs. Higgins." He looked hard-faced and stern.

Mrs. Higgins must have been going to bed when he telephoned, for her hair was tucked loosely under her hat, and her hand at her throat held her light coat tightly across her chest so her dress would not show. She came in, large and plump, with a little smile on her friendly face. Most of the store lights had been turned out and at first she did not see Alfred, who was standing in the shadow at the end of the counter. Yet as soon as she saw him she did not look as Alfred thought she would look: she smiled, her blue eyes never wavered, and with a calmness and dignity that made them forget that her clothes seemed to have been thrown on her, she put out her hand to Mr. Carr and said politely, "I'm Mrs. Higgins. I'm Alfred's mother."

Mr. Carr was a little embarrassed by her lack of terror and her simplicity, and he hardly knew what to say to her, so she asked, "Is Alfred in trouble?"[1]

In the preceding selection the narrator says that Alfred knows how his mother will act, that Mrs. Higgins does not see Alfred when she first enters the store, and that Mr. Carr feels embarrassed. This special knowledge of what is going on in all the characters' minds is not available to the *first-person narrator*. When a story is told from a first-person point of view, the narrator is one of the characters and uses the pronouns *I* and *we* to tell the story. A first-person narrator cannot know what other characters are thinking; he or she can see and understand only what a real-life person could in that situation.

---

[1]From *All the Years of Her Life* by Morley Callaghan. Copyright 1935 by Morley Callaghan; renewed © 1962 by Morley Callaghan. Reprinted by permission of the Harold Matson Company, Inc.

Model: First-person Narrator

In the following excerpt from "The Telescope," the writer, August Derleth, employs a first-person narrator; the story is told from the point of view of a teenager who wants to borrow an elderly neighbor's telescope. Why does the narrator say "he *seemed* to regret letting me come"? Why can Derleth not state directly what the old man is feeling?

> "I want to see the rings of Saturn," I said. "It's a clear night and this is the year. It won't be for fourteen years till they're like they are this winter."
>
> "The rings of Saturn," he repeated. "I remember, I always wanted to see them, too." He sighed. "Well, come in."
>
> He turned around and walked back into the room. I followed him, closing the door. The room was crowded with an old wood box, a table and some chairs, a couch, cupboards, a sink, the stove, and piles of magazines, books, and boxes that had something in them, I did not know what. Once I had got in, he seemed to regret letting me come. He stood there a little uncertainly, his pale blue eyes gazing at me, troubled, a frown on his forehead.
>
> "I don't know," he said. "Maybe you could come back tomorrow, or next week sometime. I don't know where it is."
>
> "We could look for it," I said.[1]

Good writers choose their point of view carefully. They know, for example, that choosing a twelve-year-old boy as a first-person narrator so that events are seen through his eyes influences the entire story. Written with the boy's grandmother as the first-person narrator, the same story would be very different.

Good writers also reread their stories carefully to be certain that the original point of view is maintained throughout the story. If a writer uses a twelve-year-old boy as a first-person narrator, he or she must maintain this character as the "I" telling the story. Changing the point of view in midstream makes for a confusing and sometimes incoherent narrative. What problems with point of view must be solved in the following passage?

> I opened one eye, stuck my head out from under the blanket, and blinked in the bright sunlight flooding the room. Late. It must be late, but my body seemed paralyzed. I didn't want to move. Through a fog of grogginess, I could hear my mother at the foot of the stairs.
>
> "Anna, it's nearly noon. Saturday or not, it's time to get up."
>
> Anna stretched lazily beneath the covers, trying half-heartedly to shake what seemed to imprison her. Groaning weakly, she pushed back the sheets and slid one foot toward the floor.

---

[1]From "The Telescope" by August Derleth. Originally published in *Story* Magazine. Reprinted by permission of Hallie Burnett for *Story* Magazine.

When you write your short story, consider your purpose before you decide on the point of view. If you wish one of your characters to tell the story, you will choose first person. However, if it is important for the reader to understand all the characters' thoughts and emotions, then an omniscient narrator is the best choice.

Writing Practice 5: *Changing Point of View*

1. This selection from "Miss Brill" by Katherine Mansfield is written from an omniscient narrator's point of view. Rewrite the paragraph, using a first-person narrator. Notice that you will have to change many of the pronouns to make it sound as if you are the character.

     On her way home she usually bought a slice of honey-cake at the baker's. It was her Sunday treat. Sometimes there was an almond, in her slice, sometimes not. It made a great difference. If there was an almond, it was like carrying home a tiny present—a surprise—something that might very well not have been there. She hurried on the almond Sundays and struck the match for the kettle in quite a dashing way.[1]

2. In his famous novel *The Adventures of Huckleberry Finn*, Mark Twain uses a first-person narrator, Huck Finn, to tell the story. In the following excerpt, Huck is talking with Pop, his father. Rewrite this section using an omniscient narrator point of view. Remember that changing the point of view will mean changing some of the pronouns in the selection.

     I stood a-looking at him; he set there a-looking at me, with his chair tilted back a little. I set the candle down. I noticed the window was up; so he had clumb in by the shed. He kept a-looking me all over. By-and-by he says:
     "Starchy clothes—very. You think you're a good deal of a big-bug, *don't* you?"
     "Maybe I am, maybe I ain't," I says.
     "Don't you give me none o' your lip," says he. "You've put on considerable many frills since I been away. I'll take you down a peg before I get done with you. You're educated, too, they say; can read and write. You think you're better'n your father, now, don't you, because he can't? *I'll* take it out of you."[2]

Finding Meaning in Stories

The following short story is a *fable,* a story told to illustrate a moral. What is the "message" in this fable?

Model: A Fable

A fox was trotting along a dusty road. The day was hot, and the fox was hungry and thirsty. Suddenly he spied a grapevine by the side of the road, and high upon the vine hung a bunch of fat, juicy grapes.

The fox's mouth began to water, and he licked his chops. If he could just reach those grapes, he could sit in the shade of the grapevine and eat them, satisfying his thirst and hunger.

He stood on his hind legs and stretched as high as he could, but the grapes were out of his reach. So he began to jump for them. Again and again, he leaped in the air, trying to reach the grapes.

The more he jumped, the more thirsty, tired, and hungry he became. Finally, the jumping made him so tired that he gave up trying to reach the grapes. With his tail between his legs, he slowly continued his way down the dusty road, panting wearily.

Pausing briefly, he looked back. Shaking his head, he said, "They were sour grapes, anyway." Then he continued his journey down the road.

Note: In older stories such as this one, animals are often given gender. In the traditional version the fox is male.

The purpose of the preceding fable is to illustrate the idea that when people cannot have what they want, they often try to make the goal seem less important. The expression "sour grapes" comes from this fable.

The *theme* of a story is the story's main idea or basic meaning.

When you think about what the author is trying to say about life or about people, you are expressing the theme. For example, "The Cask of Amontillado" by Edgar Allan Poe is about a perfect crime. On a carnival night, a man meets someone who has once done him wrong. He lures his enemy into a vast underground chamber, where he chains him, builds a wall around him, and leaves him to die. The crime is never discovered. That is a summary of the plot, but it is not the same as the theme—the story's meaning. The theme might be expressed in a single sentence: "It is unhealthy to nurse a grudge and seek revenge for a wrong—real or imagined." In some stories, the theme is directly expressed in a sentence or two; in others, it is implied. What were the themes in stories you have recently read?

Writing Assignment I: *A Short Story*

A. Prewriting

Making a Story Map: In previous Writing Practices in this chapter you have described a character, a conflict, and a setting for a short story. Using these descriptions, make up a story map following the diagram below. Write a brief description of the setting, the main characters, the conflict, and the resolution for a short story.

Story Title

Story Setting	Main Characters
Conflict	**Resolution (End of Story)**

Plotting the Action: Once you have mapped out the basic parts of your story, you are ready to consider how the plot will unfold. Before writing the story, make a list of the main events in the order of occurrence. Identify the point at which the climax of the story will occur. Include an ending or resolution that is unusual, surprising, or unpredictable.

B. Writing

Writing a Discovery Draft: A good story beginning is essential if you want the reader to continue reading. Professional story writers often change the beginning of a story several times before deciding on one to use. Often they discover the best beginning after they have written a large portion of the story. This is why it is important to think of your first draft as a "discovery draft." Most likely, you will discover new traits for your characters, new episodes to include, and possibly a new beginning. You may decide to begin with action that, in the first draft, occurred later in the story. You may want to start with dialogue or conversation. Read over several stories to see how they begin.

Use the story map and the list of events to write your story draft but do not hesitate to explore new directions. As the storyteller, you can make any changes you want. Include the descriptions of setting and character that you wrote in previous Writing Practices if they are appropriate.

C. Postwriting

Revising by Yourself: As you read over your discovery draft, think about your readers. Keep only the most essential and interesting parts of the story. Fill in any gaps by adding necessary details. Use the following checklist to revise your story.

Checklist for Revising a Short Story

1. Does the story begin in an interesting or unusual way?

2. Are the story's characters and setting described in detail? Does the description of the setting include the use of sensory details? Are the major characters described through their words, actions, thoughts, and physical appearances?

3. Do the main events in the plot unfold in a logical sequence? Is there a relationship between the events and the characters? Does the plot build to a climax? Is there a conflict that is resolved in the end?

4. Is the story narrated using the same point of view throughout?

5. Is the language clear and correct? Are sentences complete? Is there a variety of sentence patterns? Is the wording exact?

Use the Proofreader's Checklist at the back of this book to check your story for correct sentence structure, grammar, mechanics, and spelling.

Revising with a Partner: Share your story with a partner before you write your final draft. Ask your partner to read your story and to complete the following steps.

1. Read over the story draft the first time for content, clarity, and interest.

2. Identify the climax of the story.

3. Point out the part you found to be most interesting or exciting.

4. Suggest parts that need to be clarified or details that need to be added or deleted.

5. Read over the final draft after it has been revised. Check for correct sentence structure, grammar, mechanics, and spelling.

From Dialogue to Drama

Dialogue is the conversation between characters that goes on in stories and in drama, whether on the stage, in movies, or on television.

Dramatic dialogue helps the audience understand the characters, their actions, and the reasons behind their actions. By listening to dialogue, audiences discover why characters behave as they do and what kind of people they are.

Reading Dialogue

Perhaps you have seen the Marx Brothers—Groucho, Chico, Harpo, and Zeppo—in one of their old movies. Their movies, such as *Horse Feathers*, *Monkey Business*, and *High Society*, are full of humorous

dialogues, such as the following passage from the movie *A Night at the Opera*. In this dialogue, "Groucho and Chico Make a Deal" by George S. Kaufman and Morrie Ryskind, Groucho is asking Chico to sign a contract for an opera singer Groucho represents. As you read, look for reasons why the dialogue is humorous.

CHICO: Wait a minute. Before I sign anything, what does it say?

GROUCHO: Go ahead and read it.

CHICO (*a little reluctantly*): Well—er—you read it. I don't like to read anything unless I know what it says.

GROUCHO (*catching on*): I see. All right, *I'll* read it to you. Can you hear?

CHICO: I haven't heard anything yet. Did you say anything?

GROUCHO: Well, I haven't said anything worth hearing.

CHICO: I guess that's why I didn't hear anything.

GROUCHO (*having the last word*): Well, that's why I didn't say anything. (*He scans the contract, holding it near him and then far away. CHICO watches him suspiciously.*)

CHICO: Wait a minute. Can *you* read?

GROUCHO (*holding contract farther and farther away*): I can read, but I can't see it. If my arms were a little longer, I could read it . . . Ah, here we are. Now pay attention to this first clause. (*Reads.*) "The party of the first part shall be known in this contract as the party of the first part." How do you like that. Pretty neat, eh?

CHICO: No, that's no good.

GROUCHO (*indignantly*): What's the matter with it?

CHICO (*conciliatorily*): I don't know—let's hear it again.

GROUCHO: "The party of the first part shall be known in this contract as the party of the first part."

CHICO: It sounds a little better this time.

GROUCHO: Well, it grows on you. Want to hear it once more?

CHICO: Only the first part.

GROUCHO: The *party* of the first part?

CHICO: No. The *first part* of the party of the first part.

GROUCHO: Well, it says, "The first part of the party of the first part shall be known in this contract"—look! Why should we quarrel about a thing like that? (*He tears off the offending clause.*) We'll take it right out.

CHICO (*tearing the same clause out of his contract*): Sure, it's too long anyhow. Now what have we got left?

GROUCHO: Well, I've got about a foot and a half . . . Now, then: "The party of the second part shall be known in this contract as the party of the second part."

CHICO: Well, I don't know. I don't like the second party, either.

GROUCHO: You should have come to the first party. We didn't get home till around four in the morning. (*Slight pause.*) I was blind for three days.

CHICO: Look, couldn't the first part of the second party be the second part of the first party? Then we got something.

GROUCHO: Look! Rather than go through all that again, what do you say? (*He indicates a willingness to tear further.*)

CHICO: Fine. (*They both tear off another piece.*)

GROUCHO: Now, I've got something here you're *bound* to like. You'll be crazy about it.

CHICO: No, I don't like it.

GROUCHO: You don't like what?

CHICO: Whatever it is.

GROUCHO: All right. Why should we break up an old friendship over a thing like this? Ready?

CHICO: Okay. (*They both tear.*) Now, the next part I don't think *you're* going to like.

GROUCHO: All right—your word's good enough for me. (*They both tear.*) Now then, is *my* word good enough for *you*?

CHICO: I should say not.

GROUCHO: All right—let's go. (*They both tear*, GROUCHO *looking at the contract.*) The party of the eighth part—

CHICO: No. (*They tear.*)

GROUCHO: The party of the ninth part—

CHICO: No. (*They tear.*) Say, how is it I got a skinnier contract than you?

GROUCHO: I don't know. You must have been out on a tear last night. Anyhow, now we're all set. Now sign right here. (*He produces a fountain pen.*)

CHICO: I forgot to tell you. I can't write.

GROUCHO: That's all right. There's no ink in the pen, anyway. But, listen, it's a bargain, isn't it? We've got a contract, no matter how small it is.

CHICO (*Extending hand, Groucho clasps it.*): You betcha! Only one thing I want to know: what does this say? (*Showing last piece of contract left.*)

GROUCHO: Oh, that's nothing. That's the usual clause in every contract. It says if any of the parties participating in the contract are shown not to be in their right mind, the contract is nullified.

CHICO: What do you call it?

GROUCHO: That's what they call a sanity clause.

CHICO: You can't fool me. There ain't no sanity clause![1]

Think and Discuss

1.   What conflicts do the characters face in "Groucho and Chico Make a Deal"? Why do Groucho and Chico rip off more and more of the contract?

---

[1]From the MGM release "A Night at the Opera," copyright 1935 by Metro-Goldwyn-Mayer Corporation. Copyright renewed © 1962 by Metro-Goldwyn-Mayer, Inc. Reprinted by permission.

225

2.   What is the outcome, or *resolution*? How do Groucho and Chico resolve the conflict in the scene?

3.   This scene is a spoof on business deals. Explain how the scene makes fun of high finance and legal forms, such as business contracts.

4.   What part does *misunderstanding* play in the humor? Point out instances in the scene where the two characters completely misunderstand one another.

5.   The last line of the scene contains a *pun*. Explain the pun in the lines: *You can't fool me. There ain't no sanity clause!*

Writing a Play

A *short play*, or dramatic sketch, has the same main elements found in the short story: character, plot, setting, and conflict.

However, there are some differences between a play and a short story. Since a play is meant to be acted out on stage as if it were really happening, the writer cannot interrupt the dialogue to describe a character or tell the audience what a character is thinking or feeling. The writer must suggest a character's inner feelings through that character's speech and actions. The actors performing the play will use voice, posture, and gesture to show that a character is young, old, confident, or shy. In a play the setting is suggested by props and scenery, or the characters' speeches may tell the audience where the play is happening. For a printed play, actions are described in short stage directions in parentheses after a character's speech.

Writing Practice 6: *A Group Play*

With two or three classmates write your own short play, using the following outline.

1.   First, think of a plot—some actions and the reasons for them. You can use your personal experiences as a basis or you can create an imaginary plot. Outline your plot in writing.

2.   Next, think of the kinds of characters that you want in your play. Should they be a little stupid or very intelligent? Should they be clowns, like the Marx Brothers, or tragic heroes?

3. Write the dialogue for your play. If necessary, review the section on dialogue in Chapter 3.

4. Read your play as a group for your class.

More Creative Writing

Use the following suggestions to write more poems, stories, and plays.

1. Think about a person who is, or was, important to you. What special quality about this person makes him or her important to you, and what effect did this quality have on you? Write a poem, short story, or play about this person and the quality you admire.

2. Think of a beautiful, graceful animal; place it in a setting; and then describe the animal and setting in a sense poem. Use vivid sense images to capture the animal's actions and looks.

3. Think of an event that had meaning for you, perhaps an exciting event like a race of some sort, or a nostalgic event like the last day in your house before you moved. In a short story or a short play, write about this event and the effect it had on you.

4. Look through a telephone book until you find a name that interests you and imagine a person to go with the name. Place the person in a setting and think of a conflict he or she might have. Then write a short story around this character, setting, and conflict.

5. Using newspapers and magazines from home or the school library, find an article about an interesting person. Write a short story or play about him or her.

6. From one of the advice column letters in your local newspaper, select a letter that interests you and that involves a conflict. Think about the kind of person who wrote the letter. Then write a story about him or her and the conflict in the letter.

7. Look through your old family snapshots until you find a picture you like and then write a story or short play about it. If you like, write the story not about what really happened but about what might have been happening if the people in the picture had been different kinds of people.

8. Many artists like to focus on one sight as it changes over a period of time. The famous painter Monet, for example, painted one scene in his garden and one view of a cathedral many times over, at different times of day and in different weather. Choose a sight you find especially beautiful or interesting. Write descriptions of this place first as it looks in the morning, then at noon, and then in the evening. Then try to capture how this place looks during different types of weather. For a longer writing project, keep entries in your Notebook on how this scene changes during the seasons.

9. Perhaps you have read a short story, play, or novel about characters that were especially interesting to you, and were sorry to come to the end of their adventures. Choose one such character (or set of characters) and write another episode that begins where the short story, play, or novel left off.

10. Writers often get inspiration from ordinary conversation. For one day pay special attention to everything that is said to you. Listen to what your friends, family, and teachers say and how they express themselves. Jot down phrases that seem typical of the way these people talk, and use these phrases to help create dialogue for a short story or one-act play.

Sentence Combining:
Inserting Clauses

Using The Fact That, That, and Join Signals

For information on phrases, see pages 490-509.

The signals (*the fact that*), (*that*), and (*join*) work in the same way as (*who*), (*what*), (*why*), (*when*), (*where*), and (*how*). The signal word *something* in the base is removed and *the fact that* or *that*, followed by some part of the insert sentence, is put in its place. When you see the signal (*join*), simply place that sentence where *something* appears without adding other words. The following examples illustrate how these combinations work.

> **Base:** Vincent suspected *something*.
> **Insert:** We wouldn't be on time. (*that*)
> **Combined:** Vincent suspected *that we wouldn't be on time*.

> **Base:** I think *something* helped you to be successful.
> **Insert:** You had ambition. (*the fact that*)
> **Combined:** I think *the fact that you had ambition* helped you to be successful.

> **Base:** Nicole believed *something*.
> **Insert:** Rosa had sent her the gift. (*join*)
> **Combined:** Nicole believed *Rosa had sent her the gift*.

Exercise 1: Using The Fact That, That, and Join Signals

On a sheet of paper, combine each of the sets on the next page. When there are two or more insert sentences, combine them in the order in which sentences are given. For sets 6–10, decide whether or not to use *that* or *the fact that* to join sentences. Study the example before you begin.

Example

a. *Something* made people believe *something*.
   The *Titanic* was well constructed. (*the fact that*)
   It could never sink. (*join*)

   The fact that the *Titanic* was well constructed made people believe it could never sink.

1. Nan felt *something*.
   Shelley owed her an apology. (*that*)

2. *Something* makes me wonder about his sanity.
   He does such odd things. (*the fact that*)

3. In spite of her aptitude for science, Miranda thought *something*.
   She would never become a doctor. (*that*)

4. She didn't think *something*.
   She should join such an exclusive organization. (*join*)

5. *Something* makes me question his honesty.
   He was caught and punished for shoplifting. (*the fact that*)

6. Robin concluded *something*.
   She wanted to study ceramics in art class.

7. *Something* doesn't mean *something*.
   She hasn't called in three days.
   She doesn't like you anymore.

8. *Something* made me think *something*.
   The waves were fifteen feet high.
   We shouldn't go swimming.

9. In his speech to the visiting ambassadors, the Secretary of State said *something*.
   He wanted them to know *something*.
   They were welcome to our country.

10. Because of the many good reviews she has read, Betsy thinks *something*.
    She can safely say *something*.
    She will enjoy the film.

Inserting It . . . That

I nserting with (*it . . . that*) is very much like combining with (*the fact that*) and (*that*). In the combined sentence the signal word *something* will be replaced by the word *it*, and the insert sentence will be joined to the base by the word *that*:

Base: *Something* is false.
Insert: There will never be another ice age. (*it . . . that*)
Combined: *It is false that there will never be another ice age.*

Exercise 2: Using Various Sentence Combining Signals

On a sheet of paper, combine the following sets as the signals indicate. The first part of the exercise will signal only (*it . . . that*); the last part will combine several signals that you have already learned.

1. *Something* was clear to the spectators.
   The game would have to be called because of rain. (*it . . . that*)

2. *Something* seemed so obvious.
   We wondered how we could have missed it. (*it . . . that*)

3. *Something* happened.
   The Kangs surprised their relatives with an anniversary party. (*it . . . that*)

4. *Something* was not certain.
   The tanks would have enough fuel to finish their drive to the front lines. (*it . . . that*)

5. *Something* is thought.
   The canals on Mars were caused by expanding and contracting subsurface water. (*it . . . that*)

6. *Something* seemed clear.
   Marie didn't suspect *something*. (*it . . . that*)
   Her car had been tampered with. (*that*)

7. In place of the watering can, *something* is better.
   You use this siphoning device. (*it . . . that*)

231

8. *Something* wasn't certain.
    The tourists believed *something*. (*it . . . that*)
    They would be allowed to cross the border. (*join*)

9. *Something* was never thought.
    The old gentleman guessed *something*. (*it . . . that*)
    His nephew had cheated him out of his fortune. (*the fact that*)

10. *Something* didn't prevent the boss from believing *something*.
    The road crew worked all night. (*the fact that*)
    They would not finish the job until sundown. (*join*)

Inserting with How . . . and It . . .

The signals (*how . . .*) and (*it . . .*) operate much the same way as those in the previous two sections of this chapter. If the signal says (*how much*), (*how long*), (*how far*), and so on, place that information in the *something* slot of the base sentence.

Base:	We haven't yet figured out *something*.
Insert:	The problem will take so much time. (*how much*)
Combined:	We haven't yet figured out *how much time the problem will take*.

(*How much time* replaces *something*. Notice the changed order of words in the inserted sentence.)

Base:	We have decided *something*.
Insert:	The string should be so long. (*how long*)
Combined:	We have decided *how long the string should be*.

If the signal says (*it . . . who*), (*it . . . what*), (*it . . . where*), and so on, replace the signal *something* with the word *it* and join the insert sentence to the base with *who, what, where* and so on.

Base:	*Something* is a mystery.
Insert:	We got this far. (*it . . . how*)
Combined:	*It* is a mystery *how we got this far*.

Exercise 3: Inserting with How . . . *and* It . . .

On a sheet of paper, make the combinations in the sets on the next page. Use signals where given. Study the example before you begin.

Example

    a. *Something* matters to me.
      You sing. (*it . . . what*)
      It matters to me what you sing.

1. For the past two years *something* has been unclear to me.
   My eyes tire so when I read. (*it . . . why*)

2. Eugene Hsi knows *something*.
   He must service his bicycle. (*how often*)

3. The estimators decided *something*.
   They will judge the value of this property. (*how soon*)

4. The Chagall mural in downtown Chicago tells us *something*.
   We must take the changing seasons of the year. (*how seriously*)

5. *Something* was noticed.
   She could balance two trays, three rubber balls, and a glass
   pitcher on her nose. (*it . . . how*)

6. *Something* suddenly became clear.
   Juanita went.

7. The reporters only guessed *something*.
   The speaker would be dressed.

8. The scientist's experiment told the world *something*.
   It was important to take safety precautions.

9. *Something* now seems obvious.
   We need someone in charge.

10. *Something* became clear.
    His obligations lay.

Varying a Combination Pattern

(*Where to*), (*when to*), (*why to*), (*what to*), (*how to*), and (*who to*) are further combinations that follow the same pattern as the (*who*) and (*what*) combinations.

Base:	The doctor didn't know *something*.
Insert:	She was to operate. (*when*)
Combined:	The doctor didn't know *when she was to operate*.

Base:	The doctor didn't know *something*.
Insert:	She was to operate. (*when to*)
Combined:	The doctor didn't know *when to operate*.

Base:	I wonder *something*.
Insert:	Someone is to blame for this mess. (*who*)
Combined:	I wonder *who is to blame for this mess*.

Base:	I wonder *something*.
Insert:	Someone is to blame for this mess. (*who to*)
Combined:	I wonder *who to blame for this mess*.

Notice that when you use the (. . . *to*) combinations, the subject and the verb are dropped from the insert sentence.

Exercise 4: Making Various Combinations

The following sets contain several kinds of combinations, including the (. . . *to*) combination. On a sheet of paper, combine each of the sets. Use signals where given. Study the examples before you begin.

Examples

a. Luis could not believe *something*.
   He was told something. (*what*)
   Luis could not believe what he was told.

b. Sergeant Carlson did not say *something*.
   We are to contact someone in case of emergency. (*who to*)
   Sergeant Carlson did not say who to contact in case of emergency.

1.   Deciding *something* will be difficult.
     I am to fix dinner sometime. (*when to*)

2. Because David had no experience with painting, he did not know *something*.
    He needed so long to let the mixed paints set. (*how long to*)

3. *Something* explains *something*.
    My little toe hurts. (*the fact that*)
    I have a limp. (*why*)

4. The scout leader gave a demonstration on *something*.
    One is to give artificial respiration somehow.

5. The scout leader gave a demonstration on *something*.
    Citizens should give artificial respiration somehow.

Review: *Making Different Combinations*

For each of the following unsignaled sets of sentences, write at least *two* different versions of the combined sentences, using all the information that is given. Study the example before you begin.

Example

a. A few people were hurrying.
    Their children's hands were tucked firmly in theirs.
    They were hurrying to the big parade.

    With their children's hands tucked firmly in theirs, a few people were hurrying to the big parade.
        or
    A few people, with their children's hands tucked firmly in theirs, were hurrying to the big parade.

1. The rifle went off.
    It went off with a splendid bang.

2. Money was scarce.
    It was during the Depression years.

3. We rushed to find seats.
    We rushed frantically.
    The seats were in the stands.

4. Her acceptance speech was written.
    It was written poorly.
    It was written by a ghost writer.

5. Young Baxter ran the mile.
   He ran in less than four minutes.
   He ran on a muddy track.
   He ran effortlessly.
   He ran gracefully.

In this exercise the only signal is *something*, so combine the sentences in any way you think best. Consider the first sentence in each set the base. Write the new sentences on a sheet of paper.

6. Jason's friends invaded his parents' kitchen.
   They raided the refrigerator.
   They wiped their sticky hands on the tablecloth.
   They left mayonnaise and ketchup blobs all over the cabinet.

7. The large black dog leaped at the intruder's throat.
   It threw the man backwards.
   It tore a large chunk from his coat collar.
   It snarled viciously.

8. Zachary sat.
   He sat in the tub.
   He sat peacefully.
   He was sailing his toy ship.
   He was squishing the soap between his toes.

9. Mary told me *something*.
   She took a ride.
   She rode in the park.
   She rode on the bridle path.
   She rode bareback.

10. Don't let *something* discourage you.
    Your softball is lost.
    You may borrow mine.
    You will be able to enter the contest anyway.

11. Betty tried to figure *something*.
    She had money to buy a gift for her parents' anniversary.
    The anniversary is next week.

12. *Something* was clear at last.
    John didn't understand *something*.
    There was much work to do.

13. *Something* kept Nell from *something*.
    The telephone rang loudly.
    Nell heard *something*.
    The doorbell chimed.

14. None of the passengers knew *something*.
    The passengers were on the train.
    The noise indicated *something*.
    The noise was overhead.
    Something had produced a very dangerous situation.
    The cable contracted.

15. Scientists consider *something* important.
    The scientists do research.
    The government funds research.
    The research is for a cure for cancer.

Writing Practice: *Revising a Short Story for Sentence Variety*

Reread the short story you wrote. Check each paragraph for sentence variety. Look at the beginnings of the sentences. Do the sentences often begin in the same way? Check the length of your sentences. Is there a variety of sentence lengths? Do you need to combine parts of sentences or divide longer ones?

Make the necessary changes to improve the quality of the sentences in your short story. When you have made a final draft, share your story with a small group of classmates.

10 Writing to Persuade

Techniques of Persuasion

I n *The Adventures of Tom Sawyer*—Mark Twain's great American novel—Tom is an expert at getting others to do what he wants them to. When Tom's Aunt Polly makes him whitewash a fence, he pretends he is having such a good time doing the job that Tom's friends beg to join the "fun."

Tom used a trick to persuade his friends, but Snoopy, in the cartoon on page 239, has another method of persuasion. What is it?

When you want others to think or behave in a certain way, you can use tricks (as Tom Sawyer did) or threats (as did Snoopy). Although these methods may be effective, the first is dishonest, and the second is not generally accepted in this society.

Persuasive writing can be either effective or ineffective and honest or dishonest. In this chapter you will learn to write *effective* persuasion and to guard yourself against *dishonest* persuasion. You will learn about two types of appeals involved in persuasion: appeals to emotion and appeals to reason. You will also learn the important steps involved in all types of persuasive writing.

Learning the skills of persuasive writing will help develop your critical thinking skills, for you will practice focusing on a particular problem and then giving specific and convincing reasons to support your view. You will have to evaluate the reasons you think of, choosing those that seem soundest and most effective, and discarding others. Being able to write persuasively will also improve your ability to speak persuasively, for you will develop the skills necessary to presenting an effective argument.

Writing Practice 1: *Using Persuasion*

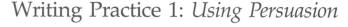

You have probably tried to persuade someone recently. Perhaps you tried to get a brother or sister to do a chore for you, or asked a parent or friend for a loan, or convinced a friend to go to a movie of your choice. Quoting the dialogue that you actually used (as nearly as you can remember), write about a time when you tried to change how someone thought, or behaved. Were you able to persuade the other person? If not, why do you think you failed?

The Appeal to Emotion

Imagine that you are sitting in a restaurant, waiting to order breakfast. The server tells you there is a shortage of menus and hands you a slip of paper that looks like the following list.

Breakfast

Choice of Orange juice or Strawberries	Choice of Bacon or Sausage
Choice of Omelet or Waffle	Choice of Toast or Rolls

Your friend, however, gets the following menu:

Breakfast

Choice of
Chilled glass of freshly squeezed orange juice
or
Plump, ripe strawberries

Choice of
Omelet made from farm fresh eggs
or
Thick, crispy waffle, served with our
own special syrup

Choice of
Crispy bacon or sizzling sausage

Choice of
Hot, buttered toast
or
Home-baked rolls, fresh from the oven

For more information on adjectives, see pages 386-413.

Which menu makes the food seem more appealing? The first menu gives the facts, but the second one attempts to persuade the reader that the food is delicious. The creators of the second menu do not want you to just *think* about the food; they want you to *feel* as though you can actually taste it. Adjectives on the second menu like *farm fresh* eggs, *special* syrup, and *home-baked* rolls do not give factual information about the food because these words may mean almost anything, but they do make the food seem more appealing. *Farm fresh* eggs may make you think that Farmer Smith gathered them at sunrise and then rushed them to the restaurant. Actually, the eggs were probably laid in a hatchery and rolled down a conveyor belt into waiting boxes to be kept "fresh" for several days by refrigeration.

Advertisers often use words that appeal to your emotions.

Most people want cars that are *elegant* or carpets that are *luxurious*, even though these words may have many meanings. People like cleaning products that are *tough* and *effective*, and they prefer *soft, gentle* products for babies.

Words can also make you respond in a negative way. A politician who calls another candidate *un-American* is trying to make you feel negatively about his or her opponent, even though the word may mean only that the two politicians do not agree on many issues. Many citizens, however, feel strongly about being American and would not vote for a politician who they think might be un-American.

Using words to appeal to emotions is not in itself dishonest. Many public service advertisements appeal to your sense of justice and fair play, trying to make you feel good about saving the world's resources or about preserving a clean environment. You should be aware, however, when words are being used to appeal to your emotions. Ask yourself what the effect will be if you allow yourself to be influenced. Sometimes, the only result may be spending a small amount of money for something you really do not need; other times, however, you may spend a great deal of money for something you later find disappointing, or you may vote for someone who is not the best candidate.

Writing Practice 2: *An Advertisement*

The adjectives in the following list are often found in advertisements. Using this list, write a magazine or newspaper advertisement for a real or an imaginary product or service. Your purpose is to sell the product by appealing to your readers' emotions.

amazing	fine	perfect
appetizing	free	pretty
compact	gentle	refreshing
creative	guaranteed	rich
crunchy	handsome	satisfying
delectable	ideal	soft
delicate	improved	special
delicious	luscious	subtle
delightful	lustrous	super
distinctive	luxurious	tender
effective	modestly priced	thrilling
elegant	mysterious	tough
exciting	natural	unbelievable
exquisite	old-fashioned	wonderful

Writing Practice 3: *Analyzing Ads*

From newspapers, magazines, or brochures, select two or three ads that sell products and two or three that promote an idea or urge people to believe in a cause. (Try to find ads that have words as well as pictures or drawings.) Then determine how effective each ad is and how each one attempts to sell a product or persuade an audience. The following questions will help you analyze the ads. You may think of other questions to add to the list as well.

1.   What audience is the ad directed to?

2.   What does the ad want the reader to do or believe?

3. Does the ad encourage anything that may be harmful to mental or physical health?

4. Does the ad try to get readers to believe or do something society considers "good"?

5. Does the ad appeal to the emotions? What specific words are used for this purpose?

6. Does the ad use factual information to persuade the audience? If so, what is it?

7. Is the visual part of the ad—the artwork, photographs, colors—more convincing or less convincing than the words in the ad? Explain.

8. Are you persuaded by the ad? Would you buy or do what the ad suggests? Why?

The Appeal to Reason

Fifteen-year-old Anna Ortega wanted an increase in her allowance. Before she talked with her parents, however, she thought of some reasons why she needed the extra money. For example, she had more expenses now that she was in high school: her lunch cost more; she had to pay a locker fee; and she had to pay to ride the city bus. Anna also reminded her parents that during the past year she had taken on more responsibility at home. Because she could now baby-sit for her younger brother, she was saving her parents money.

Anna used these *reasons* to persuade her parents to raise her allowance, but she could have tried other ways—appealing to their emotions ("If you love me, you'll raise my allowance!") or threatening them ("If you don't raise my allowance, I'll never baby-sit again!"). However, she decided to use an appeal to reason.

Persuasive writing that appeals mainly to reason is called *argumentation*.

You may think of an argument as a shouting match between two or more people. In persuasive writing, however, an *argument* is something very different. When you write an argument, you have reached a conclusion about the way people should change their thinking or behavior, and you support this conclusion with logical reasons.

Learning to Reason Well

The reasons underlying an argument must be sound. Anna's reasons for wanting an increase in her allowance were sound because she could support each with some kind of evidence. Arguments based on reasons that are supported by evidence are convincing.

Some common types of *unsound* arguments follow. You should learn to recognize them when people use them to convince you, and you should avoid unsound arguments when you are trying to convince others.

1. Reaching a quick conclusion without enough evidence to support it:

    "All bulldogs are vicious," said Martin. "I know this because my neighbor's bulldog is vicious."

    This kind of reasoning is dangerous because it allows people to draw false conclusions about groups, races, and nations. For example, a student at Grant Junior High School is in a chess tournament with the team from Washington Junior High. Two of the Washington players cheat, and the student from Grant concludes, "All students from Washington Junior High School are cheaters. I don't like cheaters, so I'll have nothing to do with anyone from Washington Junior High." On the basis of just two examples, the Grant student has condemned hundreds of students.

2. Ignoring the main point and switching the subject to something or someone else:

    "I would like my afternoons free for sports," said Jenny. "Closing schools at noon would save electricity."

    Jenny started with one point—her desire to have her afternoons free for sports—but she immediately shifted to another—saving electricity. In making this switch, she shifted the argument from its real purpose to another one.

    "You can't trust Alexandra. Her uncle is an embezzler."

    The point of the preceding argument has nothing to do with Alexandra's uncle but with Alexandra's own trustworthiness.

3. Distorting the original question or statement:

    "My mother says that I should try to enjoy my work, but if I enjoy what I do, I'm playing, not working. So why doesn't Mother let me play video games instead of making me do homework?"

243

Here the arguer has distorted the point that work should be made enjoyable. Through twisting, the arguer claims that he or she should be allowed to do what he or she enjoys.

4. Using an authority who is not an expert on the subject or who is prejudiced in some way:

"Dr. Smith, the world-famous expert on whales and dolphins, claims that potatoes are the most nutritious foods available."

Dr. Smith may be an expert on whales and dolphins, but that does not make her an authority on nutrition. Perhaps she knows no more about that subject than you do.

"The Power-Vac is the most efficient vacuum cleaner that your money can buy. I know this because a Power-Vac salesperson told me so."

A person selling Power-Vacs is likely to be prejudiced in favor of his or her product and is not a reliable authority.

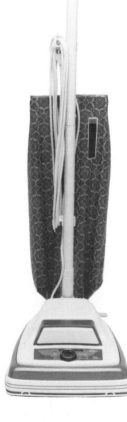

Writing Practice 4: *Identifying Unsound Arguments*

Each of the following arguments on this page and the next contains unsound reasoning. Read each carefully and then write two or three sentences explaining what is wrong with the reasoning. Then write one of your own, using unsound reasoning.

1. Smiley Sullivan, the great baseball player, says Gummo is terrific! He brushes his teeth with Gummo every day. Be like Smiley. Use Gummo every day.

2. I eat Crunchy Chewies for breakfast every morning because it is nutritious—one small serving gives me all the vitamins and minerals I need every day. I got this information from the back of the cereal box.

3. I walked to the theater last Saturday in the snow without my winter coat and gloves. That's why I have the flu now.

4. John was accused of not paying attention to the coach during practice. John said to the coach, "What did I do? You're always picking on me!"

5. Parent: You can have the car occasionally when you're sixteen and get your license.
   Teenager: Hey, Bob, my dad says I can have a car.

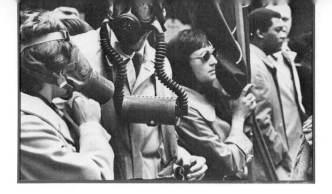

6.   Rosa used to get straight A's in English, but since she started playing soccer after school every day, she barely makes a C. If she quit soccer, her grades would surely go up.

7.   Yesterday I saw a man throw a can out of his car window, and today my neighbor burned trash outdoors. Everybody is polluting the environment. Soon we will all have to wear masks to filter the air we breathe.

8.   (Write your own argument.)

Defining Your Views for an Argument

Before you write an argumentative paper, you must be able to explain what your beliefs are and to give reasons for them.

Within your own school or neighborhood you should find many issues on which you can express your opinion. Your opinions may not be the same as those of your friends, but in a democratic society it is not important that people agree on all issues. It is important, however, that people be able to give good reasons for the ways they think or feel.

Forming a sound opinion on a particular issue depends on how much you know about the issue and how much you can learn about it. For instance, suppose your school board is considering lengthening the school day. You might be tempted to form an opinion before gathering the facts. After talking to a teacher and reading the local newspaper, you learn that, by adding another hour to the school day, students will gain an extra two weeks of vacation. Or, perhaps, the extra hour will be an optional class period for tutoring, electives, or sports activities. Knowing these facts might affect your opinion.

Your awareness and understanding of current events is important for you as an individual and as a citizen of your country. The ability to state your beliefs about major national and international events is also important. In order to do this, you need the kind of information you get from radio and television news programs, newspapers, and weekly news magazines.

Writing Practice 5: *Giving Reasons for Opinions*

From the following list select the five statements that most interest you. On a sheet of paper, write whether you agree or disagree with each statement. Then list three or four reasons why you believe the way you do about each one.

1. When the crime rate in the neighborhood rises, teenagers should be put under a strict curfew.

2. Tax money should be spent to build basketball courts and other recreational facilities in local neighborhoods.

3. Tax money should be spent to provide part-time jobs for all teenagers who want them.

4. Teenagers should not be allowed to have driver's licenses until they are eighteen.

5. All eighteen-year-olds should be required to spend a year in public service. This year could be spent in the military or working in a hospital, library, or school.

6. There should be no required subjects in high school. All subjects should be electives.

7. Ninth-grade students should be allowed to leave the school grounds during lunch and during any other free time.

8. Schools should operate on a ten-hour day, four-day week, the way many businesses now do.

Knowing Your Audience

Before a company spends millions of dollars a year to advertise a product on television, the advertising agency looks carefully at the kind of audience that is most likely to watch the show during which their product will be advertised. This is done to be certain that the audience is the kind who will buy that product.

For example, on Saturday mornings millions of children spend several hours watching cartoons. Companies that buy advertising time during these hours usually make products for children, and children persuade their parents to buy the cereal and toys that are advertised.

Like advertisements, your persuasive writing must be aimed at an audience. If it is, your argument will have a better chance of getting the result you want.

Writing Practice 6: *Persuading an Audience*

In each of the situations on this page and the next, one person attempts to persuade others to believe or behave a certain way. Select one of these situations or use the work you did in Writing Practice 5 and write a short paper in which you attempt to persuade the audience. Before you begin the paper, answer the following questions.

(a) How old is your audience? (b) How will the age of your audience affect the way you write? (c) Is your audience made up of people you know or do not know? (d) How will your familiarity with the audience affect the way you write? (e) What kind of attitude should you take toward your audience? (f) What kind of language is most appropriate for your audience?

Situations

1. You are trying to persuade an adult to give permission for something you are not ordinarily allowed to do, perhaps stay out later than usual or skip an important school assignment. Write down the dialogue that might take place between you and this adult.

2. Attendance in one of the local elementary schools has been a problem lately, and you have been invited to speak to some fifth-grade students about the importance of coming to school. Write down what you would say to these students to persuade them to attend regularly.

3.   You are trying to persuade a friend who is your age to join a school organization, such as the jazz band. Write down what you would say to persuade your friend to join this organization.

A Letter to the Editor

Most school and community newspapers have a section where letters to the editor are published. (The *editor* is the person responsible for the general content of the paper.) When people in the school or community want to react to a local event or to a story carried by the paper, they may write *letters to the editor*. Sometimes, this section will have a title, such as *Voice of the People* or *Our Readers Speak.* In the section you will usually find directions for writing these letters: where to send your letter and whether or not to sign it and include your address. Some newspapers will omit the signature when the letter is printed, but it must usually be signed before it will be published. Because newspaper space is limited, brevity is encouraged, and newspapers usually reserve the right to condense the letter.

Letters to the editor are written for many reasons: to mention a contribution a person or an organization has made to the community; to give an opinion about current events, such as elections; or to express an opinion on a news story or an editorial.

Many magazines also have a letters-to-the-editor section. Because a letter in a national magazine, such as *Time* or *Newsweek*, may be read by millions of people, such a letter must be of wide interest. For example, *Time* magazine would not publish a letter about a carwash at a junior high school (unless it was a very unusual event) because the event would not interest the magazine's millions of readers around the world. Sometimes, radio and television stations broadcast what amounts to an editorial, giving the management's point of view about local or national issues. When this is done, the station must give its audience the right to respond, by reading letters from listeners and viewers on the air or by taping a statement for broadcast.

Many times in a society as large as the United States, people feel they do not have much to say about events that happen around them. A letter to the editor, whether it is written to a school newspaper, a national magazine, or a radio or television station, gives you an opportunity to express your views. Your letter may be read by many people and, if it is well written, may have some influence on them. Effective writing helps you shape the world around you.

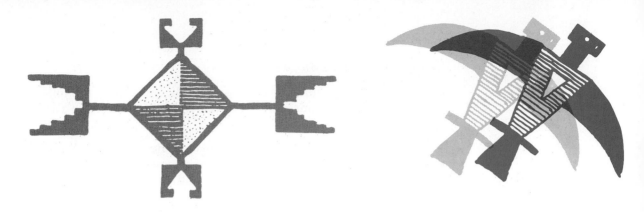

Model: *A Letter to the Editor*

The following letter to the editor was published in *Rough Rock News*, Rough Rock, Arizona, Navajo Nation, December 2, 1969. Bertha Desiderio, a young Navajo girl, argues on behalf of her culture and her language. As you read the letter, notice how the writer develops her argument with details.

I came into this world as a Navajo child. As I grew up, I learned to speak a language. This language I came to treasure, to feel at ease when I spoke it, and it brought me an identification as a true, proud Navajo. I spoke this language before I heard another language called English. My parents taught me how to pronounce the Navajo words right and taught me what they meant. I treasured the language as I went through my early youth, even though I was learning a new language that I would need as I got through life, but still, I never wanted to lose my own language.

When I conversed with this language that I treasured, I was proud because it was mine and it was given to me by my ancestors. I was never ashamed to speak my language, because it was one with my pride and joy.

Today—I hate to say this—but I am ashamed to speak Navajo in front of a group of Navajo students. The language that I was proud of has been changed into a "twisted" language. These days it seems like I can't say anything in Navajo without getting embarrassed. When I do talk in Navajo, my words are changed into dirty thoughts by people who do not realize that our language is supposed to be a value for us. Instead, they take our language as trash.

I wonder how students who twist their language into dirty thoughts feel about their culture going down the drain. Again I wonder if it ever bothers them not to take their culture into consideration. As an individual, I dread to see my culture fade just because some of us students don't care to use our language as it is supposed to be used. Are you really proud to be a Navajo? Then talk as if you took pride in your language.[1]

[1]"I came into this world . . ." by Bertha Desiderio. Originally published in *The Word-Passer*. Reprinted by permission of Bertha Desiderio-Muskett.

Think and Discuss

With your teacher and classmates discuss the answers to the following questions; or, if your teacher prefers, write the answers on a sheet of paper.

1. How does Bertha Desiderio develop her argument? (Some methods of development are personal experience, facts, reasoning, examples, and statements by authorities.)

2. Who do you think is the audience for the letter? Would the letter have widespread appeal? Was the letter convincing? Why?

3. Does Bertha Desiderio offer a solution to the problem that she discusses in the letter? What is it? Do you think it would be effective? Explain.

4. Is the conclusion to the letter effective? Explain.

Writing Assignment I: *A Letter to the Editor*

A. Prewriting

Identifying Topics: Over a period of a week, complete the following activities and make a list of at least ten possible topics for an editorial. Some of the topics may come from the work you completed in Writing Practices 5 and 6.

1. Begin reading the letters-to-the-editor section of your local newspaper (or your school newspaper). Write down the topics covered in at least three editorials.

2. Listen to your local radio or television news broadcasts or talk shows. Make a list of at least four topics about which people have strong opinions. Include topics that are of special concern to you.

3. Read the letters-to-the-editor section of a national news magazine, such as *Time, Newsweek,* or *U.S. News and World Report,* or the letters in a magazine published for teenagers. Make a list of three more topics covered in these letters.

4. At the end of the week, go over the topics you have identified and select ten that you feel strongest about.

5. In a class session, compare your list with those of your classmates. (Each student might want to list three or four on the chalkboard.) Brainstorm other current issues that concern your school or immediate community. Add those that interest you to your list.

Forming an Opinion: From your list of topics, select one that you feel strongly about. Write a topic sentence that clearly states your opinion. Then make a list of reasons, examples, facts, statements, or personal experiences supporting your opinion. If you do not have enough information, find out more about your topic by reading newspapers or periodicals, listening to the news, interviewing people, and so on.

B. Writing

A Persuasive Draft: Use your topic statement and list of reasons to write a first draft of a letter to the editor. Arrange your supporting arguments so that they build from least important to most important. In this way, the most convincing argument is presented last and leaves the reader with the strongest impression.

Direct your letter to your fellow students. Use language that is convincing and reasons that are logical. Your purpose is to persuade the audience to agree with your opinion. End your letter with a conclusion that suggests a solution or urges the readers to believe or act in some way.

C. Postwriting

Responding to Opinions: Revise and proofread your final draft using the checklists at the back of the book. Recopy your letter. If you intend to actually mail the letter, follow the form for writing a business letter in Chapter 11.

In a student response group, read four or five letters aloud. Use the following guidelines for discussing each letter.

1. Summarize the issue or topic presented in each letter and the writer's opinion about it.

2. Identify three arguments or reasons given to support the writer's opinion.

3. Discuss which argument seems to be the most convincing.

Supporting an Opinion

Because the parent-teacher group of Lincolnwood High School was concerned about the amount of time the students spent watching television, the group decided to present a panel program on the issue of restricting viewing time. Four students were asked to present the views of the students.

The president of the parent-teacher group began the meeting by expressing his opinion that television viewing time for teenagers should be limited. This opinion was partly based on his experiences with his own son and daughter. He explained that, when they first began high school, they watched television for several hours each evening and neglected their homework. As a result they did not make good grades. After television time was restricted to the weekends, however, they began studying in the evenings, and their grades improved.

Next, the president of the group mentioned the fact that high school students' national test scores began to fall in 1963, about the time television viewing became widespread. He quoted an authority on television who felt the medium was responsible for the decline in test scores. Finally, he gave two more reasons viewing time should be limited: (1) there is too much violence on television, and (2) television viewing takes time from more healthful activities, such as sports.

When the students stood up to speak, they did not know how to convince the audience of their viewpoint. Finally, they expressed their feelings and then sat down. The members of the audience respected the students' feelings but were not convinced by what they had to say because the students did not have the specific details they needed to develop their argument. The audience was more convinced by the president's speech. He began his talk by relating his personal experience with high school students and television. He also quoted a recognized authority on television and gave two more reasons for his opinion.

A good argument is developed with specific details.

Details most often used to develop argumentative writing are personal experiences, facts, reasons, examples, and statements by authorities. As in the president's speech, an argument may also be developed by a combination of these methods.

If the students in the panel discussion had given more thought to what they were going to say, their comments might have been like the following ones.

The amount of time high school students watch television should not be limited. We do not think that limiting viewing time will cause students to study more. To gather evidence for our belief, we surveyed the ninth-grade students in our school to find out whether they would study more if they could not watch television. Slightly more than 90 percent of the students said they would spend their time listening to records or to the radio if they could not watch television. We also feel that much of the time spent watching television is time well spent. There are many educational shows on television, and entertainment shows often have something to teach. For example, high school

students can choose from among shows that explore and explain ways of living in foreign countries, investigate the news and current state of national issues, or feature the arts and crafts of other people.

Finally, we feel that teenagers should take responsibility for their own actions. If television time is limited, teenagers are denied a good opportunity to learn self-discipline by making responsible choices.

This time the students gave specific details to support their belief that television viewing time should not be limited. For this reason their comments would now be more convincing to their audience.

Writing Practice 7: *Point of View*

Think of a subject about which you have a strong point of view, or select a subject and a point of view from the following list. Then, on a sheet of paper, make a list of details (facts, reasons, examples, personal experiences, statements of authority) you can use to convince your audience.

Subjects	*Points of View*
Allowance:	Teenagers should (or should not) have to help at home to earn an allowance.
Grade Average:	Students should (or should not) be required to have a B average to participate in sports, band, or cheerleading activities.

Subjects	Points of View
Part-time Jobs:	Ninth-grade students should (or should not) be able to get work permits for part-time jobs.
School Security:	For reasons of security, all students should (or should not) be required to have identification cards and show them when asked.
School Lunches:	Schools should (or should not) install snack machines.
Reading:	English teachers should (or should not) require all students to read at least one book outside of class every two weeks.
Television:	Television shows with violence of any kind should (or should not) be taken off the air.
Open Campus:	Students should (or should not) be allowed to leave the school grounds at lunch and eat at a place of their choice.

Model: A Persuasive Essay

In the following essay, entitled "Kill the Metric!", Lisa Shillinger, the writer makes an argument against the United States' converting to the metric system. As you read, look for reasons she uses to support her argument.

Miss Horsefield introduced me to the metric system in her third-grade class at DuBois School in Springfield, Ill., 25 years ago. I didn't find it awesome or difficult to understand then, and I don't now. The interrelationship of distance, volume and weight is impressive. What a pity the United States didn't adopt it 100 years ago when we joined in the signing of the International Metric Convention.

Now, however, I wonder with growing horror what lunacy propels us to go metric at this late date. Thanks to the Metric Conversion Act of 1975, . . . the metric wave is scheduled to engulf this country over the next ten years.

Whereas conversion to the metric system (or International System of Units) was accomplished by Napoleonic decree in France

and accompanied political upheavals in the Soviet Union, China and Latin America, the United States is relying on a seventeen-member Board of Metrics and public indifference to usher in the conversion.

It's "The Emperor's New Clothes" and Prohibition all over again. To oppose the metric system in the United States is to oppose progress, we are told. As soon as we learn our conversion factors and overcome our reactionary fears we shall rise up and join the great brotherhood of metric man.

Well, I disagree. Conversion to the metric system in this country is simply an exorbitantly expensive experiment in inconvenience. The primary victim, as usual, will be the American consumer.

Point one: let us accept the inherent superiority of the ISU over the English system. It is more logical and easier to learn. For Europe, which gave birth to it during the French Revolution and matured with it, the metric system has served very well. For developing nations emerging from tribal cultures, why not? But for the United States, the most industrialized and standardized nation in the world, to convert to another system of measure is sheer madness.

Point two: the American public is under the delusion that the effects of conversion will primarily hit industry and science. Media reports on conversion costs and schedules are almost exclusively concerned with heavy industry. The average American has been led to believe the primary effect upon his own life will be the obsolescence of a few old saws and literary expressions ("A miss is as good as 1.6 kilometers")—hoo-hah. What is being overlooked is the devastating effect the conversion to metrics will have on the everyday life and pocketbook of the American consumer.

Point three: examples abound. We are going to have to invest in gram scales and measures to weigh out our flour, sugar, rice, cocoa, etc. That's merely an inconvenient adjustment housewives will have to make. But what about the millions of dollars of cookbooks now on the market and in our homes, not to mention those favorite old recipes? They'll soon be obsolete. If your recipe calls for the traditional cup of whipping cream you will have to settle for a .2- or .3-liter size, since it would be a bit ridiculous to come up with a .23656-liter carton to equal our current 1-cup carton. That's not real efficient. That, of course, goes for all those convenient packages that now happen to match what a recipe calls for—like the familiar 3-ounce package of cream cheese and the fifth of wine that goes into your holiday punch. Thousands of recipes are coordinated with food items that have been commercially packaged in quarts, pints, ounces and pounds in the United States since the Year One. And, by the way, who do you think is going to absorb the cost of repackaging? It isn't General Foods.

What if you want to reframe that fine old family portrait into a new nonexistent 9- by 12-inch frame? Or perhaps you'll want to hang a mirror on the wall. Finding the studs is no big problem since studs in American homes built in the last 50 years are standardized at 16 inches apart. That means you mark off the distance in handy increments of 40.64 centimeters. Of course in the new post-metric homes we'll probably round that off to 40 centimeters and in a few years that could result in a lot of excitement when you try to locate your studs to install new wiring, insulation or whatever.

Down on the farm, the south 40 (acres) becomes the south 16.1874 (hectares). It'll be up to the farmer to figure out how many kilos of fertilizer to buy per hectare. And what about all the land and property titles to be converted?

And in the business world, we may say goodbye to the 8½-by-11-inch paper that fits your file folders and lines up with all those existing sheets. The post office can scrap all its ounce-calibrated scales and postal meters. And since the metric system will hit our printing industries with a real wallop, you may even have a slightly larger- or smaller-sized *National Geographic* to file away with all those your grandfather saved for you.

Finally, a nice little touch for travelers. Europeans vacationing in this country frequently remark on the convenience of the English system, which allows one to figure a town 45 miles away is just about 45 minutes away. I won't even attempt to convert that.

The examples of the idiocy of conversion to the metric system are infinite and all-pervasive. They permeate every phase of our lives, creating costly obsolescence in everything from shot glasses to storm doors—items that we never considered vulnerable before.

Let the scientists and industrialists continue to use whatever system they choose to carry out their international dealings. For the rest of us, let's stick with our English system. Conversion is exorbitantly expensive, inconvenient and pointless. What's more, like Prohibition, it won't work.

Where were *we* when they pushed this one through? Who's making the bucks on this one? Where is the consumer uproar? Where are our crusaders now that we need them? I say, *"Vive la différence!"*[1]

Ounce-calibrated scales **measure weight in units of ounces.**

Obsolescence **means "the process of becoming out-of-date."**

"Vive la différence!" **is a French phrase meaning "Long live the difference!"**

Think and Discuss

1. In a good persuasive essay the writer's opinion is adequately supported with details. First, Lisa Shillinger gives the reasons

---

[1]"Kill the Metric!" by Lisa Shillinger from *Newsweek*, November 8, 1976. Copyright © 1976 by Newsweek, Inc. All rights reserved. Reprinted by permission.

for her opinion that the United States should not convert to the metric system: it would be confusing, inconvenient, and expensive for the American consumer. Then she gives many examples of how the new system would be a burden for the consumer, including the cost of buying new scales and measures for the kitchen, and problems with packaging food. What are other examples the writer uses to develop her opinion?

2. A persuasive essay is more convincing if the writer deals with counterarguments, the reasons most often used to support the opposing opinion. One counterargument Lisa Shillinger treats is that the metric system is more logical and easier to learn than the system currently used in the United States. What are the other counterarguments she treats in this essay?

Writing a Persuasive Paper

In the following sections, you will learn how to write a thesis statement expressing the main idea of a persuasive essay. You will also learn to write the introduction, body, and conclusion of a persuasive paper.

The Thesis Statement

In a persuasive paper the *thesis* states the point for which you will argue, perhaps in the form of a statement such as "Television viewing time should not be limited for high school students."

The main point you argue in your persuasive paper should not be based on matters of personal taste or value judgments, which cannot be changed by logical argument. For example, "Blue is my favorite color" or "I think hamburgers should always be served well-done" are not acceptable thesis statements because they are personal preferences rather than arguable opinions. Value judgments and statements that say that one thing, person, or idea is better than another are also not acceptable as thesis statements. The statement "The Beatles were the world's most popular singing group" is a value judgment, not a belief that can be argued with logic.

The thesis statement of an argumentative paper should be

257

clearly and directly stated, often in the introductory paragraph. Professional writers sometimes do not directly make a thesis statement until later in an essay. For example, in the sample essay on pages 254-256, the thesis statement does not appear until the fifth paragraph: "Conversion to the metric system in this country is simply an exorbitantly expensive experiment in inconvenience. The primary victim, as usual, will be the American consumer."

Model: *A Persuasive Introduction*

A beginning writer may want to take a more direct approach by placing the thesis statement in the introductory paragraph, as Roger M. Williams does in the following introduction to his essay "Away with Big-Time Athletics." In your own words, what is the thesis statement in the paragraph? What would you expect to find in the remaining paragraphs?

> At their mid-January annual meeting, members of the National Collegiate Athletic Association were locked in anguished discussion over twin threats to big-time college athletic programs: rapidly rising costs and federal regulations forcing the allocation of some funds to women's competition. The members ignored, as they always have, the basic issue concerning intercollegiate athletics. That is the need to overhaul the entire bloated, hypocritical athletic system and return athletics to a sensible place in the educational process.[1]

The last sentence of the preceding paragraph is the thesis statement. Notice that this thesis does more than state the subject; it also gives the writer's point of view toward it.

Writing Practice 8: *A Persuasive Introduction*

Think of a subject about which you have a point of view, perhaps one you have already used in this chapter. Then write an introductory paragraph in which you state your viewpoint as a thesis for a persuasive essay. Make your paragraph interesting by using one of the methods for writing an introduction described in Chapter 6, *Writing an Expository Composition,* or use an introduction of your own design.

The Body

Writing a persuasive paper requires the same attention to audience and purpose that any other paper does. Before you write, it is important to consider who will read your paper because the audience you write for affects how you present your ideas. For example, suppose that your topic deals with a school problem: students need more tutors during study halls. If your audience consists of the teachers, staff, and students of your school, you can assume that they are already familiar with what a study hall is, how tutors are assigned, and so on. However, if your audience is your town or community, you will probably need to explain school terms and procedures in your paper.

The purpose of a persuasive paper is to convince the reader to believe in something, to change his or her mind about something, or to do something. Decide which of these aims fits your paper before you write. In general, writers use two basic methods of persuasion: (1) an appeal to reason or logic, and (2) an appeal to emotion.

In a logical argument your approach is to present the reader with clear and sufficient reasons supporting your point of view. For example, in Lisa Shillinger's essay "Kill the Metric!" she argues that it is too late for the United States to go metric and that going metric will be expensive for the consumer, extremely inconvenient, and confusing. Her essay supports these statements by giving examples. She asserts that, among other reasons, it is too late to go metric because the United States is "the most industrialized and standardized nation in the world."

In logical argument especially, writers use the device of mentioning opposing ideas or counterarguments that might occur to the reader. For example, Lisa Shillinger agrees from the beginning that the metric system is easier to learn than the English system. She accepts this point against her argument and deals with it by stating that the enormous inconvenience and expense outweighs the benefits of easy learning. In your own writing try to anticipate criticism or counterarguments by dealing with them in your paper.

Few essays are based entirely on logical argument; writers usually introduce emotional appeals as part of a logically argued paper. Lisa Shillinger uses emotional language when she states, "I wonder with growing horror what lunacy propels us to go metric at this late date." The words *horror* and *lunacy* are emotionally charged words; they invite the reader to share the writer's point of view. Describing the consumer as a "victim" is another example of emotional language. Look through the essay for other appeals to the reader's feelings.

Two other qualities important in persuasive writing are necessary in all essay writing: the paper must be adequately developed, and it must concentrate on the main point of the argument.

Adequate development means not only using a sufficient number of examples to support an argument but also making a thorough explanation of their importance. For example, Lisa Shillinger explains that most people are completely unaware of the tremendous effects metric conversion will have on their daily lives; her examples illustrate these bad effects.

Persuasive papers take a single-minded approach to argument: they focus on one important purpose and do not stray from it. Always keep the purpose of your paper in mind when you write. For example, if you want to persuade the reader to vote for a political candidate, do not bring in extraneous information about the history of the candidate's political party. If you want to convince the reader that solar power is the only solution to the energy problem, do not spend time writing about the history of electricity. In "Kill the Metric!" the writer uses different arguments and examples to make one basic point: metric conversion is a bad idea for the United States. Keeping your thesis statement in mind as you work on your paper will help you focus your argument and will help prevent you from straying too far from your main idea.

Writing Practice 9: *The Body of a Persuasive Paper*

Write three major reasons to support or develop the thesis statement you selected for Writing Practice 8. Using specific details, develop each of the three reasons into a separate paragraph. These three paragraphs will be the body of your paper and will follow the introductory paragraph you wrote for Writing Practice 8.

The Conclusion

The conclusion of a persuasive essay should inspire the reader to believe or act in some way. The writer may end with an emotional appeal for agreement, call for a specific course of action, or propose a solution to a problem.

Model: A Persuasive Conclusion

In Lisa Shillinger's essay, the conclusion encourages readers to protest the conversion to the metric system. It is an emotional appeal that ends with the statement "I say, '*Vive la différence!*'" Such a call to action is an effective way to conclude a persuasive paper.

> The examples of the idiocy of conversion to the metric system are infinite and all-pervasive. They permeate every phase of our lives, creating costly obsolescence in everything from shot glasses to storm doors—items that we never considered vulnerable before.
>
> Let the scientists and industrialists continue to use whatever system they choose to carry out their international dealings. For the rest of us, let's stick with our English system. Conversion is exorbitantly expensive, inconvenient and pointless. What's more, like Prohibition, it won't work.
>
> Where were *we* when they pushed this one through? Who's making the bucks on this one? Where is the consumer uproar? Where are our crusaders now that we need them? I say, "*Vive la différence!*"

Another way to conclude a persuasive paper is to predict what the future will be like if the reader does not support your point of view. This method of ending the paper may easily be combined with a call to action or an emotional appeal.

Writing Practice 10: *The Conclusion of a Persuasive Paper*

Write a conclusion for the body of the paper you wrote in Writing Practice 9. Use one of the methods you read about in this section or a combination of methods. Make your conclusion convincing by encouraging the readers to believe or act in some way.

Writing Practice 11: *Responding and Revising*

After you have completed the first draft of your persuasive paper, use the following checklist to revise it. Then rewrite the paper. Have an editing partner or a student response group help with your revision by offering constructive suggestions. Remember to follow the Guidelines for Student Response Groups suggested in Chapter 1.

Checklist for Revising Persuasive Writing

1. Does the argument use sound reasoning and focus on the main purpose throughout the paper?

2. Is the thesis statement clearly stated in an interesting introductory paragraph?

3. Is the thesis statement an opinion that can be argued with logic rather than a value judgment?

4. Is the argument logically organized?

5. Does the paper include sufficient supporting details (facts, reasons, or personal experiences)?

6. Is the language appropriate for the intended audience?

7. Does the paper end with an interesting conclusion that encourages the reader to act in some way?

8. Does each paragraph develop the thesis statement?

9. Can the reader easily move from one idea to the next?

Use the Proofreader's Checklist at the back of the book to make corrections in sentence structure, grammar, mechanics, and spelling.

Sentence Combining:
Inserting Phrases

Using *the* ing *and* pos *Signals*

For information on gerunds, see pages 493-496.

You can use (*ing*) to change a verb to a noun. For instance, in each of the following examples, the *-ing* word is a noun:

Running is good exercise.
[*Running* is the subject of the sentence.]

Her *singing* is driving me crazy.
[*Singing* is the subject of the sentence because it names *what* is driving me crazy. *Driving* also ends in *-ing*, but here it is part of the verb, *is driving*.]

For more information on possessives, see pages 302, 311-313, 505-506.

In the following examples the (*ing*) and the (*pos*) signals work together.

Base: *Something* has startled me.
Insert: Leslie shouted. (*pos* + *ing*)
Combined: *Leslie's shouting* startled me.

Base: Patricia can't put up with *something*.
Insert: Her brother whistles. (*pos* + *ing*)
Combined: Patricia can't put up with *her brother's whistling*.

263

Base: The coach insisted on *something*.
Insert: They win the game. (*pos + ing*)
Combined: The coach insisted on *their winning the game*.

Notice that in the last example, *they* in the insert sentence becomes *their* in the combined sentence. The (*pos*) signal affects pronouns in the following way.

I	becomes	*my*
she	becomes	*her*
he	becomes	*his*
they	becomes	*their*
it	becomes	*its*
you	becomes	*your*
we	becomes	*our*

Exercise 1: Using the ing *and* pos *Signals*

On a sheet of paper, make the combinations on this page and the next. Use signals where given. Study the examples before you begin.

Examples

a. *Something* made Harriet angry.
The dog barked. (*pos + ing*)
The dog's barking made Harriet angry.

b. According to my teacher, *something* is not certain.
We will pass the test.
According to my teacher, our passing the test is not certain.

1. My parents will easily understand *something*.
I want to become a singer. (*pos + ing*)

2. The pirates noticed *something*.
The submarine stalked them through the bay. (*pos + ing*)

3. The crowd praised *something*.
The police officer captured the mugger. (*pos + ing*)

4. *Something* caused it to sink.
The ship sprang a leak.

5. *Something* will prevent *something*.
   John coughs.
   He will sing in the concert.

Combining the ing *and* of *Signals*

When the (*-ing*) signal is given with words ending in *-ly*, drop the *-ly* endings.

The bees buzzed *endlessly*	becomes	The bees' *endless* buzzing
She talked *loudly*	becomes	Her *loud* talking
Angie skates *gracefully*	becomes	Angie's *graceful* skating

As you can see, this change also requires a change to possessive form.

Base: *Something* brought me awake with a shock.
Insert: The stove exploded loudly. (*pos = ly + ing*)
Combined: The *stove's loud exploding* brought me awake with a shock.

The (*of*) signal can be used in combination with the (*ing*) signal to avoid the possessive form.

Base: While I was reading, *something* made me fall asleep.
Insert: The rain dripped steadily. (*ing + of*)
Combined: While I was reading, the steady dripping of the rain made me fall asleep.

Exercise 2: Using Combinations of Signals

On a sheet of paper, combine each sentence set on the next page. Use signals where given. Study the examples before you begin.

Examples

a. Joanna praised *something*.
   Her mother sketched. (*pos + ing*)
   Joanna praised her mother's sketching.

b. After the rain, *something* prevented us from going outside.
   The leaves dripped continuously.
   After the rain, the continuous dripping of the leaves prevented us from going outside.

265

1. *Something* was a sorry thing to hear.
   Jesse admitted his guilt. (*pos + ing*)

2. I can't abide *something* when she shares my room.
   She snores heavily. (*pos = ly + ing*)

3. Do you understand *something?*
   Sarah refused to attend our party. (*pos + ing*)

4. *Something* put me to sleep.
   The surf pounded ceaselessly. (*ing + of*)

5. Does *something* keep you on edge?
   The bell rings noisily. (*pos = ly + ing*)

6. Could *something* awaken you?
   A herd of elephants trumpet loudly.

7. *Something* is the most soothing sound I hear when I'm outdoors.
   The wind whistles in the willows.

8. *Something* did not afford him the warm reception back home.
   Sir Mark retreated hastily from the enemy.

9. *Something* puts me to sleep.
   The cat purrs monotonously.

10. *Something* caused me to work carelessly so I failed the test.
    I had the flu.

Word Changes That Work Like the -ing Signal

Verbs can change their forms in ways other than adding *-ing* to become nouns.

Verbs	Nouns
explode	explosion
discover	discovery
entertain	entertainment
conclude	conclusion
describe	description

The signals for making the changes required in the next exercise work very much like the (*ing*) signal, as the following examples show.

Base: Mr. Michaels could not understand *something*.
Insert: His students discussed last Saturday's football game. (*pos + discussion + of*)
Combined: Mr. Michaels could not understand *his students' discussion of* last Saturday's football game.

Base: *Something* kept the family busy.
Insert: They entertained company frequently. (*pos + entertainment + of*)
Combined: *Their frequent entertainment of company* kept the family busy.

Exercise 3: Using Signals That Work Like the -ing Signal

On a sheet of paper, combine the following sets of sentences on this page and the next. Use signals where given. Study the example before you begin.

Example

a. Mr. Basehart's defeat in the campaign was due to *something*. Bribes were paid. (*payment + of*)

Mr. Basehart's defeat in the campaign was due to payment of bribes.

1. *Something* made them senior residents.
   The doctors were promoted. (*pos + promotion*)

2. *Something* made the room seem small.
   The chairs were arranged awkwardly. (*arrangement + of*)

3. The banker refused *something*.
   Credit was extended further. (*extension + of*)

4. It was too bad that *something* prevented her performance.
   The show was canceled. (*cancellation + of*)

5. *Something* meant that we would have to find another culprit.
   Hank denied his guilt. (*pos + denial + of*)

6. *Something* means that there will be no municipal swimming pool this year.
   Proposition 10 was defeated.

7. The record books showed *something*.
   Mom had paid the bill.

8. *Something* brought about a nationwide search.
    The priceless gems disappeared.

9. *Something* resulted in *something*.
    An ancient gas furnace exploded.
    The museum was destroyed.

10. *Something* caused the people to believe in *something*.
    His true identity was revealed.
    The witchcraft had occurred.

Variations on a Familiar Combination Pattern

The combinations (*for . . . to*) and (*it . . . for . . . to*) work very much like other (*. . . to*) combinations.

Base:	*Something* was difficult.
Insert:	Carlos mowed the tall grass. (*it . . . for . . . to*)
Combined:	It was difficult *for Carlos to mow the tall grass.*

Base:	She had always been looking (for) *something*.
Insert:	A lucky break would change her life. (*for . . . to*)
Combined:	She had always been looking *for a lucky break to change her life.*

Base:	Their injuries made *something* impossible.
Insert:	They could not continue. (*it . . . for . . . to*)
Combined:	Their injuries made *it* impossible *for them to continue.*

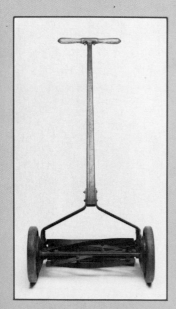

The last example demonstrates another change when the (*it . . . for . . . to*) signal is given: the following words will also change when they are used in the (*it . . . for . . . to*) or the (*for . . . to*) patterns:

I	becomes	*me*
she	becomes	*her*
he	becomes	*him*
they	becomes	*them*
we	becomes	*us*
it	remains	*it*
you	remains	*you*

Exercise 4: Using Two New Combination Patterns

On a sheet of paper, make the following combinations. Use signals where given. Study the example before you begin.

Example

a. *Something* requires much effort.
   I get up before 6 A.M. (*it . . . for . . . to*)

   It requires much effort for me to get up before 6 A.M.

1. *Something* promised to be dangerous.
    The hunters stalk the saber-toothed tiger. (*for . . . to*)

2. The customer had been waiting for a half-hour (for) *something*.
    The waiter will bring the soup. (*for . . . to*)

3. *Something* remained impossible.
    People will fly without some sort of engine. (*it . . . for . . . to*)

4. *Something* will be a difficult decision for her to make.
    The disc jockey will talk or play records. (*for . . . to*)

5. *Something* seems easy.
    The mountaineers will descend the dangerously steep cliffs.
    (*it . . . for . . . to*)

6. The frequent buzzing in my ears seemed to be a signal (for) *something*.
    I will get a hearing test.

7. The captain says (for) *something*.
    We will abandon ship.

8. *Something* will cost twenty dollars.
    You will sail across Lake Michigan and back.

9. *Something* will take very little time and effort.
    Someone will lift this rock off my foot.

10. The class is preparing (for) *something*.
    You will return.

Writing Practice: *Revising a Persuasive Paper for Sentence Variety*

Reread the persuasive paper you wrote in this chapter. Check your paper for sentence variety, using the following criteria.

1. Is there a variety of sentence beginnings?

2. Is there a variety of sentence lengths?

3. Is there a variety of sentence patterns?

11 Writing for the Business World

The Business Letter

Writing a business letter differs from writing a personal letter in several ways. Because a business letter is usually written to people you do not know, it is more formal. Most business letters, for example, do not have slang words, contractions, or many abbreviations. Also, your business letters will probably be briefer than your personal letters. You may fill your personal letters with interesting news and stories, but in a business letter you should state your purpose as clearly and concisely as possible. Finally business letters follow a conventional form that differs in several ways from the form of a personal letter.

Business letters are written for many purposes: for example, to apply for a job, to ask for information, to place an order, or to make a complaint. In the following sections you will learn how to write several types of business letters. You will also practice filling out a standardized job-application form.

The Letter of Application

If you have not already applied for a job, you may want to do so in the near future. The *letter of application* may be the first contact you have with a prospective employer.

When you write a letter of application, you want the prospective employer to think of you as a careful, reliable person who is ready to take on the responsibility of a new job. Before writing a letter of application, try to put yourself in the employer's place. For example, suppose you were the personnel manager of a grocery store who had placed the following ad in the local newspaper.

> Wanted. Hard-working, reliable high school students to stock shelves and bag groceries. Hours 5–9 P.M. M–F; 2–6 P.M. Saturdays; $3.50 per hour. Apply by letter to Ms. Joan Sheppler, Personnel Manager, Crown City Grocery Store, 121 Wiltshire Blvd., Kansas City, MO 66155.

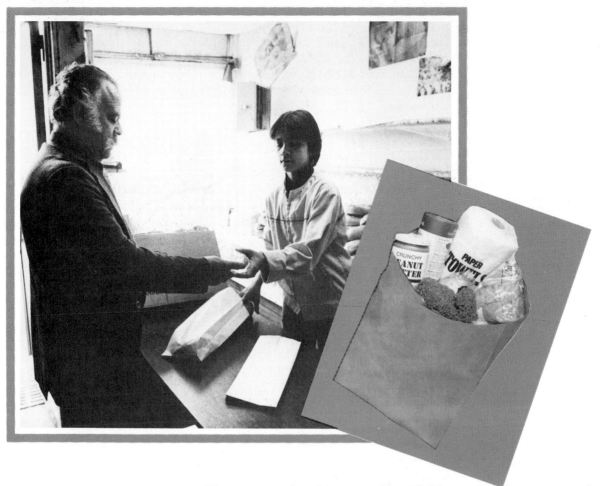

The personnel manager would probably want to know some of the following things about applicants.

1. How did the students hear about the ad?

2. How old are they, and what are their grade levels?

3. Are they hard-working and reliable individuals?

4. What previous work experience have they had?

5. Who are some people who will recommend these students, and how can these men or women be reached?

6. Are the students available for an interview? If so, when? How can the students be reached?

When you write your letter of application, give your prospective employers information they need to decide whether you would be a good candidate for the job. You can do this in your letter by answering the questions in the preceding list. Most employers want to know the names, addresses, and telephone numbers of people who can tell them that you would be a good employee. These people, called *references*, may be adult neighbors, teachers, school counselors, principals, and ministers who know about your ability to work. As a courtesy ask the people whom you plan to list as references for their permission.

Model: A Letter of Application

The following letter of application is a response to the preceding advertisement for a grocery clerk. As you read it, notice the information the writer gives about herself. Then answer the questions on the next page.

2331 Lancaster Drive
Kansas City, MO 66152
June 2, 1984

Ms. Joan Sheppler
Personnel Manager
Crown City Grocery Store
121 Wiltshire Boulevard
Kansas City, MO 66155

Dear Ms. Sheppler:

Your advertisement for help to stock shelves and bag groceries was posted on the school bulletin board. I would like to apply for one of these jobs.

I am fifteen years old and a ninth-grade student at Evans High School. I am very hard-working and reliable. Last semester I was elected secretary of our ninth-grade class.

During the past two summers, I worked in Mr. Peter Carswell's grocery store bagging groceries, stocking shelves, and waiting on customers.

My faculty adviser, Miss Maria Rodriguez, has said she would be happy to recommend me for this position. She can be reached at the school telephone, 555-6640. My neighbor, Mr. Robert Stevensen, 306 Briar Court Road, telephone 555-1632, will also recommend me. You can call Mr. Pete Carswell, at 555-1691.

I am usually home from school by 3:30 and can come in after that time for an interview.

Very truly yours,

Julie Lombach

Julie Lombach

Think and Discuss

1. In a letter of application, you are trying to sell yourself as a prospective employee. Do you think the writer of the letter has done so? Why?

2. What specific details does the writer give to show that she is hardworking and reliable?

3. Why are the people whom this student has listed as references good ones to use? What kinds of things should these people be able to tell the employer about the applicant?

4. In the third paragraph of the letter, the writer tells about her previous experience working in a grocery store. Why?

5. Is this letter clear and concise, as a good business letter should be? Does it have any information that does not relate to the job for which the student is applying?

Writing Practice 1: *Responding to a Job Advertisement*

Look through the want ad section of your local newspaper. Find an advertisement for a job that interests you. Or write your own ad after studying the following example.

> Wanted. Hard-working high school students for job in snack bar of skating rink. Must have initiative. Some work experience helpful but not essential. Hours 5–8 P.M. M–F; 4–9 P.M. Saturdays. Apply by letter to Mr. Robert Steele, Crown Rink, 101 Elm St., Chicago, IL 60606.

Write the body of a letter of application in which you respond to the ad you found or made up. Save your first draft for the next Writing Practice.

For Your Writer's Notebook

Students who leave career planning until two months before graduation may decide to enter a career such as nursing or auto mechanics, but find they have not taken the required courses in high school. Now is a good time to explore your interests and career possibilities. Write a notebook entry discussing three or four of your interests and skills. How might you use them in various careers? Think carefully about what you like to do—if you enjoy meeting people and traveling, a job with an airline might be a possibility. If you like working with numbers and organizing material neatly and carefully, you might consider accounting or computer programming.

The Form of a Business Letter

E ach of the forms, or styles, in the following examples is acceptable for a business letter. Businesses today most often use the *full block* or *block forms* for typewritten letters. The *semiblock form* is often used for handwritten letters. Regardless of the form, every business letter has six parts: the *heading*, the *inside address*, the *salutation*, the *body*, the *closing*, and the *signature*.

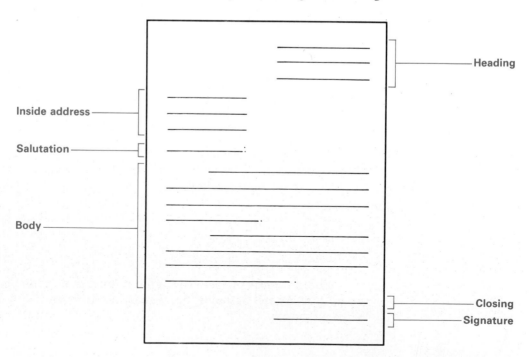

Semiblock

Block

Full block

Heading

For more information on punctuation and capitalization, see pages 548–598.

The *heading* consists of the sender's address and the date on which the letter is written. In the semiblock and block styles the heading is in the upper right-hand part of the page, about one inch from the top.

In the full block style the heading is even with the left-hand margin of the letter. The following examples show the proper form.

> 1903 Lincoln Street
> Evanston, Illinois 60602
> August 16, 1984

> Route 1, Box 586
> Gainesville, Georgia 30501
> July 4, 1984

Inside Address

The *inside address* consists of the name, title, company, and address of the receiver of the letter. If the person's title fits on the same line as his or her name, place a comma between the two; if not, write the title on the line following the name. If you do not know the name of the person to whom you are writing, use the title of the person you want to receive the letter, or use the name of the department. Regardless of the style, the inside address is even with the left-hand margin of the letter. If the letter is handwritten, skip a few spaces between the heading and inside address; if the letter is typed, skip four spaces.

Mrs. Jane Freeman, Principal
Evergreen High School
203 Clark Street
Evergreen, AL 35801

Dr. John E. Goldberg
Director of Student Services
Florida State University
662 Monroe Boulevard
Tallahassee, FL 32304

Personnel Department
Rich's Department Store
233 Peachtree Road
Atlanta, GA 30314

Salutation

The *salutation* of a business letter is more formal than that of a personal letter. Use *Dear* and the receiver's last name preceded by a title, such as *Mr., Mrs., Miss, Ms., Dr.,* or *Professor;* for example, *Dear Ms. Rodgers* or *Dear Professor Yue.* If you are writing to a firm rather than to an individual, several salutations are appropriate. For many years the customary salutation in this case was *Dear Sir* or *Gentlemen* even though the writer was not certain a man would be reading the letter. Today, however, the acceptable practice is to write *Dear Sir or Madam* or even *Dear (Name of Company or Department),* as, *Dear Personnel Department* or *Dear Sun-Times.* Write the salutation two spaces below the last line of the inside address, even with the left margin. A colon always follows the salutation.

Body

The *body* of the letter begins two spaces beneath the salutation. In the semiblock style, paragraphs are indented; in the full block and block styles, they are not. When you type a letter, skip a space between each paragraph.

Closing

The *closing* of a business letter is more formal than that of a personal letter. Customary closings are *Yours truly, Yours very truly, Very truly yours, Sincerely yours,* and *Yours sincerely.* Only the first word of the closing is capitalized, and a comma follows the closing. Write the closing two spaces beneath the body of the letter, in line with the heading.

Signature

After typing the closing, skip four spaces and type your name and then sign the letter in the space between the closing and typed name. Do not use a title when you sign your name, although women sometimes insert *Miss, Ms.,* or *Mrs.* in parentheses before their typed name to show how they wish to be addressed in a return letter: *(Miss) Sally M. Hudson.* The model business letters in this chapter show how a signed business letter should look.

Writing Practice 2: *A Letter of Application*

Select the appropriate business form from the previous examples and write a complete business letter using the body of the letter you wrote in Writing Practice 1. Be sure to include all six parts: the *heading,* the *inside address,* the *salutation,* the *body,* the *closing,* and the *signature.* Then use the Checklist for Revising Business Writing on page 287.

If you like, share your completed letter of application with a classmate, parent, or friend, or read it to a small group of classmates. Do not send the letter unless you actually intend to apply for the job.

Mailing a Business Letter

To fold a business letter place the letter on a flat surface so that the heading is at the top of the page. Think of two imaginary lines running across the page, dividing the letter into thirds.

Heading

Fold the bottom third of the page toward the heading and crease the fold. Now fold the top of the page to within ¼ inch from the bottom fold. This ¼ inch makes it easier to open the letter. Put the letter into a plain 9½ × 4½ inch envelope with the top of the page facing the back flap of the envelope.

The following sample shows the customary style for addressing a business envelope.

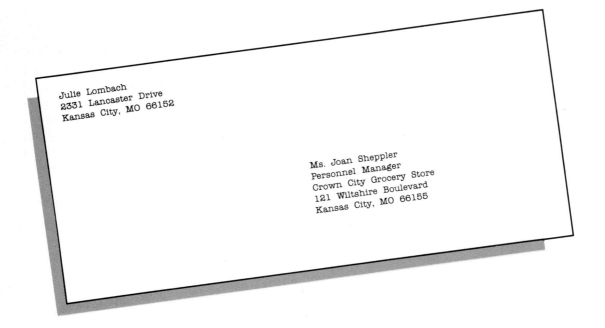

Julie Lombach
2331 Lancaster Drive
Kansas City, MO 66152

Ms. Joan Sheppler
Personnel Manager
Crown City Grocery Store
121 Wiltshire Boulevard
Kansas City, MO 66155

Writing Practice 3: *Addressing an Envelope*

Address a business envelope for the letter of application you wrote in Writing Practice 2. Enclose your letter in the envelope and give it to your teacher.

The Order Letter

An *order letter* is written to order merchandise by mail. Although many catalogues and magazine advertisements have clip-out order blanks, there will be times when you will want to write a letter to place an order for merchandise.

When writing an order letter, give precise information about the articles you are ordering: the catalogue number, if any; the color of the articles; the number or amount you want; and the price. If ordering clothes, include the size, style, and color of each article.

The order letter is written in the same general form as any other business letter. However, an order letter has several special features. Set the list of items off from the rest of the letter, placing the prices of the items so that they are in a column near the right-hand margin. Then total the amount you owe, adding postage and tax. Indicate how you are paying for the merchandise and whether the shipping address is different from your return address.

An order letter

> 1622 Hawthorne Drive
> Fort Smith, AR 72903
> August 15, 1984
>
> Davison's Department Store
> 180 Peachtree Street
> Atlanta, GA 30303
>
> Dear Sir or Madam:
>
> I would like to place the following order from your July sale catalogue:
>
> 1 red, white, and blue soccer ball,
>   plastic $ 2.98
>
> 2 lightweight wool sweaters,
>   1 size 15–33, light green,
>   pullover; the other size 16–34,
>   blue, pullover @ $6.95   13.90
>
>   Postage and Tax   1.78
>
> I am enclosing a money order for $18.66 to cover this amount.
>
>   Very truly yours,
>
>   John Hall
>   John Hall

Writing Practice 4: *An Order Letter*

In a letter to Service Record Company, 502 Meadow Road, Salem, OR 97304, order the following items: one copy of your favorite record album at a cost of $8.95; two long-sleeved shirts with pictures of your favorite singer or group in your size and in colors of your choice; one copy of the new record store catalogue at no charge. Prepare your letter for mailing. If you do not have an envelope, draw a rectangle on a sheet of paper and address it as though it were an envelope.

A Letter of Request

In a *letter of request*, you ask a company or a person to help you in some way, perhaps to send you information or a catalogue or to appear as a speaker for a class or club meeting. Like other business letters, this letter should be courteous, brief, and to the point.

Before writing a letter of request, be certain that the help you are asking for is reasonable. Some organizations, such as government agencies and chambers of commerce, are happy to fill requests for information. Representatives of government offices, such as libraries and fire and police departments, are usually willing to appear as speakers at various school functions.

Be cautious, however, about writing request letters to private individuals. Writers, for example, sometimes receive letters from students who want questions answered about the writers themselves. If they were to answer all of these requests, many writers would have little time left for their own writing. Respect the right of people to their privacy.

In your letter briefly state your reason for making the request, giving specific details about what you want. If, for example, you are inviting a speaker to your class, give the time, place, and date of the class, as well as the topic on which you would like him or her to speak. If necessary, include directions to the meeting place. Close your letter by thanking the person, company, or agency for considering your request.

A letter of request

26 Wharf Road
San Diego, CA 92109
September 26, 1984

Mr. John Hand, Director
Information Services
Sea World
1720 South Shores Road
San Diego, CA 92109

Dear Mr. Hand:

My ninth-grade class at Leon High School is planning a trip to Sea World on October 16.

Will you please send us information about the price of admission, the hours of operation, and the amount of time we should plan to spend there? We would also like to know about nearby places where we could lunch inexpensively.

Thank you for your help.

Sincerely yours,

Sharon Lee

Sharon Lee

Writing Practice 5: *A Letter of Request*

Select one of the following situations and write a letter asking for information or making some other request. When you finish, prepare your letter for mailing, using either an envelope or a rectangle drawn on a sheet of paper. Do not mail your letter unless you actually want the information.

1. Ask your state's tourist agency for information about campgrounds where you could stay during a hiking or biking trip this summer. You can find the name and address of the tourist agency in the library or telephone directory under state listings.

2. Write a letter to your local public library, inviting a librarian to speak to your English class on the facilities available in the public library. Decide on a time and date for the class.

3. Write to your local driver's license bureau, requesting information about getting a driver's manual. Find the address of the bureau in your local telephone directory.

A Letter of Adjustment

If an order is filled incorrectly or if you have received damaged merchandise, you should write a *letter of adjustment* as soon as possible. In the letter give specific information about the original order and about the problem with the merchandise.

You may also write a letter of adjustment when you are not satisfied with a product or service: a scratched record, a badly cooked meal in a restaurant, slow or discourteous service in a store. Give exact information about your dissatisfaction and state what you feel should be done in the situation, such as replacing a product or refunding your money. Most companies appreciate the opportunity to replace a defective product or improve their service, rather than lose a customer.

A letter of adjustment

23 North 6th Avenue
Gainesville, FL 32601
March 3, 1984

Highland Hobby Shop
893 Elmwood Street
Gadsden, AL 35904

Dear Sir or Madam:

In my letter of February 6, I ordered your model train catalogue at a price of $1.00. Yesterday, however, I received your stamp-collecting catalogue. I am returning the stamp catalogue. Please send me the model train catalogue.

Sincerely yours,

Jenny Wood

Jenny Wood

A Letter of Commendation

A very pleasant type of letter to write (and one that can have a powerful effect) is one complimenting a person or company on a good product or service. For example, television shows with small audiences are often replaced with other shows. Some very good programs in this situation have been saved because viewers wrote letters to television networks, telling how much they enjoyed the programs and encouraging the networks not to cancel the shows.

Writing Practice 6: *A Letter of Adjustment or Commendation*

Write a letter of adjustment or commendation for one of the following situations or for one of your own choice. You may write this letter as a follow-up to the letter you wrote in Writing Practice 4.

1. You very much like a television or radio program. Write to the station that broadcasts the program, briefly stating your reasons for liking it.

2. You very much dislike a television or radio commercial. Write to the station that broadcasts the commercial, briefly stating why you find it objectionable.

3. You recently renewed a subscription to your favorite magazine, but after seven weeks you have not received one issue. Write to the publisher.

4. The person who delivers your family newspaper has not once, in two years, failed to deliver the paper on time. Even when the weather is bad, your newspaper, carefully wrapped in plastic, arrives on time. Write to the circulation manager of the newspaper, commending your carrier.

5. You have a new person delivering your family newspaper. During the past three weeks your paper has been more than an hour late four times, and twice it was never delivered. Write to the circulation manager of the paper stating your complaint.

6. You ordered your favorite poster from Joe's Poster Shop, 1651 Richmond Avenue, Macon, GA 31201. Two days ago you received a different poster of a singer you do not like. Write to Joe's Poster Shop.

The Application Form

When you apply for a job, you may be asked to fill out an *application form*, a form used by businesses to get the information they need about a prospective employee. Most application forms ask for four kinds of information.

First is personal information: your name, address, and telephone number; the date and place of your birth; your parents' names and addresses. There may also be blanks for information about your physical characteristics, such as weight, height, and color of hair and eyes, and perhaps about your hobbies and interests.

Second is information about your education. Most application forms have spaces for you to write the names of schools you have attended and the dates when you attended them. There may also be spaces for you to write the subjects you studied and the grade average you earned.

A third kind of information is about your work experience: the names of people or companies you have worked for and how long you worked at each job. You may also have to write why you left each job. Finally, most application forms have spaces where you write information about people who can recommend you for the job. These people are the same references you may have included in your letter of application. You will be asked to state their names, addresses, and telephone numbers and perhaps how long they have known you.

The information you enter on an application form is important because it tells the employer whether or not you are qualified for the job. How you fill out the form is also important, since a messy form will leave the impression that you are somewhat careless.

To fill out an application form use a pen that does not skip or run. Try to avoid having to cross out answers. Be accurate. If you tend to forget dates, names, and addresses, write this information on a slip of paper and take it with you when you apply for a job.

Follow directions exactly. If the form says *Please print,* and you write your answers, the employer will not be impressed with your ability to follow directions. The following directions are typical ones you may encounter.

1. *Name*—The form may ask for your last name first. Put your last name in the space that says *Last Name* and your first name in the space that says *First Name.*

2. *Date of birth*—Check to see if there are separate spaces for month, day, and year of birth. If so, put the information in the proper spaces; otherwise you may write the date like this: *11/28/72*

3. *Address*—Check to see if there are separate spaces for house or apartment number, street, city, state, and ZIP code. If there are, put the items in their proper spaces.

4. *Work experience*—Many forms ask for last or present (most recent) job first. Write your first job first only if that is the only job you have ever had.

5. *Person to notify in case of emergency*—This is usually a parent or guardian.

6. *Signature*—Most application forms have a place for you to sign your name. Often this is the only part of a form to be handwritten. When you sign your name, you are stating that you have answered the questions honestly.

Writing Practice 7: *An Application Form*

On page 288 is a sample copy of an application form. Number a sheet of paper 1–18. On each line write the information called for in that section of the application. Write the information in the same order you would write it on the application form, as shown in the following examples. Do not write in this book.

1. *11/28/72   266-68-1446*
2. *Lowell   Steven   Mark*

Revising Business Writing

To revise business writing, check your letter or form against the following items. Proofread your letter or form in the same way you would any other kind of writing, using the Proofreader's Checklist at the back of this book.

Checklist for Revising Business Writing

1. Is the business letter brief, to the point, and courteous?

2. Does the letter of application include all the information an employer needs to know? Does the order or request letter include all the information needed to fill the order or to meet the request?

3. For an application form or a letter of application, are the names, addresses, and dates all correct? For an order or request letter, is the information included accurate?

4. Is the letter in the correct form for a business letter?

5. For an application form, were all the directions followed in completing the form?

An application form

APPLICATION FOR EMPLOYMENT

PERSONAL INFORMATION

1. DATE 5/20/84   SOCIAL SECURITY NUMBER 334-38-3151

2. NAME KUSKIE   JON   ALLEN
            Last   First   Middle

3. PRESENT ADDRESS 10226 ZENITH LANE   OMAHA   NEBRASKA 68154
                        Street   City   State

4. PERMANENT ADDRESS SAME AS ABOVE
                        Street   City   State

5. PHONE NO. 402-231-3376

6. DATE OF BIRTH 9/19/69 7. Height 5'6" Weight 138 lbs Color of Hair BROWN Color of Eyes BROWN

8. IF RELATED TO ANYONE IN OUR EMPLOY, STATE NAME AND DEPARTMENT   REFERRED BY MR. CHARLES SCHALZ

EMPLOYMENT DESIRED

9. POSITION SUMMER GROUNDS CREW DATE YOU CAN START 6/10/84 SALARY DESIRED 3.50/hr.

10. ARE YOU EMPLOYED NOW? YES   IF SO MAY WE INQUIRE OF YOUR PRESENT EMPLOYER? YES

11. EVER APPLIED TO THIS COMPANY BEFORE? NO   WHERE   WHEN

EDUCATION	NAME and LOCATION OF SCHOOL	YEARS ATTENDED	DATE GRADUATED	SUBJECTS STUDIED
12. GRAMMAR SCHOOL	JEFFERSON JR. HIGH BLOOMINGTON, MN	81-83	JUNE, 83	ACADEMIC
13. HIGH SCHOOL	LINCOLN HIGH SCHOOL OMAHA, NE	83-	—	ACADEMIC

FORMER EMPLOYERS (LIST BELOW LAST TWO EMPLOYERS, STARTING WITH LAST ONE FIRST)

DATE MONTH AND YEAR	NAME AND ADDRESS OF EMPLOYER	SALARY	POSITION	REASON FOR LEAVING
14. FROM 83 TO —	MRS. RICHARD LANCE 1225 N. WASHINGTON, OMAHA	3.50/hr	YARD WORK	NONE
15. FROM 81 TO 83	MINNEAPOLIS TRIBUNE MINNEAPOLIS, MN	2.00/hr	PAPER CARRIER	MOVED TO NEB.

REFERENCES: GIVE BELOW THE NAMES OF THREE PERSONS NOT RELATED TO YOU, WHOM YOU HAVE KNOWN AT LEAST ONE YEAR.

NAME	ADDRESS	BUSINESS	YEARS ACQUAINTED
16. 1. DR. CRAIG STEVENSON	208 DE KALB OMAHA, NE	VETERINARIAN	1
17. 2. MR. HOWARD DANNENBERG	535 S. FIFTH ST. OMAHA, NE	RETIRED	1
18. 3. MRS. GRETCHEN MUSICH	104 YORK LANE OMAHA, NE	BEAUTICIAN	1

Signature Jon A. Kuskie

Sentence Combining: Inserting Phrases and Clauses

Using the To + Verb Signal

For information on infinitives, see pages 500-503.

One of the uses of the (*to*) combination is to join *to* plus a verb to the base. The (*to + verb*) combination may appear at the beginning, middle, or end of the base sentence, as the following examples show.

Base: You are free (*to do*) *something*.
Insert: You go fishing. (*to + verb*)
Combined: You are free *to go fishing*.

Base: Diane urged him *something*.
Insert: He helps her. (*to + verb*)
Combined: Diane urged him *to help her*.

Notice that the verb in the insert sentence must sometimes change form to combine with *to*: *helps/to help*. Forms of *be*, such as *is*, *was*, *are*, change to *be*: *to be*.

Exercise 1: Using the To + Verb Signal

On a sheet of paper, combine the following sentence sets by using (*to + verb*). Study the example before you begin.

Example

a. I wanted *something*.
    I solve the problem quickly.
    I wanted to solve the problem quickly.

1. Ms. Donnelly meant for us (*to do*) *something*.
    We answer the question without hesitation.

2. *Something* is her greatest ambition.
    She becomes a tightrope walker.

3. Of course, we are happy *something*.
    We are selected for this great honor.

289

4. The signs warned us (to be) *something*.
   We are on the lookout for stray cattle on the highway.

5. Is it necessary (to do) *something*?
   One gets an education.

6. Chris considered Raoul *something*.
   Raoul is the candidate for this job.

7. *Something* would be an exciting experience, don't you think?
   One appears on a television game show.

8. The cars are sure (to do) *something*.
   The cars skid on the ice.

9. *Something* requires the player to have the ability (to do) *something*.
   A player wins at marbles.
   He or she smashes the opponent's glassies out of the ring.

10. *Something* is sure (to do) *something*.
    One cares too much about how one looks.
    It causes others some resentment.

A New Way to Use Two Familiar Combinations

For information on phrases, see pages 490-509.

In some kinds of sentences (*that*) and (*for*) may be used in the same way as (*to* + *verb*). Other words, such as *from* and *of*, often appear in the same manner that *for* does. Examine the sentences that follow to see how these new combinations work. Notice that in every case the (*that*) or (*for*) additions follow a describing word, such as *pleased, happy, excellent, fine,* and *afraid.*

Base:	Ms. Forsythe is happy.
Insert:	Vacation will soon be here. (*that*)
Combined:	Ms. Forsythe is happy *that vacation will soon be here.*

Base:	Worms are excellent.
Insert:	Worms catch catfish. (*for* + *-ing*)
Combined:	Worms are excellent *for catching catfish.*

Base:	Little children are sometimes afraid.
Insert:	They are left in the dark. (*of* + *-ing*)
Combined:	Little children are sometimes afraid *of being left in the dark.*

Exercise 2: *Using Familiar Combinations in a New Way*

On a sheet of paper, make the following combinations. Use signals where given. Study the example before you begin.

Example

a. The camel was terribly angry.
    It was not allowed to drink the water. (*that*)
    The camel was terribly angry that it was not allowed to drink the water.

1. The members of the group were excited.
    They had enough money to go on tour. (*that*)

2. A necklace is good.
    It dresses up a denim shirt. (*for* + *-ing*)

3. Alley cats are best.
    They catch mice. (*for* + *-ing*)
    They survive outside. (*,for* + *-ing*)
    They are good pets. (*,and* + *for* + *-ing*)

4. *Something* requires one (to do) *something*.
   One performs before the President. (*to + verb*)
   One requests an audition first. (*to + verb*)

5. You are welcome (to do) *something*.
   You visit the hospital. (*to + verb*)
   The doctor is pleased. (*,but*)
   You decided not to visit until next week. (*that*)

6. These brooms seem fine.
   Brooms sweep sidewalks.

7. My sister wanted *something*.
   She is an airplane pilot for a major corporation.

8. Inner tubes are fine.
   They slide down ice.

9. Light blue is best.
   It matches the fuchsia shades in this cloth.

10. The committee is happy.
    The publicity brought out such large crowds for the carnival.

Another Use of the -ing Signal

For information on participles, see pages 496-500.

Following a certain small group of verbs in English, *-ing* words can be used in this way:

I saw him *raiding* the supply closet.
I kept her *from raiding* the supply closet.

Huck found Jim *sitting* on the raft when he got back from shore.
Huck prevented Jim *from being* discovered by telling a lie.

Sheryl found the kitten *unraveling* the yarn.
Sheryl tried to keep the kitten *from unraveling* the yarn.

In an even more limited way you can use an *-ing* word following certain verb phrases. For example, you can say:

She just kept on *talking*.

He woke up *screaming*.

We sat *thinking* about what we had done.

Ziggy went on *humming* that same old tune.

The ring turned up *missing*.

Study the following examples to see how the combinations are made.

Base: I saw him (do) *something.*
Insert: He raids the supply closet. (*-ing*)
Combined: I saw him *raiding the supply closet.*

Base: Huck prevented Jim (from) *something* by telling a lie.
Insert: Jim is discovered. (*from + -ing*).
Combined: Huck prevented Jim *from being discovered* by telling a lie.

Exercise 3: *Using* -ing *in Another Way*

On a sheet of paper, make the following sentence combinations. Use signals where given. Study the example before you begin.

Example

a. He woke up (doing) *something.*
He screams. (*-ing*)
He woke up screaming.

1. We found our pet snake (doing) *something.*
It kills our white mice. (*-ing*)

2. Marlene caught her sister (doing) *something*.
   Her sister takes the perfume from the dresser. (*-ing*)

3. Mike liked (doing) *something*.
   He thinks up crazy new ideas. (*-ing*)
   He will settle for *something*. (*,but*)
   He will settle for using more serious ones. (*-ing*)

4. The commander spied Lasardo (doing) *something*.
   Lasardo spills the gunpowder along the walls of the fort. (*-ing*)
   He was unable to prevent Lasardo (from) *something*. (*;however*)
   Lasardo lights a match. (*-ing*)
   Lasardo sets off the explosion. (*and* + *-ing*)

5. Jeanne jumped up (doing) *something*.
   She shakes. (*-ing*)
   She saw the ape (doing) *something* through the window at her.
   (*when*)
   The ape peers. (*-ing*)
   She wondered *something*. (*,and*)
   She might prevent it (from) *something*. (*how*)
   It breaks in. (*from* + *-ing*)
   It carries her off. (*and* + *-ing*)

6. Two boys in leather jackets and sporting 1950s' hairstyles walked
   along (doing) *something*.
   They combed their slicked-back hair.

7. A large, red neon sign warned people (about) *something*.
   They walk on the damaged bridge.

8. Observers admired the artist (doing) *something*.
   The artist paints the storefront.

9. The cafeteria worker prevented me (from) *something*.
   I put too much meat on my tray.

10. The director advised us (against) *something*.
    We try to examine the model of King Kong.

A New Signal for Removing Words

For information on
phrases, see pages
490-509.

A signal for removing unneeded words from insert sentences is
an X marked through the words. In the longer combinations
in the following sections, too many X's would be confusing,
so underlining is used to indicate words that should remain in the
sentence combination. The following examples demonstrate how the
signal works.

Base: The tigers were snarling in defiance.

Insert: The tigers were <u>in the end cage</u>.

Combined: The tigers *in the end cage* were snarling in defiance.

Base: The old building has been here for a century.

Insert: It is <u>to be torn down tomorrow</u>.

Combined: The old building *to be torn down tomorrow* has been here for a century.

Base: San Diego has the most perfect climate of any place in the world.

Insert: San Diego is <u>my favorite city</u>.

Combined: San Diego, *my favorite city*, has the most perfect climate of any place in the world.

There are many sentence combinations that will require the use of the other signals you have learned, however. Look at the next two combinations and notice how they *differ* in makeup but are *alike* in meaning.

Base: The musician suffered a bad case of stage fright.

Insert: The musician was alone on stage for the first time. (*who*)

Combined:	The musician, *who was alone on stage for the first time,* suffered a bad case of stage fright.
Base:	The musician suffered a bad case of stage fright.
Insert:	The musician was <u>alone on stage for the first time</u>.
Combined:	The musician, *alone on stage for the first time,* suffered a bad case of stage fright.

Exercise 4: Combining Sentences in Various Ways

On a sheet of paper, combine the following sets of sentences. Use signals where given. When the underlining signal is given, insert the words so that they make sense in the combined sentence. Consider the first sentence in each set the base sentence. Study the example before you begin.

Example

   a. *Something* is a good bet.
      Life exists elsewhere. (*it . . . that*)
      Life exists <u>in the universe</u>.

     It is a good bet that life exists elsewhere in the universe.

1. My grandfather told jokes.
   He was a genuine character. (*who*)
   The jokes were <u>corny</u>.

   The jokes were <u>about his friends</u>.

2. *The Blood Oranges* is by John Hawkes.
   The Blood Oranges is <u>a strange title for a novel</u>.

3. The girl smiled.
   The girl <u>realized she had won</u>. (*-ing*)

   A moment later her smile faded. (*;*)
   The girl burst into tears. (*and*)

4. Fog settled in over the bay.
   Its thick darkness lay heavily over the village. (*,-ing*)
   Its thick darkness hid the comings and goings of people. (*,-ing*)
   The people were <u>anxious to find early passage out of the port</u>.

5. There stood Malcom.
    His hands were twisting the end of his shirt. (,)
    His toes were turned in. (,)
    His face was as red as a beet. (,and)

6. Yim's problem was *something*.
    He was to find a thread somewhere.
    The thread would be exactly the same color as his pants.

7. The captives pleaded with their captors.
    The captives were exhausted from the chase.
    The captors were steely-eyed.

8. Tony insisted *something*.
    He would drive the road to Nantucket.
    The road was long.
    His twin brother preferred *something*.
    They take a train.

9. The program told *something*.
    The program was special.
    Explorers do *something*.
    Explorers prevent *something*.
    Explorers collapse in weather.
    The weather is sub-zero.

10. *Something* forced her (to do) *something*.
    Caroline realized *something*.
    She would have to learn *something*.
    She cooks.
    She would die of starvation.
    She takes cooking lessons.
    The lessons are from a chef.
    The chef is famous.
    The chef is French.

Writing Practice: *Using Sentence-Combining Skills*

Choose one or more of the writing exercises on the following page. With each suggestion is a short list of sentence-combining skills you might find useful.

1. *Compare or Contrast:*
   Two sports you enjoy
   Two people whom you know very well
   Two schools you have attended
   Ways to spend a rainy afternoon
   A subject of your own choice

   Try to include in your comparison several of these sentence-combining skills:

   Combining with (*which*) or (*that*)
   Combining with (*it . . . how*), (*when*), or (*how long*)
   Combining with (*pos + -ing*)
   Combining with (*join*)
   Combining with (*with*)

2. *Describe:*
   A recent illness
   A place you know very well
   An event you recently attended, such as a game, a concert, or a play
   A very young or a very old person whom you know
   A subject of your own choice

   Try to include in your description several of these sentence-combining skills:

   Adding a series to the end of a sentence base
   Combining with (*-ing*)
   Combining with (*who*), (*what*), (*where*), (*why*), or (*how*)
   Combining with (*or*), (*and*), or (*but*)
   Combining with (*colon*), (*dash*), or (*parens*)

3. *Explain:*
   How to change the oil in a car
   How to use a simple calculator
   How to play backgammon
   How to administer CPR
   A subject of your own choice

   Try to include in your explanation several of these sentence-combining skills:

   Combining with (*how to*) or (*when to*)
   Combining with (*it . . . that*)
   Combining with (*the fact that*) or (*that*)
   Combining with (*who*), (*what*), (*why*), (*where*), or (*how*)
   Combining with (*because*), (*for*), (*then*), or (*although*)

2
Grammar and Usage

12 Nouns

Understanding Nouns

Nouns are words that name. There are three ways you can identify a noun: by its definition, by the features that distinguish it from other parts of speech, and by the classes into which nouns can be grouped. In the following sections you will study and practice each of these ways to identify nouns.

Defining Nouns

A *noun* is usually defined as the name of a person, a place, a thing, or an idea.

Joshua walked slowly and carefully.	[name of a person]
Chicago can be very cold and windy.	[name of a place]
The old *house* remained vacant.	[name of a thing]
True *beauty* lies within us all.	[name of an idea]

Exercise 1: *Identifying Nouns by Definition*

Write the sentences on the next page, underlining all nouns. Above each noun write whether it names a person, a place, a thing, or an idea.

Examples

a. Janet reads stories about Ireland.

    person   thing   place
    Janet reads stories about Ireland.

b. The zookeeper had a genuine love for animals.

      person   idea   thing
    The zookeeper had a genuine love for animals.

1. Kathleen enjoys science and geography.

2. Have you seen the band shell in Topeka?

3. In psychology we read how important it is for a parent to show love to a small child.

4. The Garcias recently moved to Cleveland.

5. Geronimo was a great leader of the Apache.

6. The coach said that fairness was more important than winning a trophy.

7. Kiyoko grows strawberries on her farm near Sacramento.

8. Seattle and Annapolis both have waterfronts, Seattle being off the Pacific and Annapolis off the Atlantic.

9. Muhammad Ali was perhaps the greatest boxer in the history of the sport.

10. Jack expected a little sympathy from Jill after his nasty fall.

Finding Nouns by Their Features

The following four features can help you identify nouns. A word that is a noun will usually have at least one of these features, and some nouns have all four.

1. Nouns often follow determiners.

Determiners—words like *a, an, the, some, this, that, these, those, his, her, my, many, one, two*—often appear before nouns. The most common determiners—*a, an,* and *the*—are also called *articles.*

some people	the Andersons
his problem	an orange
this neighborhood	those hopes

2. Nouns may be singular or plural.

Most nouns have both a *singular* and a *plural* form. The plural form is used for nouns that name more than one person, place, thing, or idea.

Singular	*Plural*
one table	three tables
one girl	six girls
one child	four children
one wolf	several wolves
one baby	two babies
one watch	many watches

3. Nouns may show possession.

Both singular and plural nouns have possessive forms that are shown by the addition of an apostrophe (') and -s or by the addition of an apostrophe only. The possessive form shows either the ownership of one noun by another or the relationship of one noun to another.

The notebook that *Kim* owns is brand new. *Kim's* notebook is brand new.	[ownership]
The windshield of the *car* had been broken. The *car's* windshield had been broken.	[relationship]

4. Nouns may be formed with a noun suffix, such as *-ation*, *-ism*, *-ment*, *-ness*, or *-ance*.

Many nouns are formed by the addition of a *noun suffix*, or ending, to a *stem*. Thus, a word such as *good* becomes the noun *goodness* when the noun suffix *-ness* is added to the stem. The endings of many words give helpful clues that the words are nouns.

relax + ation	→	relaxation
patriot + ism	→	patriotism
govern + ment	→	government
happy + ness	→	happiness
attend + ance	→	attendance

Exercise 2: Identifying Nouns by Their Determiners

Many of the nouns in the following paragraph are preceded by a determiner. Write the paragraph, underlining each determiner and the noun that follows it.

a. On our way to the game, we saw an accident involving several cars.

On our way to the game, we saw an accident involving several cars.

Some folks say that house is haunted. Before I set one foot in it, I'd like to know why my friends hear those noises in the night. And what about the lights? Many evenings when the moon is full, our neighbors have seen a lamp moving by itself from the parlor to the hallways, up the stairs, and through the attic. Those stories give me the willies.

Classifying Nouns

Nouns can be grouped into two main classes: *common nouns* and *proper nouns*.

Nouns that name specific persons, places, things, or ideas are called *proper nouns*. All other nouns are called *common nouns*.

A good *teacher* must be understanding.

The noun *teacher* is a common noun because it does not name a specific person.

Mr. Cruz is very understanding.

The noun *Mr. Cruz* is a proper noun because it names a specific person. Proper nouns are capitalized; common nouns are not.

The *city* was cool and damp.	[common noun]
San Francisco can be cool and damp.	[proper noun]
We all gazed at the *monument*.	[common noun]
We all gazed at the *Washington Monument*.	[proper noun]
The *mayor* is a clever *politician*.	[common nouns]
Mayor Byrne is a lifelong *Democrat*.	[proper nouns]

Many proper nouns are *compound nouns* because they are made up of more than one word, as in *Anne Morrow Lindbergh* (one woman) or *Kansas City, Kansas* (one place). Some common nouns also consist of more than one word, as in *fire engine* (one thing) or *landlord* (one person). Some compound nouns are written as separate words (*Julian Bond, high school*). Some are written with a hyphen between words (*father-in-law, cave-in*), and some are written as one word (*airplane, wristwatch*). Consult your dictionary if you are not certain how to write a compound noun.

Exercise 3: *Identifying Nouns by Class*

Write the following sentences, underlining each noun. Then write *C* above each common noun and *P* above each proper noun. Be certain to underline the entire noun if it is a compound.

Example

 a. Many years ago Aunt Ann studied law at Harvard University.

      C   P   C   P

 Many years ago Aunt Ann studied law at Harvard University.

1. The distance between Austin and San Antonio is almost 115 kilometers.

2. Our car had quite a road test during the tour of Yellowstone National Park that Uncle Howie planned for us.

3. The song called "Happy Birthday" was written by two sisters named Mildred and Patty Hill.

4. The flight of the spacecraft *Voyager I* revealed that Jupiter, like Saturn, has rings.

5. If you like baseball, go to Wrigley Field and watch the Chicago Cubs try to wallop the Cincinnati Reds.

6. The written form of the Cherokee language was made possible by the syllabary invented by Sequoya, who lived in Tennessee.

7. I listened to Ms. Ramos read "The Gift of the Magi," a short story by O. Henry, whose real name was William Sydney Porter.

8. When Snow White wakened in that dollhouse in the forest, she saw seven tiny men, whose names were Happy, Doc, Sneezy, Bashful, Grumpy, Dopey, and Sleepy.

9. The capitals of Czechoslovakia, Hungary, and Poland are Prague, Budapest, and Warsaw, all behind the so-called Iron Curtain.

10. The social worker Jane Addams founded a settlement house named Hull House in Chicago, and she was awarded the Nobel Peace Prize in the early thirties.

Review: Understanding Nouns

The following paragraphs from the book *A History of Women in America* describe some of the hardships women faced on the frontier. The first five nouns in the selection are underlined. Using what you have learned in the preceding sections, identify thirty additional nouns, listing them on a sheet of paper numbered 1–30. In parentheses after each noun, indicate the line on which it appears within the selection.

Example

a. women (line 1)

1.   Women drove wagons, fought prairie fires, forded streams
2. in icy water, and walked day after day across the country in
3. burning heat, in rain storms, and in early freezes. They did
4. "woman's work" as well, tending campsites and preparing three
5. meals a day. They faced births and deaths and illnesses along
6. the route. Sometimes the men died, leaving women and chil-
7. dren to continue on alone.
8.   One traveler described the scene of such a frontier death
9. on the Great Plains in 1852. "An open bleak prairie, the cold
10. wind howling overhead, bearing with it the mournful tones of
11. that deserted woman; a new grave, a woman and three children
12. sitting nearby; a girl of fourteen summers [years] walking round
13. in a circle, wringing her hands and calling upon her dead
14. parent; a boy of twelve, sitting upon the wagon tongue sobbing
15. aloud; a strange man placing a rude headboard at the head of
16. the grave."[1]

Applying What You Know

Select a paragraph at least five sentences long from a magazine, newspaper, or book you have read and identify the nouns, using the various ways you have learned in the previous sections. List the nouns on a sheet of paper and be prepared to say how you identified each one. Did you determine that it named, that it had one or more features of a noun, or that it belonged to one of the major noun classes?

[1]From *A History of Women in America* by Carol Hymowitz and Michaele Weissman. Copyright © 1978 by the Anti-Defamation League of B'nai B'rith. Reprinted by permission of Bantam Books, Inc. and the Anti-Defamation League of B'nai B'rith.

Using Nouns

The following sections will give you practice in forming the plurals of nouns, including compound nouns. You will also learn how to write the possessive forms of nouns, and you will learn how to determine which nouns are proper and must be capitalized.

Forming Regular Plurals

The plurals of most nouns are formed by adding the suffixes -*s* or -*es*. These are called *regular plurals*.

Form the regular plurals of most nouns by adding the suffix -*s*.

Singular	*Plural*
one basket	two baskets
one school	several schools
one house	many houses

Form the regular plurals of nouns ending in *s*, *sh*, *ch*, *x*, or *z* by adding the suffix -*es*.

Singular	*Plural*
one dress	three dresses
one wish	several wishes
a match	many matches
one box	some boxes
a buzz	four buzzes

Form the plurals of nouns ending in *o* preceded by a vowel by adding the suffix -*s*; form the plurals of nouns ending in *o* preceded by a consonant by adding the suffix -*es*.

Singular	*Plural*
one radio	three radios
one patio	many patios
one hero	several heroes
a potato	two potatoes

Exception: The plurals of nouns that end in *o* and have to do with music take only the suffix -*s*.

solos   pianos   trios

Exercise 4: *Forming Regular Plurals*

All the nouns in the following sentences have been *italicized*. Write the sentences and change each singular noun to its plural form by adding *-s* or *-es*. Underline the nouns that you make plural.

Examples

  a. The *cat* made the *scratch* on our *door*.
     The cats made the scratches on our doors.

  b. We put the *box* and *suitcase* on the *train*.
     We put the boxes and suitcases on the trains.

1. The *player* and the *coach* argued with the *referee*.

2. The *fox* and the *coyote* paced endlessly in the *cage*.

3. The *acrobat* drew the *crowd* to the *circus*.

4. Bring the *pass* to the *booth* before the *game* to get your *ticket*.

5. The *rider* in the *rodeo* had the *steer* roped and tied as soon as the *chute* opened.

6. The *sting* of the *lash* made the *captive* row the *boat* quickly past the *fortress*.

7. The *crystal* of the *watch* broke because the *clerk* chose the wrong shipping *box*.

8. The *tomato* on the *vine* will become tomorrow's *sauce* and *stew*.

9. After the *march* the *band* will play either the *waltz* or the *polka* for the *crowd*.

10. When the *night watch* bedded down in the *arroyo*, the *eye* of the *lynx* gazed steadily into the *wash*.

Forming Irregular Plurals

The plurals of some nouns are formed by a spelling change other than the addition of the suffixes *-s* or *-es*. These are called *irregular plurals*.

Form the plurals of most nouns that end in *y* by changing the *y* to an *i* and adding *-es*.

Singular	*Plural*
one lady	many ladies
one country	two countries
one pony	several ponies

Form the plurals of nouns that end in *y* preceded by a vowel by simply adding -*s*.

Singular	*Plural*
one day	three days
one delay	frequent delays
a journey	some journeys

If you are unsure about which plural ending to use with a noun ending in *y*, check your dictionary for the proper spelling.

Form some irregular plurals by changing a vowel sound.

Singular	*Plural*
foot	feet
goose	geese
man	men
mouse	mice
tooth	teeth
woman	women

Form the plurals of many words ending in *fe* and sometimes *f* by changing the *f* to a *v* and adding the suffix -*es*.

Singular	*Plural*	*Singular*	*Plural*
calf	calves	self	selves
elf	elves	sheaf	sheaves
half	halves	shelf	shelves
knife	knives	thief	thieves
leaf	leaves	wife	wives
life	lives	wolf	wolves
loaf	loaves		

Form the plurals of some words ending in *f* or *fe* by simply adding the suffix -*s*.

Singular	*Plural*
safe	safes
gulf	gulfs
belief	beliefs
reef	reefs

Some words have the same form for singular and plural.

We saw a *sheep* in the meadow.	[singular]
We saw three *sheep* in the meadow.	[plural]

The following words are included in this group.

bass	moose
carp	pike
deer	salmon
fish	sheep
grouse	trout

Use your dictionary to check plural forms with which you may be unfamiliar.

The plurals of some words fit no pattern. If you are unsure about the spelling of a plural, look up the singular form of the word in your dictionary. Its plural will be given after the singular spelling, usually with the abbreviation *pl* for *plural*, if the plural is irregular.

child n. pl **chil-dren**

hip·po·pot·a·mus n. pl **-mus·es** or **-mi**

ra·di·us n. pl **ra·dii** also **ra·di·us·es**

Exercise 5: *Forming Irregular Plurals*

The *italicized* nouns in the following sentences all have irregular plurals. Write each sentence, changing each *italicized* noun to its proper plural form. Underline the nouns you change.

Example

a. The *woman* placed the *knife* in the drawer.
   The <u>women</u> placed the <u>knives</u> in the drawer.

1. Look at the *hoof* of the newborn *calf.*

2. Each took *half* of the *loaf* of banana bread.

3. You use the *knife* this way to bone the *fish.*

4. When the *wolf* howled, the *sheep* bleated for help.

5. If you put your *foot* in your mouth, you're likely to knock out your *tooth.*

6. When the *leaf* fell and the wild *goose* flew, the *sheaf* of wheat frightened the *child* at night.

7. The *mouse* feared the carving *knife* of the farm *wife*.

8. Ask *yourself* whether the *elf* painted your garage *roof*.

9. The *thief* left only the *shelf* of smoked *salmon* and striped *bass*.

10. Our *canary* swallowed the *cranberry*.

Forming the Plurals of Compound Nouns

Form the plural of a compound noun that is written as one word as you would form the plural of the last word of the compound.

Singular	Plural
one drugstore	two drugstores
one teaspoonful	three teaspoonfuls
a matchbox	several matchboxes
this wristwatch	those wristwatches
one firefly	many fireflies
one toothbrush	both toothbrushes

Form the plural of a compound noun that is written as separate words or as hyphenated words by making plural the most important word in the compound.

Singular	Plural
one tennis ball	two tennis balls
this high school	these high schools
one mother-in-law	two mothers-in-law
our attorney-general	both attorneys-general

With some compound nouns it is difficult to tell which is the main word (*merry-go-round, eight-year-old, drive-in*). The plurals of these compound nouns are formed by adding the suffix *-s* to the last word (*merry-go-rounds, eight-year-olds, drive-ins*).

Exercise 6: Forming Compound Noun Plurals

Each of the following sentences contains one or more compound nouns, each in its singular form. Write the sentences, changing each compound noun to its plural form. Underline the compound nouns you make plural.

Examples

a. Up sprang the jack-in-the-box.
   Up sprang the jack-in-the-boxes.

b. Juan lent the sportcoat to his brother-in-law.
   Juan lent the sportcoats to his brothers-in-law.

1. The football sailed over the goalpost.

2. The countdown had been timed by the stopwatch.

3. Ask your sister-in-law to help you plan the housewarming.

4. Did you add the tablespoonful of raisins to the trail mix?

5. Their two-year-old hid the golf ball from the baby-sitter.

6. The student wrote the compound noun on the chalkboard.

7. The attorney-general congratulated the runner-up.

8. The delegate-at-large entered the convention hall.

9. The letter carrier tripped over the two-by-four lying on the sidewalk.

10. As the merry-go-round turned, the newlywed watched.

Forming the Possessives of Nouns

The *possessive form* of a noun shows ownership or the relationship of one noun to another. One possessive noun can do the job of several words in a sentence.

The car *owned by Tom Garcia* saves gas.
Tom Garcia's car saves gas.

The *lights of the city* shone in the valley below.
The *city's lights* shone in the valley below.

Form the possessive of a singular noun by adding an apostrophe (') and an -s.

Noun	*Possessive Form*
a novel by *Dickens*	*Dickens's* novel (*Dickens' novel* is also correct.)
the shoes of the *boy*	the *boy's* shoes
the son of the *boss*	the *boss's* son

Form the possessive of a plural noun ending in *s* by adding an apostrophe only.

Noun	Possessive Noun
the team made up of *boys*	the *boys'* team
the covers of several *books*	the *books'* covers
the hems of the *dresses*	the *dresses'* hems

Form the possessive of a plural noun not ending in *s* by adding an apostrophe and an *-s.*

Noun	Possessive Noun
the hides of the *cattle*	the *cattle's* hides
the chattering of *teeth*	the *teeth's* chattering
the zoo for *children*	the *children's* zoo

Exercise 7: *Forming Noun Possessives*

Write the following sentences, supplying the possessive form of each noun given in parentheses. Check whether the noun is singular or plural before you form its possessive. Underline the possessive nouns.

Examples

a. Is that your _____ car in the _____ driveway? (mother, Smiths)
   Is that your mother's car in the Smiths' driveway?

b. Lay _____ socks in the _____ top drawer. (Ross, dresser)
   Lay Ross's socks in the dresser's top drawer.

1. Just smell that _____ aroma! (flower)

2. Do you have the _____ permission to be in _____ class? (principal, Ms. Ling)

3. Today I'm wearing _____ letter sweater, which is better than any of the other _____ letter sweaters. (David, boys)

4. This is _____ apron for barbecuing. (Mom)

5. The _____ dog is lying in _____ flowerbed. (Cavanaughs, Mrs. Rodriguez)

6. If one _____ buzzing bothers you, imagine ten _____ buzzing. (fly, flies)

7. The _____ jumper was designed like the other _____ jumpers. (child, children)

8. The _____ picture isn't coming in very clear at all because of the _____ interference. (television, shortwave radio)

9. Did Tommy raise the handlebars on the _____ bicycles? (twins)

10. _____ pockets were full of pennies, and _____ pockets were full of holes. (Uncle Sid, Uncle Les)

Capitalizing Proper Nouns

Nouns that name specific persons, places, or things are *proper nouns* and are always capitalized.

In addition to the guidelines for capitalization that follow, there are complete rules in Chapter 25.

Capitalize the names of specific persons, places, and things.

Common Noun	Proper Noun
that man	Andrew Hatcher
our town	Joliet, Illinois
my red sled	Fearless Flyer

Capitalize all of the important words in the name of a specific building, landmark, or institution.

Note: Unimportant words (the articles *a, an,* and *the* and prepositions or conjunctions of fewer than five letters) are not usually capitalized.

Common Noun	Proper Noun
this building	the Library of Congress
that monument	the Statue of Liberty
our high school	Eleanor Roosevelt High School
my college	the University of Wisconsin

Capitalize the first word and all of the important words in the title of a book, periodical, poem, story, song, movie, or television series.

Common Noun	Proper Noun
Eliot's novel	*The Mill on the Floss*
our newspaper	the *St. Louis Post-Dispatch*
	but
	The New York Times
my magazine	*People* magazine
Markham's poem	"The Man with a Hoe"
Howe's song	"The Battle Hymn of the Republic"
Forbes' short story	"Mama and the Graduation Present"
Spielberg's movie	*Close Encounters of the Third Kind*
Lear's TV series	*All in the Family*

Note: The titles of longer works, such as a novel, periodical, movie, or continuing television series are *italicized* in print and underlined in handwriting. The titles of shorter works are placed in quotation marks.

Note: Unless it is part of a title, the word *the* is not capitalized before the title of a periodical or book, just as the words *magazine* and *newspaper* are not capitalized.

> *Newsweek* magazine
> the *St. Louis Post-Dispatch* newspaper

Capitalize the name of a team, an organization, a business firm, or a government body.

Common Noun	Proper Noun
our team	the San Francisco Giants
my club	the Girl Scouts of America
my parents' store	Flynn's Hardware
the agency	the Department of Health and Human Services

Capitalize names of national origins and religions.

Common Noun	Proper Noun
a religion	Buddhism
a native American	an Oglala Sioux
our neighbors	the Mexicans

The rules for capitalization in Chapter 25 of this book will help you with specific capitalization problems.

Exercise 8: Capitalizing Proper Nouns

Write the following sentences and capitalize the proper nouns according to the rules for capitalization. Underline the proper nouns that appear in *italics*. Circle the capital letters you use.

Example

a. My friend jean and I enjoyed *star wars* so much that we saw it first in louisville, kentucky, and then saw it again 570 kilometers away in cleveland, ohio.

My friend (J)ean and I enjoyed (S)tar (W)ars so much that we saw it first in (L)ouisville, (K)entucky, and then saw it again 570 kilometers away in (C)leveland, (O)hio.

1. While jennifer and kevin were in springfield, illinois, they visited the home of abraham and mary todd lincoln, where the young lincolns, robert, willy, and tad, grew up.

2. My friend kurt johnson attended amundsen high school on north damen avenue in chicago, illinois. While a student there, he was a member of the national honor society.

3. We saw grant's tomb on riverside drive in new york city after watching the ice skaters at rockefeller center across the street from radio city music hall.

4. Every morning the *los angeles times* is delivered to our home at 16511 chula vista in huntington beach, california.

5. We read "the story of an eyewitness" by jack london, an account of the earthquake and fire that leveled san francisco.

6. I was lent a copy of pearl buck's *the good earth* by the topeka public library.

7. We always watch dan rather on the evening news to see what may be happening anywhere in the world from albania to zambia.

8. The fans gave a mighty roar when the cincinnati reds defeated the atlanta braves 7–6 at riverfront stadium.

9. The sanchez family drove the 1,100 kilometers from tulsa, oklahoma, to new orleans, louisiana, to see jackson square in the french quarter.

10. Many of the hopi live on mesas not far from taos, new mexico.

Using Proper Nouns and Common Nouns

Some nouns may be either common or proper, depending upon their use in sentences. You need to determine which way the noun is used to know whether it should be capitalized.

Common Nouns	*Proper Nouns*
My favorite *uncle*	is *Uncle Carlos*.
The *mayor* of Sedalia	is *Mayor Lillian Jessup*.
We drove *northwest*	to see the great *Northwest*.
My only *aunt* who jogs	is my *Aunt Eleanor*.
	or
	Oh please, *Aunt*, take me along!

Capitalize a title only when it is used as part of a name or in place of a name.

I'll speak to *Judge Brady* about your case.

Excuse me, *Judge*, may I speak with you for a moment?

On what floor will I find most of the *judges?*

Capitalize words showing family relationship only when used as part of a person's name or in place of a name.

Please meet *Uncle Herman*.

May we visit *Grandma* and *Grandpa Hernandez?*

I have eight *cousins* on *Mother's* side of the family.

Capitalize geographical sections of the country but not directions.

The *Northwest* in autumn is breathtaking!

Austin is *northwest* of San Antonio.

We drove *west* to Portland to our new home in the *West*.

Exercise 9: Capitalizing Proper Nouns

Write the following sentences, capitalizing the proper nouns. Underline the nouns you capitalize.

Example

a. I invited aunt deborah and cousin marc to my bar mitzvah.
   I invited <u>Aunt Deborah</u> and <u>Cousin Marc</u> to my bar mitzvah.

1. One of my aunts, aunt sue, teaches at wayne state university.

2. You'll have to take that up with representative joan smith.

3. Did president jackson serve one term or two?

4. The ex-wife of senator john warner is the actress elizabeth taylor.

5. Having grown up in the east, I found it hard to go without an egg cream in the midwest.

6. I present to you united states ambassador shirley temple black.

7. As we drove east across nebraska, we tried to remember whether its capital is omaha or lincoln.

8. Did uncle rich ask if grandmother would be spending her vacation in the south this year?

9. I want to thank you, mayor, for this wonderful welcome to des moines.

10. When her term ended, representative barbara jordan accepted a position at the university of texas in austin.

Review: Using Nouns

Each of the following sentences is vague and general, partly because only common nouns are used. Write each of the sentences, rewording them and adding proper nouns. Be sure to capitalize the proper nouns.

Example

a. My friend and I wish we could go somewhere.
   Bobby Meyers and I wish we could go to Sea World.

1. Three of us from school went to the museum.

2. This letter is from a relative of mine who lives in a city in another state.

3. If I could be a movie star, I'd be the star of that picture we saw on television the other night.

4. I guess you know that in our state we have this governor and two senators.

5. I've got a favorite short story by a quite famous author.

6. Somebody in our house reads the newspaper or some magazine or other, but I'd rather watch my favorite show on television.

7. There are foreign countries I'd like to visit.

8. If I could see my favorite team play on their home field, I'd ask the principal to excuse me from classes at my school.

9. One member of my family knows about foods and customs from another country because our family hasn't always lived here.

10. My friend is religious and worships at a place here in town.

Writing Focus: *Using Specific Nouns in Writing*

Good writers use specific nouns to paint a clear picture for readers. For example, the noun *collie* is more specific than the noun *dog*. *Tulips* and *daffodils* are more specific than *flowers*. As much as possible, use exact nouns to make your writing more precise, informative, and clear.

Assignment: *Describing a Country*

Pretend that you live in an imaginary country of your own invention. You have just landed a job writing the copy for a brochure advertising your country for prospective tourists. In the brief brochure, you want to describe your country in as much detail as possible. Many questions that might be answered through the copy occur to you. What is the name of your country? Where is it located? What type of terrain does it have? What is the capital city like? Is the predominant way of life rural or urban? What features of your country make it a particularly desirable place to visit?

Think about the preceding questions, and write one or more well-developed paragraphs about your imaginary country. The purpose of your writing will be to describe your country as vividly as possible so that your audience of prospective tourists will want to visit. Your work will be evaluated for effective use of specific nouns.

Use the steps on the next page to complete this assignment.

A. Prewriting

Using the preceding questions to stimulate your thinking, make a word cluster that describes your imaginary country. If necessary, review the section on clustering in Chapter 1. Write the name of your country in the center of the cluster. Around the name, add words and phrases that describe the country. Connect any that are related, such as physical features, for example. From your word cluster, choose the items that you will highlight in your brochure. List these items in a logical order.

B. Writing

Use your list to write one or more paragraphs for your brochure describing the imaginary country. Start with a topic sentence that makes an important general statement about your country. Then add details from your list to support this main idea. As your write, use specific nouns to make your description precise. Create such a vivid picture of your country that tourists will flock there.

C. Postwriting

Use the following checklist to revise your work.

1. Does each paragraph have a clear topic sentence?

2. Does each supporting sentence relate to the topic?

3. Are enough specific details included?

4. Are the details grouped together in a logical and effective way?

5. Are specific nouns used effectively to make the writing precise?

Proofread your work using the Proofreader's Checklist at the back of the book. If appropriate, share your writing with your classmates by actually producing the brochure of your country using illustrations and your description.

13 Pronouns

Understanding Pronouns

Pronouns help make language more versatile and less repetitive. With only nouns, language would look and sound like this:

> Ms. Reyas asked Mr. Jones if Mr. Jones would help Ms. Reyas restore Ms. Reyas' old apartment. Mr. Jones said Mr. Jones would enjoy helping Ms. Reyas restore the apartment.

Instead of repeating so many nouns you can replace them with pronouns to make your writing more efficient and direct:

> Ms. Reyas asked Mr. Jones if *he* would help *her* restore *her* old apartment. Mr. Jones said that *he* would enjoy helping *her* restore *it*.

By learning to understand and use pronouns, you can make your writing clearer and more interesting.

Defining Pronouns

A *pronoun* is usually defined as a word that takes the place of a noun or another pronoun.

A pronoun refers to a specific noun or pronoun, called an *antecedent*. Antecedents usually come before the pronoun.

> Allison finished the *book* and returned *it* to the library.
> [*It* refers to *book*; *book* is the antecedent.]

> Most *shoppers* were using *their* charge cards.
> [*Their* refers to *shoppers*; *shoppers* is the antecedent.]

Sometimes, an antecedent follows its pronoun.

> Because *he* was honest, *Gallagher* returned the money.

> When *they* arrived at the bus station, the *Nelsons* still had to buy tickets.

A single pronoun can replace several nouns in a sentence.

Oranges, pears, and *peaches* supply energy, for *they* contain natural sugar.
[*They* refers to *oranges, pears,* and *peaches.*]

Sometimes, a pronoun replaces a word group that functions as a noun.

The *lack of money, which* sometimes bothered Joan, did not affect Alice.

A single pronoun can be used in place of an entire sentence.

Jamie thought the lion was tame. That was a mistake.

Exercise 1: Identifying Pronouns

Write the following sentences, circling each pronoun and underlining its antecedent.

Examples

a. Sharon enjoys hiking, but she doesn't care for camping.

Sharon enjoys hiking, but (she) doesn't care for camping.

b. The vacuum cleaner is a lemon; it has no suction.

The vacuum cleaner is a lemon; (it) has no suction.

1. The horse was so wild that it threw the rider.

2. Nicole wanted an A, so she studied hard.

3. Miguel wants to be an army officer, so he is attending West Point.

4. Robert likes people who are honest.

5. Thousands of people were killed in the great Chinese earthquake of 1976. That is so sad!

6. Since she wanted to run for the Senate, Nora Campbell made many speeches.

7. *Tom Sawyer, Little Women, The Heart of a Dog*—these are treasured books.

8. The students read the instructions but found them difficult to follow.

9. Take the essays home and read them.

10. Jay found the flies annoying. They are such pesky critters.

Grouping Pronouns by Classes

Pronouns can be grouped into seven main classes: *personal, possessive, reflexive, indefinite, interrogative, relative,* and *demonstrative.*

Personal Pronouns

A special group of pronouns allows speakers to refer to themselves; to the people to whom they are speaking; or to the people, places, objects, or ideas about whom they are speaking. The pronouns in this group, called *personal pronouns,* have different singular and plural forms.

Singular	*Plural*
I	we
me	us
you	you
he/she	they
him/her	them
it	they/them

When speakers refer to themselves, they use the *first-person pronouns:*

Singular	*Plural*
I drink milk.	*We* drink milk.
The cow kicked *me.*	The cow kicked *us.*

When speakers refer to other people, they use *second-person pronouns:*

You drink milk.	*You* are all drinking milk.
The cow kicked *you.*	The cow kicked both of *you.*

Speakers use *third-person pronouns* when speaking about other people, places, or objects:

He *She* } drinks milk. *It*	*They* drink milk.

The cow kicked { *him.*
 her.
 it.   The cow kicked *them.*

Exercise 2: *Identifying Personal Pronouns*

Write the following sentences, underlining the personal pronouns in each.

Examples

a. Yim tuned the car, and he listened to the motor purr.
   Yim tuned the car, and <u>he</u> listened to the motor purr.

b. Anna and Lisa went to the circus, but they didn't see Tanya the elephant.
   Anna and Lisa went to the circus, but <u>they</u> didn't see Tanya the elephant.

1. Alex couldn't get into the movie theater because he was wearing a swim suit and fins.

2. He was very annoyed at the management.

3. How could they do such a thing to him?

4. Suzie told him that he was being foolish, but he didn't listen.

5. "I wanted to see the movie," she said, "but it might be over by the time we finish dinner."

6. He wanted a salad, and she wanted a sandwich.

7. "Where can we eat?" Suzie asked. "Can you think of a restaurant that will let us in?"

8. Poor Alex. Remember, he was still wearing the swim suit. Poor Suzie. She had a new dress made especially for her.

9. No restaurant would let them in, and they were getting hungrier by the minute.

10. You can imagine her anger when Alex said, "Here I am, all dressed up with no place to go!"

Possessive Forms of Personal Pronouns

Like the nouns that they replace, personal pronouns have possessive forms; these may be either singular or plural.

Singular	Plural
my/mine	our/ours
your	your/yours
his	
her/hers	their/theirs
its	

The possessive forms of personal pronouns may be used in two ways: to replace a possessive noun and stand in front of the noun that is possessed, or to stand alone in place of a possessive noun.

Miyaro's car is expensive.
Her car is expensive.
[*Her* is a possessive pronoun replacing *Miyaro's* and modifying *car.*]

The expensive car is *Miyaro's.*
The expensive car is *hers.*
[*Hers* is a possessive pronoun replacing *Miyaro's.*]

Unlike possessive nouns, possessive pronouns are not spelled with apostrophes ('). The possessive pronouns *theirs, yours, hers, ours,* and *its* are frequently misspelled with an apostrophe before the letter *s.* When an apostrophe is mistakenly added to *its,* the word is no longer a possessive pronoun. *It's* is a contraction meaning *it is.*

Exercise 3: *Identifying Possessive Pronouns*

Write the following sentences, supplying the proper possessive pronouns to replace the words in *italics.* Underline each possessive pronoun.

Examples

a. The band didn't cry when *Jake's* drum set was stolen.
   The band didn't cry when <u>his</u> drum set was stolen.

b. *Maria's* was always the paper chosen best.
   <u>Hers</u> was always the paper chosen best.

1. *Sarah's* eyes were very green.

2. Edgar said, "This is *Edgar's* book."

3. Edgar said, "Don't take this book—it's *Edgar's.*"

4. The football team doesn't like *the team's* uniforms.

5. The women can't believe that the new stadium is *the women's.*

6. Alan, is this *Alan's* mother?

7. Mr. and Mrs. Kye asked, "How do you like *the Kye's* house?"

8. Now, Jackie, the decision is *Jackie's.*

9. The conquering heroes declared the territory to be *the heroes'.*

10. Victor wanted *Victor's* room to be *Victor's* and only *Victor's.*

Reflexive Pronouns

Reflexive pronouns are formed with the suffixes *-self* or *-selves* added to some personal pronouns. They are used to replace a noun the second time it is referred to in a sentence. See the examples below.

John Smith saw John Smith in the mirror.
John Smith saw *himself* in the mirror.

The machine destroyed the machine.
The machine destroyed *itself*.

You can help you.
You can help *yourself*.

The following reflexive pronouns can be used to refer back to the subject and repeat its meaning.

Singular	Plural
myself	ourselves
yourself	yourselves
himself herself itself	themselves

Reflexive pronouns can also be used to give emphasis to another noun or pronoun. When used in this way, they are called *intensive pronouns*. Intensive pronouns may immediately follow the noun or pronoun they intensify, or they may be moved to the end of the sentence.

I *myself* made this shirt.
I made this shirt *myself*.

King Alfred *himself* led the battle.
King Alfred led the battle *himself*.

She *herself* wrote the class constitution.
She wrote the class constitution *herself*.

Exercise 4: Identifying Reflexive and Intensive Pronouns

Write the sentences on the following page, underlining each reflexive and intensive pronoun. Label each one by writing *R* above reflexive and *I* above intensive pronouns.

Examples

a. Mary trusted herself to wake up early.

R

Mary trusted <u>herself</u> to wake up early.

b. Harriet Tubman, once a slave herself, helped other slaves to escape.

I

Harriet Tubman, once a slave <u>herself</u>, helped other slaves to escape.

1. Maureen scratched herself when she tripped and fell into the hedge.

2. Thomas believed himself to be the smartest student in our class.

3. Harry asked himself why Vivian had not asked him to the party.

4. You yourselves are responsible for the success of the party.

5. Ms. Wong and Ms. Anderson planned the entire program themselves.

6. The Supreme Court reversed itself in a later decision.

7. No one, not even Tom, knew that he could take care of himself so well.

8. Luther Standing Bear, himself a Lakota chief, wrote about the Lakotas in *Land of the Spotted Eagle*.

9. Before the collision Casey Jones ordered his crew to jump, but he himself remained with the train.

10. Jean Baptiste Point DuSable, who was the first permanent settler of Chicago, built himself a successful trading center.

Indefinite Pronouns

Indefinite pronouns do not refer to specific people or things. They may take the place of nouns in a sentence, but they often do not have antecedents.

Everyone in the neighborhood is coming to the party.

One of my friends is from South America.

On the plane I sat next to *someone* the same age as I.

Some indefinite pronouns are always singular; some are always plural.

Singular Indefinite Pronouns

anybody	everybody	nobody
anyone	everyone	no one
each	much	one
either	neither	somebody

Plural Indefinite Pronouns

both   few   many   several   others

A few indefinite pronouns can be either singular or plural, depending on the nouns to which they refer.

all   any   most   none   some

All of the mail *is* on the table.   [singular]

All of the tickets *were* sold.   [plural]

Most of the salad *has* been eaten.   [singular]

Most of my friends *have* radios.   [plural]

Exercise 5: *Identifying Indefinite Pronouns*

Write the following sentences, underlining the indefinite pronouns. Then write *S* above a pronoun if it is singular and *P* if it is plural.

Examples

a. Each of my sisters has a job.

   S
   Each of my sisters has a job.

b. None of the letters were mailed today.

   P
   None of the letters were mailed today.

1. Most of the apples were used in the salad.

2. Neither of the dogs belongs to us.

3. Each of the windows needs to be washed.

4.   All of the cars get good gas mileage.

5.   Some of the international spy movie was exciting and parts were frightening.

6.   In the front of the bus sits someone I know.

7.   Much of the movie is already over.

8.   At the end of the Shakesperean play, *Romeo and Juliet,* everyone clapped vigorously.

9.   Most of my baby pictures were saved.

10.   None of the watermelons were ripe.

Interrogative Pronouns

Interrogative pronouns, which appear in place of unnamed people, places, or things, are used in asking questions.

Interrogative Pronouns

who	whom	whose	which	what

Who will answer the question?

Whom have you invited to the party?

Whose was the book you borrowed?

Which has more room?

What caused the fire in the store?

If an interrogative pronoun is used before a noun, it is used as a modifier, not as a pronoun.

Which is softer?	[interrogative pronoun]
Which pillow is softer?	[modifier]
What is the question?	[interrogative pronoun]
What question did you ask?	[modifier]

Exercise 6: Identifying Interrogative Pronouns

Write each of the following sentences, underlining all interrogative pronouns. Circle these words when they are used to modify nouns.

Examples

a. Who wants to go to Waco with us?
   Who wants to go to Waco with us?

b. Which senator had the best attendance this year?
   (Which) senator had the best attendance this year?

1. Who is on your left?
2. What street should I take to get to the International World Fair?
3. With whom will you be going?
4. What did Carlos do with the wrenches he took from the shop?
5. Which is the correct choice?
6. Whose answer matches the one in the book?
7. From what city did the package arrive?
8. Whom have you selected as group leader?
9. What are the family's plans for dinner tonight?
10. On whose authority are you acting?

Relative Pronouns

A *relative pronoun* relates, or connects, a group of words to some other word or group of words in the sentence. The word or group of words to which the pronoun refers is the *antecedent*.

Here is the boat *that* broke the speed record.

Mari, *who* moved here from Ohio, lives down the street.

The cellist *whom* we are hearing is very famous.

Meat prices, *which* have risen for months, are declining.

The following words are used as relative pronouns *only* when they introduce a group of words within a sentence.

which	who	whose
that	whom	

Exercise 7: Identifying Relative Pronouns

The following sentences contain relative pronouns, each with a clear antecedent. Write the sentences, circling the relative pronoun in each. Underline its antecedent.

Examples

a. The employee who sells the most will receive a bonus.

The <u>employee</u> (who) sells the most will receive a bonus.

b. The cat, which is certainly the most durable of animals, is rarely caught off guard.

The <u>cat</u>, (which) is certainly the most durable of animals, is rarely caught off guard.

1. Susan preferred the clerk who was courteous.

2. Ricardo visited the aunt whom he admired.

3. I have yet to read the pamphlet that you gave me.

4. The toothpaste, which looked like any other, was supposed to bring romance into my life.

5. There is the senator whose speeches so excite us!

6. Jane Ling, whom I admire deeply, takes no notice of me.

7. Michelle called the mechanic who had helped her before.

8. Is this the house that Jack built?

9. The house, which Jack built, tumbled down some years ago.

10. I want to thank the woman whose alertness saved more than 6,000 hectares of forest from fire.

Demonstrative Pronouns

The pronouns *this, that, these,* and *those* are used to point out specific people, places, and things for special attention. When used in this way, these words are called *demonstrative pronouns.*

This costs more than you can imagine.

That costs a lot too.

If you want more than one, you might choose *these*.

However, *those* really give you more for your money.

In each of the preceding sentences, the demonstrative pronoun takes the place of the unnamed but understood antecedent. The demonstrative pronouns *this* and *that* are used to point out singular nouns, while *these* and *those* point out plural nouns.

Demonstrative pronouns are often used to avoid repeating a noun in a sentence.

My glove and *that* of my friend Ralph are similar.
[meaning: *the glove*]

Compare your drawings to *those* on the wall.
[meaning: *the drawings*]

Demonstrative pronouns take the place of their antecedents. When *this, that, these,* and *those* modify nouns, they are used as adjectives.

This is the one I want.	[demonstrative pronoun]

This camera is the one I want.	[adjective]

Exercise 8: *Identifying Demonstrative Pronouns*

Write each of the following sentences, underlining each demonstrative pronoun. (Be certain that these pronouns do not modify nouns in the sentence.)

Examples

a. That is one of the best restaurants I know.
   That is one of the best restaurants I know.

b. It would help if you would take this dog home instead of that.
   It would help if you would take this dog home instead of that.

1. These are the true pioneers of the West.

2. Would you please help me with this?

3. Given my choice, I would select that novel before this.

4. I have seen butterflies before, but those are spectacular.

5. This has been one of the happiest days of my life.

6. From these acorns mighty oaks will grow; from those nothing will grow.

7. That was truly a test of strength.

8. When I decided upon these, I thought I knew what I was doing.

9. If it had not been for those heroic women, the battle would have been lost; these could not have fought alone.

10. After buying these books, I had no money left for those.

Finding a Pronoun by Its Features

Pronouns have three features that distinguish them as a part of speech. Personal pronouns have all three of these features; most other kinds of pronouns have at least one.

1. A pronoun may be singular or plural.

	Singular	Plural
Personal:	I, you, he, she, it, me, him, her	we, you, they, us, them
Reflexive:	myself, yourself, himself, herself, itself	ourselves, yourselves, themselves
Possessive:	my, mine, your, yours, his, her, hers, its	our, ours, your, yours, their, theirs
Demonstrative:	this, that	these, those
Indefinite:	anybody, everyone, nobody, someone, each, one	both, few, many, others, several

Relative and interrogative pronouns do not show number. The same forms are used with both singular and plural antecedents.

2. Pronouns may change form to show their function in a sentence.

Personal pronouns, which are the only ones that have this feature, have both subject and object forms.

Subject	Object Forms
I, we	me, us
you	you
he, she, it	him, her, it
they	them

Subject: Tomorrow *we* are driving to Colorado.
             They hoped to study engine mechanics.

Object: Maurice is driving *us* to Colorado.
             Ms. Avraira is teaching *them* algebra.

---

3. Pronouns may show gender.

Personal, possessive, and reflexive pronouns may be masculine, feminine, or neuter.

Masculine: he, him, his, himself

Feminine: she, her, hers, herself

Neuter: it, its, itself

Some pronouns can be either masculine or feminine, depending on the speaker or person referred to.

I, me, myself, you

Some pronouns refer to groups of men or women or to mixed groups, depending on the meaning of the sentence.

we us	they them	you
ourselves	themselves	yourselves

Exercise 9: *Identifying Pronouns by Features*

Write the following sentences, underlining the pronouns you find in each sentence. Your teacher may ask you which features you used to identify the pronouns.

Examples

a. We found everything in order just as she said it would be.
   We found everything in order just as she said it would be.

b. They thought about their decision carefully.
   They thought about their decision carefully.

1.   Everyone liked her hair when she wore it that way.

2. He usually lets us ride in his car to the game.

3. Both of the choices are what I want.

4. In the dark I found myself lost in my own neighborhood.

5. All of us would be glad to help you.

6. Those are the coins I wanted to show you.

7. The boy who lives there saved my dog's life.

8. I myself prefer someone who is loyal.

9. Each of the cats ate its dinner in silence.

10. No one noticed your late entrance in our play.

Review: Understanding Pronouns

Write the following sentences, underlining the italicized pronouns. In parentheses after each sentence, identify the class to which the underlined pronoun belongs: *personal, possessive, reflexive, indefinite, interrogative, relative,* or *demonstrative.*

Examples

   a. Kimberly sent postcards to Darin and *me.*
     Kimberly sent postcards to Darin and me. (personal)

   b. Jim makes *himself* breakfast before 6 o'clock.
     Jim makes himself breakfast before 6 o'clock. (reflexive)

1. Melissa and *he* are practicing for the band concert tonight.

2. All of the students in our math class consider *themselves* whizzes at long division.

3. Mr. and Mrs. Kumamoto praised the diligence of *us* teenagers.

4. The students *whom* the committee recommended for the position are all well qualified.

5. *Who* ate all the popcorn?

6. *Those* are the most expensive flowers in the florist's shop.

7. I was pleased when the committee chose Julio and *me* to plan the school dress-up day.

8. The announcer told us *who* would be first to speak on the radio panel discussion.

9. It was *she,* Jenny, who wrote the letter.

10. Michael and *they* will do well in the upcoming track meet.

11. In rural Alabama we say, "Tell your mother and *them* hello."

12. Bonnie and Allan wore *their* best clothes to the ceremony.

13. Before class Alice reads Luis' paper for errors, and he reads *hers*.

14. Robin writes much more exciting poetry than *I*.

15. It was she *who* called us at midnight to ask the time.

16. You may invite *whomever* you wish to the party, Anna.

17. The Ortegas borrowed your lawn mower this week, but they borrowed *ours* last week.

18. Is this David Yee? Yes, this is *he*.

19. *This* is the most beautiful statue I've ever seen.

20. The person *who* painted this picture is a truly talented artist.

Applying What You Know

Using what you have learned in this chapter, identify the pronouns in a paragraph from a magazine, newspaper, or book. List the pronouns on a sheet of paper and beside each one write the class to which the pronoun belongs.

Using Pronouns

Because pronouns have so many different forms, choosing the correct form sometimes presents problems for writers. In the following sections you will study and practice the correct use of pronouns. You will also practice using pronouns to increase clarity and variety in your writing.

Agreement of Pronouns and Antecedents

A pronoun must agree in number with its antecedent. When an antecedent is singular, a singular pronoun is used to refer to it. When the antecedent is plural, a plural pronoun is used to refer to it.

The *lady* was a true magician. *She* delighted the audience.
[singular antecedent and singular pronoun]

The *boys* filled *their* knapsacks with food.
[plural antecedent and plural pronoun]

This is your *room*, and *these* are your *towels*.
[one singular antecedent and pronoun; one plural antecedent and pronoun]

Exercise 10: Choosing Pronouns That Agree in Number with Their Antecedents

Write the following sentences, supplying in each space a pronoun that agrees in number with the *italicized* antecedent. Underline the pronouns you insert.

Examples

a. *Ms. Espinosa* is an experienced teacher. _____ studied at the University of Texas.

Ms. Espinosa is an experienced teacher. She studied at the University of Texas.

b. *Terry and Wilma* play basketball. _____ team may win the championship.

Terry and Wilma play basketball. Their team may win the championship.

1. The choral *singers* perform beautifully because _____ practice often.

2. *Carol* was happy when _____ was chosen best swimmer of the year.

3. *Carlos and Tim* wrote _____ essays during study hall.

4. *Mary* believes that _____ success in sports is due to good nutrition.

5. Most art *books* are very expensive, but _____ are worth the price.

6. *Don* consoled _____ with the thought that the game would have been lost anyway.

7. The principal will see *Susan* on Monday and will ask _____ to work in the office.

8. I love *soccer!* _____ is the most exciting sport in the world.

9. *Ginny and Bob* consider _____ to be the school's best all-around dancers.

10. *Sam* writes _____ short mystery stories in the early morning hours.

A pronoun must agree in gender with its antecedent.

When a singular antecedent is clearly masculine, use the pronouns *he, him,* or *his.*

Hasn't *Jonathan* brought *his* book to class?

Juan asked if *he* could leave, but the teacher told *him* no.

When a singular antecedent is feminine, the pronouns *she, her,* or *hers* are used.

Susan did a great deal of work on *her* painting.

Maureen thought *hers* was the best entry.

When a singular antecedent is neuter, the pronoun *it* or *its* is used.

The *giraffe* stood quietly as we watched *it.*

The *mountain* cast *its* purple shadow.

Exercise 11: Choosing Pronouns That Agree in Gender with Their Antecedents

Write each of the sentences on the following page, replacing the *italicized* word with an appropriate pronoun. Above the pronoun write *M* if it is masculine, *F* if it is feminine, or *N* if it is neuter. Underline the pronoun you supply.

Examples

---

a. Sara works diligently, so *Sara's* grades are very high.

                                           F

Sara works diligently, so <u>her</u> grades are very high.

    b. Tom cut *Tom* while shaving.

                   M

    Tom cut <u>himself</u> while shaving.

1. Lee studies math because *Lee* wants to become a scientist.

2. Karen lent *Karen's* bicycle to Mike.

3. Bill found *Bill* amazed by how easy cooking really was.

4. Mr. Chang washed *Mr. Chang's* hands after working in the garden.

5. When Melissa was younger, *Melissa* loved reading mystery stories and science fiction.

6. On *Harry's* birthday Harry always eats turkey with dressing.

7. As the white oak grew, *the oak's* shadow covered the vegetable garden.

8. The house shook during the earthquake, but *the house* did not collapse.

9. Rebecca called *Rebecca* Becky, but her family never would.

10. The coach, Ms. Chu, explained *the coach's* plans to the football team.

Agreement with Compound Antecedents

When a pronoun refers to a compound antecedent, you must decide whether to use a singular or a plural pronoun.

Use a plural pronoun when referring to antecedents joined by *and*.

The *catcher* and the *pitcher* discussed the signals *they* would use.

José, Diane, and *I* passed *our* tests.

The *passengers* and the *bus driver* directed traffic *themselves*.

Use a singular pronoun when referring to singular antecedents joined by *or* or *nor*.

Either *Harold* or *Arnie* will drive *his* car to the game.

Neither *Wilma* nor *Janet* thought that *she* was at fault.

We all knew that either the *pigeon* or the *crow* would return home all by *itself*.

The singular pronoun is used because it refers to only one of the subjects, not to both of them.

When two or more plural antecedents are joined by *or* or *nor*, use a plural pronoun.

Neither the *teachers* nor the *students* thought that *they* should be charged admission.

Exercise 12: Choosing Pronouns That Agree with Compound Antecedents

Write each of the following sentences, choosing the pronoun in parentheses that agrees with the compound subject of each sentence. Underline the pronoun you choose.

Examples

a. Keith and Mike took _____ dog to the veterinarian. (his, their)
Keith and Mike took their dog to the veterinarian.

b. Either Susan or Jane will ride _____ bike in Sunday's race. (her, their)
Either Susan or Jane will ride her bike in Sunday's race.

1. Teresa and Rosemary worked hard and saved _____ money. (her, their)

2. If either Ellen or JoAnn had won, _____ would have given the prize to charity. (she, they)

3. Lois and Carmen went to the beach, but _____ didn't swim. (she, they)

4. Neither the high schools nor the colleges predicted _____ current problems. (its, their)

5. While _____ were trying out for the team, Norma and Dale learned to play better chess. (she, they)

6. Neither Guy nor Tony is expected to win _____ next game. (his, their)

7. Either Victor or Juan will lend you _____ jacket. (his, their)

8. Neither the coaches nor the players complained about _____ losing season. (his, their)

9. The French club and the speech club are holding _____ monthly meetings this afternoon. (its, their)

10. Neither cars nor buses are as efficient as _____ competitor, the bicycle. (its, their)

Agreement Between Pronouns

When the antecedent is an indefinite pronoun, you must decide whether it is singular or plural.

	Singular		*Plural*
each	everyone	someone	several
one	everybody	somebody	few
either	anyone	no one	both
neither	anybody	nobody	many
much			others

One of the restaurants serves *its* own fresh-baked bread.   [singular]

Both of the restaurants serve *their* own fresh-baked bread.   [plural]

The pronouns *all, any, most, none,* and *some* are considered singular when their meaning in the sentence is singular, and plural when their meaning is plural.

Some of the chemical had burned *its* way through the surface.   [singular]

Some of the players thought that *they* were being overworked.   [plural]

None of the women said *she* wanted to see   [singular]
the bill passed in its present form.

Of the freshmen, sophomores, and juniors,   [plural]

none thought *they* could defeat the seniors.

The gender of the antecedent may be determined by the phrase that follows it.

The *captain* of the men's team wanted the trophy for *himself*.

Each of the women had *her* own bowling ball.

Exercise 13: *Choosing Pronouns That Agree with Indefinite Antecedents*

Write the following sentences, inserting the pronoun in parentheses that agrees with the *italicized* indefinite pronoun. Underline the pronoun you select.

Examples

   a. *Each* of the girls on the swim team washes _____ own suit. (her, their)

     Each of the girls on the swim team washes her own suit.

   b. *All* of the boys on the team wore _____ uniforms in the parade. (his, their)

     All of the boys on the team wore their uniforms in the parade.

1. *Everybody* on the men's team wanted _____ coach to win. (his, their)

2. *Many* of the women won _____ gold medals in the Lake Placid Olympics. (her, their)

3. *All* of the boys in the gym class buy _____ own gym suits. (his, their)

4. *None* of the boys in the club believed that _____ could afford the dues. (he, they)

5. *No one* on the girls' team washed _____ uniform. (their, her)

6. *Most* of the girls in the freshman class spent _____ evenings doing homework. (her, their)

7. *Some* of the boys in the woodworking class thought _____ worked better with the lathe than the girls. (he, they)

8. *Each* of the women said _____ dieting would succeed only with exercise. (her, their)

9. *Neither* of the captains of the girls' team asked _____ teammates for their advice. (her, their)

10. *All* of the mathematics teachers were sure that _____ students would do well on the district-wide examination. (her, their)

Problems with Agreement in Gender

A pronoun must agree with its antecedent in gender.

Sometimes, the meaning of the sentence will tell you whether the antecedent is masculine or feminine.

Each of the men removed *his* coat.

Neither of the sisters remembered *her* key.

A singular indefinite pronoun sometimes refers to a mixed group of men and women. In such sentences many writers use the words *his or her* or recast the sentence to make the antecedent plural.

Everyone in the group voted for *his or her* favorite team.

All of the group members voted for *their* favorite team.

Neither of the doctors felt that *he or she* would have chosen another career.

The *doctors* felt that *they* would not have chosen another career.

Exercise 14: Solving Problems with Agreement in Gender

Rewrite each of the following sentences without changing its meaning, using plural nouns and pronouns to replace singular subjects and pronouns.

Examples

a. Each of the vocalists had memorized his or her song.
   All of the vocalists had memorized their songs.

b. A good player feels confident when he or she has prepared himself or herself for the tasks that he or she will face.
   Good players feel confident when they have prepared themselves for the tasks that they will face.

1. A good student prepares for his or her exams gradually.

2. Anyone who is a good driver uses his or her rearview mirror.

3. Every good attorney prepares his or her cases well.

4. Each of the students received his or her award at the annual assembly.

5. Nobody on the track team was awarded a letter unless he or she had won at least one race.

6. Everyone on the basketball team practiced his or her free throws.

7. Somebody in class always asks for special help with his or her homework.

8. As each of the contestants finished his or her event, he or she would wait with the coach for the scores.

9. As he or she waited for the storm to pass, everybody on the construction site had a well-deserved rest.

10. No one in the family had ever entered his or her livestock in the county fair until last year.

Using Subject Pronouns

The subject form of pronouns includes the personal pronouns found at the top of the next page.

Singular	*Plural*
I, you, he, she, it	we, you, they

Use a subject form when the pronoun is the subject of a sentence.

Patty and *I* live on the same street.

The Robinsons and *we* built a fence together.

When using a personal pronoun to refer to yourself, always place the pronoun that refers to you last.

Manuel and *I* share a locker.

The girls and *we* took a train ride.

Use a subject form when the pronoun follows a form of the verb *be* and renames or identifies the subject of the sentence.

The best debaters in the school are *we*.

It's *she* who started the argument.

The boy who lost his dog is *he*.

When a sentence ends in an *incomplete construction*, use a subject form of the personal pronoun.

An incomplete construction has part left for the reader to complete.

Holly is taller than *I*.	[than *I am*]
Jim can swim faster than *he*.	[than *he can swim*]

If a pronoun is joined with a noun or another pronoun, use the form of the pronoun you would use if the pronoun were alone in the sentence.

He gave the sword to Falstaff and *me*.
[He gave the sword to *me*.]

She and *I* watched the stars.
[*She* watched the stars. *I* watched the stars.]

Exercise 15: *Choosing Subject Forms of Personal Pronouns*

Write the following sentences, choosing the subject form of the personal pronoun from those given in parentheses. Underline the pronouns you choose.

Examples

a. Juanita and (she, her) bought a used car.
Juanita and <u>she</u> bought a used car.

b. Joe said that it was (him, he) who ordered the search.
Joe said that it was <u>he</u> who ordered the search.

1. Carrie and (he, him) pumped gas on Saturdays.
2. That could have been (her, she) on the elevator.
3. (We, Us) rookies never seem to play in the real game.
4. It is (I, me), the masked man, that you seek.
5. Was it the Purple Gang that did this horrible deed? Yes, it was (them, they).
6. Do you think Carlos is as nice as (me, I)?
7. (He, Him) and (I, me) never play on the same team.
8. You think Gloria swims better than (I, me).
9. Marilyn and (her, she) were the best of our school's basketball players.
10. Jimmy and (I, me) gave them the essays that (us, we) students had written about conserving energy.

Using Object Pronouns

Personal pronouns have a singular and plural object form.

Singular

me, you, him, her, it

Plural

us, you, them

Use the object form of the personal pronoun when the pronoun is the object of the verb. The object answers the question *whom?* after the verb.

Grandmother sent *me* a crocheted bedspread.

Richard and Fred saw *us* on the roller coaster.

Use the object form of the personal pronoun when the pronoun answers the question *to whom?* after the verb.

Sandra sent *me* a postcard from Florida.

Mike gave *them* the key to the house.

Use the object form of the personal pronoun when the pronoun follows a preposition, such as *by, for, with, to,* or *from.*

Kiyo came to the concert with *us*.

Carrie delivered the papers for *them*.

Exercise 16: Using Object Pronouns

Write the following sentences, choosing the correct personal pronoun from those given in parentheses. Underline the pronouns you choose.

Examples

---

a. The manager sent (they, them) out of the building.
   The manager sent them out of the building.

b. Melissa went to the airport with John and (he, him).
   Melissa went to the airport with John and him.

---

1. Uncle Ted called (us, we) when he arrived in town.

2. Mother told Michelle and (I, me) to watch my cousin.

3. The counselor gave (they, them) new schedules.

4. Yesterday Tony rode to school with Pat and (she, her).

5. Sooner or later they will see (us, we) waving to (they, them).

6. Ms. Rodriguez gave Shelly and (I, me) credit for our report.

7. At the movies we saw Raoul and (he, him) sitting in the very front row.

8. Did you find that book for (she, her) and (I, me) to use?

9. Mr. Tishiro gave (us, we) a warning about being late.

10. We thanked (they, them) for having (we, us) neighbors for dinner.

Making Pronoun Antecedents Clear

If the antecedent for a pronoun is vague, the writer's meaning may not be clear.

> Karen told Helen that she had to stay home.
> [Who had to stay home?]

> Children obey their parents because *they* love them.
> [Who loves whom?]

When a sentence has two or more possible meanings, it is *ambiguous*. Ambiguous sentences can be corrected by making certain that each pronoun has a clear antecedent.

> Karen had to stay home, and *she* told Helen so.

> Because *they* love their parents, children obey *them*.

Exercise 17: Making Pronoun Antecedents Clear

The sentences on the following page are ambiguous because of vague pronoun reference. Rewrite each sentence so that each pronoun refers clearly to its own antecedent and the meaning is clear.

Examples

a. Charlie lent Mike a dollar because he needed it.
   Because Mike needed a dollar, Charlie lent it to him.

       b. Carol called Dolores when she made the basketball team.
           When Carol made the basketball team, she called Dolores.

1. Kirk went to Dan's house because he needed help in algebra so that he would not fail.

2. Carla waved to Nicole as she drove by.

3. Luis and Estella haven't talked to the Washingtons since they were on vacation.

4. Leslie's family didn't meet Todd and Steve when they came to visit while they were camping at the lake.

5. Diane has known Barbara since she was only six years old.

6. Campers sometimes bother the bears while they are eating; they should be aware of the danger of this practice.

7. Geronimo fought General Crook bravely until his men could fight no more.

8. Dick cooks John's dinner while he talks on the telephone.

9. The police caught the criminals as they were leaving the grocery store and getting into their car.

10. Don and Suzanne enjoy seeing the Hendersons every time they visit Milwaukee.

Pronouns Without Specific Antecedents

Using pronouns to refer to a general idea instead of a specific antecedent can be confusing when the general idea is not clearly expressed. The following example illustrates the problem.

> Our climb to the top had to be well planned. We needed to pack enough food and clothing, study the terrain carefully, and select a time that promised good weather. *This* would make the difference between success and failure.

The pronoun *this* does not clearly refer to any antecedent and should be replaced by a definite noun.

> These *preparations* would make the difference between success and failure.

Sometimes, a reference cannot be corrected by merely substituting a definite noun as an antecedent. You may need to rewrite a sentence so that its meaning is clear.

Jane studied the subject, wrote the report, and presented it to the class, *which* demonstrated how competent she was.

Rewriting the sentence and removing the pronoun *which* helps to clarify the meaning.

Jane demonstrated her competence by studying the subject, writing the report, and presenting it to the class.

Sometimes, writers will use a pronoun to refer to an unstated idea that exists only in their minds.

Stephanie was good at horseback riding and had always been interested in *them.*

In the preceding sentence the pronoun *them* refers to horses, but the word *horses* is not in the sentence, so the pronoun has no clear antecedent.

Always interested in horses, she was good at horseback riding.

Exercise 18: Using Pronouns Only with Specific Antecedents

The pronouns in the sentences on the following page have no clear antecedents. Some refer vaguely to general ideas and some to unstated antecedents. Rewrite each sentence, replacing the pronoun with a definite noun or revising the sentence for clarity.

Examples

a. The wind came in violent gusts, the sky had a greenish tint, and heavy rain could be seen in the distance. It was a sign that a tornado might occur.
The wind came in violent gusts, the sky had a greenish tint, and heavy rain could be seen in the distance. These conditions were signs that a tornado might occur.

b. The children had no consideration for anyone else in the pool, which angered the lifeguards.
The lifeguards were angered by the children's lack of consideration for anyone else in the pool.

1. The students often forget to reread their essays and correct the errors, which annoys the teacher.

2. Tommy washed the dishes, cleaned the dining room, and took out the garbage. This amazed his parents.

3. We have all wanted to try sailing, but we have yet to save enough money to buy one.

4. Jonathan did well in biology and poorly in Spanish. That really surprised us.

5. Carmen spent the weekend fishing, but she didn't catch any.

6. José writes whenever he can, but none of it has been published just yet.

7. We all wore suits or long dresses, which the new principal thought old-fashioned.

8. Ted cleaned out the garage and raked the leaves; however, even this didn't satisfy his Uncle Hector.

9. Our family is very thrifty because we never spend any of it unwisely.

10. On our bike trip my bike had a flat, a squeaky brake pad, and a wobbly wheel. This put me in a bad mood.

Review: *Using Pronouns*

Rewrite each of the following sentences, correcting any problems of reference or agreement between pronouns and their antecedents.

Examples

a. Bill saw Jim after he had returned from vacation.
   After Bill had returned from vacation, he saw Jim.

b. Karen has been duck hunting for two years, but she has yet to bag any.
   Karen has been duck hunting for two years, but she has yet to bag a duck.

c. At camp each of the campers wash their own plates.
   At camp all of the campers wash their own plates.

1. Linda couldn't go water-skiing because she didn't have any.

2. Kevin didn't call Andrew when he got back to town.

3. Everyone in our dance class must show their skills during the annual recital.

4. Although he was only a tenderfoot, Luis showed Karl how to find shelter in the woods.

5. Even though they've never met one, Juanita and Kim want to study modeling.

6. Tony thinks that everyone at the party should introduce themselves to others.

7. Since she was vacuuming the hall, Lauren asked Rosalie to mow the lawn.

8. Surprisingly, nobody asked to have their money returned after the terrible movie.

9. Because she wanted to win the prize, Ellen sang with Suzanne at the talent show.

10. The class in general science will begin when everybody has taken their seats.

11. Phillip always invites Christopher to dinner when he has something of importance to discuss.

12. It will be a long time until she can afford to buy one, so Monica will have to continue to dream of scuba diving.

13. Carlos and his family always dine with the Wongs when they are in Chicago.

14. During the test no one looked up from their papers, and only the clock could be heard.

15. Kathy had made reservations for 8 o'clock, but when she arrived at 7, she seemed to have forgotten this.

16. Naomi promised to take Phyllis out for pizza when she made her first A in English.

17. George and Judy will take the twins to the beach when they finish summer school.

18. If somebody finds a fly in their soup, they should return it to the kitchen.

19. No one had swept the front walk nor picked up the old newspapers. This shocked Miles.

20. The football team is working with the basketball team to raise money for its scholarship fund.

Writing Focus: *Using Pronouns in Writing*

You can strengthen your writing by using pronouns to avoid unnecessary repetition and to vary the structure of your sentences. Be sure that the pronouns you use have the correct form and agree with the nouns they refer to.

Assignment: *Reporting a "Happening"*

When was the last time you were in a crowd watching or participating in a community event? Did you watch the Fourth of July parade or amble down the arcade at the summer fair or carnival? Perhaps you attended the opening of a new store or a club meeting. What happened at the event?

Think about the event you went to, and write one or more paragraphs telling what happened there. Pretend that you are writing a column for your school newspaper. The students at your school will be your audience, and your purpose is to report what happened at the event you attended in an informative and interesting way. Your paragraphs will be evaluated for correct use of pronouns.

Use the following steps to complete this assignment.

A. Prewriting

Make a list of community events you have attended recently. Choose one to write about that you remember well because of the impression it made on you. Use the six basic questioning method described in Chapter 1 to generate ideas for your paragraphs. Begin to jot down questions that need to be answered, questions like the following: *Who* was present at the event? *What* happened? *Where* did the event take

place? *When* did it occur? *Why* did it take place? *How* did the people react? Think of as many specific details as you can in listing your questions. On a separate piece of paper, begin to answer the questions in specific words, phrases, and sentences. When you have finished, review your answers and begin to group them into an organizational pattern that supports the telling of the event.

B. Writing

Using your answers, write one or more paragraphs reporting what happened at the event you attended. Begin with a brief overview. Then add specific details to further explain to your readers everything they need to know to understand what went on at the event. As you write, pay particular attention to the pronouns you use and their antecedents.

C. Postwriting

Revise your first draft using the following checklist.

1. Have I answered the questions *who? what? why? when? where?* and *how?* about the event?

2. Have I provided enough specific details to inform and interest my readers?

3. Have I organized my information clearly?

4. Have I used each pronoun in its correct form?

5. Does each pronoun agree with its antecedent in number and gender?

Proofread your work using the Proofreader's Checklist at the back of the book. If appropriate, share your writing with your teacher and the members of your class.

14 Verbs

Understanding Verbs

Everything you want to say about the things you do, the places you go, and the people you meet depends on verbs. Because they make a statement about the subject, verbs are the foundation of sentences. In fact, verbs are so important that they may stand alone and be meaningful. When someone says to you, "Run!" "Talk!" "Laugh!" you understand the message exactly.

Defining Verbs

A *verb* is usually defined as a word that expresses action or a state of being about a noun or pronoun.

Frank Shorter *ran* more than sixteen kilometers.	[action]
Marcia *painted* her bedroom blue.	[action]
The Phillips *are* generous neighbors.	[being]
Melissa *felt* ill last night.	[being]

Grouping Verbs by Classes

Verbs are usually grouped into three main classes: *action, linking,* and *helping* verbs.

Action verbs show physical or mental action.

Physical Action

Manuel *saddled* the horse.
Alice *plays* the leading role.
Gene *recorded* the concert.

Mental Action

Jan *remembered* my birthday.
I *understand* the formula now.
This game *decides* the champion.

Action verbs may or may not take objects. An object is a noun or pronoun that receives the action of the verb. Action verbs that take objects are called *transitive* verbs.

Manuel *saddled* the horse.   [*Horse* is the object of *saddled*.]

I *understand* the formula.   [*Formula* is the object of understand.]

Action verbs that do not take an object are called *intransitive* verbs.

The bike racer *trains* very diligently.

Racers *practice* indoors during the winter months.

Note: Some action verbs can be either transitive or intransitive, depending on how they are used in the sentence.

We rode ten miles yesterday. (I)

Mike rode his bike to school. (T)

Exercise 1: *Identifying Action Verbs, Transitive and Intransitive*

Write the following sentences, underlining the verb in each. Put a T next to the sentence if the verb is transitive; put an I if it is intransitive.

Examples

a. Kitty Connor rides the bus to school.
   Kitty Connor rides the bus to school. (T)

b. The pine trees whistled in the autumn wind.
   The pine trees whistled in the autumn wind. (I)

1. The coach scheduled our game for next Thursday.

2. The avocados froze during the long cold night.

3. A stone will sink in water.

4. Marsha and Bill demonstrated the dance.

5. My brothers and I swam across the lake.

Linking verbs do not show action; instead, they link a noun or pronoun in the first part of a sentence with a word in the second part of a sentence. Linking verbs are always intransitive.

The word that is linked to the noun or pronoun names or describes it.

These apples *are* juicy.　　Those clouds *look* threatening.

Linking Verbs

am	has been	taste	look	grow
is	have been	smell	feel	appear
are	had been	sound	become	remain
was	would be	seem	stay	turn
were	could be			
may be	should be	shall be	could have been	
can be	would have been	will be	should have been	

Note: Some words can be either action or linking verbs. You must look at the way the verb is used in the sentence to determine its type.

Action:　　Laurie *grew* watermelons in her garden.

Linking:　　The players *grew* impatient for the game to start.

Even forms of *be*, when followed by certain adverbs or adverb phrases, are not considered linking verbs.

We *have been* here before.

Exercise 2: *Classifying Verbs*

Write the following sentences, underlining the verb in each. Identify the verb as either *action-transitive*, *action-intransitive*, or *linking* by writing the label in parentheses at the end of the sentence.

Examples

    a. Julio studies law at the university.
       Julio studies law at the university. (action-transitive)

    b. Ms. Yamishi remained calm during the crisis.
       Ms. Yamishi remained calm during the crisis. (linking)

1.   Pete and Valerie are cocaptains of the tennis team.

2.   Ellen works at the pet shop after school.

3.   Dolores looks nervous about her dance routine.

4.   Kevin takes the CTA train to school.

5.   They needed money for gym uniforms.

6.   Myra grew tired of waiting for Jim.

7.   David felt the sharp points of the cactus.

8.   Beth's parents attended the band concert.

9.   Brad believes in the illusion of magic.

10.   The audience seemed bored with the performance.

Helping verbs help the main verb express action or a state of being.

Jennifer *can* play the piano and the violin.

Tonight's game *has been* canceled.

José *will* answer the phone.

Rose *should have* won the election.

Helping verbs include forms of *be* and many other commonly used words. The following is a list of helping verbs.

am	be	do	might	would
is	been	does	must	should
are	have	did	can	shall
was	has	may	could	will
were	had			

Exercise 3: *Identifying Main Verbs and Helping Verbs*

Write the following sentences, underlining each main verb once and each helping verb twice.

Example

---

a. Cynthia has run in the marathon for two years.
   Cynthia has run in the marathon for two years.

1.   Our train is scheduled for track H6.

2.   I must have left my book at home.

3.   The plane could have been delayed because of fog.

4. A good attitude can improve your success.

5. A purse was found beneath the bleachers.

6. The coats should be hung in the hall closet.

7. The guests will have arrived by 5.

8. We might paint our house this summer.

9. Jonas should have run for class vice president.

10. Ms. Alvarez will understand your problem.

Identifying a Verb by Its Features

Three features can help you identify verbs. Every verb must have at least one of these features; some have all three.

1. Verbs have *tense*.

Tense is the time expressed by a verb.

There are six tenses: *present, past, future, present perfect, past perfect,* and *future perfect*.

Present:	They *ride* the train to work.
Past:	The team *rode* the bus to the game.
Future:	The coach *will ride* on the same bus.
Present Perfect:	Sharon *has ridden* on a monorail.
Past Perfect:	Manuel *had ridden* in the first-class section.
Future Perfect:	After tonight they *will have ridden* to every game with us.

The tense of the verb is formed from the *principal parts* of the verb. Every verb has three principal parts: *present, past,* and *past participle*.

The *present* form is the form of the verb used with *to*:

(to) know   (to) bring   (to) talk

The *past* form is the same as the verb in the simple past tense:

knew   brought   talked

The *past participle* form of the verb is the form used with the helping verb *has* or *have*:

has known   have brought   has talked

Present	Past	Past Participle
go	went	gone
speak	spoke	spoken
walk	walked	walked
yawn	yawned	yawned

The following list shows how verb tenses are formed.

Tense	How Formed	Example
Present:	present form of verb (Add -s in third-person singular.)	I look he looks
Past:	past form of verb	I looked he looked
Future:	present form + *shall* or *will*	I shall look he will look
Present Perfect:	past participle + *have* or *has*	I have looked he has looked
Past Perfect:	past participle + *had*	I had looked he had looked
Future Perfect:	past participle + *shall have* or *will have*	I shall have looked he will have looked

Helping verbs are used to form the future and all of the perfect tenses. The helping verb and the main verb together are called a *verb phrase*.

I *shall look* for my history book.	[future]
I *have looked* for my history book.	[present perfect]
I *had looked* for my history book until yesterday.	[past perfect]
By tomorrow I *shall have looked* for my history book for two weeks.	[future perfect]

Exercise 4: *Identifying the Tenses of Verbs*

Write each of the sentences on the following page, underlining the verb or verb phrase. Identify the tense of each by writing *present, past, future, present perfect, past perfect,* or *future perfect* in parentheses after the sentence.

Examples

a. Many truck drivers travel at night.
Many truck drivers <u>travel</u> at night. (present)

b. Emilio has swept around the end for a touchdown.
Emilio <u>has swept</u> around the end for a touchdown. (present perfect)

1. Caroline makes a daily trip to the bank.

2. Mario has studied agriculture and agronomy as a part-time student at the university.

3. Eric will appraise the value of that stamp for you.

4. Marsha needed an excuse from economics class for her dental appointment.

5. Susan had painted the cup blue with white trim before changing her mind.

6. The newspaper will have arrived by 5 o'clock.

7. The mechanics did their best work on the car.

8. We have prepared enough food for an army.

9. Members of our club wear special uniforms.

10. John has gone to St. Louis with his family.

2. Verbs have an -ing form.

The -ing form of a verb is its progressive form. The progressive form of the verb includes a form of be and will or shall in the future tense.

I *am locking* the door.	[present tense]
I *was locking* the door.	[past tense]
I *will be locking* the door.	[future tense]

3. Verbs have a singular and plural form.

A verb in the present tense changes form to agree in number with the subject of the sentence. When the subject is singular, the ending -s or -es is added to the present tense form of the verb. When the subject is plural, the present tense form is used by itself. Helping verbs may also have singular or plural forms.

Willie *hopes* to attend college.	[singular]
The students *hope* to attend college.	[plural]
Carlos *has* painted a mural.	[singular]
We *have* painted a mural.	[plural]

Exercise 5: *Verbs in Their Progressive, Singular, and Plural Forms*

Write the following sentences, underlining the verbs or verb phrases. Identify each as singular or plural by writing *S* or *P* over the verb.

Examples

a. Daniel delivers newspapers after school.

        S

Daniel <u>delivers</u> newspapers after school.

b. Several students have a bad case of measles.

              P

Several students <u>have</u> a bad case of measles.

1. Mr. Wong selects the best music students for the spring concert band.

2. By evening we are usually tired and hungry from our afternoon workout at the gym.

3. Anthony will sing the solo quite professionally.

4. Lifeguards protect the swimmers both at the beach and at the pool.

5. Mr. Armstrong often gives us several pages of biology homework on weekends.

6. Those travelers have ignored the weather reports.

7. Helen's enthusiastic gymnastic performance pleases the audience every time.

8. She has found unusual shells off the Florida coast.

9. The usher will have shown them to their seats.

10. We are planning a surprise birthday party for Jed on Tuesday afternoon.

Review: Understanding Verbs

In the following passage from Jesús Colón's short story "The Lady Who Lived Near the Statue of a Man on a Horse," an elderly Puerto Rican woman is lost in New York City. Notice that the first verb phrase is underlined. Using what you have learned in the preceding sections, identify twenty-five other verbs or verb phrases and list these on a sheet of paper numbered 1–25. In parentheses beside each one, indicate on what line of the selection the verb or verb phrase can be found.

Example

a. did go (line 1)

1. "And where did you go to?" I inquired.
2. "I took the first bus that I could find in the neighborhood, until
3. the last stop. I left that and got into another. The main thing I wanted
4. to do was to get as far away as possible from that house where there
5. was all toil and no rest. At last I knocked at one door. A Negro man
6. opened the door. He could see that I was crying and very much
7. fatigued. He and his wife took me in. Since then, I have been living
8. with them. One of them usually takes me to different houses to work
9. a few hours here and a few hours there. Then one of the two, the
10. man or his wife, comes for me during the evening.
11.   "Yesterday morning the man took me to a house where I had
12. worked before a few hours. I finished early. Thinking that I could get
13. to the house all by myself, I did not wait for anybody. I thought that I
14. took the same bus that they would have taken if they came for me.
15. Somehow I did not get off where they always did. And, here I am,
16. having taken buses all day and all night, cold, hungry and tired."
17.   "And where is the house of this family with whom you are now
18. staying?"
19.   "All I know is that a few blocks from the house, there is a
20. statue of a man on a horse. That is all I know."[1]

Applying What You Know

From a newspaper, magazine article, book, or story you have read, select several paragraphs. Identify the verbs and verb phrases. List them on a sheet of paper, and beside each write its tense in parentheses.

---

[1]From *A Puerto Rican in New York and other Sketches* by Jesús Colón. Copyright 1982 by Jesús Colón. Published by Mainstream Publishers.

Using Verbs

Because there are so many different forms of verbs, their usage sometimes presents special problems. In the following sections you will learn to use the various tenses of verbs correctly. You will also learn to choose between the active and passive voice, to make verbs agree with their subjects, and to use commonly confused verbs correctly.

Using the Simple Verb Tenses

Form the *present tense* with the present form of the verb.

In the third-person singular (*he, she, it*) form, add *-s* or *-es* for agreement.

I follow	we follow
you follow	you follow
he	
she } follows	they follow
it	

Form the *past tense* of *regular verbs* by adding *-d* or *-ed* to the present form.

I opened	we opened
you opened	you opened
he	
she } opened	they opened
it	

Form the *future tense* with the helping verb *shall* or *will* and the present form of the verb. In formal usage the helping verb *shall* is used with first person singular and plural (*I, we*).

I shall/will invite	we shall/will invite
you will invite	you will invite
he	
she } will invite	they will invite
it	

Exercise 6: *Using Simple Verb Tenses*

Write each of the following sentences, changing the tense of the verb in each sentence to the tense given in parentheses. Underline the verbs. (Use your dictionary for help with spelling verb forms.)

Examples

---

a. Lisa and Rosa visit their aunt in the country. (past)
   Lisa and Rosa visited their aunt in the country.

b. The police officers work different shifts. (future)
   The police officers will work different shifts.

1. Miriam never agreed with her older sister. (present)

2. The assistant chefs carve the turkey. (future)

3. Katherine knew the answer to the question. (present)

4. Ramona preferred mysteries to science fiction. (present)

5. Marvin challenged Albert at the swimming meet. (future)

6. Louis struggled with his chemistry homework. (present)

7. Anna will prepare for the ski trip by exercising. (past)

8. I never played soccer on artificial turf. (future)

9. The counselors instructed the group in gymnastics. (present)

10. Rebecca received more votes than Jim in the election. (future)

Using the Perfect Tenses

The *present perfect tense* is formed with the helping verb *has* or *have* and the past participle form of the verb.

I have decided	we have decided
you have decided	you have decided
he	
she } has decided	they have decided
it	

The present perfect tense is used to express an action that begins in the past and may continue to the present or one that happened at an unspecified time in the past.

John *has studied* Spanish for two years now.

I *have wondered* many times how Houdini performed that trick.

The *past perfect tense* is formed with the helping verb *had* and the past participle form of the verb.

I had shared	we had shared
you had shared	you had shared
he she } had shared it	they had shared

The past perfect tense usually describes an action that took place at some time earlier than another action.

          past   past perfect
Before we *arrived*, Wayne *had sold* his van.

          past perfect   past
The Smiths *had eaten* when we *entered*.

The *future perfect tense* is formed with the helping verbs *shall have* or *will have* and the past participle form of the verb. In formal usage *shall* is used with the first-person form of the verb.

I shall have arrived	we shall have arrived
you will have arrived	you will have arrived
he she } will have arrived it	they will have arrived

Verbs in the future perfect tense describe a future action that will be completed before another future action takes place or before a future date.

We *will have raised* forty dollars for our trip by the time we leave for Texas.

My parents *will have been married* twenty-five eventful years this July.

Exercise 7: Using the Perfect Tenses of Verbs

Rewrite each of the sentences on the following page, changing the verb in the sentence to the perfect tense form given in parentheses. Underline the verbs you form.

Example

---

a. The jazz band will practice on Tuesdays. (past perfect)
The jazz band had practiced on Tuesdays.

1. The detectives searched the garden for a clue. (future perfect)

2. Chuck tutors other students in math. (present perfect)

3. Avocados increased in price before the drought. (past perfect)

4. Luis invited Ben and Maria to his house for dinner. (present perfect)

5. Our class discussed meteorology during Monday afternoon's science class. (future perfect)

6. This season's grapefruit taste especially sour. (present perfect)

7. The thunderstorm stopped by early evening. (past perfect)

8-10. Write three original sentences, one in each of the perfect tenses. Use the examples below as models.

Examples

Present Perfect:	I have worked on my homework all evening.
Past Perfect:	They had already eaten by the time I arrived.
Future Perfect:	We will have moved by the end of July.

Using Irregular Verbs

Irregular **verbs do not follow the regular pattern for forming the past and past participle.**

S ome irregular verbs form their past and past participle by a change in spelling; others have the same past and past participle forms. The following list gives the three principal parts for commonly used irregular verbs.

Present	*Past*	*Past Participle* (has, have, or had)
begin	began	begun
blow	blew	blown
break	broke	broken
bring	brought	brought
build	built	built

Present	Past	Past Participle
burst	burst	burst
buy	bought	bought
choose	chose	chosen
come	came	come
dive	dove *or* dived	dived
do	did	done
draw	drew	drawn
drink	drank	drunk
drive	drove	driven
eat	ate	eaten
fall	fell	fallen
fly	flew	flown
forget	forgot	forgotten
freeze	froze	frozen
give	gave	given
go	went	gone
grow	grew	grown
keep	kept	kept
know	knew	known
lay	laid	laid
lie	lay	lain
ride	rode	ridden
ring	rang	rung
rise	rose	risen
run	ran	run
see	saw	seen
set	set	set
shake	shook	shaken
shrink	shrank	shrunk
sing	sang	sung
sink	sank	sunk
sit	sat	sat
speak	spoke	spoken
spend	spent	spent
spring	sprang	sprung
steal	stole	stolen
swear	swore	sworn
swim	swam	swum
take	took	taken
teach	taught	taught
think	thought	thought
throw	threw	thrown
wear	wore	worn
write	wrote	written

Like regular verbs, irregular verbs form the six tenses from the principal parts of the verb and helping verbs.

Present Tense
(Add -s or -es in third-person singular.)

I know	we know
you know	you know
he she } knows it	they know

Past Tense
(past form)

I knew	we knew
you knew	you knew
he she } knew it	they knew

Future Tense
(shall or will + present form)

I shall/will know	we shall/will know
you will know	you will know
he she } will know it	they will know

Present Perfect Tense
(have or has + past participle)

I have known	we have known
you have known	you have known
he she } has known it	they have known

Past Perfect Tense
(had + past participle)

I had known	we had known
you had known	you had known
he she } had known it	they had known

Future Perfect Tense
(shall have or will have + past participle)

I shall/will have known
you will have known
he
she } will have known
it

we shall/will have known
you will have known

they will have known

Exercise 8: *Using Irregular Verbs*

Write the following sentences, choosing the proper verb form from those given in parentheses. Underline the verb form that you choose.

Examples

 a. Jeremy (lay, laid) the glass of apple cider on the table.
  Jeremy laid the glass of apple cider on the table.

 b. We have (drove, driven) down the coast before.
  We have driven down the coast before.

 1. The art classes (drew, drawn) covers for the programs.

 2. The hurricane-force wind has (blew, blown) the roof off the house.

 3. I hope Gary will not (forget, forgot) my advice.

 4. The bailiff (swore, sworn) in the witness.

 5. Have you (ate, eaten) at the new restaurant yet?

 6-10. Choose five verbs from the list of irregular verbs. Use each verb in a sentence. Identify the tense you have used.

Examples

bring: The mailman has brought me a package.   (present perfect)
wear: A mourning dove ate my sunflower seeds.   (past)

Using Progressive Forms of Verbs

The progressive form of the verb expresses continuing action. It consists of a form of *be* plus the *-ing* (present participle) form of the verb.

The progressive form can be used in all six tenses. Form the progressive for each tense by using the correct tense of the verb *be* with the present participle.

Progressive Form of Present Tense

I am running
you are running
he
she } is running
it

we are running
you are running

they are running

Progressive Form of Past Tense

I was running
you were running
he
she } was running
it

we were running
you were running

they were running

Progressive Form of Future Tense

I will be running
you will be running
he
she } will be running
it

we will be running
you will be running

they will be running

Progressive Form of Present Perfect Tense

I have been running
you have been running
he
she } has been running
it

we have been running
you have been running

they have been running

Progressive Form of Past Perfect Tense

I had been running
you had been running
he
she } had been running
it

we had been running
you had been running

they had been running

Progressive Form of Future Perfect Tense

I will have been running

you will have been running

he

she } will have been running

it

we will have been running

you will have been running

they will have been running

Exercise 9: *Using Progressive Forms of Verbs*

Rewrite each of the following sentences, changing the tense of the progressive form of the verb to the tense given in parentheses. Underline the verbs you form.

Examples

a. The plane is soaring above the clouds. (future progressive)
   The plane will be soaring above the clouds.

b. Carol was cleaning out the garage. (past perfect progressive)
   Carol had been cleaning out the garage.

1. Mom and Dad have been planning a vacation to Mexico. (past progressive)

2. The chorus will be singing at the shopping center. (present perfect progressive)

3. Robert was repairing the broken radio for his brother. (future progressive)

4. The dog is burying the bone in the backyard. (past perfect progressive)

5. The reporter has been writing since early morning. (future perfect progressive)

6. The children will be swimming in the indoor pool. (present progressive)

7. Michael has been sleeping all morning. (past progressive)

8. Mr. Sanchez is photographing my sister's wedding. (future progressive)

9. The faculty had been judging the tryouts. (present perfect progressive)

10. Jessica is running in the marathon. (future progressive)

Using Active and Passive Voices

A verb is in the *active voice* when it expresses an action performed *by* its subject. It is in the *passive voice* when it expresses an action performed *upon* its subject.

Active: The architect designed the building.
              [The subject performs the action.]

Passive: The building was designed by the architect.
              [The subject receives the action.]

Only *transitive* verbs (those that take an object) can be used in the passive voice. The object of an active voice sentence becomes the subject of a passive voice sentence.

                            S   O
Active: The *cab driver* assisted the *passenger*.

                            S
Passive: The *passenger* was assisted by the *cab driver*.

The verb phrase in a passive voice sentence always includes a form of *be* and the past participle form of the main verb.

When a verb is written in active voice, the subject performing the action is emphasized. When a verb is written in passive voice, the emphasis is on the person or thing receiving the action rather than on the one performing it. Passive voice is also used when the speaker or writer does not know who performed the action.

Active: Mother Teresa won the Nobel Peace Prize.
              [The emphasis is on Mother Teresa.]

Passive: The Nobel Peace Prize was won by Mother Teresa.
              [The emphasis is on the Nobel Peace Prize.]

Exercise 10: Using Active and Passive Voice

Write each of the following sentences, changing the active verbs to passive, and the passive verbs to active. (It will be necessary to rearrange each sentence.) Underline the verbs you form.

Examples

  a. Carlita found my watch in the car.
     My watch <u>was found</u> in the car by Carlita.

b. The noise from the stereo was ignored by my mother.
My mother <u>ignored</u> the noise from the stereo.

1. The movie was criticized by several reviewers.

2. The *Nutcracker Ballet* was flawlessly performed by the Joffrey Ballet Company.

3. Our family doctor reads several medical journals.

4. The marathon was sponsored by the Chamber of Commerce.

5. The paramedics rescued the woman in the burning car.

6. The farmer harvested the field of corn.

7. Sunken treasure is sometimes discovered by scuba divers.

8. Rosita mailed the important package to her brother in South America.

9. Mr. Salerno gave the class free passes to the soccer game.

10. During history class Mrs. Wong showed us a film about the Depression.

Making Verbs Agree

> The basic rule of verb agreement is a simple one: use a singular form of the verb with a singular subject; use a plural form of the verb with a plural subject.

Singular nouns and the pronouns *he, she,* and *it* take the verb form ending in *-s* or *-es.*

Singular

Denise Lee *wants* an unlisted phone number.

The doctor *reads* medical journals.

He *visits* his grandmother often.

Plural nouns and the pronouns *I, you, we,* and *they* take the verb form without an added ending.

Plural

Sam and Felicia *want* an unlisted phone number.

The doctors *read* medical journals.

They *visit* their grandmother often.

Exercise 11: Making Verbs Agree with Their Subjects

Rewrite each of the following sentences so that each subject is the noun or nouns given in parentheses. Without changing verb tense, change the form of the verb to agree with its subject. (It may not be necessary to change the forms of some verbs.) Underline the verbs in the sentences you write.

Examples

a. Sean is studying to be an accountant. (Sean and Miguel)
   Sean and Miguel are studying to be accountants.

b. The girls do the vegetable gardening at our house. (Danielle)
   Danielle does the vegetable gardening at our house.

1. We are traveling to Pennsylvania this summer. (Robert)

2. Andrew has chosen several courses for next semester. (The students)

3. The hawks nest on the side of the mountain. (hawk)

4. The campers were hiking along the river. (camper)

5. Have you ever bought a warped record album? (she)

6. In the summer Bob works at the grocery store. (Bob and JoAnn)

7. The winner of the school poster contest receives movie passes. (winners)

8. The glasses on the shelf are fragile. (glass)

9. Has Mari ever returned that library book? (we)

10. The fires burn out of control in the forest. (fire)

Problems in Agreement

The number of a subject is not changed by a phrase following it. A verb agrees in number with the subject, not with the object of a preposition.

The *robin* in the bushes *hunts* worms.

The *windows* of the building on the corner *were broken*.

Exercise 12: *Making Verbs Agree with Their Subjects*

Write the following sentences, choosing the form of the verb in parentheses that agrees with the subject. Then underline the subject once and the verb you select twice.

Example

---

a. The friend of the ladies (was, were) coming to the party.
The friend of the ladies was coming to the party.

1. The actors in the play (has, have) practiced for three months.

2. The new socks I bought yesterday (is, are) good for jogging.

3. The people responsible for the early movies in Hollywood (was, were) pioneers in a new art form.

4. The horse ridden by the cowboys in the rodeo (has, have) been carefully trained.

5. Five of the people wanting to learn Italian (was, were) adults.

6. The lawns on your street (look, looks) manicured.

7. The ship going to the Canary Islands (sail, sails) at dawn.

8. These books on architecture (serves, serve) my purpose well.

9. Even your first drawing of geometric shapes (illustrate, illustrates) your talent.

10. The jewelry on her fingers (shine, shines) in the dark.

When indefinite pronouns are used as subjects, their verbs must agree with them. Some indefinite pronouns are always either singular or plural.

Singular Indefinite Pronouns

---

each	anyone	either
one	anybody	neither
no one	someone	everyone
nobody	somebody	everybody

Plural Indefinite Pronouns

---

both	few
many	several

No one in the class *reads* more quickly than Susanne.

[singular subject, singular verb]

Both of the teachers *want* to learn to dance.

[plural subject, plural verb]

Exercise 13: Choosing Verb Forms That Agree with the Subjects

Write the following sentences, choosing the form of the verb given in parentheses that agrees with the subject. Underline the subject once and the verb you select twice.

Example

---

a. Everybody (like, likes) the new science teacher.
   Everybody likes the new science teacher.

---

1. Both of the last runners in the marathon (is, are) still trying.

2. Anyone who attends Central High (live, lives) in the southwest part of the city.

3. Several of the trucks (are, is) big enough for freight.

4. No one on the football team (fumble, fumbles) the play.

5. Somebody among the seniors (has, have) written a new school song.

6. Few of the new members (memorizes, memorize) the oath.

7. One of our best friends (are, is) working for a bank.

8. Someone among our friends (are, is) practicing karate.

9. One of the new teachers (plays, play) the guitar.

10. Many of the students (were, was) recognized for an award.

The indefinite pronouns *all, any, most, none,* **and** *some* **cause special agreement problems because they can be either singular or plural, depending on the "sense" of the sentence.**

If the pronoun refers to one person or thing, it is singular and takes a singular verb. If it refers to more than one person or thing, it is plural and takes a plural verb.

All of the yarn *has* been used.	[singular]
All of the yarns *have* been used.	[plural]
Some of the paint *is* still usable.	[singular]
Some of the paints *are* still usable.	[plural]

When the subject follows the verb in sentences beginning with *there* or *here* or in questions, the subject and verb must still agree.

There are several *menus* available.	[plural]
There is a *menu* on the table.	[singular]
Who is the *winner*?	[singular]
What are the *results*?	[plural]

Exercise 14: *Choosing Verb Forms That Agree with the Subjects*

Write the following sentences, choosing the form of the verb given in parentheses that agrees with the subject. Underline the subject once and the verb you select twice.

Examples

a. Most of the rivers (have, has) bridges.
   Most of the rivers have bridges.

b. Here (is, are) the tablecloth you asked for.
   Here is the tablecloth you asked for.

1. There (is, are) heroes in every walk of life.

2. None of the glue (stick, sticks) to this surface.

3. What (is, are) the major attractions of your city?

4. Part of this book (illustrate, illustrates) city skylines.

5. Here (is, are) the list of members you wanted.

6. There (was, were) only a few people attending the ceremony.

7. Some of the mailboxes (has, have) decorations.

8. (Was, Were) there a no-trespassing sign on the lawn?

9. All of the juice (remain, remains) in the pitcher.

10. Any of the maps (indicate, indicates) this as the fastest route.

Agreement with Compound Subjects and Collective Nouns

Subjects joined by *and* usually take a plural verb.

Manuel and *Rosita are* cousins.

The *sofa* and *chairs have been reupholstered*.

Some subjects joined by *and* act as a singular noun and therefore take a singular verb.

Macaroni and *cheese is* a nutritious dish.

The Stars and Stripes is waving proudly in the breeze.

Singular subjects joined by *or* or *nor* take a singular verb.

A *dictionary* or a *thesaurus has* the information you need.

Neither *Ted* nor *Sarah wants* to go.

Plural subjects joined by *or* or *nor* take a plural verb.

Neither the *police officers* nor the *fire fighters have agreed* to strike.

Neither the *employees* nor the *employers want* to settle their differences without benefits.

When a singular subject and a plural subject are joined by *or* or *nor*, the verb agrees with the nearer subject.

Either my *brother* or my *parents have* the house key.

Neither the *bananas* nor the *melon is* ripe.

Collective nouns can be either singular or plural.

If they refer to a group as a unit, they are singular. If they refer to the individual members of the group, they are plural.

The *group was preparing* for the hike.	[singular]
The *group were packing* their backpacks.	[plural]

Exercise 15: Choosing the Correct Verb Form

Write the following sentences, choosing the verb form given in parentheses that agrees with the subject. Underline the verb that you choose.

Examples

a. The majority of the members (is, are) in their seats.
   The majority of the members are in their seats.

b. Peanut butter and mayonnaise (is, are) a good combination.
   Peanut butter and mayonnaise is a good combination.

1. (Has, Have) the letter or package arrived yet?

2. Robin and Moor Company (is, are) always busiest at income tax return time.

3. Either the porch or the sidewalks (need, needs) to be swept before company arrives.

4. The Red, White, and Blue (represent, represents) our armed forces.

5. The orchestra (tunes, tune) their instruments before every performance.

6. Neither the teachers nor the students (object, objects) to a leisurely lunch.

7. Why (has, have) the audience become so noisy?

8. Neither the players nor the coach (was, were) in the gym.

9. Ginger, Maria, and Pam (practices, practice) swimming on Mondays.

10. Either strawberries or bananas (tastes, taste) good on cereal.

Verbs Often Confused

Three commonly confused sets of verbs are *lie/lay, sit/set,* and *rise/raise.*

The forms of *lie* express the action of relaxing in a horizontal position. *Lie* is intransitive.

lie   lay   lain   lying

Robert $\left\{ \begin{array}{l} \text{lies} \\ \text{lay} \\ \text{has lain} \\ \text{is lying} \end{array} \right\}$ on the mat to rest.

The forms of *lay* express the action of putting or placing something. (In using this verb, state the object that is being put or placed.) *Lay* is transitive.

lay   laid   laid   laying

Melissa $\left\{ \begin{array}{l} \text{lays} \\ \text{laid} \\ \text{has laid} \\ \text{is laying} \end{array} \right\}$ the hammer on the bench.

The forms of *sit* express the action of resting in a seated position or of remaining undisturbed. *Sit* is intransitive.

sit   sat   sat   sitting

Maria $\left\{ \begin{array}{l} \text{sits} \\ \text{sat} \\ \text{has sat} \\ \text{is sitting} \end{array} \right\}$ in her grandmother's rocker.

The forms of *set* express the action of putting or placing something. (In using this verb, state the object that is being put or placed.) *Set* is transitive.

set   set   set   setting

Kiyo $\left\{ \begin{array}{l} \text{sets} \\ \text{set} \\ \text{has set} \\ \text{is setting} \end{array} \right\}$ the book on the shelf.

The forms of *rise* describe the motion of someone or something that is going up. *Rise* is intransitive.

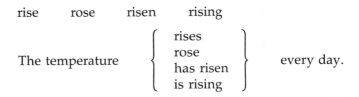

rise   rose   risen   rising

The temperature { rises / rose / has risen / is rising } every day.

The forms of *raise* mean "to lift up," "to force up," or "to bring up." (In using this verb, state the object that is being lifted, forced up, or brought up.) *Raise* is transitive.

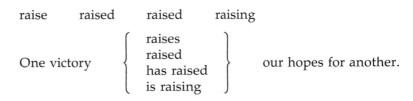

raise   raised   raised   raising

One victory { raises / raised / has raised / is raising } our hopes for another.

Exercise 16: *Using Lie/Lay, Sit/Set, Rise/Raise*

Write each of the following sentences, supplying the correct form of the verb given in parentheses. Underline the verbs you supply.

Example

a. Yesterday we _____ in the bleachers at the baseball game. (sit)

   Yesterday we sat in the bleachers at the baseball game.

1. I don't often _____ as soon as the alarm rings. (rise)

2. We _____ our compositions on the teacher's desk as we left the room. (lay)

3. We _____ our lunches on the table before going to get milk. (set)

4. Until today we thought we would never _____ the money. (raise)

5. Sally _____ the flowers on the table before she begins arranging them. (lay)

6. Michael is _____ on the sofa in the living room. (lie)

7. Danielle remembered that she had _____ awake for hours the night before, tossing and turning. (lie)

8. As winter approaches, the sun _____ later and sets earlier each day. (rise)

9. "Who has _____ in my chair?" asked Mama Bear. (sit)

10. Just as Jamie is _____ the pan on the stove, the doorbell rings. (set)

Review: Using Verbs

Write each sentence, choosing the correct verb from the pair shown in parentheses. Underline the verb you select.

Examples

a. Raymond's older brother, Jason, _____ absent most of the time. (be, is)

Raymond's older brother, Jason, is absent most of the time.

b. Last week Benjamin _____ dinner every night. (cook, cooked)

Last week Benjamin cooked dinner every night.

1. Tecumseh _____ a well-known Shawnee war chief. (was, were)

2. Who _____ that wonderful green bean, rice, and cheese casserole? (bake, baked)

3. Pamela _____ the living room window to get a little fresh air. (open, opened)

4. Last weekend Mary Anne _____ Debby to skate. (teached, taught)

5. The twenty-five small children from Miss Grumbacher's class _____ every animal that they saw in the children's zoo. (hug, hugged)

6. Our teacher always _____ at a desk in front of the class. (sits, sets)

7. Ellen never _____ in bed for more than five minutes after the alarm has sounded. (lies, lays)

8. The animal control office has issued a warning about Marilyn's dog, Coyote, who has _____ almost every letter carrier in town. (bit, bitten)

9. The student volunteers at the dance marathon for the Mothers' March Against Birth Defects _____ twenty-five liters of water. (drank, drunk)

10. The students in our gym class _____ noisy all the time. (are, be)

11. Juan, our foreign exchange student from Caracas, Venezuela, is lucky because he _____ to speak foreign languages very easily. (learn, learns)

12. Mary _____ the pot of beef stew in the center of the table. (sat, set)

13. On our fishing trip to Tehaya Lake we _____ thirty-eight rainbow trout. (catched, caught)

14. Pat will _____ this special delivery package at the post office. (leaves, leave)

15. George has _____ a delivery truck for several years. (drove, driven)

16. You've never really experienced the country until you have _____ in the straw on a lazy summer afternoon. (laid, lain)

17. Oscar, dear, don't _____ those wet clothes on the sofa, please. (sit, set)

18. After an unusually hard-fought election campaign, the freshman class has _____ Susie as its president. (chose, chosen)

19. We are getting a little worried about our prize-winning white Leghorn chickens because they haven't _____ a single egg this week. (lain, laid)

20. Celia _____ her exam on the teacher's desk and left the room. (laid, lay)

Writing Focus: *Using Vivid Verbs in Writing*

You can greatly improve your writing by including vivid verbs in your sentences. Such verbs can help *show* action precisely and clearly. Let the subject of your sentence *yell, screech, bellow, cackle, roar,* or *giggle* rather than *make a noise.* Avoid overusing such non-vivid verbs as *make, has, have, does, do, are, was, is,* and *were.*

Assignment: *Running the Rapids*

Notice the photograph on page 385 which has stopped the action of the canoe ride. Imagine that you can enter the photograph and be a part of the continuing action. You are now one of the people in the canoe. You are kneeling in the canoe, paddling through the foamy water. You feel the cold spray against your face, the muscles tensing in your arms as you raise the oar, and your heart pounding with excitement as you see what's coming up ahead.

Write one or more well-developed paragraphs telling about the canoe ride as though you are on it—right now. Pick up the action that the photograph has stopped. Use words to paint more pictures of the action-packed ride. Your purpose will be to relate the experience of being in the canoe for your audience of classmates. Your writing will be evaluated for correct and effective use of verbs.

Use the following steps to complete this assignment.

A. Prewriting

Study the photograph carefully. Use your imagination to enter the picture. Pretend that you are in the canoe, running the rapids. Take notes about what you are experiencing: what you do, what you see, what you hear, what you feel, and what you think. After you have finished, decide which notes will most effectively convey your experience. Then number them in an order that shows the action.

B. Writing

Using your notes, write one or more paragraphs relating the experience of running the rapids. Provide enough details and vivid verbs to allow your readers to be there with you, taking part in the action. Consider using the present tense of verbs to help you tell the

experience as if it were happening *now*. As you write, try to use the active voice as much as possible. Be certain to use the correct form for each of your verbs.

C. Postwriting

Revise your first draft, using the following checklist.

1. Does my account include enough specific details so that readers can imagine being in the canoe?

2. Is the action narrative presented in chronological order?

3. Do I use vivid verbs to convey a clear picture of the action?

4. Is each verb in the proper tense, and does it agree in number with the subject?

Proofread your revision, using the Proofreader's Checklist at the back of the book. If appropriate, share your writing with your classmates to enjoy each other's "trips."

15 Adjectives

Understanding Adjectives

The clothes you wear, the people you know, and the place where you live would be dull topics for conversation if you had no adjectives to describe them. Adjectives add life, color, and feeling to language. Understanding how adjectives work and how to use them effectively can make your use of language more precise and more interesting. In the following sections you will learn to identify adjectives through their definition, the classes into which they can be divided, and their features.

Defining Adjectives

Adjectives are usually defined as words that *modify* (describe or make more specific) nouns and pronouns.

The manager of the *department* store wore a *blue* suit.

The *furry Angora* kitten curled up on the sofa.

We were *eager* to start our trip.

Several houses remain *vacant* near the *old railroad* yard.

Adjectives answer the question *what kind? which one?* or *how many?* about the words they modify.

the *oak Parsons* table	[What kind of table?]
the *larger* table	[Which one of the tables?]
one table	[How many tables?]

Exercise 1: Identifying Adjectives

Write the following sentences, underlining the adjectives used to modify nouns and pronouns. Then draw an arrow from each adjective to the word modified.

Example

a. John bought woolen long underwear to wear when hiking.

John bought woolen long underwear to wear when hiking.

1. Terri bought paperback poetry books for English class.
2. The soccer coach spends the most time with the new players on the team.
3. The students usually wear casual clothes to the first dance.
4. Noriko always sends us funny cards for our birthdays.
5. While we were fishing, we caught six smallmouth bass.
6. After looking them over, Maria chose the smallest black kitten.
7. Wally reads several different auto magazines every week.
8. Coretta likes to eat in small, unknown restaurants.
9. Of the two cars we looked at, we wanted the small, blue convertible.
10. In the busy cafeteria, lunch is served on green plastic trays.

Grouping Adjectives by Classes

Many adjectives fall into one of five classes: articles, proper adjectives, common nouns acting as adjectives, pronouns acting as adjectives, and predicate adjectives. Some of the most common adjectives, such as *small, large, pretty,* and *happy,* do not fit into any special class.

The largest group of adjectives is *a, an,* and *the,* also called *articles.*

The is used before singular and plural nouns, *a* and *an* before singular nouns only.

The last several tests were difficult.

This was *a* much harder test than I expected.

Notice that other modifiers may come between the article and the noun or pronoun it modifies.

Use *a* before words beginning with a consonant sound; use *an* before words beginning with a vowel sound.

A hard rain is predicted for tonight along the northeastern coast of Maine.

Mountain climbing is *an* arduous sport even for those who are physically fit.

An hour ago you said I could leave.

Proper nouns used as adjectives (to modify other nouns or pronouns) are called *proper adjectives*.

Proper adjectives are always capitalized; some proper nouns change form to become adjectives.

Tourists love *America*.	[proper noun]
Tourists love *American* food.	[proper adjective]
They felt at home in *Alaska*.	[proper noun]
They felt at home in the *Alaskan* wilderness.	[proper adjective]
Queen Victoria ruled until 1901.	[proper noun]
The Industrial Revolution occurred in the *Victorian* Era.	[proper adjective]

Exercise 2: Identifying Proper Adjectives

Write the sentences on the next page, capitalizing and underlining proper adjectives. Circle all other adjectives in the sentence. (Not all sentences have proper adjectives.)

Examples

a. The best american cheese is either the tasty cheddar cheese or the nutlike swiss cheese.

(The) (best) American cheese is either (the) (tasty) (cheddar) cheese or (the) (nutlike) Swiss cheese.

b. Paula likes korean restaurants that serve spicy dishes, such as kimchi.

Paul likes Korean restaurants that serve (spicy) dishes, such as kimchi.

1. Our egyptian friend, Abdul, asked us to take off our muddy shoes at the door.

2. The fearless kitten attacked the japanese lantern.

3. Stormy weather made our trip on the dangerous roads a nightmare.

4. The spineless creature known as the jellyfish can deal out painful stings.

5. The dusty roads of the algerian countryside can become swamps in rainy weather.

6. The norwegian language is closely related to the swedish language.

7. Dangerous snakes can be found in the dusty plains.

8. The famous dancer was described as having catlike moves.

9. Tommy described a funny incident that took place when he was living on the indonesian island of Borneo.

10. The adventurous explorers left Maine in a balloon, carried to the east by the blustery winds of August on a trip that would make them national heroes.

Common nouns act as adjectives when they modify other nouns or pronouns.

An *ostrich* egg can weigh more than a kilogram.

The *kitchen* table had six chairs around it.

Note: Common nouns modifying nouns can easily be confused with compound nouns. In the phrase *garden hose,* for example, *garden* is a noun acting as an adjective to modify *hose; king cobra,* however, is a compound noun. Use your dictionary to determine whether a noun is a noun used as an adjective or is part of a compound noun.

Exercise 3: Identifying Nouns Used as Adjectives

Write each of the following sentences, underlining all nouns that are used as adjectives. Draw an arrow to the noun that each modifies.

Examples

    a. Mr. Chan amused the children by reciting nursery rhymes.

       Mr. Chan amused the children by reciting nursery rhymes.

    b. When we camped in the Maine woods, we felt like pioneers on the new frontier.

       When we camped in the Maine woods, we felt like pioneers on the new frontier.

1. We enjoyed the farm life when we stayed on Aunt Louise's farm.

2. Living in the Iowa countryside was really different from living in the city.

3. Our family outings frequently take us to the state park nearby.

4. It is always a good idea to turn off radio equipment when driving near a construction project.

5. When shopping for a new car, consider the business reputation of the automobile dealer.

6. Fishing near the Florida coast is a holiday treat.

7. When Maria forgot to wear her tennis shoes into the ocean, she cut her foot on an aluminum can.

8. The detective agency sent someone to the Nevada desert to investigate the casino robbery.

9. Mr. Schwartz and Ms. Espinosa are criminal lawyers who work for the county government.

10. The last meal that we had at summer camp consisted of bean soup and cheese sandwiches.

Some pronouns act as adjectives when they modify nouns or pronouns.

Demonstrative pronouns *(this, that, these, those)* act as adjectives when they modify a noun or pronoun.

This is more difficult than I thought.	[pronoun]
This test is more difficult than I thought.	[adjective]
These are the best of the group.	[pronoun]
These ideas are considered revolutionary.	[adjective]

Interrogative pronouns, *which* and *what,* act as adjectives when they modify a noun or pronoun.

Which is the correct answer?	[pronoun]
Which answer is correct?	[adjective]
What is the date of your birth?	[pronoun]
On *what* date were you born?	[adjective]

Indefinite pronouns (see list in Chapter 13) can sometimes act as adjectives, if they modify a noun or pronoun.

One can be lonely even in a crowd.	[pronoun]
One minute can seem like an hour.	[adjective]
Much can be accomplished in an hour.	[pronoun]
Much trouble can be avoided with planning.	[adjective]

Some possessive pronouns *(my, your, his, her, its, our, their)* act as adjectives to modify nouns.

Crosswalks are for *your* safety.

The seals performed for *their* dinner.

Exercise 4: Identifying Pronouns Used as Adjectives

Write each of the following sentences, underlining all pronouns used as adjectives. Draw an arrow from the pronoun used as an adjective to the noun that it modifies.

Examples

a. One person can accomplish a great deal.

One person can accomplish a great deal.

b. Neither of the new students wants any help.

Neither of the new students wants any help.

1. What kind of vegetable do you like best?

2. The teacher asked each student to recite some poetry.

3. Many people tried out for the city chorus, but few students made it.

4. Some students at Central High want to organize a student-teacher volleyball league, but some reject the idea.

5. Which type of car would you prefer, a two-door or a four-door?

6. Any student who wants to continue in school should study math.

7. Both front tires blew out, but neither passenger was hurt.

8. Many citizens of our town enjoy spending Sunday in the park, and most bring a picnic lunch with them.

9. All prepared foods now carry nutrition labels, and many consumers read them carefully.

10. Few people give any thought to their insurance until it is too late.

Predicate adjectives follow linking verbs and describe or modify a noun or pronoun in the subject of the sentence.

Sharon has been *thoughtful* and *responsible.*

The air seems *calm* and *muggy* this morning.

Exercise 5: Identifying Predicate Adjectives

Write each of the following sentences, underlining each predicate adjective. Then draw an arrow from the adjectives to the nouns or pronouns they modify.

Examples

    a. Our voices were hoarse from all of our cheering.

      Our voices were <u>hoarse</u> from all of our cheering.

    b. The cars on the lot are appealing but expensive.

      The cars on the lot are <u>appealing</u> but <u>expensive</u>.

1. The police will be careful to preserve order in the city.
2. From the scenic overlook the city seems miniature and toylike.
3. The mayor would be wise to listen to our complaints.
4. The truck felt large and clumsy compared with our car.
5. The fish I ordered was smaller and bonier than I expected.
6. The clouds coming in from the west are dark and ominous.
7. Ms. Merrick, who is always strict and unsympathetic, reprimanded me for being late.
8. The cabin looked friendly and inviting when we arrived.
9. That home computer unit appears entertaining and educational.
10. Our dog becomes irritable and nervous whenever it thunders.

Finding an Adjective by Its Features

Two characteristics, or features, can help you identify some adjectives. (Some adjectives have neither of these features; others have both.)

1. Adjectives may change form to show degrees of comparison.

Adjectives have three degrees of comparison: *positive, comparative,* and *superlative.*

Positive (modifies *one* noun)	Comparative (compares *two* words)	Superlative (compares *three* or *more* words)
warm	warmer	warmest
hungry	hungrier	hungriest
fast	faster	fastest

This is a *fresh* cucumber.	[positive]
This cucumber is *fresher* than that one.	[comparative]
This is the *freshest* cucumber in the store.	[superlative]

The regular way to make the comparative and superlative forms is to add -*er* and -*est* to the positive form. Sometimes, there will be a slight spelling change: *hungry / hungrier / hungriest*.

Some adjectives have irregular comparative and superlative forms.

Positive	Comparative	Superlative
good	better	best
bad	worse	worst
much, many	more	most

David has *much* talent in art.	[positive]
David has *more* talent in art than Michael.	[comparative]
David is the *most* talented student in art.	[superlative]

Many two-syllable adjectives and all adjectives that have three or more syllables form their comparative degree with *more* and their superlative degree with *most*.

Positive	Comparative	Superlative
careful	more careful	most careful
intelligent	more intelligent	most intelligent
superstitious	more superstitious	most superstitious

Exercise 6: *Identifying Adjectives by Degrees of Comparison*

Write the sentences on the next page, underlining only the adjectives that show one of the three degrees of comparison. Label these adjectives *P* for positive, *C* for comparative, and *S* for superlative.

Examples

a. Tom is the tallest student in the school.

  S
Tom is the tallest student in the school.

b. Joan's small dog is lazier than my large dog.

  P   C   P
Joan's small dog is lazier than my large dog.

1. I have heard many good pianists, but I think the best one is Bobby Short.

2. Raoul needs a quieter office than the one he has now.

3. One of the most destructive weapons in history is the atomic bomb.

4. Before his diet Tom was fatter than Rick, but now he is skinny.

5. There are several shades of paint available; the reddest is called *Southwest Sundown*.

6. The new police officer was more anxious than the more experienced officer.

7. The heat was bad today, but yesterday it was worse.

8. Paul may be the shortest member of the team, but he is the fastest runner.

9. Pork sausage is usually a spicier filling than hamburger.

10. The students have seen several plays, but the most dramatic scenes took place at the exciting conclusion of *Othello*.

---

2. Adjectives may be formed with suffixes.

The following list gives the most often used adjective suffixes:

Noun	+ Suffix	= Adjective
nation	+ -al	= *national* airport
child	+ -ish	= *childish* idea
care	+ -less	= *careless* move
toy	+ -like	= *toylike* village
poison	+ -ous	= *poisonous* chemical
breeze	+ -y	= *breezy* room

Exercise 7: *Identifying Adjectives Formed with Suffixes*

Write the following sentences, underlining the adjectives that are formed with suffixes. Then draw an arrow from the adjective to the noun or pronoun it modifies.

Examples

a. The boat was motionless on the calm lake.

The boat was <u>motionless</u> on the calm lake.

b. The dangerous road was too steep for bicycling.

The <u>dangerous</u> road was too steep for bicycling.

1. We took a coastal drive along the Pacific for our vacation.

2. Your remark to your sister was thoughtless and rude.

3. The honorable Judge Jacob Harding presided over the court.

4. On a windy day nothing looks lifeless.

5. The United States exports more agricultural products than other countries do.

6. My mother has a flawless reputation for keeping accurate financial records.

7. The lifelike portrait hanging over the mantel was quite dusty.

8. My younger brother always looks helpless when he's asked to do work around the house.

9. It is often rainy in the mountainous regions of South America.

10. The endless search for Bigfoot often stirs national interest.

Review: *Understanding Adjectives*

In the following selection from *Last Flight* by Amelia Earhart, the pilot records her observations during the beginning of her first Pacific flight. Notice that four adjectives in the selection are underlined. Identify and list twenty other adjectives used in the selection. Number a sheet of paper 1–20 and list the adjectives in the order they occur. In parentheses beside each adjective indicate the line in the selection on which it appears. (Do not include the articles *a, an,* and *the.* Hint: *no* in line 11 is an adjective.)

Example

6000 (line 2)

1.   Clouds were all about me from the start. I had to climb
2.   6000 feet to get over the <u>first</u> layers of <u>filmy</u> white. I could look
3.   down and see the water, dark blue and then darker blue, then
4.   black, as night came on. It was a night of stars. Stars hung
5.   outside my cockpit window near enough to touch. I have never
6.   seen so many or such large ones. I shall never forget the contrast
7.   of the white clouds and the moonlight and starlight against the
8.   black of the sea. It is interesting that I have flown over
9.   thousands of miles of water but have seen only hundreds of
10.   miles. I have been over clouds, between two layers, or actually
11.   in the formation, for hours on end, and have seen no ships
12.   excepting very near land. However, on the Pacific flight I took
13.   along a chart showing the position of every ship in the course
14.   that night. The possibility of one little airplane and one little
15.   ship passing near enough to see each other in that rather large
16.   ocean seemed ridiculous.
17.   I had been flying off the islands for about six hours when I
18.   became aware of a pink light to my right—pink in contrast to the
19.   stars. I realized I was actually seeing a ship. I couldn't see it as a
20.   ship, of course. It appeared only as <u>revolving</u> pinkish light.[1]

Applying What You Know

Using what you have learned about their definition, classes, and features, identify the adjectives in a paragraph from a book, magazine, or newspaper. Copy the selection and underline the adjectives. Then list the adjectives and write the method you used to identify each one.

Using Adjectives

In his autobiography Charles Dickens describes a warehouse where he worked as a child as a "crazy, tumbledown old house." Without adjectives the writer would not have been able to give this vivid picture of a place he detested. Although adjectives can add vitality to writing, using them sometimes creates problems because of the three comparative forms they have.

---

[1]From *Last Flight* by Amelia Earhart. Reprinted by permission of Harcourt Brace Jovanovich, Inc.

In the following sections you will study and practice using adjectives correctly.

Using Comparative and Superlative Degrees

Adjectives may change their forms to show the comparative and superlative degrees in one of three ways:

1. With -er and -est added to the positive form
2. With the words more and most used with the positive form
3. With words that are completely different from the positive form

Using -er and -est to Form Degrees of Comparison

Form the comparative and superlative forms of most one-syllable adjectives by adding -er and -est to their positive degrees.

Positive	Comparative	Superlative
low	lower	lowest
cold	colder	coldest
small	smaller	smallest
young	younger	youngest

When these one-syllable adjectives end in the letter *y*, change the *y* to an *i* before adding -er or -est. When they end in a silent *e*, drop the *e* before adding -er or -est.

Positive	Comparative	Superlative
happy	happier	happiest
easy	easier	easiest
late	later	latest
wise	wiser	wisest

For some adjectives that end in a single consonant, double that consonant before adding -er or -est.

Positive	Comparative	Superlative
big	bigger	biggest
thin	thinner	thinnest
hot	hotter	hottest

Exercise 8: Using -er and -est to Show Comparison

Write each of the following sentences, supplying the correct form of the adjective in parentheses. Underline the adjective you form.

Examples

a. Norma has a _____ vocabulary than her sister. (large)
   Norma has a <u>larger</u> vocabulary than her sister.

b. There were twenty dogs at the pound, but the _____ was the sheep dog. (fuzzy)
   There were twenty dogs at the pound, but the <u>fuzziest</u> was the sheep dog.

1. Of geography, biology, and algebra, geography is probably the _____ subject. (easy)

2. Just because it's the _____ paper of the two doesn't mean it will get a better grade. (long)

3. Since he lost thirty pounds and took up marathon running, Mike is the _____ student in our school. (fit)

4. No one really believed it, but Howard was a _____ player than Samantha. (strong)

5. Carla's vegetarian diet is certainly _____ than the junk food she used to eat. (healthy)

6. Jim is the _____ of all the attendants at the carwash. (wet)

7. Studying for a few days before a test is _____ than waiting until the last night. (wise)

8. I may be _____ and younger than my brother, but I always beat him at chess. (short)

9. Of the four flower arrangements I made, this is the _____. (pretty)

10. The movie we saw this afternoon was _____ than the one we saw last night. (sad)

Using More *and* Most *to Show Comparison*

Many two-syllable adjectives and all adjectives having more than two syllables form their comparative and superlative degrees with *more* and *most*.

Positive	Comparative	Superlative
capable	more capable	most capable
honest	more honest	most honest
terrible	more terrible	most terrible
superficial	more superficial	most superficial

Comparisons that show lesser amounts of a quality form the comparative degree with the word *less* and the superlative degree with the word *least*.

Positive	Comparative	Superlative
intense	less intense	least intense
difficult	less difficult	least difficult
bright	less bright	least bright
sharp	less sharp	least sharp

Exercise 9: *Using* More *and* Most *to Show Comparison*

Write the following sentences, supplying the correct form of each adjective in parentheses. Use the sense of the sentence to decide whether to use *more*, *most*, *less*, or *least*. Underline the modifier you form.

Example

a. It may be hard to believe, but the pig is a _____ animal than the dog. (intelligent)

It may be hard to believe, but the pig is a more intelligent animal than the dog.

1. I hope that Miss Martin's algebra test is _____ than the one she gave last week. (difficult)

2. The storm we had yesterday was terrible; in fact, it was the _____ storm we've had all year. (terrible)

3. Yours was the _____ card I received while I was sick; it helped me to feel better. (cheerful)

4. José makes better grades in drafting than I do because his blueprints are _____ than mine. (precise)

5. The heat actually felt _____ in the car than in the backyard, so I stayed in the car. (intense)

6. Sarah's hard work and talent have made her the _____ artist in the class. (accomplished)

7. My grandfather was _____ in the 1930s than in the 1920s because of the great stock market crash in 1929. (wealthy)

8. Sylvia is always _____ right before a gymnastic routine than during it. (nervous)

9. I've shopped at several grocery stores, but I like this one because it has the _____ supply of fruit. (plentiful)

10. I thought the judging was unfair because the student who won was actually the _____. (talented)

Using Irregular Comparisons

A few adjectives change their forms completely to show the comparative and superlative degrees.

Positive	Comparative	Superlative
good	better	best
bad	worse	worst
much, many	more	most

Exercise 10: Using Irregular Comparisons

Write the sentences on the following page, supplying the correct form of the adjective in parentheses. Underline the adjective you form.

Examples

a. Last week's hurricane was the _____ in five years. (bad)
   Last week's hurricane was the worst in five years.

      b. Janice had a _____ time at the carnival than I. (good)
        Janice had a better time at the carnival than I.

1. Your singing is good, but Kayo's is even _____. (good)

2. I charge _____ for baby-sitting now than I did two years ago. (much)

3. Melissa is not very good at singing, but she is the _____ organist in the county. (good)

4. We thought that Michael was a _____ player than Jim, but we were wrong. (bad)

5. One of the _____ moving speeches I have ever read is that of Joseph, Chief of the Nez Percés. (much)

6. Betty is a _____ student than an employee. (good)

7. Rosita can do _____ sit-ups than you, but Jennifer can do the sit-ups better. (many)

8. Sarah's grades were acceptable last year, but she made _____ marks this year. (bad)

9. Of the many places we have traveled, Timbuktu was the _____ unusual. (much)

10. The United States imports _____ oil than any other country in the world. (much)

Problems with Comparisons

The following are the four most common problems encountered in using adjective comparisons:

1. Using double comparisons

2. Using illogical comparisons

3. Using *less* and *fewer* incorrectly

4. Using demonstrative adjectives improperly

Double comparisons occur when two forms of comparison are used together. Only one form of comparison, *-er* or *-est*, or the word *more* or *most*, should be used.

The asterisk (*) denotes a feature that is not a part of Standard English.

*Helen is *more shorter* than I.
Helen is *shorter* than I.

*This yogurt is the *bestest* of any you have made.
This yogurt is the *best* of any you have made.

Occasionally writers will create comparisons that appear to make sense but are actually illogical.

---

*My frog Eric is a better jumper than any frog.

Eric cannot be a better jumper than *any* frog because Eric is himself a frog, and Eric cannot be a better jumper than himself.

*Janet has longer hair than anyone in her family.

Janet is also a member of her family, and her hair cannot be longer than her own hair.

Such sentences can be easily corrected with the words *other* or *else* added to the sentence.

My frog Eric can jump farther than any *other* frog.

Janet has longer hair than anyone *else* in her family.

Exercise 11: Eliminating Illogical Comparisons

Each of the following sentences has an illogical comparison. Rewrite each sentence, adding either the word *else* or *other* to eliminate the illogical comparison.

Examples

---

a. Carla is a better writer than anyone in her English class.
   Carla is a better writer than anyone else in her English class.

b. Julius Caesar is a faster runner than any dog in his pack.
   Julius Caesar is a faster runner than any other dog in his pack.

1. Henry Chan plays better soccer than any player on the team.

2. Michelle is better at remembering dates than any girl in her civics class.

3. Maria has a stronger floor exercise than anyone on her gymnastics team.

4. Corporal Rey has larger shoes than any soldier in the platoon.

5. The steer Marsha entered is heavier than any steer entered in the fair.

6. The mayor has a greater influence on the city council than anyone does.

7. Martin Luther King, Jr., was more famous than any black leader of the 1960s.

8. Michael is less dependent on weight lifting than anybody on the swimming team.

9. Some people claim that football is more violent than any sport played in the United States.

10. Ms. Washington, the biology teacher, is more eager to organize field trips than the members of the faculty.

Troublesome Adjectives

The adjective *less* is used to modify singular nouns.

I have *less* money in my pocket than he does.

The number of mistakes was *less* on the second test.

The adjective *fewer* modifies only plural nouns.

Miguel has *fewer* dimes than I do.

Your chances of winning are *fewer* if you don't practice.

The demonstrative adjectives have a singular and a plural form.

Singular	Plural
this that	these those

Difficulty often occurs when demonstrative adjectives are used to modify the nouns *kind*, *kinds*, *sort*, or *sorts*.

this kind	*this* sort	*these* kinds	*these* sorts
that kind	*that* sort	*those* kinds	*those* sorts

The demonstrative adjectives agree in number with the nouns they modify: singular adjective with singular noun, and plural adjective with plural noun.

The expressions *kind of* and *sort of* can be used when they mean "a type" or "a style."

What *kind of* dress are you making?

I throw my curve with this *sort of* motion.

We all like those *kinds of* crackers.

Do not add an unnecessary *a* at the end of such expressions. The phrases *kind of a* and *sort of a* are not features of Standard English.

In Standard English the expressions *kind of* and *sort of* should not be used to mean "rather" or "somewhat."

The asterisk (*) denotes a feature that is not part of Standard English.

*He thought the program was *kind of* long.

He thought the program was *rather* long.

Exercise 12: *Using Troublesome Adjectives Correctly*

Write each of the following sentences, supplying the appropriate word or words in parentheses. Underline the form you select.

Examples

a. Our school bookstore sells _____ books than pencils. (less, fewer)
   Our school bookstore sells fewer books than pencils.

b. Billie's report was _____ long, but it was interesting. (kind of, rather)
   Billie's report was rather long, but it was interesting.

1. The principal says that students drink _____ milk than water. (less, fewer)

2. Mitsuko is _____ shy, but she has many good friends. (somewhat, kind of)

3. No one wants _____ kinds of shoes anymore because they are not good for running. (this, these)

4. Charles asked whether that wasn't _____ long to practice. (kind of, rather)

5. At our library there are _____ works of fiction than nonfiction. (less, fewer)

6. _____ sort of outfit is now out of style, but it was popular in the fifties. (This, These)

7. We wanted to buy _____ kinds of decorations for our class party, but we couldn't afford them. (this, these)

8. Mr. Espinosa is a _____ inexperienced teacher who just started teaching at our school. (kind of, rather)

9. What _____ car would you prefer, a sedan or a station wagon? (kind of, kind of a)

10. The teacher said that our exams were _____ disappointing and that we would be retested. (kind of, somewhat)

Placing Adjectives to Modify Nouns and Pronouns

Adjectives can be used in positions other than immediately before the nouns or pronouns they modify. Using adjectives in different positions can add variety and appropriate emphasis to your writing.

Adjectives can be set off by commas immediately after the noun or pronoun they modify.

Now the castle, *dark* and *gloomy*, could barely be seen in the twilight.

Adjectives can be placed at the beginning of a sentence with several words separating them from the word they modify.

Wise and *fair* in all her decisions, Jane seemed to be the perfect judge.

Adjectives can follow both the noun or pronoun they modify and a linking verb.

Sean appears *polite* and *thoughtful*.

They hoped that their vacation would be *eventful*.

An adjective must clearly modify a noun or pronoun in the sentence.

Exercise 13: Using Adjectives in Different Places

Rewrite the following sentences, moving the *italicized* adjectives to different positions. Sometimes, you may need to add or delete words. Underline the adjectives that you move.

Examples

a. The *tired* and *weary* student, after hours of study, turned out the light.
   The student, tired and weary after hours of study, turned out the light.

b. Jane had been both *vain* and *inconsiderate* in the past but was now a different person.
   Both vain and inconsiderate in the past, Jane was now a different person.

1. The tunnel, *long* and *dark,* lay ahead of us.

2. *Hot* and *spicy,* the flavor of the Indian curry attracted us.

3. We have been *lazy* all afternoon, but tomorrow we'll work.

4. Cassius, *lean* and *hungry,* was a man to be feared.

5. *Regal* and *majestic,* the queen ruled from her bejeweled throne.

6. John was *slow* and *deliberate* in choosing a good book to read.

7. The sailors survived the wreck because they were *smart* and *hardy.*

8. *Exhausted,* the runners dropped like flies.

9. Four students, *anxious* and *nervous,* were directed to the personnel office by the receptionist.

10. The athletes had been *tired* and *defeated* only minutes before, but they were now ready for action again!

Using Commas with Adjectives

Several adjectives may be used to modify the same noun.

The *two famous, aging film* stars continued to attract large audiences.

Use a comma to separate adjectives if you could substitute the word *and* between those adjectives without changing the meaning of the phrase.

A *talented, charming* executive spoke to our class.
[A talented *and* charming executive spoke to our class.]

The *four foreign* students were studying economics.
[The *four and foreign students* changes the meaning of the phrase.]

Exercise 14: Using Commas with Adjectives

Write each of the following sentences, underlining all of the adjectives except articles. Separate the adjectives with commas when necessary. Circle the commas you insert.

Examples

---

    a. A small yellow puppy followed us through the old empty graveyard.
       A <u>small</u>(,) <u>yellow</u> puppy followed us through the <u>old</u>(,) <u>empty</u> graveyard.

    b. The many friends of the famous band leader played a concert after the long boring eulogy.
       The <u>many</u> friends of the <u>famous</u> band leader played a concert after the <u>long</u>(,) <u>boring</u> eulogy.

1. The young children who live in the old brick cottage near the lake have never visited the many public libraries nearby.

2. These unfortunate children have missed a wonderful experience because that magnificent old library is a treasure chest.

3. The old county library has a large varied collection of popular old records.

4. The old Victorian building has tall white columns with huge oak doors and is bathed in bright sunlight by long narrow skylights.

5. The sandy beach lay before us, while the mirrorlike surface of the deep cold lake called us to swim.

6. As we entered the lake, our hot dry skin was shocked by the sting of the frigid water.

7. After several painful seconds the shock passed, and a quick adjustment was made.

8. After a short brisk swim the warm radiant sun removed the chill, and the cycle began again.

9. In the third-period biology class the young inexperienced teacher forgot to take the daily attendance.

10. During the long extra-inning baseball game Mr. Durango took a peaceful nap and woke to a still-tied score.

Forming Adjectives with Suffixes

Adjectives may be formed by adding suffixes to other parts of speech such as nouns and verbs.

Noun	+	Suffix	=	Adjective
haze	+	-y	=	*hazy* afternoon
end	+	-less	=	*endless* drive
help	+	-ful	=	*helpful* hand
danger	+	-ous	=	*dangerous* road
respect	+	-able	=	*respectable* position
fool	+	-ish	=	*foolish* idea
universe	+	-al	=	*universal* symbol
sphere	+	-like	=	*spherelike* object

Verb	+	Suffix	=	Adjective
throw	+	-ing	=	*throwing* arm
play	+	-ful	=	*playful* kitten
consider	+	-ate	=	*considerate* letter
pitch	+	-ed	=	*pitched* ball
use	+	-able	=	*usable* bag
run	+	-less	=	*runless* inning
rain	+	-y	=	*rainy* week

Exercise 15: *Forming Adjectives with Suffixes*

Form adjectives from the following words and suffixes and then write a sentence using each new word you form. Underline the new adjective in each sentence that you write. Since a word's spelling sometimes changes when a suffix is added, use your dictionary to check for correct spelling.

Example

a. (health + -y)
   healthy
   Jogging can be <u>healthy</u> activity.

---

1. honor + -able

2. occasion + -al

3. train + -ed

4. score + -less

5. adventure + -ous

6. limit + -less

7. salt + -y

8. book + -ish

9. nation + -al

10. run + -ing

Review: *Using Adjectives*

Write each of the following sentences, supplying the appropriate form of the adjective in parentheses. Underline the adjective you supply.

Example

a. Of the four women Harriet was clearly the _____. (tall)
   Of the four women Harriet was clearly the <u>tallest</u>.

---

1. We all agree that Norman is _____ than Carey. (nice)

2. José, Alex, and Leroy all took the test, but Alex had studied more and received the _____ grade. (good)

3. Judging by the beauty of her work, I decided that Alice was the _____ of the two artists. (skillful)

4. Many baseball players think that Hank Aaron was the _____ hitter of all time. (great)

5. Mary and Kathy both ski, but because she has practiced more, Kathy is the _____. (agile)

6. At the county fair the judges ruled that Ann's rhubarb casserole was the _____ in the county and awarded it the prize. (delicious)

7. Lisa has not worked all semester, so her grades are the _____ in the freshman class. (bad)

8. Of all the native American leaders, Crazy Horse, who seldom lost a battle, was the _____ general. (successful)

9. The temperature now seems _____ than it was earlier today. (low)

10. His many discoveries rank George Washington Carver as one of the _____ scientists in history. (talented)

Rewrite each of the following sentences, making adjectives conform to Standard English.

Example

a. Jane is a more better swimmer than she is a diver.
   Jane is a better swimmer than she is a diver.

11. Charley is the most best swimmer in our school's history.

12. John's most longest poem won him the annual literary prize.

13. Our athletes now drink fewer milk than they did last year.

14. The art teacher is more patient than any member of the faculty.

15. The rabbit is the most importantest exhibit for the success of the experiment.

16. Carlos checked out less books from the library than I did.

17. Sharon and Michelle make better grades than their friends.

18. The play that we saw was sort of boring, but Uncle John loved it.

19. This is the most worst meal that we've ever eaten.

20. Mary Beth is a carefuler driver than her friend.

Writing Focus: *Using Specific Adjectives in Writing*

Specific adjectives can give your writing life, color, and feeling. Such adjectives add specific details of sight, smell, sound, taste, and touch. Too many adjectives as well as overused ones such as *nice, cute,* or *great,* however, can overwhelm or deaden your writing. Use precise and effective adjectives consciously in your writing.

Assignment: *A Better Time*

Some years seem just naturally better than others. This year, for example, you may have gotten your own room. Perhaps this time is better not because of a specific event, but because of the advantages of being older, meeting new people, taking new courses, or being involved in new activities.

Write one or more paragraphs describing how this year, day, or week is different from the last one. Your purpose will be to describe the situations or circumstances in both time periods in order to show why one is better than the other. Write for your classmates and teacher. Your writing will be evaluated for correct and effective use of adjectives.

Use the steps on the next page to complete this assignment.

A. Prewriting

Think about your life: today and yesterday, this week and last week, this year and last year. Choose one of the pairs to write about, the one that shows most clearly how different and better this time is compared to the last one. Begin to recall what the past time was like. Free write. (If you have questions about free writing, review Chapter 1.) Relax and let observations and memories about the time flood your mind and flow out through your pen onto the paper. Don't worry about writing correctly or rereading what you've written. Just put down words, phrases, or sentences as they occur to you. Write quickly and easily until no more ideas come. Review your free writing, and underline three or four key points or ideas that describe the situation or circumstances of the past time.

B. Writing

Write one or more paragraphs telling how one time period is different from another. Use ideas from your free writing to help you. You might begin your work with a sentence like, "This year is different from last year for several reasons." Use fresh adjectives to help provide the details.

C. Postwriting

Revise your first draft using the following checklist.

1.   Does my writing show how one time period is better than another?

2.   Have I included details to support and explain my reasons?

3.   Have I used fresh, specific adjectives?

Proofread your work, using the Proofreader's Checklist at the back of the book. If appropriate, share your writing with your classmates or family.

16 Adverbs

Understanding Adverbs

Suppose you need to explain *how* something happened—perhaps how you made the winning shot in last night's basketball game or how difficult it was taking Mr. Watkin's algebra test last period. Speaking or writing interestingly and clearly about either of these situations without using adverbs would be difficult. You could not say, for example, that the shot was made *skillfully* or that the test was *extremely* difficult. Adverbs add variety and specificity to speech and writing.

In the following sections you will learn to identify adverbs through their definition, the classes into which they can be grouped, and their features.

Defining Adverbs

Adverbs are usually defined as words that modify (describe or make more specific) verbs, adjectives, or other adverbs.

Modifying a Verb

Margaret types *quickly* and *accurately*.

The company arrived *late* for dinner.

Modifying an Adjective

The game was *very* exciting in the last quarter.

The sound on the radio was *too* low for me to hear.

Modifying Another Adverb

We bowl *rather* frequently on the weekends.

The turtles move *so* slowly that the race will never end.

Adverbs modify verbs, adjectives, and other adverbs by answering one of several questions: *how? how often? when? where?* or *to what extent?*

Ali crossed the highway *cautiously*.	[how?]
Kim runs to school *frequently*.	[how often?]
Sandi *recently* received an award.	[when?]
Most students go *home* for lunch.	[where?]
The test was *extremely* difficult.	[to what extent?]

Exercise 1: Identifying Adverbs

Write the following sentences, underlining the adverbs. Then draw an arrow from each underlined adverb to the word or words it modifies.

Example

a. John walked briskly along the corridor.

John walked <u>briskly</u> along the corridor.

1. The test was moderately difficult.
2. Tom and Sam built model cars carefully.
3. Sandra stops here for lunch.
4. Paul arrives at school late.
5. Mary was very friendly to everyone.
6. The class members often bring apples and other fruit for the homeroom teacher.
7. Carmen studies her German daily.
8. Martin arrived early for biology class.
9. Nhim reacts unpredictably to bad news.
10. Fred and Martha met there on the stoop.

Grouping Adverbs by Classes

Three classes of adverbs are *intensifiers, interrogative adverbs*, and *negative adverbs*.

Intensifiers, adverbs that modify other adverbs and adjectives, sometimes strengthen, or intensify, the meanings of the words they modify.

Martha is *very* sick.

We were *quite* relieved when it didn't snow.

Other intensifiers limit or restrict the meanings of the words they modify.

The machine is *almost* fixed.

The project is *nearly* complete.

One way intensifiers differ from other adverbs is that intensifiers cannot complete a pattern such as "She ran _____."

An asterisk (*) indicates a sentence with a feature that is not part of Standard English.

*He played very.

*We worked just.

The following words are often used as intensifiers.

almost	quite	somewhat
nearly	rather	too
pretty	really	very

When the adverbs *how, when, where,* and *why* are used to introduce a question, they are called *interrogative adverbs*.

How often do you hike here?	[modifies the adverb *often*]
When will the campaign be over?	[modifies the verb phrase *will be*]

Where are the two referees?	[modifies the verb *are*]
Why did you buy that one?	[modifies the verb phrase *did buy*]

Exercise 2: *Identifying Intensifiers and Interrogative Adverbs*

Write each of the following sentences, underlining all intensifiers and interrogative adverbs. Then draw an arrow from each adverb to the word or words it modifies.

Examples

a. Why do so many football players lift weights?

Why do so many football players lift weights?

b. John became somewhat angry when he forgot the combination to his locker.

John became somewhat angry when he forgot the combination to his locker.

1. How do really lazy people manage to graduate from high school?

2. When did JoAnn write that rather boring poem that has just appeared in the school newspaper?

3. Where is that sweater I want to wear hiking?

4. Why hasn't Ms. Carmichael distributed the report cards?

5. When will you complete that nearly impossible chemistry assignment?

6. How many of our athletes are fairly certain of making the team this year?

7. Why has the coach selected Tom, a somewhat awkward player, as co–captain?

8. Where did you hide that rather ugly statue that we gave you?

9. How often does a crowd of nearly 1,000 people attend a PTA meeting?

10. When will the new international airport and hotel complex open in our city?

The most common negative adverb is *not*.

Not, which is often part of a contraction, gives a negative meaning to the word or words it modifies.

Susan has *not* cooked dinner.

Susan has*n't* cooked dinner.

We do *not* like tuna fish sandwiches.

Other negative adverbs are *barely, hardly, never, scarcely,* and *seldom*.

Like other adverbs, negative adverbs may modify verbs, adjectives, and other adverbs.

I could *not* find the ticket.	[modifies the verb phrase *could find*]
Carmen, *never* happy without a problem, creates her own difficulties.	[modifies the adjective *happy*]
Mike paints regularly, although *seldom* skillfully.	[modifies the adverb *skillfully*]

Exercise 3: Identifying Negative Adverbs

Write the following sentences, underlining the negative adverbs. Then draw an arrow from the adverb to the word or words it modifies. (When a negative adverb is part of a contraction, underline only the adverb.)

Examples

a. John doesn't like pizza for dinner.

John doesn't like pizza for dinner.

b. Jenny has scarcely begun the painting.

Jenny has scarcely begun the painting.

1. Didn't Carmen sing a solo during the choir recital?
2. Marsha had hardly begun her new secretarial job when she was fired.
3. Moishe has never met the mayor of Gary, Indiana.
4. Isn't Amy planning the class party?
5. Hasn't Paul read the Koran before?
6. Crazy Horse, the great Sioux chief, was seldom defeated in battle.
7. The new P.E. instructor never played football for Purdue University.
8. The bus was barely full.
9. Mike and Sharon aren't the current managers of the school supply store.
10. Why didn't Patricia attend algebra class?

Finding an Adverb by Its Features

Two features can help you identify adverbs: look for words that show a degree of comparison and words that are formed by particular suffixes.

Some adverbs change form to show degrees of comparison.

Adverbs have three degrees of comparison: *positive, comparative,* and *superlative.*

Most adverbs form their comparative and superlative degrees with the words *more* and *most.*

Positive (modifies one word)	*Comparative* (compares two words)	*Superlative* (compares three or more words)
carefully	more carefully	most carefully
graciously	more graciously	most graciously
frequently	more frequently	most frequently

Janet practiced her lessons *carefully*.	[positive]
Susan practiced her lessons *more carefully* than Janet.	[comparative]
Kristine practiced her lessons *most carefully* of all.	[superlative]

Some adverbs add *-er* and *-est* to form their comparative and superlative degrees.

Positive	*Comparative*	*Superlative*
near	nearer	nearest
soon	sooner	soonest
early	earlier	earliest
fast	faster	fastest
high	higher	highest

Robert arrived *soon* after Paul.	[positive]
Paul arrived *sooner* than Robert.	[comparative]
Miguel arrived *soonest*.	[superlative]

A few adverbs form their comparative and superlative degrees in irregular ways.

Positive	*Comparative*	*Superlative*
badly	worse	worst
well	better	best
much	more	most
little	less	least
far	farther	farthest

Vickie plays volleyball *badly* in P.E.	[positive]
My volleyball playing is *worse* than Vickie's.	[comparative]
Of all my friends Bill is the *worst* volleyball player.	[superlative]

Less or least of a quality is indicated with the words *less* or *least*.

I studied *less carefully* than usual and failed the test.

The *least tiresome* job I ever had was working in a library.

Exercise 4: Identifying Adverbs That Show Comparison

Write the following sentences, underlining adverbs that show one of the three degrees of comparison. Label the adverbs *P* for positive, *C* for comparative, and *S* for superlative.

Examples

a. Kevin debates less aggressively than Ricardo.

               C

Kevin debates <u>less</u> aggressively than Ricardo.

b. Deep into the jungle marched the safari.

  P

<u>Deep</u> into the jungle marched the safari.

c. Of all the woodshop students Diane works most skillfully.

                                    S

Of all the woodshop students Diane works <u>most</u> skillfully.

1. After only a week's instruction Miranda skis better than before.

2. Carol gazed fondly at the boy sitting nearest to her.

3. This group of students listened more respectfully to the speaker than the other.

4. We must either evacuate the building more quickly or have a fire drill more often.

5. Shelly has always ridden a bicycle faster than I have.

6. Of all the chorus members Yim sings least loudly.

7. Suzanne accepted the nomination most graciously of all the candidates.

8. I usually answer questions more confidently in English class than I do in biology.

9. Our car was severely damaged in the accident.

10. Kanu draws badly, but James draws even worse.

Some adverbs may be formed with suffixes.

Many adverbs (especially those that answer the question *how?*) end in the suffix *-ly*. These adverbs are usually formed by adding the suffix *-ly* to adjectives.

Adjective	+	*-ly*	=	*Adverb*
simple	+	-ly	=	*simply* repaired
complete	+	-ly	=	*completely* confusing
quick	+	-ly	=	*quickly* thrown

Other suffixes that are frequently used as adverb suffixes are *-wards, -ways,* and *-wise.*

In the confusion the ball carrier ran *backwards*.

She placed the book *sideways* on the shelf.

The stripes ran *lengthwise* all the way to the ceiling.

Exercise 5: Identifying Adverbs Formed from Suffixes

Write the following sentences, underlining adverbs that are formed from suffixes. Then draw an arrow from each adverb to the word or words that it modifies.

Examples

---

a. Melissa walked slowly to the podium.

Melissa walked slowly to the podium.

b. The band marched about the field counterclockwise.

The band marched about the field counterclockwise.

1. Jimmy walked quietly to the front of the room to deliver his speech.

2. Luis is rarely late for school.

3. When we learned to study properly, our grades took an upward climb.

4. Marshall cooks absolutely delicious Chinese meals.

5. To open your locker turn the dial clockwise to the first number of your combination.

6. Time was rapidly running out, so we decided to concentrate on finishing our reports.

7. In search of the perfect wave, we drove westward to California.

8. Frances spoke truthfully when she said that she was bored.

9. Our car slid sideways when we hit the ice on the driveway.

10. Yoshiro paints portraits exceptionally well for a student.

Review: Understanding Adverbs

In the following selection from an autobiographical narrative, Nancy Huddleston Packer describes a childhood experience. Washington, D.C., where Nancy Packer lived, was in the grip of the Great Depression during the 1930s, but the memory of planning her first Christmas shopping trip remained with the writer. Two adverbs in the selection are underlined. Using what you have learned in the preceding sections, identify fifteen other adverbs. List the adverbs you identify on a sheet of paper numbered 1–15. In parentheses beside each adverb, indicate on what line of the selection it appears.

Examples

    a. very (line 1)
    b. closely (line 4)

1.   My brother George was five years older than I and <u>very</u> careful
2. with money. He owned a little file case in which he kept a stack of
3. IOU's signed by his friends and family. When all of us went, say, to an
4. amusement park, he chose his rides on the <u>closely</u> calculated basis of
5. ride time to money. And so it was to him I went for advice on how to
6. plan my Christmas spending.
7.   "First you make a list," he said. He would do it for me since I
8. couldn't really write. "Now you figure out how much to spend on
9. everybody by how much you love them."
10.   We commenced. By means of a private logic I cannot
11. now recall, I settled on thirty-five cents for Mother and thirty
12. for Father. Next came my brothers and sisters: Mary, George,
13. John, and Jane. Beside each name I directed George to write
14. twenty cents.
15.   "Everyone exactly the same, huh?" he said. "OK, what about
16. Ida?"

17.   Instinctively I read his meaning. If I cared no more for him than
18.   for the others, then he would make it tough for me. "I reckon you
19.   didn't even think about Ida," he said harshly. "Poor as she is, much as
20.   she loves you."
21.   Ida worked for Mother and was very important to all of us, but I
22.   hadn't thought I would buy her a present, for our parents gave her a
23.   nice one from all of us. Nevertheless I fell before George's attack and
24.   said, "Ida: twenty-five cents."
25.   George stared at me. "Twenty-five cents," I repeated. "How
26.   much have I got left?"
27.   Grudgingly he informed me that I had eighty cents left. I
28.   directed him to write down ten cents beside the names of three
29.   school friends with whom I had agreed to exchange presents. That
30.   left Walter.[1]

Applying What You Know

From a newspaper or magazine select an account of a sports event, such as a football game, tennis match, or track meet. Using what you have learned about their definition, classes, and features, identify the adverbs in three paragraphs. Copy the selection and attach it to your list of adverbs.

Using Adverbs

In the following sections you will learn how to use adverbs correctly.

Using Comparative and Superlative Degrees

Most adverbs form their comparative and superlative degrees with the words *more* and *most*.

Positive (modifies one word)	Comparative (compares two words)	Superlative (compares three or more words)
loudly	more loudly	most loudly
accurately	more accurately	most accurately

[1]From "Giving, Getting" by Nancy Huddleston Packer from *The Reporter Magazine*, December 31, 1964. Copyright 1964 by Nancy Huddleston Packer. Reprinted by permission.

Adverbs show lesser amounts with the word *less* in the comparative and *least* in the superlative degree.

Positive	Comparative	Superlative
softly	less softly	least softly
carefully	less carefully	least carefully
precisely	less precisely	least precisely

Maurice swims *more confidently* than Jonas.

Jonas swims *less confidently* than Maurice.

Jim types *most accurately* of the male students.

Cynthia types *least accurately* of all the students in her typing class.

Exercise 6: *Using Comparative and Superlative Degrees of Adverbs*

Write each of the following sentences, supplying the correct comparative or superlative degree of the adverb in parentheses. Underline the form you insert. Use the sense of the sentence to decide whether to use *more* or *most* or *less* or *least*. In some sentences either form will be acceptable.

Examples

a. Because she had more experience, Kristine rode _____ than her friend Doug. (skillfully)
Because she had more experience, Kristine rode <u>more skillfully</u> than her friend Doug.

b. Of Max, Karl, and Polly, Polly spoke _____. (loudly)
Of Max, Karl, and Polly, Polly spoke <u>most loudly</u>.
or
Of Max, Karl, and Polly, Polly spoke <u>least loudly</u>.

1. Of this year's troupe Paulette dances _____. (gracefully)

2. Eric accepted his grades _____ than his friend Moishe. (calmly)

3. As the only professional athlete in town, John was invited to give lectures _____ than anyone else. (often)

4. Carl finishes his work _____ than Peter. (promptly)

5. Of the three wrestlers the masked one wrestled _____. (ferociously)

6. Muhammad Ali fought _____ than his last opponent. (successfully)

7. Tom ate _____ than the other guests because he was on a strict diet. (lightly)

8. The _____ constructed models are also the most expensive. (skillfully)

9. Of all the members of his family, Carl felt the loss of Rover _____. (deeply)

10. As a result of years of laziness, Marsha worked the _____ of the fifty workers in her company. (slowly)

Some adverbs add *-er* and *-est* to form their comparative and superlative degrees.

Positive	*Comparative*	*Superlative*
close	closer	closest
deep	deeper	deepest
early	earlier	earliest
fast	faster	fastest
hard	harder	hardest
late	later	latest
low	lower	lowest
near	nearer	nearest
soon	sooner	soonest

Luis and Maria arrived at the New Year's Eve party *early*, before anyone else.

Luis and Maria arrived at the party *earlier* than we expected them to.

Luis and Maria arrived *earliest* of all the guests who were personally invited.

A few common adverbs form their comparative and superlative degrees irregularly.

Positive	Comparative	Superlative
badly	worse	worst
far	farther	farthest
little	less	least
much	more	most
well	better	best

Alfredo lives *far* from the baseball field.

Leroy gets angry *less* than I do.

Patti smiled *best* of those in the picture.

Exercise 7: Using the Correct Degree Forms of Adverbs

Write each of the following sentences, supplying the proper degree form of the adverb in parentheses. Underline each adverb that you supply.

Examples

a. Karl arrives at school _____ of all the freshmen. (early)
Karl arrives at school earliest of all the freshmen.

b. Marsha dives _____ than Mike. (well)
Marsha dives better than Mike.

1. Michelle's arrow hit _____ the bull's-eye than Mike's. (near)

2. Norman did badly in health class, but he did even _____ in speech. (badly)

3. Sam's family reads very little, and Sam reads _____ than any other member of his family. (little)

4. Miriam walks home _____ on rainy days than on sunny days. (fast)

5. Of the three police officers in our neighborhood, Jim shot _____ on the police firing range. (well)

6. Carlos and Mike swim the backstroke _____ than the other members of their team. (slowly)

7. Tom and his sister Martina live _____ from school than the other students. (far)

8. Dan and Ed arrived at practice _____ of the team. (early)

9. Sonja pitches _____ of the three pitchers on the team. (hard)

10. Even though your tape player is newer than mine, it plays _____. (badly)

Avoiding Double Negatives

The adverb *not* (or its contraction *n't*) gives a negative meaning to verbs. Other words such as *no, none, no one,* and *nothing* also carry negative meanings. When two words with negative meanings are used in the same sentence, the result is a *double negative,* which is not considered part of Standard English.

Double negatives can be corrected in one of two ways: one of the negative words can be removed, or one of the negative words can be changed.

The asterisk (*) denotes a sentence with a feature that is not part of Standard English.

*Henry did*n't* have *no* trouble with biology.	[double negative]
Henry did*n't* have any trouble with biology.	[correction]
Henry had *no* trouble with biology.	[correction]
*I was*n't* given none.	[double negative]
I was*n't* given any.	[correction]
I was given *none*.	[correction]

The adverbs *hardly* and *scarcely* are also negative words and should not be used with other negative words in a sentence.

*She could*n't* *hardly* believe it.	[double negative]
She could *hardly* believe it.	[correction]
*He was*n't* *scarcely* ever late.	[double negative]
He was *scarcely* ever late.	[correction]

In certain cases the word *only* can be a negative word, and when the word *but* means *only*, it can also have a negative meaning.

*We did*n't* have *but* ten cents between us.	[double negative]
We had *but* ten cents between us.	[correction]
*He had*n't* only* one other choice.	[double negative]
He had *only* one other choice.	[correction]

Exercise 8: *Correcting Double Negatives*

Rewrite each of the following sentences, correcting the double negative by either removing the negative word or by changing it.

Example

    a. Charlie doesn't like nothing better than grits and hog jowls.
       Charlie likes nothing better than grits and hog jowls.

1. Noriko doesn't think no one will ever travel to Mars.

2. There isn't nobody who plays tennis like Althea Gibson.

3. We didn't invite no one to dinner tonight.

4. When we divided up the profits, we didn't give Charlie none.

5. Jerry hasn't done nothing to help us finish painting the old fence.

6. I couldn't hardly believe that the Junior dance and the Senior prom had been canceled.

7. Tommy didn't lend Marilyn no money when she was broke.

8. Billie does not believe nothing that Bart says.

9. We hadn't driven but three miles before we were stopped.

10. Nobody who knows nothing about fishing would use lettuce for bait.

Choosing Between Adjectives and Adverbs

The guide to use in choosing between adjectives and adverbs is to remember what kinds of words each part of speech can modify.

Adjectives modify nouns and pronouns.

We had a *terrible* dinner before the movie.

The *last* one to leave the room should turn out the lights.

Adverbs modify verbs, adjectives, and other adverbs.

We ate our dinner *quickly* before the movie.

The food was *too* good to leave.

We ate our dinner *too* quickly.

Bad/Badly

***Bad*, an adjective that modifies nouns and pronouns, often follows linking verbs.**

The fish tastes *bad*.

Everyone felt *bad* about the accident.

***Badly*, an adverb that tells *how* or *to what extent* something was done, modifies verbs, adjectives, and other adverbs.**

Our quarterback threw the pass *badly*.

Her *badly* damaged car finally fell apart.

Easy/Easily

***Easy*, an adjective used to modify nouns and pronouns, often follows linking verbs.**

The test seemed *easy* at first.

Flying is an *easy* way to get somewhere fast.

Easily is an adverb used to modify verbs, adjectives, and other adverbs.

I finished the assignment *easily*.

The mistake was *easily* corrected.

Good/Well

Good is always an adjective used to modify nouns and pronouns.

We saw a *good* movie on television last night.

They were *good* for the baby-sitter.

Well can also be used as an adjective when it means "healthy" or "in good health" and follows a linking verb.

Max doesn't feel *well* today.

He looks *well* to me.

Well is usually classified as an adverb that modifies verbs, adjectives, and other adverbs.

She was injured, but she ran *well*.

José is *well* informed about current events.

Real/Really

Real, which is an adjective that means "actual" or "true," modifies nouns and pronouns.

Last night's soccer match was a *real* victory for us.

One of these stories is *real*.

Really, an adverb that means "actually" or "truly," modifies verbs, adjectives, and adverbs.

My watch made a *really* deep scratch in the table.

Are you *really* going to the picnic?

Slow/Slowly

Slow is an adjective used to modify nouns and pronouns.

We took a *slow*, leisurely walk on the beach.

She is always *slow* when it comes to eating.

Slowly, an adverb, is used to modify verbs, adjectives, and adverbs.

Drive *slowly* down this narrow street.

My brother eats vegetables *slowly*.

Sure/Surely

Sure, an adjective that means "certain," modifies nouns and pronouns.

He looked *sure* and confident in his new clothes.

It's a *sure* bet that Wayne will win the election.

Surely is an adverb that means "certainly." Use the adverb surely to modify verbs, adjectives, and adverbs only when you can substitute the word certainly.

This movie *surely* is exciting.
[This movie *certainly* is exciting.]

That horse *surely* can run fast.
[That horse *certainly* can run fast.]

Exercise 9: Choosing the Correct Adverb or Adjective

Write each of the following sentences. From the pair in parentheses, choose the adjective or adverb needed to complete the sentence. Underline your choice.

Example

a. Norma plays the saxophone _____. (bad, badly)
Norma plays the saxophone <u>badly</u>.

1. Laura is _____ that she will be elected president. (sure, surely)

2. Sam finished his crossword puzzle _____ and then read the paper. (easy, easily)

3. The bus was _____, but it was comfortable. (slow, slowly)

4. Mary is not _____; in fact, she's had a cold all week. (good, well)

5. Sammy Chu is studying _____ diligently; someday he wants to enter medical school. (real, really)

6. Pam will _____ graduate before her brother. (sure, surely)

7. Good study habits are _____ to learn. (easy, easily)

8. We always cook our bacon _____ to remove as much grease as possible. (slow, slowly)

9. Your paper seems _____ now, but read it again in a day or so. (good, well)

10. Kayo is _____ sure that she'll do well in art. (real, really)

Placing Adverbs in a Sentence

Adverbs that modify adjectives or other adverbs are always placed just in front of the words they modify in a sentence.

This soup is *very* hot.

The battle ended *rather* quickly.

Adverbs that modify verbs in a sentence can sometimes be moved from place to place without changing the meaning of the sentence.

Quietly Mary walked through the park in her dreams.

Mary *quietly* walked through the park in her dreams.

Mary walked *quietly* through the park in her dreams.

Mary walked through the park *quietly* in her dreams.

Mary walked through the park in her dreams *quietly*.

The movement of some adverbs that modify verbs is a bit more restricted. You could say that "Jane has *completely* finished her homework," or that "Jane has finished her homework *completely*," but you could not move the adverb to other positions.

An asterisk (*) denotes a feature that is not part of Standard English.

*Jane *completely* has finished her homework.

Completely Jane has finished her homework.

Exercise 10: *Placing Adverbs in Sentences*

Rewrite each of the following sentences twice by moving the *italicized* adverb to two different places without changing the meaning of the sentence. Underline the adverb in each position.

Example

a. John had *thoughtlessly* forgotten his sister's birthday.

<u>Thoughtlessly</u>, John had forgotten his sister's birthday.
John <u>thoughtlessly</u> had forgotten his sister's birthday.

1. *Painlessly* the dentist pulled my wisdom tooth.

2. Mary Ann ran *breathlessly* into the room.

3. The small child opened her birthday presents *excitedly*.

4. Patrick *patiently* waited for his driving test.

5. *Often* the officers would play football with the men.

6. The water from the tub *rapidly* overflowed onto the floor.

7. We broke the news to Brian *gently*.

8. *Carelessly* the campers scattered litter everywhere.

9. Carmen has *exactly* copied the Michelangelo painting.

10. Ms. Washington *constantly* stresses the importance of education.

Review: Using Adverbs

Write each of the following sentences. From the pair in parentheses, choose the adjective or adverb needed to complete the sentence. Underline your choice.

Example

a. Tom had a _____ accident while ice-skating. (bad, badly)
   Tom had a bad accident while ice-skating.

1. After hiking over the pass, we were _____ tired. (real, really)

2. Mary Lou won her race _____. (easily, easy)

3. The new school annex will _____ be finished by spring. (surely, sure)

4. Mark did a _____ job of painting the hallway. (well, good)

5. The hungry students devoured the hot dogs very _____. (quickly, quick)

6. Gail did _____ in biology, but she received a bad grade in English. (good, well)

7. We are absolutely _____ that she will be elected. (surely, sure)

8. This is a _____ kachina doll, made by the Hopi. (really, real)

9. We all thought the test was too _____, but we were truly wrong. (easy, easily)

10. Danielle dances _____, but Jen dances better. (well, good)

11. Because she is innocent, Lizzie will _____ be acquitted. (surely, sure)

12. Since he caught a cold, Mr. Cheng has looked _____ and felt worse. (bad, badly)

13. Has Marion _____ collected two miles of string? (real, really)

14. If we start now, we can finish the puzzle by Thursday _____. (easy, easily)

15. Conchita's artwork is very _____, especially the watercolors. (well, good)

Writing Focus: *Using Exact Adverbs in Writing*

You can make your writing more precise and varied by using exact adverbs to describe actions. Many adverbs explain *how* something happens. Consider, for example, the sentences below. In each case, the image conveyed depends on the adverb used.

> The painter worked *slowly.*
>
> The painter worked *sporadically.*
>
> The painter worked *meticulously.*

Choose your adverbs carefully to explain exactly what you mean.

Assignment: *Silence Is Golden*

Imagine a day at school when no one is allowed to talk. What would the day be like? How would the teacher conduct class? How would the students react to the teacher? How would students relate to one another?

Write one or more paragraphs describing a day at school during which no one speaks. Begin your narrative description with the sounding of the bell for the first period. Continue with a chronological account of the silent day. Describe and explain to your classmates how the school day would be. Your work will be evaluated for correct and effective use of adverbs.

Use the following steps to complete this assignment.

A. Prewriting

Think about a regular school day. Jot down a list of ordinary occurrences there—talking to friends, listening to the teacher, asking questions, laughing, and so on. Imagine a school day when no one is allowed to talk. Review your list of ordinary occurrences, and begin to think about how the silent day would be. Start another list or use a word cluster, discussed in Chapter 1, about the day. Concentrate on details that explain or describe how school activities will have to be handled and what the day will be like. Let your imagination provide you with ideas. Number your ideas to reflect the passing of the day.

B. Writing

Use your list or word cluster to help you write one or more paragraphs describing a day at school during which no one speaks. Begin your description with the sound of the bell for the first period. Continue describing in chronological order how the rest of the silent day would be. As you write, pay particular attention to your use of adverbs. Choose your adverbs carefully to help explain what you mean.

C. Postwriting

Use the following checklist to revise your first draft.

1. Does my writing actually describe a silent day at school?

2. Have I included enough specific details to make this day seem real to my audience?

3. Have I used exact adverbs to describe the day?

4. Do my ideas follow chronological order?

Use the Proofreader's Checklist at the back of the book to edit your revisions. If appropriate, share your writing with your classmates.

17 Prepositions
Understanding Prepositions

Sometimes you can say what you mean in short sentences, such as, "Tomorrow we are leaving town," or "The criminal was caught." These sentences certainly make sense, but they do not offer very much information about the situation. Prepositions and their objects can make important distinctions in the meaning of your sentences.

Tomorrow we are leaving town *on vacation.*
Tomorrow we are leaving town *for a new residence.*

The criminal was caught *on the street.*
The criminal was caught *in our front yard.*

In the following sections you will learn to identify prepositions.

Defining Prepositions

A *preposition* is a word that shows the relationship between a noun or a pronoun and some other word or words in the sentence.

Notice how the *italicized* prepositions in the following sentences relate the noun *city* to the verb *runs.*

This road runs *near* the city.

This road runs *around* the city.

This road runs *through* the city.

This road runs *into* the city.

This road runs *underneath* the city.

The noun or pronoun that the preposition relates to another word in the sentence is called the *object of the preposition.* The preposition (*P*), the object of the preposition (*OP*), and all the words that modify that object form a unit that is called a *prepositional phrase.* The prepositional phrases in the following sentences are *italicized.*

       P   OP

Winters *in the Midwest* can be severe.

                 P   OP

Gary opened the drawer *with a crowbar*.

              P   OP

He seemed confident *about his chances*.

     P   OP

People *from Indiana* are called Hoosiers.

         P   OP

She arrived *during the lecture*.

The following words are commonly used as prepositions:

aboard	beneath	inside	throughout
about	beside	into	till
above	besides	like	to
across	between	near	toward
after	beyond	of	under
against	but	off	underneath
along	by	on	until
among	down	onto	up
around	during	out	upon
at	except	outside	with
before	for	over	within
behind	from	past	without
below	in	through	

Exercise 1: *Identifying Prepositional Phrases*

Write the following sentences, underlining each prepositional phrase. Then label each preposition *P* and each object of the preposition *OP*.

Examples

a. Norma took a bus to the beach.

                   P   OP

Norma took a bus <u>to the beach</u>.

b. Nick told us about her.

              P   OP

Nick told us <u>about her</u>.

1. Sally found the sand dollar on the shore.

2. Mike is waiting for us.

3. Sue and Sarah are camping in the woods.

4. Mona always wears gloves under her mittens.

5. Uncle Otis threw the football to me.

6. Beneath them the astronauts saw the spinning, blue earth.

7. If your friends are late, we will leave without them.

8. Ms. Carbona witnessed an accident near the bus station.

9. Renee invited us to visit her home during the holidays.

10. After a delicious dinner we all went home.

Compound Prepositions

Prepositions made up of two or more words are called *compound prepositions*. The most often used compound prepositions are listed below:

according to	in addition to	on account of
aside from	in front of	out of
as of	in place of	owing to
because of	in spite of	prior to
by means of	instead of	

Compound prepositions act just like one-word prepositions, and each should be thought of as a unit.

                            P   OP

Our table was *in front of* the band.

                       P   OP

We left early *because of* the weather.

                                P   OP

George began running *prior to* the signal.

Exercise 2: Identifying Prepositional Phrases

Write the following sentences, underlining each prepositional phrase. Then label each preposition *P* and each object of the preposition *OP*.

Example

    a. An old saying is, "Don't jump out of the frying pan into the fire."

P   OP   P
An old saying is, "Don't jump <u>out of the frying pan</u> <u>into the</u>

OP
<u>fire</u>."

1. According to my calendar, your birthday is on a Tuesday next year.

2. She planted three honeysuckle bushes in front of the porch.

3. Aside from the picnic, we have no other plans for Saturday.

4. In addition to cold chicken, we also had hot Swedish meatballs at the wedding reception.

5. Instead of a big reception, the young couple had a small party after the wedding ceremony.

6. We all liked the house in spite of its chipped paint.

7. Because of her haste, Anita left the report on the table when she left for the meeting.

8. Because of the snowstorm and ice, we had to wait over an hour for the bus.

9. In spite of the mosquitoes, we all enjoyed the band concert.

10. Aside from the heat, living in Houston is fun.

Compound Objects

When a preposition has two or more objects, the objects are called *compound objects*.

P   OP   OP
After the business meeting and short discussion, they served lunch.

P   OP   OP
She enjoyed the unusual combination *of cucumbers and beets*.

Exercise 3: Identifying Prepositional Phrases

Write the sentences on the next page, underlining each prepositional phrase. Then label each preposition *P* and each object of the preposition *OP*. (Not all prepositions have compound objects.)

Example

---

a. Before Monday or Tuesday the final decision must be made.

    P   OP   OP

<u>Before Monday or Tuesday</u> the final decision must be made.

1. Just between you and me, I don't think Shelia is going to win the student council election.

2. Inside the incubator that morning, the class found six newly hatched robins.

3. Everyone is watching the fireworks except Franz and JoAnn.

4. The sailor strained hard against the wind and high waves.

5. All through the long winter, the pioneers rationed their supplies of dried corn and beans.

6. Kayo and Jennifer were among the semifinalists.

7. Atlantis, the lost continent, is supposed to have been situated beyond Gibraltar.

8. As the night grew darker, the campers drew together near the warm fire and roasting chestnuts.

9. During the hurricane and flood, trees were uprooted, and several houses lost their roofs.

10. The guests said that they heard eerie sounds at midnight.

Prepositional Phrases as Modifiers

Prepositional phrases are used as modifiers in the same way as adjectives and adverbs; they answer the same questions about the words they modify that single-word modifiers do.

Prepositional phrases act like adjectives when they modify nouns or pronouns.

The house *on the corner* is vacant.   [which house?]

I received a letter *from Joe and Jamie.*   [which letter?]

Prepositional phrases act as adverbs when they modify verbs, adjectives, or other adverbs.

We recited poetry *during class* today.   [when?]

We removed our shoes and jumped *into*

the water.   [where?]

Sometimes, the word that is modified by a prepositional phrase is the object of another prepositional phrase.

Adv.   Adj.
The book was placed at the end of the shelf.

Adj.   Adj.
The trophy on top of the mantel is my sister's.

Exercise 4: Identifying Prepositional Phrases as Modifiers

Write the sentences on the following page, enclosing each prepositional phrase in parentheses. Then draw an arrow from the prepositional phrase to the word it modifies. Above each prepositional phrase write *Adj.* if it acts as an adjective or *Adv.* if it acts as an adverb.

Examples

a. The house on the corner is green and white.

Adj.
The house (on the corner) is green and white.

b. Marilyn is standing on the front steps of the school.

Adv.   Adj.
Marilyn is standing (on the front steps) (of the school).

1. Mickey and Minnie appeared on the screen of the television.

2. The carpenter repaired the hole in the wall.

3. A skilled plumber can fix that within minutes.

4. The boy with blonde hair and brown eyes is my cousin Jason from Wisconsin.

5. Carol swam slowly toward the quiet island.

6. The swimming pool at the YMCA is always crowded on Fridays.

7. Under the house they found the lost treasure in an old chest.

8. Our cat always sleeps at the end of the bed.

9. Carlos now lives near a school with a large recreation area.

10. All of the students wear blue sweaters, white shirts, and blue pants on game days.

Review: *Understanding Prepositions*

Write the following sentences, enclosing each prepositional phrase in parentheses. Label each phrase *Adj.* for adjective and *Adv.* for adverb. Then draw an arrow from each prepositional phrase to the word or words that it modifies.

Examples

a. The Washington family lives in the house on the corner of Lincoln and Pine.

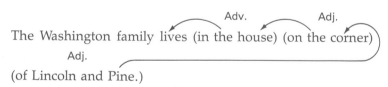

Adv.   Adj.

The Washington family lives (in the house) (on the corner)

Adj.

(of Lincoln and Pine.)

b. Mary Ann has lived in Utah for years.

Adv.   Adv.

Mary Ann has lived (in Utah) (for years).

1. Carlo divided the project into small parts.

2. The utility company brought a lawsuit against the family for their damage to the line.

3. Helen's story in the school paper caused significant changes in the lunch program.

4. David's family lives above their bakery near the fire station.

5. In spite of her hard work, Kim has not saved enough money for a new pair of jogging shoes.

6. We must bring up the subject of hall passes at our next meeting.

7. Sue called Gary during dinner in spite of his mother's request that no one should call before 7 o'clock.

8. Both Ralph Metcalfe and Jessie Owens won medals at the 1936 Olympic Games in Berlin, Germany.

9. We must throw away the food that was ruined when the freezer defrosted because of the power failure.

10. No one besides Harry has read *Dracula*, yet everyone except Naomi has read *Frankenstein*.

11. Across the river we saw towering cliffs at the edge of the water.

12. Gina leaned against the tree and waited for the parade.

13. The dogs leaped over the fence and chased the cows.

14. Nellie tagged the runner at second base, but the runner at third scored the winning run.

15. Mother says that our family has delayed our vacation for too long and that we will take a trip across the country on the train.

16. We found the shivering kitten beneath our car and brought it into our house where it warmed itself by the fire.

17. There have been other wars throughout history, but none was as devastating as the war between the Axis powers and the Allies.

18. The bubonic plague, carried by fleas from infected rats, still exists in Asia and Africa.

19. In place of junk food, our cafeteria now serves salads of fresh greens and vegetables, soups, and hot bread.

20. The steps outside the library lead visitors past the principal's office and into the courtyard near the gymnasium.

Applying What You Know

In the selection on the following page from *Medicine Man's Daughter* by Ann Nolan Clark, Tall-Girl, the medicine man's daughter, takes her first trip into the wilderness with a companion named Chanter. There are twenty-four prepositional phrases in this selection, and the first four are underlined. Number a sheet of paper 1–20 and list the remaining twenty phrases.

She remembered swinging round and round, her full skirts whipping <u>about her body</u> <u>in angry swirls</u>. Chanter uncoiled the rope slowly, slowly as she swung downward. <u>At last</u> she reached the rockshelf, slipped her feet <u>from the footloops</u> and, still holding to the rope, walked across the narrow ledge. Above her head the angry eagles circled and soared. She knelt at the edge of the great nest. Letting go of the rope, she quickly scooped handfuls of baby eagle down, eagle feathers, and small animal bones into the square of cotton. Then, tying its corners with the woven string and the bundle it made to the rope at her waist, she stood up again. Placing her feet in the loops and holding to the rope with both hands, she called to Chanter. Even slower than he had let her down, he pulled her upward again.

The sky seemed full of eagles. Their great wings almost touched the girl as she rose slowly upward. At last she reached the cliff edge. Clutching the rock, she climbed swiftly on top and stood again, her feet on ground.[1]

Using Prepositions

Because prepositions are used so often in English, it is important to learn the appropriate forms and their placement in sentences. In the next sections you will practice using prepositional phrases.

Using Pronouns as Objects of Prepositions

In Standard English only object pronouns are used as objects of prepositions.

Singular	*Plural*
me	us
you	you
him	
her	them
it	
whom	whom

Gary received a letter from *him*.

Karen divided the cards between *you* and *me*.

I sat across from Henry and *her*.

[1]Excerpt from *Medicine Man's Daughter* by Ann Nolan Clark. Copyright © 1963 by Ann Nolan Clark. Reprinted by permission of Farrar, Straus and Giroux, Inc.

Our team formed a line behind their captain and *them*.

I ran past *him* and *her*.

When compound pronoun objects appear in a sentence or when a pronoun is used with a noun object, decide the correct form to use by mentally deleting the other pronoun or the noun.

The decision is up to *him* and *me*.
[The decision is up to *him*.]
[The decision is up to *me*.]

The gift is for *us* girls.
[The gift is for *us*.]

Exercise 5: *Using Pronouns as Objects of Prepositions*

Write each of the following sentences, choosing the appropriate pronoun from the pair in parentheses. Underline the pronoun you choose.

Example

a. Mr. Schwartz sent a telegram to Mary and (me, I).
   Mr. Schwartz sent a telegram to Mary and <u>me</u>.

1. Mary and Sally received telephone calls every week from Mike and (him, he).

2. Ralph Bunche refused to let poverty come between (he, him) and a successful life.

3. The class will eat a dinner prepared by (we, us) students.

4. Besides Tom and (I, me) the only other person to know the combination to the safe is Betty.

5. Across the street from (them, they) and (me, I) stood the longest box office line that I've ever seen.

6. Beside my mother and (me, I) there appeared the most terrifying monster that ever walked the streets of Birmingham.

7. The large brass plaque in the school library was donated by (we, us) library volunteers.

8. Antoinette divided her prize money among (we, us) fellow contestants.

9. Carlos and Wendy lent their best camping equipment to Patty, Sally, and (she, her) last winter.

10. Between you and (I, me) I think this is the worst movie I've ever seen.

Using Troublesome Prepositions Correctly

Among/Between

Use *between* when referring to exactly two things and *among* when referring to more than two.

We divided the money *between* the two of us.

The treasure was divided equally *among* the six pirates.

However, *between* should be used when referring to two or more items if each item is considered individually.

We planted beans *between* the rows of corn.

The discussions *between* the countries involved eventually would have resulted in a treaty.

Beside/Besides

Beside denotes a position "next to" something. *Besides* means "in addition to" or "other than."

The police officer crouched *beside* the body.

Many others, *besides* the detective, were seeking the killer.

In/Into

The preposition *in* refers to a position and means "inside" or "within." *Into*, however, implies movement from outside to inside or from without to within.

We remained *in* the car.

George left and went *into* another car.

On/Onto

On refers to a position upon something. *Onto* implies movement toward the top of something.

We enjoyed skiing *on* the lake.

Carolyn had to be lifted *onto* the deck.

Exercise 6: Using Troublesome Prepositions Correctly

Write each of the following sentences, choosing the correct preposition from the pair in parentheses. Underline the one you choose.

Example

a. No one (beside, besides) Kate would buy more than three kinds of furniture polish.
No one <u>besides</u> Kate would buy more than three kinds of furniture polish.

1. We waited for the train (in, into) the room near the ticket counter.
2. Cousin Sue sat (between, among) Uncle Sam and Aunt Mary.
3. Donna and Jeff dropped the batter (on, onto) the hot griddle to make scones for breakfast.
4. Because Harry's seat was (besides, beside) the air conditioner, he often couldn't hear the teacher speak.
5. They walked (into, in) class after the exam had ended.
6. While sitting (on, onto) the bank of the river, we sketched the frogs and lily pads.
7. (Beside, Besides) Tom, I can't imagine who would know how to fix a toaster.
8. The home economics class parceled out the best muffins (between, among) themselves.
9. Realizing that they were outnumbered, the villains leapt (on, onto) their horses and galloped away.
10. Wires were strung (between, among) the telegraph poles from St. Louis to San Francisco.

Using Prepositions in Standard English

In this section you will learn how prepositions are used in Standard English.

about   Do not use *about* with the preposition *at*.
*I will see you *at about* 7 P.M.
I will see you *about* 7 P.M.

alongside   Do not use *alongside* with the preposition *of*.
*I parked my car *alongside of* the building.
I parked my car *alongside* the building.

at   Do not use *at* when it is unnecessary—with *where*, for example.
Where did I leave my purse *at*?
Where did I leave my purse?

behind   Use *behind* instead of *in back of*.
*For this picture the juniors will stand *in back of* the seniors.
For this picture the juniors will stand *behind* the seniors.

by   Do not use *by* to mean *with*.
*Whatever you decide is all right *by* me.
Whatever you decide is all right *with* me.

except   Use *except* (not *outside of*) when you mean "other than" or "excluding."
*There wasn't one volunteer *outside of* Terry.
There wasn't one volunteer *except* Terry.

from   Use *from* (not *than*) after the adjective *different*.
*Marathon swimming is much *different than* marathon running.
Marathon swimming is much *different from* marathon running.

Do not use *from* (or *to*) after the adjective *opposite*. Instead, use either the preposition *of* or no preposition at all.

*My desk is *opposite from* yours.
My desk is *opposite* yours.
Evil is the *opposite of* good.

in   Use *in* (not *into*) after the verb *place*.
*Carefully *place* the clock *into* that packing crate.
Carefully *place* the clock *in* that packing crate.

of

Do not use *of* as a replacement for the helping verb *have*.
*You should *of* finished that yesterday to qualify for the competition.
You should *have* finished that yesterday to qualify for the competition.

Do not use *of* when it is unnecessary.
*Tony put the groceries *inside of* the back door of the summer porch.
Tony put the groceries *inside* the back door of the summer porch.

off

Do not use *off* to mean *from*.
*John borrowed a dollar *off* me yesterday.
John borrowed a dollar *from* me yesterday.

*I slipped and almost fell *off of* the roof Thursday while painting.
I slipped and almost fell *off* the roof Thursday while painting.

on

Use the verb *blame* by itself instead of *blame it on*.
*I didn't break the side window, but he *blamed it on* me anyway.
I didn't break the side window, but he *blamed* me anyway.

to

Do not use *to* as a replacement for *at*.
*When did you arrive *to* school?
When did you arrive *at* school?

Use *to* (not *from*) after the verb *forbid*.
*I have been *forbidden from* seeing you.
I have been *forbidden to* see you.

Use *to* (not *and*) after the verb *try*.
Try and get home before dark.
Try to get home before dark.

Do not use *to* after the verb *convince*. *To* can be used after the verb *persuade*.
*She *convinced* me *to* take up another sport.
She *convinced* me *that* I should take up another sport.
She *persuaded* me *to* take up another sport.

Do not use *to* when it is unnecessary.
*That is where I am going *to* after school.
That is where I am going after school.

Exercise 7: Using Prepositions in Standard English

Write the following sentences, changing prepositions that are not features of Standard English. Underline the preposition you have chosen.

Examples

a. Whenever the Sergeant is looking for volunteers, Corporal Sinker hides in back of the taller soldiers.

   Whenever the Sergeant is looking for volunteers, Corporal Sinker hides <u>behind</u> the taller soldiers.

b. If you want to nominate me for president, it's okay by me.

   If you want to nominate me for president, it's okay <u>with</u> me.

1. Outside of the members of the football team, no one wanted to buy new body-building equipment.

2. We will begin the Halloween celebration at about midnight.

3. Swimming a mile in a pool is different than swimming it in the open sea.

4. You might of fallen into the river if you had gotten any closer to the edge of the cliff.

5. Jason couldn't remember where he had parked his car at.

6. We found our cat underneath of our car.

7. Carmen borrowed a dollar off Carl to ride the train home.

8. My mother has forbidden me from hitchhiking.

9. As we prepared to leave the campsite, we placed all the trash inside of our knapsacks and carried it home with us.

10. The city hall is opposite from the police station.

Using Prepositional Phrases as Adjectives and Adverbs

An *adjective phrase* (prepositional phrase used as an adjective) usually follows the noun or pronoun it modifies. If it does not, the meaning may be unclear. Such phrases are *misplaced.*

Mr. Sohn sends birthday cards to his grandchildren *with money in them.*	[misplaced]
Mr. Sohn sends birthday cards *with money in them* to his grandchildren	[better]

An *adverbial phrase* (a prepositional phrase used as an adverb) may be placed near the word it modifies or may be moved to the beginning or end of a sentence.

During dinner Susan frequently tells amusing stories.

Susan frequently *during dinner* tells amusing stories.

Susan frequently tells amusing stories *during dinner*.

While some adjective and adverbial phrases may be moved, you need to be certain that the meaning is clear.

The teacher told us that anyone caught cheating would be punished *on Friday.*	[unclear]
On Friday the teacher told us that anyone caught cheating would be punished.	[better]

Exercise 8: Using Adjective and Adverbial Phrases

Write the following sentences, moving adjective phrases so that the meanings cannot be confused. If the sentence contains an adverbial phrase, move it to a different position. Underline the adjective and adverbial phrases.

Examples

a. The snow was dangerous and had to be removed on the roof.
   The snow on the roof was dangerous and had to be removed.

b. Bob held a party before the election.
   Before the election Bob held a party.

1. I fell on my knee and had to have stitches.

2. Five of us sat comfortably under the shelter while the storm raged.

3. That nonfiction book is much too hard to reach with the red cover.

4. A trained seal attracted a large crowd of tourists with a fish on its nose.

5. By answering an ad in the newspaper, Carlos landed his job at the bank.

6. With great eloquence Joseph, Chief of the Nez Percés, spoke of his desire for peace.

7. Through hard work Margaret earned the money for her dance lessons.

8. There is a dangerous intersection where a light needs to be placed at the corner.

9. The needless slaughter of baby seals disturbs many people with clubs.

10. We'll stick together through thick and thin.

Review: Using Prepositions

Rewrite the following sentences, correcting all errors in prepositions and pronoun forms to conform to Standard English. (In some instances you may need to rewrite the sentence slightly.) Study the examples before you begin.

Examples

a. We divided the French fries between us seven hungry girls.
   We divided the French fries among us seven hungry girls.

b. The new students formed a line in back of Juan and I.
   The new students formed a line behind Juan and me.

c. We found the library book underneath of the notebooks us had brought home from school.
   We found the library book underneath the notebooks we had brought home from school.

1. Beside Pat, not a person in our town has ever been to the Olympics.

2. The three bank robbers jumped in their car and fled the scene of the crime.

3. Uncle Maxwell lent his fishing pole to Sandy and she for the weekend.

4. The frightened first mate jumped quickly off of the boat and on the dock.

5. Harry promised to stand among his two sisters at the awards ceremony.

6. They invited everybody but Jane and I to come at about eight o'clock.

7. The rock band was lowered on the stage by a helicopter rented by we stagehands.

8. If you place a rotten apple into a box full of fresh ones, you will not be happy with the results.

9. The goal of Martin Luther King, Jr., was to try and work peacefully for human rights.

10. We waited patiently in back of a large moving van for our friends to arrive.

11. Whatever you computer science teachers decide is all right by we students.

12. Between Navaho people the family includes those who are related on the female side.

13. Paula said that working out with us exercise fiends was different than working out alone.

14. Outside of Charles and we no one in our school likes to roller-skate.

15. The discussion on parent involvement at the PTA meeting will begin at about 8 P.M.

16. None of us students from the east side of town could of come to school if the bus drivers had been on strike.

17. The principal blamed the spoiled fruit into the cafeteria on Mr. Edelweiss and she.

18. Bonny borrowed bus fare and lunch money off the rest of her friends and I.

19. The new school regulations forbid students from eating their lunches during study hall.

20. Carl B. Stokes, Cleveland's first black mayor, tried and convince the city to clean up polluted rivers before the end of the current year.

Writing Focus: *Using* Prepositional Phrases in Writing

As a writer, you can use prepositional phrases to make important distinctions in your sentences. Prepositions and their objects add specific information and show relationships between words in sentences. Notice how the meaning of the sentences below changes with the use of different prepositions.

> Please come *to* the table.
>
> The food is *on* the table.
>
> The guests sat *at* the table.

Assignment: *A Difficult Decision*

On Monday, several of your friends invite you to an outdoor concert on Friday evening. You are really excited about going. On Tuesday, however, your mother reminds you of the surprise party on Friday night for your grandfather's eightieth birthday. You are fond of your grandfather, but you also hate the thought of missing the concert. What a dilemma! You must decide what to do. Then you must explain your decision to either your friends or your family.

After you have made a decision about your plans for Friday evening, write one or more paragraphs explaining your decision either to your friends or your relatives.

Use the following steps to complete this assignment.

A. Prewriting

Imagine two voices inside your head debating your dilemma. Record the dialogue you hear. Write it quickly, easily, and without judging the merit of the ideas. Just let it flow. You might begin with the concert and let it speak about what it can offer you. One voice might say something like, "This will probably be your only opportunity to see your favorite performer in person." The other voice might respond, "But your grandfather will turn eighty only once, and your mother has baked a triple chocolate cake." Let the two voices continue to discuss and argue their merits. Allow the dialogue to go in whatever direction it takes you until you feel you have a decision. Then write your decision on a separate piece of paper. Go back over your dialogue and underline three points that offer the most compelling reasons for your choice. Write them under your decision, leaving space between them. In the space, jot down details and more specific information to further explain your reasons. Number the reasons in this order: the second most important, the least important, and the most important.

B. Writing

Using your notes, write one or more paragraphs explaining your decision to go either to the concert or to your grandfather's birthday party on Friday night. You might highlight your reasons with words like *first, second, in the third place,* or *in addition.* As you write, use prepositional phrases to add specific details.

C. Postwriting

Use the following checklist to revise your first draft.

1.   Does my writing clearly state my decision?

2.   Have I provided adequate reasons for my choice?

3.   Have I used prepositional phrases to provide details and to show relationships?

Edit your work, using the Proofreader's Checklist at the back of the book. If appropriate, share your writing with your classmates. Discuss with them the process you used in making your decision.

18 Conjunctions
Understanding Conjunctions

Whenever you join similar ideas or names of people, objects, or events, conjunctions are the words that hold your thoughts together. With conjunctions you can express yourself more fluently.

In the following sections you will learn to identify conjunctions by their definition and function.

Defining Conjunctions

A *conjunction* joins words or groups of words.

The most commonly used conjunctions—*and, but, or, nor, for,* and *yet*—join individual words, word groups, or sentences.

When a conjunction is used to join individual words, the words usually must be the same part of speech:

Nouns: *Raoul* and his *brother* ride mopeds to school.

Pronouns: *All* of the freshmen and *most* of the sophomores have already voted.

Verbs: I usually *jog* or *exercise* for a half hour before I even step on a tennis court.

Adjectives: When I don't get enough sleep, I'm *moody* and *irritable*, no matter how well people treat me.

Adverbs: She introduced herself *politely* but *shyly*, making many constructive suggestions during the meeting.

Since pronouns take the place of nouns, conjunctions may also join nouns and pronouns.

Chris and *I* work well together.

Exercise 1: Identifying Conjunctions

Write the following sentences, circling each conjunction and underlining the two words joined by the conjunction. Study the example before you begin.

Example

a. Have you taken Algebra I or geometry?

Have you taken <u>Algebra I</u> (or) <u>geometry</u>?

1. An alligator is a unique yet dangerous pet.
2. On Saturday evenings I baby-sit or study.
3. I can't decide whether to order soup or salad.
4. The deserts have high temperatures but low humidity.
5. The surgeon operated quickly yet cautiously.
6. I wonder if that package on the table is for you or me?
7. Most of the morning we fished and swam.
8. Skydiving looks like an exciting but rather dangerous sport.
9. With a smile and a wave we left my sister at the airport.
10. For the first class, the nurse lectured and answered questions.

Grouping Conjunctions by Classes

Conjunctions can be grouped into three classes: *coordinating, correlative,* and *subordinating conjunctions.*

Coordinating conjunctions join words and groups of words. They are the most commonly used conjunctions.

Arthur lived in Boston (and) Detroit.

The message came from Dr. Wolpaw (or) his lab assistant.

Coordinating Conjunctions

and	or	so	yet
but	nor	for	

In addition to joining words and word groups, coordinating conjunctions may also join sentences.

Mary cooks lasagna, (for) it is her favorite dish.

Martha paid for the tickets, (so) John paid for dinner.

Exercise 2: *Identifying Coordinating Conjunctions*

Write the following sentences, circling each coordinating conjunction and underlining the words, phrases, or sentences joined by each. Study the examples before you begin.

Examples

a. The scouts liked and respected their leader.

The scouts <u>liked</u> (and) <u>respected</u> their leader.

b. Kai learned to develop and print color photographs.

Kai learned to <u>develop</u> (and) <u>print</u> color photographs.

1. Mary or Bruce will bring the hotdogs to the cookout.

2. Some people like to watch football, but I prefer to watch tennis.

3. John won't give a red cent for that comic book nor for your stamp collection.

4. The prices were high, yet they wanted to see the concert.

5. The band has practiced six hours, for the concert will be tomorrow.

6. The bell has rung, so the students who just came in are late.

7. I certainly won't tell that story, nor will you tell it.

8. Anna is able to read and to speak German fluently.

9. Knowing how to speak Japanese and being skilled with chopsticks, we are ready for our trip to Kyoto.

10. We were determined to watch the snowy owls, so we wore our heaviest coats.

Correlative conjunctions, always used in pairs, also join similar kinds of items.

Correlative Conjunctions

both . . . and   neither . . . nor
not only . . . but also   whether . . . or
either . . . or

Each of these pairs is thought of as one conjunction:

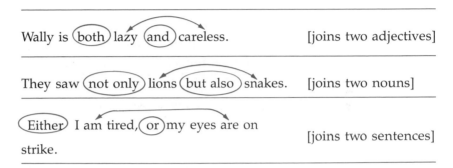

Wally is (both) lazy (and) careless.   [joins two adjectives]

They saw (not only) lions (but also) snakes.   [joins two nouns]

(Either) I am tired, (or) my eyes are on   [joins two sentences]
strike.

Exercise 3: *Identifying Correlative Conjunctions*

Write the following sentences, circling the correlative conjunctions and underlining the items joined by each. Study the example before you begin.

Example

a. Either Mary or Bob will cook dinner for the guests.

(Either) <u>Mary</u> (or) <u>Bob</u> will cook dinner for the guests.

1. Both the Army and the Marines stress physical conditioning.

2. A student may choose either the vegetarian or regular meals at most schools.

3. Carlos was not only tired but also hungry.

4. Neither the bus nor the train is the fastest way to travel.

5. Both the lazy, old dog and the frisky, young puppy were placed in the same pen.

6. Vigorous exercise not only improves the body, but also soothes the emotions.

7. Climbing stairs is not only the least expensive exercise but also the most efficient one.

8. This year John is neither running for Congress nor doing favors for his constituents.

9. It's a mystery whether the crime was committed by the cook or by the butler.

10. Neither the blue dress nor the green one is in style.

Subordinating conjunctions join groups of words called *clauses* to the rest of a sentence. A *clause* is a group of words that contains a verb and its subject and is used as part of a sentence.

Subordinating Conjunctions

after	before	unless
although	if	until
as far as	in order that	when
as if	provided that	whenever
as long as	since	where
as soon as	so that	wherever
as though	than	whether
because	that	while

A clause that begins with a subordinating conjunction is *subordinate* or *dependent* for its meaning upon the sentence to which it is joined. Most subordinating conjunctions act as adverbs by answering the questions *how? why? where? when?* and *under what conditions?* Clauses that begin with subordinating conjunctions modify verbs, adjectives, and adverbs.

John left town *before* the murder took place.   [when?]

Angelo screamed *when* I fell out of the tree.   [when?]

José looked at me *as if* I were a ghost.   [how?]

A clause containing a subordinate conjunction can also appear at the beginning of a sentence. It is separated from the rest of the sentence by a comma.

Because she was ill, Georgia went home.

Provided that it doesn't rain, the class picnic is tomorrow.

Exercise 4: Identifying Subordinating Conjunctions

Write the following sentences, underlining each subordinating conjuction and the clause it joins to the rest of the sentence. Study the example before you begin.

Example

a. Carmen left town after she read the announcement.

Carmen left town <u>after she read the announcement.</u>

1. Hank left town before his mother arrived from Austin.
2. Mary can drive us downtown if Sally Chen will go also.
3. So that we will remain healthy, we exercise regularly.
4. It always starts snowing whenever we ride our bikes to work.
5. Since he went to work for Mr. Pulaski, Carlos is much more cheerful.
6. Pam brushes her teeth as soon as she finishes her meals.
7. Good athletes can continue to exercise daily until they are extremely old.
8. The class saved thirty dollars so that we could have an invited speaker.
9. Many children leave the nest as soon as they graduate from high school.
10. When Juan was named valedictorian, we were all very pleased.

Review: Understanding Conjunctions

Write each of the following sentences, circling the coordinating, correlative, and subordinating conjunctions and underlining the items that they join. Study the example before you begin.

Example

a. Nancy painted the bedroom and the kitchen.

Nancy painted <u>the bedroom</u> (and) <u>the kitchen.</u>

1. JoAnn and Pam are planning a surprise party for Wendy.

2. Charlene won not only a blue ribbon but also a silver cup.

3. Renee can't decide whether to take Spanish or French.

4. Carmen always does her homework as soon as she gets home.

5. Until they become seniors, students in our school cannot leave campus for lunch.

6. We are painting the kitchen purple so that the color will awaken us in the morning.

7. Since Mary Lou learned to act, she has had several good roles.

8. Martin will never buy a coat as long as it is still warm.

9. Norma is certain to be elected captain, for she is the most popular player on the team.

10. Before California joined the Union, Alexander Leidesdorff built its first hotel and school there.

11. Cheryl will either get a job or attend the community college.

12. The students worked both slowly and carefully on their science projects.

13. Mary always does the laundry while her brother does the dishes.

14. Our star basketball player is both tall and skinny.

15. Provided he remembers to come home for dinner, Sam should greatly enjoy his surprise party.

16. Brenda will do well wherever she decides to attend college.

17. The police discovered the loot where the crook had hidden it.

18. Though she was skating for the first time, Sally was extremely confident.

19. Gino is saving his money so that he can visit his friend in Chicago.

20. If he doesn't arrive on time for this week's meeting, Allen will be expelled from the radio club.

Applying What You Know

Using newspapers from home or your school library, select an editorial on a subject of current interest. On a sheet of paper, list the conjunctions in the editorial and beside each one, label the conjunction *coordinating, correlative,* or *subordinating.*

Using Conjunctions

Carefully used, conjunctions can add variety and precision to writing; when overused, however, they make writing seem repetitious and dull. In the following sections you will practice replacing repeated conjunctions with punctuation and placing conjunctions for sentence variety.

Replacing Conjunctions with Punctuation

When more than two items are joined, some conjunctions can be replaced by commas.

> This store sells bolts *and* washers *and* nails.
> This store sells bolts, washers, and nails.
>
> You may select coffee *or* tea *or* milk.
> You may select coffee, tea, or milk.

Use a comma and a conjunction between the last two items in a series.

> He wore bulky ill-fitting clothes that made him appear pudgy, unkempt, *and* unconcerned about his appearance.
>
> On Saturday we plan to listen to some records, study for a while, *and* then go to a late movie.

Instead of joining two complete sentences with a coordinating conjunction, you may use a semicolon (;) as a replacement for the conjunction if the sentences are closely related in meaning.

> His intentions were noble, but it was his judgment we questioned.
>
> His intentions were noble; it was his judgment we questioned.

Exercise 5: Replacing Conjunctions with Punctuation

Rewrite each of the sentences on the following page, replacing the conjunctions *and* and *or* with punctuation wherever possible. Use a comma to link items in a series and a semicolon to link two complete sentences. Circle the punctuation you insert. Study the example before you begin.

Example

a. Who wore a suit and a top hat and sneakers to the prom?

Who wore a suit ⊘ a top hat ⊘ and sneakers to the prom?

1. Kathy and May and Sarah all volunteered to help organize the dance.

2. Norman likes Kathy and she seems to like him too.

3. The best candidate for the job would be Mary or Paul or Sue.

4. The villain in the typical western and mystery and spy story was eventually punished.

5. The grand prize will go to Vincente or Nancy or Paul, and I predict it will go to Nancy.

6. Carlos and Phillip and Joan are the best students in French and Spanish and German for this school year.

7. Norm isn't interested in chimpanzees or gorillas or dolphins, and he is certain that people will never be able to communicate with them.

8. Theodore Roosevelt and Herbert Hoover and Calvin Coolidge and Dwight Eisenhower were popular Republicans.

9. Anne has read the complete works of Ernest Hemingway, and he is now her favorite writer.

10. Was the Vice President who was elected in 1940 Henry Wallace or Harry Truman or Al Smith?

Correcting Conjunction Problems

Sentence parts joined by coordinating or correlative conjunctions must be parallel in structure. This means that the structure, or form, of each of the sentence parts must be similar. Learn to recognize *faulty parallelisms* (non-parallel structures) by comparing the sentence parts joined by the conjunction.

*Carlos loves *making* pizza and to *bake* cookies.
(different verb forms)

Carlos loves *making* pizza and *baking* cookies.
(parallel verb forms)

Carlos loves *to make* pizza and *to bake* cookies.
(parallel verb forms)

*The Oceanside Museum was an enjoyable *place* and *educational*.
(noun and adjective)

The Oceanside Museum was *enjoyable* and *educational*.
(two adjectives)

The Oceanside Museum was an *enjoyable* and *educational* place.
(two adjectives)

Exercise 6: Correcting Faulty Parallelisms

On a separate piece of paper, rewrite the following sentences, correcting each faulty parallelism. If a sentence is correct, mark it "C." Study the examples before you begin.

Examples

a. All of us want to either visit the special exhibit or we will go to the silent movie festival.

All of us want to either visit the special exhibit or go to the silent movie festival.

b. He is interested in politics and a person who enjoys fishing.

He is interested in politics and fishing.

1. Lisa knew she would enjoy either running the talent show or to design the decorations for the dance.

2. All the preparations had been carefully made and thoroughly checked, both in the house and in the yard.

3. Being very competitive and a hard worker, Richard was bewildered by people who wouldn't try to succeed.

4. Sometimes almost everyone thinks about giving up or, at least, not work so hard.

5. Allen checked all of the connections carefully, yet he couldn't find the cause for the malfunction.

Writing Focus: *Using Conjunctions in Writing*

Good writers use conjunctions effectively to connect ideas and to make their writing flow more smoothly. They use conjunctions such as *and, but, or, after, though,* and *if* to join words, phrases, clauses, and sentences. Conjunctions tell readers how one idea or event relates to another.

Assignment: *"And Then He . . . "*

Look carefully at the photograph on page 469. Imagine that you are a spectator in the crowd watching this tennis match. The photo records the beginning of an incident that goes on for some five minutes. The incident makes such an impression on you that you want to share it with your friends.

For this assignment, make up a story telling about the incident in the photograph.

Use the following steps to complete this assignment.

A. Prewriting

Study the photograph carefully. Notice what's going on. Imagine what has just happened and free write about it. (Review Chapter 1 for a discussion on free writing if necessary.) Let your imagination go. Quickly write down all the ideas that occur to you that could explain what happened before, during, and after the incident. Write until no more ideas come. Reread your free writing and underline the words you like that tell about the incident captured by the photo.

B. Writing

Using your free writing to help you, write one or more paragraphs describing the incident recorded by the photograph. Describe what happened just before, during, and after the incident. Include details that paint a moving picture of what happened for your friends. Remember that they were not present at the tennis match and will only know or "see" what you tell them. As you write, use conjunctions to make relationships between ideas clear.

C. Postwriting

Use the following checklist to revise your first draft.

1. Have I included specific details that describe the incident clearly and vividly?

2. Can I combine short sentences more effectively by using conjunctions?

3. Have I used the appropriate conjunction to show the relationship between my ideas?

Edit your story, using the Proofreader's Checklist at the back of the book. Exchange your writing with a partner who should check for the effective use of coordinating and subordinating conjunctions.

Understanding Interjections

An *interjection* is usually defined as a word that expresses a strong or sudden feeling, such as surprise, anger, or pleasure.

> *Hey!* Watch where you spray that paint.
>
> *Wow!* That was a close call.
>
> *Great!* That is the best news of the day.

Unlike other parts of speech, interjections are not related to any other words in the sentence; they merely show emotion. Some interjections such as *Dear me!* or *Goodness gracious!* consist of more than one word but are thought of as one interjection.

Almost any part of speech can be used as an interjection. The following *italicized* words, for example, are all used as interjections even though they often appear in other sentences as different parts of speech.

Nonsense! That can't be true.	[noun]
You! Come over here right now.	[pronoun]
Perfect! It is just what I wanted.	[adjective]
Forward! We have them on the run now.	[adverb]
But—! Wait just a minute.	[conjunction]

Exercise 1: *Identifying Interjections*

Write each of the following sentences, underlining the interjections.

Example

a. Well, I suppose that I could be persuaded to run for class president.

   Well, I suppose that I could be persuaded to run for class president.

1. My goodness! Your little sister has certainly grown up.

2. My, what a beautifully set table.

3. Fantastic! Our team has made the playoffs in football.

4. No! Please don't take this bus to Cuba.

5. The guard said, "Hey! Where is your identification card?"

6. Ridiculous! I'm too healthy to catch a cold.

7. Of course not! We will never sell our family farm.

8. Outrageous! I've never paid five dollars for a haircut before.

9. Oh, I don't think television is as boring as most people claim.

10. Stunning! This is the loveliest dress you have made.

Using Interjections

Interjections that express very strong or sudden feelings are usually followed by an exclamation point. Interjections expressing milder feelings are usually followed by commas.

Fire! We had better get help right now.

Well, now that's more like it.

Oh, all right, if you insist.

Commas and periods are not used immediately after exclamation points, even in direct quotations.

"Never!" he yelled back.

In the distance we heard her cry, *"Yippee!"*

The word following an exclamation point should be capitalized only when that word begins a new sentence.

Ouch! That really hurt.

Exercise 2: Punctuation and Capitalization with Interjections

Write the sentences on the following page, placing exclamation points after interjections expressing strong or sudden emotion and commas after interjections expressing milder feelings. Capitalize the first word after an interjection if that word begins a new sentence. Underline the punctuation you insert and the words you capitalize.

Example

a. Well let me know when you're coming, and I'll leave.
   Well, let me know when you're coming, and I'll leave.

1. Oops this rope is starting to slip.
2. Oh send me a dozen roses and a vase to hold them.
3. Rats I never expected Mr. Garcia to have a quiz today.
4. "Hurray" screamed the excited crowd.
5. My your house is much nicer than I had remembered.
6. The coach cried "Enough" as the opposition scored again.
7. Don't walk on that ledge. Whoops
8. Beautiful I've never seen a more gorgeous piece of sculpture.
9. Phooey I failed the test.
10. Goodness I never expected such a crowd.

Writing Focus: *Using*

Interjections in Writing

"*Good grief!*" is a typical interjection Lucy uses in the Peanuts comic strip. As this example illustrates, interjections are used to express strong emotion or sudden feeling. As such, they appear chiefly in dialogue. When you write dialogue, use interjections that are appropriate for the speaker.

Assignment: *Summer Blues*

Imagine that you are in the sixth week of summer vacation. You are bored and out of money. You and your friends are sitting around on a hot afternoon trying to think of something to do.

For this assignment, write a dialogue between you and your friends as you discuss ways to perk up your day. Your work will be evaluated for effective use of interjections.

Use the following steps to complete this assignment.

A. Prewriting

Using the brainstorming method described in Chapter 1, jot down the thoughts and feelings you and your friends might have on a boring summer day. Imagine how you might feel, what you might say, and what you could do about it. Add snippets of conversation that would be appropriate for the situation.

B. Writing

Write a short dialogue that you and your friends have about your boring situation. Begin with a few sentences describing the scene in which you meet. Then write the dialogue, using the ideas or snippets of conversation from your brainstorming list. Let the dialogue develop naturally as you discuss your boredom and things you might do. As you write, include appropriate interjections.

C. Postwriting

Revise your dialogue, using the following checklist.

1. Does my dialogue sound realistic for the situation?

2. Have I used interjections accurately to express emotion?

3. Have I punctuated and capitalized the interjections and other elements of the dialogue correctly?

Edit your revision, using the Proofreader's Checklist at the back of the book. If appropriate, work with classmates to perform your dialogue for the class.

20 Sentence Patterns

When speaking with close friends, you often use simple words and incomplete expressions to convey your thoughts. If your friends do not understand you, they can ask you to clarify your meaning by adding information. In writing, however, your audience is more distant, and you usually need to express yourself in complete sentences so that your thoughts will be clear to all readers. In the following sections you will study the basic structure and types of sentences.

Defining a Sentence

A *sentence* is usually defined as a group of words expressing a complete thought.

We stood in the rain for an hour waiting for the bus.	[sentence]
Maybe Paula and Joe can go with us.	[sentence]
The hikers sang songs around the campfire.	[sentence]

A group of words that does not have a complete thought is called a *sentence fragment*.

For an hour waiting for the bus	[fragment]
Maybe Paula and Joe	[fragment]
Sang songs around the campfire	[fragment]

Exercise 1: Identifying Complete Sentences

Some of the following groups of words are sentences; some are fragments. Number a sheet of paper 1–10. If the group of words is not a sentence, write *fragment* next to its number. If it is a sentence, write the sentence, capitalizing the first word and adding the appropriate end punctuation.

Example

a. did June finally find her book
   Did June finally find her book?

---

1. Joanie, my cousin from Lansing, Michigan
2. who is the couple on the third bleacher
3. on the chair by the front door
4. sometimes, on snowy winter afternoons
5. the laundry basket was full of clean clothes
6. is the Spanish Club meeting after school
7. is the boy with the blue T-shirt and white shorts
8. after taking my written excuse to the office
9. collected twenty cans of food for the food drive
10. for Tuesday I have math homework

Kinds of Sentences

Sentences can be classified into four types:

---

1. A *declarative sentence* makes a statement.

Edgar Allan Poe was born in 1809.

---

2. An *interrogative sentence* asks a question.

Was Edgar Allan Poe born in 1809?

---

3. An *imperative sentence* gives a mild command or makes a request.

Tell me the year in which Edgar Allan Poe was born.

4. An *exclamatory sentence* expresses a strong or sudden feeling.

What a great poet he was!

Exercise 2: *Identifying Kinds of Sentences*

Write each of the following sentences. In parentheses after each sentence, identify whether the sentence is *declarative*, *interrogative*, *imperative*, or *exclamatory*.

Examples

a. Lend me your pen, please.
   Lend me your pen, please. (imperative)

b. How bright these new students are!
   How bright these new students are! (exclamatory)

1. Mary Kay is reading a book about famous skiers.
2. Did your cousins really move to Brazil?
3. What a waste of money this hamburger is!
4. Mail your holiday gifts early this year.
5. Are you planning to attend the dance tomorrow night?
6. The rain will probably end around noon.
7. Tell the chef to finish cooking this liver.
8. Who is the best cook in our home economics class?
9. Oh, what a day for a picnic!
10. Be sure to tell your mother where we are going.

The Subject

A sentence has two basic parts: a *subject* and a *predicate*.

        S   P
My friend Janet / practices her trombone in the basement.

The *subject* of a sentence, the part about which something is being said, identifies the person, place, object, or idea that is being spoken about in the rest of the sentence.

Who will be elected president?

That ten-speed bike is my birthday present.

In the center of the ring stands *the tall ringmaster.*

(Notice that subjects need not always be located at the beginning of the sentence.)

The *simple subject* is the main word or words being spoken or written about. The simple subjects in the following sentences are *italicized.*

The old birch *trees* were covered with ice.

Each of the girls on the team is an experienced player.

Jo Ann Smith made an *A* on the test.

The *complete subject* is the simple subject plus its modifiers. The complete subjects in the following sentences are *italicized*; the simple subjects are underlined.

The small boat with only one sail is my favorite.

Movies about tornadoes and other disasters send shivers down my spine.

Exercise 3: *Identifying Simple and Complete Subjects*

Write each of the following sentences, underlining the complete subject once and the simple subject twice.

Examples

---

a. The old building behind the ivy was built in 1894.
   The old building behind the ivy was built in 1894.

b. Five members of Maria's family have studied piano.
   Five members of Maria's family have studied piano.

1. The four young police officers attended the academy together.

2. The attractive woman in the green dress is Ms. Tchan.

3. Mary Ann's favorite gerbil died yesterday.

4. Seven first-grade students from our neighborhood graduate tomorrow.

5. Many teachers in our school ride the bus.

6. Visitors to our school must stop at the principal's office.

7. Seventeen athletes in the ninth grade earned letters in track and field.

8. The congressional representative from our district was Ralph Metcalfe.

9. The most athletic students tried out for the cheerleading squad.

10. The biology teacher at your school is Carmen's cousin.

Compound Subjects

When two or more simple subjects are joined by a conjunction (usually *and* or *or*) and share the same verb, they are called *compound subjects*.

A *teller* and a *customer* prevented the bank robbery.

The *novel*, the *play*, or the *book* of short stories will make an ideal present.

Understood Subjects

The subject of a sentence can be *you* understood.

An understood subject does not actually appear in the sentence; instead, the reader understands that the subject of the sentence is *you*. The subject of an imperative sentence is usually *you* understood.

Open that crate carefully.	[*you*]
Please close the window.	[*you*]

The understood subject *you* is the simple subject of the sentence. When the name of the person or group being addressed is given in an imperative sentence, the subject is still *you* understood.

Turn the wheel to the right, Bill.	[*you*]
Sean, straighten the picture on the wall, please.	[*you*]

Exercise 4: Identifying Compound Subjects and You *Understood*

Write the following sentences, underlining the compound subjects in each. If the sentence has an understood subject, write *you* in parentheses next to the sentence.

Examples

a. Harold and Pedro are excellent students.
   Harold and Pedro are excellent students.

b. Clean your room immediately.
   Clean your room immediately. (you)

1. Buy some milk on the way home from school.

2. Nick and Nora are arriving at the station tonight.

3. The students and the teachers play an annual football game together.

4. José, Kim, and Lee are all on the honor roll this semester.

5. Turn in your reports at the final exam.

6. Buses, trains, and car pools are efficient means of transportation in metropolitan areas.

7. Kathy or Paula will probably be our new class president.

8. Prepare yourself for a terrible shock, Norman.

9. Be quiet during the assembly this afternoon.

10. Read the short story on page thirty-seven for tomorrow.

The Predicate

The *predicate* is the part of the sentence that says something about the subject.

A mild breeze *gently swayed each branch.*

Every predicate contains a verb or a verb phrase; sometimes, it will be the only word in the predicate.

An army of ants *approached.*

The verb or verb phrase in a predicate is called the *simple predicate*. Although adverbs, such as *not* or *even*, sometimes separate parts of a simple predicate, they are not part of the simple predicate.

They *should* not *be* late to the meeting.

I *can't find* my new schedule card.

The whole predicate, including the verb and any other words that modify the verb or make its meaning more definite, is called the *complete predicate*. In the following sentences, the complete predicate is *italicized*, and the simple predicate is underlined.

The angry customers *demanded their money back*.

Few of the students *have taken piano lessons before*.

Exercise 5: *Identifying Simple and Complete Predicates*

Write each of the following sentences, underlining the complete predicate once and the simple predicate twice.

Examples

a. Everyone cheered the victory of the home team.
   Everyone cheered the victory of the home team.

b. Wally will not be a very good skater.
   Wally will not be a very good skater.

1. Hank drove his mother to the airport.

2. Miriam has written several volumes of poetry.

3. My best friend sang at the annual awards assembly.

4. The blue-plate special is the best lunch at the diner.

5. The class elected Sarah homeroom repesentative.

6. The scouts walked from one side of the mountain to the other.

7. Sharon danced a hora during the folk dance program.

8. Howard and Bill are interested in local politics.

9. Everyone in our school is wearing warm clothes this winter.

10. Most of the football team will be attending the homecoming dance.

Compound Verbs

When a predicate has two or more verbs or verb phrases that are joined by a coordinating conjunction, the sentence is said to have a *compound verb*.

Each of the verbs must have the same subject.

> Dinner will begin at 7 o'clock and will end at 9.
> [compound verb: *will begin, will end*]

> Ricardo found the set of keys and received a reward.
> [compound verb: *found, received*]

Exercise 6: Identifying Simple and Compound Subjects and Predicates

Write the following sentences, underlining the simple subjects once and the simple predicates twice. (Be sure to watch for compound subjects and verbs.)

Examples

---

   a. Harry opened the door and entered the room.
      Harry opened the door and entered the room.

   b. Boys and girls rushed into the classroom and sat down.
      Boys and girls rushed into the classroom and sat down.

1. The new student reads science fiction and collects stamps for recreation.

2. Patty wrote letters or watched television in the evening.

3. Noriko mounted her bicycle and went for a ride along the lake.

4. Wally and his friends ordered hamburgers and French fries but received liver and onions.

5. Mary dove into the water and saved the terrified child.

6. Mr. Espinosa, Ms. Clarke, and Ms. Cardoza teach during the school year and go to school during the summer.

7. Ms. Lee runs, swims, and plays baseball.

8. My sister and I run or swim every morning.

9. Wendy and Michelle went to Washington, D.C., and met their congressional representative.

10. Ann replaced the broken fan belt and drove the car to the parking lot.

Sentence Patterns

Sentences may follow five different patterns, as the following list shows.

1. *S-V*
   Subject - Verb

2. *S-V-DO*
   Subject - Verb - Direct Object

3. *S-V-IO-DO*
   Subject - Verb - Indirect Object - Direct Object

4. *S-LV-PN*
   Subject - Linking Verb - Predicate Noun (or Pronoun)

5. *S-LV-PA*
   Subject - Linking Verb - Predicate Adjective

The structures following the subject and verb in a sentence pattern are called *complements*.

A *complement* is a part of the predicate that completes the thought begun by the subject and verb.

S-V *Sentence Pattern*

Some groups of words can express a complete thought with just a subject and a verb.

    S   V
Stars shine.

Even though several modifiers may be part of a sentence, a sentence might still follow the *S-V* pattern. Notice that prepositional phrases do not change the basic sentence pattern.

    S   V
The game continued into the night.

S-V-DO *Sentence Pattern*

A *direct object* is usually defined as a noun or pronoun that follows an action, or transitive, verb and answers the question *what?* or *whom?* about the subject and verb.

S	V	DO

Marie Curie discovered *radium*.   [Marie Curie discovered *what?*]

S	V	DO

Ricardo asked *me* for a ride.   [Ricardo asked *whom?*]

A sentence may have more than one direct object.

S V   DO   DO   DO
Roberta ordered a fish *sandwich*, a *salad*, and iced *tea*.

S V DO DO
Mr. Wilson thanked *him* and *me* for our help.

Direct objects receive the action of the verb or show the result of that action. They cannot follow forms of *be* or linking verbs.

Exercise 7: Identifying the S-V-DO *Sentence Pattern*

Write the following sentences, labeling the *S, V,* and *DO* parts of the sentence pattern used in each. Underline the words you label.

Example

 a. The committee slashed the budget.

    S   V   DO
  The <u>committee</u> <u>slashed</u> the <u>budget</u>.

1. We eat lunch in the cafeteria.

2. After our victory we held a celebration.

3. The police officers arrested the suspect this morning.

4. Ms. Santos is writing a novel and a play.

5. Due to the cost of insurance, we sold the car.

6. During our argument Perry insulted Sheila and me.

7. Mr. Yue is directing the band and the chorus tonight.

8. In the event of a blizzard, the district cancels classes.

9. On the school bus Mary read a book.

10. For his birthday Sam received a puppy.

S-V-IO-DO *Sentence Pattern*

An *indirect object* is a noun or a pronoun that answers the question *to what? for what? to whom?* or *for whom?* about the subject, verb, and direct object.

The indirect object always precedes the direct object.

> S V   IO   DO
> I bought *George* a book of poetry.
> [I bought a book *for whom*?]

> S   V   IO   DO
> My parents gave *me* a watch on my birthday.
> [My parents gave a watch *to whom*?]

> S V   IO   DO
> I told the *detective* everything that happened.
> [I told everything *to whom*?]

An indirect object is never part of a prepositional phrase. If the preposition *to* or *for* occurs in the sentence, the noun or pronoun that follows will be the object of the preposition, not the indirect object of the verb.

Exercise 8: *Identifying the* S-V-IO-DO *Sentence Pattern*

Write the following sentences, labeling the *S, V, IO,* and *DO* parts of the sentence pattern. Underline the words you label.

Examples

---

a. Aunt Mary mailed my family a box of grapefruit.

> S   V   IO   DO
> Aunt Mary mailed my family a box of grapefruit.

b. Mrs. Wilkinson made Pam and me new skirts.

<pre>
        S   V   IO   IO   DO
Mrs. Wilkinson made Pam and me new skirts.
</pre>

1.   Ramón mailed his cousin in the Bronx a birthday present.

2.   Mr. Chiang tells his sons and daughters long stories each night after dinner.

3.   The coach gave the runners on our team good advice.

4.   The famous chef prepared each of her customers a special treat.

5.   Mother bought Carmen and him new coats.

6.   Kuni sent her and me invitations to the party.

7.   Ms. Lorenzo read the literature class a poem about Chicago.

8.   Our state senator wrote Ann and him wonderful letters of recommendation.

9.   Ron sang our class a song from the new musical.

10. The coach has promised Dan, you, and me tickets to the baseball game.

S-LV-PN *Sentence Pattern*

A *predicate noun* or *predicate pronoun* is the noun or pronoun that follows a linking verb in a sentence and explains or identifies the subject of the sentence.

Predicate nouns and predicate pronouns are complements because they complete the meaning of the subject in the sentence.

<pre>
S   LV   PN
I might have been captain.
</pre>

<pre>
S   LV   PN
Physics is a favorite class of mine.
</pre>

<pre>
                       S   LV   PN
By winning the election, she became mayor.
</pre>

Whenever personal pronouns are used as predicate pronouns, they should always be in their subject form.

<pre>
S   LV   PN   PN   PN
The performers were Sarah, Lena, and she.
</pre>

<pre>
S   LV   PN   PN
The judges had been George and I.
</pre>

Exercise 9: Identifying the S-LV-PN Sentence Pattern

Write the following sentences, labeling the *S*, *LV*, and *PN* parts of the sentence pattern. Underline the words you label.

Example

a. The most likely winner was either Fred or I.

S   LV   PN   PN
The most likely <u>winner</u> <u>was</u> either <u>Fred</u> or <u>I</u>.

---

1.   Harry was a gentleman and a scholar.

2.   Norma became a famous newspaper editor.

3.   The best dancers in our school are Maria and I.

4.   Pauline and Carmelita are extremely skillful skaters.

5.   The new class representative will be Karen or he.

6.   Mary Lou has been a singer, dancer, and actress.

7.   Karl is a good runner but a poor swimmer.

8.   Tim has become the best debater in our school's history.

9.   Diego will be the announcer at the school assembly.

10. Three good artists are Harold, Noriko, and she.

S-LV-PA Sentence Pattern

A *predicate adjective* is an adjective that follows a linking verb and modifies the subject of the sentence.

S   LV   PA
The fabric appeared <i>worn</i>.

S   LV   PA
Our vacation had been <i>enjoyable</i> in every way.

S   LV   PA   PA
The flowers smelled <i>sweet</i> and <i>fresh</i>.

Exercise 10: Identifying the S-LV-PA Sentence Pattern

Write each of the following sentences, labeling the *S*, *LV*, and *PA* parts of the sentence pattern. Underline the words you label.

Example

---

a. The raspberries in our dessert were tart and tender.

         S   LV PA   PA

The raspberries in our dessert were tart and tender.

1. The person in the photograph looked very tall and thin.

2. Everyone was extremely excited about the upcoming dance.

3. The situation appears absolutely hopeless.

4. Dick should be very happy about his successful party.

5. The room grew dark and cold at exactly midnight.

6. The leftovers in the refrigerator smelled awful.

7. Our chances for victory became better and better as the game progressed.

8. Guillermo was calm and confident on the day of the election.

9. Ms. Chu has been very busy this week.

10. Mr. Adams will be rather surprised by his birthday present.

Review: Identifying Sentence Patterns

Write the following sentences, labeling the sentence patterns. Underline the words you label.

Example

---

a. Carmen lent me her car.

    S   V   IO   DO

Carmen lent me her car.

1. Marjorie works very diligently.

2. The first gold medal winner will be she.

3. Jeanne gave us a book about insects of the world.

4. The teachers sent Mr. Duvalier a birthday card.

5. Carolyn is a member of the athletic club.

6. Ken sings in the church choir and in the school chorus.

7. Leonard seems annoyed about his grades this semester.

8. Mike is sometimes amusing but often rather boring.

9. Michelle has been a skier for many years.

10. The committee gave Glenn the award after much debate.

11. Sarah baked Susan and him a loaf of whole-wheat bread.

12. Jerry sent most of his friends birthday cards.

13. After graduation the seniors were elated.

14. Many students find the answers only after much work.

15. The football players looked tired and disappointed.

Writing Focus: *Varying Sentence Patterns in Writing*

Good writers use a variety of sentence patterns in their writing. They vary sentence patterns in order to keep readers interested and to present their ideas in the best possible way. Choose appropriate sentence patterns and write them correctly to make your work clear.

Assignment: *Traveling Back in Time*

A time machine is ready to take you back in history. You may travel to any place at any period of time you wish—King Arthur's court, the first Olympic Games, the Wild West. To what date and place will you travel? Whom will you meet? What special sights might you see? In general, consider why you would choose a particular time and place.

A. Prewriting

Center on one period in history that appeals to you. Use the brainstorming technique, described in Chapter 1, to generate ideas about this time in history. Write down the name of your historical period and begin to list details about it. Let your thoughts flow freely, without any particular design to them. Look back over the list and begin to make associations which help explain the period's appeal to

you. For example, you may want to travel back to Egypt to see how the pyramids were built so that you can learn to be a great architect. Jot down two or three reasons for the appeal, and underline the details from your list that support or help explain them.

B. Writing

Using your list of details and reasons write one or more well-developed paragraphs explaining why you would like to visit a particular historical period. Provide specific details about the period so that you can show and explain its appeal. Write for your classmates. Your paragraphs will be evaluated for correct use and variety of sentence patterns.

C. Postwriting

Use the following checklist to revise your first draft.

1.   Is the information about my historical period accurate?

2.   Are the reasons the time period appeals to me clear?

3.   Have I included enough details to help explain my reasons?

4.   Have I used only complete sentences?

5.   Have I varied my sentence patterns?

Edit your paragraphs using the Proofreader's Checklist at the back of the book. If appropriate, share your writing with your classmates to enjoy one another's ideas.

21 Phrases

Understanding Phrases

In everyday conversation, speakers often use phrases.

"Where is she?"

"Standing by the water fountain."

"Where is it?"

"In the corner under the sign."

In Standard English, phrases of different types are often incorporated into complete sentences. In the following sections you will learn to identify the different kinds of phrases and how they are used in sentences.

Verb, Adjective, and Adverbial Phrases

A *phrase* is usually defined as a group of words that function as a single part of speech but that do not contain a verb and its subject.

A *verb phrase* is the main verb plus one or more helping verbs.

The children *are having* a good time.

Tony *should have been studying* biology.

A *prepositional phrase* (a preposition plus its object and modifiers) usually functions as either an adjective or an adverb. Prepositional phrases that function as adjectives are called *adjective phrases*; those that function as adverbs are called *adverbial phrases*. An adjective phrase modifies a noun or a pronoun within the sentence; an adverbial phrase modifies a verb, an adjective, or an adverb.

The news *about the tragedy* traveled quickly.   [adjective phrase]

The suitcase *with the broken handle* is mine.   [adjective phrase]

The governor spoke *at our school* yesterday.   [adverbial phrase]

The TV antenna was installed *on the roof*.   [adverbial phrase]

Exercise 1: *Identifying Verb, Adjective, and Adverbial Phrases*

Write the following sentences, underlining each verb, adjective, and adverbial phrase. Label the phrases *VP* for verb phrase, *Adj.* for adjective phrase, and *Adv.* for adverbial phrase.

Examples

   a. Marilyn has gone to the store.

           VP   Adv.
    Marilyn has gone to the store.

   b. Charles has been reading this book about birds.

              VP   Adj.
    Charles has been reading this book about birds.

1. Cheryl has caught a fish with big green eyes.

2. Gary will jog after school.

3. A dog from the next block was howling.

4. Ms. Neal may sing at our school.

5. The neighborhood grocer can save us two pounds of fresh smelt.

6. Our house will be a castle by the sea.

7. Bob has been arrested for car theft.

8. The distribution clerks are earning extra money through sales commissions.

9. Tom and Loc have been watching soap operas during lunch.

10. A house near the beach must be very expensive.

Appositives and Appositive Phrases

An *appositive* is a noun or pronoun that explains or identifies a nearby noun or pronoun.

> The ring contained my birthstone, *the emerald*, in the setting.
>
> These gifts are for the winner, *Mr. Angeli*.

An *appositive phrase* includes an appositive and its modifiers working together as a unit to explain or identify a noun or pronoun. An appositive phrase is usually set off by commas.

> Bowser, *our new mascot*, hasn't been seen for days.
>
> The invention, *a device for squeezing prunes*, was never patented.

Sometimes an appositive will come before the word it explains in the sentence.

> *A woman of inexhaustible energy*, our mayor has received national acclaim.

Commas are generally not used when a one-word appositive is closely related to the word it follows.

> The artist *Cristo* is internationally famous.
>
> My daughter *Ellen* has recently changed schools.

Exercise 2: Identifying Appositives and Appositive Phrases

Write the sentences on the next page, underlining each appositive or appositive phrase. Add commas wherever necessary and circle the commas you insert.

Examples

a. Mrs. Schwartz the school counselor helps students find work.

Mrs. Schwartz⊙ the school counselor⊙ helps students find work.

b. Our kitten Paws is a very playful animal.

Our kitten <u>Paws</u> is a very playful animal.

1. Our friend Dale plans to save money to buy a used car from her brother Richard.

2. Pam asked her teacher a man from Brazil about music in South America.

3. Alfredo sent the gift a large box of roses to his mother.

4. A Japanese martial art karate is Ann's newest hobby.

5. We mistook him for Ronald Reagan the President.

6. Sam brought a picture of Lassie his favorite movie star.

7. Michelangelo the great Italian sculptor and painter was born in 1475.

8. Last night we watched the movie *Bananas* for the third time.

9. My favorite place to visit is Chicago the Windy City.

10. A person of great courage the young girl survived the accident and learned to walk once again.

Verbals and Verbal Phrases

Verbals are words formed from verbs but used as nouns, adjectives, or adverbs. The three types of verbals are *gerunds*, *participles*, and *infinitives*.

When a verbal is part of a group of words that work together as a single part of speech, the group is called a *verbal phrase*.

A *gerund* is a verbal ending in *-ing* that functions as a noun.

Gerunds can be used in all the ways that nouns are used in a sentence.

Swimming is fun.	[subject]
Except for *swimming* every day, John got little exercise.	[object of a preposition]
My fondest memory is *swimming* at the lake.	[predicate noun]
I practiced *swimming* in the ocean.	[direct object]

Exercise 3: Identifying Gerunds

On a separate piece of paper, write the following sentences, underlining each gerund. Your teacher may ask you how the gerund is used in the sentence.

Examples

a. Skiing is an expensive sport.

 <u>Skiing</u> is an expensive sport.

b. Mona and David take studying seriously.

 Mona and David take <u>studying</u> seriously.

1. Running provides excellent exercise at low cost.

2. Carrie is fascinated by boxing.

3. A wonderful hobby for students is sewing.

4. Max practices diving at the community pool.

5. In addition to sweeping, I must also prepare dinner and clean my bedroom.

6. The best medicine is sleeping.

7. Mr. Giancana teaches driving at our school.

8. Most authors take pleasure in writing.

9. Dancing develops strength and coordination.

10. Hurling, a popular game in Ireland, is somewhat like lacrosse.

A *gerund phrase* is a group of words consisting of a gerund plus its modifiers or complements.

Gerunds are part noun and part verb. Like other nouns, gerunds can be modified by adjectives and adjective phrases; like verbs, gerunds can be modified by adverbs and adverbial phrases.

The *playing* of the violin lulled us to sleep. [adj. phrase: *of the violin*]

Playing in the streets can be dangerous. [adv. phrase: *in the streets*]

The complement the gerund phrase most often has is the *direct object*, a word that receives the action of the gerund.

> DO
> *Lifting* weights is strenuous work.
> [*Weights* tells *what* is being lifted; it functions as the direct object of the gerund.]

Gerund phrases can be used in all the ways that nouns are used in a sentence.

> We were excited about *camping in the mountains.*
> [gerund phrase used as the object of the preposition *about*]

> Her greatest thrill was *playing the part of Juliet.*
> [gerund phrase used as a predicate noun]

> Our principal suggested *taking a train.*
> [gerund phrase used as a direct object]

Exercise 4: *Identifying Gerund Phrases*

Write the following sentences, underlining each gerund phrase. In parentheses after the sentence, identify the function of the phrase.

Examples

a. The singing of our choir is beautiful.

   The singing of our choir is beautiful. (subject)

b. We were still hungry after eating the watercress sandwiches.

   We were still hungry after eating the watercress sandwiches. (object of the preposition)

1. Playing the guitar takes hours of practice.

2. Jean enjoyed the singing of Joan Sutherland.

3. The most difficult job in our school is being treasurer of a club.

4. We all enjoyed dancing the hora last night at Jennifer's party.

5. Ralph was sad about sinking his rowboat.

6. Listening to a good orchestra relaxes Ricardo.

7. We all awoke to the noisy chattering of an air hammer.

8. Pam delights in writing short stories.

9. Tom enjoys playing the oboe in the school band.

10. Our favorite hobby is the weaving of woolen blankets.

A *participle* is formed from a verb but functions as an adjective. Participles may be either *present* or *past*.

The *present participle* is formed with -*ing* added to the present tense form of the verb. When a present participle is used without a helping verb, it acts as an adjective.

The *singing* waiter entertained every customer.

The constantly *winding* road slowed traffic to a crawl.

A participle can appear before or after the word it modifies in a sentence.

The road, *winding* constantly, slowed traffic to a crawl.

The ambulance, *speeding* through the intersection, raced toward the accident.

Exercise 5: *Identifying Present Participles*

Write the following sentences, underlining each present participle. Then draw an arrow from the present participle to the noun that it modifies.

Examples

---

a. Our boat, leaking like a sieve, was towed into port.

Our boat, leaking like a sieve, was towed into port.

b. Tommy quieted the crying baby.

Tommy quieted the crying baby.

1. The plumber fixed the leaking faucet.

2. Ms. Aguilar is the acting principal.

3. We hid behind the crumbling wall during the snowball fight.

4. We threw the barking dog a large soup bone.

5. The squeaking door disturbed everyone in the class.

6. The building, tottering dangerously, finally collapsed into a pile of rubble.

7. The principal gives misbehaving students a second chance.

8. We fell into the freezing river when we were crossing it in the rowboat.

9. My baby sister's favorite toy is a talking telephone.

10. The wheel, squeaking crazily, fell off in the turn.

The *past participle* is one of the principal parts of a verb. The past participle of regular verbs is formed with *-d* or *-ed* added to the present tense: *walk/walked; help/helped*. The past participle of irregular verbs must be memorized or looked up.

A past participle can be used as part of a *verb phrase* or as an *adjective*. If a helping verb is used with the past participle, the past participle is part of a verb phrase; if it is used by itself to modify a noun or pronoun, the past participle is an adjective.

Fred *has practiced* the tuba.	[verb phrase]
Fred is a *practiced* musician.	[adjective]
Fred *has torn* the cloth.	[verb phrase]
Fred mended the *torn* cloth.	[adjective]

A past participle used as an adjective can appear before or after the word it modifies.

The *battered* and *worn* book gathered dust on the shelf.

The book, *battered* and *worn*, gathered dust on the shelf.

The *washed* and *waxed* floor appeared shiny.

The floor, *washed* and *waxed*, appeared shiny.

Exercise 6: *Identifying Past Participles*

Rewrite the sentences on the following page, underlining the past participles. Then draw an arrow from each past participle to the word that it modifies.

Examples

a. Mary bought a used car from her cousin Harry.

Mary bought a used car from her cousin Harry.

b. The worn belt on the car broke in the middle of rush-hour traffic.

The worn belt on the car broke in the middle of rush-hour traffic.

1. A retired executive spoke to our class about pursuing careers in business.

2. The table, polished for hours, shone like glass.

3. Grace sent the broken watch to the factory for repairs.

4. Muhammad's favorite dessert is frozen strawberries with chocolate and cream.

5. Susan is an experienced dancer with a famous ballet company in Minneapolis, Minnesota.

6. The class, bored and restless, was ready for a new assignment.

7. The battered, old sofa wore out after years of hard use.

8. The district attorney found errors in the sworn statement of the witness.

9. The cabinet, locked to ensure privacy, contains the students' records.

10. The referee gave the fallen champ the ten count.

A *participial phrase* is a participle and any complements or modifiers it may have.

Every participle is both part adjective and part verb. Like other adjectives, participles can be modified by adverbs and by adverbial phrases.

Laughing heartily, George told us what had happened.
[adverb modifying a present participle]

Injured in an accident, Betty couldn't work for a year.
[adverbial phrase modifying a past participle]

Because participles also have the properties of verbs, they can have complements, such as objects.

We heard the musicians *practicing their instruments*.
[*Instruments* is the direct object of *practicing*.]

Bringing her a small gift, Tom introduced himself.
[*Gift* is the direct object of *Bringing; her* is the indirect object.]

Exercise 7: *Identifying Participial Phrases*

Write the following sentences, underlining the participial phrases. Then draw an arrow from each participle to the noun or pronoun that it modifies.

Examples

a. The farmer, toiling in the sun, planted a whole row of beets.

The farmer, toiling in the sun, planted a whole row of beets.

b. Delivering a speech about agriculture, the President also spoke about the economy.

Delivering a speech about agriculture, the President also spoke about the economy.

1. The bus waiting at the corner is about to depart for San Francisco and Los Angeles.

2. Chopping vegetables for stew, Mark came up with the idea for his invention.

3. Many people watching the race didn't understand how the accident could have occurred.

4. Barbara Walters interviewed soldiers drafted into the army.

5. Roger lent the person teaching French II his travel posters to show the class.

6. Roasting in the sun, they never considered the danger of sunburn.

7. The stadium will give a free hat to everyone attending tonight's game.

8. The health department gives employees working in the cafeteria a yearly chest X-ray.

9. My favorite movies are the ones presenting the lives of real people.

10. Elected to the council, Sue promised to represent her class well.

An *infinitive* is a verbal, usually preceded by the word *to*, that can function as a noun, an adjective, or an adverb.

To travel was his fondest wish.	[noun]
Our chance *to win* came late in the game.	[adjective]
Marsha hurried *to catch* her train.	[adverb]

Infinitives used as nouns may function as subjects, direct objects, and predicate nouns.

To continue was out of the question.	[subject]
Both Ron and Alice wanted *to leave*.	[direct object]
Her only goal was *to succeed*.	[predicate noun]

The word *to*, which begins an infinitive, is actually part of the infinitive and should not be confused with the preposition *to* that begins a prepositional phrase. In an infinitive, *to* is followed by a verb; in a prepositional phrase, *to* is followed by a noun or a pronoun.

Infinitives	**Prepositional Phrases**
to arrive	to my school
to become	to the library
to study	to him

Exercise 8: *Identifying Infinitives*

Write the sentences on the next page, underlining the infinitives. In parentheses after each sentence, identify whether the infinitive is used as a noun, an adjective, or an adverb.

Examples

a. To succeed demands a great deal of hard work.

  To succeed demands a great deal of hard work. (noun)

   b. Harold brought us a fish to cook.

      Harold brought us a fish <u>to cook</u>. (adjective)

   c. Everyone found the roast difficult to chew.

      Everyone found the roast difficult <u>to chew</u>. (adverb)

1. Carla always tries to succeed.

2. Kim went out to eat.

3. A good carpenter is a hard person to find.

4. Ms. Peabody was the last guest to arrive.

5. Margaret's goal is to swim in the Olympics.

6. To diet calls for great discipline during the holidays.

7. Maurice and José have homework to do.

8. A good beef stew isn't easy to prepare.

9. Jacqueline played the game of racquetball too carelessly to win.

10. Carol's secret career plan for the future is to farm.

An *infinitive phrase* includes the infinitive, its modifiers, and its complements, and functions as a single part of speech.

Infinitives can have modifiers and complements.

> *To speak clearly* is difficult for some people.
> [*Clearly* is an adverb modifying *to speak*.]

> We just wanted *to relax on the beach*.
> [*On the beach* is an adverbial phrase modifying *to relax*.]

> *To tell him the correct answer* would be unfair.
> [*Answer* is the direct object of *to tell; him* is the indirect object.]

Exercise 9: *Identifying Infinitive Phrases*

Rewrite the sentences on the following page, underlining the infinitive phrases. In parentheses next to each sentence, tell whether the phrase is used as a *noun*, an *adjective*, or an *adverb*.

Examples

a. To swim across the English Channel is a great feat.

<u>To swim across the English Channel</u> is a great feat. (noun)

b. Hugh was very kind to fix dinner for us.

Hugh was very kind <u>to fix dinner for us</u>. (adverb)

1. To cross the desert on a camel is an unpleasant experience.
2. Patty always wanted to be an engineer.
3. The best place to cook meat is in the broiler.
4. Good snow tires will help you to drive during a blizzard.
5. Tina practiced to qualify for the gymnastics team from her district.
6. A musical teapot would be a perfect gift to give to Miriam for her birthday.
7. John is always careful to consider his friends' feelings before taking action.
8. Sarah's plan is to build miniature dollhouses at home and sell them in her store.
9. Many of the students in our class run to strengthen their hearts and improve blood circulation.
10. Delia wrote too slowly to finish the geography assignment before the bell rang.

While all three types of verbals can have complements, only the infinitive can have a subject.

I wanted *Jane to leave.*
[*Jane* is the subject of the infinitive *to leave.*]

If an infinitive has a subject, it will be a noun or a pronoun and will appear immediately in front of the infinitive.

Mr. Nelson asked *me to help.*
[*Me* is the subject of the infinitive.]

Infinitives that have subjects may also have direct objects.

The teacher asked *Pat to take attendance.*
[*Pat* is the subject of the infinitive; *attendance* is the direct object.]

Exercise 10: *Identifying Subjects of Infinitives*

Write the following sentences, underlining the infinitive phrases. If the infinitive has a subject, circle the subject. In parentheses next to the sentence, identify whether the phrase is used as *noun, adjective,* or *adverb.*

Examples

a. No one believed Melissa to be a great singer.

No one believed (Melissa) to be a great singer. (noun)

b. Sharon rented a car to drive her family to the beach.

Sharon rented a car to drive her family to the beach. (adverb)

1. The Smiths want their children to be happy.
2. All of the teachers want us to do our homework in looseleaf notebooks.
3. Tim needs a new suit to wear to the school dance.
4. Ms. Santos is studying to become a minister.
5. Theresa expects everyone to come to her surprise party for Maria.
6. Maurice and Flora walked slowly to conserve their energy for the dance.
7. Many athletes consider themselves to be extremely healthy.
8. To be a police officer is often dangerous.
9. Mary finally found a scarf to match her gloves.
10. The newspaper declared its basketball team to be the best in the state.

Review: *Understanding Phrases*

In the short selection on the following page, twenty-six phrases are underlined. On a sheet of paper numbered 1–25, list the underlined phrases in the order they occur. (Do not include the phrase identified in the example.) Then using what you have learned in the preceding sections, identify each phrase as adjective, adverbial, appositive, gerund, participial, or infinitive. (Hint: Identify gerund, participial, and infinitive phrases as such, regardless of their modifiers and complements.)

Example

a. *the new boy at school*—appositive phrase

Jamie, the new boy at school, should have been hurrying to gym class. Instead, he was hanging around the water fountain in the front corridor, waiting to catch a glimpse of Linda, the school judo champion and co-leader of the cheerleading squad. For Jamie, waiting in the corridor had a certain nostalgic charm. He had leaned against lockers at other schools in the hope of walking other girls to class. Smiling shyly, he would approach the girl with the lovely face he had noticed for the first time just yesterday as he sat daydreaming in class. She had blue eyes and black hair, or brown eyes and blond hair, and once, she was a redhead with such green eyes; he was certain she could see in the dark. Working his way through the 8 A.M. press of students, he would invent and discard opening lines of small talk. "I saw you at the judo match yesterday . . ." "Do you always carry a cello? . . ." "I noticed your signature on the Save the Whales petition . . ." Jamie's goal in life was to prepare for any occasion. He stood in the corridor of Central High, bracing one foot against the locker as Linda opened the front door and the final bell rang.

Using Phrases

Because they are part verb and part noun, adjective, or adverb, verbals may present special usage problems. In the next sections you will learn how to use verbals and verbal phrases effectively in your writing.

Using Possessives Before Gerunds

Like a noun, a gerund can be modified by adjectives. When a noun or pronoun acts as an adjective before a gerund, it should be in the possessive form.

I couldn't understand *Jim's failing biology*.

Our shouting disturbed the class in the next room.

The coach complimented *Joan's swimming* during the meet.

Exercise 11: Using Possessives Before Gerunds

Write the following sentences, using the correct form of the noun or pronoun in parentheses. Be careful not to mistake participles that modify nouns for gerunds that act as nouns. Underline the form of the noun or pronoun that you choose.

Examples

a. _____ skating in the ice show made her family proud. (Rosa, Rosa's)

   Rosa's skating in the ice show made her family proud.

b. Nobody predicted _____ winning the state championship. (us, we, our)

   Nobody predicted our winning the state championship.

c. The _____ singing on horseback was Gene Autry. (cowboy, cowboy's)

   The cowboy singing on horseback was Gene Autry.

1. We all enjoyed _____ retelling the story of his mishap. (Norman, Norman's)

2. _____ skipping class upset the principal a great deal. (They, Them, Their)

3. The worst mistake during the trip was _____ losing the map. (I, me, my)

4. The _____ standing at the bus stop is my Aunt Sarah. (woman, woman's)

5. The public was outraged by the _____ raising prices even higher. (grocer's, grocer)

6. We are very pleased at the _____ being repainted chartreuse. (gym, gym's)

7. _____ being offered a job in the warehouse pleased Ralph. (He, Him, His)

8. The _____ being flooded by the storm forced us to cancel the game. (field, field's)

9. The students were grateful for _____ planning of the home-coming dance. (Ms. Chiang, Ms. Chiang's)

10. The robbers were caught because of _____ calling the police promptly. (you, your)

Using Punctuation with Phrases

A participial phrase used at the beginning of a sentence is called an *introductory participial phrase* and is always followed by a comma.

Struggling with her heavy suitcase, Grandma boarded the train.

Tossed by the heavy seas, the freighter broke apart and sank.

The noun or pronoun modified by an introductory phrase should be placed immediately after that phrase in the sentence. (When it is not, the result is a *dangling modifier*.)

Dangling Modifier: Crying out in pain, the arrow was removed from his leg. [The arrow did not cry out in pain.]

Correct: *Crying out in pain,* he removed the arrow from his leg.

Dangling Modifier: Stuck in the elevator, the fire fighters rescued the children. [The fire fighters were not stuck in the elevator.]

Correct: *Stuck in the elevator,* the children were rescued by the fire fighters.

A participial phrase that adds detail but that does not change the main idea of the sentence is called a *nonessential phrase*.

Nonessential phrases are set off by commas.

The mayor, *waving to the crowd*, walked slowly to the podium.

Gene, *tired from the day's work*, collapsed on the bed.

A participial phrase that does add important information to the meaning of the sentence is called an *essential phrase*. If an essential phrase is removed, the meaning of the sentence would not be clear.

Essential phrases are not set off by commas.

The man *speaking to the newscaster* is a famous astronaut.
[*Speaking to the newscaster* identifies the man.]

All people *having coupons* will enter the movie first.
[*Having coupons* identifies the people who will enter the movie first.]

Exercise 12: Using and Punctuating Participial Phrases

All of the sentences on the following page contain participial phrases. Write each sentence, inserting proper punctuation. If the participial phrase does not clearly modify the proper word, rewrite the sentence so that it does. Underline the participial phrase and circle the commas that you insert. (Some sentences may not need any changes.)

Examples

a. Waiting for the bus I planned my day at school.

Waiting for the bus ⊘ I planned my day at school.

b. The customer recognizing a bargain grabbed the broccoli.

The customer ⊘ recognizing a bargain ⊘ grabbed the broccoli.

c. Michael discovered a crack in the ice trying out his skates.

Michael ⊘ trying out his skates ⊘ discovered a crack in the ice.

or

Trying out his skates ⊘ Michael discovered a crack in the ice.

507

1. Fighting upstream the salmon struggles onward.

2. Ms. Lewis teaching poetry to her students found they enjoyed limericks best.

3. The police officer directing traffic is my older sister Katherine Elizabeth.

4. We read the newspaper eating our breakfast cereal with milk and fruit.

5. Following too closely an accident was barely avoided.

6. The students studying hardest for the exams will receive the best grades.

7. The salesclerk tired after hours of work showed us every pair of size-eight shoes in the store.

8. Tasting lightly spiced but delicate we found the spinach crepes delicious.

9. Appearing suddenly on the horizon the ambulance passed us as though we were standing still.

10. Excited by the lecture their hands were raised for questions to the speaker.

Review: *Using Phrases*

Rewrite the sentences on the next page, making changes and adding punctuation wherever necessary. Some sentences do not follow Standard English in using possessive forms of nouns or pronouns, while others lack necessary punctuation. Some sentences contain participial phrases that do not clearly modify the proper word. (Some sentences may not need any changes.)

Examples

a. Maria singing the national anthem was a pleasant surprise to us all.

Maria's singing the national anthem was a pleasant surprise to us all.

b. Playing the lead in a new film, the audience cheered Kareem Abdul-Jabbar.

Playing the lead in a new film, Kareem Abdul-Jabbar was cheered by the audience.

1. The family was angry about him cooking all the snails for breakfast.

2. Me helping younger students with their homework has been an enjoyable experience.

3. Ms. Sanders waiting for a bus to Abilene told us about her family.

4. Reading a detective novel, an interesting idea occurred to Officer Salem.

5. Planning to travel to India Ms. Espino needed many inoculations in order to get her passport.

6. Taken from the window of the airplane Frank was proud of his remarkable photographs.

7. Tony being an athlete may have helped him in the election.

8. Mark appreciates our lending him our skates.

9. Believing her client guilty a good defense was still presented by the lawyer.

10. Wearing her new hiking boots, the glacier was not frightening to Carol.

11. Everyone was happy about Ms. Montez being named a general supervisor.

12. Intending to apologize to his sister for yelling Jiro knocked on her door.

13. Wanting to be good club members, we never missed a monthly meeting.

14. Looking for a new purple blouse Terry rode the bus to the shopping center.

15. Fascinated by Norman's talk the hour flew by.

16. Acting the part of Macbeth Tim developed a thirst for power while in office.

17. The only memorable part of the movie was Rocky knocking out the champ.

18. Seeking a cure for cancer, many problems slowed the work of the researchers.

19. Betty missing the last bus in the evening decided to take a cab home.

20. We will carefully watch Barry cooking the turkeys during the holidays.

Writing Focus: *Using Phrases in Writing*

Many different types of phrases are available to you as a writer—verb, adjective, adverbial, appositive, gerund, participle, and infinitive. To strengthen your writing style, choose appropriate phrases to add details, to combine sentences, and to vary sentences. Be sure to place and punctuate phrases correctly so that your meaning is clear.

Assignment: *Guess Who's Coming for Dinner?*

Imagine that you have a twelve-year-old younger brother or sister who wants to earn a domestic science badge from his or her club. In order to earn the badge, a member must prepare and serve a meal for the other members of the club. Your sibling has never cooked a meal and has asked for your help.

Write out instructions in paragraph form for your sibling explaining how to set the table and prepare either a breakfast, lunch, or dinner for twelve people.

Use the following steps to complete this assignment.

A. Prewriting

Think of all the meals you know how to prepare, and choose one to write about that is easy to fix. Begin a list of all the items and steps necessary to prepare it. Don't worry about the order of the steps. For now, jot down everything you can think of that will help your sibling prepare and serve the meal and set the table. Remember that your brother or sister must perform the tasks alone. Keep listing until you can't think of anything else to include. Read over your list. Group and number the steps in the order that your sibling will need to perform them.

B. Writing

Using your list, write, in paragraph form, instructions to your sister or brother for preparing and serving the meal. Begin by discussing the items that your sibling will need to assemble. Then carefully explain the step-by-step process of preparing the meal, setting the table, and serving the meal. Make sure you include everything your

sibling will need to know. As you write, use various kinds of phrases to add details, combine sentences, and vary sentences.

C. Postwriting

Revise your first draft, using the following checklist.

1. Is my vocabulary appropriate for my sibling?

2. Have I included enough information so that my sibling can complete the tasks? Could I do the tasks with these instructions?

3. Do my instructions have a logical organization? Does each step naturally follow the one before?

4. Have I used various types of phrases effectively?

5. Have I placed and punctuated each phrase correctly?

Use the Proofreader's Checklist at the back of the book to edit your instructions. Share your paragraph with a younger sibling or friend to see if he or she can understand and follow your directions.

22 Clauses

Understanding Clauses

A *clause* is usually defined as a group of words that contains a verb and its subject and is used as a part of a sentence.

<pre>
               S   V   S   V
clause [Marnie left the party] [because she was ill.] clause
               S   V   S   V
clause [I talked to Sylvia] [while Juan hid her present.] clause
</pre>

In the following sections you will learn the definition of a clause, the types of clauses, and how clauses can function in a sentence.

Distinguishing a Clause from a Phrase

A *phrase* is a group of words acting as a single part of speech that does not have its own subject and verb.

A *clause* is a group of words that has its own subject and verb.

The vase *that I bought* had a broken handle.	[clause]
I bought the vase *with a broken handle*.	[phrase]
Before the test began, Josh sharpened his pencil.	[clause]
Before the test Josh sharpened his pencil.	[phrase]
The prize will go to the person *who has the winning ticket*.	[clause]
The prize will go to the person *owning the winning* ticket.	[phrase]

Exercise 1: Distinguishing Clauses from Phrases

Write the following sentences, underlining the *italicized* words. In parentheses next to each sentence, identify the *italicized* words as *clause* or *phrase*.

Examples

> a. Our cousins living in Austin always invite us to dinner *when we are in town*.
>   Our cousins living in Austin always invite us to dinner when we are in town. (clause)
>
> b. *At Wounded Knee, South Dakota*, 300 Sioux were killed by soldiers.
>   At Wounded Knee, South Dakota, 300 Sioux were killed by soldiers. (phrase)

1. The customers *at the door at nine o'clock* were annoyed when the store opened late.

2. *Since Gail taught her brother backgammon*, he does little else after school.

3. *Skating on a frozen pond in the early morning* is one of the pleasures that reward us in the winter.

4. Naomi pulled up the covers *as she thought about walking to school in the drifting snow*.

5. The Oakdale Township High School Student Council couldn't decide *whom they should appoint chief organizer of the annual homecoming dance*.

6. *Well-known for her thriftiness*, Robin always turns off the lights when she leaves a room.

7. No one knew *who would become homecoming queen* until this morning.

8. One of the guests *leaving the party early* was a person who had attended our school.

9. *To jog four miles before breakfast* is not my idea of a relaxing morning.

10. *When he saw the flashing red lights ahead*, the driver of the big, green convertible slowed the car to a moderate speed to avoid getting a ticket.

Independent Clauses

An *independent clause* is a group of words that has a subject and a verb and that expresses a complete thought.

An independent clause is also called the *main clause* of the sentence. Independent clauses can stand alone as a sentence.

We have enjoyed our vacation since the weather has been good.

Independent Clause: We have enjoyed our vacation.

A sentence can have more than one independent clause joined by a coordinating conjuction, such as *and, but, or, nor, for,* and *yet,* or joined by a semicolon.

Juan prepared dinner, *and* Carlos washed the dishes.

You must hurry, *or* you will be late.

Joan wants to study law; her brother wants to be a farmer.

Subordinate Clauses

A *subordinate clause* (also called a *dependent clause*) is a group of words that has a subject and verb but that does not express a complete thought.

Because it is not a complete thought, a subordinate clause must be used with an independent clause for its meaning to be clear.

After the storm stopped, we cleaned up the broken branches.

Independent Clause: We cleaned up the broken branches. [complete thought that can stand alone]

Subordinate Clause: after the storm stopped [incomplete thought that cannot stand alone]

Pedro used the tennis racket that Maria let him borrow.

514

Independent Clause: Pedro used the tennis racket.
[complete thought that can stand alone]

Subordinate Clause: that Maria let him borrow
[incomplete thought that cannot stand alone]

Exercise 2: Identifying Independent and Subordinate Clauses

Write the following sentences, underlining the *italicized* words. In parentheses after each sentence label the *italicized* clause *independent* or *subordinate*.

Examples

a. This is the house *that I bought.*
   This is the house that I bought. (subordinate)

b. When Harold Yee was at Stanford University, *he studied physics.*
   When Harold Yee was at Stanford University, he studied physics. (independent)

1. *Tom always watches the news* while he cooks dinner.

2. Ed and Karen eat chicken *because they are cutting down on cholesterol.*

3. Ms. Herrera always makes us check over our work *before we turn it in for a grade.*

4. *If you save enough money,* you can buy a stereo.

5. *We found the missing bracelet* where the baby had dropped it.

6. Although the dance is still weeks away, *the organizers are already posting signs for it.*

7. *Unless Ellen studies math and science,* she will never be accepted for medical school.

8. *The Arctic explorers survived* until a rescue party located them.

9. *After we have a picnic on the bank of the river,* we will see an old movie at a nearby theater.

10. As Marlow read the Spanish exercise aloud to his class, *his teacher recorded him.*

Subordinate Clauses as Adjectives

Subordinate clauses, sometimes called *dependent clauses*, function as a unit to act as adjectives, adverbs, or nouns in a sentence.

When a subordinate clause modifies a noun or pronoun, it is called an *adjective clause*.

All of the words in an adjective clause work together to modify a noun or pronoun in the independent clause.

The game *that ended the tournament* was very exciting.

We visited the log cabin *in which Abraham Lincoln was born.*

She was the one *whose essay won first prize.*

The game of baseball, *which is considered our national pastime*, was based on the English game of cricket.

The *relative pronouns—who, whom, which, that,* and *whose*—often begin adjective clauses. These pronouns *relate* the adjective clause to the word that the clause modifies.

I was given the one present *that I wanted most of all.*

My project, *which earned an "A,"* took six weeks to complete.

Relative pronouns may be subjects or objects within the adjective clause.

She was one politician *whom we could admire.*
[*Whom* is the direct object in the adjective clause.]

That was a challenge *for which I was totally unprepared.*
[*Which* is the object of the preposition *for.*]

Ann is my neighbor *who makes pottery.*
[*Who* is the subject in the adjective clause.]

Does anyone know *whose ball fell in the water?*
[*Whose* is the direct object in the adjective clause.]

Exercise 3: Identifying Adjective Clauses

Write the following sentences, underlining each adjective clause and circling each relative pronoun. Then draw an arrow from the relative pronoun to the noun or pronoun it modifies. Your teacher may ask you how the relative pronoun is used in the clause.

Examples

a. The scientists who witnessed the explosion of the first nuclear bomb were awed.

The scientists (who) witnessed the explosion of the first nuclear bomb were awed.

b. The children whom Naomi invited to her birthday party were all in her first-grade class.

The children (whom) Naomi invited to her birthday party were all in her first-grade class.

1. Eduardo paid the newspaper carrier who came all the way up to the door every day.

2. We were quite pleased with the politicians whom we elected to public office.

3. Shizue held a thank-you party for the friends who play mahjong with her.

4. The tree that was struck by lightning must be cut down and cleared.

5. The rubble from the earthquake, which has blocked our main street, is now being cleared.

6. The cage in which we keep our sparrows was made in China nearly a century ago.

7. Everyone was admiring the drawing that John did of his old house.

8. Michelle is the woman whom the members elected president of the athletic club.

9. No one who has swum in Lake Michigan in the winter could find it pleasant.

10. I don't think this car, which is almost twenty years old, will last much longer.

When the relative pronoun *whose* acts as an adjective to modify a noun in the adjective clause, it is a *relative adjective*.

That is the man *whose car was stolen.*

This is the coat *whose zipper is broken.*

Adjective clauses can also be introduced by the relative adverbs *where* and *when*. Relative adverbs answer the question *which?* about the noun or pronoun modified.

This is the intersection *where the accident occurred.*
[At *which* intersection did the accident occur?]

I look forward to the time *when I will go to college.*
[*Which* time do I look forward to?]

Exercise 4: *Identifying Types of Adjective Clauses*

Write the following sentences, underlining the adjective clauses and circling the relative pronouns, adjectives, and adverbs. In parentheses after each sentence, identify the circled word as a *relative pronoun*, *relative adjective*, or *relative adverb*.

Examples

a. Our parents will never forget that fabulous evening when they first met.

Our parents will never forget that fabulous evening (when) they first met. (relative adverb)

b. The students helped everyone whose car had become stuck in the snow.

The students helped everyone (whose) car had become stuck in the snow. (relative adjective)

1. I have forgotten the year when Beethoven was born.

2. We looked for the place where Tammy waded in the river.

3. Norine Chiu was the student whose parents organized the after-school club.

4. The people whom we met at the airport were tourists from Egypt.

5. Norma's grandfather still lives in the house where he was born.

6. Becky often visits the park on afternoons when it is hot and humid.

7. The money that the criminals stole has been recovered by the police.

8. The student in our biology class whose project wins first prize in the science fair will receive a trip to Washington, D.C.

9. Sandy rides to work in a car whose heater no longer works.

10. The orchard where we bought the fresh apples and pears is owned by the Mendozas.

Subordinate Clauses as Adverbs

When a subordinate clause acts as a unit to modify a verb, an adjective, or an adverb, it is called an *adverbial clause.*

Adverbial clauses act like one-word adverbs and adverbial phrases to answer the questions *how? when? where? why?* or *under what conditions?* about the word they modify.

The trainer treated the lion cubs *as though they were her children.*
[*How* did she treat the lion cubs?]

Before the sun rose, Rita left for camp.
[*When* did Rita leave for camp?]

Lightning struck *where we camped last night.*
[*Where* did lightning strike?]

Because he was ill, Edward played poorly.
[*Why* did Edward play poorly?]

The bank will cash your check *if you endorse it.*
[*Under what conditions* will the bank cash your check?]

Adverbial clauses can also modify adjectives or adverbs in the independent clause to which they are joined.

Karen is taller *than I am.*

I can sing better *than she can.*

An adverbial clause is joined to an independent clause in a sentence by a *subordinating conjunction,* which begins the adverbial clause.

The words in the following list are commonly used as subordinating conjunctions. Those that include more than one word function as a one-word unit.

after	before	unless
although	if	until
as	in order that	when
as far as	provided that	whenever
as if	since	where
as long as	so that	wherever
as soon as	than	whether
as though	that	while
because	though	

The bandits entered the bank (before) it opened for business.

I asked Merle to help me so (that) I could finish faster.

Exercise 5: *Identifying Adverbial Clauses*

Write the following sentences, underlining each adverbial clause and circling the subordinating conjunction that introduces the clause.

Examples

 a. Charles has faithfully studied photography since he was ten years old.

 Charles has faithfully studied photography (since) he was ten years old.

 b. Lorraine is six inches taller than her brother Jim is.

 Lorraine is six inches taller (than) her brother Jim is.

1. Everyone attended the dance because the refreshments were free.

2. Flora left school before the snow started falling.

3. When his daughter won the race, Mr. Fong was very proud.

4. We can all play in the basketball league provided that we pass the physical exam.

5. Although he works after school, Larry still has time to do all of his homework.

6. The team played every game as if it would be the last one.

7. Frank plays backgammon every afternoon before work.

8. Diana becomes rather nervous whenever the teacher reads over her shoulder.

9. Students may use the halls between class periods as long as they carry their hall passes at all times.

10. Never again will our scout troop camp where it did last winter.

Subordinate Clauses as Nouns

A subordinate clause that acts as a noun is called a *noun clause*.

A noun clause can serve as the subject, direct object, indirect object, object of the preposition, predicate noun, or appositive in a sentence.

Whoever is best qualified should be our representative.	[subject]
I realized *that I was wrong*.	[direct object]
We will give *whoever wins* a prize.	[indirect object]
They could not see from *where they were sitting*.	[object of the preposition *from*]
My favorite saying is *that goodness always conquers evil*.	[predicate noun]
General Billy Mitchell had one thought, *that airplanes would one day rule the sky*.	[appositive]

Exercise 6: Identifying the Function of Noun Clauses

Copy the sentences on the following page, underlining each *italicized* noun clause. In parentheses next to each sentence, identify the function of the noun clause.

Examples

a. Marlene will eat *whatever you cook*.
   Marlene will eat <u>whatever you cook</u>. (direct object)

b. *Whether you get good grades* can be important.
   <u>Whether you get good grades</u> can be important. (subject)

1. Claudia can't decide *whom she should invite to her party*.

2. *Whoever ate all of the sunflower seeds* is really inconsiderate.

3. Harold knows *when the sale of shoes and clothing will start at the department store*.

4. Carmen will lend *whoever needs it* enough money for lunch.

5. The Silvas told their son he was responsible for *whatever happened in their absence*.

6. My fondest wish is *that people should be more considerate of each other*.

7. We found the sack full of money near *where the robbery had taken place*.

8. Nobody knows *whether Jane will run for class president this year or next year*.

9. Shaun may invite *whomever he wishes* to the restaurant for his birthday party.

10. Lorraine and Sheila are prepared for *whatever may happen on their winter camping trip*.

Noun clauses sometimes begin with the words *who, whom, whoever, whomever, what, whatever, that, which, when, how, where*, or *whether*. Since many of these words are also used to introduce adverb and adjective clauses, you must determine the function of the clause before deciding if it is a noun clause.

This is the doctor *that my father knows*.	[adjective clause]
My mother said *that we are moving*.	[noun clause used as a direct object]

Exercise 7: *Identifying Noun Clauses*

Write the following sentences, underlining the noun clauses and circling the word that introduces each one.

Examples

a. Whatever the coach decides is final on our football team.

(Whatever) the coach decides is final on our football team.

b. The teachers know that the students aren't really lazy.

The teachers know (that) the students aren't really lazy.

1. How we had won the basketball championship was a mystery to us all.

2. No one could believe that Mary went ice-skating on the coldest day of the year.

3. The truth of the matter is that her brother has never really been a spy.

4. A good dinner guest will eat whatever is served.

5. We won't know whom the students have elected to the student council until next Monday.

6. Television networks are often wrong about what the American people will watch.

7. The sportswriters give the award to whoever has the highest batting average in the league.

8. Whether we go to the beach or the show will depend upon the weather.

9. Jim knows who finished all of the bananas, but he won't tell anyone.

10. The company will give whoever asks an autographed picture of their mascot.

Review: Understanding Clauses

Write the sentences on the following page, underlining the subordinate clauses. In parentheses after each sentence, identify the clause as *adjective, adverb,* or *noun.*

Examples

a. The truck that is parked on the corner belongs to your uncle.
   The truck that is parked on the corner belongs to your uncle.
   (adjective)

    b. We all wondered how Tom prepared such delicious stews.
       We all wondered <u>how Tom prepared such delicious stews.</u>
       (noun)

1. You can set up this shelf wherever you think it should be placed.

2. Sarah's best friend is the student whose brother was elected to the state assembly.

3. Since it has been snowing so much, the sidewalks need shoveling now.

4. The committee planning the fall dance can't decide where it should be held.

5. Nicole paints more beautifully than any other student in the class does.

6. *Billy Budd*, which we read in English class, is an exciting novel.

7. Shizue Tanaka is visiting her aunt, who lives in Cleveland.

8. Because this package has no return address, we cannot return it.

9. Nancy could not speak with her uncle Pierre, as she had not studied French.

10. People camping in the Rocky Mountains can be surprised by blizzards that occur suddenly.

11. Tina, whom you met at the French Club dinner, is Mrs. Aguilar's daughter.

12. Nobody knows whom the students will elect president of the student council.

13. Ms. Carmichael will hire whomever the school counselor recommends to fill the position.

14. When her watch made squeaking noises, Jennifer took it apart to find out the problem.

15. If you park on a hill, you should always use the emergency brake.

16. The place where the car always stalls is near the corner of Jackson Boulevard and Michigan Avenue.

17. Corporal Jim Burns has visited many places that he would never have seen as a civilian.

18. We will help you with your chores so that you can attend the school play with us.

19. Whoever writes the best short story will have it published in the student literary magazine.

20. Upon reaching the top of Mount Everest, the famous climber skied down to the base camp, which was many miles below.

Applying What You Know

In the following excerpt from her essay "Of Man and Islands," Caskie Stinnett describes the powerful appeal of living on an island and relates her own experiences of island life. She emphasizes the positive sense of isolation and the dream of self-sufficiency that islands endorse. Many adjective, adverbial, and noun clauses are used in this selection, and the first two are underlined for you. Identify ten other dependent clauses. List them on a sheet of paper and beside each one identify it as an *adjective clause,* an *adverbial clause,* or a *noun clause.*

> For reasons that strike me as odd, I am constantly asked if I am not uneasy about living on an island alone and if I am not bored. I feel more protected by the water than I do by the doorman of the apartment house where I live during the winter months, and while I must confess to occasional boredom, I am less frequently bored on the island than in the city. There is always a changing tide to divert me, a fog-bank lifting to reveal a lobster boat cautiously working its way through the rock ledges, a totally unbelievable moon lighting up the cove, or a summer thunderstorm that rages with terrifying violence for a few minutes and then subsides apologetically into a rainbow. The man who lives on an island builds his isolation without meaning to, and sooner or later it begins to take possession of his soul; but it brings him a serenity and a sureness, a trust in himself that he may never have known before. Whether he desires it or not, he becomes the monarch of a miniature kingdom, the keeper of peace and the protector of lives, and he soon learns that he must deal with fretful winds and fickle seas and lightning and drought. This, I think, is why most island dwellers are innately humble people: They quickly learn their dependence upon nature, a lesson that is the beginning of wisdom for us all.

Using Clauses

The problem encountered most often in using clauses is punctuating them. In the sections on the following pages you will learn how to punctuate clauses.

Punctuating Independent Clauses

T wo independent clauses can be joined with a coordinating conjunction—*and, or, nor, but, for,* or *yet.* The coordinating conjunction is not considered part of either clause. A comma usually follows the first independent clause.

The death of Queen Victoria in 1901 was important, *for* it signaled the end of an era.

The evidence seemed conclusive, *yet* I was still not convinced.

Although it is never *incorrect* to place a comma after the first independent clause, writers sometimes omit this comma if the two independent clauses are short and closely related in thought.

It's 8 o'clock and I'm already up.

Another method of joining two independent clauses is to replace both the comma and the conjunction with a semicolon (;). Semicolons should be used only when the two clauses are closely related in thought.

Clara Barton was born in 1821; she died in 1912.

I called for reservations; Marion packed the suitcases.

Exercise 8: *Punctuating Independent Clauses*

Rewrite the pairs of sentences on the next page, joining them with a comma and a coordinating conjunction. If the sentences are closely related in thought, connect them with a semicolon. Underline commas and conjunctions used together and circle semicolons.

Examples

a. Paul wrote a good story about Cleveland. It won first prize in the literary contest.

   Paul wrote a good story about Cleveland ⊙ it won first prize in the literary contest.

b. Loretta has always liked to swim. Her brother Henry prefers to run.

   Loretta has always liked to swim, but her brother Henry prefers to run.

1. Francine works in New York City. She lives in Newark, New Jersey.

2. Eve will visit us on the Labor Day weekend. She may visit at Thanksgiving instead.

3. John studies English literature at Howard University. His sister Anna will join him there in the fall.

4. We all thought Reynaldo would do well in biology this semester. He failed the final exam.

5. Dale has always wanted to sing a solo. He hasn't had the chance to do it.

6. Michael must receive a high score on the test. He will become ineligible for basketball.

7. Eduardo speaks Spanish at home. He speaks English at work and at school.

8. Sandy will probably become a house painter. Most of her brothers have done so.

9. Eric intends to be a great artist. He works week after week to perfect his painting technique.

10. Keith works long hours. This hard work has led to several promotions.

Exercise 9: Using Commas and Semicolons

Rewrite the following sentences, adding commas and semicolons wherever necessary to separate independent clauses. Circle the punctuation you insert.

Example

a. Karl has bowled for ten years but he has never bowled a perfect game.

Karl has bowled for ten years‚ but he has never bowled a perfect game.

1. Noburu was terrified of the water but he applied for the job of lifeguard.

2. Martha has been studying architecture for four years she will finish her degree next spring.

3. Jennifer should study hard for the algebra test or she may receive an unpleasant surprise.

4. We arrived at the parking lot several minutes before it closed yet the parking attendants had all gone home.

5. Stephanie has never worked outdoors nor does she intend to start now.

6. Mr. Suarez has finished taking courses in business school now he intends to open his own store.

7. We asked you to bring us a pepperoni pizza but you brought something much different.

8. Mr. Friedman draws well for he just seems to have a natural talent.

9. The senior dance committee expected a huge crowd at the Halloween Hop yet no one showed up but the band and some chaperones.

10. The landlords have promised to repair the leaking faucets and they will install new screens on all of the windows.

Punctuating Adjective Clauses

An adjective clause that does *not* add information that is important to the meaning of the independent clause is called a *nonessential clause*.

Commas are used to separate a nonessential adjective clause from an independent clause.

The first American spacecraft, *which was flown by Alan B. Shepard*, was named *Mercury I.*

Alfred Nobel, *who established the Nobel Prizes,* was the inventor of dynamite.

Adjective clauses that give information essential to the meaning of the independent clause are called *essential clauses.*
Essential adjective clauses are *not* set off by commas.

The man *who invented dynamite* also established the Nobel Prizes.
[*Who invented dynamite* identifies the man and is essential.]

He made the dessert *that is my favorite.*
[*That is my favorite* identifies the dessert.]

Exercise 10: Punctuating Adjective Clauses

Write the following sentences, inserting commas to set off any nonessential clause from the rest of its sentence. Circle the commas you insert. (Some sentences may not need commas.)

Examples

a. Ms. Phillips who lives next door works for the post office.

Ms. Phillips⊙ who lives next door⊙ works for the post office.

b. The teacher whom we met at the rally was very friendly.

The teacher whom we met at the rally was very friendly.

1. The Lairds whom we invited to the party are our friends from Anchorage.

2. The runner who crosses the finish line first will be the winner.

3. Mount Baker which we climbed last summer is located in Oregon.

4. Anyone who likes jackknife clams should try eating mussels and oysters.

5. Nancy whom John met at the party for varsity athletes is a talented runner.

6. Patricia Harris who was the president of Howard University was also the head of the Department of Housing and Urban Development.

7. Everyone whom we invited to the party arrived on time.

8. A student whose grades are slipping should seek the advice of the teacher.

9. People who are kind make the world much more pleasant.

10. Marian Anderson whose singing gave pleasure to millions was the first black woman to join the Metropolitan Opera Company.

Punctuating Adverbial Clauses

When an adverbial clause appears at the beginning of a sentence, it is followed by a comma.

While the team was showering, the coach turned off the hot water.

Since we seldom see Aunt Mabel, we forgot her birthday.

When an adverbial clause appears in a position other than at the beginning of the sentence, do not use a comma in front of it.

We knew the outcome *before the ballots were counted.*
[no comma]

A comma *is* used before adverbial clauses beginning with *for, though,* and *although* when they end a sentence. A comma also precedes *as* and *since* when they mean "because."

The squirrels ate popcorn from our hands, *for* they had grown accustomed to our presence.

She seemed trustworthy, *though* I had my doubts.

We decided to make our final attempt, *as* it would be dark soon. [*As* means "because."]

Exercise 11: *Punctuating Adverbial Clauses*

Write the following sentences, adding commas wherever necessary to punctuate adverbial clauses. Circle the commas you insert. (Not all sentences need new commas.)

Example

---

a. When she finally gets into the game Clara usually plays well.

   When she finally gets into the game⊙Clara usually plays well.

1. While we were waiting for the bus we discussed our plans for the day.

2. John was not surprised by his test grades since he had not studied.

3. John will move wherever Sally wants to live.

4. Harry won the election easily although the results looked close at first.

5. Esperanza will move to Philadelphia as she has won a scholarship to the University of Pennsylvania.

6. Because he found grammar easy to learn Joe helped Tim and Sarah with their homework.

7. Wilma put a lock on the bathroom cabinet so that her baby brother couldn't play with the medicine.

8. Everyone expected Phyllis to get the job for she was the candidate with the most experience.

9. If Mary becomes a minister she will probably work somewhere in the Midwest.

10. *Moby Dick* is a fascinating novel though many people disagree about its interpretation.

Review: *Using Clauses*

Write the following sentences, adding whatever semicolons and commas are necessary to punctuate clauses. Circle the punctuation marks you insert.

Example

a. Mary likes biology her brother prefers English.

Mary likes biology⊙ her brother prefers English.

1. We must conserve energy or we may one day be out in the cold.

2. The airplane fare is one hundred dollars the train fare is only sixty.

3. When Roger was in the Navy he visited Asia, Africa, and most of Europe.

4. Groucho Marx whose real name was Julius Marx was part of a family of comedians.

5. We intend to buy new band uniforms as we have finally collected enough money from our bake sales and carwashes.

6. As soon as spring rolls around Harry will prepare the soil for the garden.

7. Because the gymnasium roof leaks basketball practice is temporarily suspended.

8. The orangutan which is found only in Indonesia is an extremely solitary animal.

9. Ruth does volunteer work in a hospital during the week her brother helps on Saturdays.

10. Though we had planned to spend the holidays with our relatives the weather kept us in Waco, Texas.

11. Bessie Smith who was one of the first American jazz singers was born in 1898 she died in 1937.

12. Our basketball team will have a difficult game with Central High's team since the visitors have the best forwards in the city.

13. So that he can save money for school Julio works at a service station.

14. Ralph's family wanted him to become a stonecutter for all of his relatives were already in the business.

15. Ralph Metcalfe who won an Olympic silver medal in 1936 was later elected to the Congress where he served until 1978.

Writing Focus: *Clauses in Writing*

You can improve your writing by using clauses to add details, to combine sentences, to show relationships, and to vary sentence structure. To decide whether a clause should be set off by punctuation, determine its position and function in the sentence.

Assignment: *What's Popular These Days?*

Within the last seven or eight years, the most popular movies in the United States seem to have been space adventures and "old time" adventures. The *Star Wars* and *Star Trek* trilogies gross millions of dollars as viewers cheer loudly at Luke Skywalker or Captain Kirk, escaping from dangerous situations. What accounts for the popularity of these films?

Write one or more well-developed paragraphs accounting for the popularity of adventure films. Center your explanation on the causes of the popularity. Write for your classmates. Your paragraphs will be evaluated for correct and effective use of clauses.

Use the following steps to complete this assignment.

A. Prewriting

Use the six basic questions technique, described in Chapter 1, to help you generate ideas. Use the questions *who? what? where? when? why?*

and *how?* to explore the adventure films from various angles. For example, questions beginning with *who?* can start you thinking about the "people" factor that may account for the popularity of the films: *Who* stars in the films? *Who* goes to the films? *Who* are the heroes and heroines in the films? *Who* are the villains? List and answer as many questions as you can for each of the six words. When you have finished, go back over your list. Notice the many different "ingredients" that might account for the popularity of the films. Choose what appear to be the major causes that explain it. Number them from the least to most important causes.

B. Writing

Using your questions and answers, write one or more paragraphs explaining why adventure films are so popular. Include the major causes that account for the popularity. Provide details about the films that support your points. As you write, vary your sentences by using clauses in different ways.

C. Postwriting

Using the following checklist, revise your first draft.

1. Have I actually accounted for the popularity of adventure films?

2. Do the paragraphs include enough specific details?

3. Are clauses used effectively to vary sentence structure?

4. Are there any sentence fragments or short sentences that can be combined by using clauses?

5. Have I punctuated each clause correctly?

Edit your revision, using the Proofreader's Checklist at the back of the book. If appropriate, share your writing with the members of your class and discuss your findings.

533

23 Complete and Incomplete Sentences
Understanding Sentences

Every sentence can be classified in one of four ways, according to the number of independent and subordinate clauses it contains: *simple, compound, complex,* or *compound-complex.*

Simple Sentences

If a sentence contains only one independent clause and no subordinate clauses, it is called a *simple sentence.*

         S   V

Everyone helped with the chores.

The subject and the verb in a simple sentence may be modified and may have complements.

              S   V

Almost *everyone helped* Floyd with the chores.

A simple sentence may have compound subjects or verbs, since a compound subject is considered one subject and a compound verb is considered one verb.

    S   S   S   V   V

Jane, Julio, and *everyone* in the area *worked* together and *helped* Floyd with the chores.

Compound Sentences

If a sentence contains more than one independent clause but no subordinate clauses, it is called a *compound sentence.*

The cars couldn't climb the hill, but *the trucks made it easily.*

The independent clauses may have compound subjects or verbs, but there must be at least two separate independent clauses and no subordinate clauses.

        S   S   V   S

The cars and *the vans could*n't *climb* the hill; the *trucks,* however,

   V   V

could and *did.*

Complex Sentences

A sentence with only one independent clause and at least one subordinate clause is called a *complex sentence*.

The subordinate clause in the following sentence is *italicized*.

As soon as I finished my homework, I fell sound asleep.

While there can be several subordinate clauses in a complex sentence, there can be only one independent clause.

After I finish my homework, I can do *whatever I want!*
[The independent clause is *I can do*.]

Compound-Complex Sentences

If a sentence contains more than one independent clause and at least one subordinate clause, it is called a *compound-complex sentence*.

     subordinate   independent
When I finally returned to school, I studied very hard,

  independent
for I had missed many classes.

Exercise 1: Classifying Sentences

Write the following sentences, underlining the independent clauses once and the subordinate clauses twice. In parentheses next to each sentence, identify its structure.

Examples

a. Jim and Bill both enjoy tennis and play to win.
Jim and Bill both enjoy tennis and play to win. (simple)

b. After we attended the banquet, Francine went home, but I did not.
After we attended the banquet, Francine went home, but I did not. (compound-complex)

1. The snow covered the sidewalks, and icicles hung from the trees.

2. We all gave Mary Ann a going-away party.

3. Our school, which was built last year, is showing some signs of wear.

4. Three of our best players suffered injuries, but they remained in the game.

5. The fact that I am only fifteen doesn't matter, and it shouldn't affect my chances of winning.

6. Whoever it was who spilled that water on the court should be responsible for cleaning it up.

7. Most of the books were old, but they were still in good shape.

8. As soon as I saw the package, I knew what it contained.

9. Whenever we travel, I take a radio with me, but I play it softly.

10. On the last leg of our trek up the steep mountainside, everyone except Terry gasped for breath and nursed each aching muscle.

Review: *Understanding Sentences*

Write the following sentences, underlining each independent clause once and each subordinate clause twice. In parentheses after each sentence, identify its structure as *simple, compound, complex,* or *compound-complex*.

Examples

a. On the table in the dining room stood a four-foot tower of presents for Brenda's birthday.
On the table in the dining room stood a four-foot tower of presents for Brenda's birthday. (simple)

b. Myron looked at me as if I knew the answer.

Myron looked at me as if I knew the answer. (complex)

1. The patterns in the water created shadows on the bottom of the pool.

2. Cortina asked her father for a map of Austria because she wanted to study its rivers.

3. The mayor listened to the panel of citizens and decided to take their advice.

4. The Sunshine Skyway, a bridge connecting Tampa and St. Petersburg, collapsed when a freighter crashed into it.

5. The new modular city will be solar powered after it is completed.

6. Felipe lives in Boston, and his cousin Juliana will visit him there at Christmas.

7. It was hot, and it stayed hot even after the thunderstorm hammered the city.

8. Ramul sent all of the invitations, but he didn't expect many people.

9. We heard whoever screamed last night three houses away.

10. If you take the subway to Fourth Street and walk one block north, you'll see the civic center on the left.

11. I wish that I could paint that landscape.

12. Consuela thought about learning to ski last winter.

13. The answer that I gave was incorrect, but the teacher gave me another chance.

14. Raoul always wanted to know more about oceanography.

15. Leroy visited the art museum where he wrote a report on the Vincent van Gogh exhibit while he sat in the lounge.

16. He had more dreams than he could ever realize.

17. You never get up in time for breakfast, but you always wish that you had.

18. How many more times will you have to write that paper?

19. Maxine has been trying to learn more about high-salaried occupations.

20. Long before daylight began to break, we were ready for the long day's hike.

Using Sentences

In the following sections you will learn to avoid two common errors in using sentences: sentence fragments and run-on sentences.

Avoiding Sentence Fragments

A *sentence fragment* is a separated part of a sentence that does not express a complete thought.

A sentence fragment results from placing a period, a question mark, or an exclamation point before a thought is completed.

Applauded the performer. [Who or what applauded?]	[fragment]
The audience applauded the performer.	[sentence]
When the truck jackknifed on the expressway. [What happened?]	[fragment]
Traffic came to a standstill when the truck jackknifed on the expressway.	[sentence]
Finishing the project. [Who is finishing the project?]	[fragment]
Alonzo had trouble finishing the project.	[sentence]

Sometimes, a fragment has a subject and a verb but still does not express a complete thought.

S V The back seat of your car is. [what?]	[fragment]
The back seat of your car is uncomfortable.	[sentence]
S V When Carl returned from college. [what?]	[fragment]
When Carl returned from college, we both found jobs.	[sentence]

Exercise 2: Making Fragments into Sentences

Rewrite each of the fragments on the next page, making it into a sentence by supplying the necessary subject, verb, or complement. (There may be many ways to make each fragment a sentence.) Place the appropriate end punctuation after your new sentence.

Examples

a. Norman always reading magazines during class

Norman is always reading magazines during class.
or
Norman always reads magazines during class.

b. While waiting for the bus

While waiting for the bus, the passengers almost froze.
or
The passengers almost froze while waiting for the bus.

1. Scrubbing the kitchen floor with steel wool

2. They're reading the comic sections

3. To run for president of the student council last year

4. Wearing white socks

5. The cat sneezing all day long

6. To eat egg rolls with their fingers

7. Sam boiling eggs for breakfast

8. Melissa driving to Miami rather frequently

9. Walking from home to school

10. Painting murals on the blank walls

Avoiding Run-On Sentences

A *run-on sentence* consists of two or more sentences separated by a comma or by no mark of punctuation.

Cheryl made a fern-stand in woodshop for her mother's birthday, then she made a bookshelf for her father.	[run-on]
Cheryl made a fern-stand in woodshop for her mother's birthday. Then she made a bookshelf for her father.	[correction]

Jim and I started a bicycle repair shop in his garage it lasted only two weeks.	[run-on]
Jim and I started a bicycle repair shop in his garage; it lasted only two weeks.	[correction]
The zoo keeper fed the hungry lions, there were ten of them.	[run-on]
When the zoo keeper fed the hungry lions, there were ten of them.	[correction]

There are four common ways to correct a run-on sentence.

1. Add punctuation at the end of each complete thought or replace commas with end punctuation.

2. Add a comma and a conjunction to join related sentences.

3. Separate the sentences with a semicolon.

4. Make one sentence into a phrase or clause.

Adding End Punctuation

My friends and I found a wallet on the street we looked inside for identification and took it to the police station, there was a reward for its return.	[run-on]
My friends and I found a wallet on the street. We looked inside for identification and took it to the police station. There was a reward for its return.	[correction]

Using Conjunctions

My sister and I wanted to find a summer job, we knew we weren't old enough to get a regular job at a store, we put an ad in the paper for odd jobs.	[run-on]
My sister and I wanted to find a summer job, but we knew we weren't old enough to get a regular job at a store, so we put an ad in the paper for odd jobs.	[correction]

Using Semicolons

Paula went to the library to research her science topic and write the report, then she typed the report and drew some illustrations.	[run-on]
Paula went to the library to research her science topic and write the report; then she typed the report and drew some illustrations.	[correction]

Using Phrases and Clauses

Many undeveloped countries have not used much of the earth's resources in the past, now they are demanding their fair share.	[run-on]
Many undeveloped countries that have not used much of the earth's resources in the past are now demanding their fair share.	[correction]

Exercise 3: Correcting Run-On Sentences

Using one of the methods discussed in this section, correct the following run-on sentences. Write the corrected sentences on a sheet of paper.

Examples

    a. After school I work at the florist shop for two hours then I go home.
      After school I work at the florist shop for two hours; then I go home.

    b. We wanted to go riding, we needed the exercise.
      We wanted to go riding because we needed the exercise.

1. From the top of the stadium, we watched the skydivers, they landed in the center of the target on the field, they were really professionals.

2. Rick and Ann visited their grandmother in the hospital, they took her some flowers, they took her some books to read.

3. The orchestra conductor bowed to the audience, then she faced the orchestra.

4. My sister is going away to college this fall, I'm helping her get ready, I'll have the bedroom to myself.

5. We took slides when we visited the Grand Canyon, I used them for my geography report.

6. I'm learning how to sew, it will save me money, I'll have more clothes.

7. I use my father's electric typewriter to prepare my school reports, my teachers say my handwriting is illegible most of the time.

8. The raging lightning storm damaged all the power lines, we were without electricity most of Sunday night, I was late for school.

9. Our dog has finally learned some tricks, it dances in a circle and rolls over then we give it a treat.

10. Carlos is a very superstitious person, he never steps on a crack, he always carries a rabbit's foot.

Review: *Using Sentences*

Some of the groups of words on the next page are sentences, some are fragments, and some are run-ons. Number a sheet of paper 1–20. If a sentence does not need changes, write *correct* next to its number. If the group of words is a fragment or a run-on, rewrite the words as a correct sentence or as separate sentences.

Examples

a. Since graduation from high school.

Charles has been a carpenter since graduation from high school.

b. Mr. Hermosa remained the principal for several years.

correct

c. The vegetable soup smelled delicious, I poured myself a bowl, I enjoyed it.

I poured myself a bowl of the vegetable soup, which smelled delicious, and then enjoyed it.

1. Hiroaki and Shizue are dancers and singers, they are the most talented students in the school.

2. On the cold winter evening even the bus terminal.

3. When the new Supreme Court judge was appointed.

4. The hardest-working students in our biology class have been Flora and I.

5. We waited in line for three hours to see the movie, we should have waited a few days, *when* the movie will be there for at least two weeks.

6. The jury found the prisoners innocent, they dropped to their knees in gratitude.

7. The principal declared Thomas Aherns the winner of the Ivy League scholarship.

8. The rabbi pronounced the couple.

9. The umpire called the runner out, the fans all booed, the coach ran out on the field.

10. Woody always finds himself hungry by 3 o'clock and stuffed by 3:15.

11. Nominated Roberto Sanchez and Bob Roy as members of the ad hoc committee.

12. Tom lent Carol money for lunch, she paid him back the next day, she bought him lunch.

13. Mike looks very nervous before every test in geometry, but he usually makes a good grade.

14. Before she reported her car stolen.

15. Ms. Fong, who sang the national anthem at the football game.

16. We were introduced to the senator by Mr. Evans, he and the senator went to college together.

17. Reynaldo met me at the bus station and helped me find my luggage at the crowded baggage claim area.

18. Notified about the tragic automobile accident at Tenth Street and Maple.

19. The cats completely unrolled the ball of yarn, and then they pulled it around the house.

20. After consulting with several doctors about his illness, John remained.

Writing Focus: *Improving*
Sentence Structure in Writing

You can strengthen your writing style by using a variety of sentence structures including simple, compound, complex, and compound-complex sentences. Make sure your sentences are, in fact, complete sentences and not fragments or run-on sentences.

Assignment: *The New Planet*

The photograph on the next page shows a strange, deserted landscape. Imagine that you are a member of a space exploration team whose spacecraft has just landed on another planet having this landscape. As the commander of the expedition, you must log your observations and feelings as you survey this new planet. How would you describe the landscape? How do you feel about this new planet?

Write one or more well-developed paragraphs describing what you see and how you feel as you observe the landscape. Write for the people back on earth who cannot see the planet's surface. You will, therefore, not only need to be vivid and specific in your description, but also relate what you see and feel to people on earth. Your paragraphs will be evaluated for correct and varied sentences.

Use the following steps to complete this assignment.

A. Prewriting

Look at the photograph carefully. Use the brainstorming technique, described in Chapter 1, to generate details about your observations and feelings. Jot down words, phrases, and sentences that occur to you as you study the photograph. Let your thoughts flow freely, without any particular order. As you brainstorm, begin to make word associations by allowing one idea to lead to another. For example, you might have listed "ribbed hills" as one detail you observed. The hills might make you think of the ribs of a prehistoric dinosaur. You may want to use this association in your paragraph by writing the following simile: "The ribbed hills surrounding us looked like the back of a prehistoric dinosaur." By associating items in your list with other ideas, you can make your description more vivid. Go over your details and associations and mark those that you think capture your observations and feelings the best.

B. Writing

Using your brainstorming notes, write one or more paragraphs describing the new planet. Include enough specific details so that your audience will be able to visualize the planet's landscape. Describe what you see and how you feel as the spacecraft lands. Then, provide a detailed description of the landscape as you explore the planet. Strive to include a variety of sentence structures in your description. When you have completed your first draft, use the checklist on the next page to revise your writing.

C. Postwriting

Revise your first draft, using the following checklist.

1. Does my description include enough specific details so that my readers can actually "see" and "feel" the planet's landscape?

2. Have I varied the structure of my sentences?

3. Are there sentence fragments that can be rewritten to form complete sentences?

4. Are there run-on sentences that should be divided into two or more sentences?

Make final corrections using the Proofreader's Checklist at the back of the book. If appropriate, share your writing with your classmates to compare descriptions.

3
Mechanics

24 Punctuation

Using Punctuation

Punctuation marks have four main uses: *to separate, to link, to enclose,* **and** *to show omission.*

1. *To separate.* A separating mark of punctuation helps readers understand that certain ideas are not run together. For example, a period (.) separates one sentence from another.

   The snow fell all night long. It glistened in the moonlight.

   By that afternoon we were home. Our vacation was over.

2. *To link.* Linking marks, such as the hyphen (-), show that words or ideas should be read as a unit.

   My brother-in-law is an airline pilot.

   This jack-o'-lantern will never last until Halloween.

3. *To enclose.* Some marks of punctuation occur in pairs and enclose what is contained within.

   "Will you help me start my car?" he pleaded.

   One of the Beatles' most famous songs is "Eleanor Rigby."

4. *To show omission.* When you use a contraction or an abbreviation in your writing, the apostrophe tells your readers that a certain letter or letters have been omitted. The apostrophe (') in the following sentence shows that the letter *o* has been omitted from the word *not.*

   Don't you know how to type?

End Marks

Three punctuation marks, the *period, question mark,* and *exclamation point,* can come at the end of a sentence.

Use a period after a sentence that makes a simple statement or a mild command.

Ellen wondered what was wrong.

Pass your papers to the front of the row.

Use a question mark after a sentence that asks a question.

Could you see him clearly?

Will it make any difference? I wondered.

Use an exclamation point after a sentence that shows excitement or that is a strong command.

How we had waited for this moment!

Stop that racket immediately!

Exercise 1: Using End Punctuation

Write the following sentences, adding the appropriate end punctuation to separate sentences and at the end of sentences. Circle the marks you insert.

Example

a. Now we're in trouble for sure

Now we're in trouble for sure(!)

1. Who ate the last banana I wanted to put it in my lunch
2. Pull over There's an ambulance behind us
3. Ian's father lives in Detroit His mother lives in Biloxi
4. Are you going to the dance Saturday There will be a live band
5. Would you like to go out to dinner, a movie, or a discotheque
6. I've caught my fingers in the window
7. Please turn the page Then do the first exercise
8. Do I really want to be class president I mused
9. What a good sport you are
10. Don't worry about it I'm really not that thirsty

The Period

Use a period after an abbreviation.

An important use of the *period* is to indicate an abbreviation.

An *abbreviation* is a word or group of words that has been shortened by omitting letters.

Abbreviation	Meaning
Mrs.	a title before a married woman's name
Ms.	a title before a woman's name
Mr.	Mister
Dr.	Doctor
A.M.	*ante meridiem* (before noon)
P.M.	*post meridiem* (after noon)
A.D.	in a specified year of the Christian era
B.C.	before Christ
etc.	*et cetera* (and so forth)
Chas.	Charles
Thos.	Thomas
Ave., St., Blvd.	Avenue, Street, Boulevard
Sgt., Supt., Gov.	Sergeant, Superintendent, Governor
Inc., Corp.	Incorporated, Corporation

Periods are not used following the abbreviations for metric units, two-letter designations for states in an address, and most government agencies.

10 kg	IL (Illinois)	NATO
153 ml	MO (Missouri)	HEW
250 cc	CA (California)	USAF

Many frequently used abbreviations, such as those for large corporations, are now written without periods. All of the following abbreviations are correctly written without periods.

CBS   TWA   am   fm   TV   YWCA   mph   rpm

Note: When an abbreviation appears at the end of a sentence, one period marks both the end of the abbreviation and the end of the sentence.

The new editor at the newspaper is Gerald Miller, Sr.

The next bus to Decatur leaves at 1:10 P.M.

Exercise 2: Using Periods

Write the following sentences, placing periods wherever they are needed to separate or end sentences or to show omission in abbreviations. Circle the marks you insert.

Examples

a. My doctor has an office in the Adler Bldg on River Road His name is Dr O'Malley

My doctor has an office in the Adler Bldg ⊙ on River Road ⊙

His name is Dr ⊙ O'Malley ⊙

b. Erin is learning to dance at Ms O'Hennessy's dancing school on Fifth St and Main

Erin is learning to dance at Ms⊙ O'Hennessy's dancing school on Fifth St⊙ and Main⊙

1. Our car became stuck in 30 cm of snow A truck driver helped us push the car back onto the highway

2. Ms Carmichael will visit China this summer

3. Henry Kissinger was born in Germany He was Secretary of State from 1973 until 1977

4. Supt Joseph Li of our school system believes that every student should receive a good education

5. Dr Death almost defeated Capt Courageous on the NBC science fiction show

6. Georgina studies classical Chinese She is translating poems that were written about AD 400

7. Mr Sammy Davis, Jr, is one of the most popular entertainers in the United States today

8. In the spring Joy's family gets up at 6 AM and goes to bed at 10 PM

9. These are the places where the job interviews will be held:

International Plastics, Inc   Polystyrene, Ltd
5800 Lake Park Blvd   3000 Madison Park Ave
Chicago, IL 60637   Seattle, WA 98168

10. You may write to Larry's father at the following address:
Mr. Larry Urago, Sr
5721 East End Pl
Tallahassee, FL 32304

The Comma

Use a comma to separate words or word groups in a series.

She wrote novels, short stories, plays, and poems about rural life.

Grant believes in telling the truth, working hard, and saving his money.

Use a comma to separate two or more adjectives when the conjunction *and* makes sense in its place.

We were being followed by a tall, dark stranger.
[We were being followed by a tall (and) dark stranger.]

A long, narrow, winding road led to the fortress.
[A long (and) narrow (and) winding road led to the fortress.]

Use a comma to separate independent clauses that are joined by the coordinating conjunctions *and, but, or, nor, for,* or *yet.*

The chicken is in the pot, and the noodles are ready to cook.

We enjoy eating fish, for it is high in protein.

Exercise 3: Using Commas

Write each of the following sentences, placing commas wherever necessary. Circle the commas you insert. Be prepared to tell why you placed commas where you did.

Examples

   a. We own a radio a television set and a tape recorder.

     We own a radio, a television set, and a tape recorder.

   b. We are having chicken for dinner but we prefer spareribs.

     We are having chicken for dinner, but we prefer spareribs.

1. Joan Grace John and Carmen are very close friends.
2. The old feeble cat barely made it to the sofa.
3. Tomorrow we can go for the meetings will have ended.
4. The President of the United States the Chancellor of West Germany and the Prime Minister of Great Britain met to discuss world trade.
5. Most of my money is spent on clothes gasoline and records.
6. The worn tattered shirts still held their color.
7. We could see a brown furry mouse in the corner of the barn.
8. We must come to an agreement or our project will never be finished on time.
9. Jamie doesn't like cold weather nor is he fond of snow.
10. The problem is that Edwina wants to study medicine practice law and become a newspaper reporter.

Use a comma to separate introductory adverb clauses, introductory participial phrases, and long introductory prepositional phrases from the rest of the sentence.

Introductory adverb clauses are followed by a comma.

     After the trial had ended, some new evidence was discovered.

     When the question was finally put to a vote, it passed easily.

Introductory participial phrases are followed by a comma.

Working as rapidly as possible, Kirsten still couldn't finish the test on time.

Covered by a thick coat of coral, the treasure did not appear to be valuable.

Long or successive introductory prepositional phrases are followed by a comma.

During the very few days of my visit, the weather has been excellent.

With five books from the library under my arm, I made my way to the bus.

Use a comma after a short introductory phrase if the sentence might be misread without it.

On the floor below, the store sold sporting goods.

Use a comma to separate some short introductory elements from the rest of the sentence.

Mild interjections and the words *yes, no, well, why, still,* and *now*—when they are used to introduce a sentence—are followed by a comma.

Oh, it wasn't that important to me.

Now, I am not saying that you definitely have the job.

Note: When these words are used as adverbs, they should not be followed by a comma.

Now we will see who has the better team. [no comma]

When a noun that is used to address someone begins a sentence, use a comma after it.

Norma, please take this check to the bank as soon as possible.

Ladies and gentlemen, let me make one thing perfectly clear.

Introductory transitional expressions, such as *however, accordingly, consequently, thus, yet, hence, therefore,* and *besides,* are followed by a comma.

However, many people still believe that the legend is true.

Thus, I can now say that my policies have been proved to be correct.

Exercise 4: Using Commas

Write the following sentences, placing commas wherever necessary. Circle the commas you insert. Your teacher may ask you to explain your reasons for using each comma. (Some sentences may not need new commas.)

Examples

a. Because he likes difficult crossword puzzles Henry always does the puzzle in the Sunday newspaper.

Because he likes difficult crossword puzzles ⊙ Henry always does the puzzle in the Sunday newspaper.

b. Yes I can fix that broken faucet next Wednesday morning.

Yes⊙ I can fix that broken faucet next Wednesday morning.

1. Although reception is terrible in our town we enjoy many good programs on television.

2. Having worn only a light sweater to school I was happy about the arrival of spring.

3. From our roof the top of the monument is visible.

4. Charles I'd like you to meet my cousin Laura.

5. Therefore our school holds a study hall in the early evening.

6. Across from our school were several old movie theaters.

7. Yes the French club will sponsor a series of bake sales.

8. Buried beneath a mountain of snow and ice the car was completely invisible.

9. When he returns from San Francisco Mr. O'Dea will bring some sourdough bread.

10. By 3 o'clock in the afternoon of the third day of our stay the sun had not yet appeared.

Use a comma to separate contrasting words, phrases, and clauses introduced by the word *not*.

To challenge me in court you must have facts, not suspicions.

This carton must be opened from the top, not from the bottom.

Use a comma to separate direct quotations from the rest of the sentence.

Dan said, "The soup is boiling."

"Turn off the stove," shouted Johanna.

Note: A comma is not used unless a person's *exact* words are being quoted.

Dan said that the soup was hot. [no comma]

Exercise 5: Using Commas

Write the following sentences, placing commas wherever necessary. Circle the commas you insert. (Some sentences may not need commas.)

Examples

a. Cairo is a city in Illinois not a city in Indiana.

Cairo is a city in Illinois, not a city in Indiana.

b. Rita said to me "This Chinese tea is delicious."

Rita said to me, "This Chinese tea is delicious."

1. The bicycle is the most efficient form of transportation not the car.

2. Carol whispered "Who is the man in the blue overcoat?"

3. Noel said that the goldfish food is in the kitchen cupboard.

4. The best tomato soup is made with milk not with water.

5. Larry explained that his boxing lessons were inexpensive.

6. Our class makes field trips to museums not discotheques.

7. Ramona announced "All freshmen may go to the head of the line."

8. The best way to cook bacon is to broil or bake it not to fry it.

9. Tim muttered "No one really wants to write a paper during vacation."

10. Why John is dressed like a clown from the circus!

Use a comma to separate parts of geographical names and to separate the name of a street, city, and state in an address.

Las Vegas, Nevada

Paris, France

4473 Stollwood Drive, Carmichael, CA 95608

Note: Do not use a comma between a state and a ZIP code. A comma is used to separate the last part of a geographical name or an address from the rest of the sentence.

The pony express operated between Sacramento, California, and St. Joseph, Missouri.

We sent the letter to 758 Third Avenue, New York, New York 10017, early this morning.

Use a comma to separate the day of the week, the day of the month, and the year in a date.

Thursday, May 18, 1949

Christmas Day, 1979

Note: A comma is used to separate the date from the rest of the sentence.

On Thursday, April 5, I hope to leave for California.

The use of the comma is optional when only a month and the year are given.

Use a comma to separate a person's name from a degree, a title, or an affiliation that follows it.

Daryl Thompson, Ph.D.

Clarence Fleugal, Jr.

Lieutenant Marjorie Woodard, USMC

Note: When used in a sentence, the degree, title, or affiliation is also followed by a comma to separate it from the rest of the sentence.

The President gave Karen Anderson, M.D., an award honoring her research.

Exercise 6: Using Commas

Write the following sentences, placing commas wherever necessary. Circle the ones you insert. (Some sentences may not need commas.)

Examples

a. Mary Lou lives at 7555 Caldwell Avenue Chicago Illinois.

Mary Lou lives at 7555 Caldwell Avenue, Chicago, Illinois.

b. The Declaration of Independence was signed on July 4 1776.

The Declaration of Independence was signed on July 4, 1776.

1. Jessica and Lisa are visiting their relatives in San Antonio Texas.
2. On September 1 1967 we moved to Fresno California.
3. Melissa is engaged to marry Elwood Fleet Jr.
4. Private Richard Bowler USMC reported to Camp Pendleton for duty.
5. Yolanda's new address is 4750 South Lake Park Champaign Illinois.
6. December 7 1970 is the date on which I was born.
7. Naomi's new furniture was delivered on Labor Day 1980.
8. We plan to visit our cousins in Ogden Utah and Boise Idaho.
9. The senior class visited Missoula Montana in May 1981.
10. Rufus T. Firefly Ph.D. will teach a course on the need for comedy in the modern world.

Paired Commas

Some phrases, clauses, and expressions require commas both before and after them in order to set them off from the rest of the sentence. The following section discusses the use of *paired commas*.

Use paired commas to enclose nonessential phrases and clauses.

Nonessential phrases and clauses are those that could be omitted without changing the meaning of the sentence.

| The cake, *decorated in our school's colors*, was placed in the center of the table. | [nonessential participial phrase] |
| The school, *which was built in 1939*, has an excellent reputation. | [nonessential adjective clause] |

Essential phrases and clauses are not set off by commas.

The cake *decorated in our school's colors* was prettier than all the other cakes in the contest.

The school *that was built in 1939* has a better reputation than the newer one.

Place one comma before a nonessential phrase or clause that appears at the end of a sentence.

The eagle made its nest in that tree, the tallest in the forest.

My favorite aunt was Pauline, who cared for me when I was young.

Use paired commas to enclose nonessential appositives and appositive phrases.

Nonessential appositives and appositive phrases could be removed without changing the meaning of the sentence.

| Jim Steeger, *our trusted guide*, led us through the jungle wilderness. | [nonessential] |
| *Pheidippides*, an Athenian courier, was sent back to the city with news of the victory. | [nonessential] |

When an appositive distinguishes the noun it explains from other members of the same group, the appositive is essential and is not set off by commas.

| The poet *Byron* became the most popular writer in Europe. | [The appositive is essential because it identifies a specific poet.] |
| My friend *Paul* is a demon for housework. | [My friend Paul, not my friend Ron or Toni or Daniel] |

Note: Place one comma before a nonessential appositive appearing at the end of a sentence.

I once lived on a delta, land deposited at the mouth of a river.

Use paired commas to enclose parenthetical and transitional expressions.

Parenthetical expressions are those that interrupt the flow of the sentence and can be removed without changing its meaning.

We will finish, *I think*, by Friday.

Only through hard work, *it is said*, can one achieve greatness.

Transitional expressions, such as *therefore, for example, then, on the other hand*, and *however*, should be set off by commas when they merely interrupt the flow of the sentence.

Our most important game, *then*, would also be our last game.

It is up to the people, *however*, to select their own rulers.

Note: When transitional expressions are used as adverbs and adverb phrases, they are not set off by commas.

We *then* played our most important game. [adverb]

Note: When a parenthetical or transitional expression appears at the beginning or at the end of a sentence, use one comma to set it off.

To tell the truth, I haven't given it much thought.

Our biggest hurdle lay ahead of us, *however*.

Exercise 7: *Using Paired Commas*

Write the following sentences, placing commas wherever they belong. Circle the commas you insert. (Some sentences may not need commas.)

Example

---

a. George Jackson whom I met in high school is a great singer.

George Jackson ⊙ whom I met in high school⊙ is a great singer.

1. The lady who taught me to play the piano is my aunt Flo.

2. School buses which are almost always painted yellow are often driven by retired schoolteachers.

3. Your plan it seems to me is a very good one.

4. Last week's math test which covered the first three chapters of the textbook was not very difficult.

no 5. The truck that my cousin uses on the farm has four-wheel drive.

no 6. The only person who will listen to Joe's boring stories is Sam.

7. Our friend from Minneapolis Carol Lee Chen has relatives in China.

no 8. To be completely frank I haven't understood a word you've said.

9. Ms. Adams our English teacher has promised to take us on a field trip to the zoo.

10. A baseball game as a general rule lasts longer than a basketball game.

The Semicolon

The *semicolon*, a stronger mark of punctuation than the comma, is sometimes referred to as a "weak period."

Use a semicolon to link independent clauses that are closely related.

Never before had such a project been undertaken; never had anything like it been considered.

Some of the boys went home; others stayed until the bitter end.

Use a semicolon to link independent clauses when the second independent clause begins with a transitional adverb, such as *besides, however, instead, moreover,* or *nevertheless.*

The tickets were just too expensive; besides, there were not enough seats.

There were many obstacles in our way; however, we pressed onward anyway.

Note: A semicolon is also proper when the second independent clause begins with a transitional phrase, such as *in fact, of course, on the other hand,* or *on the contrary*.

> Their record was not impressive; on the other hand, neither was ours.

Use a semicolon to separate items in a series when one or more of the items contains commas.

> The winners are from Gary, Indiana; Fort Dodge, Iowa; and Geneva, Illinois.

> In order to qualify, a student must be able to speak Spanish, French, or German; to play a musical instrument; and to write a play, short story, or poem.

Exercise 8: *Using Semicolons*

Write the following sentences, placing semicolons where they belong. Circle the marks you insert.

Examples

---

a. The soup scalded my tongue it was too hot.

The soup scalded my tongue(;) it was too hot.

b. My tongue was sore however, I continued to eat.

My tongue was sore(;) however, I continued to eat.

1. Alcatraz is an island in San Francisco Bay moreover, it was once a federal prison.

2. Puerto Rico is an American territory it is not a state.

3. We will be attending the concerts given by Beverly Sills, September 1 Nathan Milstein, September 15 Glenn Gould, October 9 and Ravi Shankar, October 27.

4. The Jordan River flows through Salt Lake City it empties into the Great Salt Lake.

5. The winters in South Dakota are terrible nevertheless, its residents love their state.

6. Read pages 5–8, 11–15, and 30–32 answer the questions on page 9, 16, and 33–35.

7. My uncles live in Des Moines, Iowa Salmon, Idaho Palos Verdes, California and Fairview, Utah.

8. American rivers have always been used as highways of commerce consequently, they have been important in the growth of this nation.

9. The curtain rose on the stage the audience became silent.

10. Booker T. Washington was born in 1856 he died in 1915.

The Colon

A *colon*, used to separate elements within a sentence, acts like an arrow pointing forward, calling attention to the word, phrase, or list that follows.

Use a colon to separate a list of items from an introductory statement that contains the words *as follows, the following, these,* **or a specific number.**

Among the items we brought were the following: beach towels, umbrellas, bathing suits, and swim fins.

These are the characteristics that made him great: perseverance and imagination.

There were three things to consider: weather, terrain, and equipment.

Note: A colon is generally *not* used following the words *for example, that is, such as, namely,* or *for instance.* Do not place a colon between a verb and its direct object or after a preposition.

Use a colon to separate an introductory statement from an explanation, an appositive, or a quotation.

The officers thought his excuse was valid: self-defense.

The importance of action is stressed in the writing of Thoreau: "What is once well done is done forever."

The colon also has three conventional uses that have grown out of custom and tradition.

Use a colon to separate a salutation from the body of a business letter.

My dear Mrs. Mitchell: Dear Sir:

Use a colon to separate the hour and minutes in expressions of time.

11:45 A.M.   the 7:20 train

Use a colon to separate chapter numbers from verse numbers in references to passages from the Bible.

Genesis 6:10   1 Corinthians 13:4–7

Exercise 9: Using Colons

Write each of the following sentences, placing colons where they belong. Circle each colon you insert. Your teacher may ask your reason for using each colon.

Example

a. For the party I bought the following items noisemakers, paper hats, and some new records.

For the party I bought the following items(:) noisemakers, paper hats, and some new records.

1. The main parts of an automobile are the following engine, frame, body, wheels, and transmission.

2. Does this term describe Malcom a rebel without a cause?

3. The lunch whistle always blows precisely at 1200 noon.

4. Our social studies teacher's opinion of the mayor is as follows she works hard.

5. Our rabbi asked us to memorize Proverbs 22 6.

6. Take these items with you a guidebook, travelers' checks, and suntan lotion.

7. We don't eat dinner until nearly 730 P.M. at our house.

8. We had what seemed to be an impossible dream to win an Olympic gold medal.

9. I can think of only one word to describe television commercials annoying.

10. In cold weather you should pay extra attention to the following your head, your hands, your feet, and any other exposed part of your body.

The Dash

Acting like an arrow pointing backward, the *dash* calls attention to the word or group of words that come before it.

Use a dash to separate an introductory series or thought from the rest of the sentence.

Red, blue, and yellow—these are the primary colors.

Collecting stamps—that's my favorite hobby.

But the snow—if it continues, we'll be stranded.

Use a dash to separate a sudden or unexpected change in thought from the rest of the sentence.

I agree—but let me stress one other point.

I started to fall—yes, it's all coming back to me now.

Use a dash to show omission of words in dialogue. The dash indicates a sudden break in a person's speech.

"But how will I ev—?" he began.

"I won't rest until you're—" she started.

Exercise 10: Using Dashes

Write the sentences on the following page, placing dashes where they belong. Circle each dash that you insert and be prepared to give reasons for using each one.

<u>Examples</u>

   a. To swim the English Channel that is my goal in life.

     To swim the English Channel ⊖ that is my goal in life.

   b. I'd like a beef sandwich no, make that a bowl of chili.

     I'd like a beef sandwich ⊖ no, make that a bowl of chili.

1. Running five miles before breakfast that's the way to start the day.

2. Home economics, wood shop, and auto mechanics those are just a few of the many practical courses at our school.

3. Hank said but let me try to recall his exact words.

4. Volunteer work in a child center that's important work.

5. A new gymnasium that's what we need at our school.

6. "But no one will ever find" he began.

7. To become the mayor that is the ambition of all three candidates.

8. A very rare thing that's a legal parking place.

9. We couldn't have seen the trouble coming who could have?

10. I can't imagine what happened to Sarah.

Paired Dashes

Use *paired dashes* in the following situations.

Use paired dashes to enclose phrases or clauses that show a sudden break in thought or an abrupt change in tone.

   She wants all our term papers finished—listen to this—by next Friday.

   We all knew—or should have known—that trouble was brewing.

Use paired dashes to enclose appositive phrases that need a stronger pause than that for commas or that might be misread if commas were used.

The bush—the one in the corner of the yard—is dying.

Our national parks—forests and prairie preserved forever—should be part of everyone's vacation plans.

Use paired dashes to enclose nonessential or parenthetical phrases that contain commas.

Five states—California, Oregon, Washington, Alaska, and Hawaii—border the Pacific Ocean.

Some primitive tools—the knife, for example—have changed little over the centuries.

Use paired dashes to enclose nonessential or parenthetical expressions that are sentences in themselves.

Governor Thompson—folks around here call him "Big Jim"—seems to enjoy political life.

The truly veteran lawmakers—some of them have been in Congress for decades—hold the positions of greatest power.

(Parentheses may also be used for nonessential information.)

Exercise 11: Using Paired Dashes

Write the following sentences, placing paired dashes where they properly belong. Circle the dashes you insert.

Examples

a. My friend Tom everyone thinks he's so shy is a vicious competitor in tennis.

My friend Tom⊖ everyone thinks he's so shy⊖ is a vicious competitor in tennis.

b. We should indeed, we must win the game against Central High on Friday night.

We should⊖ indeed, we must⊖ win the game against Central High on Friday night.

1. Carlos the student who's just getting off the school bus will be the best center in our team's history.

2. The location of the family reunion picnic unless it gets rained out again will be the park at the edge of town.

3. Your favorite cities Denver, Chicago, New York, and Los Angeles all have serious air pollution problems.

4. Mr. Dee's market everyone in the neighborhood calls it "Mr. Disease" has the lowest prices on chicken and fish.

5. Most petroleum-powered vehicles cars, buses, and trucks will be obsolete by the end of the century.

6. The late hour at which the local television station shows my favorite movies 12:30 A.M. makes me furious.

7. My sister Sharon the sister with the Air Force in Germany sent us a crystal vase.

8. Ms. Anderson has assigned we are still in shock over this a fifty-page research paper on the dangers of noise pollution.

9. Anyone with a solid knowledge of modern physics thus, any one of thousands of people could construct an atomic bomb.

10. An experienced cyclist your cousin Jim Walsh is a good example can ride one hundred miles per day without too much difficulty.

The Hyphen

The *hyphen* is used to link the parts of some compound words and the part of a word begun on one line with the part finished on the next.

Use a hyphen to link the parts of compound nouns that begin with the prefixes *ex-*, *self-*, and *all-* or that end with the suffix *-elect*.

> ex-judge, ex-president
> self-starter, self-control
> all-star
> president-elect

Note: The prefix *great-* is also followed by a hyphen when it is part of a family relationship.

> great-grandfather, great-aunt

Use a hyphen to link the parts of a compound noun that include a prepositional phrase.

---

daughter-in-law, jack-o'-lantern, man-of-war

Note: Remember that many compound nouns are not hyphenated at all. Some are written as two separate words (*swimming* pool, *tennis* ball); others are written as a single word (*newspaper, basketball*). Check your dictionary for the proper spelling of compound words.

Use a hyphen to link the parts of a compound adjective that is made up of an adjective and a noun.

---

hot-air balloon, short-term loan

Use a hyphen to link the parts of a compound adjective when the last word is a proper noun.

---

un-American ideas, pre-Egyptian artifacts, pro-Chicago fan

Use a hyphen to link the parts of a compound adjective when one part is a number and the other is an adjective or a noun.

---

a ten-pound weight, a one-hundred-dollar bill

Use a hyphen to link the parts of a compound adjective that is a fraction.

---

one-third fare, a three-fifths majority

Note: The hyphen may be omitted when the fraction is used as a noun.

Two thirds of our class are absent.

Use a hyphen to link the parts of a compound adjective when the second part is a participle and the compound adjective precedes the noun it modifies.

---

earth-shattering news, hair-raising story, old-fashioned clothes

Note: Do not use a hyphen between the parts of a compound adjective when the first part is an adverb ending in *-ly*.

a finely tuned instrument, a slowly moving storm

Use a hyphen to link the parts of compound numbers between twenty-one and ninety-nine.

forty-nine cents, twenty-two players

Use a hyphen between syllables when a word is begun on one line and finished on the next.

I found two of the items I was looking for beneath the counter.

The missing library books had been mistakenly placed in my bookcase.

Note: Because a hyphen can be placed only between syllables, one-syllable words are not hyphenated. Also, do not hyphenate a word if doing so would leave just one letter on either line. A word that already contains a hyphen should be divided only at the hyphen.

*We watched and waited, wondering who would come thr-
ough the door.
[*Through* should not be hyphenated.]

*The only thing I really feared was being left a-
lone in the cabin.
[*Alone* should not be hyphenated.]

*We listened politely, but the candidate's old-fash-
ioned ideas didn't impress us.
[*Old-fashioned* should only be divided at the hyphen.]

An asterisk (*) denotes a feature that is not part of Standard English.

Exercise 12: Using Hyphens

Write the sentences on the next page, placing hyphens where they belong. Circle the hyphens you insert. Your teacher may ask you to explain your reason for using each hyphen. (Some sentences may not need hyphens.)

Examples

a. Susan is very fond of her sister in law.

Susan is very fond of her sister ⊙ in ⊙ law.

b. Juanita is an ex champion in her sport.

Juanita is an ex ⊙ champion in her sport.

1. Carlos is Nancy's brother in law.
2. The school counselor tried to explain the importance of self guidance.
3. The class decided to have a post Halloween party.
4. Sally Chen declared herself sergeant at arms for the student government.
5. Eleanor's younger brother is twenty two years old.
6. Senator Thurmond is an ex Democrat who moved to the Republican party.
7. Ms. Rosario gave us a one third share of her garden plot.
8. To not love Mom and apple pie is considered un American.
9. The counselor told me I should work on my self image.
10. John's great aunt is the president elect of the stamp club.

The Apostrophe

The *apostrophe* is used to show the omission of letters or numbers, to form the plurals of letters or numbers, and to form possessive nouns.

Use an apostrophe to show that a letter or letters have been omitted from contractions.

Sharon *doesn't* want to go.	[does + not]
They're the same ones we have.	[They + are]

Note: An apostrophe is also used in the word o'clock, which is actually a contraction meaning *of the clock*.

571

Use an apostrophe to show that the first two numbers have been omitted from a year.

---

the blizzard of *'79*

the class of *'67*

Use an apostrophe to form the plural of letters or numbers.

Make sure you have dotted all the *i*'s and crossed all the *t*'s.

The temperature will be in the *20*'s or *30*'s.

Note: An apostrophe is also used to form the plural of a word that is referred to as a word. An apostrophe is optional when making the numbers of centuries or decades plural.

Your last sentence had too many *that*'s in it.

The 1960s were more turbulent than any decade in the 1900s.

Add an apostrophe and an *s* to singular nouns to show possession.

Singular Noun	*Possessive Noun*
Tom	Tom's book
the company	the company's budget
the Jones family	Mr. Jones's house

When a plural noun does not end in *s*, add an apostrophe and an *s* to show possession.

Plural Noun	*Possessive Noun*
women	women's rights
children	the children's playroom
teeth	his teeth's roots

When a plural noun ends in *s*, add only an apostrophe to show possession.

Plural Noun	*Possessive Noun*
both tables	both tables' tops
a forest of trees	all the trees' branches
two horses	two horses' limbs

Exercise 13: Using Apostrophes

Write the following sentences, placing apostrophes where they belong. Circle the apostrophes you insert. Your teacher may ask you to explain your reason for using each one. (Some sentences may not need apostrophes.)

Example

a. The mans name was Smith.

The man⊘s name was Smith.

1. Did that giant toad eat our cats favorite food?
2. Ms. Scrooges firm was profitable.
3. The Presidential elections of 76 were exciting.
4. On her quizzes Yolanda scored two 100s and an 85.
5. All five students papers received Ds and will be rewritten.
6. If you dont listen carefully, youll miss the point of this story.
7. Freeways that arent crowded are very rare in California.
8. The telephones purpose is to make conversation easy and convenient.
9. A cut roses petals will wilt rather quickly.
10. In 86 my daughters high school career will end, and shell be ready for college.

Parentheses

Parentheses, used to enclose material within a sentence, have two important uses.

Use parentheses to enclose parenthetical expressions that have no real connection with the rest of the sentence and to enclose supplemental items that are used to explain or illustrate.

The town of Oswego (it has had several names in its history) was founded in a curious way.

A few state capitals (Indianapolis, for example) were selected solely because of geography.

According to Dr. Douglas Moews (1901–1978), anyone can become bald.

Use parentheses to enclose letters or numbers that designate listed items within a sentence.

The student may then (a) ask for a schedule change, (b) elect to take an additional course, or (c) find another means of transportation.

In setting off parenthetical elements, you may use (1) paired commas, (2) paired dashes, or (3) parentheses.

Exercise 14: Using Parentheses

Write the following sentences, placing parentheses where necessary. Circle the parentheses you insert. (Your teacher may ask you to explain your reasons for using each set of parentheses.)

Examples

---

a. The YMCA Young Men's Christian Association offers recreational programs for both men and women.

The YMCA (Young Men's Christian Association) offers recreational programs for both men and women.

b. The principal has instructed all teachers to a take roll, b send all tardy students to the office, and c lecture all students on the importance of promptness.

The principal has instructed all teachers to (a) take roll, (b) send all tardy students to the office, and (c) lecture all students on the importance of promptness.

1. The Seven Years' War (1756–1763) pitted England and Prussia against the combined armies of Austria, France, Russia, Sweden, and Saxony.

2. The college application requested (1) a picture, (2) a transcript of high school grades, and (3) at least three recommendations.

3. The state of Michigan (the name is derived from the Algonquian word meaning "great water") has a population of over 8 million people.

4. Feodor Dostoevski (his name is sometimes spelled Dostoyevsky) wrote two of the world's greatest novels: *Crime and Punishment* and *The Brothers Karamazov.*

5. Dan plans to sail his large catamaran (a boat with two parallel hulls) from Miami, Florida, to Caracas, Venezuela.

6. George Washington (who never really chopped down any cherry trees) was President of the United States from 1789 until 1797.

7. The zoo officials were very excited when the first okapi (an African animal related to the giraffe) was born in captivity.

8. Liz began talking to the waiter in Spanish (she had, after all, studied in Bogotá), but the waiter made no reply.

9. Stir two cups of boned chicken (for a description of how to bone a chicken, see pages 10–13) into the mixture of cooked onions and apples, cover with broth, and simmer for twenty minutes.

10. Combine flour, water, and lard (not butter or margarine) to make the best possible pie dough.

Quotation Marks

Quotation marks, which often occur in pairs, are used most frequently to enclose direct quotations and the words in some titles.

Use quotation marks to enclose the exact words that are spoken or written. Such words are called *direct quotations*.

"We ran all the way. Have we really missed the bus?" Jamie cried.

"I'm sorry," the clerk explained, "but it left five minutes ago."

"What a pickle!" she muttered. "When does the next one leave?"

This writer states, "What we lack is a thirst for excellence."

Notice that the quotation marks appear at the beginning and end of the words that are quoted exactly, even if those words are more than one sentence in length. Expressions such as *Jamie cried, the clerk explained,* or *the writer states* identify the speaker or writer whose words are being quoted. These expressions are not enclosed in quotation marks.

Note: Quotation marks are not used unless a person's *exact* words are quoted.

Jamie told me that she missed the bus this morning.

The following rules will help you to use capital letters and other punctuation correctly with quotation marks.

1. A quotation usually begins with a capital letter.

   Sandy commented, "Those oily rags are a fire hazard. We should dispose of them."

Note: Brief quotations that are obviously incomplete sometimes begin with a small letter.

I wonder who first called this nation "the land of the free."

2. When a quotation is interrupted by an expression identifying the speaker (*they pleaded, she announced*), the second part of the quotation begins with a small letter.

   "If the rain stops by noon," they pleaded, "will we still have the picnic?"

   "We have canceled the picnic," she announced, "because of the bad weather."

3. The quotation itself is separated from the rest of the sentence by a comma, a question mark, or an exclamation point.

   "If I could find something decent to wear," he sighed, "we could leave."

   "Where did I put that sweater?" he muttered, rummaging in the drawer.

   He cried, "I've found it!" as he yanked a crumpled bundle from the drawer.

Note: Notice that *two* commas are used when words that are not part of the quotation appear in the middle of the sentence.

4. Commas and periods at the end of a quotation appear inside the closing quotation mark. Colons and semicolons at the end of a quotation appear outside the closing quotation mark.

   "I think you're wrong," Dan said.

   He added, "Look at this information."

Dan said, "I think you're wrong"; he asked us to reexamine our information.

There are two solutions to this "thirst for excellence": an increase in funds for education and improvement of library resources.

5. Question marks and exclamation points are placed inside closing quotation marks when only the quotation itself is a question or an exclamation. In other situations they are placed outside the closing quotation marks.

She cried, "Please stop at once!"

How I laughed when he said, "The Packers will win the Super Bowl"!

Mom asked, "Did you see the dentist today?"

Who asked, "Isn't this unfair"?

Note: In the last example both the quotation and the entire statement are questions, but only one question mark appears at the end of the statement.

Another use of quotation marks is to enclose the titles of short stories, essays, short poems, songs, individual episodes of television programs, magazine articles, and parts of a book.

"The Purloined Letter" and "The Gold Bug" are my favorite short stories.

Our assignment was to read Thoreau's essays "Civil Disobedience" and "Walking."

The band finished its performance with "The Stars and Stripes Forever."

My favorite episode of *All in the Family* is titled "Edith Strikes Back."

Note: The following kinds of titles are underlined rather than enclosed with quotation marks:

Books, long plays, and book-length poems	When the Legends Die
	The Miracle Worker
	The Song of Hiawatha

Newspapers, magazines, and pamphlets	<u>The New York Times</u>
	<u>Newsweek</u> magazine
	<u>How to Raise a Garden</u>

Note: Do not underline *the* unless it is part of the newspaper title, as it is for *The New York Times*.

Films, radio and television series	<u>The Empire Strikes Back</u>
	<u>All Things Considered</u>
	<u>Nova</u>
Paintings, sculptures, record albums, ballets, operas, musicals, and long works of instrumental music	<u>Still Life</u>
	<u>Venus de Milo</u>
	<u>A Hard Day's Night</u>
	<u>Swan Lake</u>
	<u>Madame Butterfly</u>
	<u>My Fair Lady</u>
	<u>An American in Paris</u>
Ships, aircraft, and spacecraft	<u>Queen Elizabeth 2</u>
	<u>Air Force One</u>
	<u>Mariner</u>

In printed matter underlined titles are *italicized: Lord Jim.*

Exercise 15: Using Quotation Marks

Write the following sentences, placing quotation marks where they belong and underlining titles that need it. Circle the quotation marks you insert. (Some sentences may not need new punctuation.)

Examples

a. Jeff said, I would really like to visit Venice.

   Jeff said, ⊙I would really like to visit Venice. ⊙

b. Sharon says that she will be absent tomorrow.

   Sharon says that she will be absent tomorrow.

c. The last good book that I read was Michaelmas by A. J. Budrys.

   The last good book that I read was <u>Michaelmas</u> by A. J. Budrys.

1. Elvira shouted, I'll never eat in this restaurant again!
2. Thomas said that he would lend me his bicycle.
3. Salvador Dali's unusual painting, The Flaming Giraffe, hangs in the Art Institute in Chicago.
4. I would be glad to drive you to school, Raoul replied.
5. Ralph admitted that he has never read James Baldwin's essay Fifth Avenue, Uptown.
6. Well, he said, I guess we won't be going to the fair after all.
7. Very few people have a vocal range high enough to sing The Star Spangled Banner.
8. Ms. Swenson asked us to read the second chapter, Life from Life, and to be prepared for a quiz on the first chapter, Biology—What Is It All About?
9. I enjoyed Carol Burnett's sketch titled As the Stomach Turns.
10. Our game plan, the coach announced, is to try to keep the ball on the ground.

Single Quotation Marks

Single quotation marks, also used in pairs, are used to enclose items that appear inside double quotation marks.

Use single quotation marks to enclose direct quotations that are inside other direct quotations.

Our teacher asked, "Who said, 'To thine own self be true'?"

Helen said, "I heard him call, 'Please help me!'"

Use single quotation marks to enclose the titles of short stories, essays, short poems, songs, television episodes, magazine articles, and parts of a book when these items appear inside a direct quotation.

The teacher announced, "Read 'Thanatopsis' and 'A Forest Hymn' for Monday's class."

"But I couldn't find it in either Chapter 10, 'The Solar System,' or Chapter 11, 'The Universe,'" I argued.

Exercise 16: Using Single Quotation Marks

Write the following sentences, adding pairs of single quotation marks where they belong. Circle the marks you insert. (Your teacher may ask you to explain why you have used each pair of single quotation marks.)

Example

a. Lawrence muttered, "Tom's last words were, Take care of my turtles, Larry."

Lawrence muttered, "Tom's last words were, ⊘Take care of my turtles, Larry.⊘"

1. The teacher announced, "I want you all to read a short story by Hemingway called After the Storm."

2. Father repeated, "I said, Put your toys away, children."

3. "The President's exact words were, We must all make conservation a part of our daily lives," Sally announced.

4. "My favorite poem by Melvin B. Tolson is entitled The Birth of John Henry," Ms. Washington said.

5. Tommy Hendricks blurted out, "Why does everyone need to memorize The Rime of the Ancient Mariner?"

6. Eleanor whispered, "Tommy always says, That's a good question when he doesn't know the answer."

7. Bob thought suddenly, "I shouldn't have used the phrase cloth-eared fool when I shouted at Kevin."

8. "The melody for the song John Brown's Body was used in The Battle Hymn of the Republic," our music teacher informed us.

9. "Everyone should watch How It All Began, a special episode of *The World at War* on Channel 32," Ms. Carbona advised.

10. The announcer said, "Be sure to tune in for The Bob Hope Special, next Thursday at 9 P.M."

Review: Punctuation

Write the following sentences, placing punctuation marks wherever necessary. Some of the sentences can be correctly punctuated in several different ways, so be prepared to explain the placement of each mark you use. Circle the marks you insert.

Example

a. But you promised to take us to the fair James cried.

But you promised to take us to the fair(!)* James cried.

1. Ive always wanted to become a movie star said Mary

2. Why dont you just say Im sorry

3. The Drama Club will hold a dress rehearsal tonight for its production of Shaws play Major Barbara the play will open on Monday night

4. The Adventures of Huckleberry Finn was written by Mark Twain his real name was Samuel Clemens who also wrote a short story titled The Man That Corrupted Hadleyburg

5. What is the square root of fifty two Harold asked

6. Karl wants to study the social life of the wasp (Why he should be interested in wasps social life is beyond me)

7. Why must we read the poems A Morning in the Office, Ode to a Hall Monitor, and Study Hall Blues

8. If you want to be prepared for tomorrow's discussion of Poe's short stories the teacher said be sure to read The Tell-Tale Heart and The Black Cat

9. What sort of person would paint a picture like this I asked

10. At that moment the waiter shouted Is there a doctor in the house

11. When interviewing the President you shouldn't ask silly questions like What is your favorite color

12. Joans car runs well for one that has been driven over 100,000 miles 162,500 km

13. I knew that I was in trouble when the principal said Come to the office immediately

14. Bill runs one half mile every morning (though he would probably prefer to sleep in instead)

15. Do you think that Jill was serious when she asked May I try that

16. Jim Spence (didn't his brother attend our high school) has been elected our states representative

17. When it had stopped raining the scout leader said Lets light a new campfire

18. Dorothy asked respectfully Didnt you say that the battle took place in AD 1066

19. Why cant you just admit youre wrong asked Clara

20. Marilyn whispered Would you like to read the poem Autumn Breezes

Writing Focus: *Improving Punctuation in Writing*

Punctuation marks are like road signs that writers use to guide readers through their writing. The marks can slow readers down, make them stop, and even point out items of interest. Like drivers who must learn to read and follow road signs, writers must use punctuation to avoid confusion and to make their writing flow smoothly.

Assignment: *What a Great Idea!*

For many hours every day, Americans of all ages sit in front of their TV sets and watch cartoons, game shows, the news, movies, situation comedies, soap operas, specials, sports, police shows, talk shows, mysteries, and westerns. And yet, even with the many selections possible, the networks always need new programs to meet increasing demands from viewers and network executives.

Imagine that you receive a questionnaire in the mail asking for new ideas for TV shows. You come up with a great idea for a "sure hit" TV show. Write a letter to a network executive explaining and describing your idea so that he or she will buy it. You'll want to be as detailed and specific as possible in your letter in order to convince the executive. Your writing will be evaluated for correct punctuation.

Use the following steps to complete this assignment.

A. Prewriting

Think about all the TV programs you have watched over the years. Begin to free write about shows you have liked or ideas you thought have worked well on TV. Using your imagination, create a new "sure

hit'' show. Write down whatever occurs to you in five or ten minutes. Don't worry about writing correctly. Then reread your free writing, underlining ideas that might work. Choose one idea that has possibilities and do another free writing on it. Add details, facts, names, or examples that help develop your idea. Reread your new free writing, underlining the details you wish to use in your letter.

B. Writing

Write a letter to a network executive selling your idea for a new sure hit TV show by describing or explaining it. Use your free writings to help you. Follow the guidelines for letter writing. Make the body of your letter as detailed as possible so that your sure hit is fully explained or described.

C. Postwriting

Use the following checklist to revise your first draft.

1.   Have I provided details to explain and describe my show?

2.   Is my letter in the correct form?

3.   Is my punctuation correct for the letter format?

4.   Is my punctuation correct in each sentence?

Use the Proofreader's Checklist at the back of the book to edit your work. Create a *TV Guide* using student ideas for new shows.

25 Capitalization

The Uses of Capitalization

The uses of capitalization can be divided into two parts: capitalization of groups larger than one word and capitalization of single words, most of which are proper nouns and proper adjectives.

Capitalization of Word Groups

Capitalize the first word of a sentence.

> The tall, thin man walked off the train carrying a cane.
>
> Everyone on the platform noticed his military bearing.

Capitalize the first word of a direct quotation, whether it is a complete sentence or a fragment.

> The members of the crowd all shouted, "Welcome home, Jeffrey!"
>
> "At least I'm remembered," he said. Then he added, "By some people."

Note: When a direct quotation is interrupted, however, capitalize only the word that begins the direct quotation, not the word that begins the second part of that quotation.

> "I'll be home," she promised, "before nightfall."
> [The words *she promised* interrupt the direct quotation "I'll be home before nightfall."]

Exercise 1: *Capitalizing the First Word*

Write each of the following sentences, using capital letters where they are necessary. Underline the words you capitalize.

Examples

a. the last man to leave the room was Mr. Wilson.
  The last man to leave the room was Mr. Wilson.

b. "the last train for Yuma just left," Milton muttered. "there won't be another one until tomorrow."
  "The last train for Yuma just left," Milton muttered. "There won't be another one until tomorrow."

1. all the younger students loved to dance.

2. June said, "the waltz is the most exciting dance of all."

3. "the waltz," Maurice replied, "is too old-fashioned for me."

4. "the only problem with the waltz," Danielle said, "is that you have to be too close to your partner."

5. "the older students think that is the best part about waltzing," said Mr. Younger.

6. "there is one problem with the waltz, however," argued Mrs. Younger. she then continued, "one major problem."

7. "few bands have waltzes in their repertoires," she explained.

8. "have you ever heard the Rolling Stones play a waltz?" asked John.

9. Ms. Schwartz, the school band teacher, said, "the waltzes of Johann Strauss were the best."

10. "the rich and elegant music of Strauss," she said, "brings back the feelings and sensations of another era. how I wish that era would come again!"

Capitalize the first word of each complete line of poetry.

> He went like one that hath been stunned,
> And is of sense forlorn:
> A sadder and a wiser man,
> He rose the morrow morn.

Capitalize the first word, the last word, and all other important words in the titles of works of art.

Note: The preceding rule applies to the titles of books, chapters, short stories, poems, plays, newspapers, magazine articles, musical works, paintings, sculptures, movies, radio and television programs, and student themes. Do not capitalize prepositions and conjunctions with fewer than five letters.

> *The Clash of the Titans* is a good film.

> *Love Among the Ruins* is a well-known book.
> [*Among* is a preposition, but it has five letters.]

> My report is titled "Lights I Can't Seem to Turn Off."
> [The last word in a title is capitalized no matter what part of speech it is.]

Exercise 2: *Capitalizing Titles*

Write each of the following sentences, capitalizing the titles according to the rules in the previous section. Underline the words you capitalize.

Examples

a. Jules Verne wrote the science fiction thriller *twenty thousand leagues under the sea*.
   Jules Verne wrote the science fiction thriller <u>Twenty Thousand Leagues Under</u> the <u>Sea</u>.

b. Mozart wrote the famous opera *the marriage of figaro*.
   Mozart wrote the famous opera <u>The Marriage</u> of <u>Figaro</u>.

1. Chris should read a book about the Panama Canal titled *the path between the seas*.

2. Bernice went to see the old movie *the enemy below*.

3. Penny's favorite film is *the day of the jackal*.

4. We will be studying Faulkner's *as I lay dying*.

5. W. Somerset Maugham's most famous novel is *of human bondage*.

6. Sholokhov's famous novel, *and quiet flows the Don*, was the inspiration for the folk song "where have all the flowers gone?"

7. The title of my theme is "the new me."

8. The article "out from under the snow" fascinated me.

9. The ballet *appalachian spring* was choreographed by Martha Graham.

10. Chapter Four in our textbook *rise of the american nation* is titled "the start of an american way of life."

Capitalization of Single Words

Most of the single words that must begin with a capital letter are proper nouns and proper adjectives. *Proper nouns* are the names of specific persons, places, or things; *proper adjectives* are formed from proper nouns.

Capitalize the names of specific people.

Jean McGillicuddy was elected class president.

The reports were read by George, Tom, and Alice.

Capitalize a title preceding a person's name or a title used in place of a person's name.

The class is taught by Professor Reilly.

You should ask Ms. Smith if you can leave.

Tell me, General, how should we meet that challenge?

Note: The words *President* and *Vice President* should be capitalized only when they precede a person's name. They may also be capitalized when they refer to the highest offices in the United States government.

We studied the speeches of President Lincoln.

In today's press conference the President spoke about the national budget.

Capitalize words that show family relationships when they precede a person's name or when they are used in place of a person's name.

I think that Uncle Chuck is my favorite uncle.

Along one side of the table sat Mother, Father, and my aunt.

Capitalize a title appearing with a person's name or the abbreviation for a person's name.

I went to see Dr. T. A. Henderson for my checkup.

The council was composed of Rev. Smith, Ms. Lindquist, and Tom Parker, Jr.

Exercise 3: Capitalizing Names and Titles

Write the following sentences, using capital letters wherever necessary. Underline the words or letters you capitalize.

Examples

a. Juan asked tina louise to dance the polka with him.
   Juan asked Tina Louise to dance the polka with him.

b. The former mayor of Minneapolis became senator hubert h. Humphrey and later vice president humphrey.
   The former mayor of Minneapolis became Senator Hubert H. Humphrey and later Vice President Humphrey.

1. Tina rodriguez was elected secretary of our club.

2. Sam asked miss tanaka to help him with his chemistry homework.

3. Lillian's favorite relative was always aunt mildred.

4. The health teacher, ms. garcia, invited dr. hemmings to talk about the importance of dental hygiene.

5. The best English teacher at the university was professor hank catchem.

6. The national reporters always attend press conferences called by the president.

7. Does uncle jack live in Anaconda, Montana, with cousin mary alice?

8. We had expected mother to invite senator reese to dinner, but we were shocked when we saw several other senators as well.

9. Frank ryan, jr., is not as famous as his father.

10. The president of our class, carey massey, will give a report on plans for the picnic.

Capitalize the names of specific places.

On our trip to Europe, we visited England, France, and Spain.

My aunt lives on the corner of Park Avenue and Third Street in Geneva, Ohio.

Note: The names of compass directions are not capitalized unless they are part of the name of a specific region or of an address.

We have traveled through the Northeast and stayed in northern Vermont.

Many people from the East and the Midwest travel south for the winter.

Turn west on Prairie and drive one block to 700 South Seventh Street.

Capitalize the names of languages and proper adjectives formed from the names of specific places.

Most students in our school speak only English, but some also speak Chinese, Japanese, or Spanish.

During our European trip we didn't eat any French fries or Swiss cheese.

Capitalize the names of buildings, monuments, institutions, businesses, organizations, and their abbreviations.

In Washington, D.C., we saw the White House, the Washington Monument, and the National Air and Space Museum.

Last week the Chicago Symphony Orchestra performed on the campus of Ohio Wesleyan University.

Investigators for the NLRB are looking into the strike by the AFL-CIO against TWA.

Note: The abbreviations *A.D., B.C., A.M.,* and *P.M.* are capitalized, but *am*, *fm*, and abbreviations for measurements *(kg, ft., sec.)* are not.

Capitalize the names of planets, stars, and other heavenly bodies.

For most of this decade, Neptune will be farther from the sun than Pluto.

During our study of the Milky Way, we learned about the path of Halley's comet.

Note: The words *sun*, *moon*, and *earth* are seldom capitalized. They are never capitalized when they follow the word *the*.

The sun is a major source of energy.

The moon is earth's only satellite.

Exercise 4: *Capitalizing Place Names*

Write the following sentences, using capital letters wherever necessary. Underline the words you capitalize.

Examples

a. On our vacation we visited indianapolis, indiana, and louisville, kentucky.
   On our vacation we visited Indianapolis, Indiana, and Louisville, Kentucky.

b. Many of the people in our neighborhood speak arabic as well as english.
   Many of the people in our neighborhood speak Arabic as well as English.

1. Mother was born in kalispell, montana, while Father was born in baltimore, maryland.

2. In her third year of college, Cindy studied french, spanish, and norwegian.

3. Sarah and Harriet walked from the essex hotel to the lincoln memorial.

4. While living in the southwest, Wilma learned to speak navaho, ute, and apache.

5. Many science fiction writers have composed fictional accounts of life on mars, but scientists say that the earth is the only planet capable of supporting life in our solar system.

6. The job of translating at the united nations is one of the most demanding in the world.

7. Miriam discovered the joys of french perfume and british woolens when her family visited europe.

8. Leaving portland, maine, at dawn, we drove west for three days before we reached southern california.

9. If you can locate the big dipper in the sky, you'll always be able to find your way.

10. In china, the city of peking is located in the northeast; the city of kwangchow (formerly called canton) is located in the southeast.

Capitalize the names of races, nationalities, and religions.

Paul is Catholic, and Alice is Jewish.

Our school has many South American and Asian students.

Capitalize words referring to holy books, including the Bible and the Koran, to parts of holy books, and to the Deity.

The Koran is the sacred text of Islam.

People of different religions praise God in different ways.

Muhammad was visited by Allah in the desert.

Note: When you refer to the gods of ancient mythology, do not capitalize the word *god* but do capitalize the individual names.

Some of the gods were concerned about the trouble between Athena and Zeus.

Capitalize the names of months, days of the week, and holidays.

I will arrive on Monday, November 4, 1982.

Last year Christmas and Hanukkah fell on the same day.

Note: The names of the seasons (spring, summer, fall, winter) are not normally capitalized.

Capitalize the names of historical periods and movements.

The debtors' prisons during the Industrial Revolution were similar to those in the Dark Ages.

The Restoration followed the reign of Oliver Cromwell.

Capitalize the names of special events.

The Superbowl is played every year, while the Olympic Games are held every four years.

We attended both the Louisiana State Fair and Chicagofest.

Exercise 5: *Using Capital Letters*

Write the following sentences, using capital letters wherever necessary. Underline the words you capitalize.

Examples

---

a. Marion , a protestant, but his uncle is a catholic.
Marion is a Protestant, but his uncle is a Catholic.

b. If you cook dinner on new year's day, I'll cook on thanksgiving day.
If you cook dinner on New Year's Day, I'll cook on Thanksgiving Day.

1. The asian countries of ceylon and malaysia produce wonderful tea.

2. The bible says that god turned Lot's wife into a pillar of salt.

3. Mother has promised to visit us on february 14 (saint valentine's day).

4. The stone age was the period when stone tools and utensils were first used.

5. The indiana state fair is an event that you shouldn't miss.

6. Some of the roman emperors (augustus, for example) were declared to be gods after they died.

7. Traveling on european trains is much more pleasant than traveling on american trains.

8. On memorial day (the last monday in may) we honor our nation's war dead.

9. The war between the states ended at appomattox on april 9, 1365.

10. The world series decides the best baseball team in the country.

Capitalize the names of school subjects when they are formed from a proper noun, are followed by a number, or name a special course.

Freshmen are allowed to take English, Spanish, art, American history, home economics, or Latin.

I have decided to take Chemistry IV, biology, Math 401, physical education, or a course called Heroes and Heroines.

Note: Most nouns that are followed by a number or a letter designation are generally capitalized.

Some of the teachers from School District 308 will be meeting in Room 17.

Please read Chapter 14 and Chapter 15 in Unit III.

Capitalize the names of political parties (but not the word *party*) and the names of government agencies, departments, and bureaus.

Many members of the Democratic party voted for the Republican Presidential candidate in the last election.

The Energy Research and Development Administration is a part of the Department of Energy.

Capitalize the names of specific ships, trains, airplanes, and spacecraft.

The U.S.S. *Constitution* is, perhaps, the country's most famous battleship.

Many Boeing 747s now cross the Atlantic Ocean in a fraction of the time it took the *Spirit of St. Louis*.

Capitalize the name of a specific product—that is, its trade name, brand name, or trademark.

Words that name a general class of products or a specific product are not capitalized.

The brand of aspirin we use is Filmore's Aspirin.

The only colas that this store carries are Foamy Cola and Poppa-Cola.

Capitalize the first word and each noun in the salutation of a letter. Only the first word in the closing of a letter is capitalized.

Dear Mrs. Baxter,   Sincerely yours,   My dear Cousin,

Capitalize the pronoun *I* and the formal interjection *O*.

This is a matter that I will discuss later.

We praise thee, O most wondrous of wonders.

Note: The common interjection *oh* is not capitalized unless it appears at the beginning of a sentence.

The hours went by but, oh, so slowly.

Exercise 6: Using Capital Letters

Write each of the following sentences, using capital letters wherever necessary. Underline the words you capitalize.

Examples

---

a. Teddy has signed up for the following courses: algebra I, drafting, english literature, and physical education.
   Teddy has signed up for the following courses: Algebra I, drafting, English literature, and physical education.

b. The republican party seldom receives many votes in the city of Chicago.
   The Republican party seldom receives many votes in the city of Chicago.

1. Rosaria did very well in typing I and biology, but she has had problems with american history and health.

2. Ms. Washington works for the department of health and human services.

3. The world's first atomic-powered submarine was the u.s.s. *nautilus.*

4. The jumbo jet in which i was riding cruised high above the rocky mountains, and they were a beautiful sight!

5. Cousin Betty's pet store sells only kitty's pride brand cat food.

6. The letter began impersonally, "dear occupant" and closed with "very best wishes, The Management."

7. Mr. Christian led the mutiny that took place on the h.m.s. *bounty*.

8. James Earl Carter, Jr., the democratic candidate in the 1976 presidential election, promised to streamline many government departments and bureaus.

9. Ms. Everett teaches biology II in room 111, but she teaches chemistry in room 221.

10. In chapter 3 and the following chapter we learned that it is dangerous to fly light planes into electrical storms.

Review: Capitalization

Write the following sentences, using capital letters wherever necessary. Underline the words you capitalize.

Example

a. At the democratic national convention in new york city during the summer of 1980, president jimmy carter accepted the nomination of the democratic party.

At the Democratic National Convention in New York City during the summer of 1980, President Jimmy Carter accepted the nomination of the Democratic party.

1. Dear uncle larry, to get to our house, turn left from highway 62 onto south boulevard and continue south until you reach poplar st. Our house is on the corner. good luck, jenny.

2. In one afternoon during our visit to chicago, we heard people on the street speaking italian, hebrew, and chinese!

3. My grandfather says that the bien brand of french cream cheese is the best.

4. The zoroastrian religion was the religion of the persians before they converted to islam, a religion started by the prophet muhammad in the seventh century a.d.

5. To the south a beautiful constellation called the southern cross is visible.

6. This year i want to take algebra, biology 101, spanish, social studies, english literature, and, oh, the new course called people and their institutions.

7. Please announce that the lincoln high history club will meet after school in room 303 to discuss the french revolution and its effect on current french culture.

8. In greek mythology the goddess of wisdom is athena, and her roman counterpart is called minerva while the greek god apollo was sometimes called Phoebus.

9. On the first tuesday of each month, except for december, the aurora businesswomen's league holds a meeting at the regency hotel on peachtree street.

10. *Glamorous glynnis* was the name that the famous pilot chuck yeager gave to his jet.

11. The federal bureau of investigation, or fbi, attained great power under the direction of j. edgar hoover during and after world war II.

12. When the astronauts landed on the moon in *apollo 11,* they watched the sun rise over the earth.

13. The calgary stampede with its exciting chuck wagon races is a popular annual rodeo that takes place each july in alberta, canada.

14. The local republicans wanted to create a special agency for pollution control, but the public works department remains in charge.

15. During the second world war the allied forces in europe used a supply train called the *redball express* to transport equipment to the troops.

16. The company that makes jack and the beanstalk beans uses a picture of a boy climbing a beanstalk as its trademark.

17. The high school basketball elimination games are called the sweet sixteen because sixteen teams participate.

18. Last winter we went to the chinese new year celebration in san francisco's chinatown.

19. The planet venus is the brightest planet we have in our solar system.

20. The bible, in the book of genesis, says that god created the world in seven days.

Writing Focus: *Improving Capitalization in Writing*

In English, many words and word groups are capitalized. The convention of capitalization helps both writers and readers recognize the beginnings of sentences, the titles of books, and the names of specific people, places, and things. Using correct capitalization will help keep your writing clear and precise.

Assignment: *A Trip of a Lifetime*

Imagine that oil has been discovered on your property. Now that money is no object, you decide to see something of the world. You begin to plan a trip that will last six months. Where will you start? What cities, states, countries, or continents will you visit? What landmarks will you see? Will you take anyone with you? Will you visit anyone?

Write one or more paragraphs telling about your proposed trip. Include details about the places, sights, and people you intend to see. Present your itinerary in chronological order. Write for your classmates, telling them as much as you can about your upcoming journey. Your work will be evaluated for correct capitalization.

Use the steps on the following page to complete this assignment.

A. Prewriting

Imagine having enough time and money to travel extensively throughout the world. Make a list of all the places you have ever thought about visiting. Don't stop to consider the practicalities involved in such a long journey. Just let your imagination and desire guide your choices. Add the names of any sights or people you would like to visit. When your list is complete, go back over it and begin to plan your itinerary. You might use a globe or atlas to help you decide the best way to proceed.

B. Writing

Use your list to write one or more paragraphs telling about your trip of a lifetime. Don't just list the places, sights, and persons involved. Present your plans in a conversational, detailed way. Help your readers visualize your journey and be as excited about it as you are. As you write, pay particular attention to correct capitalization.

C. Postwriting

Revise your first draft using the following checklist.

1. Is my work an interesting account of a proposed journey rather than a list of places, sights, and people?

2. Have I included details to make the places, sights, and people seem real?

3. Have I used capital letters correctly?

Edit your work using the Proofreader's Checklist at the back of the book. If appropriate, share your paragraphs with your classmates. Draw a map and plot your journey on it.

4
Language Resources

26 Using the Library

Since libraries have a vast amount of material, they need an efficient system for organizing their resources. Most libraries use one of two systems to organize and arrange books: the *Dewey decimal system* or the *Library of Congress system*. The Dewey decimal system, which was developed by the American librarian Melvil Dewey, is the older of the two systems and is used by most school libraries today.

This chapter explains the Dewey decimal system and the Library of Congress system. The chapter also discusses the card catalogue, reference books, and other resources in a library.

The Dewey Decimal System

The *Dewey decimal system* organizes the library's collection of nonfiction (books about real people and real events) into ten subject areas. The following are the ten subject areas and the range of numbers assigned to each.

000–099 General Works:	Includes encyclopedias, atlases, periodicals, book lists, and other reference books.
100–199 Philosophy:	Includes the fields of psychology, conduct, and personality.
200–299 Religion:	Bibles and other religious texts; theology books; and mythology.
300–399 Social Sciences:	Includes civics, economics, education, etiquette, fairy tales, folklore, legends, government, and law.
400–499 Language:	Grammars and dictionaries of different languages, including English.
500–599 Science:	Includes animals, astronomy, biology, botany, chemistry, geology, general science, mathematics, anthropology, and physics.

600–699 Technology:	Includes agriculture, aviation, business, engineering, health, home economics, manual training, and television.
700–799 The Arts:	Includes movies, painting, photography, sculpture, recreation, and sports.
800–899 Literature:	Includes poetry, drama, essays, criticism, and history of literature.
900–999 History:	Includes geography, travel, history, and collective biography.

Each subject area is subdivided into smaller categories. For example, *300–399*, the Social Sciences, is subdivided as follows:

300	Social Sciences
310	Statistical methods and statistics
320	Political science
330	Economics
340	Law
350	Public administration
360	Welfare and recreation
370	Education
380	Commerce
390	Customs and folklore

Because decimals are used to make each subdivision more and more precise, the system is named the Dewey *decimal* system. For example, the *320* subdivision for political science is further divided as follows:

320	Political science
320.9	History of political science
320.942	History of political science in England
320.954	History of political science in India

Each number indicates a category in which a book belongs and is called *Dewey decimal classification number*.

Exercise 1: Using Category Names and Numbers

Assume that you are interested in locating the library books listed on the following page. Using the category names and numbers in the preceding section, decide the range of numbers you would look under to find each book. Write the numbers on a sheet of paper.

Example

a. *A Child's Book of Anthropology*
   500–599

1. *An Introduction to English Literature*

2. *The Complete Book of Baseball*

3. *Greek Philosophy Before Socrates*

4. *A Career in Agriculture*

5. *Encyclopaedia Britannica*

6. *A Dictionary of Old English and Old Norse*

7. *Mathematical Games for a Rainy Afternoon*

8. *Do-It-Yourself Sculpture and Welding*

9. *A History of the Punic Wars*

10. *Psychology for High School Students*

The Call Number

The *call number* is a book's individual number, one that is not shared with any other book in the library. The Dewey decimal classification number is the first part of the call number, followed by the *author number*. The *author number* is made up of the first letter of the author's last name and a unique number attached to that book. Finally, the author number may be followed by the first letter of the first major word in the title. These numbers make up the book's *call number*, as the following example shows.

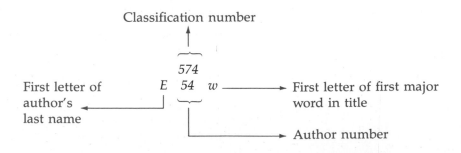

Biographies and Autobiographies

Biographies are books about the lives of real people. *Autobiographies* are the writers' lives in their own words. Under the Dewey decimal system biographies and autobiographies are treated in a special way. A book combining the biographies of two or more people is called a *collective biography*. The call number for collective biographies consists of the number *920* and the first letter of the author's or editor's last name. For example, a collective biography of American Presidents edited by John Dyer would have the call number $\frac{920}{D}$.

Individual biographies and autobiographies are usually kept in a separate section of the library. They may be assigned the letter *B*, with the first letter of the last name of the book's subject appearing under the letter *B*. The call number for a biography of Abraham Lincoln would be $\frac{B}{L}$.

In some libraries individual biographies and autobiographies are assigned the number *921*. Under the *921* is the first letter of the last name of the book's subject. Thus, a biography of Abraham Lincoln would, in some libraries, have the call number $\frac{921}{L}$.

Fiction

Books of fiction are kept in a separate section and are not classified according to the Dewey decimal system. Instead, they are arranged alphabetically by the author's last name and then by his or her first name. If there is more than one book by the same author, those books are arranged alphabetically by the first major word in the title.

Exercise 2: Arranging Books by Authors' Names

Assume that the library at your school has a biography of each of the following famous people. Make a list of these people, placing the names in the same order in which they would be found on the shelf.

1. Thomas Jefferson
2. Sarah Boone
3. Mary McLeod Bethune
4. Ernest Hemingway
5. Thomas Paine
6. Anne Bradstreet
7. Harriet Tubman
8. Georgia O'Keeffe
9. Clare Boothe Luce
10. Samuel Rayburn

The Library of Congress System

The *Library of Congress system*, a method of organizing books that is newer than the Dewey decimal system, is now used by many school libraries. This system separates knowledge into twenty classes, designated by letters of the alphabet:

A	General Works	N	Fine Arts
B	Philosophy	P	Language and Literature
C	History	Q	Science
D	General History	R	Medicine
E–F	American History	S	Agriculture
G	Geography, Anthropology, Recreation	T	Technology
		U	Military Science
H	Social Sciences	V	Naval Science
J	Political Science	Z	Library Science
K	Law		
L	Education		
M	Music		

Categories within each class are indicated by the addition of a second letter. The *D* class, standing for *General History*, for example, is divided into these subclasses:

D	General History
DA	Great Britain
DE	Mediterranean Region Greco-Roman World
DP	Spain, Portugal
DS	Asia
DT	Africa
DX	Gypsies

Categories are made more precise by a number that follows the letters, indicating the class and subclass. For example, the following call number for the book *Worlds Within Worlds* by Thomas C. Emmel is a Library of Congress call number.

QH308.2
E48

In the Library of Congress system, most biographies are catalogued under the letters *CT*. Fiction is classified under *P* and then put into subclasses according to the original language in which it was written.

The Card Catalogue

T he *card catalogue*, the guide for finding books in the library, is a series of cards, filed alphabetically in drawers. These drawers are arranged in a cabinet according to the headings of the cards they contain. For example, the headings of five drawers in the card catalogue might be these:

A–As   B–Do   R–Sa   So–Th   Ti–Z

From time to time, as cards are added or taken away, the headings will change.

In the card catalogue you will find four types of cards: the *author* card, the *title* card, the *subject* card, and the *see* or *see also* card.

The Author Card

The heading for the *author card* is the author's name, with the last name first, then the first name, then the middle name or initial. If the author's last name begins with *Mc*, as in *McCluskey*, the card will be filed as though the name were spelled *MacCluskey*. Under the author's name you will find the book's title. If the author has written more than one book, there will be a separate card for each book, arranged alphabetically by the first major word in the title. The call number of nonfiction books is in the upper left-hand corner of the card. Using the author card, you can locate a book even when you do not know the title.

```
944.025
T888

Tuchman, Barbara Wertheim.
    A distant mirror : the calamitous 14th century / Barbara W.
Tuchman. — 1st trade ed. — New York . Knopf, 1978.

    xx, 677 p., [20] leaves of plates : ill.; 25 cm.

    Bibliography: p. [599]-617.
    Includes index.
    ISBN 0-394-40026-7 : $15.95


    1. France—History—14th century.  2. Coucy, Enguerrand de, 1340-1397.
3. France—Nobility—Biography.  I. Title.
    DC97.5.T82  1978          944.025              78-5985
                                                   MARC

Library of Congress          78
```

The Title Card

The heading for a *title card* is the title of the book. A title card is filed alphabetically by the first major word in the title. *A*, *an*, and *the* are not considered major words. The pronoun *I* is, however. For example, the book *A Bell for Adano* is filed under *B* for *Bell*. The book *I Never Promised You a Rose Garden* is filed under *I*. The author's name is directly under the title of the book, and the call number for nonfiction books is in the upper left-hand corner of the card.

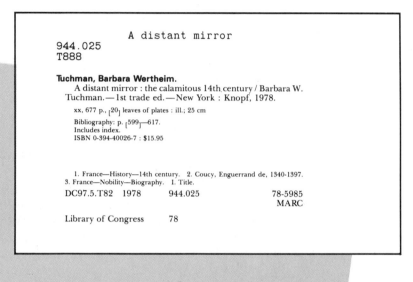

```
                        A distant mirror
          944.025
          T888

          Tuchman, Barbara Wertheim.
              A distant mirror : the calamitous 14th century / Barbara W.
          Tuchman.— 1st trade ed.— New York : Knopf, 1978.

              xx, 677 p., [20] leaves of plates : ill.; 25 cm

              Bibliography: p. [599]—617.
              Includes index.
              ISBN 0-394-40026-7 : $15.95


              1. France—History—14th century.   2. Coucy, Enguerrand de, 1340-1397.
          3. France—Nobility—Biography.   I. Title.
          DC97.5.T82   1978        944.025                    78-5985
                                                                 MARC

          Library of Congress        78
```

The Subject Card

The heading of the *subject card* is the general subject of the book. Arthur C. Clarke's book *The Challenge of the Sea*, for example, is listed under *Ocean*. Many books are listed under more than one heading, but there should be at least one subject card for every nonfiction book in the library. When you are writing a report or when you have a special interest in a particular area, these cards help you locate books on your subject, even when you do not know authors and titles. Directly under the subject heading you will find the author's name and the book's title. The call number of nonfiction books is in the upper left-hand corner of the card.

```
        FRANCE – HISTORY – 14th CENTURY

944.025
T888

Tuchman, Barbara Wertheim.
     A distant mirror : the calamitous 14th century / Barbara W.
Tuchman.—1st trade ed.—New York : Knopf, 1978.
     xx, 677 p., [20] leaves of plates: ill.; 25 cm.
     Bibliography: p. [599]-617.
     Includes index.
     ISBN 0-394-40026-7 : $15.95



     1. France—History—14th century.   2. Coucy, Enguerrand de, 1340-1397.
3. France—Nobility—Biography.   I. Title.
DC97.5.T82   1978        944.025              78-5985
                                               MARC

Library of Congress        78
```

Each of the preceding three cards lists the author, title, and call number of the book, if the book is nonfiction. These three types of cards also give you such important information as the place of publication, the publisher, and the copyright date of the book. They may also tell you the number of pages in a book, whether the book has illustrations or maps, and whether the illustrations are in color. Sometimes, you will find a summary of the book's contents at the bottom of the card.

The See and See also Cards

The *see* and *see also* cards are cross-references that refer you to another card or cards with the information you need. For example, the real name of the famous baseball player known as Babe Ruth was George Herman Ruth. If you were to look up a subject card for *Ruth, Babe,* you would find a card with the following information:

Ruth, Babe

see Ruth, George Herman

The *see also* card gives additional headings under which you can find information about a subject.

Exercise 3: Using the Card Catalogue

Assume that you are looking up the authors, titles, and subjects on the next page in the card catalogue and that each of the boxes below represents one drawer of the catalogue. On a sheet of paper, list each drawer as a separate column and list the authors, subjects, and titles that belong in that column.

Example

Drawers

A-As	B-Do	R-Sa	So-Ti

Subjects, Authors, Titles

Sailing	*A Bell for Adano*
Animal Stories	*The Red Badge of Courage*
A. Conan Doyle	Jonathan Swift

A-As	B-Do	R-Sa	So-Ti

A-As	B-Do	R-Sa	So-Ti
Animal Stories	A Bell for Adano	The Red Badge of Courage	Jonathan Swift
	A. Conan Doyle	Sailing	

Drawers

A-Bo	Br-Chi	Chr-Da	H-J	P-R	S-Th

Subjects, Authors, Titles

Samuel Taylor Coleridge	*An Introduction to Bowling*
Agatha Christie	*I Always Wanted to Be Somebody*
Aviation	*Profiles in Courage*
Heidi	*A Tale of Two Cities*
The Pigman	Animals

Exercise 4: Using Author Cards

Look in the card catalogue of your library and list any books by the following authors. If there are no cards filed for an author, write *none* by that number on your paper.

1. Arthur Conan Doyle
2. Isaac Asimov
3. Robert Louis Stevenson
4. Charlotte Brontë
5. Emily Dickinson
6. James Baldwin
7. Willa Cather
8. Rachel Carson
9. James Thurber
10. Maya Angelou

Exercise 5: Using Subject Cards

Look in the card catalogue of your library and list any books on the following subjects. If there are no books listed on the subject, write *none* by that number on your paper.

1. Baseball
2. Etiquette
3. Automobile repair
4. The Revolutionary War
5. Slavery
6. Running
7. Special effects in films
8. The moon
9. Astronauts
10. Camping

Finding Information in Magazines and Periodicals

One guide that helps you find information in magazines and periodicals is a series of books called the *Readers' Guide to Periodical Literature*, found in the reference section of your library. The books are published twice a month, except in July and August when only one volume is published.

Because most magazines are published weekly, every other week, or monthly, they are likely to be your best source of up-to-date information. The *Readers' Guide* serves as a card catalogue to help you locate articles, stories, and poems in magazines and periodicals.

The *Readers' Guide* is organized in much the same way as the card catalogue. Information in this reference series is organized alphabetically by author and by subject. Author entries list magazine and periodical articles according to the last name of the person who wrote them; subject entries list the articles according to the subject treated in the article. Only stories from magazines are listed by their titles.

Cross-referencing is widely used in the *Readers' Guide,* as you can see in the sample column on page 611.

Under the subject heading "WILDLIFE Conservation," two articles are listed. However, preceding the information about the two articles is a "See also" reference. This reference tells you which additional places you can look to find more information about the subject. In this instance "See also" means that for other articles you should look under the headings "Bird sanctuaries" and "Helicopters in wildlife conservation."

Under the author entry "WHITE, Timothy" is a "See" reference. This reference tells you to look under the heading "Rather, Dan" for complete information about that article.

Abbreviation Key to the Readers' Guide

To save space the *Readers' Guide* contains many abbreviations, the meanings of which are listed in two sections at the beginning of each book. The section titled *Abbreviations of Periodicals Indexed* lists the abbreviations for the names of periodicals. The section titled *Abbreviations* lists the meanings of other abbreviations used in the entries. By using the information in these sections, you can translate abbreviations in the entries into readable English sentences. The following subject entry has been "translated."

> WIGS
> From chemotherapy patients to Carol Channing, no one's bigger in wigs than Ralph Molliea. C. Burns. il pors People 15:77 + Ap 6 '81

An article titled "From Chemotherapy Patients to Carol Channing, No One's Bigger in Wigs Than Ralph Molliea" by C. Burns can be found on page 77 (continued on later pages in the same issue) of Volume 15 (April 6, 1981) of *People* magazine. The article is an illustrated portrait of Ralph Molliea.

Author entries may be similarly translated.

> WICKERS, David
> Growing food without a garden. il Flower & Gard 25:62-3 + F/Mr '81

An illustrated article titled "Growing Food Without a Garden" by David Wickers can be found on pages 62–63 (continued on later pages of the same issue) of Volume 25 (February/March, 1981) of *Flower and Garden* magazine.

WHITE, Timothy
  (int) See Rather, Dan. Hard act to follow
WICK, Charles Z.
  Odyssey that led Wick to Washington. por Bus W p44-5 Mr 23 '81 *
WICKERS, David
  Growing food without a garden. il Flower & Gard 25:62-3 + F/Mr '81
WIGS
  From chemotherapy patients to Carol Channing: no one's bigger in
    wigs than Ralph Molliea. C. Burns. il pors People 15:77 + Ap 6 '81
WILD burros. See Burros, Wild
WILD duck [drama] See Ibsen, Henrik
WILD rice
    See also
  Cooking—Wild rice
WILDLIFE   Africa
    See also
  Gorillas
                            Rwanda
  Imperiled mountain gorilla. D. Fossey. il map Nat Geog 159:500-23 Ap
    '81
WILDLIFE conservation
    See also
  Bird sanctuaries
  Helicopters in wildlife conservation
  To the rescue! P. Steinhart. il Nat Wildlife 19:4-11 F/Mr '81
  Wildlife [Environmental Quality Index] Nat Wildlife 19:30 F/Mr '81
                            Florida
  From the jaws of death [clearing loggerhead turtles out of Canaveral
    Channel, Fla.] J. Rudloe. il map Sports Illus 54:60-4 + Mr 23 '81
WILDLIFE introduction. See Animal introduction
WILDLIFE rescue. See Wildlife conservation
WILDLIFE sanctuaries
    See also
  Bird sanctuaries
WILEY, William Thomas
  Lament for a Zen cowboy. T. Albright. Art News 80:191 2 + Mr '81 *
WILL, George F.
  [Column] See issues of Newsweek
WILLEY, Margaret
  Missing mother [story] il Redbook 156:27 + Mr '81
WILLIAMS, Kit
  Fairy tale adults can dig. L. Langway and L. Donosky. il por Newsweek
    97:87 Mr 30 '81
WILLIAMS, Stanley
  Quality of the moment: Stanley Williams. T. Tobias. il pors Dance Mag
    55:74-83 Mr '81 *
WILLIAMS, Sylvia
  Sylvia Williams makes it big. S. Gayle. il por Essence 11:15-16 + Mr '81
WILLIAMS Electronics (firm)

  Tilt? [Xcor International's spinoff] M. Barnfather. il Forbes 127:42 Mr
    2 '81
WILLS
  Taxes and wills [dancers] M. Horosko. il Dance Mag 55:96 + Mr '81
WILSON, Janet
  Philadelphia has to be discovered. il Art News 80:160-5 Mr '81
WILSON, John Anthony Burgess. See Burgess, Anthony, pseud
WILSON, Paul
  Jingling all the way to the bank. il pors Ebony 36:81-2 + Mr '81 *
WILSON, R.C.
  America's first woman scientist. il Mankind 6:33 + F '81
WINCHESTER rifles. See Rifles
WINDMILLS
  Wind energy: can it cut your utility bills? G. Erickson. il Bet Hom &
    Gard 59:25 + Mr '81
WINDOW curtains and draperies. See Curtains and draperies
WINDOW greenhouses. See Greenhouses
WINDOW shades
  Window shades that change your point of view. il Glamour 79:214 Ap
    '81
WINDSHEAR monitors. See Air navigation—Aids and devices
WINDSURFING. See Surfing
WINFIELD, Dave
  Yankees in Florida—all this and Winfield too. V. Ziegel il por N Y
    14:63-4 Mr 23 '81 *
WINKFIELD, Trevor
  Trevor Winkfield at Blue Mountain. C. North. il Art in Am 69:131 Mr
    '81 *
WINTER
    See also
  Snowstorms
  My own West [excerpt from Winter brothers] I. Doig. il Blair &
    Ketchums 8:58-9 Mr '81
WINTER flying. See Aviation—Winter flying

Once you have found a promising article, you must then find out whether or not your library has the publication in which it appears. If your library does not have a posted list of available magazines and journals, ask a librarian for help.

In some libraries older magazines may be available only on *microfilm* or *microfiche*, two types of film on which print is reduced and stored. If this is the case, ask your librarian how to find the issue you need and how to use the machine to read it.

Exercise 6: Translating the Abbreviations in Readers' Guide

Locate each of the following entries in the sample *Readers' Guide* column on page 611. Then, using the key to abbreviations found in the *Readers' Guide*, write each entry in sentence form.

1. WICK, Charles Z.
2. WILLS
3. WINDMILLS
4. WILDLIFE
   Rwanda
5. WILDLIFE conservation
   Florida

Exercise 7: Using the Readers' Guide

Using the *Readers' Guide* in your library, find at least one article on each of the following subjects. Copy down the entry and then write it in sentence form. Check also to see whether or not your library actually has the periodical for each of the articles that you find.

1. Ecology
2. Solar energy
3. Gas mileage in cars
4. Trains
5. Astrology
6. Nutrition
7. Sharks
8. Fire safety
9. Music
10. Congress

Finding Information in Pamphlets

Pamphlets are small books, usually only a few pages in length. They are published by the U.S. Government Printing Office, by businesses and industries, and by educational and religious organizations, on every topic from *Child care* to *Gardening* to *Automobile repair* to *How to start a small business*. Because they are brief and usually very specific, pamphlets are an excellent source of information. Your library's collection of pamphlets is probably kept in folders in a cabinet called a *vertical file*. Ask your librarian to help you find information in the vertical file.

Reference Books

Reference books are a source of specialized information. The *Readers' Guide to Periodical Literature* is a reference book, as are encyclopedias, dictionaries, atlases, and almanacs.

Reference books are normally kept in a special place in a library, called the *reference section*, and usually cannot be checked out. In some libraries a reference librarian works only with those books.

Encyclopedias

Encyclopedias contain relatively short articles on any number of subjects. Because encyclopedias treat so many subjects, however, the information will usually be very general. An encyclopedia will give you a basic idea of your subject, but this reading should be followed by a search for more specific information in books and periodicals.

Most encyclopedias are made up of many volumes. Like the drawers of a card catalogue, each volume of most encyclopedia sets has letters on the spine to indicate the subjects covered in that particular volume. A volume labeled *A–An* would have articles on the *aardvark*, a mammal from Africa, as well as on the *antelope*.

Because most subjects are treated in several articles in different volumes of the encyclopedia, some way of listing the articles by subject is necessary. The *index*, which is usually a separate volume, is an alphabetical listing of all the subjects in every volume. By checking the index, you can be certain that you have found all the information in the encyclopedia on your subject.

Since encyclopedias are not revised every year, the information in them can quickly become dated, so most encyclopedias also have *yearbooks* for each year after the original publication date, which help keep the encyclopedia current.

The encyclopedias most commonly found in school libraries include the following titles.

Collier's Encyclopedia   *Encyclopaedia Britannica*
Encyclopedia Americana   *World Book Encyclopedia*

One-volume encyclopedias contain far less information than the many volumes in the preceding sets of encyclopedias. However, since one-volume encyclopedias provide a large amount of information in a small space, they are especially convenient for checking facts and figures. A well-known one-volume encyclopedia is *The Concise Columbia Encyclopedia.*

Exercise 8: Using an Encyclopedia

Look up one of the following subjects or one of your own choosing in the index of an encyclopedia in your library (except a one-volume encyclopedia). From the list of entries about your subject, select two. As you read them, make notes about the information you find. Then write a one- or two-paragraph summary of what you learn.

1. Olympic games
2. Astrology
3. Mandan Indians
4. Women's suffrage
5. Druids

6. Basques
7. Solar energy
8. Icebreaker
9. Gabriela Mistral
10. Passover

Dictionaries of Synonyms

Dictionaries of synonyms can help you increase your vocabulary and make your writing more precise. When you cannot think of the exact word you need, you can use a dictionary of synonyms to find a word with just the right meaning. However, you must be careful in using this dictionary, for no two words have exactly the same meaning. You cannot substitute *condominium* for *apartment*, for example, just because you think the longer word sounds better. You must use words that give as nearly as possible the exact meaning you need.

Roget's Thesaurus is a commonly used dictionary of synonyms in which words are grouped into large classes and smaller categories. *Abstract relations* is a class; *time, organic matter,* and *communication of ideas* are categories. Each category is divided into smaller numbered categories, as you can see in the sample entry from *Roget's Thesaurus* on page 615.

To find a synonym in *Roget's Thesaurus*, locate the word in the index, where you will find the number of the category in which the word will be found. Categories are arranged in numerical order throughout the book, and the numbers of the categories on each page are at the top outer corner of the page. For example, suppose you want to find a synonym for the word *grandeur. Grandeur*, in category *904 (904.5)*, is followed by thirty synonyms. The ones in **boldface** type will also be listed under their own headings. Words that are not used in Standard English are identified as *coll.* (colloquial) or *slang.*

What are the synonyms for the word *grandeur*? Which of those words is not used in formal English?

Exercise 9: *Using* Roget's Thesaurus

Select five words from the following list and look up each in *Roget's Thesaurus* or in another dictionary of synonyms. On a sheet of paper, write out five synonyms listed for each word. Indicate when the synonyms are not used in Standard English by writing out *coll.* (colloquial) or *slang* or whatever other term the dictionary uses.

1. superiority
2. product
3. clothing
4. travel
5. food

6. plunge
7. strength
8. death
9. fragrance
10. silence

904. OSTENTATION

.1 NOUNS **ostentation**, ostentatiousness, ostent; **pretentiousness, pretension, pretense**; loftiness, lofty affectations.

.2 **pretensions**, vain pretensions; **airs**, lofty airs, vaporing, highfalutin *or* highfaluting ways [informal], side, swank [informal].

.3 **showiness, flashiness**, flamboyance, panache, dash, jazziness [slang], jauntiness, sportiness [informal], gaiety, glitter, glare, dazzle, dazzlingness; extravagan/a; **gaudiness**, gaudery, **tawdriness**, meretriciousness; gorgeousness, colorfulness; **garishness**, loudness [informal], **blatancy**, flagrancy, shamelessness, brazenness, luridness, extravagance, sensationalism, obtrusiveness, vulgarness, crudeness, extravagation.

.4 **display, show, demonstration**, manifestation, **exhibition, parade**, *étalage* [Fr]; **pageantry**, pageant, **spectacle**; vaunt, fanfaronade, blazon, flourish, flaunt, flaunting; daring, brilliancy, éclat, bravura, flair; dash *or* splash *or* splurge [all informal]; figure; **exhibitionism**, showing-off; theatrics, histrionics, dramatics, staginess; false front, sham 616.3.

.5 **grandeur**, grandness, grandiosity, **magnificence**, gorgeousness, **splendor**, splendidness, splendiferousness, resplendence, brilliance, glory; nobility, proudness, **state, stateliness, majesty**; impressiveness, imposingness; **sumptuousness, elegance, elaborateness, lavishness, luxuriousness**; ritziness *or* poshness *or* plushness *or* swankness *or* swankiness [all informal]; **luxury**, barbaric *or* Babylonian splendor.

.6 **pomp**, circumstance, pride, **state**, solemnity 871, formality 646; **pomp and circumstance**, "pride, pomp, and circumstance" [Shakespeare]; heraldry, "trump and solemn heraldry" [Coleridge].

Entry for "ostentation" (pp. 706–708) from *Roget's Thesaurus*, Fourth Edition (T. Y. Crowell). Copyright © 1977 by Harper & Row, Publishers, Inc. Reprinted by permission of Harper & Row, Publishers, Inc.

27 Using the Dictionary

Few people devote thirty-five years of their lives to a task, but James Murray, the son of a Scottish tailor, was one man who did. Almost from birth James Murray was captivated by words. By the time he was eighteen months old, he knew the letters of the alphabet. He never lost his love of words, although at various times in his life he was a schoolteacher, a farm worker, and a bank clerk. At age forty-two James Murray had such a widespread reputation as a language scholar that he was offered the job of editing the *Oxford English Dictionary*. Although he had other people working with him, the main responsibility for the dictionary was his, and his determination to make this dictionary the best ever published meant committing the rest of his life to the work. When Murray died in 1915, he had spent almost every waking hour of thirty-five years working to compile the world's longest and most complete dictionary. In 1929 this massive work, the *Oxford English Dictionary*, was published in its then complete form of ten volumes, a total of 15,487 pages.

James Murray's contribution to the study of language was an important one. Earlier compilers of dictionaries listed only what they believed to be the best words of the language. Murray, however, insisted on listing all the words in the English language, thus showing that language is something shaped not only by a few people but by all who speak and write.

Most people know that definitions and spellings can be found in dictionaries, but many people do not know about the many other uses of dictionaries. In this chapter you will read about the many kinds of information contained in dictionaries and about how to find and use that information.

Finding a Word in the Dictionary

The words listed in the dictionary are organized in alphabetical order. To help you find the word you want, two *guide words*, the first and last words on the page, are listed at the top of each page. The following example shows guide words.

relic   1200   **rely**

Words that come between *relic* and *rely* are found on page 1200 of this dictionary. These include such words as *relief, relieve, religious, relish,* and *reluctant*.

To find a word, turn to the part of the dictionary that lists words beginning with the same letter as your word. Then find the page with your word by looking at the guide words.

Exercise 1: Using Guide Words

The major skills you need to find a word in the dictionary are alphabetizing and using guide words. For this exercise you are given sets of guide words and a list of twenty-four words. First, divide a sheet of paper into five columns, making each of the five sets of guide words a heading. (Each column of your paper is now like a page in the dictionary.) Next, alphabetize the list of words. Then list the words under the guide words where they would appear in a dictionary.

Example

a. **inarticulate–incense**
inaugural
inboard
Inca
incapacity
incarcerate
incarnate

Guide Words

1. **inlaid–innoxious**

2. **infective–influx**

3. **indoor–industrial**

4. **installment–instrument**

5. **invention–invisible**

Words

innkeeper	inferno	induct
instead	inventory	Indus
infinite	inning	instruct
invincible	instinct	invert
inner	infield	induction
infest	indulge	innards
instill	institute	instant
invest	inlet	inferior

Word Entries

Words listed in alphabetical order in the dictionary are called *main entry words*. Each main entry word is printed in **boldface** type and begins a space or two to the left of the column.

al·ba·tross (al′ba trôs′, -träs′) *n., pl.* **-tross′es, -tross′**: see PLURAL, II, D, 1 [altered, prob. after L. *albus*, white < Sp. *alcatraz*, lit., pelican < Port., pelican, orig. bucket < Ar. *al qādūs*, water container < Gr. *kados*, cask, jar; prob. < Heb. *kad*, water jug] **1.** any of several large, web-footed birds (family Diomedea) related to the petrel and found chiefly in the South Seas: they have long, narrow wings and a large, hooked beak in which, like the pelican, they were formerly reputed to carry water

The main entry word itself shows the correct spelling and syllabication (division into syllables). Following the main entry word is information about the word's pronunciation, usage, history, and meaning. This information, together with the main entry word, is the *main entry*.

Spelling

When a word has two or more spellings (*variant spellings*), all spellings are listed in the dictionary. Dictionaries do this in several ways.

Sometimes, when a word has two spellings, both spellings are listed as main entry words. In such cases both spellings are acceptable in Standard English.

the·a·ter, the·a·tre

Sometimes, the variant spellings follow the main word entry and are introduced by the abbreviation *also sp.* In this case the variant spellings are also correct but are used less often than the spelling of the main entry word.

Syllables

The main entry word also shows how a word is divided into syllables. Dictionaries divide words into syllables for two reasons: to indicate pronunciation and to indicate where a word should be divided at the end of a written line.

Syllables are usually indicated in main word entries with a raised dot. For example, a dictionary entry for the word *laryngitis* looks like this: **lar·yn·gi·tis.**

Laryngitis has four syllables: *lar, yn, gi,* and *tis.*

When you must divide a word at the end of a written line, divide it between syllables and use a hyphen to show the division.

The doctor told Vesna that her case of *laryn-*
gitis was the result of her playing in the snow.

Do not divide a word of only one syllable and do not divide a word in such a way as to leave only one letter on a line, even if the syllables are divided this way in a dictionary. The word *alone,* for example, is divided into the syllables *a* and *lone* but should not be divided at the end of a line.

Exercise 2: *Dividing Words into Syllables*

Look up the following words in your dictionary. On a sheet of paper, divide these words into syllables by placing a raised dot (·) between syllables. Place a slash mark (/), rather than a dot, in syllable breaks where the word cannot be divided at the end of a line.

Examples

a. mimeograph
   mim·e·o·graph

b. eliminate
   e/lim·i·nate

1. experiment
2. academic
3. gymnasium
4. mathematics
5. elementary

6. historical
7. explanatory
8. respiratory
9. representative
10. everybody

Pronunciation

The pronunciation of a word appears in parentheses after the main entry word in a dictionary.

wor·ry   (wur/ē)

Diacritical Marks

To show a word's pronunciation dictionaries use a set of marks called *diacritical marks* above vowels. These are diacritical marks:- ‾ ¨ ^ ˘.

A *pronunciation key* shows how to pronounce the vowels with diacritical marks. Sometimes, the key is at the bottom of every other dictionary page. Here is a sample pronunciation key from the bottom of page 265 of *Webster's New World Dictionary*[1]:

fat, āpe, cär; ten, ēven; is, bīte; gō, hôrn, tool, look; oil, out; up, fur; get; joy; yet; chin; she; thin, then; zh, leisure; ŋ, ring; ə for *a* in *ago*, *e* in *agent*, *i* in *sanity*, *o* in *comply*, *u* in *focus*; ' as in *able* (ā'b'l); Fr. bâl; ë, Fr. coeur; ö, Fr. feu; Fr. mon; ô, Fr. coq; ü, Fr. duc; r, Fr. cri; H, G. ich; kh, G. doch. See inside front cover. ☆Americanism; ‡foreign; *hypothetical; <derived from

In this key each of the sounds is shown in a word you already know how to pronounce. Read the key in the following way.

Read the symbol *a* as the sound of *a* in the word *fat*.

Read the symbol *ā* as the sound of *a* in the word *ape*.

Read the symbol *ä* as the sound of *a* in the word *car*.

Read the symbol *e* as the sound of *e* in the word *ten*.

By reading the rest of the key, tell how each of the following sounds is pronounced.

1. ē
2. i
3. ī
4. ō
5. ô

6. o͞o
7. oo
8. oi
9. ou
10. ū

You may also find a more complete key in another part of the dictionary. On page 621 for example, is a complete pronunciation key from the front of *Webster's New World Dictionary*.

Simplified Spellings

In addition to diacritical marks, dictionaries use *simplified spellings* to indicate pronunciation. In the simplified spelling, letters that are not pronounced are omitted; thus, the simplified spelling for the word *cleave* is (klēv). Because the *a* and the final *e* in *cleave* are not pronounced, they are omitted in the simplified spelling. Using the pronunciation key, you can see that *ē* is pronounced like the first *e* in *even*.

---

[1]All entries from *Webster's New World Dictionary*, Second College Edition. Copyright © 1984 by Simon & Schuster. Reprinted by permission.

Also, consonants are often written as they sound in the simplified spelling. The letter *c* in *cleave* sounds like *k* and is, therefore, represented by *k*.

Exercise 3: *Using the Pronunciation Key*

Using the full pronunciation key on this page, pronounce each of the following words. Then tell how each word is really spelled.

Example

Simplified Spelling	Word
a. māk	make
b. fōk	folk

1. pät		6. fīl	
2. fānt		7. hook	
3. tōn		8. skôr	
4. kāj		9. trik	
5. ôl		10. yir	

Pronunciation Key

Symbol	Key Words	Symbol	Key Words
a	asp, fat, parrot	b	bed, fable, dub
ā	ape, date, play	d	dip, beadle, had
ä	ah, car, father	f	fall, after, off
		g	get, haggle, dog
e	elf, ten, berry	h	he, ahead, hotel
ē	even, meet, money	j	joy, agile, badge
		k	kill, tackle, bake
i	is, hit, mirror	l	let, yellow, ball
ī	ice, bite, high	m	met, camel, trim
		n	not, flannel, ton
ō	open, tone, go	p	put, apple, tap
ô	all, horn, law	r	red, port, dear
ōō	ooze, tool, crew	s	sell, castle, pass
oo	look, pull, moor	t	top, cattle, hat
yōō	use, cute, few	v	vat, hovel, have
yoo	united, cure, globule	w	will, always, swear
oi	oil, point, toy	y	yet, onion, yard
ou	out, crowd, plow	z	zebra, dazzle, haze
u	up, cut, color	ch	chin, catcher, arch
ur	urn, fur, deter	sh	she, cushion, dash
		th	thin, nothing, truth
ə	a in ago	th	then, father, lathe
	e in agent	zh	azure, leisure
	i in sanity	ŋ	ring, anger, drink
	o in comply	'	[see explanatory note,
	u in focus		p. xi, and also *Foreign sounds* below]
ər	perhaps, murder		

An abbreviated form of this key appears at the bottom of every right-hand page of the vocabulary. A fuller explanation of the symbols will be found on pages x-xi of the Guide to the Use of the Dictionary.

Accent Marks

When you say words of more than one syllable, one syllable is always spoken more loudly than the others. This louder syllable is called the *stressed* or *accented syllable.* Some dictionaries show the accent with a heavy mark before the accented syllable; other dictionaries place a heavy mark after the accented syllable.

Dictionaries that place the mark in front of the accented syllable usually use a mark that looks like an exclamation mark without the dot: ('). Dictionaries that place the mark after the stressed syllable usually use a slanted mark: ('). For example, the word *camera* may be marked either (kam'ər ə) or ('kam ər ə). Information about how the dictionary marks accented syllables is usually found in the front of the dictionary.

A difference in stress can make a difference in the meaning of a word. For example, you cannot know the meaning of the word *present* until you know which syllable is stressed. When the first syllable is stressed, the word can mean "a gift," as in the sentence, "I think the *present* is one of the nicest gifts I have received." When the second syllable is stressed, the word can mean "to give something," as in the sentence, "We voted to *present* the principal with an award."

Other words where the stress makes a difference in meaning are *record, conduct, permit.* What does each of these words mean when the first syllable is stressed? When the second is stressed? What are other words for which stress makes a difference in meaning?

Some words of three syllables or more may have two stressed, or accented, syllables. In such cases one of the accented syllables is always spoken more loudly than the other. This louder syllable has the *primary* stress or accent; the other syllable has the *secondary* stress or accent. Both stressed syllables are spoken more loudly than syllables without an accent mark.

Dictionaries differ in the way they show primary and secondary accents. As with primary accents some dictionaries place the secondary accent before the syllable and some after. Some dictionaries use a lower mark for the secondary accent than for the primary accent. Other dictionaries use a lighter mark for the secondary accent. For example, the secondary accent for the word *accelerator* could be marked in either of these ways:

ac·cel·er·a·tor   ək 'sel ə 'rāt ər
                     ək sel'ə rāt'ər

The Schwa

When you speak a word with more than one syllable, you often find vowels that have no distinct sound. These vowels are found in most unaccented syllables. To represent these indistinct sounds dictionaries use an upside down *e* called the *schwa* (ə). Look at the pronunciation key on page **621** to see how the schwa is pronounced. When the schwa is followed by an *r*, it is pronounced like the *er* in *perhaps*.

Exercise 4: Finding Primary and Secondary Accents

Look up each of the following words in a dictionary. On a sheet of paper, write the word, dividing it into syllables. Using the same method your dictionary uses, mark each word for primary and, if necessary, secondary stress. When you finish, read each word aloud several times to listen for the primary and secondary accents and for the schwa sounds.

Example

a. pesticide
   pĕs' tə sīd'

1. captivate
2. defoliate
3. mediocre
4. reiterate
5. meander

6. laconic
7. abstruse
8. ponderous
9. docile
10. supercilious

Parts of Speech

The eight parts of speech are *noun, verb, adjective, adverb, pronoun, preposition, conjunction,* and *interjection.* Many words may be more than one part of speech, depending on their use in a sentence.

Harry scored the winning *run* for his team.	[noun]
The *run* metal poured easily into the mold.	[adjective]
I usually *run* two miles every day.	[verb]

Abbreviations in the main entry show the parts of speech a word may be. Here are the most common abbreviations that dictionaries use for the parts of speech:

n.	noun	*pron.*	pronoun
v. or *vb.*	verb	*prep.*	preposition
adj.	adjective	*conj.*	conjunction
adv.	adverb	*interj.*	interjection

Dictionaries also use the abbreviations *v.t.* and *v.i.*, which stand for *transitive verb* and *intransitive verb*. (*Transitive verbs* are those that take objects. *Intransitive verbs* are those that do not.)

In most dictionaries any verb without an object is listed as an intransitive verb. Thus, linking verbs such as *be, seem,* and *become* are intransitive. Certain verbs may be either transitive or intransitive.

I *run* from school to the lake.	[intransitive]
I *run* the store when Aunt Martha is away.	[transitive]

The abbreviation for part of speech appears in the entry before the definition. If a word can be used as more than one part of speech, all meanings for one part of speech are given first, followed by the abbreviation for the second part of speech and those meanings. For example, here is a main entry for the word *spin:*

spin (spin) *vt.* **spun** or archaic **span, spun, spin'ning** [ME. *spinnen* < OE. *spinnan*, akin to G. *spinnen* < IE. base **(s)pen(d)-*, to pull, draw, spin, whence Lith. *spéndžiu*, to lay a snare & (prob.) L. *pendere*, to hang] **1.** *a)* to draw out and twist fibers of (wool, cotton, etc.) into thread *b)* to make (thread, yarn, etc.) by this process **2.** to make (a web, cocoon, etc.) from a filament of a viscous fluid that is extruded from the body and hardens on exposure to the air: said of spiders, silkworms, etc. **3.** to make or produce in a way suggestive of spinning *[to spin a tale]* **4.** to draw *out* (a story, etc.) to a great length; prolong; protract **5.** to cause to whirl or rotate swiftly *[to spin a top]* **6.** to cause (wheels of a vehicle) to rotate freely without traction, as on ice or in sand **7.** to extract water from (clothes) in a washer by the centrifugal force of swift rotation —*vi.* **1.** to spin thread or yarn **2.** to form a thread, web, etc.: said of spiders, etc. **3.** to fish with a spinning reel **4.** to whirl or rotate swiftly **5.** to go into or descend in a spin: said of an aircraft **6.** to seem to be spinning from dizziness **7.** to move along swiftly and smoothly **8.** to rotate freely without traction *[wheels spinning on ice]* —*n.* **1.** the act of spinning or rotating something **2.** a spinning or rotating movement **3.** a moving along swiftly and smoothly **4.** a ride or pleasure trip in a motor vehicle **5.** any descent in which an airplane comes down nose first along a spiral path of large pitch and small radius **6.** any sudden, steep downward movement **7.** *Physics a)* the intrinsic angular momentum of an elementary particle or photon, produced by rotation about its own axis *b)* the total angular momentum of a nuclide —*SYN.* see TURN —**spin off 1.** to produce as an outgrowth or secondary benefit, development, etc. **2.** to get rid of

Here, the word *spin* has seven meanings as a transitive verb, eight meanings as an intransitive verb, and seven meanings as a noun.

Exercise 5: *Finding Parts of Speech*

Look up the following words in a dictionary. On a sheet of paper, list the parts of speech that each word may be. Use the abbreviations already given.

Example

a. beat

beat: vi., v.t., n., adj.

1. raise
2. work
3. chord
4. concern
5. dilemma
6. myriad
7. perfunctory
8. plebian
9. serve
10. third

Usage Labels

A word may have many meanings. You may, for example, *kick* a football and *kick in* your share of money to buy a gift.

You may talk or write about kicking a football in any situation because *kick,* in the sense of striking something with a foot, is standard usage. You would not, however, write about *kicking in* money if you were writing a formal paper or making a formal speech because *kick in* is slang usage.

To show when it is appropriate to use a word, dictionaries have *usage labels.* Usage labels and their abbreviations may vary slightly from dictionary to dictionary. One reason for this is that language is in a constant state of change. The following are some of the most common usage labels and the abbreviations often used for them.

Colloquial (Colloq.):	Suitable for informal speech and writing
Slang:	Suitable for very informal speech
Archaic:	No longer used, except in legal, religious, or other special languages
Obsolete (Obs.):	No longer used, but found in older writing
Poetic (Poet.):	Suitable in certain types of poetry
Dialect:	Suitable only in the areas of the country where commonly used

Any word that has no usage label is suitable for speech and writing if it has the meaning you want to express. Usage labels are found in the main entry before meanings relevant to them.

Word History

Dictionaries also give information about the history, or *etymology*, of many words, in square brackets usually following the pronunciation and the usage label.

A word's etymology tells how the word came into the modern English language. To understand this history, however, you must know the abbreviations and symbols used in dictionaries. These are usually listed in the front of the dictionary. For example, the following main entry is for the word *oil*.

> **oil** (oil) *n.* [ME. *oile* < OFr. < L. *oleum*, oil, olive oil < Gr. *elaion*, (olive) oil, akin to *elaia*, olive] **1.** any of various kinds of greasy, combustible substances obtained from animal, vegetable, and mineral sources: oils are liquid at ordinary temperatures and soluble in certain organic solvents, as ether, but not in water **2.** *same as* PETROLEUM **3.** any of various substances having the consistency of oil **4.** *same as: a)* OIL COLOR *b)* OIL PAINTING **5.** [Colloq.] smooth, hypocritical flattery —*vt.* **1.** to smear, lubricate, or supply with oil **2.** to bribe —*adj.* of, from, like, or yielding oil, or having to do with the production or use of oil —**pour oil on troubled waters** to settle quarrels, differences, etc. by calm, soothing methods —☆**strike oil 1.** to discover oil under the ground by drilling a shaft for it **2.** to become suddenly wealthy —**oiled** *adj.*

To read the etymology of the word *oil*, you must know the following abbreviations and symbols.

ME.	Middle English	Gr.	Greek
OFr.	Old French	<	Derived from (comes
L.	Latin		from)

The main word entry is the Modern English form of the word. The first language abbreviation in brackets is the language from which the word comes into Modern English. Each following language abbreviation traces the word further back in history, and the words in *italics* show the spelling of the word in each language. The meanings of the word in older languages may also be given. The etymology for the word *oil* reads as follows:

> *Oil* comes into Modern English from the Middle English word *oile*. The Middle English word *oile* is derived from Old French. The Old French language got its word for oil directly from the Latin word *oleum*, meaning "oil" or "olive oil." The Latin language borrowed the word from the Greek language where it was *elaion*, meaning "olive oil."

Exercise 6: Finding Word Histories

Select five of the following words and find their etymologies in your dictionary. On a sheet of paper, write the history of the five words you have chosen. Underline as shown in the example.

Example

a. sleep
   The word sleep comes into Modern English from the Middle English word slepe. Slepe is derived from the Old English word slæp.

1. routine
2. embroider
3. block
4. Colorado
5. cure

6. emerald
7. field
8. fire
9. ghetto
10. Cheyenne

Definitions

Most words have many meanings or *definitions.* To help you find the right one, dictionaries organize definitions by parts of speech, so that if you know how the word is used in a sentence, you can easily find its meaning. Suppose you want to find the meaning of the word *bear* in the sentence "The old bridge cannot *bear* the weight of heavy trucks." In this sentence *bear* is used as a transitive verb. On this page is a main entry for the word *bear*.

This entry gives twenty-five definitions for the word *bear* and for *bear* with other words. Since only the first sixteen definitions are for *bear* as a transitive verb, you can limit your search to those definitions.

Now you must consider the context of the sentence in which your word is used. In the sentence "The old bridge cannot bear the weight of heavy trucks," the word *bear* is used with *weight.* The third definition of *bear* is "holding firm under a heavy load." *Load* means "weight," and you can guess that the correct definition of *bear* in your sentence is the third definition.

To help you see how words are used in a context, dictionaries often use the words in sample sentences or phrases, sometimes for each definition. After the third definition for *bear,* for example, is the sentence "The columns bear the weight of the roof." The meaning of the sample sentence is like the meaning of your sentence, so you know you have chosen the correct definition.

bear[1] (bâr), *v.*, **bore** or (*Archaic*) **bare; borne** or **born; bear·ing.** —*v.t.* **1.** to give birth to: *to bear a child.* **2.** to produce by natural growth: *a tree that bears fruit.* **3.** to support or to hold or remain firm under (a load): *The columns bear the weight of the roof.* **4.** to sustain or be capable of: *His claim doesn't bear close examination.* **5.** to press or push against: *The crowd was borne back by the police.* **6.** to manage or conduct (oneself, one's body, one's head, etc.): *to bear oneself erectly; to bear oneself bravely.* **7.** to suffer; endure or tolerate: *He bore the blame. I can't bear your nagging.* **8.** to warrant or be worthy of: *It doesn't bear repeating.* **9.** to carry; bring: *to bear gifts.* **10.** to carry in the mind or heart: *to bear love; to bear malice.* **11.** to transmit or spread (gossip, tales, etc.). **12.** to render; afford; give: *to bear testimony.* **13.** to have and be entitled to: *to bear title.* **14.** to exhibit; show: *to bear a resemblance.* **15.** to accept or have, as an obligation: *to bear the cost.* **16.** to possess, as a quality, characteristic, etc.; have in or on: *to bear traces; to bear an inscription.* —*v.i.* **17.** to tend in a course or direction; move; go: *to bear west.* **18.** to be located or situated: *The lighthouse bears due north.* **19.** to bring forth young or fruit: *Next year the tree will bear.* **20. bear down, a.** to press or weigh down. **b.** to strive harder; intensify one's efforts. **c.** to approach rapidly, as a ship or opponent. **21. bear on** or **upon,** to affect, relate to, or have connection with; be relevant: *This information may bear on the case.* **22. bear out,** to substantiate; confirm: *The facts bear me out.* **23. bear up,** to endure; face hardship bravely. **24. bear with,** to be patient; be forbearing. **25. bring to bear,** to concentrate on with a specific purpose. [ME *bere(n)*, OE *beran*; c. D *baren*, Icel *bera*, Goth *bairan*, G *(ge)bären*, L *fer(re)*, Gk *phér(ein)*, Skt *bhar(ati)*]

Following the definitions for the word *bear* are several more definitions for the word in special phrases. These phrases are in **boldface** type and are listed separately because you cannot know the meaning of the phrase from the parts. For example, consider the sentence "Harold bears with his brother's constant complaining without a word." Definition 24 in the main entry for *bear* is for the phrase "bear with." This definition, "to be patient," fits with the context of the sentence: "Harold *is patient* with his brother's constant complaining."

Exercise 7: Distinguishing Among Definitions

Look up each of the following *italicized* words or groups of words in your dictionary. On a sheet of paper, copy the definition that best fits the way the word or phrase is used in each sentence.

Example

a. The general *dispatched* a messenger with orders for her commanders.
   to send off or out promptly, usually on a specific errand or official business

1. The students *dissented* from the new dress code at their high school.

2. Edgar *thumbed* through the new books at the school library looking for unusual pictures.

[1]From *The Random House College Dictionary,* Revised Edition. Copyright © 1982 by Random House, Inc.

3. The track team runs at the *break* of dawn.

4. The police *dragged* the bottom of the lake in search of the dog's missing body.

5. The sergeant changed the *green* recruits into skilled soldiers.

6. At this rate our plans for winter outings for our ski club will never *get off the ground.*

7. Before the tornado the teachers *herded* the students to a safe place.

8. Everyone in my family learned to swim in this swimming *hole.*

9. Mark tried to *badger* his parents into buying him a new football helmet and jersey.

10. The beginning of the concert was marked by a drum *roll.*

Facts in the Dictionary

In this chapter, you have learned the many uses of a dictionary. But it is also possible to find many interesting facts in a dictionary. Did you know that:

1. It is possible to *run out* a clock?

2. The name *David* originally meant "beloved"?

3. The word *gnu* (large African antelope) does not have a *g* sound?

4. You can cook a *pièce de résistance* or you can nail one together?

5. Several hundred years ago you could have said, "This is awful," and it would have been a compliment?

6. *Little Corporal* was Napoleon Bonaparte's nickname?

7. In the third century B.C., a wall 1,500 miles long was built in China ?

8. The word *robot* comes from the Czech language and means "forced labor"?

9. *Earl of Sandwich* was the title of an English nobleman who asked that his dinner meat be put between two slices of bread so that he could continue playing cards as he ate?

10. In some parts of the Arctic and Antarctic, the sun is still visible at midnight during the summer?

28 Understanding Your Language

The story of English began more than 2,000 years ago in *Britannia,* the country known today as England. At that time the great Roman Empire, under the leadership of Julius Caesar, began a series of invasions of the island. Eventually the Romans conquered the *Celts,* the native people of Britannia, and ruled their country as a colony.

For several hundred years the Celts and Romans lived side by side, but in A.D. 410 the Romans abandoned the colony. Without Rome's protection the Celts were helpless against attacks by tribes from nearby Scotland and Ireland. For assistance, the Celts looked across the North Sea to what is now Denmark, Germany, and the Netherlands. At that time those countries were inhabited by three Germanic tribes known for their fierceness—the Angles, Saxons, and Jutes. These tribes sailed across the North Sea to help the Celts and never returned. Instead, they drove out the Celts and took Britannia.

The Angles, Saxons, and Jutes each spoke a dialect, or form, of a Germanic language. Once the Celts were conquered, those dialects became the language of Britannia. Old English, or Anglo-Saxon as it is also called, resulted from a merging of the dialects. Even the name *England* came from a word meaning "Land of the Angles."

Old English does not look familiar to you today because the alphabet, vocabulary, and grammar have changed over the years. Many of the words you use every day, however, are from Old English stock, even though they have changed appearance.

This chapter discusses the history of English, variations in English, and ways in which words are added to the language.

The History of English

Old English

If you had lived in the year A.D. 900, you would have used a form of English that looks like the following passage.

Eft hē āxode, hū ðǣre ðēode nama wǣre þe hī of cōmon. Him wæs ġeandwyrd, þæt hī Angle ġenemnode wǣron. Þā cwǣð hē, "Rihtlīce hī sind Angle ġehaten, forðan ðe hī engla wlite habbað, and swilcum ġedafenað þæt hī on heofonum engla ġefēran bēon."

Although the preceding passage is written in English, it probably looks very strange to you. These words do not look familiar because they were written in the earliest form of the English language, a form called *Old English*. The following word-for-word translation shows the English you would use today.

Again he asked what the nation's name was that they from came.
Eft hē āxode, hū ðǣre ðēode nama wǣre þe hī of cōmon.
To him it was answered that they Angles named were. Then said he,
Him wæs ġeandwyrd, þæt hī Angle ġenemnode wǣron. Þā cwǣð hē,
"Rightly they are Angles called for they angels' fairness have, and
"Rihtlīce hī sind Angle ġehaten, forðan ðe hī engla wlite habbað, and
for such it is fitting that they in heaven angels' companions be."
swilcum gedafenað þæt hī on heofonum engla ġefēran bēon."[1]

To become the English you recognize today in books, magazines, and newspapers, Old English changed in three ways.

1. *Pronunciation.* For example, in Old English the *a* was pronounced like *ah* in: "Ah, I see." This changed to an *o* sound in Modern English, so the Old English *haldan* became the Modern English *hold*.

2. *Word-Stock* or *Vocabulary.* For example, the Old English word *wiotana*, meaning "wise men," is no longer a part of English vocabulary. The Modern English word *astronaut* was obviously not a part of the Old English vocabulary.

3. *Sentence Structure.* The word order of the first Old English sentence on this page is "Again he asked what the nation's name was that they from came." The Modern English sentence would read, "Again he asked what the nation's name was that they came from."

Language constantly changes. Several hundred years from now the English language your descendants speak and write might be as different from today's English as Modern English is from Old English.

---

[1]Adapted from *Problems in the Origins and Development of the English Language.* Second Edition by John Algeo. Copyright © 1972 by Harcourt Brace Jovanovich, Inc. Reprinted by permission of the publisher.

Exercise 1: Finding Old English Words

Each of the following words in Modern English is derived from an Old English word. Number a sheet of paper 1–10. Look up each Modern English word in your dictionary and write the Old English word from which the Modern English word is derived.

Example

Modern English Word	Old English Word
a. sock	socc

Modern English Words

1. take	6. glitter
2. beet	7. odd
3. holy	8. lily
4. sky	9. cap
5. pear	10. sly

From Middle English to Modern English

The Old English period formally ended in 1066 when the French invaded England. At this time the English language began to change rapidly in spelling, grammar, and vocabulary, as the following passage, written by Geoffrey Chaucer in the late 1300s, shows.

> This straunge knyght, that cam thus sodeynly,
> Al armed, save his heed, ful richely,
> Saluteth kyng and queene and lordes alle,
> By ordre, as they seten in the halle,
> With so heigh reverence and obeisaunce,
> As wel in speche as in contenaunce,
> That Gawayn, with his olde curteisye,
> Thogh he were come agayn out of fairye,
> Ne koude hym nat amende with a word.

The language that was written and spoken from 1066 to about 1500 is called *Middle English*.

If you try, you can probably recognize many of the words in Geoffrey Chaucer's description, but you can see that the spelling, vocabulary, and grammar of English continued to change before it became the language you know today.

Even though the English that was written and spoken from 1500 on is called *Modern English*, the early form of the English of this period still looks quite different from the English of the twentieth century. By the first part of the seventeenth century, however, English speakers were writing a language that does not appear modern but that most modern readers can understand. For example, the following famous passage was written by John Donne in the early 1600s. As you read his words, think how you would "translate" John Donne's writing into the English of today.

> The bell doth toll for him that thinks it doth; and though it intermit again, yet from that minute that that occasion wrought upon him he is united to God. Who casts not up his eye to the sun when it rises? but who takes off his eye from a comet when that breaks out? Who bends not his ear to any bell which upon any occasion rings? but who can remove it from that bell which is passing a piece of himself out of this world? No man is an island entire of itself; every man is a piece of the continent, a part of the main. If a clod be washed away by the sea, Europe is the less, as well as if a promontory were, as well as if a manor of thy friend's or of thine own were. Any man's death diminishes me, because I am involved in mankind, and therefore never send to know for whom the bell tolls; it tolls for thee.

When the first English settlers came to the United States, they brought with them the English language of John Donne and his contemporaries. For many reasons, the language of the Colonists gradually changed until it became a distinct form of British English, called *American English*. Native Americans and the many settlers who arrived from other countries made their own contributions to the language until American English became the rich language you use today.

Exercise 2: *Reporting on the History of English*

Each of the following people played a significant role in the development of the English language. Select one of these historical figures and prepare a short report in which you discuss the contribution he made to the development of the English language.

1. Alfred, King of Wessex
2. Caedmon
3. William the Conqueror
4. St. Augustine
5. Julius Caesar

Variations in English

No two speakers of any language speak exactly the same language. When you speak English, your own version of the language differs from everybody else's. Your pronunciation, word choice, and sentence structure will always be at least slightly different from that of any other speaker.

Regional Dialects

Even though no two people speak exactly alike, groups of people share language customs. These groups of people are called *dialect groups*, and the language customs they share are called *dialects*. American English is made up of many dialects.

Like other users of English, you belong to a *regional dialect group* and you speak a *regional dialect*. Regional dialects are dialects shared by groups of people in different regions, or parts, of the country. The first English settlers who came to the United States were from different parts of England and spoke different dialects of British English. For many years there was little communication between groups of settlers scattered throughout the colonies, and the differences were preserved.

One regional dialect differs from another in pronunciation, vocabulary, and grammar.

If you have ever listened to a person with a distinct regional dialect, you know that one of the ways regional dialects differ is in pronunciation. Depending on the part of the country from which you came, you may or may not pronounce the *r* distinctly in words such as *car* and *water*. If you have a Southern or New England dialect, these words are likely to sound like *cah* and *wattuh* or *wawtuh*. If you have a Midwestern or Western dialect, you are more likely to say *car* and *water*.

Regional dialects also differ in vocabulary. Depending on the region of the country, people drink *soda pop, soda, soft drinks, sody pop, soda water,* or *pop*. In various areas of the United States, you will find all the following words used to denote a creature with which everyone is familiar: *earthworm, angleworm, fishing worm, fish bait, bait worm, mudworm, eaceworm, angledog, ground worm, red worm, dew worm.*

Differences in grammar are not as noticeable as differences in pronunciation and vocabulary, but they do exist. For example, if you have a Midland dialect, you are likely to say you are sick *at, of, to,* or *in* your stomach. If you have a Northern dialect, you probably say you are sick *to* your stomach. With a Southern dialect you are likely to say you are sick *at* your stomach.

If you and your classmates speak different regional dialects, you are likely to have different answers to questions such as these:

1. Do you pronounce the word *creek* as *krik* or as *kreek*?

2. Do you pronounce *greasy* with the sound of *s* or *z*?

3. Would you carry water in a *bucket* or a *pail*?

4. Does your family prefer sitting on the *porch*, the *verandah*, or the *stoop*?

5. What meal do you eat at noon: *lunch* or *dinner*? At night do you eat *dinner* or *supper*?

6. Do you ever ride in an *auto*, or do you always ride in a *car*?

7. Does your family buy groceries at the *store* or the *market*?

8. In your house do you have a *sofa*, a *couch*, or a *settee*?

9. Is the sofa, couch, or settee in the *living room*, the *parlor*, or the *sitting room*?

10. Do you hike down the *gulch*, the *hollow*, or the *arroyo*?

Model: Regional Dialects

Writers often transcribe regional dialects to capture the flavor of a particular region and to create a vivid character, as Mark Twain does in his story, "The Celebrated Jumping Frog of Calaveras County." In the following passage from this story, Simon Wheeler describes a man named Jim Smiley who bets on almost anything. The story is set in a mining camp in Calaveras County, California, during the 1800s. As you read, look for the distinct features of vocabulary and grammar that mark this regional dialect.

> There was a feller here once by the name of *Jim* Smiley, in the winter of '49—or maybe it was the spring of '50—I don't recollect exactly, somehow, though what makes me think it was one or the other is because I remember the big flume wasn't finished when he first came to the camp; but anyway, he was the curiousest man about always betting on anything that turned up you ever see, if he could get anybody to bet on the other side; and if he couldn't he'd change sides. Any way that suited the other man would suit him—any way just so's he got a bet, *he* was satisfied. But still he was lucky, uncommon lucky—he most always come out winner. He was always

ready and laying for a chance; there couldn't be no solit'ry thing mentioned but that feller'd offer to bet on it, and take any side you please, as I was just telling you. If there was a horse-race, you'd find him flush, or you'd find him busted at the end of it; if there was a dogfight, he'd bet on it; if there was a cat-fight, he'd bet on it; if there was a chicken-fight, he'd bet on it; why, if there was two birds setting on a fence, he would bet you which one would fly first; or if there was a camp-meeting, he would be there reg'lar, to bet on Parson Walker, which he judged to be the best exhorter about here, and so he was, too, and a good man. If he even see a straddle-bug start to go anywheres, he would bet you how long it would take him to get to wherever he was going to, and if you took him up, he would foller that straddle-bug to Mexico but what he would find out where he was bound for and how long he was on the road. Lots of the boys here has seen that Smiley, and can tell you about him. Why, it never made no difference to *him*—he would bet on *any*thing—the dangdest feller. Parson Walker's wife laid very sick once, for a good while, and it seemed as if they warn't going to save her; but one morning he came in, and Smiley asked how she was, and he said she was considerable better—thank the Lord for his inf'nit mercy—and coming on so smart that, with the blessing of Prov'dence she'd get well yet; and Smiley, before he thought, says, "Well, I'll risk two-and-a-half she don't anyway."[1]

When people go to school for many years, or when they move from one area to another, they are likely to lose part of their regional dialects or to speak with a blend of regional dialects. In many parts of the country, however, you will still find the distinct regional dialects that are an important part of the heritage of the English language.

Exercise 3: *Spotting Regional Dialects*

From a song, newspaper article, story, poem, or other source, find an example of a regional dialect. Your teacher may ask you to point out features of pronunciation, vocabulary, and grammar that mark the dialect.

Formal and Informal English

Regardless of dialect, language varies in its style. Everyone uses formal language in formal situations and less formal language at other times. For example, which of the following situations calls for the most formal language? Which calls for the least formal?

---

[1]From *Sketches New and Old* by Mark Twain. Reprinted by permission of Harper & Row, Publishers, Inc.

A wedding ceremony

A talk with friends

A letter to a friend

A job interview

A talk with your teacher

Very formal language is used most often for governmental and legal documents, and for ceremonies, such as inaugurations, weddings, baptisms, and bar mitzvahs. Your language tends to be more formal when you are writing than when you are speaking, and more formal when you are speaking or writing to people you do not know well than to friends. For these reasons, a wedding ceremony probably calls for the most formal language and a talk with your friends the most informal.

The different sorts of language available to speakers and writers for different purposes are called *levels of usage*. These levels identify the formal and informal language of educated people and the language of the uneducated.

Formal Usage	Informal Usage	Uneducated Usage
I shall not return.	I won't come back.	I ain't comin' back.
They are highly intelligent.	They're very smart.	They're sharp.

The term *level of usage* does not necessarily mean that one level is "higher" and somehow better than another. Nothing in language is good or bad out of context. "Good" language used for one audience and one purpose can become "bad" language for another audience and for another purpose. For example, if you are attending a religious service, the words *thou, thy,* and *canst* may be appropriately used, especially in a prayer. Suppose, however, you are asking a friend to help you load a heavy object onto a truck. In this situation, using the same words might be humorous: "I ask thy help, George, for thou hast strong muscles wherewith thou canst aid me."

Model: Formal English

Formal language often has long and complex sentences. This kind of language does not use contractions or the various types of slang or colloquial words or phrases common today. Very formal language, especially that used for ceremonies, often has *archaic* words, old words no longer in common usage. Very formal language is solemn and, for that reason, is often used to add dignity and purpose to solemn occasions.

Formal language is the language in which Martin Luther King, Jr., gave his famous "I Have a Dream" speech:

> I have a dream today.
>
> I have a dream that one day every valley shall be exalted, every hill and mountain shall be made low, the rough places will be made plain and the crooked places will be made straight, and the glory of the Lord shall be revealed, and all flesh shall see it together.
>
> This is our hope. This is the faith with which I return to the South. With this faith we will be able to hew out of the mountain of despair a stone of hope. With this faith we will be able to transform the jangling discords of our nation into a beautiful symphony of brotherhood. With this faith we will be able to work together, to pray together, to struggle together, to go to jail together, to stand up for freedom together, knowing that we will be free one day.
>
> This will be the day when all of God's children will be able to sing with new meaning:
>
>> My country 'tis of thee,
>> Sweet land of liberty,
>> Of thee I sing.
>> Land where my fathers died,
>> Land of the pilgrims' pride,
>> From every mountainside
>> Let freedom ring.
>
> And if America is to be a great nation, this must become true. So, let freedom ring from the prodigious hilltops of New Hampshire. Let freedom ring from the mighty mountains of New York. Let freedom ring from the heightening Alleghenies of Pennsylvania. Let freedom ring from the snowcapped Rockies of Colorado. Let freedom ring from the curvaceous slopes of California. But not only that, let freedom ring from Stone Mountain of Georgia.
>
> Let freedom ring from Lookout Mountain of Tennessee.
>
> Let freedom ring from every hill and molehill of Mississippi.
>
> From every mountainside, let freedom ring. When we let freedom ring, when we let it ring from every village, from every hamlet, from every state and every city, we will be able to speed up that day when all of God's children, black men and white men, Jews and Gentiles, Protestants and Catholics, will be able to join hands and sing in the words of the old Negro spiritual: "Free at last! Free at last! Thank God almighty, we are free at last!"[1]

---

[1]From "I Have a Dream" by Martin Luther King, Jr. Copyright © 1963 by Martin Luther King, Jr. Reprinted by permission of Joan Daves.

Model: *Informal English*

Informal language has varied sentence structure and length. Sentences may be simple or complex, long or short. This kind of language uses contractions and, if the situation is very informal, colloquial words and phrases. If the speaker or writer has a regional dialect or highly personal idiolect, these features are often present in informal language.

an idiolect is a personal dialect

Informal language is the language used by most educated people in everyday speech and writing. This is the language eighteen-year-old Bill Lahr of Skokie, Illinois, used in an interview with Studs Terkel:

> Too many of my fellow students are interested in appearance. Tomorrow night is our senior prom. I think the prom is a fine idea, don't get me wrong, I'm not opposed to it. But for the last seven weeks, you hear nothing but, ''Where are you going prom night?'' ''What's going on prom night?'' If you're not going to a beautiful restaurant, if you're not going down to do something really posh, why then you just aren't in at Niles East. I just can't go along with that.
>
> The important thing for them is to be ''neat.'' Do something everybody else does, you're ''neat.'' If you do what they do you're considered ''neat.'' And who is ''they'' I don't know. I suppose ''they'' is the class in general. They never consider themselves as individuals. They're a ''neat'' group, they do things together. If you wear a madras shirt, that's ''neat,'' because everybody wears madras shirts.
>
> I was guilty of this for a long time. The important thing in my life was what other people thought of me. Was I well liked? All of a sudden, this year, I realized the important thing was whether I was well liked by myself. It's a big change.
>
> My mother, who is interested in the social life herself, is always glad when I take an individual stand. I'm afraid she's glad whether it's good or bad. (Laughs.) She just likes an individual stand. For instance, she's bragging this week that her son *isn't* going to the prom. ''He doesn't even care for that kind of stuff.'' So it's funny. (Laughs.)[1]

Exercise 4: *Finding Examples of Formal and Informal English*

Cut out articles from a newspaper that are examples of both formal and informal English. Bring them to class and be prepared to explain what language features in the examples make them either formal or informal.

---

[1]''Bill Lahr'' from *Division Street: America* by Studs Terkel. Copyright © 1967 by Studs Terkel. Reprinted by permission of Pantheon Books, a Division of Random House, Inc., and Penguin Books, Ltd.

Usage Labels

One of the ways your language varies is in the words and phrases you use in different situations. Some words and phrases are appropriate in formal language but not in informal; other words and phrases are appropriate in informal language but not in formal. *Usage* in language has to do with particular words in particular situations. To indicate when certain words and phrases are appropriate, dictionaries use *usage labels*. Two usage labels you should be familiar with are *colloquial* and *slang*.

Colloquial words and phrases are used in informal speech and writing, but not in formal.

> When the goldfish flopped out of its bowl, we thought it was a *goner*.
>
> Mary Ann is a snob; she's always trying to *put on the dog*.
>
> Don't be so angry. That was nothing to *fly off the handle* about.
>
> The suspect insisted that he had been *framed*.

Dictionaries use the colloquial label to describe words and phrases such as the italicized ones in the preceding four sentences. Although those words are used widely, they are appropriate only in very informal situations. If you are not certain whether a word or phrase is appropriate for formal speaking or writing, look up the word in the dictionary. If the definition of the word or phrase you want to use has a colloquial label, you know that it is not appropriate.

Slang words, used by members of a group, are also out of place in formal language.

When a slang term appears in highly formal context, the result is humorous:

> We shall request that the principal grant us permission to hold a *bash*.
>
> As the convicted criminal stood before her, the judge pronounced sentence: "I hereby sentence you to ten years in *the joint*."
>
> My friend treated us to dinner at the most expensive restaurant in town. The *grub* was great, and the service was marvelous, but the prices were outlandish.

The use of slang words marks the speaker as a part of a group, people who share common interests or occupations. Among Air Force recruits, for example, new enlistees are called *rainbows*. Once they have been issued their green fatigues and have been given haircuts, the recruits are called *pickles*. After the next stage, during which the recruits are issued name tags, the new Air Force members are known as *canned pickles*.

Most slang words do not remain in common usage for very long because members of each new group adopt new words to identify themselves. During the past fifty years, for example, teenagers have used the words *the bees' knees, swell, keen, fab, groovy, cool,* and *super* to describe things they like. In the 1920s *flappers* were the *rage*. They drove *jalopies* and said, *"Oh, you kid."* In the 1950s teenagers did the *bebop*. If one person danced especially well, someone might say, *"Dig that crazy cat, man."* In the 1960s *hippies rapped* with each other, often saying something like, "I want to do my own thing."

If you are not certain whether or not a word or phrase is slang, look up the expression in the dictionary. If the dictionary gives a slang label to the meaning of the word or phrase, use it only in very informal speaking and writing.

In a story, slang and colloquial words and phrases may be appropriate if you are using them as part of a character's speech.

Exercise 5: *Identifying Colloquial and Slang Words*

In the following excerpt from *Ordinary People* by Judith Guest, the main character, Conrad Jarrett, and his friend Jeannine have a bowling date. The dialogue begins with Jeannine asking Conrad about the date. As you read, look for slang and colloquial words that would be out of place in a more formal situation. If your teacher asks you to, list those words on a sheet of paper.

"You didn't talk to me all week in choir. I thought you might have changed your mind."

"I haven't changed my mind," he says. "Have you?"

Abruptly, she laughs. "This is dumb. I haven't changed my mind, I want to go, but I just hate to go and do something that'll make me look silly—"

"You won't look silly," he promises her. "I'm a great teacher, you'll look like you belong to a league in twenty minutes, okay?"

"Okay."

And it is all right after that. She is right, she's a lousy bowler but a good listener, a quick learner. He gives her all the tips he can, and she absorbs them easily, trying very hard. And besides she looks terrific up there, no matter what happens to the ball. He notices that she is wearing the blue skirt she wore the first day he saw her at school. And he notices how she sits with her legs tucked back, half on the seat, her hair a smooth river of silk.

"You were a natural," he tells her, across the table at McDonald's, afterward.

"Oh, sure, I'm also a Gemini, so be careful."

"Why?"

"Because. We are two-faced and unpredictable. And what are you?"

"January tenth."

"Capricorn. Good. That's a good sign."

"Is it?"

"Sure. Dutiful. Responsible. Serious. Capable."

"Boring."

She grins. "Late-bloomers."

He laughs. "For sure." He looks around at the people, begins to play an old game: Instant History. "See that guy there? Divorced. That's his daughter with him. He gets to see her once a week. He'd like to take her someplace fancy—Diana's, The Red Carpet. She only likes McDonald's. Every week they come here for dinner—"

"Uh uh. That's not her daddy," Jeannine says. "Sugar daddy, maybe. Okay, my turn. There's a couple. It's their first date. She's afraid of getting fat, so she just has a burger, no roll, and a cup of coffee, but he's not, so he has two Big Macs—" she rolls her eyes "—what a pig! And he's been dying to ask her out. For months he put it off. Finally he got up his nerve. He called her on the phone and said, 'Say, I was wondering—'" She giggles.

"Oh, all right." He mimics her soft soprano. "And what did she say? 'Who, me? On a date? With you?'"

"Well, I was shocked," she says. "You took long enough."

"I thought I was pretty swift."

"September to February? Is swift?"[1]

Jargon

Another kind of special language people often use is *jargon*. The word *jargon* has several meanings: (1) strange, confused, unintelligible language; (2) language used by a particular group, such as physicians; (3) obscure language used to confuse. If you think about the second meaning, you will realize that every sport has its jargon:

Football:	punt, conversion, touchback, onside kick, huddle
Baseball:	switch-hitter, bunt, homer, shortstop, three-bagger
Hockey:	goalie, puck, crease, wrist shot, left wing

[1]From *Ordinary People* by Judith Guest. Copyright © 1976 by Judith Guest. Reprinted by permission of Viking Penguin, Inc.

Occupations and professions also have their jargon:

English Teacher:	levels of usage, dialect, participle, adjectival
Lawyer:	tort, felony, continuance, hearing, post-mortem
Carpenter:	mortise, jointer, coping saw, block plane

Jargon can have a purpose. When members of a profession or other group speak to one another, their jargon may be a common vocabulary denoting special features of their profession, such as tools, instruments, or concepts. Sometimes, however, jargon is used to confuse an audience or to make the user appear important, as often happens when members of a profession or other group speak or write in jargon to an audience that does not know the jargon. If these speakers or writers really wanted to communicate, they would use everyday language the audience understands.

Exercise 6: Identifying Jargon

Choose a profession, sport, or hobby with which you are familiar and make a list of terms that are part of its jargon. If you are not familiar with a field in which jargon is used, read the sports page of a newspaper or a hobby magazine. Then make a list of terms that are part of the jargon of one sport or one hobby, such as model railroading or stamp collecting.

Cliché and Gobbledygook

A *cliché* (klee SHAY) is an overused, stale term.

Using clichés gives the impression that the writer is not thinking but is merely using predigested thought and language. See if you recognize the following clichés.

> After *burning the midnight oil*, I *hit the hay*. I had *kept my nose to the grindstone* for five hours, and I was *dead tired*. All too soon the alarm clock rang, and I got out of *the sack* to *put my shoulder to the wheel* for another day. *Bright and early* I was on the job, *bushy tailed and eager*. When the boss asked us for suggestions, you can be sure that I *put in my two cents' worth* because I believe that *God helps those who help themselves*. I had hoped at this point in my career to *set the world on fire!* At break time I didn't have any refreshments because I believe that *a penny saved is a penny earned*.

Gobbledygook is wordy language that is needlessly hard to understand.

Speakers of gobbledygook often use big words when smaller words would do as well. This kind of language is sometimes used to hide a user's real ignorance about a subject or to create a false impression of importance.

Exercise 7: *Listing Clichés*

Make a list of all the clichés you can remember. You might enjoy working with your classmates to compile a *Dictionary of Familiar Clichés*. You can use Bartlett's *Familiar Quotations* as a model for organizing your cliché dictionary.

Exercise 8: *Translating Gobbledygook*

The following are gobbledygook versions of common sayings. Use your dictionary to look up words you do not know and translate the gobbledygook into everyday language. Write your translations on a sheet of paper. When you translate the sayings out of gobbledygook, you will find that they are clichés.

Examples

a. One should not enumerate one's domestic fowls while they are still in the ovate stage.
   Don't count your chickens before they hatch.

b. A minimal unit of currency preserved for future use is the equivalent of a minimal unit of currency accrued.
   A penny saved is a penny earned.

1. An avian creature manually secured is of more value than two that are unsecured in any sort of low, densely branched shrub.

2. Harvest your silage before unfavorable weather sets in.

3. Absence of sound is of the quality of a precious nonferrous metal.

4. Melvin was as completely occupied as an apian creature.

5. Tallulah is as canny as a small, wild creature of the canine species vulpine genus.

6. Put aside sufficient assets for an inclement day.

7. The event in question is merely H_2O that has already made its way under a structure that allows passage over bodies of water.

8. One should avoid causing a cylindrical mass of tallow or any other fatty substance to undergo combustion at both ends of the mass.

9. The member of the class Aves appearing near the beginning of the morning is prone to capture the invertebrate with the flattened body.

10. The gentleman is of the nature of having the same keen edge as the miniature nail.

Edited Standard English

Sometimes, people tend to favor one dialect over another. For example, early in the history of the United States, certain areas, such as New England, became cultural centers of the nation. For this reason a form of the New England dialect was, and for many people still is, a *favored* or *prestige dialect*.

The most widely used prestige dialect in English is often called *Standard English*. From your study of language, you know that no one dialect is better than any other dialect. In many situations, however, you will find that Standard English is the appropriate dielect to use because it marks the user as an educated person. Also, most employers and other people who have the power to affect your future prefer Standard English.

The Grammar and Usage part of this text covers the grammar features that mark the written form of Standard English, called *Edited Standard English*.

Additions to English

Borrowed Words

Whether or not you have studied a foreign language, you know many "foreign" words and use them often. That is because many English words have been borrowed from other languages. You probably know and use words from the list that follows; however, you may not be familiar with the language from which the words originally came.

egg	Old Norse (Norwegian)
cigar	Spanish
moose	Natick (a native American language)
rodeo	Spanish
sauerkraut	German
kimono	Japanese
scene	French
spirit	Latin
robot	Czech
khaki	Hindi (a language of India)
meteor	Greek
algebra	Arabic

The list could be made longer, for thousands of English words have been taken from other languages. Sometimes, English-speaking people borrowed the word and kept it in its original form (as *rodeo*, *sauerkraut*, and *egg*); other times, the word was changed slightly when it was adopted into English (as *robot* changed from *robota* and *cigar* changed from *cigarro*). In the following sections you will read about how many of these words came into our language, a story that begins almost 2,000 years ago.

Latin Influences on English

As long ago as 55 B.C., the Roman emperor Julius Caesar sent an expedition of soldiers to *Britannia*, an island that later came to be called England. Eventually the Romans built colonies and ruled much of the island.

During the approximately 500 years of occupation, the Romans made many changes in Celtic life. They built highways leading from the Celts' largest town, London (its modern name), to outlying villages. They also built fortresses, temples, bathhouses, and theaters, set up a system of government modeled on the Roman system, taught the Celts their arts and crafts, and introduced their methods of trading, including the use of metal coins.

One important contribution of the Romans was their Latin language. Although the Celts had their own language, they adopted many Latin words that later came into English, such as the Latin word *castra*, for *camp*, which became in Old English *ceaster*. *Ceaster*, a common term in Old English for *town* or *enclosed community*, today can be found in many British place names, such as *Chester, Manchester,* and *Worcester.*

Latin words came into English in indirect ways also. The Romans had contact with people living on the European continent, sometimes through war and sometimes through trade. These early German-, Dutch-, French-, and Spanish-speaking people picked up Latin words, made them part of their languages, and later contributed these words to English through contact with English-speaking people. The words *battle, banner, wall, cheap, mile,* and *commerce* all came into English that way.

Another Latin influence on English vocabulary was the Roman Catholic Church. In the eighth century A.D., St. Augustine and a group of forty monks came to England to convert the British to Christianity. Before long, Latin, (the official language of the Church), made another great impact on the English language. As you might expect, words having to do with religion, such as *altar, candle, disciple, mass, priest,* and *angel*, were the first to be changed and adopted as part of the English vocabulary. Because the Church maintained schools in England, words like *grammar, school,* and *verse* were also adopted by the Celts, in changed form, of course.

Exercise 9: Identifying Latin Words

Each of the following words came into English from Latin. Look up each word in your dictionary. On a sheet of paper, write the Latin word from which the English word came.

Example

a. English Word	Latin Word
flask	flasca

1. kettle	6. pear
2. pillow	7. beet
3. chalk	8. disciple
4. cap	9. lily
5. radish	10. school

Scandinavian Influences on English

A major historical event to affect English vocabulary was a series of invasions and raids by the Vikings, a group of seafaring, adventurous people from the area in northern Europe now known as Sweden, Norway, and Denmark. By the ninth century A.D. Vikings had established control over parts of England. Gradually their languages mixed in with English and contributed to the vocabulary.

Most of the words borrowed from the Vikings such as *skin, scrub, raise, race, take, steak, sky, ill, odd, sly,* and *scout*, had to do with ordinary, everyday things.

The Scandinavian language spoken by the Vikings, called *Old Norse*, also contributed to English a large number of place-names, such as *Derby* and *Rugby*, and personal names, such as *Stevenson* and *Johnson*.

French Influences on English

An important period of growth for English vocabulary began with the *Norman Conquest*. The Normans were from a part of France called *Normandy*. Their ruler, William, claimed the English throne after defeating the English King Harold at the Battle of Hastings in 1066.

As William the Conqueror, the new king made many changes in the British way of life. He gave land, castles, and noble titles to his Norman followers and filled important positions in the Church and government with Normans. Their language, French, became the official language at the king's court, in the law courts, in government offices, in schools, and in the Church. Any native speaker of English who wanted to get ahead socially or politically had to learn to speak French as well as English. For this reason the two languages remained side by side in England for many years—French spoken by the ruling class and English spoken by the common people.

Naturally, many French words came flooding into the English language. In fact, English frequently has two words, one taken from French and one from the older English language, that refer to the same thing. For example, the words *calf* and *veal* both mean meat from a very young cow. The word *calf* comes from English; the word *veal* was taken from the French word for the same thing. Other pairs of words that exist side by side are *ox* (English) and *beef* (from French); *sheep* (English) and *mutton* (from French); *swine* (English) and *pork* (from French).

Because the French rulers were so influential, many words that relate to business, church, state, and social affairs were added to English. The following list shows the kinds of words English borrowed from French.

Government Words:	office, treasurer, governor, coroner
Words of Rank:	noble, duke, count, duchess, sir, madam
Church Words:	sacrament, baptism, lesson, parson
Words in Law:	justice, crime, bar, plea, jury, fine
Military Words:	peace, battle, siege, retreat, guard
Fashion Words:	gown, robe, cape, coat, veil
Words for Food:	toast, tart, spice, roast
Words for Social Life:	dance, carol, juggler, leisure, recreation
Words in Medicine:	physician, surgeon, pain, plague, pulse
Words for Art:	art, sculpture
Words for Learning:	study, grammar, logic

Exercise 10: *Identifying French Words*

Each of the following words comes into English from French. Look up each word in your dictionary. On a sheet of paper, write the French word from which the English word is derived.

Example

a. English Word	French Word
princess	princesse

1. prison		6. poison	
2. spy		7. closet	
3. collar		8. lamp	
4. cream		9. color	
5. sugar		10. poet	

New Words

Have you ever used any of the following words?

radar   astronaut

laser   brunch

Nike   rayon

motel   miniskirt

supercalifragilisticexpealidocious

Each of the preceding words is proof that the English language can add new words to the language, for each of them is a made-up word, not originally in the language and not borrowed from some other language.

Some new words are made up of parts of different words. *Radar* is a means of determining the presence and location of an object with radio waves. The word *radar* is made up of the first letters of the words *radio detecting and ranging*.

Advertisers frequently contribute new words to the language. Those words often begin as a reference to specific products and later become general terms used to refer to any similar product. The word *mimeograph*, for example, was once a trademark for one kind of copying machine. *Aspirin, escalator, nylon,* and *zipper* were also once brand names.

Another source of words for the English language is people's names, those of mythical and legendary characters or those of historical or living people. You probably know that *Atlas* was the Greek demigod who was given the task of holding up the heavens and was stationed on a mountain in Africa to keep heaven and earth apart. A sixteenth-century mapmaker published a collection of his maps showing a picture of Atlas with a globe on his back on the title page. Since then an *atlas* has come to mean "a book of maps."

Exercise 11: Finding the Origin of New Words

The following list is of words that are derived from the names of people. Look up each word in your dictionary or in an encyclopedia. Write two or three sentences, describing the origin of each.

Example

a. Panic

The word panic comes from the name of the Greek god Pan. Pan was known for his habit of frightening unsuspecting travelers. Panic means "fright."

1. Boycott
2. Teddy bear
3. Mason-Dixon line
4. Cereal
5. Bartlett pear
6. Volcano
7. St. Bernard dog
8. Big Ben
9. Braille
10. Cardigan

29 Vocabulary and Spelling Skills

Your mastery of vocabulary and spelling affects both your writing ability and your reading ability. By enlarging your knowledge of the meanings and spellings of words, you become better equipped not only to express yourself in writing but also to comprehend the writings of others. This chapter discusses a number of ways to learn the meanings of new words; it also covers some basic spelling rules.

Developing Vocabulary Skills

Finding Meaning Through Context

Very often the context of a word gives clues, called *context clues*, to its meaning.

The most common context clues are *experience clues, definition or paraphrase clues, example clues,* and *comparison clues.*

Experience Clues

Sometimes, you can guess the meaning of a word simply because you have had experience with the situation. For example, in the sentence "The principal admonished the students about being late for assemblies," you may not know the exact meaning of the word *admonished*; however, you know from experience what happens when students are late for assemblies and so can guess the word has something to do with "warn" or "scold."

You may not know the meaning of *voraciously* in the sentence "Hungry children eat *voraciously*," but you know from experience how hungry children eat. You can guess that *voraciously* means "eagerly."

Definition or Paraphrase Clues

Sometimes, writers simply tell you what a word means by defining the word or by restating (*paraphrasing*) it. Such clues are often used in science or social studies books, where many terms must be defined.

Sometimes, the definition or paraphrase immediately follows the word and is set off by commas; other times, the definition or paraphrase comes later in the sentence or even in another sentence. What is the definition or paraphrase clue in each of the following sentences?

The sergeant told her company, "Soldiers, there will be no *malingering*, better known to many of you as goofing off, in this outfit."

The *jerboa*, a small leaping rodent, is found most often in North Africa and Asia.

Elaine's course in car repair was difficult, but she studied *assiduously*. This constant and careful attention to her work resulted in a high grade.

Example Clues

Writers may give you *examples* of unfamiliar words that can help you determine their meanings.

For example: "John works in a clinic where people are treated for phobias. Some of the phobias he has encountered are the fear of flying, the fear of high places, and the fear of spiders." These examples tell you that a *phobia* is a fear of something. Words like *for example, for instance, such as, like,* and *other* often introduce example clues.

What are the example clues in the following sentences?

My room was painted *heliotrope,* but I don't like it. I don't think I would like any other color with purple in it any better.

Most *crustaceans*—such as shrimps, crabs, and lobsters—are edible, although some—such as barnacles—are not.

From the example clues you can guess that *heliotrope* is one example of a color with purple in it and that *crustaceans* probably live in the water and have shells.

Comparison Clues

A *comparison clue* may liken or contrast one point with another.

In the sentence "Joanne looks pallid today, with none of her usual rosy coloring," Joanne's appearance today is contrasted with her usual bright coloring. You can guess, then, that *pallid* means the opposite of bright coloring: Joanne looks pale today.

Words like *but, however, instead, although, though, on the other hand,* and *still* often introduce comparison clues that contrast. Words like *and, another, like,* and *as* often introduce clues that point out likenesses.

What are the comparison clues in the following sentences?

Although she wanted to *divulge* her secret, Susan kept it hidden.

Joan's *debilitating* disease left her feeling like an infant.

In the first sentence above, *although* Susan wanted to *divulge* a secret she did the opposite by keeping it hidden. Since the opposite of hiding a secret is revealing it, *divulge* means "reveal." In the second sentence Joan's disease left her feeling *like* an infant. Infants are helpless and weak, so you can guess that a *debilitating* disease is one that leaves the patient feeling that way.

Exercise 1: Using Context Clues

In the following passages from *Hannah's Daughters, Six Generations of an American Family: 1876–1976,* the writer records some of Hannah Lambertson's memories of her youth. Using context clues, write a definition for each underlined word. Then write down other words or phrases in the passages that led you to this definition. When you have finished, check your definition with a good dictionary.

But I guess I should say we was contented. We all had a job. We had our food, we had enough to wear. We wasn't wealthy, but we had enough to feed our stock. We had stock to butcher for our meat. And we had corn in the crib. We had enough and we had a surplus. We had several hogs and we had beef too. And all the chicken we wanted to eat. We drank warm milk night and morning; Dad would come in from the milking and we'd just stand in line and hold our cups out.

Sarah was a formidable looking woman: Black & Clarkson's, photographers of Jefferson Street in Hastings, Michigan, took a portrait of a woman in her sixties, hair pulled back tightly behind large ears and fastened at the crown. Her nose is Roman, her mouth small. Two deep lines on either side of her mouth, like those on a ventriloquist's dummy, separate her chin from the rest of her face. Her eyes stare straight ahead in disapproval.

I never asked my daddy any questions. Even now, old as I am, how I wish I'd asked questions. There was so many things I wanted to know about. I wish I had asked my poor daddy about my mother more. One time he told me that I looked an awful lot like my mother. I didn't question him. I didn't contradict. But I had been told that my mother was a beautiful woman. And I was far from a beautiful woman. I didn't consider I was pretty.

In those days women wore hoop skirts and they wore bustles. My, a dress looks pretty when it's draped over a bustle. Daytimes, around the home, the women wore small hoops. But when they'd dress up to go anywhere, they wore bigger ones. I was just a kid, so I didn't have a hoop, but I used to make believe. I'd drape material over my finger the way the big folks wore their bustles.

I've never been in York State, but that's where my grandma was born. I heard her tell how her people died when she was quite young. There was an epidemic of cholera and her folks died all in the same week. Whatever room a sick person died in, they were carried out the window. They weren't taken through the rest of the house where the well people were. And they had so many to bury that week, they didn't bury them very deep. There was one young woman buried, and the next day she came walking home. That dirt had drawed the cholera right out of her.

Now another time I was looking at Charlie Mixer. He was an elderly man and, oh, he was a statuesque man. Tall. Straight. He was wearing some spectacles and I was looking at him because there wasn't no glass in them. Grandma wore glasses, so I knew what they were. Well, Grandma thought I was looking at Charlie Mixer's nose and she gave me a twist on the arm. I didn't know it, but he had a false nose made from a mold, out of wax. And the spectacles were to hold the nose on. He'd had cancer, you see, but he'd cured himself with red clover blossom tea.

You had to know your job to be a river driver. You can get crushed if the logs jam up. And if you fall in between them you can drown. And when you get in the rapids it's pretty dangerous. Dad had to do that because he had my brother to support. Of course you didn't get much in those days—sometimes not over ten dollars a month. But you had your bed and you had your meals.

My granddaddy had an awful big farm. There were about forty acres of woods and I roamed right through it. I used to spend my time in the woods and eat all the wild stuff I could find. I always knew when the sassafras bark was tender to eat. I was always watching for the beech leaves to chew them. Eating. I was always eating. I knew when the wintergreen was coming up, because I watched for the berries. And the mandrake! Grandma told me one time. She says, "When the mandrake comes up with just two leaves on it, that's the male." I didn't know what a male was, but I knew it didn't have any apples on it. But then the other would come up and it would have a little curl on it and a big cream-colored blossom. That was the female and it had the apples. I could smell the mandrake just as far as they could be, and I got the first ones every time. I'd get an apronful of them and go along and eat them.[1]

---

[1]From *Hannah's Daughters* by Dorothy Gallagher. Copyright © 1976 by Dorothy Gallagher. Reprinted by permission of Harper & Row, Publishers, Inc., and the Julian Bach Literary Agency.

Denotation and Connotation

The dictionary definition of a word is its *denotation*.

Webster's New World Dictionary, for example, defines *flag* as "a piece of cloth . . . used as a national or state symbol. . . ."

Words also have *connotative* meanings, meanings that carry emotional overtones.

Denotative and connotative meanings differ, as the following two definitions of *American flag* show.

Denotative: A piece of cloth, varying in size, with thirteen alternating red and white stripes and fifty white stars on a blue background

Connotative: America; patriotism; loyalty to the government; pride; a feeling of oneness with other Americans; being an American

Advertisers are aware of the effect word connotations have on consumers. Cleaning products are often given names such as *Sparkle* or *Glisten*, which give purchasers feelings of cleanliness. Until the energy crisis made smaller cars more fashionable, automobiles were given names such as *Hawk* or *Panther* with connotations of power and fierceness.

Exercise 2: Identifying Connotative Meanings

The following list is of words and their denotative meanings. On a sheet of paper, write the connotative meaning for each word—the feelings you associate with it.

	Word	Denotative Meaning
1.	Church	A building set aside for public worship
2.	Home	A place where a person, number of persons, or family lives
3.	Book	A number of sheets of paper with numbers or printing on them, fastened along one edge
4.	School	A place or institution where teaching and learning take place

5. Automobile   A passenger car, usually four-wheeled, pro-pelled by an engine or a motor

6. Democracy   A government in which the people hold the ruling power

7. Prison   A place where people are confined after they have committed a crime

8. Death   Permanent ending of life in a person, an animal, or a plant

9. Spring   That season of the year when plants begin to grow, days become longer, and the temperature rises

10. A lion, Viking, bulldog   Your school's symbol

Exercise 3: *Using Connotative Meanings*

The following list is of products that do not exist but may be developed in the future. Imagine that you are an advertiser and must think of a name with a connotative meaning that will make people want to buy the product. On a sheet of paper, write a name for each product.

1. A stereo set the size of a pencil eraser

2. A battery-operated car for one person that can travel hundreds of miles without recharging

3. A memory pill that makes studying easier

4. A robot especially designed for teenagers, programmed to clean rooms and do after-school chores

5. A toothpaste that absolutely prevents tooth decay when used regularly

6. A breakfast cereal that never gets soggy no matter how long it soaks in milk

7. A two-way wristband TV like Dick Tracy's

8. A typewriter that types what you speak into it

9. A four-ounce drink that gives you all the food value you need for the entire day

10. A shampoo that attracts the opposite sex

Choosing the Specific Synonym

Synonyms are words that have nearly, but not exactly, the same meanings.

Sometimes, the difference in meanings between synonyms is one of specificity. Suppose a writer wants to describe the way a group of hikers, lost for two days in the desert, react to a drink of water when they are rescued. The writer could say, "The weary hikers *drank* the water gratefully." A synonym for the word *drank* is *gulped*. In this situation the word *gulped* is a better choice. "The weary hikers *gulped* down the water gratefully" is a more specific (and colorful) way to describe what the hikers' action was in drinking the water.

Because of the variations in meaning, synonyms cannot always be substituted. Which of the following sentences does not seem "correct"?

The car *hit* the barrier with a crash.

The car *punched* the barrier with a crash.

Hit and *punch* are synonyms because both words share the basic meaning of striking something. *Punch*, however, has a more specific meaning—"striking with a closed fist." Because of this specific meaning the sentence "The car *punched* the barrier" does not sound "right."

Exercise 4: *Choosing Synonyms*

Write the sentences on the next page, selecting from the two synonyms in parentheses the one that better fits the meaning of each sentence. Underline the synonym you select. (Your teacher may ask you to explain your reasons for choosing the word you did.)

Example

a. As Mark _____ at the low grade, he determined to study in the future. (stared, gazed)
As Mark <u>stared</u> at the low grade, he determined to study in the future.

(Although *gaze* and *stare* share the basic meaning of looking at something, the word *stare* has the specific meaning of looking at someone or something long and hard. *Gaze* has the specific meaning of looking at someone or something casually. Because Mark was concerned about his grade, he was more likely to *stare* at it.)

1. The principal ———— at the students who were standing in the path of the oncoming train. (howled, shouted)

2. Muslims must try to make at least one ———— to Mecca in their lives. (journey, pilgrimage)

3. We were all worried when Martina told us she had a ———— that would make us all rich. (plan, scheme)

4. The hucksters ———— the young couple by charging for roof repairs that had not been done. (tricked, cheated)

5. Since the suit was too large, we had it ———— to fit a size twelve. (altered, transformed)

6. In spite of her excitement over receiving the award, Joan ———— slowly up to the stage. (walked, ambled)

7. One of the greatest difficulties Arctic explorers encounter is the ———— weather conditions. (frigid, cold)

8. Oil slicks are dangerous for birds because the oil ———— their feathers, and they cannot fly. (covers, coats)

9. The large jets require a powerful ———— of energy to get them off the ground. (thrust, push)

10. The angry man ———— his papers to the floor and stormed out of the meeting. (flung, dropped)

Synonyms and Connotations

Synonyms differ in connotations, the feelings that they convey. *Automobile* and *car*, for example, refer to the same object, but *automobile* sounds more formal than *car*.

A word and its synonyms may have *favorable, unfavorable,* **or** *neutral connotations.*

Words that people feel good about have favorable connotations; words to which people have negative reactions have unfavorable connotations; and words that cause no emotional reaction have neutral connotations.

To avoid hurting people's feelings, speakers and writers often choose synonyms with favorable rather than unfavorable connotations. Clothes for very large women are called *queen-sized* clothes; thin people are referred to as *slender* instead of *skinny*; and a janitor may have the title *sanitary engineer*.

Words also have *formal* and *informal connotations*.

When you speak with or write to older people or those you do not know well, you are likely to use words with more formal connotations. With your friends you are likely to use words with less formal connotations. For example, consider the synonyms *dismiss*, *fire*, and *can*. Each word has the basic meaning of removing someone from a job, but the words differ in their connotations. Which one of these words would be most appropriate for each of the following situations?

1. A worker has just been told she will no longer have a job. The boss told the worker, "I'm very sorry, Gail, but business has been poor lately, and I have to _____ several of you in the shipping department."

2. Gail is explaining to her high school counselor why she will no longer need to leave school early for her afternoon job. She says, "I was _____ because business is slow."

3. Gail is somewhat bitter about losing her job. She tells a friend, "They _____ me."

These situations differ because of the relationships between the people and because of the feeling the speaker wants to communicate. In the first situation the boss probably does not know Gail personally and seems to have a neutral feeling about her. The likely word to be used in this situation is the more neutral and formal *dismiss*.

In the second situation Gail probably feels less formal with her high school counselor. Because she does not feel neutral about her experience, she would probably use the word *fired*.

The most informal situation is the last one. Gail feels bitter about her experience and might communicate that feeling to her friend by using the word *canned*.

Exercise 5: *Identifying Connotations*

Each of the words on the next page has either a favorable or neutral connotation. For each word think of a synonym with an unfavorable connotation and write it on a sheet of paper.

Example

a. laugh
   snicker

1. walk
2. plan
3. sing
4. thrifty
5. eat

6. youth
7. determined
8. intelligent
9. observant
10. friendly

Exercise 6: *Using Connotations*

Select two of the words with favorable or neutral connotations from the preceding exercise. First think of a situation in which each word might be used and write two or three sentences using the word in context. Then think of a situation in which the synonym with the unfavorable connotation of the word might be used and write one or two sentences, placing the synonym in context.

Example

Favorable:	Ralph's speech was a great success. Everyone in class *laughed* at his witty remarks, and the teacher gave him an A.
Unfavorable:	When Ralph began his speech, a few students in the back of the room began to *snicker*. The teacher asked the students to apologize for their rude behavior.
Favorable:	When the young teacher *smiled*, the frightened first-graders were comforted.
Unfavorable:	When he saw Bob's low grade, John *smirked*. He was happy to see his former friend disgraced.

Finding Meaning Through Structure

The meaning of a word can often be determined by its *structure*, that is, by the way the word is put together.

Each word in the following list has another word inside it. What are these "hidden" words?

unfearful
repayable
unselfish
restless
discounting

unthinkable
disclaim
preview
regain
insane

The "hidden" words in the preceding list are *fear, pay, self, rest, count, think, claim, view, gain,* and *sane.* The groups of letters that are added to these words to make the words you see above are called *affixes.* The affixes in the previous list are *un-, -ful, re-, -able, -ish, -less, dis-, -ing, pre-,* and *in-.*

The following list is another of words with affixes. How does this list differ from the previous one?

repeat	insulate
presume	width
proceed	baker
postpone	union
biennial	activity
annual	tolerable

The affixes in the preceding list are *re-, pre-, pro-, post-, bi-, an-, in-, -th, -er, -ion, -ity,* and *-able.* When you remove these affixes, however, you do not have words.

Affixes **are groups of letters that always carry the same, or nearly the same, meaning.**

Affixes are attached to *roots*, **which may or may not be whole words.**

Many common English roots and affixes come from Latin and Greek and carry the same meaning they did in the original language. When you know the meanings of roots and affixes, you can often determine the meanings of many words you would not otherwise know.

For example, knowing that the affixes *in-, dis-, im-, il-,* and *un-* all carry the general meaning of *not* helps you to determine the meanings of words with one of these affixes.

His mother was *displeased* with his schoolwork.

That letter is completely *illegible*.

His high winnings were *unprecedented* in the history of the lottery.

Eliza's *immature* behavior often got her into more confrontations than other girls her age.

Affixes are divided into two groups: (1) those that are attached to the beginning of a root and (2) those that are attached to the end of a root. Affixes that come before the root are *prefixes*; affixes that follow the root are *suffixes*.

Prefixes

Prefixes come before the root to which they are attached.

In the following list are some of the most common prefixes in the English language and the meanings they most often carry. (Prefixes sometimes change their spelling when added to a root.)

Prefix	Meaning
anti-	against
bi-	two
co-	equal
dis-	not
ex-	former
extra-	beyond
il-, im-, in-	not
inter-	between
intra-	within
mis-	wrong
post-	after
pre-	before
re-	again

Exercise 7: *Using Words with Prefixes*

Write each of the following sentences, supplying the appropriate word from the list below. Underline the prefix in each of the words you use.

disloyal	inattentive	misunderstand	rearrange
unpleasant	illegal	dissemble	disallow
impractical	extracurricular	immobile	immoderate

Example

a. _____ eating is the best way to gain weight.
   Immoderate eating is the best way to gain weight.

1. Suffering from poison ivy is an _____ experience.

2. It is _____ to steal, rob, or burgle.

3. Nora spends less time on her classes than on her _____ activities.

4. A good friend always stands up for his or her other friends and is never _____.

5. The teacher kept us awake by calling on _____ students.

6. Sometimes, a careless choice of words will cause others to _____ you.

7. The witness in the case had been known to _____, so the attorney sought to trap him in his own lie.

8. The books on the shelf were out of order, so Miriam decided to _____ them to make things easier to find.

9. Trying to fix a broken axle with a piece of wire is possible but certainly _____.

10. Mary knew that the IRS would probably _____ her tax deduction, but she included it anyway.

Suffixes

Suffixes follow the root to which they are attached.

Some suffixes add meaning to the root, and some change the part of speech to which a word belongs. For example, when the suffix *-er* is added to the root *paint*, the new word is *painter*, or "one who paints." When the suffix *-al* is added to the root *nation*, the new word is *national*, and the word changes from a noun to an adjective. When the suffix *-ity* is added to the root *national*, the new word is *nationality*, and the word changes from an adjective to a noun.

In the following list are some common suffixes in the English language and the meanings they usually carry.

Suffix	Meaning
-ish	like, similar to
-ful	full of
-able	able to
-er	one who
-fy	to make
-less	without

Exercise 8: Using Suffixes

Using the suffixes in the preceding list, determine the word that fits the following definitions. Write each word on a sheet of paper.

Examples

a. one who swims
   swimmer

b. to make terror
   terrify

1. similar to a fool
2. to make horror
3. one who sails
4. without pity
5. full of wrath

6. to make glory
7. one who designs
8. able to break
9. like a brute
10. full of sorrow

Developing Spelling Skills

In this section you will learn basic rules of spelling, some of which have exceptions. Learn each rule and then concentrate on its few exceptions.

Words with ie *or* ei

If the word is spelled with the combination *ie* **or** *ei* **and is pronounced with a vowel sound like the long** *e* **in** *beet***, write** *ie* **except after the letter** *c***. Write** *ei* **after the letter** *c***.**

ie: believe, relieve, chief, thieves

ei: receive, deceive, receipt, ceiling

Exceptions:. neither, either, seize, sheik, leisure

If the word is spelled with the combination *ie* **or** *ei* **but is pronounced with a vowel sound other than long** *e***, write** *ei***.**

ei: eight, rein, weigh, foreign, counterfeit, height, their

Exceptions: friend, mischief, handkerchief

665

The seed *Sound*

Words with a syllable that is pronounced like the word *seed* **are spelled in one of three ways:**

1	*2*	*3*
supersede	exceed	accede
	proceed	concede
	succeed	intercede
		precede
		recede
		secede

Exercise 9: Spelling Words with ie *or* ei

Write the following sentences, supplying the missing *ie* or *ei* in each underlined word. Underline the completed word. Be ready to explain why you spelled the word as you did.

Examples

   a. The demon was accompanied by two f___nds and a goblin.

   The demon was accompanied by two fiends and a goblin.

   b. The silence in the house made us suspect that the baby was up to misch___f.

   The silence in the house made us suspect that the baby was up to mischief. [Mischief is an exception to the second grammar rule on the previous page.]

1. A football f___ld is one hundred yards long.

2. The c___ling of the room was made of tile.

3. The fr___ght train left the station at midnight.

4. We all bel___ve that Ryan is innocent of the charges.

5. The rel___f pitcher came in and struck out the batter.

6. Diego ach___ved the highest grade of all his classmates on the biology tests this year.

7. A truly conc___ted person is rarely able to see his or her own faults.

8. N___ther Jane nor Eduardo went to the movies.

9. Daniel studied to be a pr___st at a well-known seminary.

10. The police s___zed their suitcases as evidence.

Adding Prefixes

Whenever a prefix is added to a word, the spelling of the word remains the same.

il- + legal	It is *illegal* to swim in the polluted river.
im- + mortal	A person who is *immortal* will live forever.
dis- + satisfied	The teacher was *dissatisfied* by the students' answers.
mis- + spell	Nadia was careful not to *misspell* any words in her essay.
re- + new	After the first year we asked to *renew* the lease.
over- + react	A team manager should never *overreact* to a crisis.

If a prefix is added to a proper noun or a proper adjective, a hyphen follows the prefix. The prefix is not capitalized.

anti-Nazi	pro-American
un-American	pre-Christian

When the prefix *re-* is used to mean "again," use a hyphen after the prefix if the word could be confused with a similarly spelled word.

re-collect	=	to collect again	recollect	=	to remember
re-cover	=	to cover again	recover	=	to get back or to get well
re-count	=	to count again	recount	=	to tell

Exercise 10: Spelling Words with Prefixes

Write the following sentences, supplying the word that has the same meaning as each phrase in parentheses. The word you should supply is the combination of one of the prefixes listed below and the *italicized* word that follows each sentence. Underline the word you form.

Prefixes

anti-	in-
dis-	mis-
il-	over-
im-	re-

Examples

    a. John's handwriting was _____ to everyone but his class-room teacher. (not *legible*)

       John's handwriting was illegible to everyone but his class-room teacher.

    b. Some fans might find soccer an _____ sport. (not *American*)

       Some fans might find soccer an un-American sport.

1.   We were _____ with the terrible dinner at the restaurant. (not *satisfied*)

2.   Some people _____ because they are bored with their lives. (*eat* too much)

3.   During the American Revolution many colonists were _____. (against the *British*)

4.   When Joan claimed that she was perfect, we had to _____. (not *agree*)

5.   After the assembly the workers _____ all of the chairs in the hall. (*arranged* again)

6.   Most people would agree that kidnaping is _____. (not *moral*)

7.   The mayor wants to be _____ for a third term. (*elected* again)

8.   The team that lost the game had been _____ by the sports-writers. (*rated too highly*)

9.   Martina wanted to _____ her old apartment, but her landlord wouldn't let her do it. (*decorate* again)

10.   Melissa and Carmen _____ the old sofa that the police had recovered from the burglars. (*covered* again)

Adding Suffixes

Drop the final _e_ before adding a suffix beginning with a vowel. If the suffix begins with a consonant, keep the final _e_.

love	+ -able	The cocker spaniel is _lovable_.
fame	+ -ous	Abraham Lincoln is a _famous_ name.
imagine	+ -ary	Norman has an _imaginary_ enemy.
force	+ -ible	The criminals were charged with _forcible_ entry.
hope	+ -less	The score was 31 to 4; the prospects looked _hopeless_.

Exceptions: mileage, peaceable, noticeable, judgment, advantageous, ninth, argument, duly, truly, wholly

When adding a suffix that begins with any letter other than _i_ to a word ending with -_y_ (pronounced with an _ee_ sound), change the _y_ to _i_. When adding a suffix that begins with -_i_, keep the final -_y_.

carry + -ed	= carried	We _carried_ equipment in our backpacks.
crazy + -ness	= craziness	This _craziness_ must stop.
lazy + -est	= laziest	Button is the _laziest_ of the kittens.

Exceptions: ladylike, ladyship, babyhood

Words ending with -_y_ preceded by a vowel keep the final -_y_.

joy + -ful = joyful

boy + -hood = boyhood

display + -ed = displayed

Exercise 11: Spelling Words with Suffixes

Write the sentences on the next page supplying the correctly spelled form of each word and suffix in parentheses. Underline the new word you form.

Examples

a. Henrietta's patience with children was _____. (envy + -able)
   Henrietta's patience with children was enviable.

b. Morris was _____ his hair when you called. (dry + -ing)
   Morris was drying his hair when you called.

1. Ms. Wallace is _____ the papers on a scale of one to ten. (grade + -ing)

2. Sally Wu is _____ a hard worker. (tru + -ly)

3. What was the _____ shown on the odometer when we began this trip? (mile + -age)

4. The _____ of the curry shocked the diners. (spicy + -ness)

5. Mr. Narrow's _____ was cut short by tragedy. (boy + -hood)

6. My grandfather is more than _____ years old. (nine + -ty)

7. Louise _____ the piano at the recital. (play + -ed)

8. Our dog is busily _____ a soup bone. (bury + -ing)

9. Harry is _____ the worst singer I've ever heard. (possible + -ly)

10. One of the hardest things to learn is good _____. (judge + -ment)

Double the final consonant before a suffix beginning with a vowel when both of the following conditions exist.

---

a. The root word has one syllable or the accent is on the last syllable.

b. The root word ends with a single consonant preceded by a single vowel.

   plan + -ing   *Planning* the delivery route is part of her work as a dispatcher.

   stir + -ed   Mike added salt and *stirred* the chili vigorously.

If both of these conditions are not met, do not double the final consonant before a suffix.

---

gal'lop + -ed   The wild horses *galloped* freely across the fields. [accent is on the first, not the last, syllable]

| look + -ing | Anna is *looking* for a used car. [word ends with a single consonant preceded by a double vowel] |
| re′fer + -ence | How many *reference* books did you check? [accent shifts from the last syllable to the first when the suffix is added] |

Exercise 12: *Spelling Words with Suffixes*

Write the following sentences, supplying the properly spelled form of each word and suffix in parentheses. Underline the word you form.

Examples

    a. Henry rarely _____ to his old friend Joe. (refer + -ed)
       Henry rarely referred to his old friend Joe.

    b. Felicia accidentally _____ the brick on Maurie's right foot. (drop + -ed)
       Felicia accidentally dropped the brick on Maurie's right foot.

1. Billy Joe is _____ to attend college in Massachusetts. (plan + -ing)

2. Angela is _____ the picnic due to the bad weather. (cancel + -ing)

3. Warm weather is _____ to cold weather if you live in California. (prefer + -able)

4. All of the students _____ from the new gym. (benefit + -ed)

5. Our boat's _____ became tangled in the lily pads. (propel + -er)

6. We found that selling newspapers could be _____. (profit + -able)

7. Most of the students _____ oranges to apples. (prefer + -ed)

8. The _____ of the picnic disappointed everyone who had counted on a warm Saturday get-together. (cancel + -ation)

9. We _____ our job applications to the company that makes woolen coats. (submit + -ed)

10. Roscoe _____ the serve over the net, but Ilie managed to return it. (slam + -ed)

30 Speaking and Listening Skills

Preparing to Speak Before an Audience

On an average day 70 percent of your waking time is spent communicating—either reading, writing, speaking, or listening. Most of this time, almost 8½ hours a day, is occupied either speaking or listening. With so much time devoted to just two activities, you might think that speaking and listening are easy. After all, you have had almost a third of your life to practice sending and receiving oral messages. However, when you express yourself, how effective are you in getting people to understand your ideas, feelings, and experiences? When you listen to others, how well do you comprehend their messages?

The effectiveness of your communications depends on your speaking and listening habits.

One way to learn good speaking and listening habits is to practice speaking in front of your class. The ability to organize your thoughts, support your statements, express yourself clearly, and listen effectively are all important benefits of public speaking that will help you in school and in later life. In this chapter you will study and practice one form of public speaking—the speech. Through reading and practice you will learn how to choose a topic, gather materials, and organize your thoughts. You will also learn the important listening skills that will help you benefit the most from your classmates' speeches.

Determining Your Speech's Purpose ·

When you speak, you should have an idea of how you want your listeners to respond. When you ask your teacher to postpone a test, your goal is for your teacher to agree, and his or her response determines the success of your message. When you tell a joke, the success of your communication depends on a positive response from your audience.

When preparing a classroom speech, determine how to approach your topic by first understanding the purpose of your speech and the response you want from your audience. Your speech's purpose will determine the material you gather, the organization you follow, and the style of delivery you practice. Your speech will probably have one of the following three purposes.

1. **To inform**

    When your primary aim is to share information, as you do when giving instructions, directions, descriptions, or demonstrations, you are speaking informatively. An informative speech is your opportunity to teach your classmates a new idea. Since your aim is to increase your listeners' knowledge, the response you want from your audience is, "I didn't know that before, but I do now."

    Your responsibility in an informative speech is to be clear, accurate, detailed, and organized. Informative speaking is more than just giving out information; it means presenting it so that your listeners can easily understand and remember it.

2. **To persuade**

    When you try to convince your parent to give you an advance on your allowance, you are using persuasion. A lawyer tries to convince a jury of a client's innocence by speaking persuasively. Television advertisements rely on persuasive appeals to convince you to buy certain products.

    A persuasive speaker tries to change a listener's beliefs or actions by convincing him or her that the speaker's opinions are the most reliable. Subjects for a persuasive speech should be arguable. You cannot argue the fact that the first *Star Wars* film grossed more money than *Gone with the Wind*, for example. In choosing a topic, be certain that you have reasons to support your side of the issue. If you expect your listener to change a belief or to act in a certain way, you must give him or her reasons to do so.

3. **To entertain**

    The primary purpose of speaking to entertain is to relate ideas, experiences, events, or stories for the enjoyment of an audience. You will find that most entertaining speeches are built on the speaker's personal experiences. Relating funny or exciting incidents, pet peeves, or mysterious tales can be highly entertaining. Everyone likes to hear a good story told well, and that is the purpose of an entertaining speech.

Exercise 1: Writing for a Specific Purpose

Choose a commercial from radio or television and rewrite it in one of two ways. Using only facts, make the commercial informative instead of persuasive. Or, rewrite the commercial to be entertaining, changing the material so that it is lighthearted in nature. Then present your commercial to your classmates.

Exercise 2: *Speaking for a Specific Purpose*

Choose one of the following informative, persuasive, or entertaining topics or make up one of your own. Then give a one-minute speech based on that topic.

Informative

Describe and show the proper way to sneeze.

Describe and show the proper way to eat various foods with chopsticks.

Explain and show how to change a tire.

Describe and show how to do your school yell.

Explain and show how to extinguish a grease fire.

Persuasive

Convince listeners that a woman should be elected the next President.

Convince listeners that a house is not complete without a Venus's–flytrap.

Convince listeners that every man needs to learn how to cook.

Convince listeners that the voting age should be increased or decreased.

Convince listeners that students should be responsible for cleaning schools.

Entertaining

Explain what it's like to be a professional alligator wrestler.

Describe your life as a dog, cat, or bird.

Explain what it's like to be a tube of toothpaste.

Tell about a day in the life of Superman, Tarzan, or your principal.

Explain what it's like to be a garbage can or a garbage disposal.

Choosing a Topic

Deciding on a topic is the first step in preparing a speech. A topic's worth is determined by the extent to which the speaker and his or her listeners can become involved in the message. Your chances of selecting a worthwhile topic can be improved by following the guidelines in this section.

Choose a topic that interests you.

If you cannot become involved with your topic, then your listeners are not likely to either. To avoid this possibility, consider choosing a topic from your own experience. For example, if you are a trivia buff, choose the topic "Trivia," or choose a topic that you have always wanted to investigate, perhaps the history of your own family or community.

Choose a topic that is likely to interest your listeners.

To make a topic interesting to listeners, you must make it relevant to their experience. Ask yourself what your listeners might like to know about a certain subject. If you can come up with an answer, then use that subject; if you cannot, then begin looking for a new idea.

Choose an original idea to present a familiar subject.

Think of all of the subjects that tend to make you yawn because you have heard about them so many times before. You may be tired of hearing about the energy crisis or about capital punishment because no one says anything new or different about either subject.

Choosing an original idea may mean nothing more than giving a new twist to an old idea; or it may mean choosing a topic that your listeners do not know much about. For example, telling your classmates about how baseball is played would probably be an old idea, but telling them about how baseball was invented or how it has gained popularity in foreign countries might be the new angle the subject needs.

Exercise 3: Listening for Speech Topics

Listen to programs on radio or TV that interest you. On a sheet of paper, list five or more possible speech topics from these sources.

Exercise 4: Locating Speech Topics in the Media

Leaf through several newspapers or magazines to find ideas for speech topics in articles or advertisements. On a sheet of paper, list five or more ideas that interest you and that you think would interest your classmates.

Exercise 5: Finding Speech Topics in the Library

In your school library locate a trivia quiz book, an almanac, a book of lists, or a book of records. Skim the table of contents in one of these books, selecting an interesting subject heading. Read that section in the book and, on a 3 × 5 note card, jot down topics that you could develop further in a speech. For example, you may find trivia concerning the invention of ice cream, barbed wire, zippers, toothpaste tubes, or Ferris wheels.

Taking Inventory

A good speaker realizes that a speech is far from complete when a topic is chosen. The next important step is to take inventory.

Finding out what you know and do not know about a subject is called *taking inventory*—a process you might begin by brainstorming.

If you choose to inform your listeners about superstitions, begin your research by brainstorming to recall the bits and pieces of information you have heard or seen about the subject. To brainstorm ideas, write the word *superstition* in large letters on a sheet of paper. Then let your mind run freely over this subject, jotting down all of the ideas that come to you about it.

You might recall that a black cat crossing your path is bad luck. You might also remember that breaking a mirror causes seven years of bad luck. Or is it six? Maybe it is thirteen, because you remember that there is something superstitious about that number. These bits and pieces are important because they help you to think of questions to ask about your subject—questions such as the following:

How did the number thirteen become so unlucky?

Why should people be frightened of a black cat? Why not a calico cat? Why a cat at all?

Who believes in these superstitions?

How many superstitions are there?

How did superstitions begin?

Is there any truth in them?

How do you define a superstition?

Asking questions, your next step in taking inventory, will give you some strong leads in searching for material on your subject.

Exercise 6: Brainstorming

By yourself or in a group of four or five classmates, brainstorm about one of the following topics. Keep a list of the information you gather, and use this list to write a series of questions to ask about your subject.

Alligators	Emotions
Animal instincts	Endangered seals
Balloons	Families
Bermuda Triangle	Homecoming
Buried treasure	Hurricanes
Crimes	Magic
Dating	Optical illusions
Diets	Space exploration

Using Outside Sources

The next step in taking inventory about a topic is to use outside sources. Begin by taking an inventory of the information about your subject that can be found at your school or community library. Locate any books, magazine articles, newspaper stories, pamphlets, filmstrips, phonograph records, tapes, vertical files, and reference books about your subject. Taking inventory of the available published material will help you to answer the questions you asked earlier.

People can also be resources, and you can take inventory of their knowledge. Interviews with friends, parents, teachers, and neighbors might shed new light on the subject. They may add interesting personal anecdotes that will help to enliven your speech.

Once you have gathered your sources, the next step is to survey each source individually. Look for examples, quotations, explanations, statistics, descriptions, definitions, or brief stories that say something about your subject. These details are important because the more information you have, the easier your speech will be to develop and the greater your chance will be of saying something new and interesting.

Recording the information is the last step in taking inventory. You may not use all the information you find, but you will have a convenient record from which to choose important points. Using note cards, write one fact or piece of information about your subject on each card. In the upper left-hand corner, write a subject heading to label the detail recorded on that particular card; this heading will help you organize the information later. On the bottom of the card, write the source of the material so that you can return to it later, or so that it will be available for others.

Exercise 7: Using Outside Sources

Using a subject of your choice, survey library materials or talk with people who have had some experience with your subject. From these sources cite at least one of each of the following kinds of information: an example, a quotation, a statistic, a brief story, a definition, and an explanation relevant to your subject. Then write each one of these six details (in your own words) on a different note card.

Limiting a Topic

Once you have gathered information, the next step is to limit the topic. You may have many details, but that does not mean that you can use them all in one speech. If you have only five minutes to speak, you may find that your topic is too broad to cover in that time. Superstitions, for example, is too broad to deal with adequately in five minutes. If this were your topic, you would need to narrow its scope, perhaps limiting yourself to kinds or origins of superstitions. It is always better to discuss a limited topic with specific details than to cover a broader topic and skimp on the important details that make a speech interesting for your listeners.

Exercise 8: Limiting a Topic

Select five of the broad subjects on the next page or make up five of your own. Then, for each of the five, suggest a limited topic that you could discuss in detail during a five-minute speech.

Driving	Improving public transportation
Dating	Improving schools
Taking tests	Planning a party
Watching soap operas	Finding a part-time job
Serving in the armed forces	Exercising

Outlining Your Speech

All speeches include an introduction, a detailed discussion, and some concluding thoughts about the topic. These speech divisions are known as the *introduction*, *body*, and *conclusion*. As you prepare your speech, decide what you will say in each of these divisions, and how you will organize them. Listeners usually do not have the patience to follow a speech that is disorganized. If you expect listeners to stay with you, to hear what you have to say, and to understand your thoughts, you must be organized.

The first step in organizing a speech is to outline the body.

Outlining means arranging details in a logical, organized way, drawing a blueprint for the development of your ideas. Since the body of the speech is where you explain your topic in detail, it is necessary to arrange your details carefully. Listeners justifiably become confused and annoyed when a speaker throws in unrelated ideas, expecting them to do the sorting. Take responsibility for organizing your details by following the guidelines in this section.

Write a controlling statement.

When you write a controlling statement, you are actually specifying the purpose of your speech and indicating what you will say in it. This statement will help you to determine what you need to outline in the body. For example, if your speech topic is *Kinds and Origins of Superstitions*, a controlling statement might be, "I want to inform my audience about some facts concerning the kinds and origins of superstitions."

Find the main points.

A main point is the largest division of your topic. For a persuasive speech, main points might be reasons for your opinion. For an informative speech, main points might explain, describe, or give facts about the topic. If you are entertaining an audience by telling a story, main points might be the major events that happen in the incident.

These divisions, or main points, support the topic stated in your controlling statement by giving specific details about it. The main points are not the most specific points you can say about your topic, but they are the link between the general topic and its most specific details. A speech always has at least two main points, and it can have as many as five. The exact number depends on the speech's length, but five main points usually is the maximum because listeners have trouble remembering more than that. If you speak about superstitions, for example, your major divisions might be arranged in the following way:

Facts About Superstitions

I.   Kinds of superstitions
II. Origins of superstitions

Exercise 9: *Identifying Four Main Points*

The following is a list of musical instruments. Identify the four main points (or types of instruments) in the list under which the other instruments could be grouped.

Trombone	Saxophone	Percussion
Clarinet	Tuba	Cello
Violin	Woodwinds	Flute
Brass	Bassoon	French horn
Drums	Trumpet	String bass
Oboe	Cymbals	Strings

Exercise 10: *Identifying Two Main Points*

The following list is of ideas on the subject *Ways to Exercise*. Identify the two major points in this list under which the other points would be grouped.

Indoor team sports	Softball
Football	Basketball
Baseball	Individual sports
Outdoor individual sports	Volleyball
Team sports	Bicycling
Jogging	Weight lifting
Hiking	Outdoor team sports
Indoor individual sports	Tennis

Find the minor points.

Minor points are specific details about a main point. If your main point is a reason, a minor point explains that reason in greater detail. Minor points about the topic *Superstitions* would be arranged in the following way.

Facts About Superstitions

    I.   Kinds of superstitions

        A.   Taking-action superstitions

        B.   Sign-reading superstitions

    II. Origins of superstitions

        A.   Outgrowth of a historical event

        B.   Outgrowth of people's fears

In this outline the minor points are labeled with the capital letters *A* and *B*.

Find the details of the minor points.

You can become more specific by dividing minor points into minor details. The only rule is that the division must be more specific about the heading or topic immediately above it, as the following outline listing minor details shows.

Facts About Superstitions

    I.   Kinds of superstitions

        A.   Taking-action superstitions

            1.   Acting to ensure good luck

                a.   Throwing rice at wedding

                b.   Carrying baby upstairs first

            2.   Acting to prevent bad luck

                a.   Eating right foods to prevent birthmarks

                b.   Not starting trip on the 13th

        B.   Sign-reading superstitions

            1.   Foretelling good luck

        a.   Horseshoe

        b.   Four-leaf clover

    2.   Foretelling bad luck

        a.   Broken mirror

        b.   Spilt salt

II.   Origins of superstitions

    A.   Outgrowth of historical event

        1.   Plague

        2.   World War I

    B.   Outgrowth of people's fears

        1.   Insecurities about present time

        2.   Uncertainties about future

Notice that the minor details are listed under Arabic numerals (*1, 2, 3*) and that minor details that are further divided are labeled with lowercase letters (*a, b, c*).

Exercise 11: Writing the Main and Minor Points of an Outline

Using the list of details about *Musical Instruments* on page 680, prepare an outline showing the main and minor points.

Exercise 12: Adding Minor Details in an Outline

Using the list of details for the subject *Ways to Exercise*, prepare an outline, including minor details as well as main and minor points.

Exercise 13: Preparing an Outline

Using a topic of your choice, develop two to five main points that each have at least two minor points. Under one minor point include at least two minor details. Prepare an outline showing these details.

Planning an Introduction

Plan an introduction with two goals in mind: to capture your listeners' attention and to introduce your subject. Any of the following methods can help you meet these goals.

Use an illustration or story

By using an example or a story or a series of examples or stories, you can capture your listeners' attention and introduce them to your subject. Of course, the examples or stories you choose must directly relate to your topic, since you want a good lead-in for your speech.

Use a quotation

If you read over the notes you gathered for your speech, you will probably find that you copied down a quotation. An interesting quotation can be a good opener for a speech, if it relates to your subject.

Define your topic

If your audience is not likely to know much about your topic, you might begin by defining the terms in that topic. You can also point out what you will and will not cover in your speech. This is a rather direct approach, and it immediately lets your listeners know the purpose of your speech.

Refer to your audience

Immediately appealing to the needs and interests of your audience will often capture their attention.

Make factual statements

Beginning with a fact or a series of facts about your topic is another good method. If you use this approach, remember that your purpose is to present fresh information so that your listeners' response will be, "I didn't know that."

Combine methods

You might find that one method alone is not enough to accomplish your purpose. The only guideline for using a combination of methods is to remember that your ideas must tie together clearly and smoothly.

A sample introduction for a speech on the subject *Superstitions* is found on the next page. The speaker uses a combination of methods to capture the listeners' attention and to introduce the subject. As you read, look for the methods the speaker uses and decide whether or not he or she is successful in planning a good introduction.

683

Waking up early one morning, you sleepily wander into the bathroom, where you carelessly knock a mirror to the tile floor, shattering the glass to pieces. Do you believe this means bad luck for seven years? Walking to school that same morning, you see a black cat in your path. Do you walk the other way? While sitting in the grass, you find a four-leaf clover. Do you pick it and keep it? If you react in any of these ways, you may be superstitious.

When you believe that a broken mirror or a black cat will bring you bad luck or that a four-leaf clover will bring you good luck, you are putting faith in a superstition. In other words, you are believing that an action foretells an event, when there is actually no connection between the two.

To really understand this topic you need to know something about the kinds of superstitions and the origins of superstitions. I hope to share some of that information with you today.

Exercise 14: *Writing an Introduction*

Using one of the six methods you read about in the preceding section, write an introduction for a speech on a topic of your choice. If you like, use a topic for which you have already gathered information.

After developing the introduction, deliver it before a classmate and keep it to use later.

Planning a Conclusion

The conclusion is the final impression with which you leave your audience. Plan a conclusion that redirects your listeners' attention to the central purpose of your speech and leaves them with a sense of finality.

The best way to begin your conclusion is to summarize your main idea. Summarizing can be done in one of two ways:

Main point summary. In your outline, identify your major topic divisions with Roman numerals. If you use a main point summary in your conclusion, state those "Roman numeral" ideas once again for your listeners. Such a statement helps your listeners review the important ideas of your speech; it is also a good way to begin your concluding remarks.

Single idea summary. The second way to begin your conclusion is to state once more your speech's controlling idea and purpose. A single sentence leading into your wrap-up is all that is necessary.

The final part of your conclusion should be your wrap-up. The wrap-up gives listeners a final, positive impression and a definite ending. The best way to wrap up a speech is to return to the method you used in the introduction. For example, if you used a quotation to begin your speech, refer to that quotation in your conclusion.

The following conclusion was written by the same speaker who wrote the introduction to the *Superstition* speech.

> Now I hope that you have a better understanding of the kinds of superstitions people believe in and the origins of those superstitions. So, if you feel anxious when you break a mirror or cross paths with a black cat, or if you are pleased when you find a four-leaf clover, you'll know a bit more about where those feelings come from.

As you can see, this speaker began with a main point summary and referred to the introduction's opening remarks to give the listeners a sense of completion.

Exercise 15: Writing a Conclusion

Using a speech topic of your choice, write a conclusion. (If you like, use a topic you have already used in this chapter.) Use either a main point or single idea summary to begin your conclusion and return somehow to your introductory remarks for your wrap-up. Then save your conclusion for later use.

Delivering Your Speech

Aspeaker's manner of presentation, or delivery, determines to a great extent the success of the speech. If you want your speech to be successful, you should analyze your delivery because your listeners will pay as much attention to *how* you give your speech as to *what* you say.

Your delivery consists of how you "print" your message, both verbally and nonverbally.

Verbal "printing"

Verbal "printing" is the speech equivalent to the words you write on paper. Just as it is difficult to read very small print, so it is difficult to listen to a voice that is not "printing" the message loudly enough to keep your interest. To avoid poor verbal printing, check your delivery with questions such as the ones on the next page.

a. **Do you project your ideas loudly enough?**

Some speakers are so softspoken that their listeners have to strain to hear them; such speakers forget to turn up the volume so that everyone in the room can hear. Sometimes, speakers also have the tendency to begin loudly and fade out at the end. Good projection means that there is sufficient volume for everyone to hear every word.

b. **Do you articulate clearly?**

Perhaps you speak loudly enough, but you may mumble so badly that the words sound blurred and indistinct. Each sound or word you project must be clear. Boldly "print" your words by slowing down and by not running sounds together.

c. **Is your voice energetic?**

Very few people will listen long to someone who sounds tired or bored. Changing the volume level, the speed with which you speak, or your voice's musical pitch will help to make the speech lively; otherwise your speech will sound monotonous and flat. Work on trying to make your speech sound conversational, and you will find that you naturally vary your volume, rate, and pitch.

d. **Do you use too many "catchall" words?**

Many speakers punctuate their speech by using a certain word or phrase over and over again. For example, whenever they pause, they throw in meaningless expressions, such as *um, uh, okay, all right, you know,* and *stuff like that*. See if you tend to use these catchall words; if so, work at eliminating them from your speech.

e. **Do you speak too quickly?**

When people are nervous or excited, they tend to speak quickly. If this happens to you, take a deep breath and slow down. Rushing will cause you to feel more nervous and to lose your audience's attention.

Exercise 16: Repeating Tongue Twisters

Try saying some of the following tongue twisters quickly but clearly. Then repeat each three times rapidly.

1. Five wives wearily weave bright red rugs.

2. He sawed six, slick, slender, slim, sleek saplings.

3. Lemon liniment

4. Tim, the thin, twin tinsmith

5. Does this shop stock short socks with spots?

6. Fanny Fowler fried five floundering fish for Francis Finch's father.

7. Betty Botter bought a bit of butter. "But," she said, "this butter's bitter. If I put it in my batter, it will make my batter bitter. But a bit of better butter will make my batter better." So Betty Botter bought a bit of better butter, and it made her batter better.

8. The prickly, primal pear picker picked three pecks of prickly, primal pears from the prickly, primal pear trees on the pleasant prairies.

9. Robert gave Richard a rap on the rear because Richard roasted the rabbit too rare.

10. A big, black bug bit a big, black bear.

Exercise 17: Writing and Saying Your Own Tongue Twister

Write your own two-line tongue twister and memorize it. Then say it to your classmates, but with your back turned so that they cannot see your lips. Repeat your tongue twister and have your classmates write down what they hear. Did they hear every sound correctly? Were you loud enough?

Exercise 18: Pantomiming

Pair up with someone in your class and think of a situation in which two people would be talking. For example, you might choose a situation where you just ran into the back of a police car and the police officer is approaching you to discuss what happened. Pantomime the action but carry on the dialogue by using only letters of the alphabet, numbers, or nonsense sounds. See if you can get the meaning of the situation across by varying your voice's volume, rate, and pitch. After you have practiced your pantomime, perform it for your classmates to see if they understand the event and the dialogue.

Nonverbal "printing"

Your speech involves more than what you say and how you say it. Every movement you make "speaks" to your listeners and delivers a nonverbal message. Every movement can enhance or detract from the words you speak. The key to nonverbal "printing" is to make this body language say what you want it to say. Help yourself do this by thinking about questions such as the following ones.

a.   **How do you appear to your listeners?**

Your posture or your stance communicates more than you may think. Standing stiffly in front of your listeners may convey tension and may make them feel uncomfortable. Leaning on the lectern or standing carelessly may give an impression of awkwardness or even laziness. However, standing with your weight on both feet in a relaxed manner helps your audience see the confidence with which you approach your speech.

b.   **Do your movements become distracting?**

Your listeners will follow whatever movements you make when speaking. When you fidget with jewelry, pace back and forth, or gesture too much or too little, you may be distracting your listeners. Before long they will be focusing on your movements instead of on your thoughts.

Try to make your gestures and body movements meaningful and definite. Do only what is natural and what reinforces the words you speak.

c.   **Does your facial expression reflect what you are saying?**

Your facial expression lets your listeners know your attitudes toward yourself, toward them, and toward your topic. Your expression can tell your listeners that you really believe what you are saying, or it may tell them just the opposite.

Listeners will read your facial expressions as they listen to your words and will make judgements about your speech based on what they see. If you tell your listeners about an exciting trip with a deadpan expression, they are more likely to believe what they see than what they hear.

d.   **Do you develop eye contact with your listeners?**

Developing eye contact with your listeners gets them involved with your speech and keeps them involved. It also gives you a chance to read your audience's reaction to your ideas.

Try to avoid reading your speech from your notes. Also, try to avoid staring out into space. Select people to look at and look at them as you talk. Establishing good eye contact is one way to establish an easy and sincere relationship with your listeners.

Exercise 19: Exaggeration

Select a newspaper or magazine advertisement to read to your classmates. Then decide on one emotion, such as love, hate, anger, sadness, frustration, joy, or fear, and read your ad, expressing that one emotion to your classmates. Exaggerate your facial expressions, body movements, and voice to create the desired emotional effect.

Exercise 20: Telling a Children's Story

Write a one- to two-minute children's story for an audience of five-year-olds. Imagine that your classmates are those children and tell the story to them. Exaggerate your facial expressions and body movements, to make the story come alive. Change your voice for different characters. Also use your voice to express moods.

Preparing Your Speech Assignment

To deliver a speech, begin by choosing a topic you have already worked on in this chapter or select a new topic. Then write a controlling statement, giving the purpose of your speech.

Once you determine your purpose, continue your preparation by taking an inventory of your topic. Gather all the sources and details you can find and turn in that material on note cards to your teacher. Next, prepare an outline, an introduction, and a conclusion for your speech.

Once you have made your outline, you probably will want to jot it down on note cards to use when giving the speech. A good idea is to limit yourself to two note cards; otherwise, your speech might become an exercise in how well you read.

Your final step is to practice. Practice in front of others or in front of a mirror so that you can work on both the verbal and nonverbal aspects of your speech. If you have access to a tape recorder, another good way of preparing is to tape your speech.

Exercise 21: Developing a Speech

For this activity use a speech topic that you have already developed in preceding exercises, or select a new one. Then develop a five-minute speech by using these steps:

1. Prepare note cards, listing details and sources.

2. Prepare an outline, an introduction, and a conclusion.

3. Jot down your outline on note cards to use when giving the speech.

4. Practice the speech.

Consult your teacher before delivering your speech before your classmates.

Listening to Speeches

Your job as a member of a speaker's audience is to reach some conclusion about what the speaker says. This requires concentration and thought on your part. In turn, the rewards for paying attention to a speech are the development of good listening and evaluating skills, and the betterment of your own speaking skills. Following are a few guidelines to help you become a better listener.

Prepare yourself.

You must prepare yourself to listen just as you prepare yourself to speak. A speaker's message demands your full attention, so you must resist distractions and concentrate completely on the speaker. Do not pay attention to those around you, and do not allow yourself to think about anything other than the speaker's words. Settle comfortably in your seat, look at the speaker, and concentrate solely on his or her voice.

Catalogue what you hear.

Your second listening guideline is to catalogue what you hear by training yourself to mentally outline the speech's structure. Identifying the speech's purpose, main points, and minor points will help you make critical decisions about the speaker's topic.

Since a good introduction will contain the speaker's purpose and topic, listening carefully at this point will help you focus on that purpose and topic. Once you are certain of the speaker's intent, you will be able to see how he or she supports the speech's purpose. In the body of the speech, try to separate major points from the supporting, specific details.

You can check your cataloguing by listening carefully to the speech's conclusion. Usually, in a conclusion a speaker will restate the speech's purpose and may also summarize main ideas. If your mental notes match the speaker's final words, then you will be adequately prepared to make decisions about the speech.

Review what you hear.

Reviewing what you hear means mentally repeating the ideas of the speech. For example, if a speaker says that a superstition is often an outgrowth of a person's fear, you should silently repeat this idea to yourself. In doing so, you have a better chance of remembering what the speaker says. Reviewing will also help you to keep your attention on the speech.

Evaluate what you hear.

As a listener you have the responsibility to determine how you will respond, which you can do only if you honestly and critically evaluate the ideas you hear. Evaluating means asking questions such as the following:

Does the speaker know the topic well?

Is the topic relevant to the needs and interests of the audience?

Is the speech's purpose clear?

Is the speaker specific and to the point?

Does the speaker clearly present well-organized ideas, or is he or she hard to follow?

Does the speaker rely mostly on facts rather than opinions?

Are all the facts accurate?

Is the speaker being truthful?

Is the speaker's voice loud and clear?

Does the speaker articulate clearly and distinctly?

Is the speaker's voice energetic and interesting?

Does the speaker avoid using many "catchall" words?

Does the speaker avoid speaking too rapidly?

Does the speaker have good posture? Good movement? Good facial expression? Good eye contact?

Exercise 22: Concentrating

Have someone read a story or a magazine article to the entire class. Have that same person ring a small bell five or six times as he or she reads. When the bell rings, class members should immediately write down the idea being expressed at exactly that moment. Check to see how well everyone concentrated on the message.

Exercise 23: Cataloguing and Reviewing

Choose one of the speeches given by your fellow classmates and outline the main and minor ideas on paper.

691

Glossary of Terms

Abbreviation A word or group of words that has been shortened by omitting letters

Abstract noun A noun that refers to a feeling or an idea that exists in a mental, not in the physical, world

Action verbs Verbs that show physical or mental action

Active voice The form of the verb that expresses action performed by its subject

Adjective clause A subordinate clause used to modify a noun or pronoun

Adjectives Words that modify (describe or make more specific) nouns and pronouns

Adjustment letter A letter written to give specific information about the original order and about the problem with the merchandise

Adverb clause A subordinate clause that acts as a unit to modify a verb, an adjective, or an adverb

Adverbs Words that modify (describe or make more specific) verbs, adjectives, or other adverbs

Almanacs Books useful for finding information about facts and figures that relate to both current and historical people, places, and events

Anecdote A brief story about a single incident sometimes used to develop a paragraph

Antecedent A word or group of words to which a pronoun refers

Application forms A form used by businesses to get the information they need about a prospective employee

Apostrophe A punctuation mark (') used to show the omission of letters or numbers, to form the plurals of letters or numbers, and to form possessive nouns

Appositive A noun or pronoun that explains or identifies a nearby noun or pronoun

Appositive phrase An appositive and its modifiers working together as a unit to explain or identify a noun or pronoun

Articles The largest group of adjectives (*a, an,* and *the*)

Atlases Primarily collections of maps but also having much information about such matters as climate, population, geography, and ethnic distribution

Author card A library card filed by the author's last name

Autobiography A true story about a part of the writer's life

Base sentence The sentence that remains as it is when others are added to it in a series

Bibliography A list of sources that have been used in preparing a report

Brainstorming Letting thoughts wander freely over the subject to discover ideas

Business letter A formal letter having six parts (heading, inside address, salutation, body, closing and signature)

Call number A book's individual number, according to the library in which it is found

Card catalogue The "road map" for finding books in the library, a series of cards filed alphabetically in drawers

Characters The actors in a literary work

Chronological organization The arrangement of events as they happen in time

Clause A group of words that contains a verb and its subject and that is used as part of a sentence

Clear writing Writing that can be easily understood by readers

Cliché An overused, stale term

Coherence The quality of being logically connected

Colon A punctuation mark (:) used to separate elements within a sentence by pointing forward, calling attention to the word, phrase, or list that follows

Comma A punctuation mark (,) used to separate elements within a sentence

Common nouns All nouns other than those that name specific persons, places, things, or ideas; common nouns are not capitalized

Complete subject The simple subject plus its modifiers

Complex sentence A sentence with only one independent clause and at least one subordinate clause

Composition A short paper usually consisting of several paragraphs on a single topic

Compound-complex sentence A sentence that contains more than one independent clause and at least one subordinate clause

Compound prepositions Prepositions made up of two or more words

Compound sentence A sentence that contains more than one independent clause but no subordinate clause

Compound subject Two or more subjects, sharing the same verb, that are joined by a conjunction

Compound verb Two or more verbs or verb phrases that are joined by a coordinating conjunction and have the same subject

Concrete nouns Nouns that stand for things that exist in the physical world

Conflict A struggle within one person or a struggle involving more than one person

Conjunction A word that joins words or groups of words

Connotation Meaning that carries emotional overtones

Context The "setting" of a word; language that surrounds a word and helps to make its meaning clear

Coordinating conjunctions The most commonly used group of conjunctions, those that join words, groups of words, and sentences

Correlative conjunctions Conjunctions always used in pairs to join similar kinds of items

Dash A punctuation mark (—) that points backward, calling attention to the word or group of words that comes before it; a sentence connector used to show a sudden change in thought

Declarative sentence A sentence that makes a statement

Demonstrative pronouns Pronouns used to point out specific people, places, things, and ideas for special attention

Denotation The dictionary definition of a word

Dewey decimal system The older of the two systems that libraries use for organizing books

Dialogue The exact words spoken by a character; the conversation between characters that goes on in stories and in drama

Double negative The result of using two words with negative meanings in the same sentence

Edited Standard English The written form of Standard English

Encyclopedias Works usually made up of many volumes that contain relatively short articles on any number of subjects

End marks Three punctuation marks—the period, question mark, and exclamation point—that come at the end of a sentence

Essential clause An adjective clause that gives information essential to the meaning of the independent clause and so should not be set off by commas

Exclamatory sentence A sentence that expresses a strong or sudden feeling

Expository paragraph A paragraph that conveys information or an explanation

Expository writing Writing that explains thoughts, explores ideas, and presents information

Fable A story with animal characters told to illustrate a moral

Faulty parallelism The (incorrect) use of conjunctions to join dissimilar parts of speech.

Figurative language Language that is not literally or actually true; imaginatively represents one item in terms of another

Final draft A rewrite of the first, or rough, draft

Formal outline An outline that divides topics into major headings marked by Roman numerals and subheadings marked by capital letters

Gerund A verbal, ending in -*ing*, that functions as a noun

Gerund phrase A group of words consisting of a gerund plus its modifiers or complements

Gobbledygook Wordy language that is needlessly hard to understand

Haiku A Japanese verse form that does not rhyme but has a fixed number of syllables

Hyphen A punctuation mark (-) used to link the parts of some compound words and the part of a word begun on one line with the part finished on the next

Idiomatic expression An expression whose non-literal definition has become fixed

Imperative sentence A sentence that gives a command or makes a request

Indefinite pronouns Pronouns that do not refer to specific people or things and that often do not have antecedents

Independent clause A group of words that has a subject and a verb and that expresses a complete thought

Infinitive A verbal, usually preceded by the word *to*, that can function as a noun, adjective, or an adverb

Infinitive phrase A group of words that contains the infinitive, its modifiers, and its complements, and functions as a single part of speech

Informal outline An outline that shows the arrangement of major ideas and supporting details

Insertion Building sentences by taking part of one sentence and putting it into a base sentence

Intensifiers Adverbs modifying other adverbs and adjectives that strengthen, or intensify, the meaning of the word they modify

Interjection A word that expresses a strong or sudden feeling, such as surprise, anger, or pleasure

Interrogative adverbs The adverbs *how*, *when*, *where*, and *why* when they are used to introduce a question

Interrogative pronouns Pronouns that appear in place of nouns referring to unnamed people, places, or things, and are used in asking questions

Interrogative sentence A sentence that asks a question

Irregular plurals of nouns Plurals of some nouns, formed by a spelling change other than the addition of the suffix *-s* or *-es*

Irregular verbs Verbs that do not follow the regular pattern for forming the past and past participle

Jargon Strange, confused, or obscure language that is not intelligible or is used by a particular group

Letter of application A letter written to apply for a job

Letter of commendation A letter complimenting a person or company on a good product or service

Letter of request A letter written to ask a company or a person for help

Levels of usage The different sorts of language available to speakers and writers for different purposes

Library of Congress system A method of organizing books that separates knowledge into twenty classes

Linking verbs Verbs that link a noun or pronoun in the first part of a sentence with a word in the second part of that sentence

Main entry words Words listed in alphabetical order in the dictionary

Metaphor A comparison of items made without the use of *like* or *as*

Middle English The English that was spoken and written from 1066 to about 1500

Modern English The English spoken from 1500 on

Negative adverbs Adverbs that give a negative meaning in the word modified

Nonessential clause A clause that does not add essential information and so should be set off by commas

Noun The name of a person, place, thing, or idea

Noun clause A subordinate clause that acts as a noun

Old English The earliest form of the English language written

Omniscient narrator An "all-knowing" storyteller

Order letter A letter written to order merchandise by mail

Parentheses Punctuation marks () used to enclose within a sentence material that has no real connection with the rest of the sentence or that designates listed items within a sentence

Participial phrase A participle and any complements or modifiers it may have

Participle A word formed from a verb but functioning as an adjective

Parts of speech The eight classes of words

Passive voice The form of the verb that expresses an action performed upon its subject

Perfect verb tenses The present perfect, past perfect, and future perfect tenses of the verb

Period A punctuation mark (.) used at the end of a sentence or to mark an abbreviation

Personal pronouns A group of pronouns that allows speakers to refer to themselves, the people to whom they are speaking, or the people, places, objects, or ideas about which they are speaking

Personification The assigning of human qualities or characteristics to inanimate (nonliving) things or ideas

Phrase A group of words that functions as a single part of speech but that does not contain a verb and its subject

Plot The relationship between events in a story and the reasons for their happening

Point of view The position from which the events of the story are observed; way of thinking about things

Possessive form of a noun A word that shows ownership or the relationship of one noun to another

Precise writing Writing that is specific, not general or vague

Predicate The part of the sentence that says something about the subject

Prefix One or more syllables attached to the beginning of a word to change or modify its meaning

Preposition A word that shows the relationship between a noun or a pronoun and some other word or words in the sentence

Prepositional phrase A preposition plus its object and modifiers that usually functions as either an adjective or an adverb

Progressive form of verbs The form of the verb that expresses continuing action

Pronoun A word that takes the place of a noun or other pronoun

Proper adjective A proper noun used as an adjective (to modify another noun or pronoun)

Proper noun A noun that names a specific person, place, thing, or idea, and is therefore capitalized

Punctuation Marks that have four main purposes: to separate, to link, to enclose, and to show omission

Quotation marks Punctuation marks (" ") used most frequently in pairs to enclose direct quotations and the words in some titles

Reference book A source of specialized information normally kept in a special place in a library

Reflexive pronouns Personal pronouns formed with the suffix *-self* or *-selves*

Regional dialects Language customs shared by groups of people in different regions of the country

Regular plurals of nouns Plurals of most nouns, formed by adding the suffix *-s* or *-es*

Relative pronoun A pronoun used to introduce a subordinate clause

Report A factual account

Rough draft The first copy of a piece of writing

Run-on sentence Two or more sentences separated by a comma or by no mark of punctuation

Semicolon A punctuation mark (;) stronger than the comma that shows the relationship between two sentences

Sense poems Poems describing people, places, or events through their *look, feel, taste, smell,* and *sound*

Sensory details Details perceived through the observer's senses that have the effect of making writing more vivid

Sentence A group of words expressing a complete thought

Sentence fragment A group of words punctuated as a sentence but that does not express a complete thought

Setting The time, place, and whole background in which the story takes places

Simile An imaginative comparison, that uses the word *like* or *as*, between two basically different items that share some characteristic

Simple subject The main word or words being spoken or written about

Simple verb tenses The present, past, and future tenses of the verb

Single quotation marks Punctuation marks (' ') used most frequently in pairs to enclose items that appear inside double quotation marks

Specific nouns Nouns that refer to only one or a few things in the physical world

Standard English The most widely used prestige dialect in English

Subject The part of a sentence about which something is being said

Subject card   A library card whose heading is the general subject of the book

Subject matter   The particular characters, actions, settings, and properties or things that the story, poem, or play is about

Subordinate clause   (also called a *dependent clause*) A group of words that has a subject and a verb but that does not express a complete thought

Subordinating conjunctions   Conjunctions that join groups of words called *clauses* to the rest of a sentence

Subordinators   A group of connecting words that joins ideas of unequal importance by making the words that follow them less important than the rest of the sentence

Suffix   A letter or group of letters attached to the end of a word to change its part of speech or modify its meaning

Symbol   Something that stands for, or represents, something else

Synonyms   Words that have nearly, but not exactly, the same meanings

Theme   The story's main idea or basic meaning

Thesis statement   A statement of the purpose of a paper that gives it focus, direction, and sharpness in purpose

Title card   A library index card filed alphabetically by the first major word in the title

Topic sentence   A sentence that states the main idea of a paragraph

Transitional devices   Words and phrases that show relationships between ideas and act as bridges between parts of the paragraph

Understood subject   The subject of a sentence understood by the reader to be *you*

Verb   A word that expresses action or a state of being

Verb phrase   The main verb plus one or more helping verbs

Verbals   Words formed from verbs but used as nouns, adjectives, or adverbs

Writer's Notebook   A record of important events in the writer's life

Index of Authors and Titles

Index

organization, **84**, **88–90**
selecting, **86–87**, **89–90**
sensory, **36–37**, 87, **131**
specific, **30–35**, **113–114**
in speeches, **681**
Determiners, **301–303**
Dewey decimal system, **600–601**
Diacritical marks, **620**
Dialects, **634–636**
Dialects of Middle and Modern
English, **632–633**
Dialogue
details of **92–94**
dramatic, **223–225**
writing, 226–228
Diction. *See* Language
Dictionaries
abbreviations in, **624**
checking spelling in, **618**
content and arrangement,
616–618
definitions in, **627–628**
etymologies, **626–627**
facts, 629
finding word origins in, 626–
629
guide words, **616–617**
Oxford English, **616**
parts of speech, **623–625**
pronunciation in, **619–622**
schwa, **623**
spelling in, **618**, **620–621**
syllables, **618–619**
of synonyms, **614–615**
usage labels, **625–626**
using, **616–629**
word entries, **618**
Direct object **483–484**
Direct observation. *See* Observation
Direct quotations
capitalizing, **584–585**
enclosed by quotation marks,
575–576
enclosed by single quotation
marks, **579**
Directions, giving, **106**
Documentation in research
paper, **162–165**
Double comparisons, **402–403**
Double negatives, avoiding,
428–429
Drama
characters in, **211**

dialogue in, **223–225**
conflict in, **212–213**
plot in, **209–210**
setting, **226**

E

Each, number of, **340**
Easy, easily, **430–431**
Editing marks, **17–18**
Editor, letters to, **248–249**
Ei, ie, rules for, **665–666**
Either, number of, **340**
Either/or, **26**
-Elect, hyphen with words end-
ing in, **568**
Emotions, appeal to, 239–241
in advertising, **240–241**
Employers, letters of application
to, **270–273**
Encyclopaedia Britannica, 613
Encyclopedia Americana, 613
Encyclopedias, **613–614**
using, 614
End marks, **548–549**
exclamation point, **549**
period, **549**, **550–552**
question mark, **549**
English language
borrowed words, **645–646**
development of, 645–651
history of, **630–633**
English language. *See* Language
Edited Standard English, **645**
formal, **636–637**
informal, 636–**637**
new words, **650–651**
Standard English, **645**
Entertainment, as goal of
speech, **672–674**
Enunciation, during speech,
685–687
Envelope, of business letter, 278
Essay. *See* specific type of composition
Etymology, **626–627**
borrowed words, 645–651
in dictionaries, 626–627
Everybody, number of, **340**
Everyone, number of, **340**
Evidence in persuasive composi-
tion, 251–253
Ex-, hyphenation of words beginning with, **568**

Example clues, **653**
Examples, developing paragraphs with, **58–59**
Except, usage, **450**
Exclamation point, **549**
after sentence showing excitement, **549**
after strong command, **549**
with interjections, **471–472**
with quotations, **577**
Exclamatory sentence, defined,
476
Experience clues, **652**
Expository composition, **128–145**
arranging ideas for, **118–119**
body, **134–138**
choosing and limiting subject,
113–115
coherence, **53–56**
conclusion, **138–139**
considering the audience,
119–121
gathering information, **115–**
116
guidelines for revising, **140**
introduction, **131–133**
model composition, 135–137
outlining, informal, **118–119**
paragraph development,
50–71
paragraph patterns, **62–69**
prewriting, 112–119
proofreading, **140**
purpose, **106–110**
revising, **140**
searching for a subject, **112–**
113
thesis, **128–130**
used to explain opinions, **108**
used to explain a process, **106**
used to form definitions, **109**
used to give directions, **106**
used to make reports, **106**
used to present information
through facts or data, **108**
uses of, **106–109**
writing, **106–122**
Expository paragraphs
checklist for revision, **70**
coherence in, **53**
combining chronological and
spatial organization in, **53**
developing with details, **56**
developing with examples,
58–59

705

developing with reasons,
60–61

developing through anecdote,
70–71

developing through comparison and contrast, **66–69**

patterns in, **62–66**

supporting sentences in, **50**

topic sentence in, **50**

transitional devices in, **54–56**

unity in, **50**

Expository writing, purpose of,
106–110

External conflict, **212–213**

Eye contact, **688**

F

Facial expression, **688**

Facts, **87**

  in dictionary, 629

  used in expository writing,
108

Family relationships, capitalization, **587**

Feminine pronouns, **333, 337,
342**

Few, number of, **340**

Fewer, less, **404**

Fiction

  arrangement in library, **603**

  comparisons, **194–195**

  in poetry, 193–199

Figurative language, 193–199

  metaphor, **195–196**

  personification, **196**

  simile, **194**

Figures of speech. *See* Figurative
language

First-person narrator, 218–219

First-person pronouns, **322**

Focus, in description, 36–39

Folding a business letter, 277–
278

Formal English, 636–645

  clichés, **643**

  colloquial words and phrases,
640

  gobbledygook, **643**

  jargon, **642–643**

  slang words, **640–641**

Formal outline for reports, 160–
162

Fragments. *See* Sentences, fragments

Free writing, **10, 42–43**

French influences on English,
648–649

From, **450**

Full block form of business letter, **274–275**

Future perfect tense, 358–359,
365

  forming, **365**

  progressive form, **371**

Future tense, 358–359, **363**

  forming, **363**

  progressive form, **369–370**

G

Gathering information

  six-question system, **9–10**

  about topic, **115–116**

Gender of pronouns, **333**

  agreement in, **337**

Geographical names, capitalizing, **589**

Gerund phrase, **493–496**

Gerunds, **493–496**

  modifiers, **505**

  possessives preceding, **505–
506**

Gobbledygook, **644**

Good, well, **431**

Guide words, **616–617**

Guidelines. *See* Checklist

H

Haiku, 191–193

Hardly, **418, 428**

Heading of business letter, 274–
275

Helping verbs, 357, **364–365**

  list of, **357**

"Hidden" words, **661–662**

His or *her*, agreement of pronoun and antecedent, **342**

Historical periods and movements, capitalizing, **591**

History of words, **626**–627, 629,
646–649

Hyphen, **568–570**

  and prefixes, **667**

  between words at end of line,
570

  linking parts of compound adjectives, **569**

linking parts of compound
nouns, **568–569**

linking parts of compound
numbers, **570**

uses of, **568–570**

with *ex-, self-, all-*, or *-elect*,
568

I

I, capitalizing, **594**

Ideas

  brainstorming, **5–7, 676**

  clustering, **4–5**

  main, of paragraph, **50–52**

  for writing, gathering, **3–4,
40–41**

Ie, ei, rules for, **665–666**

Illogical comparisons, **403**

Imperative sentence, **475**

In, into, **448, 450**

Incident. *See* Anecdote

Indefinite pronouns, 322, **326–
327**

  agreement, **375–377**

  features, **326–327**

  list of, **327, 340**

  number of, **327, 340**

Independent clauses, 514, **534–
535**

  comma separating, **552**

  linking with semicolon, **526**

  punctuating, **526–527**

Indirect object, **484–485**

  never part of prepositional
phrase, **484**

Infinitive phrase, **501–504**

Infinitives, **500–503**

  distinguished from preposition *to*, **500**

  function of, as noun, adjective, or adverb, **500**

  having subjects, **502**

  modifiers and complements,
502

  subject, **502**

Informal language, 636–**639**

Informal language. *See also* Formal English

Informal outline, **118–119**

Informal (personal) essay. *See*
Narrative, personal

Information

  on application form, **285–286,**
288

710

question mark, **549**
quotation marks, **575**–**581**
with quotations, **575**–**579**
replacing conjunctions with,
   465–**466**
semicolon, **561**–**563**
Pun, **181**–**182**
Purpose in writing, **11**–**12**,
   110–112

Q

Question marks, **549**
   with quotations, **577**
Questions
   for gathering information, 35,
      158
   in developing report, 158
   as introduction to paper, **132**
   six basic, 9–10
Quotation marks
   single, **579**
   uses of, **575**–**579**
Quotations
   colon setting off, **563**
   direct, **584**–**585**
   direct, inside other direct quo-
      tations, **579**
   direct, quotation marks with,
      575–**577**
   punctuation with, **576**
Quoting sources, in research
   paper, **158**–**159**, **162**–165

R

Raise, rise, **381**
*Readers' Guide to Periodical Litera-
   ture*, **609**–611, **613**
Real, really, **431**–**432**
Reason, appeal to, **242**
Reasoning, learning, **243**–**244**
Reasons
   developing paragraphs with,
      60–62
   in persuasive writing, **245**–**246**
   order of importance, 61
Reference books, **613**–615
References, **613**
   in *Readers' Guide*, **609**–612
Reflexive pronouns, **325**
Regional dialects, **634**–636
Regular plurals of nouns, 306
Relative adjective, **518**
Relative adverb, **518**

Relative pronouns, **329**, 518
   beginning adjective clauses,
      516
   who, whom, etc., 329
Repetition, as transitional device, **55**
Reports, **106**–107, **146**–171
   asking questions, **158**
   bibliography, **171**
   bibliography cards for,
      156–157
   choosing a subject, **153**
   documentation, **162**–165
   example of, 165–167
   final draft, 165–167
   limiting a subject, **154**–**155**
   model, 165–167
   organization in writing, 153
   outline, formal, **160**–162
   parenthetical documentation,
      162–165
   prewriting steps, 153–165
   quoting sources, 158–**159**,
      162–163
   revision, checklist for, **169**
   rough draft, **162**, **168**
   subjects for, **154**
   using encyclopedia for, 155
   writing, 153
Request, letter of, **280**–281
Requests (questions), punctuation of, **549**
Research on topic, **677**–678
Research paper. *See* Reports
Restricted topic sentence, **62**
Restriction of topic, **154**–**155**
Revision, **16**–17
   of business writing, **287**
   checklist for, **20**
   editing symbols, **17**
   of expository paper, checklist,
      140
   personal narrative checklist,
      83
   of reports, checklist for, **169**
Rhyme, **186**–187
Rise, raise, **381**
*Roget's Thesaurus of English Words
   and Phrases*, **614**–615
Roots, **662**
   followed by suffixes, **664**–665
   prefixes in front of, **663**–664
Rough draft of report, **162**, **168**
Run-on sentences, **539**–542

S

Salutation of letter, 274, **276**
   colon in, **276**
Scandinavian influences on En-
   glish, **648**
Scarcely, **418**, **428**
School subjects, capitalizing, **593**
Schwa, **622**–**623**
Seasons, names of, 591
Second-person pronouns, **322**
-Sede, -ceed, -cede, spelling rule,
   666
-Seed sound, **666**
See and *See also* cards, **607**, **610**
Self-, hyphenation of nouns be-
   ginning with, **568**
-Self, -selves, pronouns ending
   in, **325**
Semicolon
   before connecting adverbs,
      561
   linking independent clauses,
      561
   as sentence connector, 46–49,
      541
   to separate items in a series,
      562
   and transitional adverbs, **561**
   uses of, **561**–562
Sense poems, writing, **189**–193
Sensory details, **131**
   in poetry, **190**–191
Sentence combining. *See* Combining sentences
Sentence combining methods,
   24–27, 46–49, 72–77, 100–
   105, 123–127, 141–145, 172–
   179, 200–207, 229–237, 263–
   269, 289–298, 544–546
Sentence outline, **160**
Sentence patterns, **482**–488
Sentences, **474**–489, **534**–546
   base, 75–77, **123**
   classes, **534**–536
   combining, 24–27, 46–49,
      72–77, 100–105, 123–127,
      141–145, 172–179, 200–207,
      229–237, 263–269, 289–298
   complements, **482**
   complex, **535**
   compound, **534**
   compound-complex, **535**
   declarative, **475**
   direct object of, **483**
   exclamatory, **476**

Skills Index

Writing

Business Writing

adjustment, 282–283
application, 270–274
commendation, 283–284
forms, 274–277, 285–286
mailing, 277–278
order, 278–280
request, 280–282
revising, 287

Expository Compositions

body, 134–138
checklist for revising, 140
conclusion, 138–139
introduction, 131–134
purpose, 128–131

Expository Writing

finding subject matter, 112–115
informal outlines, 118–119
organizing information, 115–116
planning, 117–118
purposes, 106–112
readers, 119–122

Paragraphs

checklist for revision, 57, 70
coherence, 53–54
definition and features, 100
descriptive, 36–39
developing through anecdotes,
    70–71
developing by comparison and
    contrast, 66–69
developing with details, 56
developing with examples,
    58–59

developing with reasons, 60–62
topic sentence, 50–53, 58–61
transitional devices, 54–56
TRI pattern, 62–71
unity, 50–53
variations in patterns, 62–66

Personal Narrative

central theme, 78–81
character description, 95–98
checklist for revision and proof-
    reading, 83–99
dialogue, 92–94
elements, 78–81
organizing, 84
selecting details, 86–89
spatial organization, 89–90

Persuasion

audience, 247
letters to the editor, 248–250
papers, 257–262
points of view, 245, 251–254
thesis statement, 257–259
using emotion, 239–242
using reason, 242–245

Poems

figurative language, 193–199
haiku, 191–193
humor, 180–182
mood and feeling, 183–184
rhyme, 186–187
sensory descriptions, 189–191
sounds of words, 185–189

Prewriting Techniques

brainstorming, 5–7
clustering, 4–5
free writing, 10–11
purpose and audience, 11
six basic questions, 9–10

Proofreading

personal narrative, 83

Research Reports

asking questions, 158–
bibliographies, 156–162, 171
final drafts, 169–
footnotes, 162–165
formal outlines, 160–170
gathering information, 146–157
rough drafts, 162, 168–169
subjects, 153–155
summarizing, 147–152
taking notes, 158–160

Revising

business writing, 287
expository paragraph, 57, 70
expository composition, 140
personal narrative, 83
research report, 169

Short Stories and Plays

character, 211–212
conflict, 212–213
definition of a play, 226
dialogue, 223–226
plot, 208–210
point of view, 216–219
setting, 214–216
theme, 220

Writer's Notebook

concrete and abstract nouns,
    43–44
different points of view, 45
free writing, 42–43
observations, 28–30
using sensory details, 36–42
using specific details, 30–33

Language Resources

Dictionary

Speaking and Listening

Spelling

Vocabulary

Checklist for Revision

1. Did I express my ideas in a clear and interesting way?

2. Should I add new details, examples, or information?

3. Can I omit or leave out unnecessary details?

4. Is the content organized clearly?

5. Does each paragraph include a main idea with supporting sentences that develop this idea?

6. Have I used a variety of sentence patterns and lengths?

7. Are my sentences clear and complete?

8. Did I link sentences and ideas by using transitional words and phrases?

9. Are there better word choices I can make (concrete nouns, descriptive adjectives, and active verbs)?

10. Does the style of my writing reflect my own ideas?

11. Does my writing form a circle by showing a relationship between the introduction, the body of the composition, and the concluding statement?

12. Am I satisfied with my writing?

Proofreader's Checklist

1. Have I indented each paragraph?

2. Did I use capital letters where they were needed?

3. Did I punctuate each sentence correctly?

4. Have I corrected any sentence fragments or incomplete sentences?

5. Do related verbs, nouns, or pronouns in each sentence show agreement in kind and number?

6. Are all words spelled correctly?

7. Can my writing be read easily?

Acknowledgments

Credits

Key: (t) top, (c) center, (b) bottom, (l) left, (r) right.

Page 1, Gregg Eisman; 3(l), 3(r), 5, 7, Jean-Claude Lejeune; 9(l), Vito Palmisano; 9(r), Steven E. Gross; 10, Thomas Hooke Photography; 13(l), Jean-Claude Lejeune; 13(r), Bruce Powell; 15, Jean-Claude Lejeune; 16, Bruce Powell; 19, Jean-Claude Lejeune; 21, Vito Palmisano; 24, Jean-Claude Lejeune; 26, Thomas Hooke Photography; 27, Jean-Claude Lejeune; 28, Thomas Hooke Photography; 29(l), 29(r), Jean-Claude Lejeune; 30, Thomas Hooke Photography; 31, Vito Palmisano; 32, Frank Siteman/The Marilyn Gartman Agency; 33(l), Thomas Hooke Photography; 33(r), Vito Palmisano; 34, Jean-Claude Lejeune; 35, Frank Siteman/The Marilyn Gartman Agency; 36, Thomas Hooke Photography; 37, Bruce Powell; 40, Frank Siteman/The Marilyn Gartman Agency; 41, Thomas Hooke Photography; 42, Bruce Powell; 43, John Weinstein; 45, Vito Palmisano; 50, Thomas Hooke Photography; 51(l), Vito Palmisano; 51(r), Thomas Hooke Photography; 52, V. Lee Hunter; 53, Bruce Powell; 56, Thomas Hooke Photography; 58, 60, Jean-Claude Lejeune; 63(l), Gregg Eisman; 63(r), Vito Palmisano; 65, 66, Thomas Hooke Photography; 68, Jean-Claude Lejeune; 71(l), 71(r), Thomas Hooke Photography; 74, Jean-Claude Lejeune; 77, Frank Siteman/The Marilyn Gartman Agency; 78, Thomas Hooke Photography; 79(l), Nawrocki Stock Photo; 79(r), Vito Palmisano; 80, Nawrocki Stock Photo; 85, Jean-Claude Lejeune; 87, Frank Siteman/The Marilyn Gartman Agency; 88, Thomas Hooke Photography; 94, Jean-Claude Lejeune; 97, Thomas Hooke Photography; 99(all), Jean-Claude Lejeune; 105, Vito Palmisano; 106, Thomas Hooke Photography; 107(l), Gregg Eisman; 107(r), Thomas Hooke Photography; 108, Jean-Claude Lejeune; 109, 110, Thomas Hooke Photography; 111, Vito Palmisano; 113, Thomas Hooke Photography; 114, Jean-Claude Lejeune; 117, Gregg Eisman; 120, 124, Jean-Claude Lejeune; 127, Thomas Hooke Photography; 128, Gregg Eisman, W.C.H.M.; 129 (l), D. Shigley; 129(r), Gregg Eisman, W.C.H.M.; 130, Vito Palmisano; 132, 133, 134, 136(l), 136(r), 137, 139, Gregg Eisman, W.C.H.M.; 140, Jean-Claude Lejeune; 141, Vito Palmisano; 143, John Weinstein; 144, Jean-Claude Lejeune; 146, Thomas Hooke Photography; 147(l), Gregg Eisman; 147(r), Jean-Claude Lejeune; 149, Bruce Powell; 153, Jean-Claude Lejeune; 155, Springer/Bettmann Film Archive; 158, Sea World Photo; 167, John Chellman/Animals, Animals; 168, Jean-Claude Lejeune; 170(l), W.B. Finch/Stock, Boston; 170(r), Cary Wolinsky/Stock, Boston; 173, Vito Palmisano; 174, Steven E. Gross; 177, Jean-Claude Lejeune; 180, Bruce Powell; 181(l), Jean-Claude Lejeune; 181(r), Frank Siteman/The Marilyn Gartman Agency; 182, 184(l), Bruce Powell; 184(r), 186, 188(l), 188(r), 190, 192, 194, 196, Jean-Claude Lejeune; 197, 198, Vito Palmisano; 203, Thomas Hooke Photography; 204, Vito Palmisano; 206, Jean-Claude Lejeune; 208, Thomas Hooke Photography; 209(l), John Weinstein; 209(r), Steven E. Gross; 211, Bruce Powell; 213, Vito Palmisano; 214, 217, Jean-Claude Lejeune; 218, Thomas Hooke Photography; 223, 224, 225, Culver Pictures, Inc.; 227, Jean-Claude Lejeune; 230, Vito Palmisano; 233, John Weinstein; 236, 237, Jean-Claude Lejeune; 238, Thomas Hooke Photography; 243, Gregg Eisman; 244, Thomas Hooke Photography; 245, Jean-Claude Lejeune; 246, Frank Siteman/The Marilyn Gartman Agency; 253, Gregg Eisman; 255, Thomas Hooke Photography; 258, Jean-Claude Lejeune; 261, Gregg Eisman; 263, Jean-Claude Lejeune; 268, 270, Thomas Hooke Photography; 271(l), Bruce Powell; 271(r), Thomas Hooke Photography; 273, Bruce Powell; 280, Thomas Hooke Photography; 282, Jean-Claude Lejeune; 284, Movie-Still Archives; 286, 287, 291, 292, Jean-Claude Lejeune; 293, Steven E. Gross; 295, Jean-Claude Lejeune; 297, Thomas Hooke Photography; 298, Gregg Eisman; 319, Steven E. Gross; 352, 353, Jean-Claude Lejeune; 385, Mark Antman/Stock, Boston; 412, 413, 437(l), 437(r), Jean-Claude Lejeune; 456, Frank Siteman/The Marilyn Gartman Agency; 457, Bruce Powell; 469, Photo Researchers, Inc.; 473, Frank Siteman/The Marilyn Gartman Agency; 489, Vito Palmisano; 511(l), 511(r), Gregg Eisman; 533, Movie-Still Archives; 545, Vito Palmisano; 546, Movie-Still Archives; 547, Gregg Eisman; 583, 597, Jean-Claude Lejeune; 598, Steven E. Gross; 599, Gregg Eisman.

1 2 3 4 5 6 7 8 9 0—93 92 91 90 89 88 87